Internet Bible, 2nd Edition

Brian Underdahl and Keith Underdahl

IDG Books Worldwide, Inc.
An International Data Group Company

Foster City, CA ✦ Chicago, IL ✦ Indianapolis, IN ✦ New York, NY

Internet Bible, 2nd Edition

Published by
IDG Books Worldwide, Inc.
An International Data Group Company
919 E. Hillsdale Blvd., Suite 400
Foster City, CA 94404
www.idgbooks.com (IDG Books Worldwide Web site)

ISBN: 0-7645-3469-6

Printed in the United States of America

10 9 8 7 6 5 4 3

1B/SX/QU/QQ/FC

Distributed in the United States by IDG Books Worldwide, Inc.

Distributed by CDG Books Canada Inc. for Canada; by Transworld Publishers Limited in the United Kingdom; by IDG Norge Books for Norway; by IDG Sweden Books for Sweden; by IDG Books Australia Publishing Corporation Pty. Ltd. for Australia and New Zealand; by TransQuest Publishers Pte Ltd. for Singapore, Malaysia, Thailand, Indonesia, and Hong Kong; by Gotop Information Inc. for Taiwan; by ICG Muse, Inc. for Japan; by Intersoft for South Africa; by Eyrolles for France; by International Thomson Publishing for Germany, Austria, and Switzerland; by Distribuidora Cuspide for Argentina; by LR International for Brazil; by Galileo Libros for Chile; by Ediciones ZETA S.C.R. Ltda. for Peru; by WS Computer Publishing Corporation, Inc., for the Philippines; by Contemporanea de Ediciones for Venezuela; by Express Computer Distributors for the Caribbean and West Indies; by Micronesia Media Distributor, Inc. for Micronesia; by Chips Computadoras S.A. de C.V. for Mexico; by Editorial Norma de Panama S.A. for Panama; by American Bookshops for Finland.

For general information on IDG Books Worldwide's books in the U.S., please call our Consumer Customer Service department at 800-762-2974. For reseller information, including discounts and premium sales, please call our Reseller Customer Service department at 800-434-3422.

For information on where to purchase IDG Books Worldwide's books outside the U.S., please contact our International Sales department at 317-596-5530 or fax 317-572-4002.

For consumer information on foreign language translations, please contact our Customer Service department at 800-434-3422, fax 317-572-4002, or e-mail rights@idgbooks.com.

For information on licensing foreign or domestic rights, please phone +1-650-653-7098.

For sales inquiries and special prices for bulk quantities, please contact our Order Services department at 800-434-3422 or write to the address above.

For information on using IDG Books Worldwide's books in the classroom or for ordering examination copies, please contact our Educational Sales department at 800-434-2086 or fax 317-572-4005.

For press review copies, author interviews, or other publicity information, please contact our Public Relations department at 650-653-7000 or fax 650-653-7500.

For authorization to photocopy items for corporate, personal, or educational use, please contact Copyright Clearance Center, 222 Rosewood Drive, Danvers, MA 01923, or fax 978-750-4470.

Library of Congress Cataloging-in-Publication Data

Underdahl, Brian.
    Internet Bible / Brian Underdahl and Keith Underdahl. --2nd ed.
        p.   cm.
    ISBN 0-7645-3469-6 (alk. paper)
    1. Internet (Computer network) 2. World Wide Web. 3. Web sites. I. Underdahl, Keith. II. Title.
TK5105.875.157 U52   2000
004.67'8--dc21   00-027452

Internet Bible, 2nd Edition

ABOUT IDG BOOKS WORLDWIDE

Welcome to the world of IDG Books Worldwide.

IDG Books Worldwide, Inc., is a subsidiary of International Data Group, the world's largest publisher of computer-related information and the leading global provider of information services on information technology. IDG was founded more than 30 years ago by Patrick J. McGovern and now employs more than 9,000 people worldwide. IDG publishes more than 290 computer publications in over 75 countries. More than 90 million people read one or more IDG publications each month.

Launched in 1990, IDG Books Worldwide is today the #1 publisher of best-selling computer books in the United States. We are proud to have received eight awards from the Computer Press Association in recognition of editorial excellence and three from Computer Currents' First Annual Readers' Choice Awards. Our best-selling ...For Dummies® series has more than 50 million copies in print with translations in 31 languages. IDG Books Worldwide, through a joint venture with IDG's Hi-Tech Beijing, became the first U.S. publisher to publish a computer book in the People's Republic of China. In record time, IDG Books Worldwide has become the first choice for millions of readers around the world who want to learn how to better manage their businesses.

Our mission is simple: Every one of our books is designed to bring extra value and skill-building instructions to the reader. Our books are written by experts who understand and care about our readers. The knowledge base of our editorial staff comes from years of experience in publishing, education, and journalism — experience we use to produce books to carry us into the new millennium. In short, we care about books, so we attract the best people. We devote special attention to details such as audience, interior design, use of icons, and illustrations. And because we use an efficient process of authoring, editing, and desktop publishing our books electronically, we can spend more time ensuring superior content and less time on the technicalities of making books.

You can count on our commitment to deliver high-quality books at competitive prices on topics you want to read about. At IDG Books Worldwide, we continue in the IDG tradition of delivering quality for more than 30 years. You'll find no better book on a subject than one from IDG Books Worldwide.

John Kilcullen
Chairman and CEO
IDG Books Worldwide, Inc.

Eighth Annual
Computer Press
Awards ≥1992

Ninth Annual
Computer Press
Awards ≥1993

Tenth Annual
Computer Press
Awards ≥1994

Eleventh Annual
Computer Press
Awards ≥1995

IDG is the world's leading IT media, research and exposition company. Founded in 1964, IDG had 1997 revenues of $2.05 billion and has more than 9,000 employees worldwide. IDG offers the widest range of media options that reach IT buyers in 75 countries representing 95% of worldwide IT spending. IDG's diverse product and services portfolio spans six key areas including print publishing, online publishing, expositions and conferences, market research, education and training, and global marketing services. More than 90 million people read one or more of IDG's 290 magazines and newspapers, including IDG's leading global brands — Computerworld, PC World, Network World, Macworld and the Channel World family of publications. IDG Books Worldwide is one of the fastest-growing computer book publishers in the world, with more than 700 titles in 36 languages. The "...For Dummies®" series alone has more than 50 million copies in print. IDG offers online users the largest network of technology-specific Web sites around the world through IDG.net (http://www.idg.net), which comprises more than 225 targeted Web sites in 55 countries worldwide. International Data Corporation (IDC) is the world's largest provider of information technology data, analysis and consulting, with research centers in over 41 countries and more than 400 research analysts worldwide. IDG World Expo is a leading producer of more than 168 globally branded conferences and expositions in 35 countries including E3 (Electronic Entertainment Expo), Macworld Expo, ComNet, Windows World Expo, ICE (Internet Commerce Expo), Agenda, DEMO, and Spotlight. IDG's training subsidiary, ExecuTrain, is the world's largest computer training company, with more than 230 locations worldwide and 785 training courses. IDG Marketing Services helps industry-leading IT companies build international brand recognition by developing global integrated marketing programs via IDG's print, online and exposition products worldwide. Further information about the company can be found at www.idg.com.   1/26/00

Credits

Acquisitions Editor
David B. Mayhew

Project Editors
Christopher C. Johnson
Michael Christopher

Technical Editor
Earl Jackson

Copy Editors
Marti Paul
Lane Barnholtz
Nancy Rapoport

Media Development Specialist
Jake Mason

Permissions Editor
Lenora Chin Sell

Media Development Manager
Stephen Noetzel

Project Coordinators
Linda Marousek
Joe Shines

Graphics and Production Specialists
Robert Bihlmayer
Jude Levinson
Michael Lewis
Victor Pérez-Varela
Dina F Quan
Ramses Ramirez

Proofreading and Indexing
York Production Services

Cover Illustrator
Andreas Schueller

Book Designer
Drew R. Moore

Illustrator
Mary Jo Richards

About the Authors

Brian Underdahl is the well-known, best-selling author of over 48 computer books including several current titles from IDG Books Worldwide: *Windows 98 One Step at a Time, Teach Yourself Microsoft Office 97, Teach Yourself Windows 2000 Professional, Teach Yourself Microsoft Office 2000,* and *Opera Web Browser For Dummies.* Brian spends most of his time at the keyboard writing about personal computing. When he finds the time he enjoys taking in the view from the home he and his wife Darlene built in the mountains 2000 feet above Reno, NV. He tries to find the time to attend Mensa meetings whenever possible, and has become a fairly decent gourmet cook in recent years, too.

Keith Underdahl is an author living in Albany, Oregon. He has served as writer or technical editor on dozens of books, including IDG's *Teach Yourself Microsoft Word 2000, Teach Yourself Microsoft Office 97,* and *Internet Bible.* Keith is also a development team manager for Ages Software, where he specializes in electronic preservation and publication of historic Christian literature. When he is not goofing off with computers, Keith is the Pacific Northwest editor for *Street Bike,* a print and online magazine serving motorcyclists in the western United States.

Kathy E. Gill is a communications consultant specializing in Web design, writing, and training; she "speaks" Macintosh, Windows, and Linux (in that order). Her first IDG project was on *Webable: Making Web Sites Accessible to People With Disabilities.* She has worked with Boeing and AT&T Wireless, teaches at Seattle-area community colleges, and is an adjunct professor at Pacific Lutheran University. When not lecturing or tip-tapping at her keyboard, she can be found motoring around Washington State on her BMW R65.

John Preisach has worked on numerous IDG projects including the *Internet Bible, Teach Yourself Windows 2000,* and *Windows 98 One Step At A Time.* He is currently a tank commander for the Nevada National Guard and works as a technical instructor for a major software and hardware manufacturer.

*This book is dedicated to some very special people in my life:
Darlene Underdahl, Bobbie Gaudette, Sue Chapweske,
Jean Stokes, Chris Raible, DeForest Underdahl, and in loving
memory of Laurie Choate.*

—*Brian Underdahl*

*I dedicate all of my work to my sons Soren and Cole, who
graciously agreed to pose for pictures throughout this book.*

—*Keith Underdahl*

Preface

An acquaintance of ours has long been a fan of a well-known author. For years he wondered if a literary society might exist that devoted itself to this writer's life and work. He checked reference books, asked at libraries, wrote a few letters — all without success. Perhaps such a group didn't even exist! Then along came the Internet. Literally within minutes of getting wired, he found the academic society for which he had been searching for ten years. He's now assistant editor of the society's journal.

The Internet can easily open doors like this, connecting people and ideas across the globe or across the street. The Internet is a huge place with many interesting things to do and intriguing places to go. And it's a lot of fun, too.

But the Internet can also be confusing and mysterious. If you want to know what's out there and how to get the most from the Internet, you need a top-quality guide — the *Internet Bible,* 2nd Edition. This book is here to open the Internet's many doors for you — including a few new ones you may not know about.

We produced this book to provide you with the best resource for Internet-related information you can find anywhere, regardless of what kind of computer you are using. Whether you're just thinking about getting on the Internet or if you're a seasoned Internet surfer, you'll find not only what you need but also a few surprises in the pages that follow.

What You'll Find in This Book

Part I, An Internet Primer, gives you a quick overview of everything you need to get started on the Internet. (In the rest of the book, we greatly expand on the information you find in this section.) Here you learn how to sign up for Internet service and then see how you can begin browsing the Internet for yourself. You also see how you can find what you're looking for amid the vast amount of information sources. Later in this part you learn how to use the Internet to send and receive messages quickly, and even how you can become a part of the Internet by creating your own Web pages.

Part II, Connecting to the Internet, begins by helping you choose your Internet service provider. You learn about some of the national service provider options and what you need to consider so you can be satisfied with your choices. You have a chance to learn about your options for speedier Internet access, and you will also learn how to keep everyone online if you are one of the growing number of small-network owners.

Part III, Browsing the Web with Browsers, shows you your options for browsing the Web and also helps you learn how to get the most from whichever Web browser you prefer. This part shows you how to manage your Web sessions so you can get more done in less time.

Part IV, Using Easy and Effective E-mail, has everything you want to know about sending and receiving messages across the Internet. You learn how to make certain your messages are private and secure, how to choose e-mail software, how to organize your e-mail, and even how you can get e-mail service free. This part also shows you how to send and receive files along with your e-mail. In addition, you learn what you can do to avoid junk e-mail.

Part V, Finding Everything You Need on the Web, cuts through the confusion and shows you how to find what you want. You will learn how to find cool software, graphics, movies, and music on the Web, locate old friends, and conduct research. And if you're looking for other people on the Internet, this part also shows you two exciting options — chat and newsgroups.

Part VI, Web Directory, is your guide to hundreds of interesting Web sites. Go ahead and open any page listed here and you'll find yourself drawn to places you might not have found on your own. You're bound to discover hours of enjoyment in these pages!

Part VII, Creating Your Own Web Content, shows you everything you should know to create exciting Web sites that people will want to visit. You learn how to create a simple Web site and how to enhance your site with all sorts of fancy additions. You also see how you can use digital cameras and photo manipulation software to make your Web site a lot more interesting.

Part VIII, Living in Cyberspace, introduces you to some of the most exciting things you can do on the Internet. You learn how you can safely shop online, find and play games online, and how to do business and even hold meetings over the Internet. You will also learn about some of the security and privacy problems you could encounter online, and learn what to do about them. And on the same note, we'll show you some tools that you can use to protect your family while they use the online world.

Finally, the appendixes show you some of the bits and pieces you should know to understand how the Internet got to where it is today. You also learn about the software on the *Internet Bible* CD-ROM.

Conventions Used in this Book

We want the *Internet Bible* to be easy to use and informative, so we follow several conventions to help you understand just what you're seeing. For example, when you need to make a series of selections from a menu, we show the commands like this:

File➪Open

This tells you that you need to select the **File** menu first and then choose the **Open** option from that menu.

When you need to type something exactly as shown in the text, we present the text you should enter in bold. Here's an example:

Type these exact words

We also used several icons in the margins to alert you to special information that will be important. These icons include the following:

Tip   This shows you a special tip or trick that can help you do things like an expert.

Note   Notes are important information that amplify a subject. They provide special information you won't want to miss.

Caution   If there's a danger you need to know about, we display a caution to alert you so you don't accidentally do something that causes a problem.

The entire *Internet Bible,* 2nd Edition team hopes you enjoy the book. We feel it's your best source of up-to-date information about the Internet.

Acknowledgments

A project as large as the *Internet Bible,* 2nd Edition is the result of a lot of hard work by many different people. We'd like to be able to thank each of you personally, but that's simply not possible because so many people contributed. Here are some of the special people who helped make this book possible:

- ✦ **Walt Bruce, David Mayhew,** and **Andy Cummings** at IDG Books Worldwide for giving me the chance to do this book.

- ✦ **Chris Johnson** for his ability to make sense of our work.

- ✦ **Marti Paul, Michael Christopher, Lenora Chin Sell, Carmen Krikorian**, and dozens of other wonderful people at IDG who all worked so hard to help us complete this book on time.

- ✦ **Kathy Gill** and **John Preisach**, our fellow authors who worked many long hours expertly writing sections of the book.

- ✦ **Earl Jackson** for his technical review of the manuscript.

- ✦ The **Opera Software** team, especially **Håkon Wium Lie, Sandra Thorbjørnsen, Lars Frelsoy, Shae McKean,** and **Rikard Gillemyr** for doing so much to make this book possible and for creating my favorite Web browser.

- ✦ **Tom Beardmore** at **iDOT Computers** for providing the BeOS PC so we could get screen shots in more than just Microsoft Windows. **Dan Bonfitto** at **iDOT Computers** for providing technical support.

- ✦ **JudeAnn Smith, Dave Brown, Tom Maddox, Victoria,** and **Sylvie** at Be.

- ✦ **mr. zenn (thanks Joe)** at VA Linux, **Asha Clayton-Niederman** at **Deja.com, Brian M. Brotschi** and **Joe Farinella** at **NetworkICE, Frederic Pare** at **Copernic Technologies, Jennifer Iacullo** and **Angelica Mkok** at **Panda, Lucy Stokstad** and **Krissy Petersen** at **Web3000.com,** Nenad Koncar at **Translation Experts, Ltd, Leslie K. Palmer, Salena Goudreault, Heather L. Stern,** and **Carrie Reeves** at **Intel, Robert Savage** at **1Jump, Bud Baker** at **Spinnerbaker, Michael Burford** at **HeadLight Software, David Weinlader** at **Kaylon Technologies, Steve Thomas** at **Webroot Software, Stephen LeHunte, Manuel Schmidt** at **Manitu,** and **Francois Crevola.**

- ✦ Our **families** and **friends**, who provided support through the long hours and tireless work required to make the *Internet Bible* a reality.

We appreciate all the help everyone provided, and we're sorry if we missed any of you here.

Contents at a Glance

Contents

Part II: Connecting to the Internet   49

Chapter 5: Choosing Your Service Provider 51

Chapter 6: Speeding Up Your Connection 63

Part VI: Web Directory   369

Part VII: Creating Your Own Web Content   473

Starting Fast: An Internet Primer

You already know the Internet is new, exciting, and bursting with all sorts of good things. That's why you bought this book — to learn about every nook and cranny of the dot-com world. Well, there's no reason to wait. It's time to dive right in!

In this part, you'll get connected to the Internet fast. In no time you'll be surfing the web, using e-mail, and creating a simple Web page. So power up your computer and get started!

Getting Connected Fast!

These days the Internet seems to be everywhere. It's on TV, in the newspapers, and even in the movies. E-mail has quickly become a major form of communication, Wall Street is going crazy over Web-based business, and it's hard to find a company nowadays that hasn't added ".com" to the end of its name. If you've picked up the Internet Bible because you would like to be part of the excitement, this chapter will help you get connected fast. To make things easier, you'll even find the software you need on the CD right in the back of this book. There's nothing to stop you. Just sit back, follow along, and get connected!

Finding What You Need to Get Connected

Okay, so you want to get connected to the Internet, but where do you begin? How do you get connected? Do you have to know someone special, or is there some secret ritual involved in becoming a part of the great Internet community? Actually the answers are pretty simple and you're going to find that it's easier than you thought.

To become a part of the Internet community, your PC must be physically connected to the Internet. You have many ways to do this, but you'll probably use a modem — a device that enables your computer to talk with other computers — and a telephone line. You might have other connection possibilities, such as your local cable company or your company network, but a modem and a plain old telephone line is still the most common way to hook up to the Internet.

Who Owns the Internet?

Even though you pay an ISP to access the Internet, that doesn't mean the ISP owns the Internet. In fact, no one owns the Internet; it belongs to everyone. What you have to pay your ISP for is the use of their computers, modems, and other expensive hardware to access the Internet. You aren't really paying to use the Internet—you're paying someone to provide a connection to it.

In addition to your modem and phone line, you also need an Internet Service Provider, or "ISP." An ISP is an organization that has a high-speed connection to the Internet and sells Internet access. You can usually find an ISP in your local area by looking in your phone book under "Internet" or "Internet Service Providers." Local computer retailers can also help you find a provider in your area.

Note

If you bought your computer as part of a package that included a contract for Internet service, the software and hardware are probably already configured for online use. Look for an icon for your new ISP on the computer's desktop area.

Checking out your hardware

Your modem is such an important part of getting connected to the Internet that it's important to make certain your modem is working correctly. If you've already used your modem and know everything is okay, you can skip forward to the next section. If you haven't installed your modem yet, you'll want to follow along to make sure your modem is installed and working properly.

It's easy to check your modem for problems. Start by verifying that the telephone cord is firmly plugged into both the "Telco" (or "Line") jack on your modem and into the phone jack on the wall. If you own an external modem, make sure it's plugged into an electrical outlet, confirm the cable between your computer and your modem is firmly attached at both ends, and look to see if the lights at the front of the modem are lit. You may need to turn on a power switch.

Once you're sure the hardware is plugged in, you then need to make sure your modem is talking to your computer. This means you need to check that the software is installed and working with your operating software.

Connecting with Windows

If you're using Windows, checking to see that your modem is working properly is easy. Here's what you need to do:

1. Turn on your computer and launch Windows, if you have not done so already.

2. Click the Start button and choose Settings ⇨ Control Panel.

3. Double-click the Modems icon to display the Modems Properties dialog box shown in Figure 1-1. You use this dialog box to add, remove, configure, or test your modem.

Depending on which version of Windows you have, if your modem is not yet installed you might see the Install New Modem wizard instead of the Modems Properties dialog. This wizard is described in the next step.

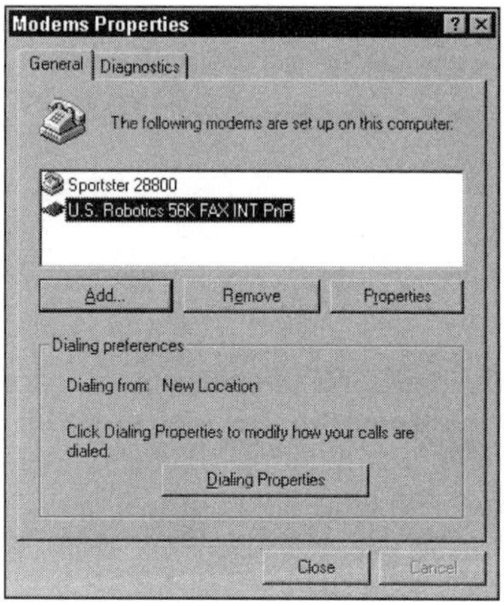

Figure 1-1: Use the Modems Properties dialog box to make sure your modem is working correctly.

4. If your modem is shown in the list, click the Diagnostics tab.

If your modem isn't shown in the list, you need to install modem software, also called a modem "driver," which should have been included with your new modem. Click the Add button and, when the Install New Modem dialog box appears, follow the installation steps.

If you have to install new modem software, just follow through the dialog boxes and accept the default settings. In most cases, Windows already knows enough to find and identify your modem, so you simply have to confirm what it finds.

5. Select your modem from the list on the Diagnostics tab.

The Diagnostics tab list also shows any com (communications) ports installed on your system. Be sure to select the correct port — the one that lists your modem — before continuing.

6. To test your modem, click the More Info button. After a brief wait, the More Info dialog box should appear, similar to the one shown in Figure 1-2. If you see the More Info dialog box, your modem is working correctly.

Note

Don't worry! While the More Info dialog box displays a lot of technical-looking information, you're don't need to do anything. This box is simply used as a reference to tell you that your modem is working.

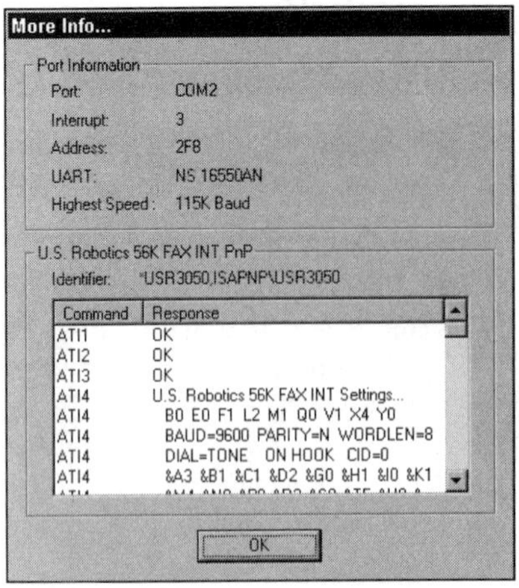

Figure 1-2: The More Info dialog box shows that your modem is working.

```
More Info...
┌─ Port Information ──────────────────┐
│   Port:          COM2               │
│   Interrupt:     3                  │
│   Address:       2F8                │
│   UART:          NS 16550AN         │
│   Highest Speed: 115K Baud          │
└─────────────────────────────────────┘
┌─ U.S. Robotics 56K FAX INT PnP ─────┐
│   Identifier:  *USR3050,ISAPNP\USR3050 │
│                                      │
│   ┌─Command─┬─Response──────────────┐│
│   │ ATI1    │ OK                    ││
│   │ ATI2    │ OK                    ││
│   │ ATI3    │ OK                    ││
│   │ ATI4    │ U.S. Robotics 56K FAX INT Settings... ││
│   │ ATI4    │ B0 E0 F1 L2 M1 Q0 V1 X4 Y0 ││
│   │ ATI4    │ BAUD=9600 PARITY=N WORDLEN=8 ││
│   │ ATI4    │ DIAL=TONE  ON HOOK  CID=0 ││
│   │ ATI4    │ &A3 &B1 &C1 &D2 &G0 &H1 &I0 &K1 ││
│   └─────────┴───────────────────────┘│
└─────────────────────────────────────┘
              [    OK    ]
```

If the More Info dialog box doesn't appear, or if you see a message telling you that your system is unable to communicate with the modem, you'll need to troubleshoot to find out what's wrong. Both Windows 95/98 and Windows 2000 include detailed troubleshooters that can help you pinpoint the problem. To find the modem troubleshooter, click the Help button on the Diagnostics tab of the Modems Properties dialog. When the Help dialog box pops up, click Modem in the list of troubleshooters. This option displays the modem troubleshooter, which should help you discover and correct the problem by following some simple troubleshooter steps.

Connecting with a Macintosh

If you are using a Macintosh, connecting to the Internet can be very simple or somewhat difficult. Most modern Macs have internal modems preinstalled and configured. Internal modems are standard on all new iMacs, iBooks, and PowerBooks, but are optional on the Power Mac G4. If your computer includes an internal modem, you should be ready to go.

But if you have a G4 or an older Mac that does not include a modem, you can still use an external modem that is compatible with your Macintosh. Consult a local computer store that specializes in Macs to make sure you get one that will work with your system. Once you have obtained a modem, you need to do the following:

✦ Make sure that you plug the modem into the correct port on the back of your case. Depending on the modem, you'll probably use a round 8-pin connector (hardware handshaking cable), or a trapezoid-shaped 9-pin serial cable.

✦ Check the modem's documentation to see if any configuration is necessary. Some Mac modems, such as those offered by U.S. Robotics, require you to set some DIP switches on the device before installation.

Connecting with Linux

Getting online is a bit more complicated if you are using the Linux operating system, because various releases of Linux require steps that are a bit different from each other. For now, we'll assume that you are using a common "flavor" of Linux (such as Red Hat), you wish to connect using a modem, and you're familiar with the X Window System.

First, determine which COM port your modem is connected to. Disconnect all serial devices (except the modem), log on as the *root* user. If you are not authorized to log on as *root* on your system, find out who is (it is probably your system administrator). Only the *root* user can install a new modem in Linux. Now do the following:

1. At a command prompt, type `statserial /dev/cua0` to determine the status of the device attached to cua0 (the UNIX equivalent of COM1).

   The *statserial* command runs and provides you with the status of any device connected to that port. Note the output values for CTS and DSR.

2. Repeat step 1 for cua1, cua2, and cua3, noting the output for CTS and DSR in each case. The value for each should be 0, except for the port that actually has the modem attached. So, if the CTS and DSR values for cua2 are 1, then you know that your modem is on COM3.

When you have determined which serial line the modem is attached to, you can give this information to Linux and check to ensure that it is configured properly. Start the X Window System, and in the Control Panel click the Modem Configuration button to open the Configure Modem dialog box, which is shown in Figure 1-3.

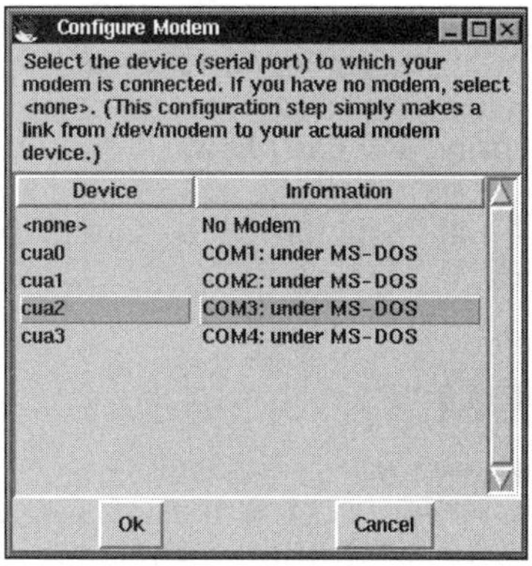

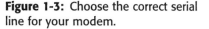

Figure 1-3: Choose the correct serial line for your modem.

Once you've selected the correct serial line, you can configure Linux to connect to your ISP account:

1. Click the Network Configuration button in your Control Panel.

2. In the Nameservers box, type the DNS (*Domain Name Server*) numbers provided to you by your ISP.

3. Click the Interfaces tab and click Add.

4. Choose PPP and click OK. You'll see the Create PPP Interface dialog, where you should enter the ISP's dial-up phone number as well as your login name and password. Click Done when you have entered the required information.

5. Click Save to close Network Configuration.

You should now be ready to connect to the online world. But just to be safe, let's test your connection. Type the following command into your terminal emulator:

```
/sbin/ifup ppp0
```

You should hear your modem dialing up and connecting to your Internet connection. If so, congratulations! Otherwise, some more troubleshooting may be necessary. Consult a Linux-specific book, such as *Red Hat Linux Bible* by Christopher Negus, for more information about setting up your connection.

If all is well, go ahead and log off your connection by giving the following command:

```
/sbin/ifdown ppp0
```

Trying out an Internet Service Provider

Now that your modem is running properly, it's time to find an ISP. There are a lot of ways to find an ISP: You can look in your phone book to see who is offering Internet service; scan the ads in computer magazines; or check to see if your long distance or cable company provides Internet access. There are a lot of options out there, but in order to help you get started quickly, the CD-ROM that comes with this book provides software for two national ISPs: MindSpring and EarthLink.

Cross-Reference
For more information on how to find an ISP that's right for you, be sure to check out Chapter 5, "Choosing Your Service Provider."

Using the Internet Bible CD-ROM

MindSpring is a national Internet Service Provider whose access software for Macintosh or Windows you'll find on the *Internet Bible* CD-ROM. If you want to check out MindSpring, you won't need to go searching for software, phone numbers, or anything else—it's all right there at the back of this book.

The MindSpring software included on the *Internet Bible* CD-ROM is based on Internet Explorer. If you prefer Netscape Navigator, you'll still need to install Internet Explorer to set up your MindSpring account, but once your account is established, you can use whichever browser you prefer. If you like, you can even uninstall the browser you don't use. Versions of Internet Explorer and Netscape Communicator for Windows and Macintosh are available on the *Internet Bible* CD-ROM.

The following example will show you just how easy it is to set up MindSpring as your ISP using the software on the *Internet Bible* CD-ROM. Here's what you need to do:

1. Make certain the *Internet Bible* CD-ROM is in your CD-ROM drive.

2. To launch the MindSpring setup program in Windows, open the My Computer icon on your desktop, double-click the CD-ROM drive, and then open the ISPs folder. Find the mis4011.exe file and double-click it to run the program.

   If you are using a Macintosh, copy the file Install_MindSpring4_01.sit to your desktop, and then double-click to launch the setup program.

   When you run the setup program, you'll see the MindSpring Internet Software Installer, as shown in Figure 1-4.

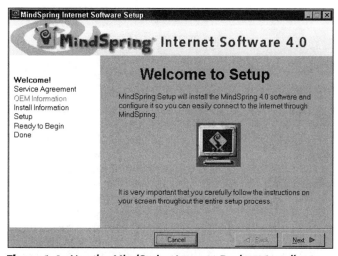

Figure 1-4: Use the MindSpring Internet Desktop Installer to set up your MindSpring account.

3. To begin installation, click Next. Follow the instructions on-screen to complete installation. Once you've completed the sign-up process, you'll be ready to surf the Internet! In addition to MindSpring, software for EarthLink is also provided on the *Internet Bible* CD-ROM, which you can also find in the ISP folder. Follow the same basic instructions as outlined above if you want to give that service a try.

Are you ready to find out what's in cyberspace? Check out Chapter 2, "Taking a Quick Tour of the Internet."

Considering other Internet Service Providers

Along with MindSpring and EarthLink, which you can install using software provided on the CD-ROM at the back of this book, Table 1-1 lists telephone numbers of some national ISPs.

Table 1-1 Some National ISP Options to Consider	
Internet Service Provider	**Telephone**
America Online	1-800-827-6364
CompuServe	1-800-848-8990
Concentric Network	1-800-939-4262
EarthLink	1-888-EARTHLINK ext. 3500
MindSpring Internet	1-888-MSPRING
Prodigy Internet	1-800-PRODIGY
UUNET	1-800-488-6384

Although each ISP has its own membership plan, you'll find that you can try them out with very little risk. Many offer free trial memberships. Others will provide a refund if the service doesn't work out for you. Be sure to ask for all the details, and also ask about any optional service plans. Although most ISPs now offer an unlimited access option for about $20 to $25 per month, you may find one of the more limited options a better buy — especially if you don't spend a lot of time online.

You should also know that some service providers — such as AOL and CompuServe — are actually *online services*, rather than true ISPs. They offer an extensive network of information and services that are only available to members, and some parts of the Internet (like newsgroups and IRC chat) may not be available at all. Further distinguishing them from other service providers, AOL and CompuServe have their own software for Web browsing and e-mail.

Caution   If you want to give a service like AOL or CompuServe a test drive, check around to make sure their software won't impact any other Internet accounts that you already have. For instance, depending on the setup options you choose, AOL 5.0 can take full control of all dial-up settings on your computer. *Windows Magazine*, among others, has reported that they were unable to use their other accounts after installing the AOL 5.0 software.

You may also want to consider signing up with a local ISP. Unfortunately, it's not possible to recommend specific local ISPs in the *Internet Bible*. If you are considering this option, you may want to ask a few of your friends about their experiences with local ISPs before you sign up for service.

Summary

Getting connected to the Internet really won't take very long, but before you start sending e-mails and surfing the Web, you need three things:

✦ A modem and modem software

✦ A telephone line

✦ An Internet Service Provider

Once you're connected, you'll be ready to find out why everyone is talking about the Internet!

✦   ✦   ✦

Taking a Quick Tour of the Internet

I f you've never surfed the Internet you're probably eager to get going and see what all the excitement is about. Surfing the Net is a lot of fun, and it's easy, too. Once you jump a few minor hurdles and get your system connected to the Internet, you'll be ready to go.

Note   Chapter 1 provided you a quick start for connecting to the Internet. This chapter requires that you have access. If you don't already have an account with an Internet Service Provider (ISP), you need to set one up before you complete this chapter.

On the CD-ROM   To help you get started quickly, software for two national ISPs, EarthLink and MindSpring, can be found on the CD-ROM in the back of this book. You'll also find copies of Netscape Communicator, Microsoft Internet Explorer, and Opera on the CD-ROM as well. If you would like to know more about selecting an ISP that will meet your needs, take a look at Chapter 5, "Choosing Your Service Provider."

Getting Ready to Surf

Your Internet Service Provider (ISP) will give you the information you need to connect to the Internet. Some of the settings are pretty standard, and the default settings will probably work just fine. Some of the information, such as the phone number and your account name, is pretty important—you won't be able to connect without it. Be ready to write it down!

Here are three basic items you'll need to access your ISP account:

✦ A *dial-in phone number*—the phone number your computer must call to connect to the Internet. If you're using a national ISP rather than a local one, make sure the number you receive isn't a toll call.

✦ Your *user name*—this is how you will be identified by your ISP and may or may not be case-sensitive. This is sometimes called your *account*.

✦ Your *password*—this provides secure access to your ISP account and prevents others from logging on under your user name. Your password should be known only by you. It may or may not be case-sensitive, too.

 Caution Watch out for 800 or 888 toll-free access numbers. The phone call may be free, but ISPs usually charge a premium rate for using one of these numbers to access the Internet.

You'll generally need to enter your account information once, the first time you connect to the Internet. However, it's a good idea to have all of your account information available before you attempt to connect. Your ISP's technical support line should also be a good problem-solving resource.

 Caution For security purposes, memorize your User ID and password! Don't write them down on a yellow notepad and stick them on your computer for all the world to see. A lot of computer hackers would love to access your account and cause serious mischief. Don't make it easy for them by advertising your personal access information.

Surfing for the First Time

These days it seems like everyone wants to browse—or surf—the *World Wide Web*. The *Web* is just one part (albeit the most popular part) of the larger phenomenon known as the Internet. The Internet also encompasses things like e-mail, Usenet newsgroups, chat rooms, and much, much more. But for now, let's stick to the Web (no pun intended). In this section you'll learn how to take your first steps onto the World Wide Web and embark on your journey into the online world.

To surf the Web you need a *Web browser*—a program that enables you to view the contents of pages on the Web, the graphical portion of the Internet. These days most people use Microsoft Internet Explorer or Netscape Navigator as their Web browsers, although Opera is making some inroads here. All three do an excellent job of displaying most Web pages. These browsers have a few minor differences, but in most cases choosing a Web browser is simply a matter of personal preference. You don't really have to choose just one Web browser, either. There's no reason (other than a lack of disk space) why you can't try each and make your ultimate choice based on your own experiences. In this section we'll use Internet Explorer, but if your choice is Netscape Navigator or Opera you'll be able to follow along easily.

Tip

Unless your computer is connected to the Internet through your work or school's network, your computer has to be connected to the Internet through your modem.

If you have a single telephone line that you use for both voice and modem calls, you won't be able to make or receive voice calls while you're surfing the Internet. Also, if someone picks up an extension phone while you're using the Internet, it's quite likely that your connection will be disrupted. Keep these factors in mind and free up the telephone line when you're not actively surfing the Internet. Finally, be sure to disable call waiting for the line connected to the Internet. An incoming call will break your connection.

No matter which Web browser you choose, you'll probably enjoy Web browsing more if you don't have to constantly scroll up and down or left and right to see the Web pages you visit. One thing that can help reduce the amount of scrolling you need to do is to set your screen resolution to either 800 × 600 or, if your monitor is large enough, to 1024 × 768. If you have a very large monitor you may even be able to use a higher resolution setting.

Starting your Web browser

No matter which Web browser you choose, the first time you open the program you'll probably have to go through several steps to configure your Internet service. In Chapter 1 you saw one example of doing just this, so here we'll assume that your account is already set up and that you're ready to surf. If this isn't the case, please go back to Chapter 1 and make certain your Internet account is ready to go.

Launching a Web browser is no more complicated than starting any other program on your computer. You'll probably find an icon on your desktop for either Internet Explorer, Netscape Navigator, or possibly even Opera. You'll also probably find a Start or Apple menu item you can use to load your browser. Choose your favorite method and start your Web browser now.

Once you've launched your Web browser, it should automatically detect your Internet connection settings and dial your ISP's phone number. While it is doing this, you may see a dialog box showing information about your progress in making a connection to the Internet. In most cases you won't have to respond to the messages, although if you haven't configured your system to connect automatically you may have to click a Connect button to initiate the connection.

Note

One of the most frustrating experiences you may encounter in attempting to browse the Web is the inability to connect reliably to your ISP. If you can success-fully connect some of the time, but are unable to connect at other times, the prob-lem may be that your ISP has too many customers and not enough equipment and staff. If the problem persists, you may want to consider trying a different ISP. Many of the national ISPs, such as those featured on the *Internet Bible* CD-ROM, offer new customers a free trial period. You may find that simply selecting a new ISP solves most (or even all) of your connection problems.

Once your account has been verified (that is, checked against your user name and password), your browser loads and displays a "home page," which is a Web page your browser first loads after it is launched. If you are using Internet Explorer, the home page will probably look similar to what is shown in Figure 2-1. Keep in mind, however, that the information shown on Web pages is constantly being updated, so your start page will certainly display different information.

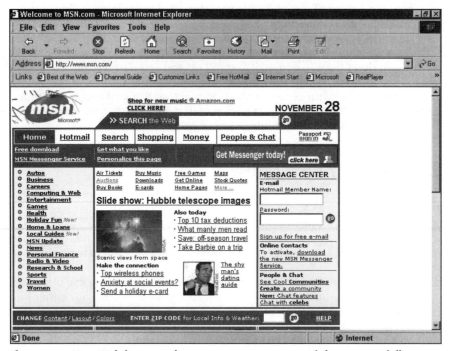

Figure 2-1: Your Web browser shows your start page once it has successfully connected to the Internet.

Browsing the Web

Now that you've connected to the Internet and have loaded your first Web page, take a moment to look at the toolbar buttons found at the top of the Browser window. The toolbar for Internet Explorer is shown in Figure 2-2. These are the tools you'll most often use to move around the Web.

Move your mouse around the screen and notice when the pointer changes to a hand. The hand indicates that you're pointing to a *link*, which is usually a connection to another Web page. Linked text is usually underlined and highlighted with a different text color to distinguish it from regular text.

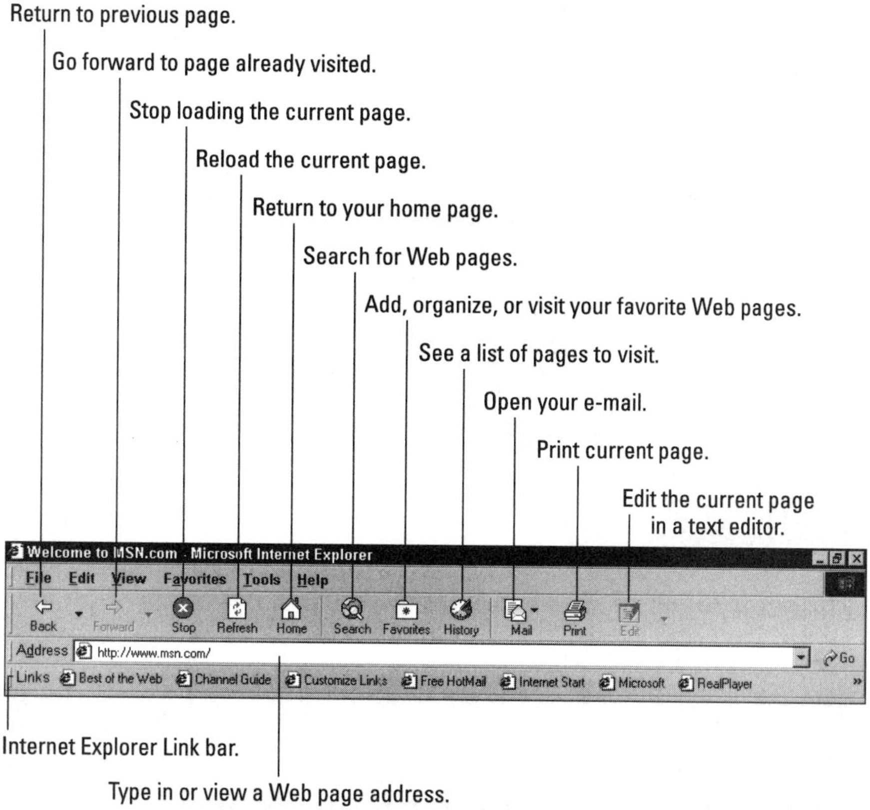
Return to previous page.
Go forward to page already visited.
Stop loading the current page.
Reload the current page.
Return to your home page.
Search for Web pages.
Add, organize, or visit your favorite Web pages.
See a list of pages to visit.
Open your e-mail.
Print current page.
Edit the current page in a text editor.
Welcome to MSN.com - Microsoft Internet Explorer
File Edit View Favorites Tools Help
Back Forward Stop Refresh Home Search Favorites History Mail Print Edit
Address http://www.msn.com/
Go
Links Best of the Web Channel Guide Customize Links Free HotMail Internet Start Microsoft RealPlayer
Internet Explorer Link bar.
Type in or view a Web page address.

Figure 2-2: The toolbar buttons in Netscape Navigator and Opera are similar to those in Internet Explorer—the names may be a little different, but you'll still be able to accomplish similar tasks.

On the MSN Web page (`www.msn.com`), click the Shopping link, which you'll find at the top of the page. The MSN shopping page should appear. It serves as an index to shopping for items in a variety of categories. To see how this site works, click the Books & Magazines link to display the list of related subcategories, as shown in Figure 2-3. When you click this link, you might also see various links to books and other related sites. If you had selected one of the other major categories, the links would have reflected the category you selected.

Most Web pages provide additional links you can click to take you to many different sites on the Web. Maybe now it's becoming a little clearer why this is called a Web. Given all the links you can click to jump from one place to another, the Web is truly interconnected just like a spider's web. If you don't find yourself spending hours visiting Web sites at random, you've got a lot more willpower than most people!

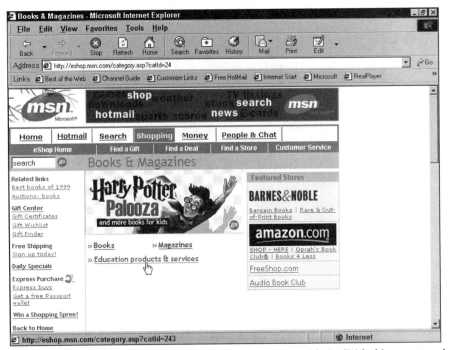

Figure 2-3: Like many online directories, this shopping guide is divided into categories.

Doing a Quick Search on the Web

You'll probably find the Internet to be a bit confusing at first. The Web has no road maps, and it's constantly changing. You'll run into a lot of dead ends, but you may well find several paths that all lead to your destination. In the following sections you'll learn how you can find what you need on the Web.

Understanding Web addresses

One of the keys to finding things on the Web is to understand how Internet addresses work. When you know this, your searching becomes much easier.

Everything on the Internet is identified by an address called a *URL* — a Uniform Resource Locator. Some people call them "earls." Either way, URLs are your tickets to Internet surfing, enabling your computer to locate the Web pages you want to see. URLs take the following form:

```
protocol://server_address/document_name
```

This may look a little complicated, but it's really pretty simple. For example, the following URL locates the home page of IDG Books Worldwide:

```
http://www.idgbooks.com/
```

In this case, `http://` signifies *HyperText Transfer Protocol,* which is the way Web pages are transmitted (this indicates the protocol you're using). The next part of the URL, `www.idgbooks`, identifies the IDG Books Worldwide Web server. As you might already know, the `.com` portion (often called "dot-com") stands for "company" (or "commercial" depending on who you ask) and identifies IDG as a commercial enterprise. The final part, the forward slash (/), simply says you want to load the default page.

If you skip the trailing slash it's automatically assumed you want to load the default page on the server. If you skip the protocol indicator, most browsers will assume you mean `http://`. To learn more about the ins-and-outs of URLs, see Appendix A, "What's This URL Stuff?"

Don't make the mistake of using the backslash (\) in place of the forward slash (/) in Web addresses. Backslashes may be more familiar on PCs, but because the Internet uses UNIX naming conventions, you must use the forward slash rather than the backslash in Internet addresses.

Finding things on the Web

Finding what you want on the Web would be virtually impossible if it weren't for the existence of *search engines* — services that index the sites on the Web and automatically search through their indices at your request.

You can use any of several well-known search engines, including Yahoo, AltaVista, Excite, and so on. The good news is that using these search engines is free. The not-so-good news is that you may need to try more than one search engine to find what you're looking for. Still, if something exists on the Web, one or more of the search engines will almost certainly find it for you.

In this example you'll see how to conduct a very simple Web search. To learn more about doing Web searches, check out Chapter 16, "Using Search Engines."

To practice finding Web sites — in this case the IDG Books Worldwide Web site — try the following:

1. Start your Web browser and connect to the Internet, if you haven't already done so.

   In this case, we're using Internet Explorer and continuing from the previous examples in this chapter. You, of course, can use your favorite Web browser.

2. Click the Search button on the toolbar to load the search toolbar (or search page, depending on your browser settings).

   The search page provides links to several search engines. These search engines use *keywords* you enter to find Web pages. You may need to get creative in figuring out which keywords will identify the correct Web pages.

3. Type **"IDG Books"** in the keyword text box — the box next to the Search button on the search page.

   Be sure you include the opening and closing quotation marks when you enter the search phrase. When you enclose the keywords in quotation marks, most search engines treat the keywords as a single phrase rather than separate words to find. If you omit the quotation marks, the search looks for sites that have either "IDG" or "books," which would probably match many more sites that might not be of interest to you.

4. Click the Search button next to the text box — not the Search button on the toolbar — to begin looking for Web pages that include the keywords you entered.

   When you click the Search button, the search engine sifts through its index to find Web sites that match your request. These may include exactly the Web site you'd like to find, and they may include many others where it also finds the keywords. If you're lucky, your keywords will narrow the search enough so that you can easily find just the site you want.

5. To visit one of the sites found by the search engine, click the link.

6. To see the entire IDB Books Worldwide Web site, click the Close button on the Search bar.

Tip   You can also go to a Web page by typing the URL in the Address text box yourself. To go directly to the IDG Books Worldwide Web site, type `http://www.idgbooks.com` in the Address text box. In many cases you don't have to type the entire address. You could, for example, just type `www.idgbooks.com` rather than `http://www.idgbooks.com`.

Because different search engines index Web pages quite differently, you may discover that some search engines find very few pages that match your keywords, while others may find so many it's hard to know which to visit. You may want to try out several different search engines to see which of them produces the best results in finding the Web sites you seek. In addition, Web pages quite often include links to related sites. If you click those links you'll probably find other quite interesting pages that may not show up when you use one of the search engines.

Keeping Track of Your Favorite Sites

As you browse the Web, you'll discover Web pages that are very interesting and worth a repeat visit. But how do you get back? You could just try to remember how you got to your favorite pages, but there's a much easier way to keep track of the sites you like.

You can tell your Web browser to remember the addresses for your favorite pages so that, when you're ready for a return visit, you can simply pick out the page from your list of favorites. For example, let's say you check the snow report for your local ski areas every day during the winter. Clicking the ski report's name from your list is much easier than entering a long and hard-to-remember URL. You'll be on the slopes that much faster!

Internet Explorer and Netscape Navigator enable you to store a list of your favorite Web site addresses. In Internet Explorer, the list of your favorite Web site addresses is called *Favorites*; in Netscape Navigator it's called *Bookmarks*, and in Opera it's called a *Hot List*. It really doesn't matter what the list is called — it's a useful feature that makes it fast and easy for you to go back and visit your favorite sites.

Keeping track of your favorite Web sites is easy. Here's how you can add the IDG Books Worldwide Web site to your list of favorite Web sites:

1. Start your Web browser.
2. Type the following text in the Address box: `http://www.idgbooks.com`.
3. Press Enter to go to the IDG Books Worldwide home page.
4. Click Favorites (or Bookmarks, if you're using Navigator).
5. Select Add To Favorites to display the Add Favorites dialog box, as shown in Figure 2-4.

   You'll see a different dialog box in Netscape Navigator or Opera, of course, but the procedure is similar.

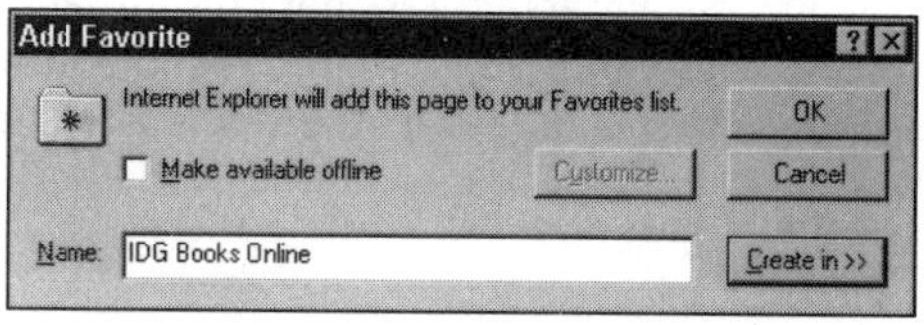

Figure 2-4: Use the Add Favorites dialog box to add a Web site to your favorite Web site list.

6. Click OK to add the page to your list of favorite Web sites.

7. Click the Favorites button on the toolbar to display the list of your favorite Web sites.

8. Scroll down the list until you highlight IDG Books Online.

9. Click the IDG Books Online item in the drop-down list to quickly return to the Web site as shown in Figure 2-5.

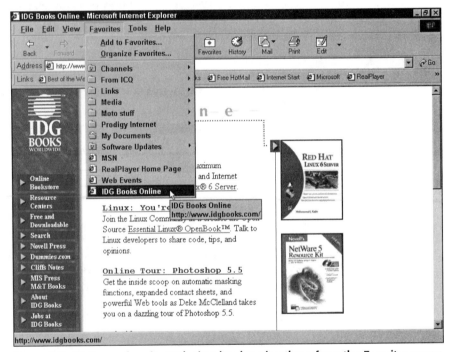

Figure 2-5: Visit your favorite Web sites by choosing them from the Favorites menu.

Tip

If you use Windows 98, you can also display an address bar on your Taskbar. Right-click a blank space on the Taskbar, choose Toolbars from the shortcut menu that appears and select Address. Type a Web address in the address bar and press Enter to go to the Web site.

Summary

Now that you've read this chapter, you have the basic tools you need to surf the Web. You should now be able to launch your Web browser, connect and log in to your ISP, use links to move from one Web page to another, conduct a simple search for a Web site, and create a list of your favorite Web sites.

Surfing the Web is pretty easy, and now that you know how to find those interesting sites, you'll probably spend hours seeing what's out there to enjoy.

✦   ✦   ✦

Getting Started With E-mail

No matter how much hype you hear about all the rest of
the Internet, surveys have shown that more people use
the Internet for *e-mail*—electronic mail—than for any other
purpose. People like e-mail for lots of reasons—it's fast, it's
cheap, and it's very convenient. After all, who couldn't like
something that enables you to send a message halfway around
the world in an instant for far less than the cost of an old
fashioned first-class postage stamp?

What is e-mail? What do you need in order to use it? How can
you send and receive messages? If you're asking yourself these
questions, you've come to the right place for the answers.

Understanding How E-Mail Works

Knowing what e-mail is makes it a lot easier to understand
how e-mail works. At the most basic level, e-mail is simply a
file that's sent from one computer to another. In virtually all
cases, that file is sent across a *network* that connects the two
computers. You may not realize there's a network involved,
but it's usually there anyway. (The Internet, of course, is really
just a huge network that connects millions of computers—
including yours.)

Of course, e-mail messages are meant to be read by someone.
Most e-mail only consists of text, but there's nothing to stop
you from sending other types of files as part of your e-mail
messages.

Well, *almost* nothing can stop you from sending other types of
files as a part of your e-mail. It turns out that the Internet has a
lot of funny little idiosyncrasies. Because the Internet started
on UNIX, a popular operating system that has been used for

running networks since the 1970s, all files need to be *encoded* on the sending end, and then *decoded* into its original form on the receiving end. In most cases, you won't know your files were encoded and decoded, but sometimes the automatic process breaks down and you receive a message full of garbage. If this happens to you — and it may — you have several choices.

 To learn more about what to do about encoded files, see Chapter 14, "Doing More with E-Mail."

E-mail necessities

Not surprisingly, you'll need a few things before you can send or receive e-mail from your computer. Here are the most important:

✦ A computer, modem, and a phone line with which you can access the Internet. (And by the way, although some new cellular phones have limited e-mail services built in, you're on your own if you want to use one of those for your e-mail.)

✦ E-mail software, which you can use to write, edit, send, and receive your e-mail messages. Here, too, you'll find plenty of choices.

✦ An account with an Internet Service Provider (ISP) or an account with a free e-mail service. The *Internet Bible* CD-ROM has several ISP options you can choose from — these are covered in more detail in Chapter 5.

 Actually, you don't even need an e-mail program for some Web-based e-mail services. Some services, such as Hotmail, enable you to receive and send e-mail from any computer that has a Web browser installed. This means that you could check your mail on a Web-connected computer at your local library or at a friend's house.

 To learn more about Web-based e-mail services, see Chapter 13, "Using Web-Based E-Mail Services."

The technical e-mail information you need

Your ISP or e-mail service provider should furnish a list of technical information you need so you can access your mail account. At the very least, this list includes the following information:

✦ The *dial-in phone number* — the phone number your computer must call to connect to the Internet.

✦ *Your user name* — this may or may not be case-sensitive. If it is case-sensitive, you'll need to use the correct combination of upper and lower case characters to connect. If your ISP account offers multiple e-mail boxes, you will need a separate name for each box.

✦ *Your password*—this may or may not be case-sensitive. Passwords are more likely to be case-sensitive than the user name. Again, if you have multiple mail boxes each one should have a unique password.

✦ *The mail server*—this may be two names, one being the *SMTP* (Simple Mail Transfer Protocol) *outgoing host*, the other being the *POP* (or IMAP) *server host*. If you are using a Web-based e-mail service you will probably receive an HTML account server name instead.

Tip   If you can't access your ISP directly, perhaps because you're on vacation, you can always access your e-mail by specifying your user name, password, and mail server if you log on to someone else's Internet account. Just remember to change these settings back to their original values when you're done accessing your mail, so the person who loaned you an account can get his or her mail—not yours.

Try to get all of the preceding information in writing, and keep it on a piece of paper in a safe place. Print it out if you need to. If you aren't sure you understand part of the information, check it out before you go on. It's a lot easier to enter the correct information in the first place than to figure out later what is causing problems.

Understanding e-mail addresses

Any time you send a letter to someone you have to put the correct delivery address on the letter so the mail can be delivered to the right person. E-mail is no different— it has to be addressed correctly or it won't be delivered.

For now you don't need to worry about what all the pieces of an e-mail address really mean, but it is important to have a general understanding so you can be pretty sure you've used a valid e-mail address.

E-mail addresses generally look something like this:

```
bunderdahl@idgbooks.com
```

Here's a simple explanation of the various parts of the address:

✦ *bunderdahl* is the name of the recipient. Often this is the person's real name, but it can also be a nickname or even a set of numbers.

✦ @ is a separator between the recipient's name and the rest of the address. E-mail addresses can't include any spaces, so the @ sign lets the mail system know when the recipient's name is complete.

✦ *idgbooks* is the mail server's *domain* name. That's just a fancy way of saying you don't have to type out the IP address for the recipient's mail server — you can use the name of the mail server rather than a string of numbers.

✦ *.com* is the type of mail server. The increasingly ubiquitous .com is used for commercial organizations, but the mail server could also be denoted by a *.net*, *.edu* (for an educational organization), or *.org* (for a nonprofit organization). The exact meaning of each combination is not all that important, as long as you type them correctly when you are addressing outgoing messages.

E-mail addresses usually aren't case-sensitive. If someone tells you that their e-mail address is BobSmith@Smith.Net, you'll probably be just as successful sending him a message at BOBSMITH@SMITH.NET or bobsmith@smith.net — or even bObSmItH@sMiTh.NeT. In the early days of Internet e-mail, some mail servers were a little picky about this sort of thing, but you probably don't have to worry about it.

Tip   When someone sends you an e-mail message, right-click the return address and choose Add to Address Book in Outlook Express to quickly save the e-mail address in your address book. This will save time and you won't have to worry about typing errors, either.

Quickly Sending E-Mail

Now that you know e-mail basics, you're just about ready to give e-mail a try. If you're using Windows 98 or Internet Explorer 4+, you probably already have Outlook Express loaded on your system. If you want to use a different e-mail program, you can still follow along with this section, although you may have to hunt a bit more to find some of the commands.

Cross-Reference   To learn about the features of some other well-known e-mail programs, check out Chapter 12, "Choosing an E-Mail Client and Using E-Mail."

Setting up a mail account

If you're using Windows, Outlook Express may or may not already be installed. Check to see if there is an Outlook Express icon next to the Start button. If there isn't, you may want to install it so you can follow along with the examples. You don't have to keep using Outlook Express if you prefer a different e-mail program, but you may want to give it a try for now. If it's already installed, skip ahead to step 7.

To install Outlook Express in Windows:

1. Click the Start button to display the Windows Start menu.

2. Select Settings ➪ Control Panel.

3. Double-click the Add/Remove Programs icon.

4. Click the Windows Setup tab.

You use the Windows Setup tab to add or remove the optional Windows elements.

5. Select Outlook Express as shown in Figure 3-1. It should show up in the list if you have installed Internet Explorer 4 or 5.

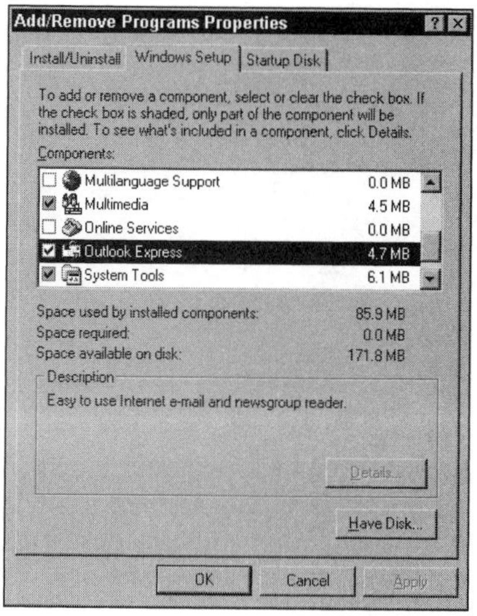

Figure 3-1: To install Outlook Express, select it from the list in the Windows Setup tab of the Add/Remove Program Properties dialog box.

6. Click OK to continue.

You may need to insert your Windows CD-ROM to complete the installation. Some PCs have all of the Windows installation files stored on the hard disk and don't require the CD-ROM to install additional components.

7. Once Outlook Express is installed, double-click its icon on your desktop, or click Start ➪ Programs ➪ Outlook Express.

If this is the first time you have used Outlook Express, you may see the first screen of the Internet Connect Wizard.

8. If the wizard appears, answer the questions it asks, as shown in Figure 3-2, clicking Next after each screen is complete.

Outlook Express first asks for your display name. This is the name that recipients will see when you send them mail, so choose carefully. The rest of the information in the wizard should have been provided by your ISP, including your e-mail address, the type of server you use for incoming mail, the mail server names, and your account name and password.

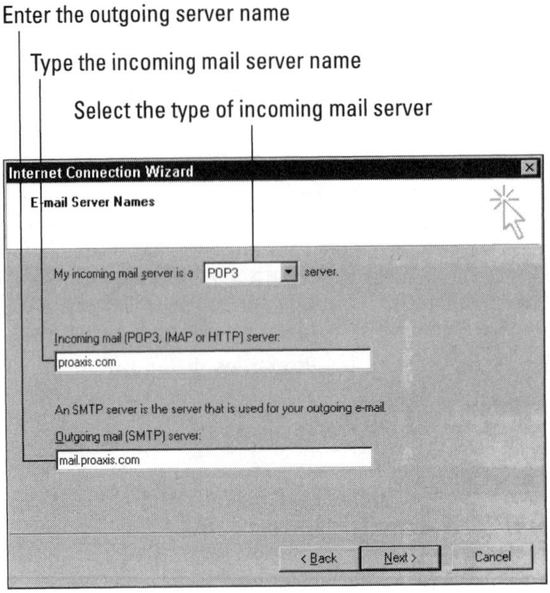

Enter the outgoing server name

Type the incoming mail server name

Select the type of incoming mail server

Figure 3-2: Answer the questions on-screen to set up
your e-mail account.

After you finish the wizard, Outlook Express will open and, if necessary, will
attempt to dial your Internet connection. Now you're ready to begin exchanging
some mail!

> **Note**   If you have never connected to the Internet with the computer you're using, you
> may be sent directly to the Internet Connection Wizard after you have finished
> installing Outlook Express. To learn more about setting up your connection, take a
> look at Chapter 1, "Getting Connected Fast!"

Creating a quick message

Once Outlook Express is set up, you're just a few minutes away from sending some
e-mail. If you've never used e-mail before you may be surprised at just how quickly
and easily you can send a message. This is one instance where the world is literally
right at your fingertips!

> **Note**   One characteristic that e-mail shares with ordinary mail may surprise you. Even
> though your e-mail messages may travel halfway around the world in seconds,
> there's no guarantee about just when the recipients will see your message. The
> reason for this is simple — unless they log on and retrieve their messages, your
> message could sit on their mail server for hours, days, or longer. What this means
> to you is that if the message is truly urgent, e-mail is no substitute for a good old-
> fashioned phone call.

To create and send a quick message in Outlook Express:

1. Launch Outlook Express. When the program opens, it will display a window similar to Figure 3-3.

   Outlook Express is customizable, so your screen may look a little different than Figure 3-3. Don't worry about any differences — they won't affect your ability to create and send a message.

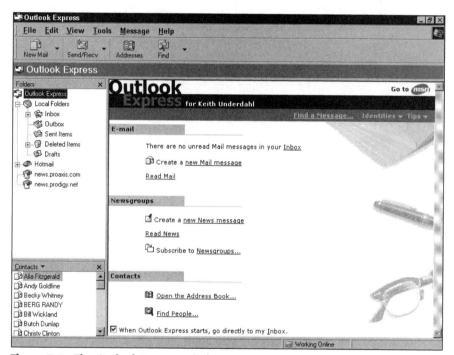

Figure 3-3: The Outlook Express window

2. Click the New Mail button on the toolbar to open a new message window.

3. Type the recipient's e-mail address in the To: text box.

   If you don't happen to know anyone else's e-mail address, type your own e-mail address to send the message to yourself.

4. Type a short description in the Subject text box.

   It's a good idea to make certain the subject gives the recipient a good feel for the content of your message — especially if you're sending your message to a busy person!

5. Type your message in the message section, as shown in Figure 3-4.

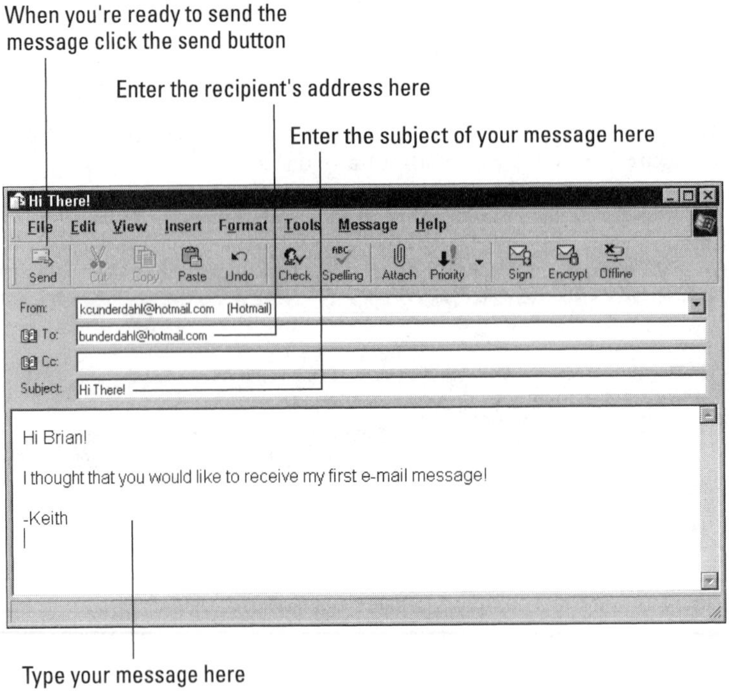

When you're ready to send the
message click the send button

Enter the recipient's address here

Enter the subject of your message here

Type your message here

Figure 3-4: Use the new message window to create your e-mail message quickly.

6. Click the Send button to send your message.

7. Depending on your Outlook Express settings, you may (or may not) see a dialog box advising you that your message has been placed in the "Outbox" and that it will be sent the next time you click Send and Receive. If so, click the OK button to return to Outlook Express.

8. Click the Send and Receive button (located near the top of the Outlook Express window) to send your new message.

If you sent the message to yourself, it may be delivered immediately or you may have to log on a second time to receive the message, depending on your mail server. Messages you send to other people will probably take a few minutes (or maybe even hours) because they're often routed through several computer systems on their way to the destination system.

Receiving Your E-Mail

Everyone likes to receive mail, as long as it isn't from your credit card company or part of a bulk mailing campaign! Most people enjoy getting e-mail, too.

Note

Well, okay, all e-mail isn't welcome. Some people send out unsolicited mass mailings that are generally called *spam*. Fortunately, effective measures to counteract the "spammers" are being developed, and many large Internet service providers (such as AOL and CompuServe) have even canceled the accounts of some privacy-invaders who send out spam. For more information on how you can avoid spam, see Chapter 15, "Taking Charge of your E-Mail."

Receiving your e-mail is pretty easy. In fact, when you log on to send messages, your e-mail software automatically checks to see if you have any incoming messages. You can check for new messages any time you like. In Outlook Express, just click the Send and Receive button.

Automating your e-mail

It's rather easy to get wrapped up in a project and just plain forget to click that Send and Receive button. But unless you check frequently, your incoming messages won't get to you very quickly. There has to be a better way!

Most e-mail software does offer a better way to check your e-mail. In Outlook Express, for example, you can tell the program to automatically check for messages at specified intervals. That way you don't have to remember to check for new mail.

To tell Outlook Express to automatically check for new mail, select Tools ➪ Options to display the Options dialog box shown in Figure 3-5. Make certain the *Check for new messages every xx minute(s)* checkbox is selected, and that the time interval is short enough so your messages aren't delayed too long.

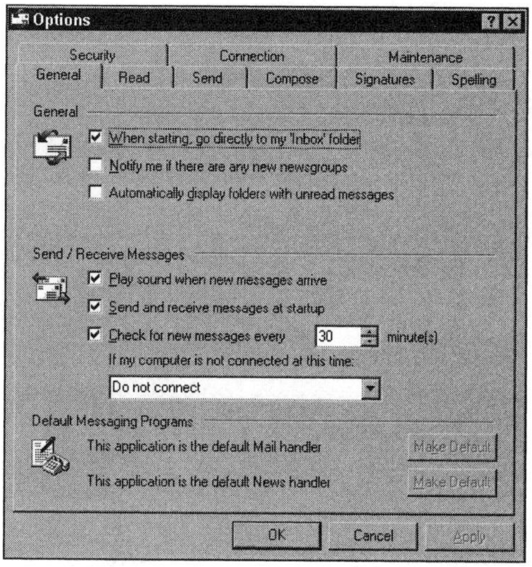

Figure 3-5: Using the Options dialog box, you can tell Outlook Express to automatically check for new messages.

> **Tip**   While you have the Options dialog box open, you may want to check out some of the other settings. To find out more about one of the options, click the question mark icon near the upper right corner of the dialog box to change the mouse pointer into a question mark, and then click an option. When you click an item with the question-mark pointer, a short explanation of the item is displayed.

Reading your e-mail

To read your incoming messages in Outlook Express, open the Inbox folder (depending on how you have Outlook Express configured, the Inbox may be opened automatically when you start Outlook Express). If the Inbox isn't already open, click the Inbox icon in the Folder list along the left side of the Outlook Express window.

Figure 3-6 shows the Outlook Express Inbox. Your incoming messages are listed in the upper pane of the Inbox, and the currently selected e-mail message appears in the lower pane.

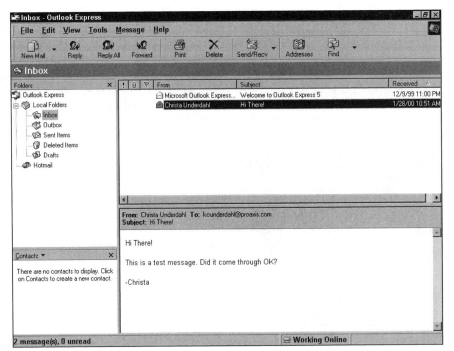

Figure 3-6: Use the Inbox to read your e-mail.

> **Tip**   If the preview pane in the Inbox isn't big enough for you, double-click a message in the message list to open it in its own window.

If you want to reply to a message you've received, click the Reply button to send a reply only to the person who sent you the message. To send your reply to everyone who received a copy of the message, click the Reply All button. You can also forward a copy of the message by clicking the Forward button. When you reply to a message, your reply automatically contains a copy of the text in the original message. When you forward a message, the forwarded message includes not only the original text but also any file attachments.

Summary

In this chapter you've seen a brief introduction to sending and receiving e-mail. You've learned what e-mail really is, what you need so you can use it, how the e-mail address works, how to quickly send an e-mail message, and how to receive and read your e-mail.

Of course there's a lot more to using e-mail effectively than what could be covered in one short chapter. To see how you can really take control of your e-mail, be sure to spend some time with the chapters in Part 4, "Using Easy and Effective E-Mail."

✦   ✦   ✦

Creating a Web Page in Ten Minutes

Just looking around on the Internet isn't nearly as much fun as actually having your own Web site. When you create your own Web site, people can come to visit you and see what you have to offer. You can be famous!

Believe it or not, creating your first Web page isn't hard. You can have your page ready in about ten minutes or so — even if you've never created anything more complicated than a simple memo!

This chapter is a bit of a teaser, too. By showing you how quickly and easily you can create a simple Web site, we hope to pique your interest in learning a lot more about the possibilities for your Web site. In later chapters you have a chance to do just that, especially in Part VII, "Creating Your Own Web Content," where you'll learn how to make your Web site the one everyone wants to see.

Doing Basic Web Design

The World Wide Web has come to dominate the way we think about the Internet. It's more dynamic, more informative, and usually more entertaining than e-mail and Usenet. The Web has become such a valuable tool because anyone with the ability to get online can create their own Web pages, thus adding to the collective content of the online world. Here, we'll focus on Web page basics — the information you need to begin making a Web page of your own.

Understanding HTML basics

The Web is the graphical part of the Internet. It's a place with lots of colors, graphics, images, sounds, video, and a whole bunch of other exciting stuff. The Web is colorful because Web pages are programmed using *HTML* — HyperText Markup Language. Web browsers — programs such as Internet Explorer, Netscape Navigator, and Opera — translate HTML into the fancy-looking pages you see when you surf the Web.

Does this mean you have to learn HTML to create a Web page? Do you have to get a pocket protector and a bunch of leaky ballpoint pens? No, you don't have to learn HTML just to create a good-looking Web page. It's quite possible (and even easy) to create Web pages without ever seeing any HTML code, or even being aware that your page is programmed in HTML.

So just what does this HTML look like? Figure 4-1 shows some of the HTML code that makes up a simple Web page. Even though this code is pretty simple, it's obvious that the Web wouldn't be nearly so popular if you had to put up with viewing the HTML code rather than seeing the end result!

```
index.htm - Notepad
File  Edit  Search  Help
<html><head><style type="text/css"> <!--TD { font-family: Verdana,
Arial, san-serif; font-size: 10pt; }// --></style><title>Underdahl
Online</title></HEAD><BODY>
<CENTER>
<h1>Underdahl Online</h1>
<img src="chair.jpg" alt="The boys">
</center>
<h2>Contents</H2>
<ul>
        <li><a href="family.htm">Family Page</A></li>
        <li><a href="resume.htm">Keith's Resume</A></li>
        <li><a href="links.htm">Links</A></li>
<p><i>Last updated January 16th, 1999</></p>
<p><a href="mailto:kcunderdahl@proaxis.com">Send us an e-mail!</A></p>
</body></html>
```

Figure 4-1: It's a good thing your Web browser automatically converts HTML code into graphics.

After you've created some Web pages the easy way, you may want to learn some HTML. For one thing, learning HTML will help you to handle more complex tasks, such as programming your Web page to recognize the types of Web browsers visitors to your page are using. This information is vital if you want to get really fancy, because tricks that work well with one Web browser may not work at all with a different browser.

 You can learn more about some of the fancy things you can do with Web pages in Part VII, "Creating Your Own Web Content."

Are you curious about what the HTML code you saw in Figure 4-1 looks like when seen through a Web browser? If so, have a look at Figure 4-2.

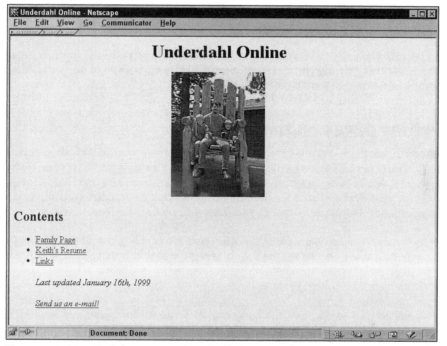

Figure 4-2: Your Web browser automatically converts the HTML code in Figure 4-1 into this Web page.

Creating your Web pages

So just how does an ordinary person create Web pages without all the fuss and mess of programming in HTML? One way is to use a graphical Web page editor, such as Microvision's Web Express, Netscape Composer, or FrontPage from Microsoft. Graphical Web page editors enable you to concentrate on the appearance of your Web page without forcing you to deal with a new programming language such as HTML.

Later in this chapter you'll see how you can use Netscape Composer to quickly create Web pages. Composer is a program offered free by Netscape and comes as part of the Netscape Communicator package.

You've probably heard the term *Web site* and may be wondering how a Web page and a Web site are related. A Web site is just a collection of one or more Web pages that are *linked* together so you can quickly move from one page to another.

Typically this means you would have a *home page* (an introductory page to the rest of your site) on a Web site that contains *links* that a visitor can click to visit the rest of the pages that make up the Web site. For example, if you were creating a Web site for a small business, you might have a Web page devoted to each of the company's products, or a page with information on how customers could reach various departments such as customer service.

You create each page of a Web site individually and then add the links as needed. There's nothing wrong with starting your Web site with a single page and then adding additional pages as you need them.

Putting pages on the Web

Once you create your Web site, you'll want to put it out on the Web so everyone can see it. Normally this means you must transfer the files that make up your Web site to a Web server. In many cases, the Web server you'll use will be one that belongs to your Internet Service Provider (ISP). If you're making a company Web site and your company has its own Web server, you'll need to place your files on that server.

Tip   If your ISP or company doesn't provide Web server space, consider publishing your Web site on one of the free Web servers available online, such as GeoCities. Free Web servers are described in greater detail in Chapter 25, "Applying Intermediate Web Design Features."

To make certain no one else changes your Web site without your permission, special access controls limit who can change the files on the Web server. Although you may only need your regular user name and password, it's best to check with your ISP (or your company Web site administrator) before you attempt to place your files on the Web server. This way you'll be prepared if you need to enter a special password for the Web server.

When you place your Web site on the Web server, it's important to remember that you need to include all related files. If your Web site includes graphics, such as pictures or photos, that are in separate files, those graphics files must also be placed on the Web server. Otherwise, visitors to your Web site will be greeted with a *broken link* and won't be able to view the pictures. Likewise, if your Web site has more than one page, each Web page file must be located on the server, too.

Using Netscape Composer

If you have Netscape Communicator installed, you probably also have Composer —even if you haven't noticed it yet. Composer is an excellent entry-level Web-site editor that let's you get started creating simple, attractive Web pages in just a few minutes. Other editors offer a more complete set of advanced features, but you won't miss them when you are creating your first Web page.

Note

If you have only the Netscape Navigator Web browser, you may not have Composer. If you don't have Composer, install Netscape Communicator 4.7 from the *Internet Bible* CD-ROM, as described in Appendix C, "Using the Internet Bible CD-ROM." Doing so will install all components of Communicator, including Composer.

If you don't have Netscape Communicator installed, you'll need to do so before you can continue with this chapter. Remember that versions of Netscape Communicator for Windows and Macintosh PowerPCs are available on the *Internet Bible* CD-ROM, which can be found at the back of this book. To open Composer, follow these steps:

✦ **Windows** – Click Start ➪ Programs ➪ Netscape Communicator ➪ Netscape Composer.

✦ **Macintosh** – Open the Apple menu, and choose Applications. Locate Communicator and launch it, then choose Composer from the Communicator menu.

✦ **Linux** – The exact procedure will vary depending on your installation of Linux. If you use one of the common Windows-like interface managers, click Start ➪ Programs ➪ Networking ➪ Netscape Communicator. Then choose Page Composer from the Communicator menu.

Creating your basic Web site

Although surfing the Internet can be a lot of fun, creating your own Web pages for other people to view makes the Internet even more fun. You can't learn everything about creating fancy Web sites in just a short chapter, of course. But this quick overview can give you a taste of what it takes to design simple Web pages. Then, if you decide you'd like to do something a bit fancier, you can learn how in Part VII, "Creating Your Own Web Content."

Netscape Composer has a *wizard* that makes creating a Web page pretty easy. The wizard guides you through a series of questions and uses your answers to quickly build a Web page. Once you've created a Web page, you can use Composer to further modify the page to suit your needs, or you can use the page as it is.

To create your first Web page using Netscape Composer:

1. Launch Composer. When Composer is open, you should see a blank document window with toolbars that resemble those in most word processors. But as you can see in Figure 4-3, some buttons are unique to a Web page editor as well.

2. To begin creating a new Web page using the Netscape Composer Wizard, select File ➪ New ➪ Page.

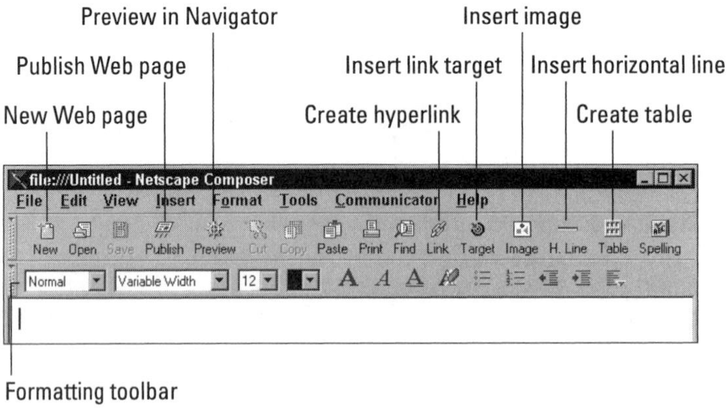

Preview in Navigator

Publish Web page

New Web page

Insert image

Insert link target

Create hyperlink

Insert horizontal line

Create table

Formatting toolbar

Figure 4-3: The Netscape Composer screen has a lot of tools you can use to make your Web page look just the way you'd like.

The Wizard will actually open in Netscape Navigator, and you will be prompted to connect to the Internet.

3. Read the introductory information for the Netscape Page Wizard and click Start (you may have to scroll down a bit to see the Start button).

   The wizard links you to a wide selection of free artwork, which is part of the reason why you must be connected to the Internet to use it. Throughout the process, the wizard will give you instructions on what to do next. It is important to read them, because it is possible that the wizard has changed slightly since this book was written.

4. Click the link to give your page a title, and name your site. Click Apply when you are done typing a name. Notice that the Preview page will now show your title at the top of the page.

5. Now click the link to type an introduction to your site. Type an introductory sentence or two and click Apply again.

6. Click the link to add some "hotlinks."

   This step allows you to add some links to other Web pages. If you don't know what you want to link to, try linking to the IDG Books Web site. Type **IDG Books Worldwide** in the Name field and `http://www.idgbooks.com/` in the URL field. Now click Apply.

7. Continue clicking the links in the wizard to add various elements to the Web page. You can even change background and text colors, modify the style of bullets used in lists, and give the horizontal lines a different look.

8. When you are ready to view your finished Web page, scroll all the way to the bottom of the left-hand pane and click Build. The page will appear in Netscape Navigator as it was meant to be viewed.

9. To save your Web page to your local hard drive, click File ➪ Edit Page. This step will download it and all graphics to your local hard drive and open it in Composer as shown in Figure 4-4. Note that in Composer the page will not look exactly the same as it does in your Web browser.

Figure 4-4: The page you created with the wizard will look strange in Composer.

10. Once the page is open in Composer, you can save it locally. In Composer click File ➪ Save As and choose a location for the page. If this is going to be your main page, we suggest that you call it **index.html** or **home.html**.

Tip

It's a good idea to create a separate folder on your hard drive in which to store all of your Web page files, including graphics and pictures.

11. To make sure that everything looks okay, click the Preview button on the Composer toolbar. Notice that the page shown in Figure 4-5 looks better than it did in Composer.

Note

The Web page wizard described here is not the only way to create a Web page in Composer. You can simply open Composer from the Communicator menu in Netscape Communicator and begin adding elements to your page.

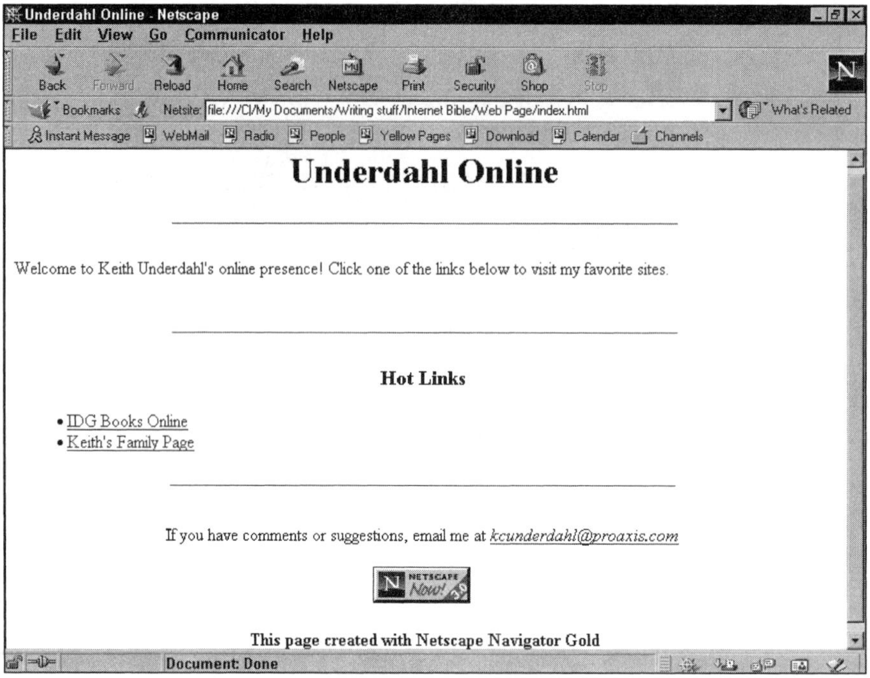

Figure 4-5: Make sure that your Web page looks okay by previewing it in Navigator.

Personalizing your Web site

Once you've created a basic Web page, you're ready to put your personal touches on the page. In Figure 4-5, for example, the page includes a statement at the bottom that says, erroneously, "This page created with Netscape Navigator Gold" and includes a link button to download Netscape Navigator 3. You may want to remove these items, add a picture, and possibly reword the introduction you wrote previously.

Editing your Web page in Composer is very similar to working on a document in a word processor. You can change the text in your Web page by simply selecting the old text and typing your new text. You can edit items by selecting them and modifying them with commands on the formatting toolbar.

Tip It's often better to create relatively small Web pages — at least as the top page of a Web site — and link to your more complex pages. That way people who visit your Web site won't have to endure long delays while your entire Web site loads.

If you wish to add images, sound, or other items, open the Insert menu, as shown in Figure 4-6.

Figure 4-6: Personalize your Web page using the options on the Insert menu.

You may be tempted to add all sorts of fancy things to your Web page, but some restraint may be warranted. For instance, you may be tempted to insert dozens of very large pictures, but too many will make your page slow to download on computers using slower dial-up connections. You also need to make sure that all of the pages and graphics you use don't exceed the storage space allowed by your Web server.

Don't forget to save your page often as you work!

Publishing Your Web Page

Once you've created your masterpiece, you'll probably want other people to be able to see it (just a hunch). You aren't likely to want to limit the viewing of your Web site to people who come to gaze rapturously at your computer, so you'll want to publish your site on the Internet. This generally means placing the files that make up your Web site on the Web server belonging to your ISP.

Note

You don't have to use your ISP as the host for your Web site—you have a lot of other options. Many companies provide Web-hosting services you may want to consider, especially if your Web site will be for your business. Web-hosting services offer several advantages compared to placing your Web site with your ISP. When you use a dedicated Web-hosting service, you generally can have your own *domain name*, which can make it a lot easier for people to find your Web site. In addition, a Web-hosting service may provide speedier access for visitors than is possible through some local ISPs. Of course, using Web-hosting services does tend to be more expensive than simply placing your Web site on your ISP's Web server. You'll have to decide for yourself whether the extra cost is worthwhile.

Because you used Netscape Composer to create your first Web page, it makes sense to use Composer to help place your site on the Web server. The Publish feature in Composer makes it easy to transfer files to the server, but you need to answer some basic questions before you can proceed with this step. Check with your ISP (or whoever owns the server where you will be publishing) to obtain the following pieces of information:

✦ **The FTP or HTTP address of the Web server**.

✦ **Your user name and password for the server**. If you are using your ISP's server, the name and password will probably be the same ones you use for other account services.

Once you have all the necessary information, follow these steps to publish your Web pages:

1. Open your main page in Composer if it isn't already.

2. Click Publish to open the Publish dialog. Enter the required destination and user information for the Web server you will use, as shown in Figure 4-7.

3. Click OK continue. The pages and related files will be transferred to the Web server.

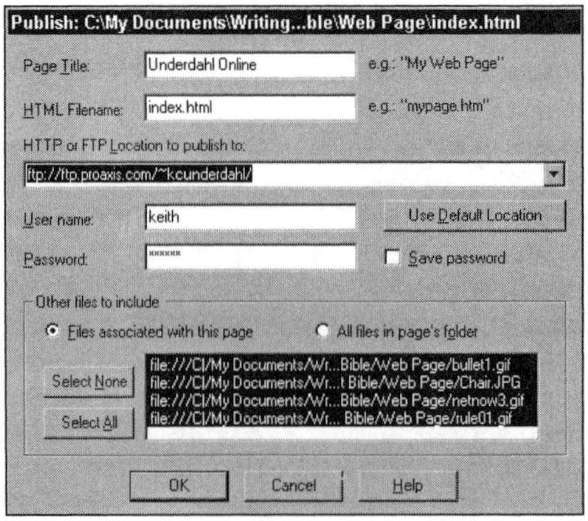

Figure 4-7: Enter the server address and user information before you publish.

Note Some Web servers do not allow the types of commands issued by Composer's Publish feature. If this is the case, you may see an error message stating that the server does not allow the *PUT* command or something to that effect. If so, contact the ISP and find out what procedure you need to use in order to publish the files. If you need to use an FTP program such as WS_FTP, take a look at Chapter 24, "Doing Basic Web Design."

When you're done, close Composer, open your Web browser, and navigate to the URL for your new Web page. The first part of the URL will be provided by the Web server, and it will be followed by the file name for the page you just published. For instance, if you publish a page called `index.html` in the server location `http://www.myserver.com/~username/`, the URL for the site will be `http://www.myserver.com/~username/`.

Summary

This chapter has shown you that it really is possible to publish your own Web site in just a few minutes. You probably found out something else about publishing your own Web site—it's kind of fun, too! When you're ready to move up to more advanced Web publishing, go to Part VII , "Creating Your Own Web Content," and become your very own Webmaster!

✦   ✦   ✦

Connecting to the Internet

P A R T

✦ ✦ ✦ ✦

In This Part

Chapter 5
Choosing Your
Service Provider

Chapter 6
Speeding Up Your
Connection

Chapter 7
Getting Online with
Your Small Network

✦ ✦ ✦ ✦

There's all sorts of stuff to know driving on the Internet highway. Getting connected is the first step, and you may already have a few questions, such as: What do I need to get connected? How much does it cost? Who do I have to call? and How fast can I go?

In this part, you learn how to choose an Internet service provider, find the hardware you need to surf the Web, and discover how to connect a small network of computers to the Internet using a single connection.

Choosing Your Service Provider

Before you can use the Internet, you need to connect to it. At your place of business, you may already be connected to the Internet. Many companies tie their employees' computers together on a Local Area Network (LAN), and then connect that LAN to a high-bandwidth connection to the Internet.

If you want to access the Internet from home or your small businesses, you'll need to find your own Internet connection. This usually means making arrangements with an *Internet Service Provider* (ISP). Fortunately, you have a lot of choices when it comes to choosing an ISP. In fact, a bunch of ISPs are out there right now ready to fight for your business.

Tip If you are not sure whether you already have a connection to the Internet, start up your Internet browser (Netscape Communicator, Internet Explorer, or Opera) and try to display the IDG Books Web page (www.idgbooks.com) from the Internet. If the page appears, you have a working connection to the Internet. If you don't have a working connection, see Chapter 1, "Getting Connected Fast!" to learn how to get connected quickly.

The most common way for an individual to connect to the Internet is by using a modem (probably built into your computer) that dials a local telephone number to the ISP. Usually the ISP provides you with a setup program that configures your computer to connect properly. Then, each time you want to use the Internet, you start up the connection (usually by starting your browser or opening a connection icon).

Finding an Internet Service Provider

ISPs want you to use their services. Makers of Internet software want you to find ISPs so that you can use their products. With ISPs eager for your patronage, finding them shouldn't be that difficult. Here are some ways you can go about finding an ISP that's right for you.

Let Windows help you

If you have Internet Explorer set up on your computer, you can use IE's Internet Connection Wizard to help you find an ISP. You'll need a modem connected to a phone line to do this. To launch the Internet Connection Wizard:

1. In Windows 95/98, open the Start menu, select Programs, and click Accessories ➪ Internet Tools ➪ Internet Connection Wizard.

2. When the Internet Connection Wizard dialog box appears (Figure 5-1), choose the option to sign up for a new Internet account. Click Next.

Figure 5-1: The Internet Connection Wizard makes it easy to sign up for a new online account.

3. The wizard will automatically dial a toll free number for a referral service, and download a current list of providers. When the download is complete, you should see a list similar to that shown in Figure 5-2.

4. When you have settled on a provider, click Next. You will then be prompted to enter personal information about yourself. It is important that you provide accurate information here. Click Next when you are done.

5. Depending on the service you choose, you should see a list of billing and account options. Make a selection and click Next.

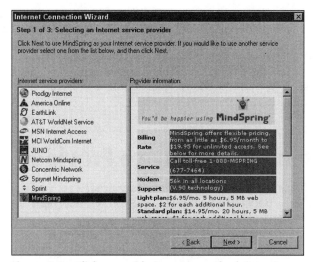

Figure 5-2: Click a provider's name on the left to view a description of its services on the right.

6. Now you have to enter billing information. Sorry, if you don't have a valid credit card number the wizard simply won't proceed past this point.

7. Click Next. The Wizard will dial-up a number for the ISP.

Beyond this point you will be presented with a series of screens that vary depending on the service provider you choose. All of the ISPs will ask you to help find a local dial-up number; this is an important step, because if you choose a dial-up number that is a long-distance phone call from your location, your phone bill could skyrocket.

Local resources

To find ISPs that serve your community, you can draw on local resources. Check your local Yellow Pages directory for ISPs. They may be listed under either "Internet" or "Computers — Networking." Check with your friends and neighbors to see what services they use and whether or not their experiences have been positive. Local newspapers, especially those that are computer-oriented or business-oriented, usually list ISPs serving your area. Even billboards are touting ISPs these days!

Published lists and evaluations

Just as you'll find no shortage of ISPs, you'll run into no shortage of opinions about which ISPs are best. Many magazines and Web sites regularly evaluate ISPs and rate the quality of their service, costs, and other features.

A number of Web sites can help you find an ISP. ZDNet offers a guide to ISPs at `http://www.zdnet.com/products/internetuser/isp.html`. If you are into quantity when you make your important life choices (such as choosing an ISP), then The List is for you (`http://thelist.internet.com/`). The List is a compilation of almost 10,000 ISPs around the world. Using this page, you can locate ISPs based on telephone area codes or by country codes. Specific lists are also available for the United States and Canada.

Evaluating an Internet Service Provider

Most likely several local and national ISPs serve your area. If so, you can be selective in the one you choose. To help you make your choice, here are some of the issues you should consider.

Cost

The going rate for individual, unlimited (or virtually unlimited) dial-up connection time to the Internet is approximately $14.95 to $25.00 per month in the United States. If you plan to use the Internet more than a few hours per month (usually more than about ten hours), you will probably want to go for the unlimited rate. Though the features associated with this price can vary, this rate typically provides:

✦ An Internet connection 24 hours a day, every day

✦ An e-mail account

✦ Access to the World Wide Web

✦ Space on a Web server to host Web pages

Be aware, however, that there may be limitations to service or additional charges for services not included in an ISP's basic rate. These may include:

✦ A fee to use your own computer to host Web pages

✦ Extra charges for high-speed connections

✦ Long distance charges, if the ISP's number is outside your calling area

✦ Fees for the use of the ISP's 800 number (ironic, but true)

✦ Additional charges for exceeding the allotted space on the ISP's Web server or for your Web site exceeding a certain amount of traffic

✦ Use of CGI scripts and other technical supports for specialized Web sites

When you compare ISPs — even those that have the same basic rate — make sure you know what the rate includes (and doesn't include). Often an ISP starts you off with a free month or several months at a reduced rate, but raises the rate later.

Free Computers?

You may have seen the advertisement from your local computer superstore touting incredibly low prices for new computers. Some even claim to offer computers for free. Are these deals too good to be true?

Yes and no. In most cases, these super-low prices reflect your purchase price after what is called an *Internet Discount* or *ISP Rebate*. To get the rebate – which usually totals hundreds of dollars – you must agree to a service contract with an ISP that the retailer has a partnership with. The contract typically lasts two or three years, which means you must maintain an account with that ISP for the duration of the agreement. If you cancel the service before the end of the contract period, you have to repay the rebate you originally received when you bought the computer.

Whether or not this sounds like a good deal probably depends on whether or not you already have an ISP that you are happy with. If you already have service and don't want to switch, this type of rebate is probably not worth the trouble. Also, if you aren't sure that the ISP specified in the rebate will be the right one for you, you probably don't feel comfortable obligating yourself to them for such a long period of time. On the other hand, if you already have an account with the ISP in question, or if you were planning to switch over to them anyway, this could be an excellent way to get a great deal on a powerful new machine.

Local access

If you are paying a monthly rate to get on the Internet, you don't want to pay extra for a long-distance telephone call to reach the ISP. That's why the first criteria for choosing an ISP is to find one that has a local telephone connection.

Most national ISPs (AT&T, EarthLink, MindSpring, and others) have local dial-up connection points for many cities and towns across the United States. When you sign up with the ISP, they'll probably ask for your ZIP code or telephone number so they can tell you if they have a local telephone number to reach their service.

Tip   The advantage of a national ISP is that they have many local access numbers across the country. If you are traveling with your notebook computer, you may be able to use a local phone number to check your e-mail while you are on the road. Some also have toll-free dial-up numbers, but these usually have an associated per-minute charge from the ISP.

Reliability

Anyone who has used an unreliable ISP knows that encountering a lot of busy signals and disconnects can be very frustrating. If you are paying for unlimited connection time, you expect an error-free connection any time of the day. Most ISPs are reliable enough that you shouldn't have to wait to connect under normal circumstances.

In general, you should be able to connect on the first try more than 90 percent of the time. Highest demand for dial-up connections occur during the evenings, with business hours being the next busiest.

Connection type and speed

When connecting with an ISP using a telephone line, the typical connect speed is between 28.8 and 50 kilobytes per second (Kbps). For most individuals, this is sufficient for viewing most Web pages. At this speed, however, you may have to wait a bit for a graphic to be displayed, a video to be played, or a file to be downloaded.

Though every ISP should support 28.8K connections, most support higher-speed connections as well. Modems that support speeds of 56K are common. If you have one, check to see that your ISP supports it. You should also make sure that your telephone line can support a faster connection.

Cross-Reference

To learn more about high-speed connections, see Chapter 6, "Speeding Up Your Connection."

Support

Technical support is an important consideration when choosing an ISP. As a subscriber, you want to know you can speak to a live person when necessary. Waiting for some anonymous Webmaster to answer your e-mail can be frustrating when you need help in a hurry. An ISP with good support offers some or all of the following services:

✦ **FAQ**. A frequently-asked-questions document often answers the most common questions you have about using the ISP.

✦ **Chat Support**. There may be a chat room with people from the ISP, or just helpful people who like to hang out and answer questions. Type in your question and you should get a few good ideas to try.

✦ **Newsgroup**. Some ISPs have a newsgroup where you can ask support questions. Be forewarned — you may not get your answer immediately.

✦ **E-mail**. Even the leanest ISP should have e-mail technical support. Responses can take a few days, so this option won't be best for your "right now" types of problems. Often, technical support questions should be directed to the Webmaster user name at the ISP site.

✦ **Bulletin board**. When problems or changes occur with your ISP, often they post the new information on a bulletin board or help desk. For example, the ISP may have a new access number or a change to the mail server that they want to post.

✦ **Support pages**. Many ISPs offer Web pages that offer tutorials and other support information online. These often include information about taking advantage of some of the ISP's advanced features or extras, such as Web hosting and CGI scripting.

Besides the support services mentioned previously, a good ISP also provides easy ways for doing common tasks. For example, it might offer a simple way to change your password or to download updated software.

Internet services

Web browsing and e-mail are the most popular uses for the Internet, but the Internet has a lot more to offer. Although you may not be aware of it, there a lot of other Internet services that your ISP may or may not fully support.

For starters, thousands of newsgroups are available on the Internet, though no ISP carries all of them on its news servers. Certain international newsgroups and those that cover controversial topics may not be offered. If you want a particular newsgroup, you may wish to check that it is available from your ISP.

The Internet service that requires the most consideration is Web hosting. If you want to have your own Web page and have it hosted with your ISP, you will want to do some comparison shopping. A whole section is devoted to Web hosting later in this chapter.

Free stuff

One way that ISPs are distinguishing their services from others is by offering special discounts, gifts, or member-only content to subscribers. Many ISPs offer you a free month or several discounted months of Internet connection time for signing on with them. Most ISPs offer some free software, which contains at least an Internet browser and software for setting up the connection to the ISP. Free software "extras" may be included as well. MindSpring offers several unique tools, including an antispam tool and a browser plug-in that filters objectionable content.

Special member-only content is a particularly big draw for ISPs that began as self-contained online service providers (such as America Online and CompuServe). Telephone companies sometimes offer special Internet services to their regular telephone customers.

Web hosting

Most ISPs offer Web hosting services. Web hosting provides you with a place to put your Web content so it can be seen by others on the Internet. The ISP provides disk space and a Web address for your site.

If you plan to ask the ISP to host your Web site, you'll still need to provide the content for the site, by either creating the Web pages yourself or paying the ISP (or an independent Web Design firm) to create the content for you.

To learn more about personal Web hosting, take a look at Chapter 30, "Hosting a Personal Web Server."

If you want to sign on with an ISP that will host your Web pages, evaluate the service carefully. Some ISPs give you a limited amount of disk space with your Internet connection account. If you just want to create a personal Web page without any bells and whistles, the 5 to 10MB of space the ISP usually provides may be fine.

If you need to create a Web site that is bigger or you expect a lot of traffic, you will probably have to pay more for your Web site.

Part VII, "Creating Your Own Web Content," describes some of the issues you should consider when publishing online.

Choosing an ISP

One of the first decisions you make when choosing an ISP is whether you want to use a national ISP or a local ISP. Local ISPs can offer a service that is more tailored to a community. They may have a support staff that you can speak to in person. They may combine their service with information that supports the local community. On the other hand, national ISPs usually offer additional free software tools, and most offer local dial-up numbers across the country that you can use when you travel.

Because of the nature of this book, descriptions of particular local ISPs are not really feasible. Instead, the remainder of this chapter describes some of the better national Internet Service Providers. Some of these ISPs are strictly Internet-related businesses (such as EarthLink and MindSpring), while others (like AT&T) provide a wide array of communication services. Also, keep an eye out for special offers or price changes. The prices shown here were current as of this writing, and do not reflect any temporary discounts.

Tip

You may also want to check with your local telephone company or cable service. Many now offer Internet service, sometimes with much higher access speeds than you can get from the ISPs mentioned here.

AT&T WorldNet Service

Some nice extras come your way when you have AT&T WorldNet (http://www.att.net/) as your ISP. The service comes with discounts on various products and some members-only content. Add those features to the very reliable physical network that AT&T has dedicated to Internet service and AT&T WorldNet becomes a strong contender in the ISP field.

As with most other ISPs, AT&T offers a $19.95 dial-up service that allows up to 150 hours of online time per month. AT&T has a sizeable network, so you should be able to find local access numbers across most of the United States. However, we should mention that it is the only service listed here that does not have a local dial-up number for our test city, Albany, Oregon.

AT&T often offers discount packages on long distance calling if you sign up for the AT&T WorldNet Service. Check their Web site for details and to see if this offer is still available.

America Online

Instead of beginning as an ISP, America Online (`http://www.aol.com`) started as an online service provider, offering proprietary content on a proprietary network. While still maintaining its members-only content, AOL now offers millions of subscribers Internet connectivity.

The price of a standard account with unlimited access is $21.95 per month, although a discount is available if you pay for a whole year up front. Lighter plans are available, starting as low as $4.95 per month for three hours of access time.

AOL distinguishes itself from other ISPs by continuing to offer a service that is more like a community than just a bunch of modems and wires. It also makes chatting with friends and colleagues easy with an instant messaging program.

CompuServe

CompuServe (`http://www.compuserve.com`) has been around longer than any other ISP. It was formed in 1969, and began offering "online" services in 1979, where members could exchange e-mail and other data. CompuServe is now owned by AOL, but maintains a separate identity within the corporation.

Like AOL, CompuServe offers its own Web browser and a network of content that is available only to members. They offer a $19.95 unlimited account, or you can sign up for 20 hours per month at just $9.95. If you only plan to access the Internet occasionally, this deal might be worth your consideration.

EarthLink

The EarthLink (`http://www.earthlink.com`) unlimited connection plan goes for $19.95 (plus a $25 start-up fee, which may be waived if you register online or come over from AOL).

You don't have to search far to get help from EarthLink. Links from its home page let EarthLink members connect to a newbies page (for first-time users), *bLink* online (EarthLink's online newsletter), and Internet & Web help site. Also, under the

Explore heading, you can select a topic that interests you (such as news, music, kids, shopping, sports, or travel, to name a few) to find links to related information on the Web. You can find setup software for EarthLink on the *Internet Bible* CD-ROM.

MindSpring

MindSpring (http://www.mindspring.net) offers a variety of dial-up programs to which you can subscribe. It is also available on this book's CD-ROM. With the Light plan, you get five hours of connect time per month for $6.95. The Standard plan gives you 20 hours per month for $14.95. For Unlimited Access and three e-mail accounts, you pay $19.95 per month. The Works, for $26.95 per month, is similar to Unlimited Access except that you also get 10MB of space for a personal Web page and five e-mail accounts.

Prodigy

Prodigy (http://www.prodigy.com) is another ISP that has been around for a few years, and boasts a wide network of local dial-up numbers. Their unlimited plan costs $19.95 per month. A 10-hour plan is available for $9.95. Members enjoy access to private Prodigy communities as well as toll-free 24-hour technical support.

UUNET

Of the large ISPs competing for Internet subscribers, UUNET Technologies (http://www.uunet.com), is one of the oldest and offers an access area that extends outside of the United States. UUNET was founded in 1987. Today, local access to the UUNET backbone is available from more than a thousand locations around the world. Figure 5-3 shows the UUNET home page.

UUNET Technologies, which is now a subsidiary of WorldCom, Inc., has networks in 26 countries around the world. Its Internet backbone extends fiber optic cabling between North America, Europe, and Asia.

UUNET offers individual subscriber services. The company's focus, however, is more toward business customers. Individuals and small businesses can take advantage of standard 28.8 modem connections or higher-speed ISDN connections. For companies that need full-time connections, UUNET has Frame Relay and T-1/E-1 connections, as well as other connection types.

Web hosting is also available, along with a variety of options. Your Web sites can incorporate secure transactions and electronic commerce. You can have CGI scripting as well as traffic and usage reporting. UUNET claims it can offer these services more cost effectively and reliably than customers can by hosting Web sites themselves.

Figure 5-3: UUNET offers worldwide local access to the Internet.

Summary

Selecting an Internet Service Provider is the first important decision you make when you decide to use the Internet. With literally hundreds of ISPs available today, choosing the one that is best for you requires some scrutiny. This chapter described some of the many features you should consider when you choose an ISP. If you want to do more than just dial up the Internet on occasion, you may want to look into additional features. For example, can your ISP host your Web site for you? Can you rely on the ISP to be there when you absolutely need reliable support? If you need to choose an ISP, the descriptions of each in this chapter should have given you a good start on evaluating their services.

✦ ✦ ✦

Speeding Up Your Connection

◆   ◆   ◆   ◆

In This Chapter

Considering a faster connection?

Connecting super-fast over the telephone system

Using cable modems

Surveying wireless options

◆   ◆   ◆   ◆

There's a maxim in the computer industry: Whenever there's more than a ten-second lag between a user entering a command and an action taking place, the procedure can't be called interactive. If that's true, then the Internet isn't nearly as interactive as its boosters would like you to think. The delay between calling up a Web page and seeing the complete page on your screen is usually a heck of a lot longer than ten seconds. Other activities suffer, too. Online audio plays in fits and starts and video often looks like a slide show.

The transmission of data between the source and your computer can be delayed for a lot of reasons, but traditionally the biggest bottleneck has been your own modem and the phone line it is connected to, limited to around 28.8 kilobytes per second (and usually actually handling a lot less). But if you're serious about your Internet surfing, and you have the cash, solutions are out there . . . if you happen to live in the right place!

Considering High-Speed Access?

The first question to ask yourself before spending money to obtain high-speed access to the Internet is, "Do I need it?" To figure this out, ask yourself a few questions:

1. Is the Internet my primary source of information?

2. Do I use the Internet two or more hours a day?

3. Do I access a lot of graphic, sound, or (especially) video-intensive sites, such as sites that show video clips? (See Figure 6-1.)

4. Do I play a lot of games over the Internet?

5. Do I use the Internet less than I'd like to because I have limited time, and it just takes too long to find what I need?

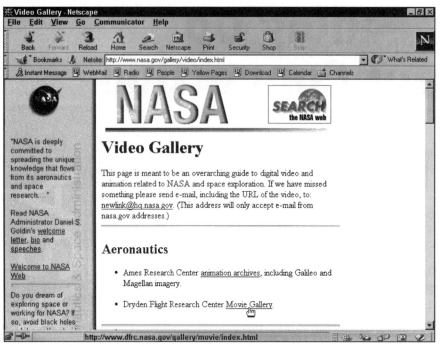

Figure 6-1: If you spend a lot of time downloading multimedia clips such as those available in NASA's Video Gallery, high-speed access will seem like a godsend.

If you answered "yes" to most of the preceding questions, high-speed access is probably worth investigating.

That Doesn't Look Like 30 Mbps to Me!

One word of caution before we proceed: A big difference exists between how fast a given technology can theoretically provide data and how fast that data actually moves. There's even a formula for it:

Theoretical speed - Bottlenecks = Real-world speeds

Bottlenecks are anything that limit speed, and you don't have control over many of them. It doesn't do you any good to have a theoretical connection speed of 30 Mbps (megabits per second) if your Internet Service Provider is connected to the Internet backbone by a T1 line, which is limited to 1.5 Mbps — and shared by who knows how many users.

Still, even with bottlenecks, many of these technologies can provide you with a noticeable increase in speed over what you're probably using now — especially if what you're using now is a 28.8 Kbps analog modem!

Note

Internet access technology is changing rapidly. To ensure that you have the most up-to-date news, check out the various specialist Web sites mentioned throughout this book.

Achieving High-Speed Phone Line Access

It seems like there's an acronym for everything in the world of the Internet. Did you know, for example, that right now you're probably connecting to the Internet using POTS? Don't get excited, it's not some peripheral you didn't know you had. POTS is engineer-speak for "Plain Old Telephone System."

The Plain Old Telephone System has proved remarkably resilient and flexible over the years. If you live in an older neighborhood, the twisted copper wires over which you carry on telephone conversations, send and receive faxes, and connect to the Internet were probably installed decades ago — back when nets were used for catching fish, webs were spun only by spiders, and a mouse was something you set out traps for.

These copper wires still function adequately, but the Internet and other modern technologies are pushing the limits of how much information they can transmit. POTS wires represent the primary bottleneck in connection speed today, and these old copper wires are simply too slow to keep up with the ever growing need for faster throughput. The state of the art today is fiber optic cable, and eventually fiber will probably completely replace copper, at least in North America — but don't hold your breath. The process is ongoing but could take years to complete.

In the meantime, the copper cable is going to be called on to carry more and more data faster and faster. Amazingly, thanks to the genius of telecommunications engineers, it seems to be up to it.

Alexander Graham Bell would be pleased.

56K Modems

Not too long ago, some experts were predicting that 33.6 kilobytes per second (Kbps) was as fast as modems would ever get. At that speed, they were approaching the theoretical limit of the amount of data that could be sent through most phone lines (because of filters that are designed to reduce noise on the line — unfortunately, they tend to interpret data as noise!). Yet, today almost all new modems are capable of 56 Kbps. What gives?

Well, for one thing, they very rarely live up to their name. If your telephone line goes through one of those voice-enhancing filters mentioned previously, then 33.6 Kbps is all you can hope for. Even with a 56K modem, 33.6 Kbps is also the best you'll do if the signal between your Internet Service Provider and the telephone company's switch has to be converted from analog to digital more than once. The distance between your physical location and the telephone company's switch also affects the quality of the signal and, thus, transmission speed. If you are located more than two miles from the switch, forget about ever achieving 56 Kbps on an analog line.

Until recently two operating standards existed for 56K modems: x2, developed by U.S. Robotics, and K56flex, developed by Rockwell and Lucent. Early in 1998, however, the International Telecommunications Union decided on a new standard, called V.90. Most of the major manufacturers of modems offer free (or at least cheap) upgrades to their older 56K modems to make them conform to the new standard, and all new 56K modems use V.90. Most ISPs now offer 56K V.90 service, although you usually have to pay a few dollars extra each month to get it.

If you already have a 28.8K or 33.6K modem, whether you'll notice much difference when you upgrade to a 56K depends on the quality of your phone line. If you want to go really fast, though, you have to look for another solution.

Integrated Services Digital Network

Of all the new technologies offering higher-speed access to the Internet, Integrated Services Digital Network (ISDN) is the oldest. In fact, it's been around for years: It just hasn't been easy to get your hands on, at least not if you're an ordinary residential user.

ISDN sends data digitally over the phone line, unlike a conventional modem which converts the binary code of a computer into analog format. If the data can be sent digitally all the way, there's no need for this conversion.

The ISDN adapter has a number of advantages over an analog modem. It connects quietly and quickly, and it never loses data to static or line noise. What's more, it's highly adaptable. An ISDN BRI (Basic Rate Interface) — which is what you'd get if you were to start using ISDN on your home computer — has three separate channels, two labeled B (for "Bearer"), which carry data at up to 64 Kbps, and a signaling channel labeled D (for "delta" — no, we don't know why they didn't label it S for "signaling"!). The B channels can be used together, giving you a possible 128 Kbps connection — four times as fast as a 28.8 modem — or for two simultaneous tasks, which means you could stay connected to the Internet at 64 Kbps while making a phone call or sending or receiving a fax at the same time!

Unfortunately, this flexibility has also meant that ISDN is a bit more complicated to set up. To do so, you need to know several things:

1. The directory number (a standard seven-digit telephone number) for each of the two B channels.

2. The Service Profile Identification (SPID) for each B channel. This is a string of numbers that encompasses both the line's directory number and information about its installed options.

3. The type of switch used at your phone company's central office. Several different types are commonly used across the United States, and not all adapters support all of them, although some can detect the switch type automatically and adjust themselves accordingly.

Armed with this information, you can install your ISDN adapter. The adapter's setup software should provide the necessary drivers; you'll also have to check with your Internet Service Provider to learn how to configure the software that connects you to it.

Speaking of your ISP, before you can even think of upgrading to ISDN you need to find out if your ISP supports it, and if it does, how much the service costs. ISDN service is usually more expensive than analog service — rates typically begin at about $40 per month for 128 Kbps access, but prices can range much higher.

Finally, you need to make sure that your phone company supports ISDN, and that the quality of your phone line is able to handle it. Contact your local phone company to find out if ISDN will work for you. ISDN Zone (`www.isdnzone.com`) is a good place to find more information about ISDN.

Asymmetric Digital Subscriber Line

Even at its best, ISDN is only about three or four times as fast as a typical analog modem connection. But ISDN isn't even close to the fastest method of transmitting data over the phone lines. That honor goes to something called Digital Subscriber Line (DSL).

Various sorts of DSL are used for various purposes, but residential computer users need only concern themselves with one: Asymmetric Digital Subscriber Line (ADSL). ADSL modems bring in data much faster downstream than they send it upstream, but they're so fast that you're not likely to notice the discrepancy — if you're fortunate enough to live in an area where you can actually get ADSL.

ADSL can pump data as fast as 9 Mbps over existing phone lines, although in practice the speeds offered by providers is much less. Nevertheless, the minimum speed offered with most ADSL accounts is 256 Kbps, which is at least twice as fast as ISDN.

One of the biggest advantages of ADSL is its ability to coexist with regular telephone service on the same line. That means you can be surfing the Web at high speed while carrying on a phone conversation over the same line. That's possible because ADSL uses three separate frequency channels at the same time: one carrying telephone conversations, one carrying information upstream from your computer to the Internet (at anywhere from 16 to 640 Kbps) and one carrying information downstream from the Internet to you.

ADSL requires that the wire between your premises and the telephone company's central office is less than 18,000 feet (about 3.4 miles). Furthermore, you must purchase a special ADSL modem, and you usually have to pay an installation fee. But the good news is that ADSL accounts often don't cost much more than typical dial-up accounts, with the going rate for a basic, unlimited usage account beginning as low as $30 as of this writing. Prices do vary widely depending on your location and the speed of the connection, with some services costing hundreds of dollars per month. This makes ADSL one of the best deals going in Internet access for some, so long as you can actually get it.

ADSL makes such effective use of those old twisted copper wires that, under ideal conditions, an ADSL-equipped home could theoretically watch four movies stored in MPEG format and transmitted at 1.5 Mbps on separate TVs, hold a video conference at 384 Kbps, download data files from a server at 128 Kbps via ISDN, and carry on a telephone call with the neighbors, all at the same time!

That' not all. Once you're hooked up to ADSL, you're online whenever your computer is turned on: you don't have to dial up to access the Internet. This makes it easier to keep abreast of breaking news, to be notified immediately when new e-mail arrives, and so forth.

If you'd like to learn more about ADSL, visit the ADSL Forum at `www.adsl.com`. You can also locate a DSL provider in your area using the 2Wire Web site at `http://www.2wire.com/`.

Multilink PPP

PPP stands for "Point to Point Protocol." It enables a variety of different devices with different sorts of links to the Internet to talk to each other—but as its name indicates, it's intended for fairly simple links from one point to another, which means it enables only one physical link—say, from your computer to your ISP's computer—at a time.

Multilink PPP, as its name implies, does away with this restriction and enables several physical links to be combined into one virtual link that can carry much more data than any one of the physical links could on its own.

Multilink PPP has a lot of uses for networks everywhere. For the home Internet user, however, its biggest advantage is that, if you're able to take advantage of it, you can achieve speeds with ordinary modems equal to that of an ISDN line, at much less cost.

The first requirement, of course, is that your ISP support Multilink PPP. A few do; many don't. The second requirement is that you have two available phone lines and two modems in your computer, each hooked up to a different line. Because it requires two lines, this option should only be considered if ADSL is not available to you.

Using Cable Modems

Of course, there's another way to get data into our homes, one we use all the time (though we may not think of it that way) — coaxial cable. That's the cable that brings television programs to millions of people in the United States and Canada.

Coaxial cable is capable of carrying huge amounts of data — it's already handling full-motion video, remember! — so it's not surprising that it's also being tapped by cable companies to provide high-speed Internet service.

Note   CATV CyberLab, a Web site dedicated to the cable TV industry, provides a great deal of information on cable modems, cable telephony, and other cable-related issues.

How high speed? Well, theoretically coaxial cable could pump the Internet into your computer at 30 Mbps — not that your computer could handle receiving it that fast. A more realistic figure is between 3 and 10 Mbps. Data could be sent from your computer to the network at up to 10 Mbps, but most cable modems are, like ADSL and ISDN modems, asymmetric — there's so much less traffic from you to the Internet than the other way around that a more typical upstream speed is between 200 Kbps and 2 Mbps.

To use the Internet over coaxial cable, first you obviously need to sign up with a cable company that offers high-speed Internet access. They'll provide you with a cable modem. You'll also need a cable outlet close enough to your computer to let you use it, and an Ethernet card in your computer (usually supplied by the cable company as part of its set-up package). For some cable companies, you may also need a regular modem and a phone line, because cable systems weren't originally designed for two-way communication — upstream communication may be sent by phone, while downstream communication comes via cable (although some cable companies try to address that situation by replacing coaxial networks with systems that combine coaxial cable and fiber optics).

ADSL's Achilles' heel, as mentioned earlier, is the fact that the signal attenuates as you get farther away from the central office. Cable modems have a different problem: because you are sharing a data pipeline with everyone else in your neighborhood, speed decreases drastically if you all log on at once and start downloading files. Of course, a 30 Mbps data stream can handle a lot of users simultaneously before you would experience a measurable performance hit.

The typical cost for a cable modem installation is around $100, with monthly charges of about $40. Cable modems share ADSL's advantage of providing a full-time Internet link; when your computer is on, it's also online.

Connecting with Wireless Connections

Some companies are now offering high-speed Internet access that doesn't involve any wires at all — copper, coaxial, or fiber optic. For people in rural areas with no access to either ADSL or cable, wireless connection, as a viable alternative, offers hope for a speedier Internet experience.

Satellite

Just as satellites can beam television programming directly to your TV via a small, inexpensive dish antenna, they can beam Internet data to your computer. Of course, sending signals the other way is more problematic, because two-way satellite communication equipment is expensive to buy and maintain, hard to operate, and not very secure. Companies that offer satellite Internet services therefore rely on ordinary analog modem connections to Internet Service Providers for the upstream link.

A major satellite Internet provider, Hughes Network Systems' DirecPC (www.hns.com), can deliver up to 400 Kbps downstream, more than three times as fast as ISDN, though nowhere near cable modem or potential ADSL speeds. Eventually, however, satellite transmission could deliver Internet data at 92 Mbps — once computers are available that can accept data at such a speed! Currently the dishes cost on average between $300 and $400, depending on the features you choose. The more expensive units can be used both for Internet access and satellite TV reception.

Internet service rates are quite reasonable. If you want to stick with your existing ISP, you can get 25 hours of 400 Kbps access for as little as $19.99 per month. You can choose from plans that offer more time, and you can also opt to discontinue your current ISP and use DirecTV's service instead. A 100-hour "Family Surfer" plan costs $49.99 per month. That may sound like a lot for an account that doesn't offer unlimited access, but keep in mind that with such fast data transmission rates you won't have to spend nearly as much time online anyway. On the other hand, perhaps having such easy high speed access will cause you to spend even more time online, not less!

Cellular Digital Packet Data and Personal Communications Systems

Cellular Digital Packet Data (CDPD) and Personal Communications Systems (PCS) are two technologies that can carry data to "Internet appliances," such as smart pocket phones and hand-held PCs. To learn more about the CDPD system, visit CDPD.org at http://cdpd.org/cdpd/.

Stacking Them Up

Okay, enough talk. How about some hard data? Table 8-1 compares the theoretical speed of various types of Internet access methods (remember that real-life speed depends on the bottlenecks encountered on the Internet) and the time required to download a 10-megabyte file, assuming you're actually able to realize the theoretical top speed. If you're like us, the results will immediately have you hankering for high-speed access!

Table 8-1
Theoretical Speeds of Various Access Methods

Type	Theoretical Speed	Ideal Transfer Time for a 10-Megabyte File
14.4 modem	14.4 Kbps	1.5 hours
28.8 modem	28.8 Kbps	46 minutes
33.6 modem	33.6 Kbps	40 minutes
56K modem	45 Kbps	29.6 minutes
ISDN	128 Kbps	10.4 minutes
Satellite (DirecPC)	400 Kbps	3.3 minutes
ADSL	256 Kbps–9 Mbps	5.2 minutes–8.9 seconds
Cable modems	10 Mbps–30 Mbps	8 seconds–2.7 seconds

Only you can answer the question of which service to use. You must consider which services are available in your area, what kind of equipment you need to buy, how much the service will cost per month, and whether the speed justifies the expense and trouble.

Summary

As you can see, you aren't necessarily limited to your current 28.8 or 33.6 Kbps access speed. Now 56K modems are readily available (though they rarely manage 56 Kbps); ISDN is widely available (though it can be expensive to obtain and difficult to set up); cable modems are fast but still not very common; ADSL is a good value if you can get it in your area; and satellite access costs just a bit more but is available anywhere.

It's not easy sorting out which of these competing methods of high-speed access is best for you. We hope, though, that this chapter has helped.

✦   ✦   ✦

Getting Online with Your Small Network

✦ ✦ ✦ ✦

In This Chapter

Determining if you
need a network

Sharing an Internet
connection on your
network

Pondering proxy
server software

✦ ✦ ✦ ✦

You no longer open books like this and read that PCs are creeping into our lives; they've already crept. According to the U.S. Department of Commerce, nearly half of all American households have access to a computer, and the percentage grows daily. A more interesting trend is the growing number of households with more than one computer. PCs have been around long enough that many people are on their second, third, or even fourth upgrade.

If you have a couple of computers around the house, or if you run a small business, you may be a candidate for setting up your own small network. Networks have many advantages, among them is the ability to share a single Internet connection with several computers. In this chapter, we'll describe why you may or may not want your own network, as well as show you how to use a network to share an Internet connection with several computers.

Considering a Network?

Networks aren't just for large corporations anymore. If you've ever found yourself carrying dozens of floppy disks back and forth between computers, or swapping printer cables, or wishing everyone in your home or office could share a single Internet connection, a small network might suit your needs quite well.

A basic understanding of networking is important before you can think about setting one up. Usually, networked computers each contain an expansion card specifically designed to connect to a network. Most small networks today connect each card to a hub using a cable. The hub serves as the physical link between all of the computers on the network.

Ethernet (10Base-T) and Fast Ethernet (100Base-T) networks have become the de facto standards in networking today. Ethernet cards are readily available for less than $25, and five-port Ethernet hubs can be had for as little as $40. Apple equips virtually all of its new computers with built-in Ethernet adapters, making networking doubly easy if you are of the Macintosh persuasion.

In addition, many companies now offer networking "kits" that make it easy for you to get your network up and running. Some kits offer wireless options, transmitting data via radio waves instead of a cable. Other kits utilize existing phone lines in your building.

Note Showing you how to set up and configure your computers in a network is beyond the scope of this book. Most networking hardware includes documentation to help you get started, and we also recommend that you check out *Home Networking Bible* by Sue Plumley to learn more. For now, we'll assume that you have the bugs worked out and that all of your computers are properly networked.

Sharing an Internet connection with the network

Sharing a single Internet connection with other computers on your network is relatively easy, and it can solve many of the problems you may encounter when multiple users need or want Internet access. Some advantages of a shared connection include

✦ Simultaneous, multiple-user Internet access without taking up more than one phone line

✦ Reduced equipment costs when several computers share one modem

✦ Easier administrator control of other network users

But just because you *can* share a connection, don't assume that you always *should*. Before you decide to share a connection, consider the following potential drawbacks:

✦ Bandwidth could suffer dramatically, especially if several people on the network want to use the Internet at the same time.

✦ Your network could become vulnerable to Internet-borne viruses and hacker attacks.

The second concern generally can be addressed by using up-to-date antivirus software, and you can protect your system from outside hacking with software such as BlackICE (see Chapter 32, "Maintaining Your Online Privacy and Security).

But bandwidth concerns are not so easily resolved. If your typical connection speed is less than 50 Kbps, you will probably find that Web browsing is unacceptably slow when two or more computers are trying to use the Internet at once.

Cross-Reference If you plan to use a shared connection regularly with many simultaneous users, we suggest that you take advantage of one of the high-speed connection solutions described in Chapter 6, "Speeding Up Your Connection."

Using Internet Connection-Sharing with Windows

Let's assume that you have your network up and running and that you have decided that a shared connection is the right thing for you. Now you need software that will facilitate the shared connection. This type of program, called *proxy server software,* has been around for years.

Whether you need special software or not depends on your operating system. When Microsoft released Windows 98 Second Edition in June 1999, it included a new feature called Internet Connection Sharing (ICS). ICS enables your Windows 98 machine to be a proxy server for the whole network, without the need to purchase any additional software. ICS has since been incorporated into all subsequent operating systems from Microsoft.

Tip If you have a Microsoft operating system older than Windows 98 Second Edition, you'll have to purchase an upgrade from Microsoft to take advantage of ICS. Windows upgrades are available at virtually any computer or electronics retailer, although you may want to check Microsoft's Web site (www.microsoft.com). As long as you have Windows 95 or higher, the online upgrade from Microsoft is fast, effective, and often cheaper than buying it elsewhere.

The computer that will actually connect to the Internet must have ICS installed. This will be your *sharing computer* (also called the *host*), and once configured you can set up the rest of the computers on your network as *clients.* Fortunately, any computer that is networked with the sharing computer and is running at least Windows 95 can be a client.

Setting up the sharing computer

Your first step in using ICS is to configure the sharing computer. The sharing computer has the modem/connection adapter in it and facilitates the actual connection. Make sure that the Internet connection on your sharing computer works properly before proceeding.

To configure the sharing computer:

1. Insert your Windows CD in the sharing computer's CD-ROM drive and click Start ➪ Settings ➪ Control Panel.

2. Open the Add/Remove Programs icon and select the Windows Setup tab. Select Internet Tools and click Details.

3. Place a check mark next to Internet Connection Sharing, as shown in Figure 7-1. Click OK twice to close the dialog boxes and install ICS.

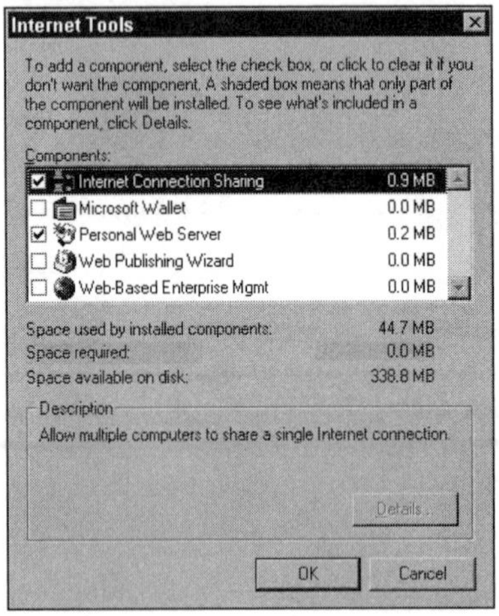

Figure 7-1: Select Internet Connection Sharing in the Internet Tools dialog box.

4. When the files are done copying, the Internet Connection Sharing Wizard should appear. To continue installation, click Next.

5. In the next wizard box, select the adapter you use to connect your computer to the Internet, not the network. Notice that in Figure 7-2, we have selected the Dial-up Adapter. Click Next to proceed.

6. *Now* you can select the adapter you use to connect your computer to the rest of the network, and then click Next.

   In the next step, you will be prompted to create a client disk. This disk will be used to configure the other "client" computers on your network. Be sure you have a blank, formatted floppy disk ready for this step.

7. Insert a disk in the floppy drive and click Next. When the client disk is created, remove it and click OK. Click Finish to complete the Wizard and restart the computer when you are prompted to do so.

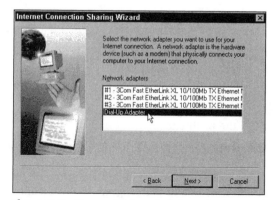

Figure 7-2: Be careful to select the adapter used for connecting to the Internet, not your network.

Configuring the rest of your network

You have configured the sharing computer, but the time for celebration is not yet at hand. To set up the other computers on the network so that they can access the Internet through the sharing computer, you'll need to do the following:

1. Take your client disk and put it in one of the other computers on your network. Again, be sure that your network is up and running or this won't work.

2. Click the Start button and select Run.

3. In the Open box, type **a:\icsclset.exe** and click OK.

4. When the Browser Connection Setup Wizard begins, click Next. The wizard tells you that it's going to review — and possibly change — some browser settings. Click Next to proceed.

5. When the final wizard screen appears, place a check mark next to the option that asks whether you want to try connecting to the Internet, and then click Finish.

Your browser should open, and you may or may not achieve success. Chances are, you won't on the first try. You'll probably see an error screen that says something like, "The page cannot be displayed." If this is the case, try the following:

✦ Locate a link on the browser's error page that says "Detect Network Settings" and click it. Sometimes you need to click it more than once. We have seen the connection finally work after clicking this link more than ten times.

✦ Try closing the browser and reopening it.

✦ Confirm that your network is working properly by opening the Network Neighborhood icon on your desktop and browsing the contents of the host computer. If you cannot browse the host computer, there is something wrong with your network connection.

✦ Determine if you have hacker countermeasure software running on your network. Countermeasures usually block the type of TCP probe that ICS must conduct in order to facilitate a connection. Try disabling the countermeasures temporarily to see if that solves the problem.

✦ Go to your sharing computer and make sure that it's connected to the Internet.

If a countermeasure program, such as BlackICE, proves to be the source of your problem, you can usually work around it by telling the program that the client computers are "trusted." You will need to determine the IP address for the network cards in each client computer by doing the following:

1. Click Start ➪ Run, and type **winipcfg** in the Open box. Click OK.

2. In the IP Configuration dialog box shown in Figure 7-3, select the network adapter from the drop-down list near the top.

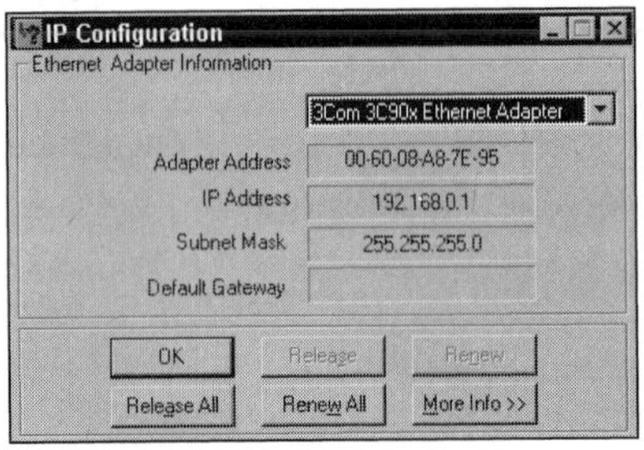

Figure 7-3: The IP Configuration dialog box will tell you the IP address for each client computer.

3. Write down the IP Address for the client computer's network adapter.

   The first several digits should be 192.168.0, but the last digit will be unique to each computer on the network. The number 192.168.0.1 is always assigned to the sharing computer.

4. Click OK when you have recorded the IP Address. Now open the configuration manager for your countermeasures program. If you are using BlackICE, right-click the BlackICE icon in the system tray (near the clock) and choose Configure BlackICE.

5. Find an area that allows you to identify trusted IP addresses. As you can see in Figure 7-4, the IP address for a client computer on our network has been entered on BlackICE's Trusted Addresses list.

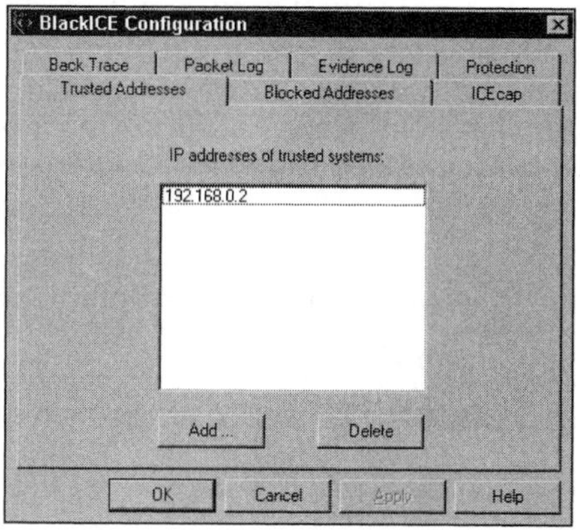

Figure 7-4: Identify your client computers to the countermeasures software to ensure that ICS will function properly.

If you're still having trouble getting ICS to work, try using Microsoft's ICS Troubleshooter on their Web site, located at `http://support.microsoft.com/support/`.

Using your shared connection

Assuming you can get ICS running correctly, using the Internet on a client computer is really no different than on the host. You can open your Web browser, mail program, or other Internet software as usual, but rather than connecting to the Internet with a local modem, the sharing host computer is called to duty. If a connection isn't already in place, the host computer will automatically establish one.

Note If your ISP provides special dial-up software, it may or may not dial your connection automatically when a client computer tries to get online. If this is the case, you may need to go to the host and establish a connection manually.

When you are using a shared connection, you will notice a couple of things that are unique to this situation. First of all, you will not see a connection icon in the system tray of the client computers, so unless you are actually at the host computer, you won't know for sure if an Internet connection is still in place or not. Furthermore, expect download times to slow dramatically if two or more people are online at the same time. No matter how many computers you have on your network, they must all drink through the same straw of your Internet connection.

Pondering Third-Party Proxy Servers

Windows' Internet Connection Sharing is neat, but doesn't suit every need. ICS was designed primarily with the home network user in mind, so it lacks some server features that small business owners often need. Furthermore, it doesn't work on computers that run Linux, the Macintosh OS, or any other operating system.

If you demand more, you should probably consider one of the many proxy server programs available commercially. Features offered by most proxy servers include

✦ Internet connection sharing

✦ Firewall security to prevent unauthorized intrusions into your network

✦ Usage tracking and content filtering for all network users

✦ Provisions for secure remote access to the network by telecommuters and other remote users

✦ Cross-platform networkability

The best place that we have found to locate proxy server software is a Web site called Tucows (www.tucows.com). Tucows lets you browse software by operating system and software type. Look for listings under Proxy Servers, Miscellaneous Servers, Modem Utilities, and other similar categories.

Summary

Computer networking used to be the domain of large corporations, universities, and the government, but now small networks are appearing in homes and small businesses everywhere. Small networks become especially useful if you wish to share a single Internet connection with many users. In this chapter, you learned how to share Internet connections with all of the computers on your small network.

✦   ✦   ✦

Browsing the Web with Browsers

◆ ◆ ◆ ◆

◆ ◆ ◆ ◆

L ick your finger and flip the page: It's time to do some browsing! If you think you have to use the browser that came installed with your computer, think again. In this part, you learn how to use three different Web browsers: Microsoft Internet Explorer, Netscape Communicator, and the new, yet powerful alternative: Opera.

By the time you've finished perusing the next few pages, you'll be an expert at surfing the Web.

Choosing and Installing Your Internet Browser

I f it weren't for browsers, the World Wide Web as we know it would not exist. *Browsers* are computer programs that enable you to view the HTML documents, graphics, and other multimedia that make up a Web site. The very first browser with a graphical user interface, Mosaic, was largely responsible for turning the World Wide Web from a research tool for high-energy physicists into the powerful communications, entertainment, and education medium it is today. Mosaic is long gone from the front lines of the browser wars, replaced by Netscape Communicator, Microsoft's Internet Explorer, and a handful of other smaller offerings including recent upstart Opera. This chapter compares the latest versions of the two most popular browsers, and Opera too, for good measure, to help you decide which one to use.

Using Netscape versus Explorer

Let's get to the bottom line: For the average user, the latest versions of Netscape and Explorer are both excellent browsers, superior to their ancestors, that will serve you well in your day-to-day Web-surfing adventures.

Either one will do the job, and each is available on this book's CD-ROM, with versions available for both Macintosh and Windows. But let's compare them feature-by-feature.

Browsing

There wouldn't be much point in a browser that couldn't browse, so let's begin with both programs' *raison d'être*.

Netscape Communicator 4.7 and Internet Explorer 5 represent great advances over their previous incarnations, adding new features without becoming much more complex — which means if you're familiar with older versions of either, you can move up to the latest version without fear.

As of this writing, Internet Explorer 4.5 is the latest version available for Macintosh systems. Although we describe Version 5 for Windows here, the two are similar in most respects. Current versions of Communicator and Internet Explorer for Windows and Macintosh are available on the *Internet Bible* CD-ROM.

The two programs are alike in a couple of major ways:

✦ Both automatically fill in the necessary prefixes and suffixes when you enter URLs. In other words, if you just type in `www.yahoo.com`, both Communicator and Explorer automatically add the `http://` in front of the URL to make it a valid Web address.

✦ Both programs also attempt to match the URL you're typing to recent URLs you've entered, as illustrated in Figure 8-1. If the program gets it right, you're saved several keystrokes. (Of course, if you're entering a URL that's only similar to one you've typed in before, this won't do you any good, but you can simply type over the suggested URL, so it doesn't slow you down, either.)

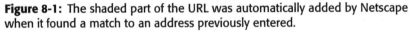

Figure 8-1: The shaded part of the URL was automatically added by Netscape when it found a match to an address previously entered.

The two programs do have differences, browsing-wise. For one thing, although they generally follow the supposed Internet standards, they both deal differently with some scripting languages — such as Java and Dynamic HTML — which means that the same page won't necessarily look the same on each browser.

Netscape Communicator

Some of Communicator's other features include the following:

✦ **Powerful History tools.** You can search the history file for words in the URL or document title, as well as reordering the file by time, title, URL, or even number of times a site has been visited. Communicator's History file is illustrated in Figure 8-2.

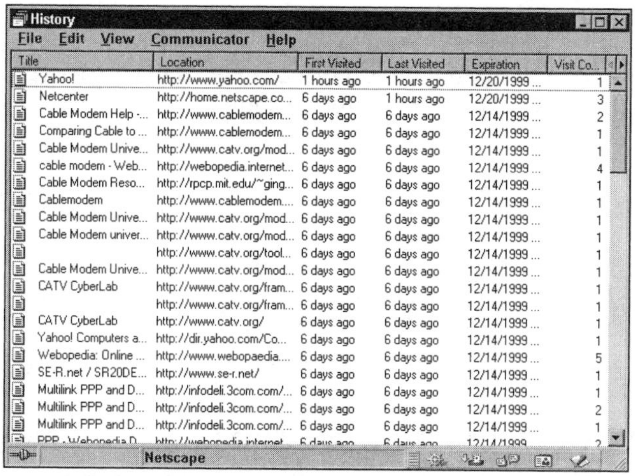

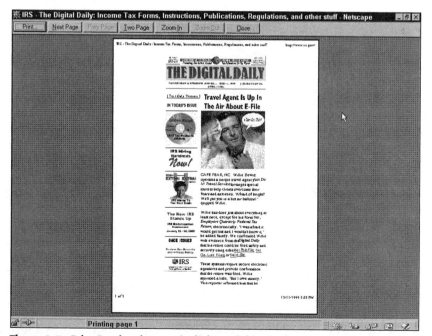

Figure 8-2: Communicator's History file can be quickly reorganized and just as easily searched.

✦ **Print Preview.** As Figure 8-3 shows, Communicator enables you to view on-screen what the Web page will look like printed, before you print. This will help save precious ink, paper, and time.

Figure 8-3: Print Preview is a particularly useful feature in Netscape Communicator. Print Preview is only available in version 5.5 of Internet Explorer.

✦ **OLE Support.** Netscape Communicator now supports Object Linking and Embedding, which means you can use it to open and edit any document from an application that also supports OLE, such as Excel (assuming you have the application on your computer, of course).

Internet Explorer

Some of Internet Explorer 5's interesting browser features include the following.

✦ **A Full Screen mode.** Clicking View ➪ Full Screen (or pressing the F11 key) removes most of the side and bottom navigation bars, leaving only a small strip of tools at the top of the screen, as shown in Figure 8-4. You'll particularly appreciate this if you use a laptop or have a small monitor.

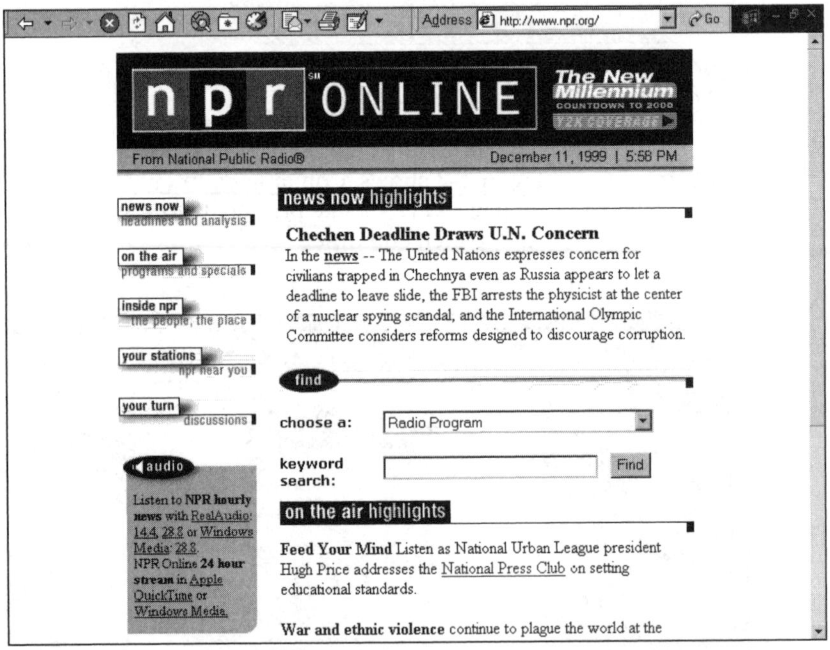

Figure 8-4: Explorer's Full Screen button lets you get the most out of your monitor.

✦ **An improved History function.** Clicking the History button brings up a left-hand pane, which is illustrated in Figure 8-5. This area shows your most recently viewed pages by date, and lists all the pages within a site that you visited in a hierarchy similar to the one you see when you browse your own hard drive. Like Netscape, Internet Explorer 5 has the ability to search the history file.

✦ **Two-window Search.** Clicking Search enables you to conduct a search in a left-hand pane, while viewing the results in the main browser pane at the right.

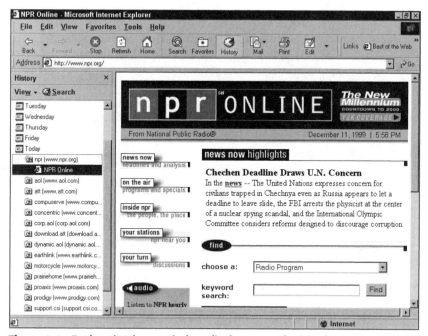

Figure 8-5: Explorer's History window displays recently visited URLs in an easily browsable format.

✦ **Greater multimedia support.** Internet Explorer 5 auto-installs ActiveX controls and comes with Windows Media Player 6, an advanced player for many different types of media, including streaming audio and video.

✦ **Print Preview (in IE 5.5 only).** The print preview feature is similar to the one offered by Netscape Communicator. It allows you to view on-screen what a Web page will look like when it is printed.

E-mail and newsgroups

There's more to the Internet than just the World Wide Web, of course, and good browsing software has to recognize this reality by providing support for the Internet's other functions — especially e-mail and Usenet newsgroups.

Not so long ago, you needed to buy a special stand-alone e-mail program to really get the most out of the Internet's e-mail capabilities, but the e-mail support that comes with both Netscape and Explorer today makes that entirely unnecessary.

Netscape's e-mail program is called Messenger; Explorer's is called Outlook Express. They have several e-mail features in common:

✦ Both support the vCard standard, which enables users to send and receive electronic business cards.

✦ Both enable you to digitally sign outgoing messages, as well as send and receive encrypted e-mail.

Cross-Reference   To learn more about certificates and encryption, take a look at Chapter 32, "Maintaining Your Online Privacy and Security."

✦ Both enable you to create and view HTML-based e-mail, which means you can send e-mail as richly formatted as a Web page, complete with graphics and links (provided, of course, that your recipient's e-mail program also supports it!).

✦ Both enable you to filter messages based on the sender's name, the message's subject matter, or the message's size. They will also allow you to forward, respond, or delete those messages as you see fit.

Of course, Messenger and Outlook Express also have some differences. Most of them are detail differences in the way the interface works, and thus open to personal preference. But Outlook Express does have two significant advantages over Netscape Messenger:

✦ Outlook Express enables you to configure an unlimited number of mail server accounts and identities. This means you can set up Outlook to check mail on your home and work e-mail accounts, and you can configure many different "identities" for each. In contrast, Netscape Messenger limits you to a single incoming mail server account if you have a POP (*Post Office Protocol*, the most common type of mail server in use today) mail account, and you can only have one identity.

✦ If you have a Web-based e-mail account, such as Yahoo! Mail or Hotmail, you can use Outlook Express to send and receive mail from that account. Web-based e-mail utilizes HTML mail servers, and Messenger does not support those.

On the other hand, Outlook Express has been susceptible to some recent e-mail virus issues that haven't affected Messenger. Whether this is because Outlook Express is less secure or is simply targeted more often by people who don't like Microsoft is anybody's guess.

Tip   If you share a computer with several people (members of your family, for example), you'll probably want to use Outlook Express to send and receive e-mail. Unlike Netscape Messenger, Outlook Express allows you to set up individual e-mail accounts for each user. This way, you can share your computer without sharing your mail.

Active desktop

Internet Explorer has one other major capability that Netscape Communicator lacks. If you have Windows 98 or higher, you can add Web page items to your desktop. Figure 8-6 shows a Web cam that has been added to a Windows desktop so that the conditions at a local mountain pass can be easily checked.

Figure 8-6: You can add an item from a Web page to your Windows desktop. This item is from the Web site of the Oregon Department of Transportation.

Introducing Opera: The New Kid on the Block

The new buzz in the browser wars is called Opera. This fast and friendly Web browser hails from Opera Software, based in Kjeller, Norway. Opera is unique in a number of ways:

✦ **It's small.** It's around 1 megabyte (MB) in size, which means your download can be measured in minutes rather than hours — and it's less than 2MB installed, a real boon for anyone who's short of disk space (and who isn't?).

✦ **It's fast.** Because it's small, it doesn't need to use very much of your machine's memory to run, leaving more room free for caching and rendering Web pages. As a result, pages tend to load and display faster than on Explorer or Netscape, especially on slower machines with less RAM.

✦ **Single window displays multiple Web pages.** Unlike Explorer and Netscape, which display separate Web pages in RAM-eating separate windows, Opera displays separate Web pages in windows that can be tiled or cascaded within a single Opera window (see Figure 8-7). Again, this means separate pages can be displayed more quickly and are also more stable. Each page can be configured differently, too, as to which fonts and graphic options they use, and what size they are.

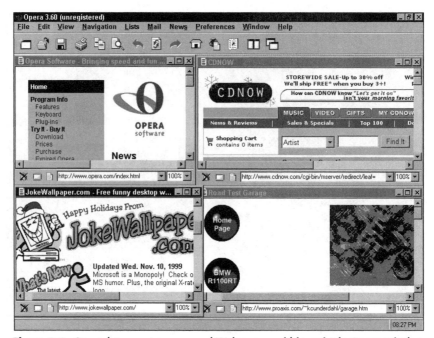

Figure 8-7: Opera lets you open several Web pages within a single Opera window.

✦ **Highly configurable.** You can configure Opera any way you wish. It looks completely different from the other browsers, but you can make it look more like Explorer or Netscape if you want.

✦ **Versions available for most operating systems.** Opera is available for virtually any operating system in use today, including Windows, Macintosh, Linux, UNIX, BeOS, Epoc, and OS/2.

On the downside, Opera has stayed lean by not supporting VRML, Java, ActiveX, DHTML, cascading style sheets, and some of the other latest and greatest tricks of the Web designer's toolbox. (It does, however, support some of the most popular plug-ins, such as Macromedia Shockwave and the Adobe Acrobat Reader.) Opera does not include an e-mail program, although Opera Software does host a Web-based mail service called OperaMail (www.operamail.com).

Opera's speed alone makes it worth a look. Who knows? You may find you prefer it to Netscape and Internet Explorer put together — at least for everyday browsing.

Which browser should I use?

Netscape 4.7 and Explorer 5 are free (and available on the CD-ROM in the back of this book), so there's no reason not to take them both for a spin. A registered copy of Opera is about $35, but a free 30-day trial version is also available on the CD-ROM. All three browsers are available for Windows and the Macintosh, but only Opera and Netscape Navigator (the browser component of Communicator) is available for UNIX and Linux.

For the average user, the differences probably aren't that significant. Use the one you feel most comfortable with. Like a new pair of shoes, sometimes you don't really know what you think about a piece of software until you've broken it in.

Installing Netscape

Netscape Communicator for Windows and for PowerPC (Macintosh) is available on this book's CD-ROM. To install Netscape:

1. Locate the Netscape installation file on the *Internet Bible* CD-ROM. For more information on using the CD-ROM and finding files on it, see Appendix C.

2. If you are running Windows, double-click the file `cc32d47.exe` to begin installation. If you have a Macintosh, double-click the Start Here icon.

3. Follow the instructions on each screen that the installer program presents. You'll be asked to read and agree to a license agreement, decide where you want to install the software, and to choose or create a folder for the program.

4. If you have a previous version of Netscape and you install the new one into the same folder, the old version will be overwritten, but your current bookmarks, preferences, and settings will be assigned to the new browser. If you don't want to overwrite your old version, just create a new folder and install the new version into it.

5. Once you're told that installation is complete, you can launch Netscape by clicking the Navigator icon on your desktop, or you can go to the folder where you installed your new browser and double-click the Navigator icon located there.

Installing Internet Explorer

Internet Explorer for Windows and PowerPC (Macintosh) is available on this book's CD-ROM. To install Internet Explorer:

1. Locate the Internet Explorer installation file on the *Internet Bible* CD-ROM. For more information on using the CD-ROM and finding files on it, see Appendix C.

2. If you are running Windows, double-click the file `ie5setup.exe` to begin installation. If you have a Macintosh, copy the Internet Explorer folder from the CD-ROM to your hard disk and remove the CD from the drive. Then double-click the Internet Explorer Installer icon in the folder you just copied.

3. Follow the instructions on each screen that the installer program presents. You'll be asked to read and agree to a license agreement and decide where you want to install the software. You'll also be asked whether you want to install just the browser, perform a standard installation, or install everything.

Internet Explorer has three setup options:

✦ **Browser Only**: Includes Internet Explorer 5.01, Java Support, the Microsoft Internet Connection Wizard, and multimedia enhancements.

✦ **Standard**: Adds Microsoft Outlook Express, True Web Integration, and Microsoft Wallet to the Browser Only installation.

✦ **Full**: Adds Microsoft NetMeeting, Microsoft Web Publishing Wizard, and Microsoft Chat 2.0 to the Standard installation.

Once you've made your decision, setup installs the browser and all the components you've chosen to your computer. Double-click the Internet Explorer icon on your desktop to open your new browser.

Installing Opera

Trial versions of Opera for Windows and Linux are available on this book's CD-ROM. To install Opera for Windows from the CD-ROM:

1. Locate the Opera installation file `o362e32.exe` on the *Internet Bible* CD-ROM and double-click it. For more information on using the CD-ROM and finding files on it, see Appendix C.

2. Follow the instructions on each screen that the installer program presents. You won't actually be presented with any options, unless you consider declining the terms of the license agreement an option.

The version of Opera for Linux that you will find on the *Internet Bible* CD-ROM is a technology preview, which means that there are still some bugs that need to be worked out. To install Opera for Linux:

1. Log in to your system as the *root* user. If you are not authorized to log-in as *root*, find out who is (it's probably the network administrator).

2. Place the *Internet Bible* CD-ROM in the CD drive and mount it using the following command: `mount /dev/cdrom /mnt/cdrom`

3. Move to the local directory where you want to install Opera. It will probably be `/usr/local`.

4. Create a new folder for Opera by typing `mkdir opera`.

5. Copy the Opera installation file `opera_0125.tar.gz` from the CD-ROM into the new folder. The command you type should look like this:

   `cp /mnt/cdrom/browsers/opera/opera_0125.tar.gz /usr/local/opera`

6. If you aren't in the local `opera` folder you created in step 4, go there now. Decompress the installation file by typing:

   `gunzip opera_0125.tar.gz ; tar xvf opera_0125`

7. Run the installation program by typing `./runnow`. Answer "Y" when you are asked if you decompressed and tarred the files. As with the Windows version, the only choice you will have during setup is whether or not you accept the terms of the license agreement. When you've completed installation, use the command `./opera` to run the browser.

Setup takes just a few seconds and Opera is ready to use immediately. During the trial period a message will be displayed each time you open the program to remind you how much time is left until expiration.

Summary

Netscape Communicator and Internet Explorer are powerful tools for exploring the World Wide Web. Explorer holds a slight edge in terms of features, but you won't be disappointed in either one. In the end, the choice between them boils down to which one you feel most comfortable with — and if you find both of them bloated and slow, maybe you should consider going another route entirely and join the chorus of critics praising the slim and speedy Opera.

✦   ✦   ✦

Using Internet Explorer 5

Can you imagine what it might be like if you were expected to get into some strange new vehicle that was quite unlike anything you've seen before, and were expected to immediately drive off in it? You'd probably like to have a bit of an orientation before you slipped out into heavy traffic on a rainy night, wouldn't you?

If you're going to use Internet Explorer as your Internet browser, this chapter is your orientation ride. Here you not only learn the basics of Internet Explorer, but you also learn how to configure the Internet Explorer options to suit your needs — sort of like adjusting the seat, steering wheel, and mirrors before you head out into traffic.

Internet Explorer 5 is really pretty fantastic, especially if you compare it to the ancient Web browsers of just a few years ago. In the early days of Web browsing, most people were happy just to see a bit of color or the occasional graphic image. No one expected to see live video newscasts, to hold meetings over the Internet, or to make secure purchases using a credit card. Now all of these and many more tasks are not only possible, but are becoming common.

Learning the Basics of Internet Explorer

Internet Explorer is a Web browser — a program that enables you to view the contents of pages on the World Wide Web, the graphical portion of the Internet. Web pages are constructed in HTML — the language Web browser programs understand. Internet Explorer 5 is available for Windows, and Internet Explorer 4.5 is available for Macintosh systems.

Note To make full use of Internet Explorer, you need access to the Internet. For most people, this means that you must open an account with an Internet Service Provider, or ISP; that you have a modem; and that you have access to a telephone line. If you have direct access to the Internet through your network, you won't need the ISP, modem, or telephone line. Internet Explorer will work well as your Internet browser no matter what type of equipment you use to access the Internet.

Web browsers do more than simply display graphical information on your screen. They also play sounds, show animation, screen movies, let you choose the Web sites you want to visit, keep track of Web sites you've visited, enable you to buy items online, and much more. In addition to HTML documents, Web pages often include graphics images, sounds, videos, Java applets, ActiveX controls, and a whole host of other optional components. The task of your Web browser is to integrate all of those bits and pieces seamlessly into the pages you see on your screen.

Internet Explorer is easy to launch — especially if you use Windows. Figure 9-1 shows four easy ways to start Internet Explorer in Windows 98. You can:

✦ Click the Internet Explorer icon on your desktop.

✦ Choose Internet Explorer from the Start menu.

✦ Select the Internet Explorer icon on the Quick Launch toolbar.

✦ Enter a Web address in an address toolbar.

Tip To display the address toolbar as part of your Windows 98 Taskbar, right-click the Taskbar, and choose Toolbars ⇨ Address.

To start Internet Explorer using a Macintosh:

✦ Double-click the Internet Explorer desktop icon.

✦ Select the Internet Explorer icon from the Applications list in the Apply menu.

Although you can use Internet Explorer for some offline tasks, such as viewing offline Web pages or other HTML documents, launching Internet Explorer generally also starts your connection to the Internet. If you haven't used Internet Explorer before or if you haven't already set up your Internet access, you'll have to configure your Internet account the first time you use Internet Explorer. Before you launch Internet Explorer, make certain you're ready to connect to the Internet with your modem turned on (if your modem is an external modem) and with your telephone line available.

Cross-Reference To learn more about making your connection, read Chapter 1, "Getting Connected Fast!"

Double-click the desktop icon   Use the Start menu shortcut

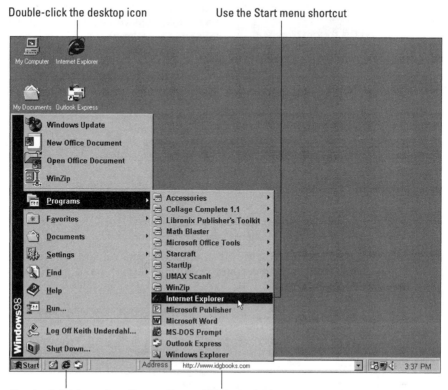

Use the Quick Launch toolbar   Enter a URL in the Address bar

Figure 9-1: Launching Internet Explorer in Windows is easy using one of several methods.

To start Internet Explorer, follow these steps:

1. Launch Internet Explorer using one of the techniques just described. Internet Explorer loads and displays the Dialing Progress dialog box shown in Figure 9-2.

   If you haven't used Internet Explorer before, you won't see the Dialing Progress dialog box at this point. Instead, you'll see a series of screens asking for information about how you'd like to connect to the Internet. You might want to refer to Chapter 1, "Getting Connected Fast!" and Chapter 5, "Choosing Your Service Provider," for more information if you need to set up an Internet account.

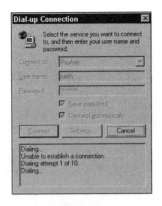

Figure 9-2: The Windows Dialing Progress dialog box keeps you informed while your PC connects to the Internet.X

2. Once your account has been verified, Internet Explorer loads and displays a start page similar to Figure 9-3.

   Web pages are constantly being updated. The page you see when you launch Internet Explorer will certainly look quite a bit different than Figure 9-3.

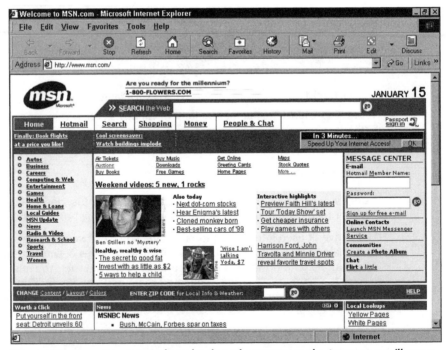

Figure 9-3: Once Internet Explorer loads and connects to the Internet, you'll see a Web page like this one.

3. Move your mouse around the screen and notice when the pointer changes to a hand.

When the mouse pointer changes to a hand, you're pointing to a *link* — a connection to another Web page. If you click one of the links, Internet Explorer displays the page connected to the link.

4. Click the Close button or choose File ⇨ Close (or File ⇨ Exit on a Mac) to exit Internet Explorer.

You may be asked if you wish to disconnect from your ISP when you close Internet Explorer. If not, you may need to disconnect manually.

Tip
Web pages generally don't look too good if your screen is set to the 640 × 480 VGA resolution setting. You may want to set your screen to a higher resolution setting, such as 800 × 600 or 1024 × 768, before you start Internet Explorer so you can see more of each Web page without so much scrolling.

Introducing the Internet Explorer 5 Screen

The Internet Explorer screen can be a pretty busy place. It has menus, buttons, links, and an address box — and all this is just what sits at the top of the screen even if you aren't visiting any Web sites. You'll also find a status line and scroll bars plus lots of different options for changing the appearance of the screen.

Figure 9-4 shows how the Internet Explorer 5 screen may appear if you display all of the toolbars and opt for text labels on the buttons. Of course, it may not look quite like this figure on your computer, especially if you've moved the toolbars around to make better use of your screen space.

Tip
To move the menu bar or the toolbars, point to the left edge of the menu bar or toolbar, hold down the left mouse button, and drag the bar to a new location.

The Title bar

The Internet Explorer title bar does more than just show the name of the program; it also shows you the name of whatever Web site you happen to be visiting. In Figure 9-4, for example, the title bar shows that we're visiting a site named "CJs Birthday."

The Web site name generally isn't the same as the Web site address. Rather, it's usually the title line from the top of the Web page.

Title bar   Menu bar   Standard toolbar   Address bar   Links toolbar

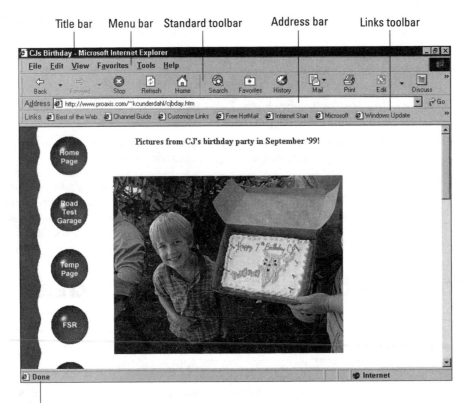

Status bar

Figure 9-4: The Internet Explorer screen gives you a lot of tools for browsing the Internet.

The Menu bar

The menu bar provides access to all Internet Explorer commands through drop-down menus. Most of these commands are duplicated on the toolbars if you'd rather navigate using the mouse.

> **Tip** To devote all of your screen to viewing a Web page, select View ➪ Full Screen, or press F11. Press F11 again to quickly return the elements to the top of your screen.

Here's a brief summary of the menus on the Internet Explorer menu bar:

✦ **File** — Provides commands for opening, saving, and printing Web pages. You'll also find a useful option for sending a Web page or link via e-mail when you'd like to share a Web page with someone.

✦ **Edit**—Provides commands that enable you to copy all or part of a Web page to your Clipboard, to edit a local HTML file, and to search for a text string on the current page.

✦ **View**—Enables you to control the appearance and various other aspects of the Internet Explorer screen. The Text Size submenu enables you to change the default size of text on Web pages you view. In addition, View ➪ Source enables you to view the HTML programming code that generates a Web page. If you want to learn how a particularly fancy element on a Web page was programmed, View ➪ Source enables you to see all the gory details.

✦ **Favorites**—Enables you to manage all of the favorite Web site links you've saved and to subscribe to specific information services. Use Favorites ➪ Add to Favorites to make it easy to return to specific Web sites.

✦ **Tools**—Enables you to link to your mail program, or set up synchronization features for viewing content offline. The Internet Options dialog, which controls virtually every aspect of your browsing experience, can be found here.

✦ **Help**—Provides help with Internet Explorer, program updates, and access to help resources on the Internet. Use Help ➪ About Internet Explorer to find out if your copy of Internet Explorer is the international version with 40-bit security, or the U.S. and Canada-only version that is more secure because it uses higher-level security features. With 40-bit security, it's easier to break into a message from the international version of Internet Explorer—the U.S. and Canada-only version uses a 128-bit encryption key that's much harder to break.

The Standard toolbar

The standard button toolbar provides quick one-click shortcuts to the most common Internet Explorer tasks. In fact, you'll probably find yourself ignoring the menus most of the time because it's so much faster and easier to simply click one of the buttons.

> **Tip** Once you're familiar with the toolbar buttons, click View ➪ Toolbars ➪ Customize, and change the Text Options item so that no Text Labels are shown. Without the text labels, the standard button toolbar takes a small fraction of the space it requires when the labels are visible.

Table 9-1 explains how to use the toolbar buttons as you browse the Web.

> **Tip** If you have text labels turned off, hold the mouse pointer over a button for a few seconds to see a description of the button.

Don't forget that you can drag the toolbars to new locations in the area just below the title bar. When you turn off the text labels, for example, it's possible to nest the menu bar and the three toolbars in two rows rather than the four rows needed if each bar has its own row.

	Table 9-1	
	The Standard Button Toolbar	
Button	*Button Name*	*Click to Do This*
⇦ Back	Back	Return to the previous page you visited during the current session. Click the small down-arrow to the right of the Back button to select a page to return to.
⇨ Forward	Forward	Go forward to a page you've already visited during the current session (this button is enabled only after you've used the Back button). Click the small down-arrow to the right of the Forward button to select a page to go forward to.
⊗ Stop	Stop	Stop loading the current page. This option is most useful if the current page seems to be loading very slowly and you don't need to see the remaining page elements.
🗐 Refresh	Refresh	Reload the current page. Use this button if an error occurs that prevents all page elements from loading, or if you click the Stop button in error.
🏠 Home	Home	Return to your start page.
🔍 Search	Search	Use an Internet search engine to locate Web pages based on keywords you enter.
⭐ Favorites	Favorites	View the favorites pane so you can add, organize, or visit your favorite Web pages.
🕐 History	History	View the history pane so you can quickly review or return to Web sites you've already visited.
📧 Mail	Mail	Send or receive an e-mail message using your mail program.
🖨 Print	Print	Print the currently displayed Web page.
📄 Edit	Edit	Open the current page in an HTML editor, such as FrontPage or Notepad.

The Links toolbar

The links toolbar enables you to visit Web sites with a quick mouse click. When you first install Internet Explorer, the links toolbar has several predefined links that take you to one of several Microsoft Web sites.

As handy as it may be to visit those Microsoft Web sites with a quick click of your mouse, you can probably think of plenty of other Web sites you'd rather visit. For example, you might want to change one of the links so you can quickly jump right to `http://www.idgbooks.com` so you can always be on top of the latest books published by IDG Books Worldwide.

To add a Web page you are currently visiting to the Links bar, drag the Web page icon from the address bar to the Links toolbar. You can also make a few changes to an existing link, such as updating the URL or giving it a different name, by right-clicking (on a Mac click and hold) the link—you can also delete links. Click the Customize Links button to visit a Microsoft Web page that discusses methods of customizing the links even more.

The Address toolbar

You use the address toolbar to enter an address, or URL (Uniform Resource Locator), of a Web page you'd like to visit. The address toolbar also shows the current Web site address when you click a link and jump to a new page.

Tip   New in Internet Explorer 5: When you start typing a URL in the address bar, the program automatically reviews your browsing history to see if anything matches what you are typing. Possible matches will appear below the Address bar, and, if you see one that you want, just click it rather than continuing to type the whole URL.

To return to some of the Web sites you've already visited, click the down-arrow at the right edge of the address box. Choose the site you'd like to visit again from the drop-down list.

The Status bar

The Status bar provides information about Web sites that you visit. When you click a link or enter a Web address, you'll see a message, "Finding site," that tells you Internet Explorer is attempting to locate the Web site. As the Web site begins to load, you'll see messages that tell you how many objects remain to be downloaded. Later you'll see a message that says Done to tell you the download is complete.

The status bar also provides information on the security status of a Web site. You wouldn't, for example, want to send your credit card number to a nonsecure site, and you'd probably want to be very careful about the types of files you might download from sites you don't completely trust.

Cross-Reference   For more information on Internet security issues, take a look at Chapter 32, "Maintaining Your Online Privacy and Security."

Playing with the Internet Explorer Options

Even though a lot of careful planning went into the design of Internet Explorer, the program may not always work just the way you'd like. Fortunately, Internet Explorer is extremely flexible, so if you don't like something about it, you can probably customize an option to better suit your needs.

You've already seen that you can change the appearance of Internet Explorer by moving, hiding, or resizing the toolbars. The Internet Options dialog box enables you to make even more profound changes in the way Internet Explorer functions. In the following sections you'll see how important the Internet Options dialog box can be in customizing Internet Explorer to your tastes.

To view the Internet Options dialog box, select Tools ➪ Internet Options. Each of the tabs on this dialog box has quite a number of settings, so the following sections each cover the options on one tab of the dialog box.

Modifying the general options

Figure 9-5 shows the General tab of the Internet Options dialog box. The options on this tab primarily deal with appearance issues, such as colors and fonts, but you can also use it to set your home page, control your temporary files, and adjust the History folder.

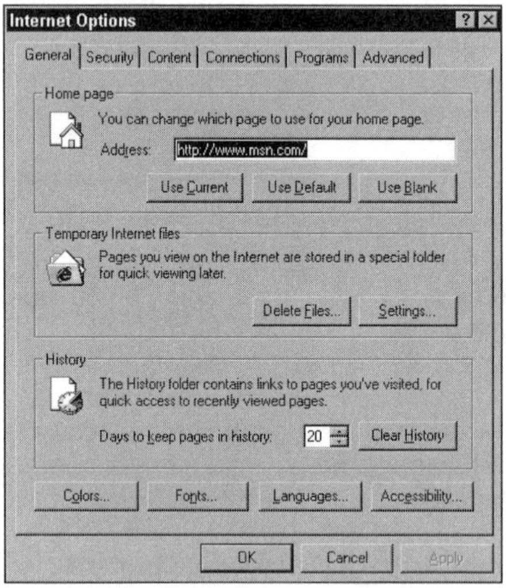

Figure 9-5: The General tab enables you to control the appearance of Internet Explorer.

Setting home page options

Use the Home page section of the General tab to control which Web page appears when you start Internet Explorer. You can enter an address in the Address text box, but it's usually easier to visit the Web site you want to use as your home page and then click the Use Current button. When you click this button, the URL for the currently displayed page is inserted in the Address text box, and this page will be set as your new Home Page from now on. To return to the original setting for your home page, click Use Default. If you don't want to automatically display any Web page when Internet Explorer is launched, click Use Blank.

Caution

Because Internet Explorer stores copies of Web pages you've visited on your hard disk, it's pretty easy for someone to snoop around and see where you've been on the Internet. If you need to maintain your privacy, be sure to click both the Delete Files and Clear History buttons just before you close Internet Explorer. Keep in mind, however, that this option does not remove any tracking of your Internet activities by third-party programs, such as Cyber Sentinel.

Configuring temporary Internet files options

The Temporary Internet files section controls the Internet Explorer *page cache* — the way pages you visit are stored on your hard disk. By storing Web pages on your hard disk, Internet Explorer can display those pages more quickly the next time you visit the page because unchanged items won't need to be downloaded again. Of course this improved performance does come with a price — some of your hard disk space is used to store the files. You can delete the current page cache files by clicking the Delete Files button. Although this removes the files currently in the page cache, new files will start to fill the cache as soon as you start browsing again. If you're concerned about disk space, you'll probably want to use the Settings button to display the Settings dialog box shown in Figure 9-6.

Figure 9-6: Use the Settings dialog box to control the page cache settings.

Use the option buttons at the top of the Settings dialog box to control how often Internet Explorer should check to see if Web pages have been updated. Here's what the four options do:

✦ **Every visit to the page** — Checks for changes every time you go to a page, even if you're just returning to a page you just visited. This setting makes moving around the Web pretty slow because Internet Explorer has to check a lot of pages that probably haven't changed much in a few minutes.

✦ **Every time you start Internet Explorer** — Checks for changes once per session. If you return to a page you just visited, Internet Explorer doesn't need to check for changes and the page will load much faster. This setting is generally the best for most browsing because it represents a good compromise between speed and making certain the current versions of Web pages are displayed.

✦ **Automatically** — If you have previously visited a page during the current day or Internet Explorer session, the program will not check for updated pages if you choose this setting.

✦ **Never** — Doesn't check for changes unless you click the Refresh button. This setting isn't a very good choice, because the time you save by always using the cached pages is offset by the need to click Refresh often and the likelihood that you'll miss important changes.

Use the *Amount of disk space to use* option to control how much room is allocated to the page cache. You'll probably want to keep the page cache size pretty small — the minimum size is 1 percent of the total disk space.

Tip

If you have more than one hard disk (or more than one partition on your disk) you may want to use the Move Folder button to place the page cache on a different drive. This may be especially true if you're running out of space on your primary hard drive.

When you finish making changes in the Settings dialog box, click OK to return to the General tab of the Internet Options dialog box.

Changing history options

The History section of the General tab of the Internet Options dialog box controls how long your system retains the links to Web sites you've visited. These links make it faster to return to the same sites in the future.

Modifying color options

Click the Colors button to display the Colors dialog box shown in Figure 9-7. You can use this dialog box to adjust the colors that Internet Explorer uses for text, background, and links.

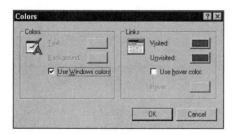

Figure 9-7: Use the Colors dialog box to control the color settings.

You may want to adjust the colors if you find it difficult to see the standard color choices. One option in this dialog box, *Use hover color*, is especially useful because it helps you determine when your mouse pointer is correctly located over a link by changing the color of the link.

Remove the check from the *Use Windows colors* checkbox first if you want to change the text or background colors. Otherwise you won't be able to adjust these options.

When you finish making changes, click OK to return to the General tab of the Internet Options dialog box.

Changing font options

Click the Fonts button to display the Fonts dialog box shown in Figure 9-8. The Fonts dialog box enables you to control the fonts that Internet Explorer uses to display Web pages.

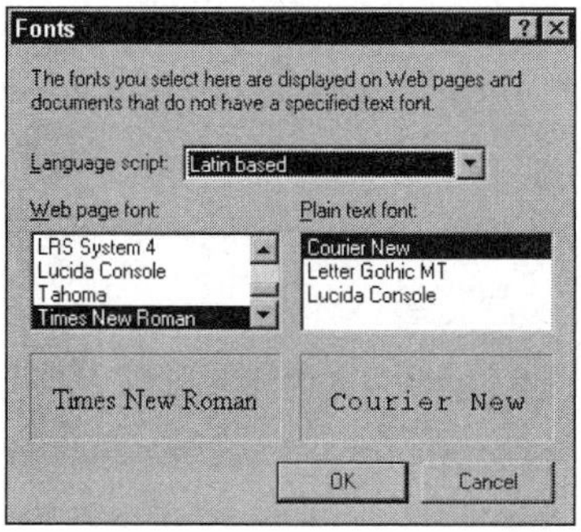

Figure 9-8: Use the Fonts dialog box to change the fonts used to display Web pages.

You may need to change the character set if you visit a lot of foreign-language Web sites. In most cases the default fonts should be acceptable, but you may want to play around with Web page fonts if you prefer a different typeface. Unfortunately, if you want to change the size of fonts you cannot do it here. For that you will have to close the Internet Options dialog and choose View ➪ Text Size.

Click OK to return to the General tab of the Internet Options dialog box.

Configuring language options

Click the Languages button to display the Language Preference dialog box shown in Figure 9-9. You can use this dialog box to add additional languages that can be used to display multilanguage Web sites.

Figure 9-9: Use the Language Preference dialog box to change the language used when displaying multiple language Web pages.

In most cases the Language Preference dialog box shows only one option — your current language selection. To add another language to your list, click the Add button and choose a language from the Add Language dialog box. Once you've added additional languages to the list in the Language Preference dialog box, use the Move Up and Move Down buttons to specify which languages you prefer. When you visit a multilanguage Web site, Internet Explorer uses the language highest in the preference list to display the site.

Tip Adding a language to the Language Preference dialog box can be very helpful for someone who is studying a foreign language.

Click OK to return to the General tab of the Internet Options dialog box.

Setting accessibility options

Click the Accessibility button to display the Accessibility dialog box shown in Figure 9-10. You can use the options in the Accessibility dialog box to direct Internet Explorer to ignore HTML commands that may make text hard to read.

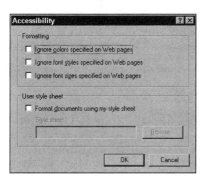

Figure 9-10: Use the Accessibility dialog box to control the appearance of Web pages to assist visually impaired users.

Web site authors can use HTML programming to control the appearance of their pages, but the choices they select may not always be the best for viewing by visually impaired visitors.

Click OK to return to the General tab of the Internet Options dialog box.

Modifying the security options

Figure 9-11 shows the Security tab of the Internet Options dialog box. The options on this tab deal with security issues for the different types of Web sites you may visit.

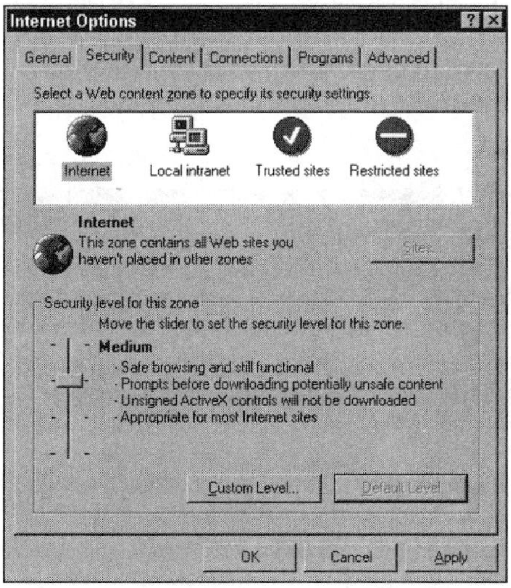

Figure 9-11: The Security tab enables you to control the security settings for Internet Explorer.

Internet Explorer has four different security *zones*—groups of related types of Web sites—for which you can define security levels. These zones are defined as follows:

✦ **Internet zone**—All sites on the Internet that you haven't specifically defined as being part of another zone.

✦ **Local intranet zone**—Your computer, your local network, sites that the network administrator allows to bypass a proxy server, or Web sites you specifically define as being part of this zone.

✦ **Trusted sites zone**—Only those Web sites you specifically define as being part of this zone. This should only include sites you're certain will not include damaging content.

✦ **Restricted sites zone**—Web sites you specifically define as sites you don't trust. Use this zone to prevent these sites from sending you damaging content such as computer viruses.

You can use one of the four predefined security levels in the lower half of the Security tab or set up your own custom security level for any of the zones. The level you choose should reflect the level of trust you feel for particular sites. For example, you probably don't worry about catching a computer virus from a Web site you've created on your computer, but you might well be concerned about an obscure Web site that discusses the creation of viruses.

If you feel you understand the various objects that can be a part of Web pages well enough, you may want to click the Custom Level button to display the Security Settings dialog box shown in Figure 9-12. This dialog box enables you to make dozens of specific settings to control how ActiveX, Java, cookies, scripting, and many other types of objects function.

Click OK to return to the Security tab of the Internet Options dialog box.

A Security Hole in IE5

Internet Explorer 5 includes a security bug that, although minor, deserves your attention. By default, the setting for the security option "Allow paste operations via script" is enabled in all but the highest security levels. This innocent-looking option enables a remote Web server to paste items to their own system from the Windows clipboard on your computer.

Think about it. What is the last thing you copied or cut in a Windows program? Was it your credit card number? A file containing your formula for cold fusion? A harmless icon graphic? The launch codes for the nation's nuclear arsenal? Whatever is contained in the Windows clipboard can be pasted to a remote server without your knowledge.

If you have set your security level to High, paste operations are disabled. But if you are using any other security level, we strongly urge you to change the "Allow paste operations via script" option to Prompt or Disable.

Make sure that this isn't enabled

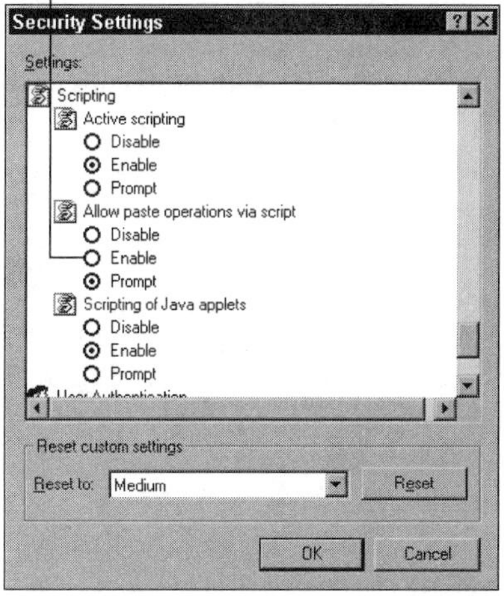

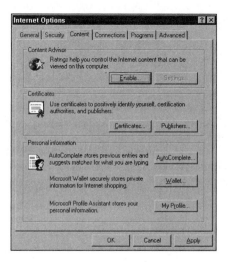

Figure 9-12: The Security Settings dialog box gives you the ultimate level of control over the security settings.

> **Tip**
>
> Although cookies do not present a virus hazard because they only contain plain text, they can be an intrusion of your privacy as described in Chapter 32, "Maintaining Your Online Privacy and Security." If you don't want Web sites to write cookies to your hard drive, change your cookie preferences here.

Modifying the content options

Figure 9-13 shows the Content tab of the Internet Options dialog box. The options on this tab deal with the types of sites you want to visit as well as issues of secure identification of yourself and the sites you visit.

Figure 9-13: The Content tab controls content and identification issues.

Note   The Internet can be a really nasty, dangerous place to visit. Its crevices and gutters not only hide criminals who would love to steal your credit card numbers, but many Web sites also peddle raw adult material and extreme political viewpoints. No matter what built-in tools such as the Content Advisor and certificates you enable, ultimately it's up to you to use some common sense in protecting yourself and your family while you're browsing the Web. To learn more about this important issue, see Chapter 33, "Protecting Your Kids on the Internet."

Using the content advisor

The Internet Explorer Content Advisor uses a voluntary rating system that Web sites can use to rate their content. Because this system is completely voluntary, many sites do not participate in the rating system. You can choose to block sites that aren't rated, but doing so also blocks the vast majority of inoffensive sites that simply haven't bothered to rate their content.

To use the Content Advisor:

1. Click Enable to display the Content Advisor dialog box.

2. Click one of the Category keys to display the current rating, as shown in Figure 9-14.

3. Drag the Rating slider to the right or left until you are satisfied with the setting. Continue on to set each of the categories to your preference.

4. Click the Approved Sites tab.

    If there is a Web site that you want to let your family view, but it is not rated, you can add it here.

5. Click the General tab.

    For the most complete protection against material you feel may be objectionable, deselect both the *Users can see sites that have no ratings* and the *Supervisor can type a password to allow users to view restricted content* check boxes. Remember, if you clear both check boxes, you won't be able to visit unrated Web sites.

Caution   The Web site rating system is voluntary, so be forewarned that a few sites may rate themselves falsely — the Content Advisor may let these sites pass as acceptable to you, when really it isn't.

6. Click the Advanced tab.

    If you wish to use a third-party rating system, you can specify the system you wish to use here. Some rating systems are continually updated by a special Web site that lists changes to Web page ratings. If you use one of these rating systems, you can specify the rating update page in the Rating Bureau text box.

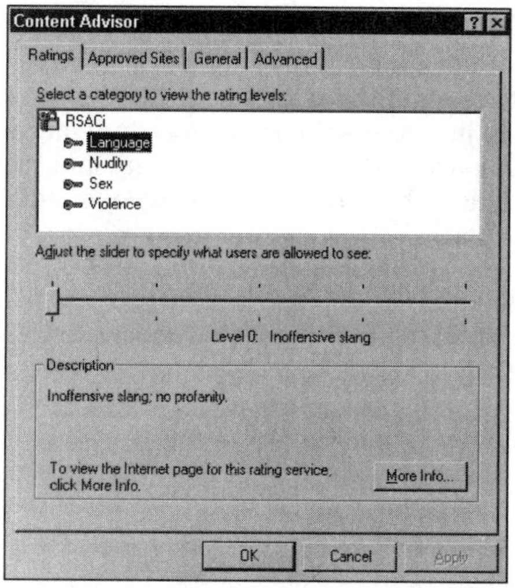

Figure 9-14: Use the Content Advisor to set the options for the types of Web sites you can visit.

7. Click OK to apply any changes and close the dialog box.

   If you haven't set up the Content Advisor before, you'll see the Create Supervisor Password dialog box in place of the Supervisor Password Required dialog box.

8. Type the password in the Password text box.

   Make certain you remember the password you type, because otherwise you won't be able to change any of the settings in the future.

9. Click OK to enable the Content Advisor.

Using certificates

Certificates are electronically encoded document files that provide proof that someone is who they say they are. You might think of certificates as being similar to the driver's license or check cashing card you use as identification when you cash a check. But because you also need assurance that the Web sites you visit are legitimate, certificates are also used to identify Web sites.

The Certificates section of the Content tab includes two items:

✦ **Certificates** — For certificates you've obtained so you can prove your identity. Most Web sites don't require you to provide a personal certificate, but you'll need a certificate for some sites that require client authentication.

✦ **Publishers** — Enables you to examine and configure the settings for Web sites you trust. For example, when you visit certain Web sites, Internet Explorer might need to download certain pieces of software such as ActiveX controls. You can accept a publisher's certificate that says you'll always accept downloads from the certificate holder. That way you won't need to verify every download from that certificate holder.

Setting up your personal information

The Personal information section of the Content tab enables you to store information about yourself so you don't have to re-enter the same text each time you want to share the information. You can store just your shipping address or you can include complete contact information. You can also store your credit card information in password protected storage so you don't have to enter your account number every time you want to buy something online.

Note   You must have Microsoft Wallet installed to securely store your credit card information. If you haven't installed Microsoft Wallet, use the Windows Setup tab of the Add/Remove Programs dialog box to install the program first.

You can enter your complete contact information by clicking the My Profile button. In addition, you can specify your digital ID using this option. The information you enter here can be supplied to Web sites that request visitor information. Use the Wallet button to specify your credit card information for Microsoft Wallet.

The AutoComplete button enables you to modify AutoComplete settings for Internet Explorer. You can choose to have Internet Explorer AutoComplete data in Web forms, Web site URLs in the Address bar, and user name and password information at various Web sites. If you want to ensure that none of your personal information remains on the computer, click the Clear Forms and Clear Passwords buttons in the AutoComplete dialog box.

Modifying the connection options

Figure 9-15 shows the Connections tab of the Internet Options dialog box. You can use the options on this tab to control the methods your PC uses to access the Internet.

Click the Setup button to set up a new connection to the Internet. You might use this option if you have a laptop PC and need to create a new connection when you're traveling and are unable to access your normal ISP, for example.

If you already have an Internet connection, select it in the Dial-up Settings list and click Settings to modify it. If you have more than one connection configured, select the one that you want to be the default and click Set Default. You can also choose whether you want Internet Explorer to automatically dial your default connection or not when you aren't online.

Finally, if you are using Internet Connection Sharing you can change settings for that here as well. The Sharing button enables you to choose how your computer connects to the Internet, and how it connects to your network (if applicable).

Your company may have established policies regarding Internet access. If so, your network administrator may have created an automatic configuration option so you don't have to set up Internet Explorer manually. Click Configure to select this option.

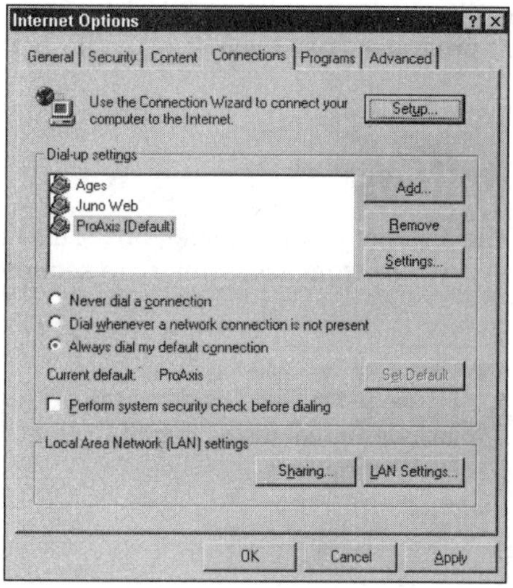

Figure 9-15: The Connections tab enables you to specify how you want to connect to the Internet.

Configuring the programs options

Figure 9-16 shows the Programs tab of the Internet Options dialog box. You can use the options on this tab to control which programs you'd like to use for news, mail, and so on.

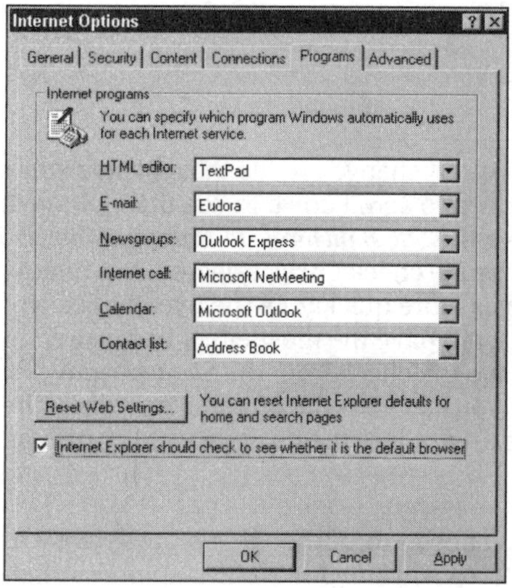

Figure 9-16: Use the Programs tab to specify the programs you want to use for Internet functions other than browsing.

The programs listed here should be the ones you use the most. For instance, if you use Eudora for e-mail and have selected it here, that is the program that will open if you click the Mail button on the Internet Explorer toolbar. You should be able to choose virtually any registered program here, even if it isn't sold by Microsoft. You can see in Figure 9-16 that non-Microsoft programs have been selected for both the HTML editor and e-mail program.

Modifying the advanced options

Figure 9-17 shows the Advanced tab of the Internet Options dialog box. This tab includes a large number of options for everything from accessibility to security to Java settings.

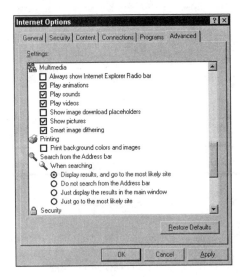

Figure 9-17: The Advanced tab includes a real mixed bag of Internet Explorer options.

As an example of some of the options you can change on this tab, consider the seven items in the Multimedia section (you'll need to scroll down to see the Multimedia options). In most cases you want to leave the *Show pictures, Play animations, Play videos, Play sounds,* and *Smart image dithering* check boxes selected, but removing the checks enables you to view Web pages more quickly. Of the five, the Show pictures check box is the one that is likely to have the most effect because so many Web pages include graphics. If you remove the check from the *Show pictures, Play animations,* or *Play videos* check boxes, you can view the pictures or videos after the page has loaded by right-clicking on the area where the image should appear and selecting Show picture.

You'll find dozens of options on the Advanced tab. Although it's pretty easy to understand the way that particular options will affect Internet Explorer, others are a bit more obscure.

Using The Best Internet Explorer Add-Ons

Internet Explorer 5 seems pretty complete all by itself, but that can be a little deceptive. Internet Explorer was designed to enable new capabilities to be added simply by loading the right *add-on* — a software component that enables Internet Explorer to handle new types of data files or to perform a new function that isn't built into Internet Explorer itself.

Note   Strictly speaking, not all add-ons enable Internet Explorer 5 itself to do more. Some add-ons, such as RealPlayer G2, are really stand-alone programs that don't require Internet Explorer to function. But because these add-ons enhance your use of Internet Explorer, it's appropriate to mention them in a discussion of Internet Explorer 5 add-ons.

Many Internet Explorer add-ons — also referred to as plug-ins — enhance the browser's ability to handle various multimedia elements on Web pages. For instance, if you want to watch a video of a movie trailer, you may need to use Apple QuickTime. Or if you want to listen to a streaming broadcast, such as Art Bell's *Coast to Coast AM* radio show, you need to use Real Network's RealPlayer. And if you want to read IRS tax form instructions, you'll have to have Acrobat Reader from Adobe. All of these programs act as plug-ins to Internet Explorer, enabling you to access document types that Web browsers aren't normally designed to open.

Other add-ons are much simpler in nature. Microsoft provides links to a variety of plug-ins at `http://www.microsoft.com/Windows/IE/WebAccess/default.asp`. The Web Accessories offered here include:

✦ **Surf Monkey Explorer Bar**. Once installed, this bar lives at the bottom of the Internet Explorer window, and offers tools that help make Web browsing safer and more enjoyable for your kids. Surf Monkey includes a content filter, as well as links to various kid-safe sites and directories hosted by Surf Monkey.

✦ **The New York Times Explorer Bar**. This add-on provides (surprise) a steady stream of up-to-the-minute news from *The New York Times*. It provides information in a ticker-style format, and includes quick links to financial news and stock quotes.

✦ **Alta Vista Power Tools**. AV Power Tools offers not only a quick way to perform Web searches, but also a place where you can quickly translate text between five major languages. This tool is useful to have on-screen if you visit a lot of foreign language Web sites.

✦ **Web Accessories**. Microsoft offers a package of accessories that add a few useful features to Internet Explorer. Most of them add functions to shortcut menus that you can open by right-clicking on a Web page in Windows. One of the most interesting is the ability to open individual frames in a new window, similar to the way Opera allows you to open pages in separate document windows.

Summary

Internet Explorer 5 is a popular Web browser, but even the most experienced Internet Explorer user probably doesn't realize all of the advanced features and options it contains. In this chapter you've learned a bit more about Internet Explorer 5 and perhaps some tricks and techniques you didn't know. You've also learned how to configure Internet Explorer so it works just the way you like.

✦   ✦   ✦

Using Netscape Communicator

Few names are as synonymous with the Internet as Netscape. Beginning in 1994, Netscape evangelized both the Web and the browser; its young entrepreneurs ushered in an era of "internet frenzy" in the financial markets. Acquired by America Online (AOL) in 1998 in a complex deal that involved Sun Microsystems, Netscape Navigator now shares the market with rival Microsoft Internet Explorer. The upstart browser called Opera lags in market share, but has a loyal following. Netscape Communicator, however, remains the only browser available for all major computing platforms: Macintosh, Windows, and UNIX.

As browsers have matured, they have evolved into a "Swiss army knife" of Internet tools. You can use a browser to view the Web, read e-mail, participate in newsgroups (Usenet), and conference with business associates or friends. The browser portion of Netscape Communicator is called Navigator, and it is this component that is the focus of this chapter.

Note At press time, Communicator was shipping in version 4.7; version 5.0 is slated for delivery the first quarter of 2000. Version 5 will be a total rebuild of the software. The latest version can be downloaded (or a CD-ROM can be ordered) from the Netscape Web site, `http://www.netscape.com/`—look for the download link. To check on the progress of the open source process, see `http://www.mozilla.org/`.

Netscape Communicator Version 4.7 (available for Macintosh and Windows) includes Navigator, Messenger, Composer, AOL Instant Messenger 3.0, Netscape Radio, RealPlayer G2, Winamp (Windows only), PalmPilot Synch tools (Windows only), and multimedia plug-ins. It is available in 23 different languages (from Brazilian Portuguese to Turkish).

Exploring the Communicator environment

Netscape Communicator is an Internet suite containing several useful online tools. After you have installed Communicator, you can launch by doing one of the following:

✦ Double click the Netscape Communicator or Netscape Navigator icon on the desktop.

✦ For Windows users, click the Start button and choose Programs ➪ Netscape Communicator ➪ Netscape Navigator.

By default, the application assumes that you want to browse the Web when you first launch the program. You may be prompted to connect to the Internet; details on how to configure your communications software can be found in Chapter 2, "Taking a Quick Tour of the Internet."

> **Tip** Macintosh users can easily add the Netscape icon to the Apple Menu. Highlight the icon on the desktop; make an alias by pressing the Ô-m keys. Drag this new alias into the Apple Menu folder, which is nested in the System Folder.

The Component bar

You can access the different features of Communicator by using the free-floating toolbar called the Component bar (Figure 10-1). By selecting the appropriate icon (Navigator, Inbox, Newsgroup, Address Book, or Composer) you can switch quickly between applications. The Component bar works much like Apple's floating application bar, introduced with System 8.5. You minimize the bar by clicking the Window Shade Widget (the lines in the upper-right hand corner). Change the shape from a vertical bar to a horizontal one by clicking the button second from the top right corner. To move the floating bar, click any portion of the border and drag to a better location on the desktop. To close, click the Close box in the upper left-hand corner.

—— Launches the Navigator Web browser

—— Launches the Netscape Messenger e-mail client

—— Launches the Collabra news group agent

—— Launches the address book

—— Launches Composer to let you create and edit your own Web pages

Figure 10-1: The Component bar offers five handy shortcuts.

Navigator elements

The Netscape Navigator window has three sets of easy-to-use elements — a menu bar, a status bar, and tool bars — as shown in Figure 10-2.

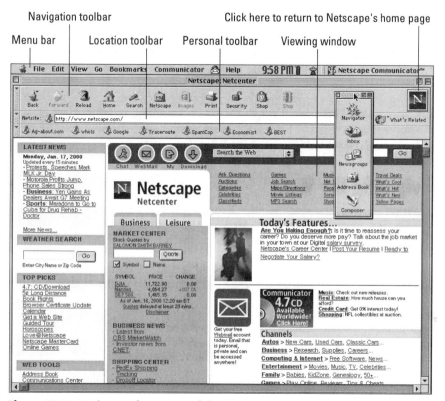

Figure 10-2: Navigator elements and the Netscape Home Page

Like all Macintosh and Windows applications, Navigator's menu bar is located along the top of the browser window and provides access to all program features.

Located just below the menu bar are three distinct toolbars:

✦ A **Navigation toolbar**, which provides basic Web browsing tools for moving around the Internet.

✦ A **Location toolbar**, which shows the URL of the current Web page. It also contains the Bookmark icon for recording new bookmarks and the "What's Related" feature, which will find Web pages related to the one that's currently loaded.

✦ The **Personal toolbar**, which you can customize for quick access to your favorite online spots.

Finally, Navigator's status bar is located along the bottom of the browser window. It supplies information about the current Web page, such as download progress and the Web page URL.

> **Tip**
>
> If you need to maximize the space available to view a Web site, minimize any toolbar by clicking the vertical arrow on the left. The toolbar disappears, and the arrow now aligns horizontally. Click the button again to restore toolbar contents.

The Navigator window functions like any other application window. For Macintosh users, this means you close the window by clicking the top left button; minimize the window by clicking the top right button; and change the shape of the window by clicking the second button from the top right.

Navigating the Web

Navigating, surfing, cruising the information highway — whatever you want to call it — Navigator makes exploring the World Wide Web an enjoyable experience. Web browsing is America's new favorite pastime, and Navigator can take you anywhere you want to go on the Web. The first time you launch Navigator, you'll probably see the Netscape home page. It contains links to Netscape-related items, as well as current news, a Web directory, a shopping channel, and a customizable section called My Netscape.

If your Internet Service Provider (ISP) provided you with your browsing software, it may have set its home page as the startup page to its Web site. For example, if your ISP is Mindspring, it will set your browser's home page as `http://www.mindspring.com/`. It's easy to customize the home page selection — whether that is your favorite search engine, ESPN, or your broker's site with daily stock reports. We'll cover that a little later in this chapter.

Browsing smart

The basics of browsing on the Internet are covered in Chapter 3, but Netscape Navigator has a unique tool, called Smart Browsing, that will make your Web surfing experience easier. When the Internet Keywords feature is enabled (it's the default setting), Smart Browsing enables you to type common words or brand names in the Location toolbar and Navigator will try to find the Web page for you. For example, if you type "Apple computer" in the location field, Navigator will find Apple Computer's home page (`http://www.apple.com/`). Type only "Apple" and Navigator will find a bushel of apple-related Web sites, as you can see in Figure 10-3.

When you have "What's Related" enabled, Navigator will use its search feature to try to find Web pages that are "like" the one currently loaded in the browser window.

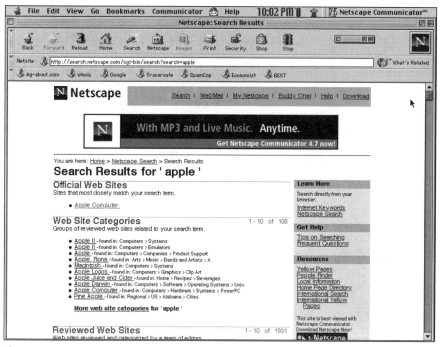

Figure 10-3: Navigator's Keyword search seeks out Web sites based on common words and names.

To explore these concepts, try the following:

1. Launch Navigator, connect to the Internet, and load the Netscape homepage (www.netscape.com).

2. To test Internet Keywords, type **IDG Books** into the Location toolbar and press Enter.

3. When the Netscape Keyword Search results screen appears, click on http://www.idgbooks.com/. The IDG Books Online Web site will load, as shown in Figure 10-4.

4. Click one of the book cover images. A new page loads with information on that book.

5. To go back to the IDG Books Online home page, click the Back button on the Navigation toolbar.

6. Want to see that book again? Click Forward.

Cover images link to book information

These buttons link to other sections of the Web site

Underline text links to other pages

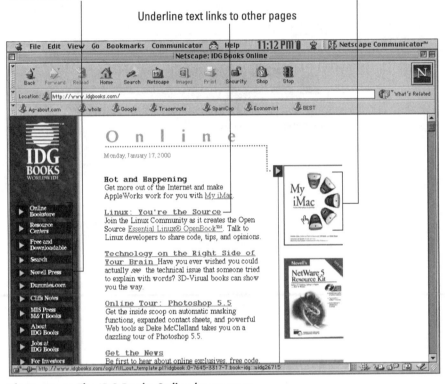

Figure 10-4: The IDG Books Online home page

7. Want to return to a Web page you visited earlier? Click the Back button to visit Web pages you visited during the current surfing session. You can also select Go on the menu bar and hold the mouse button down. Notice that a shortcut menu appears, like the one shown in Figure 10-5, showing a history of the Web pages you have visited. With your mouse button still held down, move down the list, select a Web site, and release the mouse button. The Web page you selected should open again.

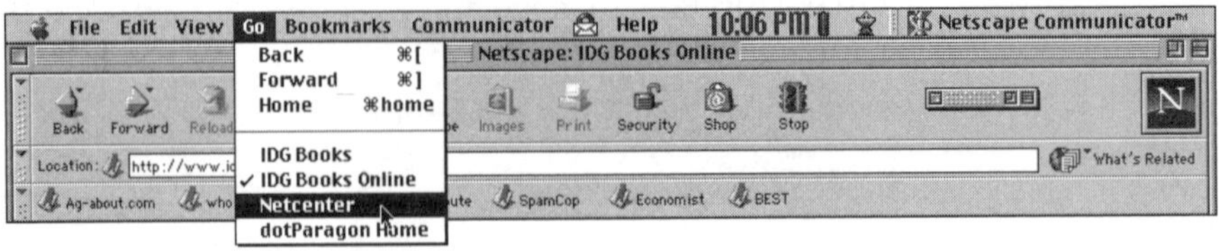

Figure 10-5: The Go pull-down menu makes it easy to jump back to previously visited Web sites.

As you can see, moving around the Web using Navigator is easy. The most important controls needed to browse the Internet appear on Navigator's Navigation toolbar. To help, the features of the Navigation toolbar are detailed in Table 10-1.

Table 10-1	
Navigation Toolbar Controls	
Button	**Description**
Back	Takes you to the previously visited page.
Forward	Takes you forward again after you have clicked the Back button.
Reload	Reloads the current page; use this as a "reset" button if the page is loading too slowly (press stop first!).
Home	Takes you to your home page.
Search	Launches a search engine such as Lycos or Excite to search the Internet. Netscape has nine embedded search engines.
Netscape	Takes you to a customized start page on the Netscape Web site.
Images	Loads all images on a non-framed Web page. Enabled when Auto load images is turned off. Selecting this button will load all images on a non-framed Web page.
Print	Prints the current Web page.
Security	Reviews security information on the current Web page, as well as Navigator security settings.
Shop	Takes you to Shop@Netscape, an online shopping directory.
Stop	Stops the current Web page from loading.

Searching the Internet

The best feature of the Internet is that you can use it to find information about almost anything. However, because information on the Web is not arranged in an orderly manner (unlike libraries with their Dewey decimal system), it can be difficult to find what you're looking for. Fortunately, Web site *search engines* help you search the Internet in a variety of ways.

Cross-Reference Searching is discussed in greater detail in Chapter 16, "Using Search Engines." In addition, a list of search engines is included in the Web Directory section of this book.

Netscape Navigator has built in several tools to help you search the Web. The most basic is the Search button on the Navigation toolbar. When you click this button, Navigator loads the Netscape search page (`http://home.netscape.com/escapes/search/`) and selects a search engine at random from a list of nine engines (About. Com, Excite, Google, GoTo.Com, HotBot, LookSmart, Lycos, Netscape, and Snap. Com). You can then type your query into the "Search the Web" box. If you don't like the search engine that appears when you click the search button, choose another one from the list that appears on the left side of every Net Search window, which is shown in Figure 10-6. Or if you have a favorite, check the "Keep" *this guide* "as my search engine" box.

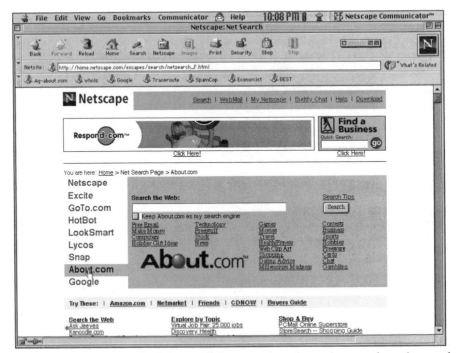

Figure 10-6: Netscape's built-in search feature selects from nine search engines and directories.

Navigator Search also contains resources for finding people (including NetCenter members) and businesses. This Open Directory Project is run by volunteer editors who choose which sites to review, add, and maintain in one or more categories.

Tip   What if you want to find something specific on a Web page? Use the search feature! From the menu bar, select Edit ⇨ Find in Page, which will open the Find dialog box, enabling you to search for a word or a string of words within the currently loaded Web page. You can also specify if the search should be case-sensitive. To search through a Web page's HTML source code, you must use the keyboard shortcut ⌘-f (for Macintosh) or Ctrl+f (for Windows).

The Netscape Guide (`http://directory.netscape.com/`) also gives you a great jumping off point if you want to surf the Web for interesting sites. The "What's New" (`http://home.netscape.com/netcenter/new.html`) and "What's Cool" (`http://home.netscape.com/netcenter/cool.html`), which is shown in Figure 10-7, are updated daily. These are great places to get ideas for Web site design and content. Sites in "What's New" may not be in the "cool" section, but they are new to the net and have something unique going for them to be listed here.

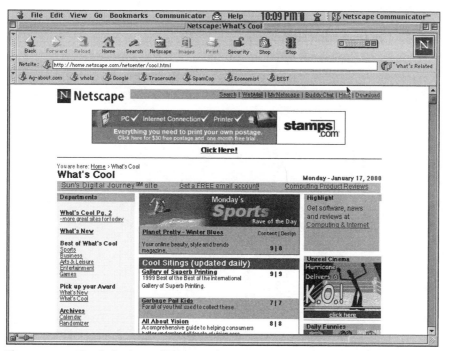

Figure 10-7: The "What's Cool" features keep you up-to-date on cutting-edge Web sites.

Another wonderful tool bundled with Navigator is an alphabetical, customizable bookmarks directory. Access it by clicking the "Bookmarks" button on the menu bar. You will see a menu of Web sites by category. This bookmark listing is handy because it provides a directory similar to what many search engines provide, but you can add or subtract sites based on your likes and dislikes! We explain how to customize the bookmark files later in this chapter.

Customizing Communicator

Netscape has built in many ways to customize Communicator so that the program fits your needs. You can change the way the program functions and change how Web sites look and act when you visit them. This section explores some of the ways to customize Netscape Navigator.

Startup options

If you use the desktop icon to open Netscape Communicator, you probably notice that Navigator launches first. What if you would rather check e-mail first? Or what if you want to check your calendar? No problem! To customize the Netscape start-up sequence:

1. Launch Communicator.

2. On the menu bar, choose Edit ⇨ Preferences. The Preferences dialog box appears.

3. In the Category listing on the left, select Appearance (it's first in the list), as shown in Figure 10-8.

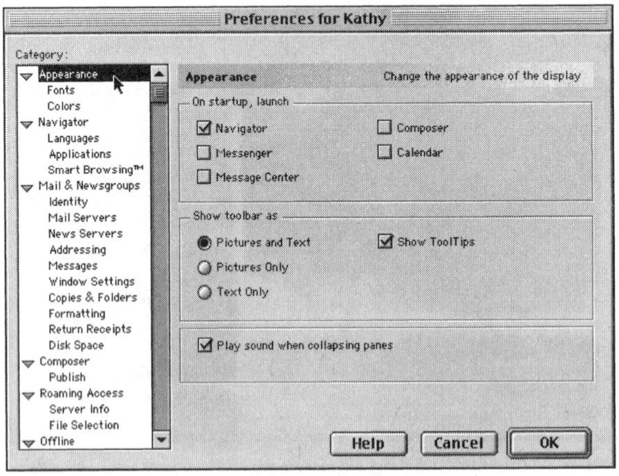

Figure 10-8: Choose which components you want to launch on startup.

4. In the *On startup, launch,* section place a check next to each component you want to launch when Communicator opens.

5. Click OK when finished.

You can choose as many or as few options as you wish (at least one must be selected). You may find this a handy option, especially if you do a lot of important correspondence via e-mail or newsgroups.

The appearance tab also enables you to modify the appearance of the Navigator button bar — it can be viewed as text only, text and icons, or icons only. Macintosh users can also turn tool tips on or off.

Changing your home page

When you launch the Navigator component of Communicator, the Web page that opens is called your home page. The default home page in Navigator is the Netscape home page (`http://www.netscape.com/`); your ISP may have substituted its homepage for the Netscape home page.

Many people like to set their personal Web page as their home page. Or you might want to use your company's home page or the home page of your local newspaper. You can even set Navigator so that it opens with whatever page you were viewing the last time you were browsing. To set your favorite Web site as your home page, do the following:

1. From the menu bar, select Edit ⇨ Preferences.

2. Select Navigator from the Categories box, which can be seen on the left side of the Preferences dialog box, as show in Figure 10-9.

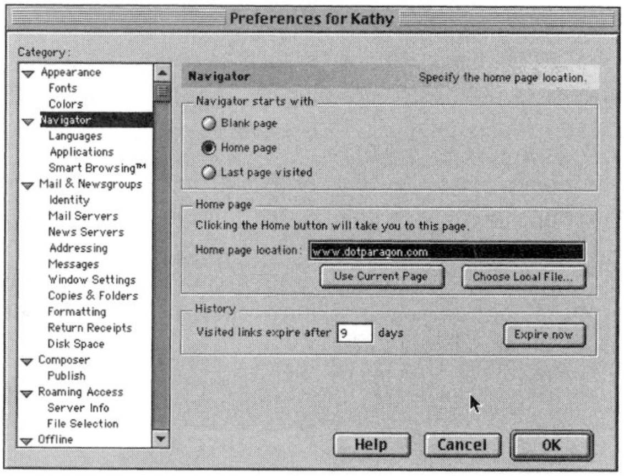

Figure 10-9: Customize your home page options.

3. Under *Navigator starts with*, select *Home page*. However, if you prefer that no page load on startup, select *Blank page*. Or if you want the last page visited to load, click *Last page visited*.

4. To customize the page that loads as the home page, make sure you've selected *Home page* and then enter the full URL (you must include the http://) in the Home page location box.

5. Click OK when finished.

The page you set as the home page is what will load each time you click the "Home" button on the Navigation toolbar.

Navigator view options

Don't like the way Navigator looks? It's very easy to change. First, let's deal with those pesky toolbars. As you know, Navigator has three separate toolbars that are displayed above the viewing area. If you find you don't use all of those bars, a temporary solution is to minimize them as described earlier. To hide them from view, go to the menu bar and choose View ➪ Show. When the Show submenu appears, as illustrated in Figure 10-10, deselect the elements that you do not want to see (this includes the floating toolbar).

Figure 10-10: You can modify how Navigator looks, such as hiding the toolbars from sight, with a simple command.

You can also use the Preferences option to change the formatting of the Web pages you view, such as the type and size of text, link colors, and so on. These options are also accessible under Appearances in the Preferences dialog box (Edit ➪ Preferences ➪ Appearance). To change the color of the background or text in the Web pages you view, including underlining, select Colors. To change font type and size, select Fonts. The Fonts dialog box can be seen in Figure 10-11.

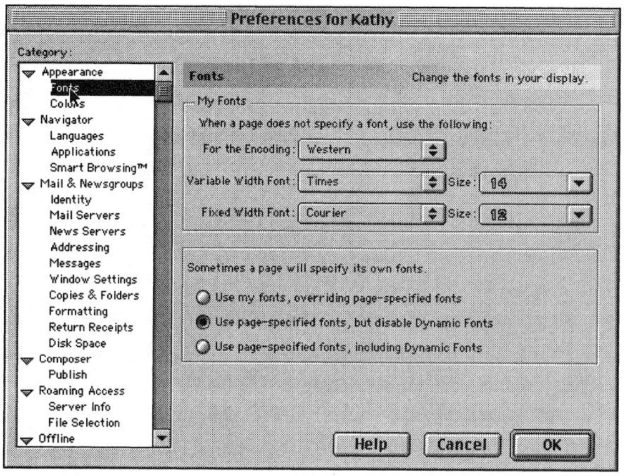

Figure 10-11: Customize text font and size.

You can customize your browser in many other ways. For example, you can tell it not to load Java or not to automatically load images (a good idea if you have a slow connection, perhaps when you are travelling and have a slow dial-up connection). Table 10-2 describes additional options that are accessible through the Preferences dialog box.

Table 10-2 Communicator Options		
Option	**Category**	**Description**
Toolbar buttons	Appearance	Toolbar buttons display as text, icons, or both text and icons.
Automatically Load Images	Advanced	Default is selected. Turn off if you have a slow dial-up connection; you will only see images if you click the images button on the toolbar.
Java and Javascript	Advanced	Default is selected for both. Turn off if you have security concerns.
Cookies	Advanced	Enable or disable cookies, or receive cookie warnings (see Chapter 15 for more on managing cookies).

Nice Web page! How do they do it?

Are you an aspiring Web publisher? If so, you have an easy-to-use Web mill integrated with the browser, called Netscape Composer. Composer is a light-featured but easy-to-use graphical editor that can help you create a basic Web page.

But what if you want to have more sophisticated (or HTML-compliant) designs? This means you need to learn HTML. A great way to learn HTML is to look at other Web sites and study the code they used to create their pages. To look at the source code for a Web page you are viewing, click View on the menu bar and then choose Page Source. A source window will open, as shown in the figure below, which displays all of the code used to create that page. To save the page for offline study, close the source code page, and select File > Save As. You will need to select "source" as the format if you want to see the code. Give the file a name (with the.html extension!) and save to your hard drive or a floppy disk, as shown in the figure on the following page.

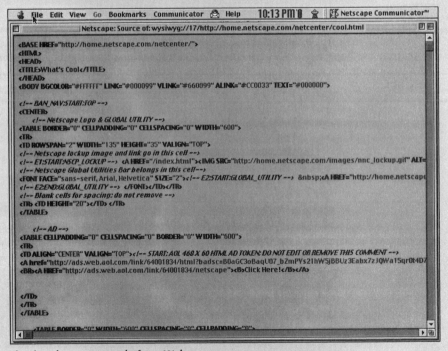

Viewing the source code for a Web page

Saving the source code for a Web page

One warning: Although viewing source code can help you learn more about writing HTML, you should never copy code directly for use in your own Web page. Programming code is protected by the same copyright laws that protect other published work, such as this book. For more on copyright issues and the Web, visit the U.S. Copyright office at http://www.loc.gov/copyright/faq.html.

Bookmarking your favorite Web sites

It doesn't take long to find Web sites you'd like to revisit (or visit regularly), but trying to remember the URLs of your favorite sites can be taxing on the memory banks! The easy way is to bookmark the site for a return visit.

Accessing bookmarks

Navigator has a set of bookmarks pre-installed with the browser and your ISP may have added or modified the list, but because you have your own special tastes and preferences, you'll be glad to know it's easy to add and modify the listings.

To access your bookmarks, select *Bookmarks* from the menu bar. (For Windows users, Bookmarks can be found on the Location toolbar.) When the list of bookmarks appears, like the one shown in Figure 10-12, scroll down to the list and select the Web site you want to visit.

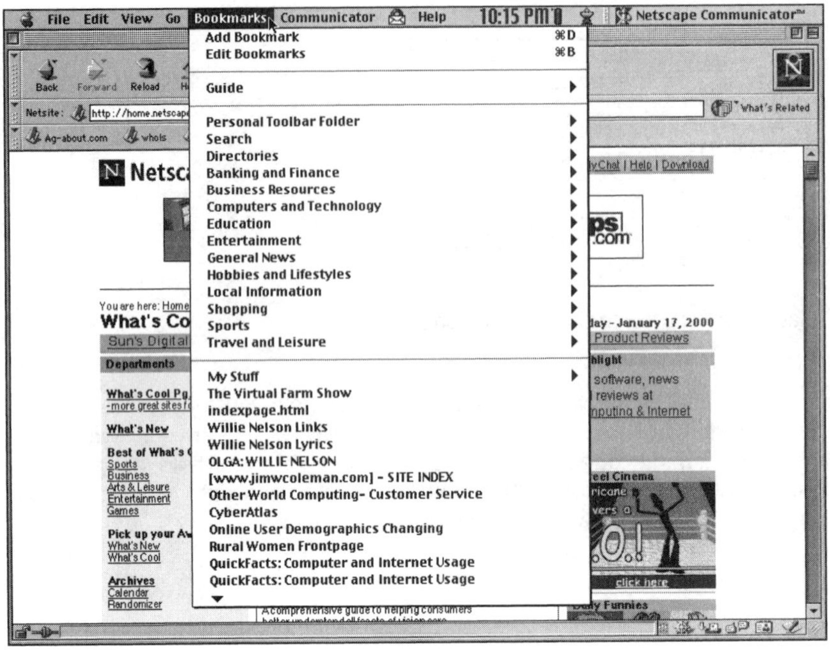

Figure 10-12: Viewing Navigator bookmarks with a Macintosh computer

Creating a bookmark

Creating a new bookmark is simple. To bookmark the Web page you are currently viewing, simply press ⌘-d (Macintosh) or Ctrl+d (Windows). If you prefer to use the mouse, go to the menu bar and select Bookmarks ⇨ Add Bookmark. Or click the bookmark icon that is immediately to the left of the location box (it looks like a little ribbon).

The Web site name (the name that appears above the menu bar) and URL will be saved in your bookmarks file. Make sure that you are on the Web page you want to set as the bookmark. For instance, suppose that you really like the NASA home page and you want to bookmark it. However, if you happen to be reading an article about the Mars mission when you set the bookmark, each time you select the bookmark, it will open to Mars, not the home page.

Tip   If you are on a framed site, it is usually possible to bookmark only the home page frameset. This is because the only URL that appears in the location bar is that of the "main frameset." You can try to circumvent this by asking the browser to open your current page in a new browser window. To do this, place your mouse inside the frame you'd like opened in a new window; avoid those hypertext links! Then, either right-click (with a multibutton mouse) or click-and-hold (with a single-button mouse). Select "New Window With This Frame." Depending upon how the developer has coded the Web site, you might get lucky and be able to create a bookmark that goes deep into the framed Web site. If the frame opens in a new window, the URL in the location bar will have changed. Now you can bookmark the page.

Managing bookmarks

An unordered bookmark list can quickly get out of hand. Your bookmarks may be as difficult to navigate as the Web! To solve this problem, you can organize your bookmarks by creating folders and then drag bookmarks of related sites—"Shopping" or "Extra-Terrestrial," for example—into the appropriate folders. To do this, select Bookmarks ➪ Edit (or use ⌘-B for Macintosh). This will launch a window, like the one shown in Figure 10-13, that contains all your bookmarks.

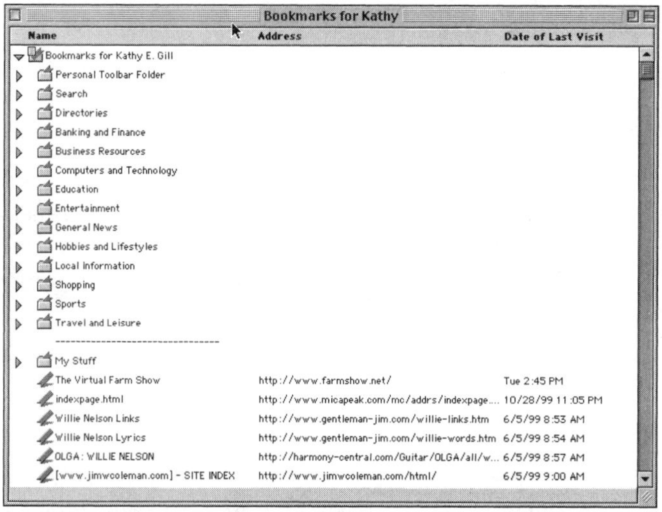

Figure 10-13: Viewing Navigator's Edit Bookmarks window

To add a new bookmark directly into the appropriate folder, you must first open the Edit Bookmarks window. The easiest way to add the bookmark is to drag the Bookmark Icon to the appropriate folder and drop it where you want it to reside. If you want to create a bookmark from scratch, first copy the page URL (highlight the URL in the location bar and select Edit ➪ Copy from the menu bar). Then highlight the folder and select File ➪ New Bookmark from the menu bar. Paste the URL into the location box and give the bookmark a descriptive name.

To create a new folder or bookmark:

1. Open the Edit Bookmarks window and select Bookmarks ➪ Edit (or press ⌘-b on a Macintosh).

2. To open an existing folder, double-click it; the new folder or bookmark will be nested inside this folder

3. On the menu bar, select File ➪ New Folder or File ➪ New Bookmark.

4. When the Properties dialog box opens, like the one shown in Figure 10-14, type something descriptive but short in the Name text box. The bookmark information dialog box also needs the Web page URL.

5. Click OK when finished.

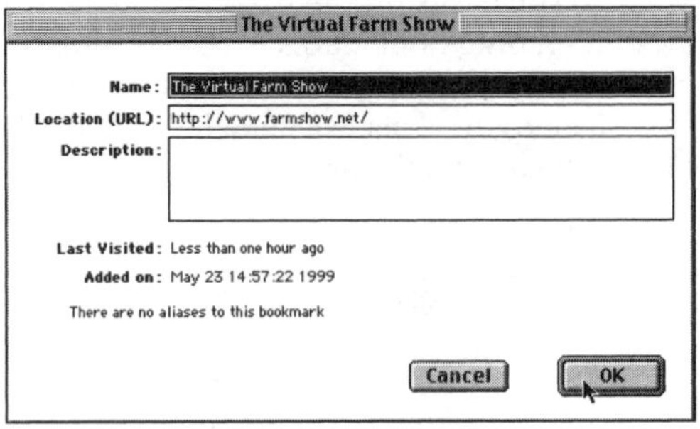

Figure 10-14: Editing a bookmark

If you want to rename an existing bookmark, highlight the bookmark and select Edit ⇨ Get Info from the menu bar (or click ⌘-I for Macintosh). You can change the URL or the bookmark name, and you may add notes (Figure 10-16). This window tells you when you created the bookmark and the last time you accessed it.

To move a folder or bookmark, click and hold the mouse button on the item you want to move, drag it to the desired location and release the mouse button. To delete a folder or bookmark, highlight the folder or bookmark and press the delete key.

Managing your bookmarks is important because it ultimately makes Navigator easier to use. Don't forget that you don't need to keep all of the Web sites and folders that Netscape included with Communicator when you first installed it. You can also get third-party bookmark management software, such as URL Manager Pro 2.6 (`http://www.url-manager.com/`) for the Mac and Powermarks 3.07 (`http://www.kaylon.com/`) for Windows.

Customizing the Personal toolbar

If you have a favorite site you visit every day — a new Web site, for example — and you don't like hunting through your bookmarks to find it, add it to the Personal toolbar. If you don't like the sites that Netscape has added to Navigator, just delete them! (Or move them to another section of the bookmarks.) The Personal toolbar is exactly what the name implies: a place to personalize your access to a select group of Web sites. Because it is limited in space, use the Personal toolbar only for those sites you visit often. Also, make the names as short as possible (edit them using the previously described procedure, if needed) so they won't take up too much space on the toolbar.

Adding Web sites to the Personal toolbar is easy. Try this:

1. Go to a Web site you want to add to your Personal toolbar.

2. Open the Edit Bookmarks window (select Bookmarks ⇨ Edit).

3. To open the Personal Toolbar folder, double-click it.

4. Drag the Bookmarks Icon from the left side of the location box onto the Personal Toolbar folder.

5. The new bookmark will be last in the series. Drag it to another location or edit the name to further customize the Personal Toolbar.

To help your surf a little faster, Table 10-3 shows a list keyboard shortcuts you can use in Netscape Navigator.

| Table 10-3 | | |
| Keyboard Shortcuts | | |
Macintosh	*Windows*	*Description*
⌘-b	Ctrl+b	Edit bookmarks window
⌘-d	Ctrl+d	Create bookmark
⌘-f	Ctrl+f	Find word or phrase on Web page
⌘-h	Ctrl+h	Open history window
⌘-p	Ctrl+p	Print Web page or frame
⌘-s	Ctrl+s	Save Web page or frame

Tracking your browsing habits

Like it or not, Netscape Communicator keeps a running record of your browsing habits. Every Web page you visit, every file you download, every image you view may be recorded for posterity. Knowing what records Navigator keeps and how you can control those records can be very helpful.

History

The Navigator History feature records the Web pages you visit. This can be helpful if you need to return to a Web page you viewed earlier in the day but can't remember its address. To review the history file, select Communicator on the menu bar and choose History (⌘-h for Macintosh, Ctrl+h for Windows), which will open a History window like the one shown in Figure 10-15. For Macintosh users, the History only records pages visited while the Communicator suite remains open. If you quit Netscape Communicator, the history information vanishes. Windows users have a longer history period, which you can customize by opening Preferences from the Edit menu.

Figure 10-15: The History window records browsing habits.

Notice that individual pages are listed, and there is an "add to bookmarks" button. You can revisit any page in the history list by double-clicking it. This is so helpful, especially during long browsing/search sessions, and is very good for people with slower connections.

Cache

The cache (pronounced "cash") is the space on your hard drive reserved for Internet files. Each time you access a Web page, various HTML, GIF, and JPEG files used on that page are downloaded to your hard drive cache. They remain on your hard drive cache until they are replaced by other files.

The cache helps make your Web browsing operate more efficiently, especially Web pages that you visit more than once. If you are visiting the good old NASA home page, you might read an article about Asteroid 1997 XF 11 and then click Navigator's Back button to return to the NASA home page. Rather than download all the files required by the home page again, Navigator reuses the files stored in cache. Files stored on your hard disk can be accessed much more quickly than over the Internet, so this can make some browsing operations run much faster.

Normally, the cache is something that operates in the background, and there's not a lot you need to do with it. However, if you are concerned about how much disk space the cache is taking up, you can make some adjustments. Check your current settings by following these steps:

1. From any Communicator window select Edit ➪ Preferences from the menu bar to open the Preferences dialog box.

2. In the Category list on the left, expand the Advanced category by clicking the plus sign (if necessary).

3. Select Cache to view the cache preferences.

4. You can see settings for Memory Cache and Disk Cache in Windows and Disk Cache only in Macintosh. Adjust the amount of hard disk space allotted for the cache by changing the number next to Disk Cache.

5. If you wish to clear the cache, click *Clear Disk Cache.*

Normally, you should be able to stick with the default settings. But if you do feel that adjustments are needed, or if you wish to clear the cache, this is the place to do it.

Tip

Mac users with extra Random Access Memory (RAM) can speed the performance of Navigator by creating a RAM disk and selecting the RAM disk as the location for the cache files.

To create the RAM disk, from the Apple menu select Control Panels ➪ Memory. When the Memory dialog box appears (Figure 10-16), turn RAM disk on and then allocate a percentage of your RAM to the disk (usually 3MB is sufficient; use more if you surf a lot and you have lots of RAM). To have the change take effect, you must reboot your computer. To tell Navigator to use the RAM disk for the cache, go to the menu bar and select Edit ➪ Preferences ➪ Advanced ➪ Cache. Make the size of the cache the same as the size of the RAM disk; use the browse feature to identify the RAM disk as the place to save cache files.

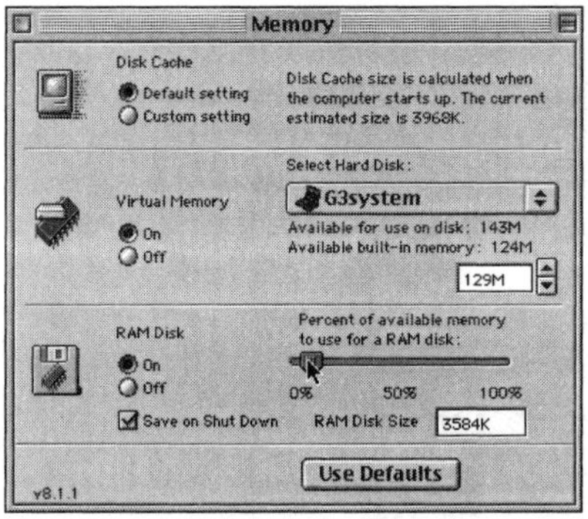

Figure 10-16: The Memory dialog box

Finding and using plug-ins

Netscape Communicator is an excellent product for exploring the online world. Its Web browser, Navigator, enables you to view a huge variety of files, from simple Web pages to images and sound. But as wonderful as Navigator is, it can't do everything. Sometimes it needs a little help from add-on programs called *plug-ins*. Such plug-ins work with Communicator to provide enhanced capabilities.

The most common plug-ins enable you to view videos or listen to audio. Other plug-ins let you create professional-looking presentations on and around the Internet, view images, or manage compressed files. This chapter describes where to find the best plug-ins for Netscape Communicator, how they're installed, and how to use them.

Tip

Whenever you download a program from the Internet and install it on your computer, you risk exposing your system to software viruses. Only download plug-ins from trustworthy sites. Better yet, check the downloaded program with virus scanning software before installation.

Browser plug-ins are easy to find; an excellent place to start is with the Netscape home page (`http://home.netscape.com/`). When you load Netscape's Browser Plug-ins page, it should look similar to the one shown in Figure 10-17. Select "Downloads" and then "Browser Plug-Ins."

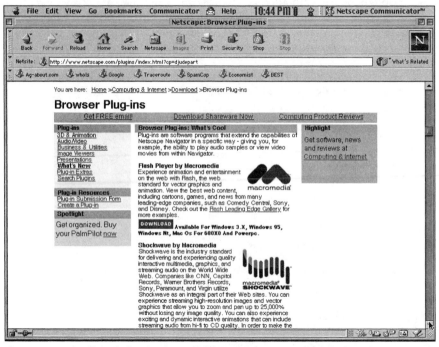

Figure 10-17: A list of plug-ins is available on the Netscape Web site.

Many of the plug-ins are products you must purchase; others are free, but the software used to develop the media must be purchased (such as Macromedia Shockwave). As you can see, plug-ins cover a wide range of uses, from simple image viewers to high-tech business and utility software. Other possible sources of plug-ins include

✦ The Yahoo! directory: `http://dir.yahoo.com/Computers_and_Internet/Software/Internet/World_Wide_Web/Browsers/Plug_Ins/`

✦ TUCOWS, `http://www.tucows.com/`

✦ c|net, `http://www.download.com/`

When you upgrade your version of Communicator, you are often given the choice of adding plug-ins at that time. Otherwise, you will probably install plug-ins on an "as-needed" basis. That is, when you like a Web site so much you are willing to go through the hassle of downloading and installing a plug-in. The following are some popular plug-ins that you may consider installing.

Flash

Macromedia's Flash enables Web developers to exert a high degree of control over Web site appearance. Flash is a versatile tool, enabling the developer to create animations, build interactivity, and add sound to Web pages using very little bandwidth. To view these files, the site visitor must have the Flash plug-in. However, like the RealPlayer plug-in (to be discussed), Flash is included with Communicator upgrades. If you do not have Flash, you can download it from the Netscape Web site or from Macromedia, `http://www.macromedia.com/support/flash/`.

Macromedia is pushing Flash as a Web standard for vector graphics. To that end, the company has undertaken many initiatives, including opening the Flash file format, releasing the Flash Player code for free licensing, and allowing redistribution of the Flash Player. You can find Flash on sites by Comedy Central, Sony, and Disney. Check out the Flash Leading Edge Gallery (`http://www.macromedia.com/software/flash/leadingedge/`) for more examples.

Net2Phone

Turn your computer into a telephone! Use Net2Phone (`http://net2phone.netscape.com/english/download.html`) to place a call from your computer to any phone, anywhere in the world. With Net2Phone, you can surf the Web and talk on the phone at the same time; your computer must have a sound card. With Net2Phone software, you can call anywhere within the United States for just 4.9¢ per minute. You initiate your call from your computer; it then goes through Net2Phone's telephone switches. These switches relay the call to its destination.

RealPlayer

With RealPlayer, the leading name in audio plug-ins, you can play real-time audio, video, animations, and multimedia presentations on the Web. RealPlayer can be seen in Figure 10-18. Features like Presets and Channels give you one-click access to music, entertainment, sports, and news. RealPlayer Plus, the commercial version of the RealPlayer has the ability to record streamed broadcasts and offers the option of telephone support. It is also preset with 150 radio stations!

You can get the free player at the Netscape plug-in download center, or you can buy the commercial version from RealNetworks (`http://www.real.com/`). Both versions play streamed audio and video files. A *streamed* file plays "live" over your Internet connection, as contrasted with a file that must first be downloaded before being played from your hard drive. Because audio and video files are much larger than text files, the streaming feature enables the site visitor to hear (and see) content before the download is complete.

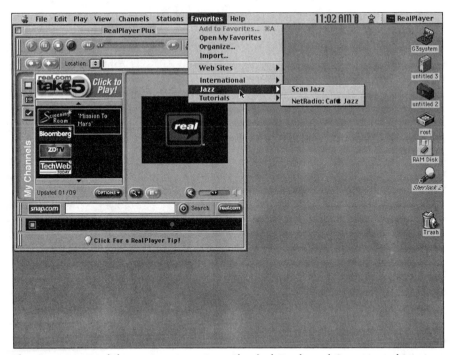

Figure 10-18: RealPlayer can stream Jazz, Classical, Rock, and Country—whatever fits your musical taste.

In addition to playing streamed audio and video from Web sites, RealPlayer offers its own programs too. When you open RealPlayer in Normal view, you will see buttons in the middle of the window with names like News, Biz/Tech, and Sports. These are destination buttons, and each is a direct link to a variety of online information.

Quicktime

With the advent of QuickTime4, Apple acknowledged the benefits of streaming technology. QuickTime has long been an acclaimed cross-platform tool for viewing video; adding the streaming capability brings this tool to the Web. More than 15 million Mac and Windows users downloaded the preview release, and a growing list of online publishers — such as the BBC, Fox News Online, Fox Sports Online, HBO, NPR, and The Weather Channel — are making QuickTime a popular streaming technology.

In addition to the traditional controls you would expect on a TV — like volume controls, pause, and play – the QuickTime4player, shown in Figure 10-19, has enhanced controls for online movie playback (like fast forward and fast rewind). One of the most famous QuickTime4 movies of 1999 was the trailer for *Star Wars: The Phantom Menace*! Apple is also taking aim at RealPlayer, as QuickTime4 is capable of playing music via music videos.

Figure 10-19: QuickTime enables you to catch the latest movie trailers on your computer desktop.

You have two ways to store the movies you want to watch again and again: stash them in the Favorites Drawer or opt for what may be the ultimate storage solution — let someone else handle it! The secret? Bookmarks. A user in Alaska, for instance, can bookmark movies, audio, and related QuickTime files stored on a server in Taiwan — and access them instantly, at will. Check out the examples at the Apple Web site QuickTime showcase: http://www.apple.com/quicktime/showcase/.

Others

This chapter can only tap the surface of the plug-ins available for Navigator. From the Adobe Acrobat Reader (to read Acrobat PDF files) to the ichat Plug-in (for chat) . . . from eCoin Wallet Manager (for online commerce) to 3M PostIt Notes . . . there are hundreds of specialized plug-ins that enable you to make Navigator a truly custom browser.

Summary

Netscape Communicator is a versatile, easy-to-use Internet suite that offers a full range of Internet products. Using the Web browsing techniques for the Navigator component discussed here will help you browse productively and enjoyably. Expand upon the customization techniques discussed here by adding various plug-ins to Communicator as you need them.

✦　　✦　　✦

Making The Web Sing With Opera

Microsoft's Internet Explorer and Netscape's Communicator had better watch out — there's a new Web browser out there that should give those two quite a bit to think about. Opera is smaller, faster, much more fun to use, and available for far more types of computers than either of those other guys.

If you're going to surf the Internet, you probably don't want to waste any time. Sitting around waiting while Web pages dribble slowly onto your screen is no fun. Because Web site designers are continuing to add more graphics, animation, video, audio, and interactive elements to their sites in order to make them more attractive, more pages load slowly, and this is becoming a bigger and bigger problem. Unless you are one of the lucky few with a high-speed Internet connection, you'll welcome anything that will allow you to surf the Web faster. If so, the Opera Web browser certainly deserves a closer look!

Learning the Basics of Opera

If you have used another Web browser, the chances are good that you will have an easy time using Opera. Just as all word processors have similarities, all Web browsers share similarities, too. After all, there are certain functions that anyone browsing the Web will need, so each Web browser must have those functions. For example, it's important for a Web browser to include a text box where you can type the URLs of Web pages that you would like to visit.

Opera is cross platform

Opera is available for more types of computers than any other browser. Operating systems that are compatible with Opera include:

✦ 32-bit Windows versions, such as Windows 95, Windows 98, Windows NT 4, and Windows 2000

✦ 16-bit Windows versions, like Windows 3.x, where Opera will run on something as simple as a 386SX computer with 4MB of memory

✦ Linux

✦ BeOS

✦ EPOC (Psion)

✦ Macintosh OS

Opera is multilingual

If all of those different types of PCs aren't quite enough for you, Opera is also available in many languages. Opera will be available in more languages in the future. Here's a list of languages in which it is currently available:

✦ Afrikaans

✦ English

✦ French

✦ German

✦ Italian

✦ Norwegian (Bokmål)

✦ Norwegian (Nynorsk)

✦ Portuguese

✦ Romanian

✦ Spanish (European)

✦ Spanish (Latin American)

✦ Swedish

Note

A free, 30-day evaluation copy of Opera is available for download from the Opera Software download page at `http://www.opera.com/download.html`. You can purchase a registered copy for $35.

Opera uses your internet connection

Once you've installed Opera, it will automatically use your existing Internet connection. If you do not already have one, you'll need to obtain an account with an Internet Service Provider (ISP) and some type of physical connection to the Internet, which is typically a phone line and a modem.

Cross-Reference

To learn how to find an Internet Service Provider and obtain a connection to the Internet, take a look at Chapter 5, "Choosing Your Service Provider," and Chapter 6, "Speeding Up Your Connection."

Before you use Opera, you should have your ISP account set up and your connection tested and functioning. Opera does not provide a *dialer*—it uses your existing means of making the connection to the Internet.

Understanding the Opera Screen

Even though Opera shares a number of features with other Web browsers, it also has a number of unique features. Figure 11-1 shows how Opera looks running on BeOS—a free alternative to the Windows and Mac operating systems. Other versions of Opera look similar to the BeOS version, although each operating system does have its own characteristics (which generally don't have much affect on how you use Opera).

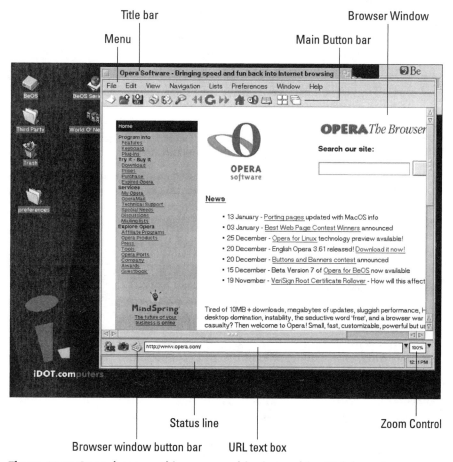

Figure 11-1: Opera has everything you need for fast and fun Web browsing.

The basic screen elements

Opera has a number of basic elements that you will probably find familiar.
These include:

✦ A *title bar* that displays the title of the currently active Web page. The title
that appears may be completely different from what you see on the Web
page because the title is determined by the HTML <TITLE> *tag,* which
you normally do not see.

✦ A *menu,* which includes commands that you can use to control how Opera
functions. The menus vary slightly between different versions of Opera, but
the differences are due to operating system considerations — not any desire
to make Opera more complex.

✦ A *main button bar,* or *toolbar,* that provides one-click access to many of the
more commonly used commands. Opera comes with several different sets of
buttons, which you can use to customize the appearance of your button bars.

✦ A *browser window,* where you view Web pages or other documents that you
open in Opera. You can open as many different browser windows as you
like — a feature unique with Opera.

✦ A *browser window button bar,* which has a set of buttons, such as back,
forward, and reload, that you can click in order to issue commands for
the active browser window.

✦ A *status line,* which shows you error messages, the URL of links that are
under the mouse pointer, and the current time.

✦ A *URL text box* that shows the address of the current document or Web page.
While a Web page is loading, status indicators replace the URL text box and
inform you of the download progress.

✦ A *zoom control,* which enables you to zoom in or out on a Web page. You can
set the zoom level between 20 percent and 1000 percent of normal size.

Browsing With Opera

Using Opera to browse the Web can be a lot of fun. If you're used to one of those
other browsers, switching to Opera can make it seem as though you suddenly
upgraded to a high-speed Internet connection. Web pages load far faster in Opera
than they do in either Internet Explorer or Communicator because Opera is able
to make better use of your existing Internet connection.

Using Opera's Hot List

One of the easiest ways to begin browsing with Opera is to try some Web site links
that are already in Opera's Hot List. This will give you a feel for just how many sites
come preloaded in the Hot List.

Opera's Hot List comes loaded with more than a thousand interesting links that you can use immediately to find a variety of great Web sites. Want to find out more about Trondheim in Norway? How about the Field Museum of Natural History? How about the InfoGranny's Tips site? Or maybe the Underground Music Archive? These are just a few of the links that you'll find in the Hot List.

Note
The Hot List window may appear as a separate window, as it does in Figure 11-2, or it may be a part of the main Opera window. Where the Hot List window appears is a function of your operating system, but the Hot List works the same, regardless of how it looks on your computer.

In addition to using the links that already appear in the Hot List, you can add you favorite Web sites in much the same way that you would add Communicator bookmarks or Internet Explorer favorites. Because Opera's Hot List is so large to begin with, you will probably want to make certain that you know where you are adding new links — otherwise, you may not be able to easily find them later.

Tip
To display the Hot List, select View ➪ Hot List. You can also use the keyboard shortcut listed on the View menu in order to toggle the display of the Hot List.

To open a link in the Hot List, follow these steps:

1. In the upper pane of the Hot List, select the folder that you want to open. Opera uses folders to organize the Hot List into categories so that specific links will be easier to locate. Because Hot List folders often contain subfolders, you may need to open additional folders in order to find the link that you want.

2. Double-click a link in the lower pane in order to open that link in an Opera Browser window, as shown in Figure 11-2.

3. To add a link in the currently displayed Web page to the active Hot List folder, select Lists ➪ Add Active to Hot List.

There actually are several methods of adding items to Opera's Hot List. You can:

✦ Open the Lists menu, navigate to the folder where you want to add the link, and choose Add Current Document Here to display the Item Properties dialog box.

✦ If your operating system supports the use of the right mouse button, you can right-click a Web page and choose Add Document to Hot List from the pop-up menu. This also displays the Item Properties dialog box, but it places the link in the active Hot List folder, rather than letting you choose one from the Lists menu.

✦ Some versions of Opera include a menu between the two Hot List panes. From this menu you can choose New ➪ Add Current to display the Item Properties dialog box. You can then add the link to the active Hot List folder.

No matter which method you prefer for adding items to the Hot List, you probably will find it easy to manage those links. Moving links between folders is probably done most easily using the drag-and-drop method, but the Edit ➪ Cut, Edit ➪ Copy, and Edit ➪ Paste commands can be used, as well.

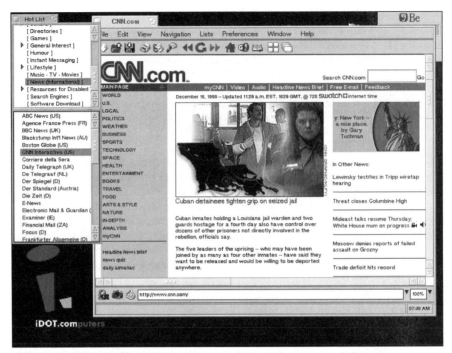

Figure 11-2: Double-click a link in the Hot List in order to open it in Opera.

Tip
The Opera Hot List has a neat feature that makes the Hot List even easier to use. When you close the Hot List, Opera remembers which folders you left open and which folder was the active folder. The next time you reopen the Hot List, the same folders will be open and the same folder will be active. If you use the keyboard shortcut to toggle the Hot List display, you can devote maximum screen space to browsing and still have the convenience of having the Hot List remain just the way you left it.

Using direct URL entry

The Opera Hot List may have well over a thousand links preloaded, but there are millions of Web sites on the Internet. You will almost certainly want to visit Web sites that are not already in the Hot List. Here are two ways you can do this:

✦ Enter an address directly into the URL text box that appears at the bottom of each Opera browser window, and press Enter.

✦ Use the Navigation ⇨ Open Remote command or click the Direct input of remote address (URL) button in order to open the Direct URL addressing dialog box, enter the Web page address, and click OK.

Figure 11-3 demonstrates both of these methods.

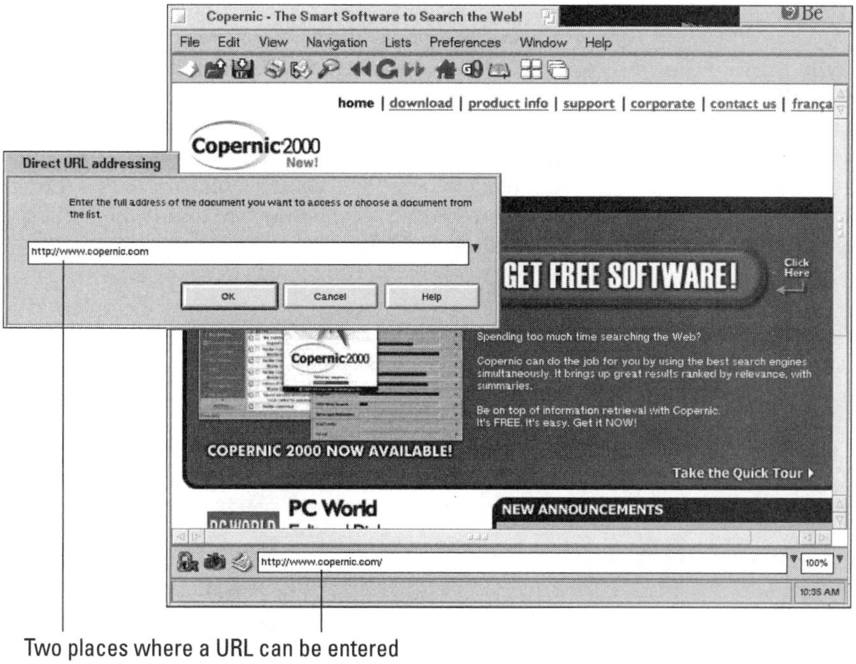

Two places where a URL can be entered

Figure 11-3: Enter URLs directly in order to view Web sites.

You can enter many Web page addresses without including the entire address. If you leave off the http:// part, Opera will automatically add that to the beginning of the address. If you type a single word, Opera will search for a site beginning with http://www., your word, and .com. You can use the Preferences ⇨ Advanced ⇨ Name Completion command, as shown in Figure 11-4, to control how Opera attempts to automatically complete incomplete addresses that you enter. Remember, though, that name completion will only display the main page on a Web site. If you want to go to a different page on the site, you must enter that address yourself.

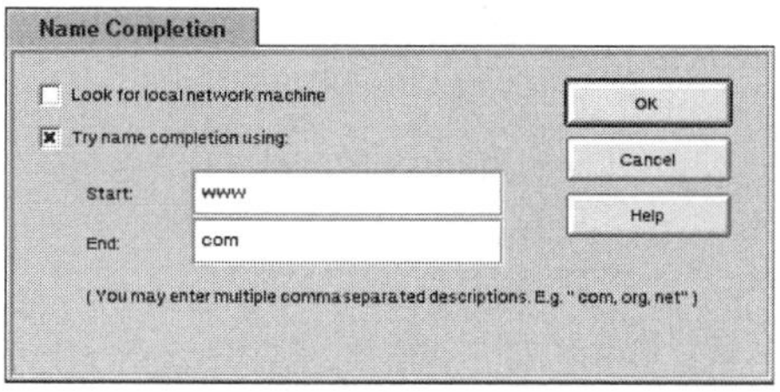

Figure 11-4: Control the prefix and suffix Opera uses to complete a URL.

Using links and navigation buttons

As you browse the Web, you will almost certainly find interesting links on Web pages. Just as in Communicator or Internet Explorer, you can click those links to visit them in Opera. In addition, Opera has the standard navigation buttons for returning to links that you have already visited, for jumping back to your home page, and for reloading a document. You can use Opera's history list to return to Web pages that you have previously visited. To display the history list, click at the right side of the URL text box, as show in Figure 11-5.

Reload current document button

Next button

Previous button   Home button

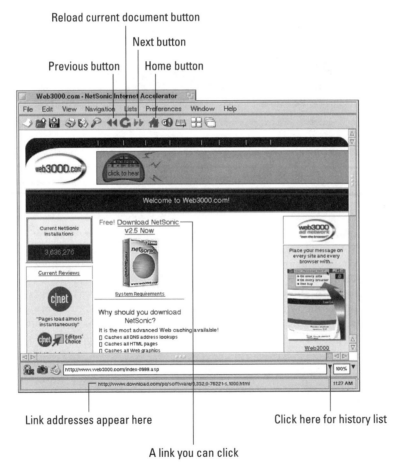

Link addresses appear here   Click here for history list

A link you can click

Figure 11-5: Click links and use the navigation buttons for browsing.

Browsing in multiple windows

One of the features that makes Opera unique among Web browsers is its ability to simultaneously open multiple Web sites. This makes it easy to view one site while another is loading, compare search results from different search engines, or monitor your stock market investments while you browse other Web sites.

You can open a new browser window by selecting File ➪ New or by clicking the New button at the left end of the Opera button bar. In most instances, however, the easiest way to open a new browser window is to hold down the Shift key when you click a link. Figure 11-6 shows two browser windows that are simultaneously open in Opera.

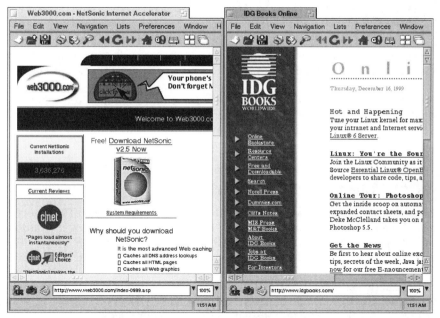

Figure 11-6: Open multiple browser windows in order to simultaneously view several Web sites.

Note

The arrangement of Opera's browser windows is controlled by your operating system. In Figure 11-6, the browser windows appear as though they are separate instances of Opera because this is how BeOS displays separate windows. On Windows-based PCs, the separate browser windows open within a single instance of Opera.

When you have multiple Opera browser windows open, you can use the Tile and Cascade buttons at the right end of the Opera button bar to control the window layout. You can also use the commands on the Window menu to control the layout. In addition, you can drag the windows to move or resize them.

Caution   Each browser window opened in Opera has its own history list, and this list is not shared between browser windows. As a result, it may seem as though your browsing history is lost when various browser windows are closed. In reality, though, Opera does keep a *global* history that you can easily access using the Window ⇨ Special Window ⇨ Global History command. The global history window makes it easy to find when you last visited each of your links, and it makes it easy to return to those Web pages — just click the link.

Making Opera Work Your Way

Opera has so many different configuration options that it's possible to fine tune the way Opera works to suit almost anyone's taste. If you can't find a configuration that meets your needs, it's likely that no Web browser would ever make you happy.

All of Opera's configuration options are accessed through the Preferences menu. You'll probably never use all of the options — some are simply overkill for most users. In the following sections, we'll have a brief look at some of the more common and useful settings.

Setting the generic options

The first options you will want to inspect are the generic options. To inspect them, select Preferences ⇨ Generic. As Figure 11-7 shows, you can set several options that control Opera's appearance, the size of the history buffer, the way Opera starts, the exit confirmation, and your personal information.

Of the generic settings, the size of the global history buffer and your personal information are the options that you will most likely want to change. The default settings for the remaining options will likely fulfill your needs.

The global history setting specifies the number of lines that will be saved in the global history window. Two hundred lines are plenty, but you may want to increase the global history setting to a much larger number — depending on how far back you want to go in order to view links that you have visited in the past.

The personal information settings allow you to specify information that Opera can automatically enter into online forms. This way, you won't have to retype the same information each time you fill out a form. Your information is made available only when you authorize it to be released, and you control the amount of information provided each time

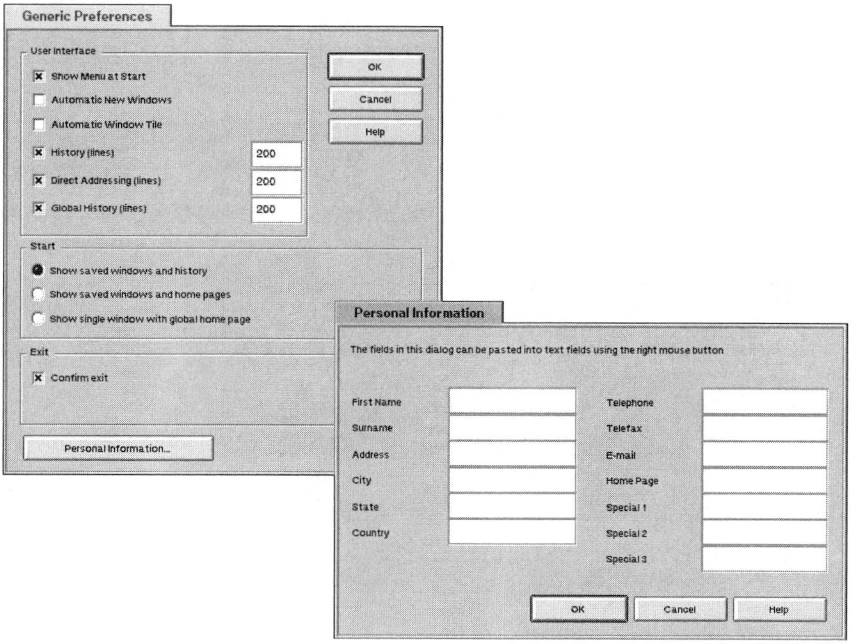

Figure 11-7: Use the generic options to set your personal information and control the history settings.

Caution

Personal information you enter into Opera's Personal Information dialog box is not encrypted, so it's not a good idea to include items like credit card numbers.

Controlling the buttons and bars

The next set of options that you may want to adjust are the button and bar settings. Select the Preferences ⇨ Button- and Statusbar in order to adjust these options. Figure 11-8 shows the Button- and Statusbar dialog box.

Most of the default settings in this dialog box work quite well. You may, however, be interested in making adjustments to a few of the settings:

✦ To change which buttons Opera uses on the button bar, click the browse button (the button with three dots) below or to the right of the Image set list box. Then choose the set you prefer by browsing to the folder containing the buttons that you want to use, selecting the buttons.ini file, and clicking OK You can slightly reduce the space used by the button bar, and thus increase the room available for browser windows, by choosing the small button set.

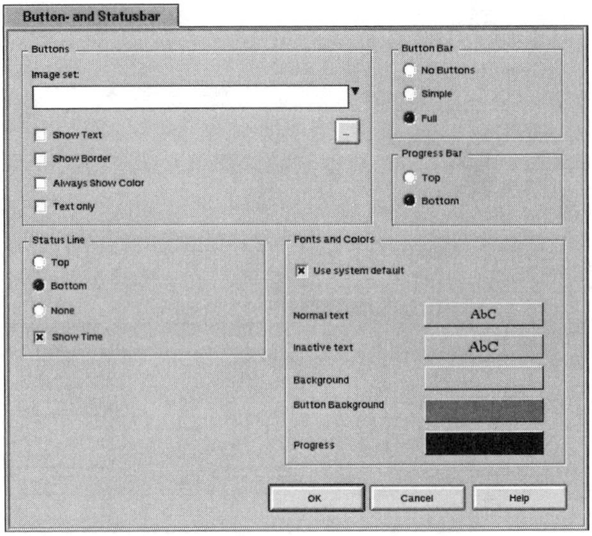

Figure 11-8: Control the buttons and bars with the
Button- and Statusbar dialog box.

✦ Select the Show text option in order to add text labels to Opera's buttons.
This is a good option to choose if you are new to Opera and still haven't
learned which button does what.

✦ Select the Text only option if you only want text labels on the buttons. This
will reduce the size of the button bar by removing the graphics that normally
appear on the buttons.

✦ Deselect the Use system default option if you want to set your own colors and
fonts for Opera's menus and controls. You might choose this option if your
screen is hard to read and you could use a little extra help seeing the
commands.

✦ If you don't like using a mouse, select the No buttons option. This will also
increase the space available for the browser windows by removing the Opera
Button bar.

Setting the advanced options

The next group of important settings is the advanced options. Choose Preferences ⇨
Advanced in order to modify these options. I'm skipping over the Hot List and
document window options because in most instances the default settings for those
two are adequate. Figure 11-9 shows the Advanced Preferences dialog box.

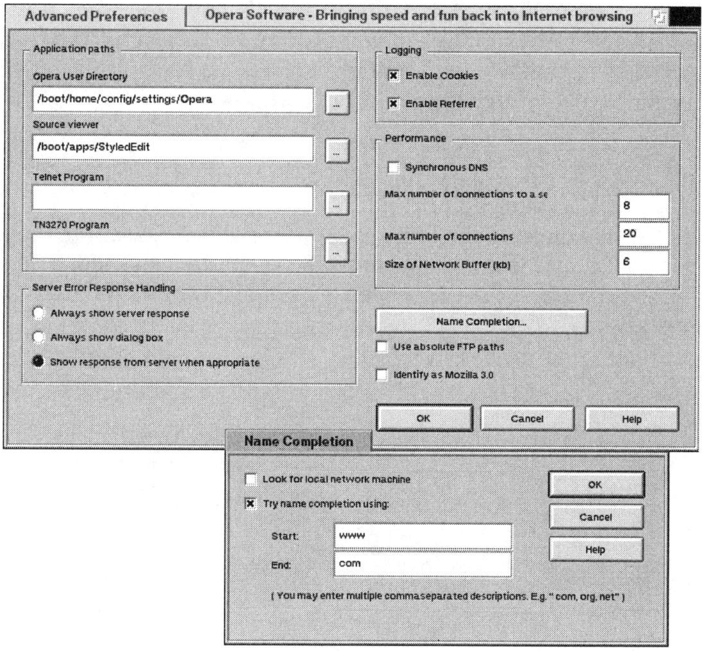

Figure 11-9: Control cookies, performance, and name completion using the advanced options.

The Advanced Preferences dialog box has several options that you may want to choose:

✦ The Enable Cookies option will determine whether Opera will accept *cookies* from Web sites. A cookie is a small text file that Web sites use to record personal information about you.

Cross-Reference

You may want to check out Chapter 32, "Maintaining Your Online Privacy and Security," in order to learn more about the implications of accepting or rejecting cookies.

✦ The Enable Referrer option controls whether a Web site will be able to determine where you came from when you arrive at the site. Deselecting this option prevents Web sites from tracking this information and affords you a bit more privacy.

✦ Selecting the Synchronous DNS option may prevent some crashes that can occur when you simultaneously are loading several Web pages or are loading a Web page that includes a large number of graphics and other elements. By default, Opera simultaneously loads many different pieces, but this can overload the system services on some computers. Selecting this option slows Opera's performance, but it may be worth trying if Opera crashes often.

If you click the Name Completion button, you can specify how Opera will fill out incomplete Web site names. For example, if you visit .org sites more often than .com sites, you may want to specify **org, com** in the End text box. Opera tries the items in the order that they are entered in the text box.

Choosing the link appearance

Next, you may want to skip down to the link appearance options. Select Preferences ➪ Link Presentation in order to access these options. You can use these options to format links so that they can be more easily seen. Figure 11-10 shows the Link Presentation dialog box.

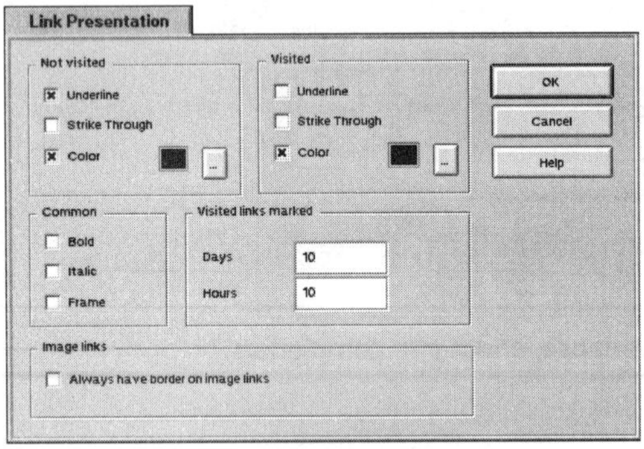

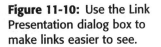

Figure 11-10: Use the Link Presentation dialog box to make links easier to see.

Opera normally uses contrasting colors to indicate links. One color is used for links that you have visited and a different color is used for unvisited links. Unfortunately, simply using contrasting colors does not always make links stand out because the same colors might also have been used for some nonlinked text. You might want to try other options that make links more distinct. For example, unvisited links could be shown with an underline and visited links using strikethrough.

Tip   If you often revisit the same Web sites to check for new content, you might want to reduce the Visited links mark settings so that links will change back from visited to unvisited appearance more quickly.

Choosing your multimedia options

The multimedia options control the nontext elements that appear on Web pages, such as graphics and animation. The Multimedia dialog box includes three sections of options: The Images section controls graphics; the Enable Multimedia section controls more sophisticated items, such as animation; and the Extensions section deals with frames. Figure 11-11 shows the Multimedia dialog box.

In most cases, you can ignore the multimedia options. However, these settings may be important if you have a slow connection and need to improve your browsing performance. If you would like to access the multimedia options, choose Preferences ➪ Multimedia.

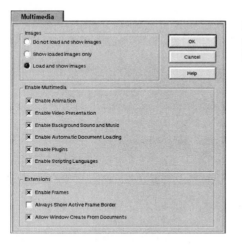

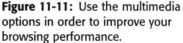

Figure 11-11: Use the multimedia options in order to improve your browsing performance.

The Images section allows you to control how the browser loads Web page images. The Load and show images button is the default setting. If it is chosen, Opera will show all images on a Web page. However, this option can slow load time. If a Web page is loading slowly, you might want to select one of the other two Images options, which should speed up the process.

> **Tip** If you choose not to automatically load images, you can still view any image on a Web page by right-clicking the image and choosing Show Image from the pop-up menu.

Deselecting options in the Enable Multimedia section of the Multimedia dialog box will also speed up your browsing. Unfortunately, this will also reduce the excitement that the multimedia add-ons bring to Web pages.

You can probably ignore the options in the Extensions section of the Multimedia dialog box, unless you use a screen reader to assist with a visual impairment. Because frames can be difficult to look at when you use a screen reader, you may want to deselect the Enable Frames option.

Setting your security options

The next group of settings that you will likely want to adjust are the security options, which you can access by selecting Preferences ➪ Security. These options help protect confidential information that you might send over the Internet. Figure 11-12 shows the Security Settings dialog box.

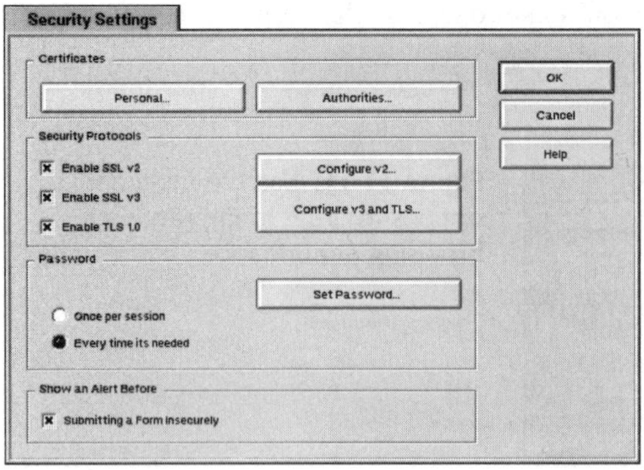

Security Settings

Certificates

| Personal... | Authorities... |

OK

Cancel

Help

Security Protocols

☒ Enable SSL v2   Configure v2...

☒ Enable SSL v3   Configure v3 and TLS...

☒ Enable TLS 1.0

Password

Set Password...

○ Once per session

⦿ Every time its needed

Show an Alert Before

☒ Submitting a Form Insecurely

Figure 11-12: Use security options to protect yourself online.

Cross-Reference

See Chapter 32, "Maintaining Your Online Privacy and Security," for information on obtaining and using certificates for secure digital identification.

Certificates are digital signatures that confirm a party's identity. If you want to use a certificate to prove your identity online, you can add a certificate that you have obtained by clicking the Personal button in the Security Settings dialog box. Opera will then display the Personal Certificates dialog box so you can choose which certificates you want to use.

Tip

If you want to use certificates with Opera, make certain that you use Opera when you visit the *certificate authority* to obtain your certificate — otherwise it is unlikely that the certificate will be valid in Opera.

By default, Opera has all of its security protocols enabled and set to accept the highest possible encryption levels. Unless you have a very good reason for doing so, it's best to leave these settings alone so that your browsing will be as secure as possible. The only reason to change these settings might be to accommodate a Web site that fails to connect correctly when all of the protocols are available.

Extending Opera with Add-ons

No Web browser can handle by itself every possible type of content that might be found on Web pages. As new types of content are developed, new ways to extend the capabilities of Web browsers through the use of various add-ons are introduced. These add-ons come in several different types, but whether they are a plug-in or a separate program isn't that important. After all, what difference does it make if you listen to music on a Web site through a browser plug-in or through a separate program that is opened by the browser? Of course, Internet Explorer and Communicator can sometimes handle content that Opera cannot handle, that is, until you install a plug-in. But then, Opera is a 1.3MB download, and those others can easily take more than 25MB to download.

Note
When you are looking for Opera plug-ins, make certain you obtain plug-ins that are compatible with your operating system. For example, plug-ins that are designed for Windows-based PCs will not be very useful if your PC runs BeOS, Linux, or the MacOS. Because Opera has been available for Windows longer than other operating systems, the largest number of Opera add-ons are available for Windows-based PCs. This situation is changing as other versions of Opera are becoming available.

Using Netscape plug-ins

While a few plug-ins have been specifically designed for Opera, Opera was designed to use most Netscape-compatible plug-ins, thereby giving users a wide variety of plug-ins to choose from. However, Netscape-compatible plug-ins sometimes need a little extra help when working with Opera. In some cases when you don't have a Netscape browser already installed, you must trick the plug-in into installing. Other times, you'll need to copy a file or two to a location where Opera can find it. The best source of current information on making plug-ins work with Opera is the Opera plug-ins Web page at http://www.opera.com/plug_in.html.

Once you have installed a plug-in, you need to tell Opera that the plug-in is available. To do so, select Preferences ⇨ Associate, which will display the Associate dialog box shown in Figure 11-13. Then click the Find Plugins button. Opera will display a message box that tells you the new plug-ins have been activated. To begin using the plug-ins, close the dialog boxes, close Opera, and then restart Opera. In some cases, plug-ins will work without closing and restarting Opera, but it is usually more reliable to close and restart.

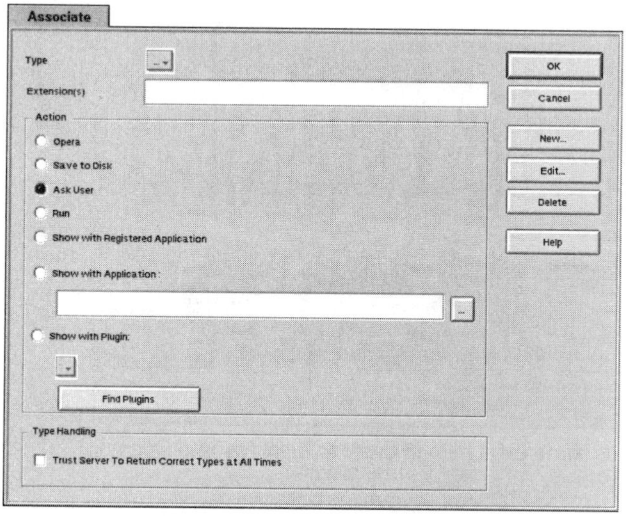

Figure 11-13: Activate new plug-ins by clicking the Find Plugins button.

The best Opera add-ons

There are quite a few great add-ons that can make your Web browsing a bit faster, more fun, or simply more organized. The Opera plug-ins page at http://www.opera.com/plug_in.html is the best place to find out about the broad range of what is available. The following sections discuss some of the best add-ons.

The Java plug-In

Java is a programming language that is used extensively on the Web to provide many different types of content. Java programs run in a special environment called a *Java virtual machine,* which is supposed to isolate those programs from the rest of your computer. This isolation is intended to prevent Java programs from inadvertently harming your system, making it safe for you to run Java programs that are found on Web pages.

Figure 11-14 shows what happens when Opera encounters content that it cannot handle on its own. Rather than showing the content, Opera displays a gray box with a message that tells you a suitable plug-in cannot be found.

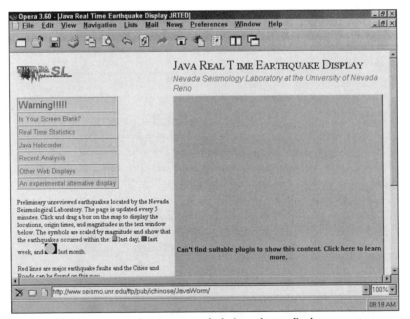

Figure 11-14: Opera needs some extra help in order to display some types of content.

In the situation in Figure 11-14, clicking the gray box would result in a message informing you that Opera needs a Java plug-in. In fact, the Java plug-in is by far the most important plug-in available for Opera. If the Java plug-would have been installed, Opera would have had no trouble showing the content missing in Figure 11-14, a real-time display of earthquake activity in Nevada, as shown in Figure 11-15.

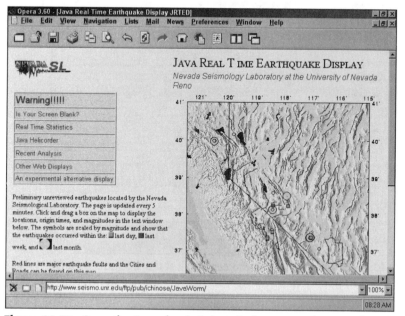

Figure 11-15: Once the Java plug-in is installed, you can view Java-based Web content.

The Java plug-in was designed to work with Netscape browsers. By following the directions available at the Opera plug-ins Web page, you can easily install the Java plug-in and use it with Opera.

Powermarks bookmark manager

Powermarks is a bookmark manager that simultaneously handles links from Opera, Communicator, and Internet Explorer. But in addition to enabling all three programs to share the same links, Powermarks makes it easy to search for links on specific subjects. With Powermarks, you can use key words to narrow your list of links until you have just a few relevant links left to choose from. Figure 11-16 shows Powermarks.

You can find a link to the Powermarks download site on the Opera plug-ins Web page.

NetSonic

NetSonic is another Opera add-on that you can find on the Opera plug-ins Web page. NetSonic, which actually works with any browser, is a program that can speed up your browsing by supercharging Opera's disk cache, therefore, enabling Opera to more efficiently handle a large disk cache. This means that items are more likely to be found in the cache. As a result, they won't have to be downloaded each time you want to visit the same Web page.

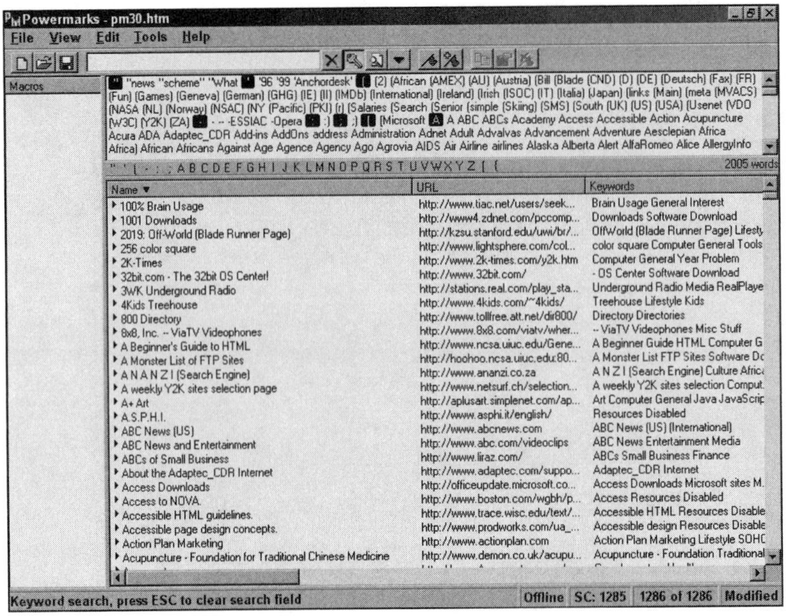

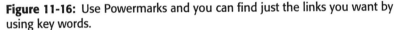

Figure 11-16: Use Powermarks and you can find just the links you want by using key words.

Like many other browser add-ons, NetSonic is available in several versions. You can download a free version, or you can upgrade to a registered version by paying a registration fee. The free version has more limited configuration options and adds advertisements to Opera's title bar. The advertisements aren't too intrusive, but the lack of the advanced configuration options may convince you to upgrade if you determine that NetSonic is improving your browsing performance.

Copernic

Copernic boosts your Internet searching ability by enabling you to create a search phrase that is then submitted to a number of different search engines. The results from the search engines are then ranked according to their relevance to your query. You then can use Opera (or another Web browser) to visit the most promising links.

Figure 11-17 shows the results of a Copernic search. In the example in Figure 11-17, Copernic searched for the phrase "Brian Underdahl" in the Web category and found sixty-six Web sites.

You can download a free copy of Copernic from http://www.copernic.com. The program is available in three versions. The free version is supported by advertising and does not allow you to select all of the categories, but it is still an excellent tool for searching the Internet.

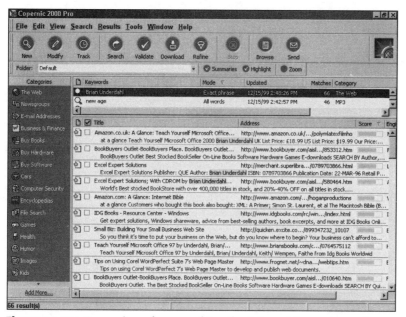

Figure 11-17: Copernic makes searching the Internet far easier and more productive.

Summary

Although Opera is not yet as well known as the browsers from Microsoft and Netscape, Opera is certainly well worth a try. Opera is far faster than any Microsoft or Netscape browser, and as you've seen in this chapter, Opera is also a top contender in every way.

Opera is a little different from those other browsers, so this chapter showed you the important elements of the Opera interface. You also learned how to configure Opera so that it works as you want to work. Finally, you learned about some great add-ons that can make Opera even more useful.

The next chapter introduces you to e-mail and discusses how to choose the right e-mail program for your needs.

✦   ✦   ✦

Using Easy and Effective E-mail

The hardest thing about writing and sending a letter is waiting for the reply. And of course the next hardest thing is that long walk to the mailbox. Well, if you use e-mail, you can often receive a reply to your message the same day and you don't even have to get off your butt to get it.

In this part, you learn everything you need to know about Internet e-mail. You start by deciding what kind of e-mail client you want to use. Then you find out about signing up for free Web-based services, using HTML mail, attaching files to your e-mail, keeping your e-mail organized, and finally, warding off all that annoying junk e-mail.

Choosing an E-mail Client and Using E-mail

If you've been on the Internet any time at all, chances are that you've checked into e-mail. And if you haven't done it yet, you will soon. E-mail gets it there fast. No postage. No phone charges. No waiting on a response three or four days from now. You want an answer to that question this afternoon, even though your client is in Sri Lanka? With e-mail, it's possible.

As you begin investigating e-mail programs, you will discover that a whole variety of offerings are out there. You might want something simple such as Eudora Light or something that does everything except write the message for you, such as Outlook 2000. This chapter introduces you to a number of popular e-mail programs and helps you learn some of the basic tasks you'll accomplish with your e-mail client.

Where Do You Get an E-mail Client?

If you don't already have an e-mail program, or you're just want a change from the program you've been using, you'll be happy to know e-mail software is easy to find.

If you wish, you can use a mail client packaged with your favorite Web browser. Internet Explorer comes with Outlook Express, while Netscape offers its own mail client, Netscape

Messenger, as part of the Communicator package. Microsoft Outlook (a different program entirely) is included with Office 2000 from Microsoft. Other stand-alone e-mail packages are available from a variety of sources. In this chapter we take a look at Eudora, one of the more popular stand-alone e-mail clients.

On the CD-ROM Versions of Internet Explorer (which includes Outlook Express) and Netscape Communicator (which includes Messenger) for Windows and Macintosh are available on this book's CD-ROM. You must install those programs to use the e-mail clients that come with them.

For now, let's take a look at these e-mail clients and find out how they stack up against each other. Table 12-1 provides the URLs for the various programs, in case you want to investigate them online yourself.

Table 12-1 Finding E-mail Clients		
E-mail Client	*Operating System*	*URL*
Outlook Express	Windows, Macintosh, UNIX	http://www.microsoft.com/windows/oe/
Outlook 2000	Windows	http://www.microsoft.com/office/outlook/
Netscape Messenger	Windows, Macintosh, UNIX/Linux	http://home.netscape.com/communicator/messenger/v4.0/
Eudora	Windows, Macintosh	http://www.eudora.com/

Tip Table 12-1 is by no means comprehensive. If you want to see what other e-mail clients might be available for your operating system, visit a software site such as Tucows (http://www.tucows.com/) and look for a list of e-mail clients.

How Do You Install an E-mail Client?

If your Web browser or office software doesn't come with an e-mail program, don't worry. You can get a lot of stuff from the Web nowadays, including e-mail programs. All you have to do is visit one of the Web sites mentioned in Table 12-1 to download the e-mail program of your choice.

Downloading the program

Your first step is to figure out which e-mail program you want. The information in this chapter can help you decide that, but you should also check out the Web sites listed in Table 12-1. Each site probably has several options, and there are two important things to consider when you choose which program to download:

✦ Make sure you choose a program specifically designed for your operating system. Eudora, Messenger, and Outlook Express all have version for Windows and Macintosh, and the latter two are even available for UNIX-based systems.

✦ Be aware of any trial periods or restrictions that may apply to the program. Free trial programs often expire after a certain amount of time, while others (such as Eudora 4.3) allow you to use the program for free as long as you don't mind a few advertisements in the program window.

When you have chosen a program and jumped through all the hoops that the download site requires, you can begin the download, as shown in Figure 12-1. Don't forget which folder you saved it in! When the download is complete, a message appears on-screen telling you so. Next, you need to install the software so you can use it. Follow the instructions on the Web site to complete installation.

Tip If you are using Windows, the file you downloaded probably has the .exe extension. If this is the case, navigate to the location where you saved it using My Computer and double-click it to begin installation.

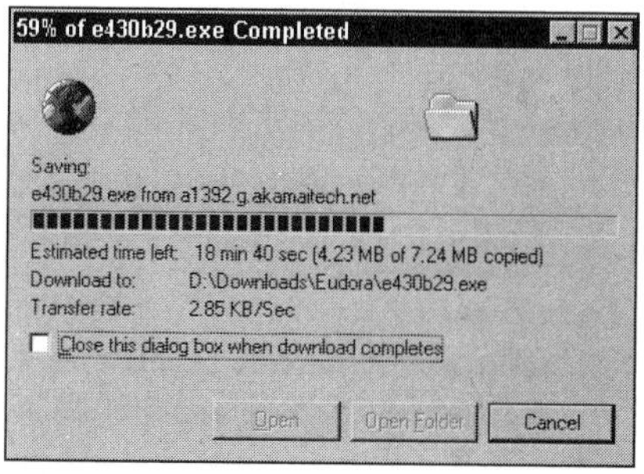

Figure 12-1: The download process will probably take several minutes.

Outlook Express

Outlook Express, which is shown in Figure 12-2, is the mail client offered along with Internet Explorer. It's simple, friendly, and easy-to-use, offering things like a menu bar, tool bar, and tiled but easy-to-navigate windows that will be familiar to almost any Windows user.

In spite of the name similarity, Outlook Express is not a knockoff or "light" version of Outlook. They are quite different, a fact that becomes evident after you spend a few minutes using either one. It's true that both can function as e-mail clients and that Outlook contains features like a personal calendar and journal that Outlook Express doesn't have. But Outlook Express can perform two very important functions that Outlook 2000 cannot: Outlook Express can function as a news client for reading and participating in Usenet newsgroups, and it can handle HTTP mail server accounts such as Hotmail.

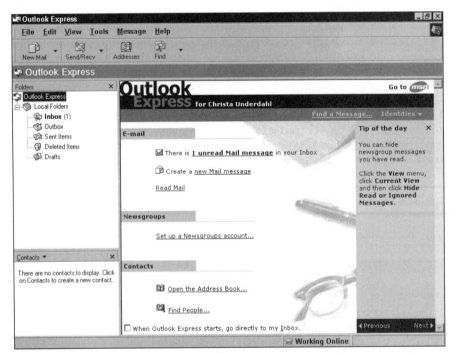

Figure 12-2: Outlook Express puts a fairly simple face on e-mail.

If you have Windows 98 or higher, Outlook Express is usually installed automatically when you first set up Windows on your computer. If Outlook Express is not already installed, select Settings from the Start menu, click on Control Panel, and open the Add/Remove Programs icon in the Control Panel window. In the Add/Remove Program Properties dialog box, click the Windows Setup tab to bring it to the front, find Outlook Express in the Components list, and place a check mark next to it. If you have another operating system, such as a Macintosh, Outlook Express will be installed with Internet Explorer.

Note   Internet Explorer 4 for Macintosh (which is included on the *Internet Bible* CD-ROM), includes Outlook Express 4. Outlook Express 5 is available for Macintosh systems, and can be downloaded from the site listed in Table 12-1.

Outlook Express features

If you haven't already, open Outlook Express by double-clicking its icon on your desktop. If you have not previously opened the program or set up a mail account, Outlook Express has a wizard to help you do that.

Cross-Reference   To learn how to configure your e-mail account quickly, take a look at Chapter 3, "Getting Started with E-mail."

A number of features in Outlook Express distinguish it from its competitors:

✦ A familiar Windows interface, which makes the program easy-to-use.

✦ Support for multiple e-mail accounts and identities. This feature is especially important for people who have both personal and business e-mail accounts but want to use one program for all of them.

✦ HTML format support, enabling you to set fonts, sizes, colors, and more as you compose e-mail messages.

✦ Support for all major e-mail technologies, including HTTP mail servers for Web-based e-mail. Outlook Express also supports HTML formatting in messages.

Note   HTML (HyperText Markup Language) is now a common feature in most popular e-mail programs. If your e-mailer supports HTML, you can send and receive e-mail messages displayed in HTML format, the format of pages on the Web. This means you can see tables as they would appear on the Web, display the fonts, colors, and sizes of text in their original Web form, and send messages with graphics and even animations in place.

Getting mail with Outlook Express

To get your mail using Outlook Express, simply click the Send/Recv button on the toolbar. The e-mail client goes out to search your mail server. If it finds any messages, they are downloaded to your Inbox. If you use Windows, Outlook Express lets you know when you have mail waiting by displaying a little mail icon on the System Tray (next to the clock). You may also hear a little musical chord when the incoming mail is received.

To read your new mail, click the Inbox icon, which is located in the folder list on the left side of the Outlook Express window. The Inbox contains a preview pane at the bottom of the window where you can read a selected message, or you can double-click a message header to open it in a new window.

Tip   The main screen of Outlook Express that appears when you first open the program isn't very useful. Because you'll probably spend most of your time in the Inbox, consider placing a check mark next to the option "When Outlook Express starts, go directly to my Inbox."

Setting up multiple identities in Outlook Express

One of the most significant advantages that Outlook Express has over most of its competitors is the ability to configure multiple e-mail accounts. This is especially important today because so many people have more than one account. You can configure an unlimited number of accounts in Outlook Express, even if they are on separate mail servers.

Besides being able to handle separate e-mail accounts, you can also create multiple e-mail identities for the same account. As you may know, when you send an e-mail message, the message identifies you based on the name—or screen name—you provided Outlook Express when you set up your account. But what if you want to be identified differently to different recipients? For instance, you may want to use an informal screen name when communicating with friends and family, but in more formal situations you may find that your full name is preferable.

The procedure for setting up additional e-mail accounts or identities is the same. Launch Outlook Express and follow these steps:

1. On the menu bar, click Tools ➪ Accounts.

2. In the Internet Accounts dialog, click Add ➪ Mail.

3. The Internet Connection Wizard should open. In the first screen, type your Display Name. This is the name that recipients will see when you send them mail.

   Click Next when you have entered a name.

4. In the next box, type the e-mail address that has been provided by your ISP or network administrator for your e-mail account. Alternatively, if you want to sign up for a free Hotmail account, choose the lower option.

   Click Next after the correct e-mail address is entered.

5. In the wizard screen, which is shown in Figure 12-3, choose the type of incoming mail server that your account uses and type in the server names. Again, this information is provided by your ISP.

6. Click Next, and enter the account name and password information for your account. Click Next again, and then click Finish.

You can repeat these steps over and over again to set up additional e-mail accounts and identities. If you are creating a new identity for an existing account, you will enter the same information for the e-mail address, server names, account name, and password, changing only the display name. Figure 12-4 shows the Mail tab of the Internet Accounts dialog, with three e-mail accounts. The first one uses an HTTP mail server and an account with Hotmail. The other two are actually separate identities for the same e-mail account.

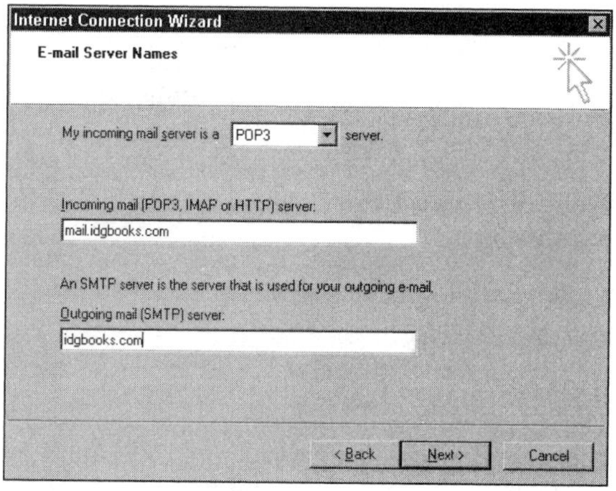

Figure 12-3: Select the type of incoming server you use, and enter the server names here.

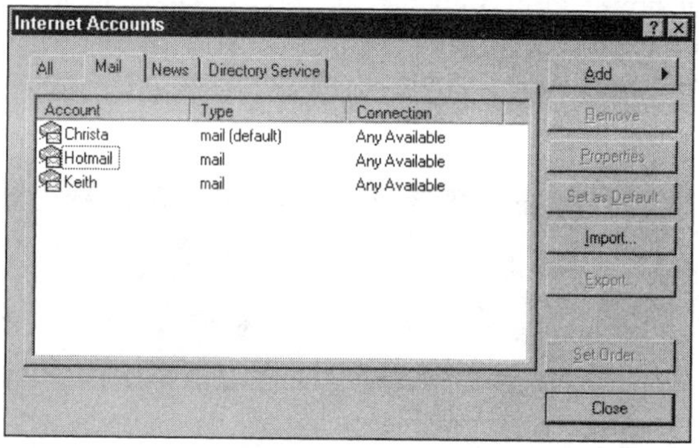

Figure 12-4: Three e-mail accounts have been configured in Outlook Express. Keith and Christa are actually separate identities for the same account.

Tip

If you don't like the account name listed under the Account column in the Internet Accounts dialog, select the account and click Properties. Type a new name on the General tab of the Properties dialog and click OK.

Using multiple identities in Outlook Express is easy. When you are composing a new message, notice that the *From* field in the message header contains a drop-down menu. Click the down-arrow and choose an identity before you send the message.

Outlook 2000

Microsoft Outlook 2000 is a full-featured contact manager, also called a PIM (Personal Information Manager) that helps you keep track of all kinds of things — from e-mail to journal entries to your daily schedule to a far-reaching calendar. If you have information and you need to organize it, you can use Outlook to do so.

Outlook is included with all versions of Microsoft Office 2000. If you have used previous versions of Outlook, or if you have used an earlier product such as Microsoft Exchange, Outlook will be familiar.

Note   Although Outlook 98 was reasonably stable, Outlook 97 was a deeply flawed product. It included numerous bugs and is generally confusing to use. If you have an earlier version of Outlook, consider upgrading to Outlook 2000. You'll find it easier to use and a lot more stable.

The Outlook interface was created to make it easy to find your way around a feature-laden program. Even though the capabilities of the program are complex, the program itself looks pretty simple at first glance, as you can see in Figure 12-5. Of course, when you go scouting through the various menus, you quickly uncover new features that give a broader picture of Outlook's capabilities.

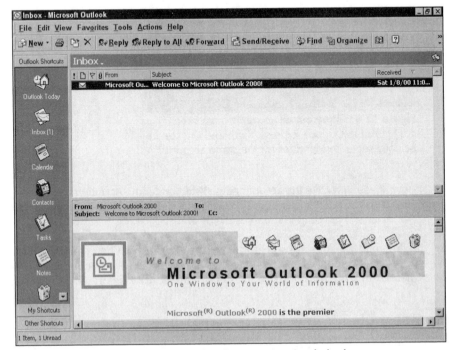

Figure 12-5: The Outlook 2000 window has a pretty simple look.

Features of Outlook 2000

Basic features of Outlook 2000 enable you to create and send e-mail, organize phone contacts, keep journal entries, set up meetings, and more. Features include:

✦ An Organize tool, which helps you create folders and organization rules

✦ A Preview pane that helps you evaluate e-mail quickly so you know which messages to read first

✦ The ability to use a word processor, such as Word 2000, as your e-mail editor

✦ HTML support for sending and receiving e-mail messages, and the ability to change formatting "on the fly"

✦ Full Java support

✦ The ability to create your own distribution lists for mass mailings

✦ A Rules Wizard, which helps set up rules for organizing, highlighting, and filtering e-mail

✦ Enhanced browser integration and the ability to view Web pages in Outlook

✦ A Meeting Planner that enables you to schedule meetings, interviews, and NetMeeting conferences

Getting started with Outlook 2000

Checking your e-mail with Outlook is a simple process. When you first launch the program, a wizard will take you through the process of configuring Outlook 2000. You will have to perform several important tasks:

✦ Decide whether you want Outlook to import data and settings from other e-mail programs, such as Outlook Express or Eudora. If you do this, messages, folders, contacts, and various settings will be carried over from those programs into Outlook.

✦ Determine the types of e-mail services you want to configure. If you connect to the Internet only through a modem, you can probably choose the Internet Only option. But if you get mail via a network, choose the option that configures both network and dial-up services. You can also choose to use Outlook solely as a schedule and contact manager, but for now we'll assume that you do want e-mail services.

✦ Set up your mail account. When you click the button to do this, a property sheet opens. Make sure you check every tab of the sheet to input information such as your name, e-mail address, server names, account name and password, and the method you use to connect to the mail server.

The information you need to configure your mail account should be provided by your ISP or network administrator. Once you've configured Outlook to receive mail, click Send/Receive on the Outlook toolbar to check for new messages. Outlook will automatically dial your Internet connection, if that is the method you use to connect to your mail server.

Note   To control how often Outlook checks your server for new mail, open the Tools menu, choose Options, and select the Internet E-mail tab. You can also use the Options dialog box to control how Outlook handles your dial-up connection.

Setting up multiple accounts in Outlook 2000

As with Outlook Express, Outlook 2000 makes it easy to configure multiple mail accounts. You can check for mail in multiple accounts, but unfortunately you cannot pick-and-choose an identity for outgoing messages as you can with Outlook Express.

To configure another mail account:

1. Click Tools ⇨ Services.

2. In the Services dialog, click Add. The Add Service to Profile window opens, as shown in Figure 12-6.

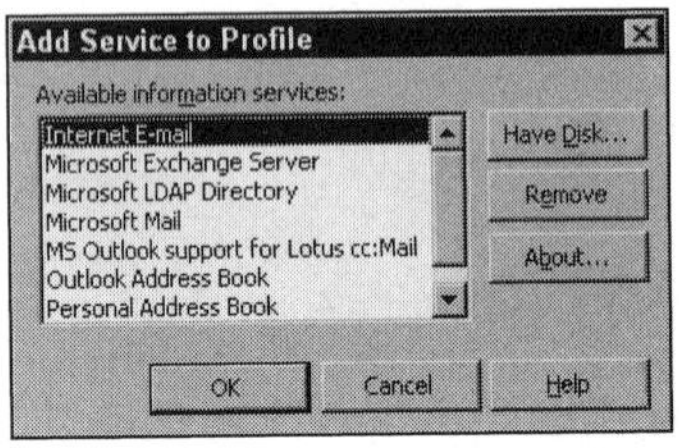

Figure 12-6: Select a service to add to your Outlook profile.

3. Select a service—in this case Internet E-mail—and click OK.

4. Configure the new account, as you did when you first set up Outlook.

5. Restart Outlook to make your new account take effect.

Netscape Messenger

Netscape Messenger is the mail component of the Netscape Communicator package. In this respect it is similar to Outlook Express because it comes as part of a browser package, and, like Outlook Express, it also serves as a newsgroup reader.

Netscape Messenger's greatest strength is its simplicity, which you can see in Figure 12-7.

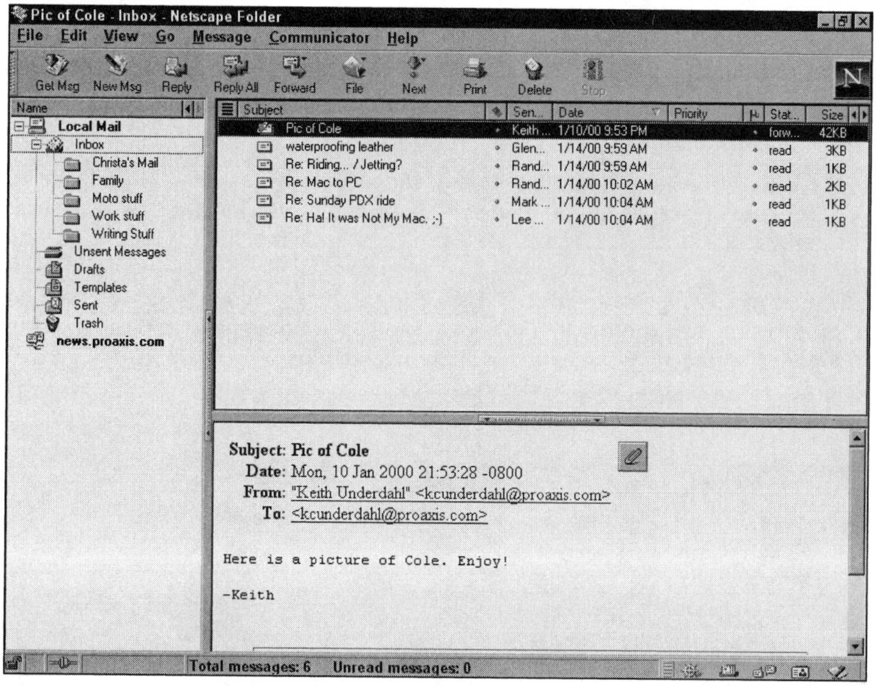

Figure 12-7: Netscape Messenger puts a friendly face on e-mail.

Features of Netscape Messenger

Messenger provides more than a simple look—it offers a list of features that will appeal to many Internet mail users. The features of Messenger packaged with Communicator include:

✦ Open and close tabs so you can display or hide your own toolbars

✦ A Sort capability for mail folders, which enables you to organize your messages

✦ A spelling checker

✦ The ability to thread messages so responses are grouped according to subject

✦ Hot hyperlinks so you can move from links in messages directly to the Web

✦ A Security Advisor feature that lets you know whether a message is secure

✦ Versions that are compatible with Windows, Macintosh, and Linux

Getting mail in Netscape Messenger

When you are working in Netscape Navigator (the Web browser), you can open Messenger quickly using the Inbox button on the Netscape Component bar. Alternatively, you can click Communicator ➪ Messenger.

To retrieve your mail using Messenger:

1. Open Communicator.

2. Click Get Msg on the far left side of the Messenger toolbar. Messenger checks for new messages. If you have new mail, the messages are downloaded to your Inbox.

New unread messages appear in boldface in the Inbox. When you select a message in the message list, the body of it appears in the preview pane and the message is no longer boldfaced. You can also double-click a message in the list to open it in a separate window, as shown in Figure 12-8.

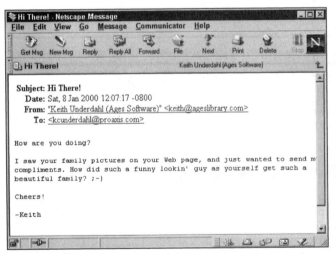

Figure 12-8: When you double-click a message, it opens in a separate window.

Controlling the timing of mail checks

How often do you want Netscape to check for messages? Some people check hourly; others check every few minutes. Messenger can go out and scan the server without interrupting your work in other programs; you need only set the time increment for the checks. Here's how:

1. Launch Messenger if it isn't already open.

2. Open the Edit menu and choose Preferences. When the Preferences dialog box appears, click Mail Server in the Category frame, as shown in Figure 12-9.

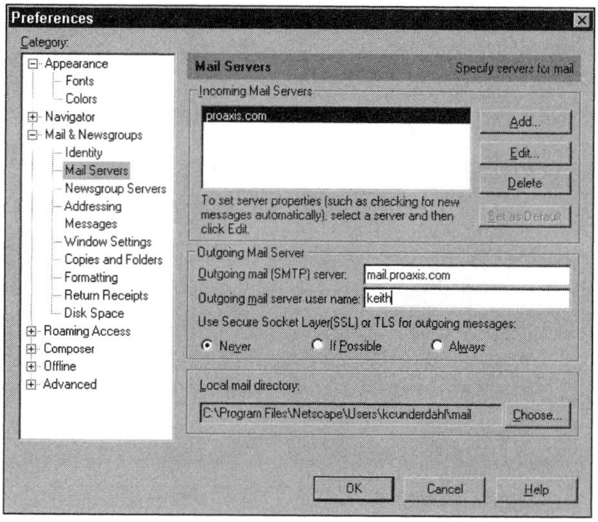

Figure 12-9: Use the Preferences dialog box to edit information about your mail server.

3. Select your mail server and click Edit. The Mail Server Properties dialog box appears, as shown in see Figure 12-10.

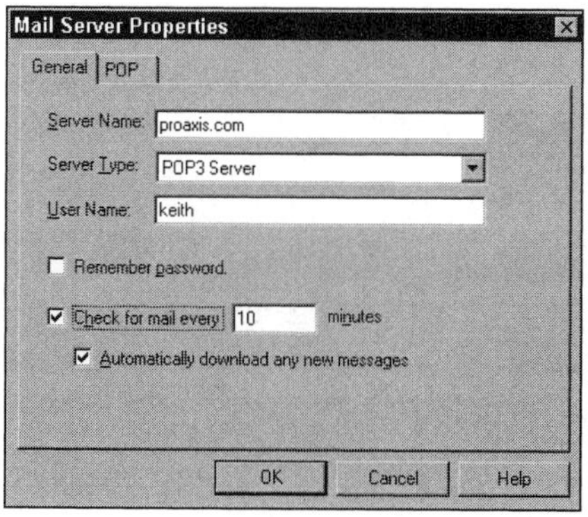

Figure 12-10: Set the timing for mail checks in the Mail Server Preferences dialog box.

4. Click the *Check for mail every* text box and type the number of minutes you want to elapse between the times Messenger checks for mail.

5. Click OK twice to close the Preferences dialog box and return to Messenger.

Caution   If your computer has limited Random Access Memory (RAM) — say, 16MB or less — enabling Messenger to check mail in the background while you work on other things could cause errors and system crashes. Consider disabling Messenger's automatic mail checks if you find yourself in this situation.

Eudora

Unlike Outlook Express and Netscape Messenger, Eudora doesn't come with a sponsoring Web browser: Eudora is a stand-alone mail program offered by Qualcomm, and you can download a free version of it from www.eudora.com. Eudora boasts millions of users worldwide and has products available in several incarnations. Many people have been die-hard Eudora fans since e-mail first began eking out an existence for itself — and one of the biggest reasons for user loyalty is this: Eudora is friendly and easy to use. Figure 12-11 illustrates the Eudora 4.3 window.

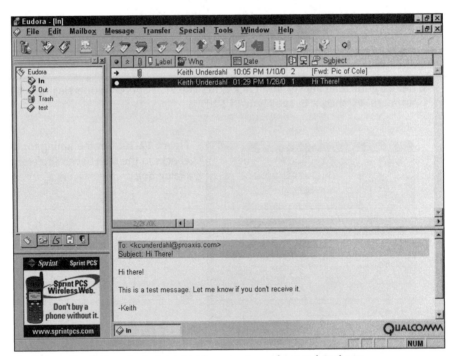

Figure 12-11: Eudora is designed to be easy to understand and use.

You can download a free version of Eudora (Version 4.3 is shown here) from Qualcomm's Web site at `http://www.eudora.com`. The free "sponsored" version includes a window in the lower left corner that displays advertisements. If you are willing to pay $39.95, you can eliminate the advertisements, or you can use the "Light" mode without advertisements. The full version offers the following capabilities that Eudora Light does not have:

✦ Spelling checker

✦ Ability to configure multiple e-mail identities and accounts, as well as multiple signatures

✦ Special stationery for richly-formatted messages

✦ Advanced message filtering

Eudora 4.3 features

Eudora has been wildly popular in all its releases, and Version 4.3 builds on its already impressive list of features, including:

✦ A New Account setup wizard, which you can use to set up your account easily

✦ HTML support

✦ A new multiple personalities feature that enables more than one user to work with your computer

✦ Filters, which you can easily create and apply to weed your mail

✦ A "sponsored" mode that enables you to use the full version of Eudora for free

✦ Voice e-mail capability, if another user has the Qualcomm PureVoice plug-in

✦ Spelling checker enhancements that enable you to check only underlined words

Getting e-mail in Eudora

The process of getting your e-mail in Eudora is simple. You need, of course, to install and set up Eudora and establish a dial-up connection. Once you are online:

1. Start Eudora by double-clicking the Eudora icon on your desktop.

2. Open the File menu and choose Check Mail. (You can also press Ctrl+M or click the Check Mail button on the toolbar, if you prefer.)

Eudora then goes out to retrieve e-mail from your server. Any e-mail retrieved is placed in your Inbox.

Cross-Reference To learn about other e-mail features that can save you time and trouble — such as configuring your e-mail program to filter out messages, warding off junk mail (spam), and a lot more — check out Chapter 14, "Doing More with E-Mail" and Chapter 15, "Taking Charge of Your E-Mail."

Composing, Sending, and Replying to E-mail

This chapter doesn't bore you to death by listing the procedures for composing, sending, and replying to e-mail for each of the programs introduced in this chapter. Nor would you want that, of course. But this example uses Netscape Messenger to illustrate the various e-mail procedures. You'll get the basic idea — but you'll need to adapt the procedures on your own system if you are using a different e-mail program.

Please note that within each of the sections earlier in this chapter, where we discussed the various features of the e-mail program, you learned how to retrieve your mail with that particular utility. This section picks up where those left off by explaining how you can create and send messages of your own.

Composing e-mail

Starting a new e-mail message is a lot like taking out a blank sheet of paper to begin a new letter. Start your e-mail program and locate a button that says New Message, New Mail, or something to that effect. When you click this button, a message composition window appears, like the one show in Figure 12-12, in which you can enter the information for the message.

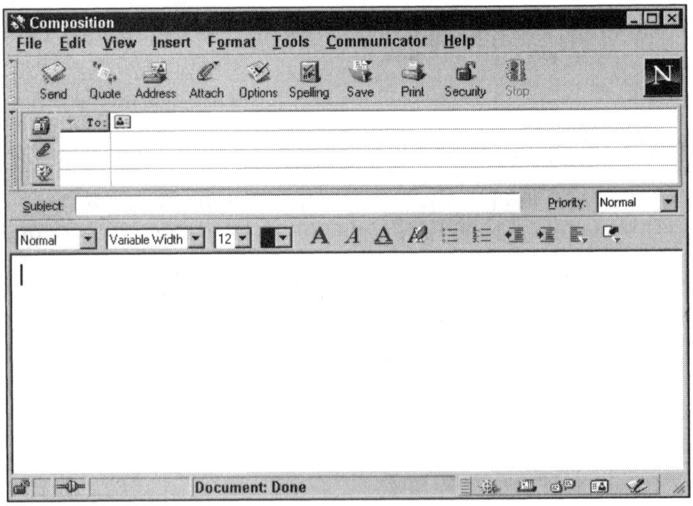

Figure 12-12: You create the new e-mail message in a message composition window.

Understanding the message composition window

Message composition windows vary only slightly between the various programs. If you are using any of the e-mail programs discussed in this chapter, your program will have most of the basic elements that we will discuss here.

Most mail program composition windows have a toolbar, which provides an array of buttons to help you carry out composition tasks easily. Table 12-2 shows you some of Netscape's buttons and gives you a brief description of each.

Table 12-2
Toolbar Buttons in Netscape's Message Composition Window

Button	Name	Description
Send	Send	Click this button when you are finished composing and are ready to send the message.
Attach	Attach	Use this button when you want to attach a file to your current document.
Address	Address	Click this button to access the program's address book.
Spelling	Spelling	Click this to check spelling.
Security	Security	If you want to encrypt or attach a digital signature to a message, click this button.

Below the toolbar you will see header information for the message. The *To* field is where you enter the e-mail address for the person to whom you are sending the message. Often you can click the To button to access your address book.

Tip

If you are sending a message to more than one person, most programs let you separate multiple e-mail addresses with a semicolon. In Netscape Messenger, just press Enter to move to the next line and enter another address.

Most mail programs have a Cc line where you can enter the e-mail addresses of people to whom you wish to send a copy of the message. In the case of Netscape Messenger, simply click and hold the To button next to each address, and select whether you want the person to be a primary recipient (To), a carbon copy recipient (Cc), or a blind carbon copy recipient (Bcc). If you send someone a blind carbon copy of a message, the other recipients will not know about it.

The Subject line gives you a place to enter a few words that describe the content of your message. Some people prefer to use cryptic, funny, or attention-getting subject lines. You'll quickly learn that, especially in business, if you want your e-mail message to get read, you should use a concise Subject line that lets your recipient know the message is worth reading.

Writing the e-mail message

When you are ready to create the body of the e-mail message, simply click in the message window in the lower portion of the window and begin typing. Most e-mail messages start off with a traditional salutation like:

```
Dear Smedley,
```

It's not necessary to enter a full header as you would on a business letter, such as the name and address information. Just click and type away.

For best results, press Enter twice at the end of a paragraph. Don't use Tab to indent a paragraph as you might in a typical word-processed letter. Tabs can act squirrelly in documents sent over the Net—so it's better not to use them.

Sending e-mail

When you're finished composing the message, you're ready to send it. In Netscape Messenger, as in virtually all other mailers, you simply move the mouse pointer to the Send button and click it. If you prefer, you can open the File menu and select Send Now. Assuming that your online connection is already established, the message goes out to your mail server, and a copy is placed in the Sent folder. (This folder may be called something else, depending on which e-mail program you are using.)

Replying to e-mail

When you receive a message, you have several options:

✦ You can delete it (but ordinarily you would read it first, unless it's junk mail or spam)

✦ You can read it

✦ You can read it and respond to it

As you know, you read an e-mail message by selecting it and opening the message window. If you want to reply to the e-mail message, click the Reply button on the Message window toolbar. When you click Reply, the Message Composition window appears.

Ten Tips for Effective E-mail

1. Be brief.

2. Be clear.

3. Be careful with humor—especially if you don't know the recipient very well.

4. Be patient (some people don't check e-mail every day).

5. Be thorough (don't assume the recipient remembers from your last e-mail what you're referring to).

6. Be friendly but cautious. E-mail is somewhat more informal than traditional business correspondence, but don't overdo it.

7. Be complete. Don't send five short e-mail messages when you could send one longer one. Try to capture all necessary thoughts in the current message so you don't litter the recipient's Inbox with mail.

8. Be aware of formatting. Skip lines or use bullets to help emphasize your point and give the reader's eyes a rest.

9. Be straightforward with your subject lines.

10. Be careful about copies. Don't Cc everyone in your address book just because you found a funny article on the Web. Send copies sparingly. Your peers will thank you for it.

In the example shown in the Figure 12-13, notice that the text of the original message has automatically been placed in the message, and it has been indented slightly with a line along the left margin. Most mail programs also place a header above the original message, which includes information about the author and the date and time the message was sent.

Besides a basic reply, you usually have two other options:

✦ **Reply All**. If the original message had multiple recipients, Reply All will send your reply to everyone on the original recipients' list.

✦ **Forward**. You can redirect a message to someone else by clicking Forward. When you click Forward, you will have to enter an e-mail address for your new recipient.

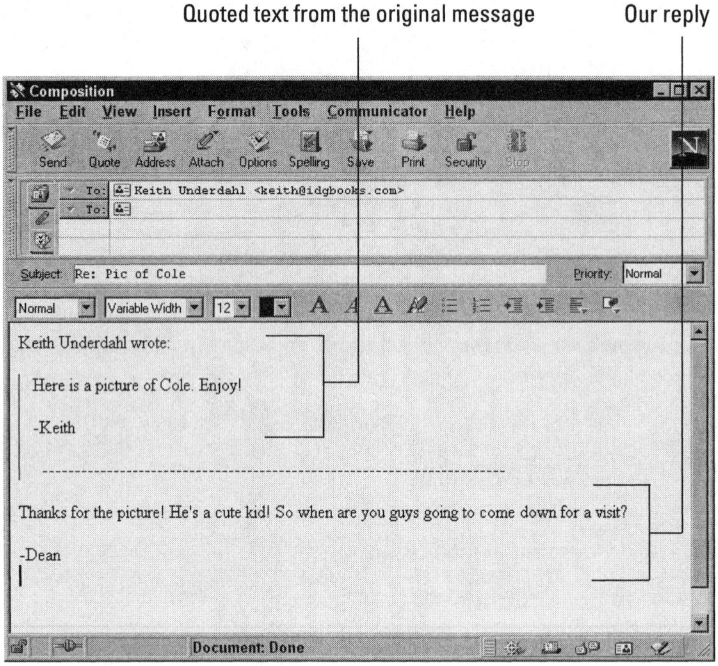

Quoted text from the original message   Our reply

Figure 12-13: Replying to an e-mail message copies the original message into your response.

Summary

In this chapter, you've learned where to find an e-mail client and discovered what to do with one once you've found it. You also took a look at several popular e-mail programs — Outlook Express, Outlook 2000, Netscape Messenger, and Eudora — and explored the basics of composing, sending, and replying to e-mail messages.

✦   ✦   ✦

Using Web-Based E-mail Services

In the previous chapter, you learned about a number of e-mail clients, software that you install on your computer and use to log on to your mail server and download your e-mail. This chapter focuses on two different types of e-mail features — free Web-based e-mail and e-mail forwarding services — that can make your e-mail life a whole lot easier and enable you to get your messages from almost anywhere, using almost any computer.

Defining Free E-mail

The term *free e-mail* is a little misleading, but it is true. It is *free*, but that's not all it is. The free part comes from the fact that you don't pay anything for it; advertisers do. E-mail providers such as Hotmail or Yahoo! Mail exist by selling space to advertisers, and when you log on to their site to send or receive e-mail, you are met with ads that are targeted to your own interests.

The e-mail services offer this targeted marketing feature to advertisers because as part of their sign-in process they ask you a number of questions about yourself: what you like, what hobbies you have, what type of computer system you use, and so on. They gather this information and then make it available to the advertisers, who then know which ads you are most likely to respond to. The advertiser makes money, the e-mail service makes money, and you get free e-mail.

Note One thing we've noticed is that many of the Web-based mail services discussed here take their servers offline to perform system upgrades for an hour or two after midnight on Saturdays. If you try to check your e-mail during these hours, you may get an error message or a note advising you to try later.

Finding Free E-mail Services

This section spotlights a number of free e-mail services that are currently popular on the World Wide Web. Most of these services are Web-based, as opposed to traditional e-mail, which operates independently of the World Wide Web. Web-based e-mail utilizes HTTP mail servers, whereas a standard e-mail account generally uses a POP or IMAP server for incoming mail and an SMTP server for outgoing mail.

 Cross-Reference   To learn more about HTTP, POP, and IMAP mail servers, take a look at Chapter 12, "Choosing an E-mail Client and Using E-mail."

Hotmail

Hotmail is Microsoft's Web-based e-mail service. You'll find Hotmail at `http://www.hotmail.com`, as shown in Figure 13-1. Hotmail is Web based, which means it uses an HTTP server.

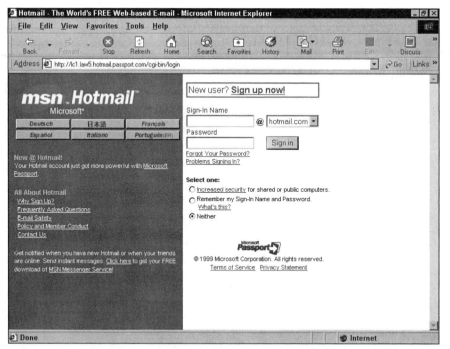

Figure 13-1: Hotmail is Microsoft's contribution to Web-based mail service.

To use Hotmail, you don't have to download software, which means it doesn't add to the drain on your system resources. Messages can be sent and received using nothing more than a Web browser, which means you can easily check your mail from virtually any computer with Internet access. Unlike some other free mail accounts, Hotmail does allow you to send and receive message attachments. But storage space is limited to 2MB, so make sure you delete old messages often.

 Tip   If you use Outlook Express for e-mail, you can sign up for a free Hotmail account by clicking Tools ➪ New Account Signup ➪ Hotmail. Outlook Express can be configured to access your Hotmail HTTP mail account.

Signing up with Hotmail

If, after surveying the various free e-mail offerings, you decide Hotmail is the one for you, follow these steps to sign up:

1. Point your browser at `http://www.hotmail.com`, and click "Sign up now!" near the top of the window.

2. Read through the terms of service — note the points that mention that you are agreeing to be honest, accurate, and current in your reporting of information about yourself. At sign-on, all this information Hotmail gathers is considered "Registration Data." If you accept the terms of service, click the I Accept button at the bottom of the page.

3. Fill in the Hotmail Registration form as completely as you can. After you fill in the necessary information, click Sign-Up to complete registration. If someone else has already chosen your user name or if there are any other problems, you will be prompted to update your information.

In the future, when you want to access your e-mail account from a Web browser, visit the Hotmail Web site and enter your user name and password. This will take you to your Hotmail Inbox, as shown in Figure 13-2.

To read the e-mail message, simply click the link in the From column. The message is displayed in the mail window. The mail window contains buttons that let you reply, forward, delete, or close the message.

Sending a Hotmail message

When you want to send an e-mail message, you have two options: You can respond to a message you've received or you can create a new message. If you want to respond to a message, simply read through the e-mail and then click the Reply button that appears both before and after the message text. Doing so displays a message window in which you can type your response.

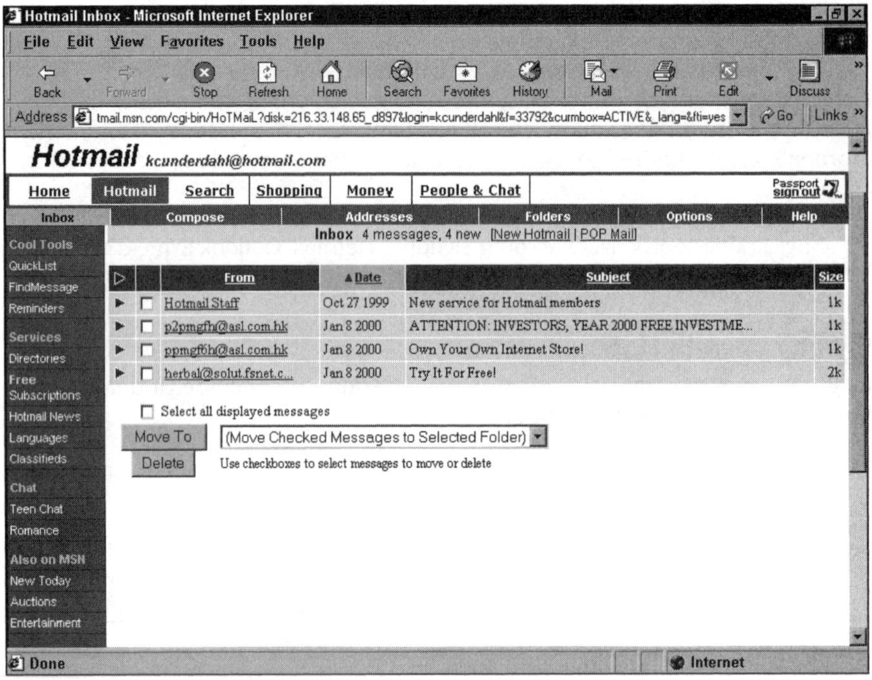

Figure 13-2: The Hotmail Inbox

Similarly, the process for creating a new message is simple:

1. Go to the Hotmail Web site at http://www.hotmail.com.

2. Enter your user ID and password to access your account.

3. Click the Compose link in the Inbox window. The Compose window appears, like the one shown in Figure 13-3, and you can enter information about the recipient of your message.

> **Tip**
>
> Do you hate spam? If so, consider obtaining a free e-mail account — such as one from Hotmail — that you can use whenever a Web site asks for your e-mail address. Reserving your free e-mail account for online registrations and such will help keep spam out of your regular account.

GeoMail

GeoMail is another Web-based e-mail program. You can find GeoMail at http://www.geomail.com. GeoMail offers to do it all on the Web — let you check your mail, store your mail, respond to your mail — all without downloading anything to your computer. In fact, GeoMail says you don't even need a computer to use GeoMail!

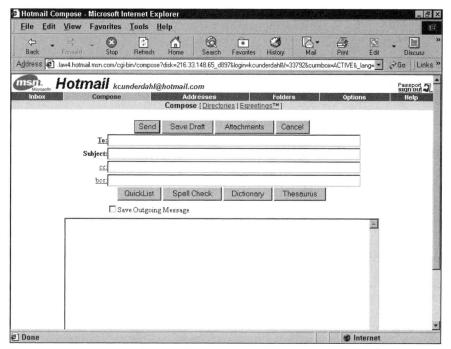

Figure 13-3: Hotmail enables you to compose messages in any Web browser.

GeoMail is unique in that it offers a number of vanity domain names for your e-mail account. Sure, you can opt for something simple like `keithunderdahl@geomail.com`, or you can choose one of their vanity names. For instance, if you're a fan of a popular southern rock band, you can choose an e-mail address like `keithunderdahl@lynyrd-skynyrd.com`, or if you drive a 240Z choose `keithunderdahl@datsun.com`. As of this writing, ten unique domain names are available.

One good point GeoMail makes is that changing e-mail addresses is a drag—when you start a new job, your corporate e-mail address changes. If you change Internet Service Providers, you get a new e-mail address. If you move or leave school, you've got it—another e-mail address. With GeoMail, or any of the Web-based e-mailers, for that matter, you have the option of using only one address. And because it stays in the same place on the World Wide Web, you don't have to worry about changing it just because your life changes.

On the down side, GeoMail's free service does not allow you to send or receive attachments, although you can purchase service upgrades that add this capability. Also, free accounts are limited to 2MB of storage space, so you should check and delete mail frequently. If your storage space fills up, additional messages sent to that account will be rejected.

Signing up with GeoMail

To sign up with GeoMail:

1. Point your browser to `http://www.geomail.com`.

2. Click the New user sign up link.

3. You are asked to sign a service agreement, which requires you to acknowledge and accept the terms of service. The agreement includes information about how GeoMail will use your personal data, how you are expected to handle the content of your e-mail messages, and more. After you have read the agreement and accepted its terms, click I Agree to continue.

4. Choose an e-mail address. Notice that you can choose a special domain name from the drop-down list. Click Continue Creating Profile when you are done typing an e-mail address. If someone else has already chosen that address, you will be prompted to choose something else.

5. Fill out the registration form as prompted. Click Save Registration Profile when you are finished. You will be prompted for an alternate e-mail address, which is an important step because the password for your GeoMail account will be sent to that address. You won't be able to use your GeoMail account until you have obtained the password that is automatically generated by GeoMail's server.

Logging in and reading your mail with GeoMail

You can access your GeoMail account by visiting the GeoMail Web page and entering your e-mail address and password. Make sure that you select the correct domain name for your account, and keep in mind that the password is case-sensitive.

GeoMail has a *frames* and *non-frames* mode. Frames divide a Web page into separate windows, creating in effect several separate Web pages all displayed in a single browser window. Not surprisingly, the no-frames mode loads faster. If you use frames, a list of options will appear along the left side of the window, with a list of actual messages front and center. If you chose no frames, options will appear across the top of the window. To read a message, click the blue link for it in the From column.

Likewise, if you want to create a new message, click Compose. Sound familiar? GeoMail's interface is similar to Hotmail's.

Logging off GeoMail

When you're ready to leave GeoMail, just click the Logout link on the right side of the window. You are taken back to the home page for GeoMail. This step is especially important if you are accessing your GeoMail account from a computer that isn't yours.

Yahoo! Mail

Another Web-based free e-mail offering is Yahoo! Mail, available at `http://mail. yahoo.com`. Similar to the other free e-mail programs discussed in this chapter, Yahoo! Mail enables you to send and retrieve e-mail messages entirely from the Web whether you are using only Yahoo! Mail or working also with other e-mail clients in your home or business. All you need to use Yahoo! Mail is a Web browser.

Signing up for Yahoo! Mail

Like the other free e-mail services, signing up with Yahoo! Mail is easy:

1. Point your browser to `http://mail.yahoo.com`.

2. Follow the instructions on-screen to select an e-mail name and register. If you have previously signed up for a Yahoo! Identity, such as Yahoo! Messenger or a Yahoo! Club area, the sign-up process will only require you to enter your password. If you do not have a Yahoo! Identity, click Sign Up Now to register.

Note

Once you've set up your Yahoo! Mail account, you can access your Yahoo! Mail inbox by visiting the Yahoo! home page (`www.yahoo.com`) and clicking the Check Mail icon at the top of the screen. Naturally, you will be prompted for your user name and password.

Reading Yahoo! Mail

To read the mail in your Inbox, simply click the Inbox link. When the Inbox appears, click the linked phrase in the Subject column to display the message. The message appears in the Message window. After reading the note, you have the option of replying, saving, printing, deleting, forwarding, or moving the message.

Yahoo! Mail provides 3 megabytes of disk storage space for each account. This is a fair amount of space, especially for e-mail, but if you are receiving a large number of messages with attached files, that storage space can be used up pretty quickly. To conserve storage space, download or delete your messages regularly.

Sending e-mail with Yahoo! Mail

You can use Yahoo! Mail to send free e-mail to friends, relatives, coworkers, clients, or anyone else. To create and send mail with Yahoo! Mail:

1. Log on to Yahoo! Mail by entering your user ID and password.

2. On the left side of the mail window, click Compose. The Compose Mail window appears.

3. Click in the *To* box and enter the e-mail address of the person to whom you are sending the message. If you don't have an e-mail address for someone you need to contact, click the *People Search* link to try to locate them using the Yahoo! People Search site.

4. In the body area of the Message window, type the message you want to send.

5. Click Send and the message is transmitted over the Internet.

> **Tip**
>
> Do you want to keep track of the e-mail you have sent? You can have Yahoo! Mail (and the other free e-mail utilities, as well) put a copy of your sent message in the Sent folder in your Yahoo! Mail folders by clicking the option "Save copy of outgoing message to Sent folder." This gives you a record of what you have sent and gives you the option of downloading and/or printing each message for your files.

Logging off Yahoo! Mail

When you are ready to leave Yahoo! Mail, simply click Sign Out on the left side of the Yahoo! Mail window. A page showing other Yahoo! options is displayed, giving you the choice to return to e-mail if you wish and thanking you for using Yahoo! Mail.

Net@ddress

Net@ddress is a free e-mail service offered by USA.NET. Like the other free e-mailers, Net@ddress is Web-based e-mail that enables you to send and receive messages from any computer that has access to the Web. The service supports the use of all popular browsers, enables you to send attached files, and has a strong antispamming policy. One thing that distinguishes Net@ddress is that it promises not to sell your profile information to third-party companies. Before you make your free e-mail decision, check out Net@ddress at `http://www.netaddress.com`.

OperaMail

Opera Software, makers of the Opera Web browser, offers their own Web-based e-mail service called OperaMail (`http://www.operamail.com/`). OperaMail's interface, which is shown in Figure 13-4, is unique in that it looks very much like an e-mail program, even though you are accessing it through a Web browser.

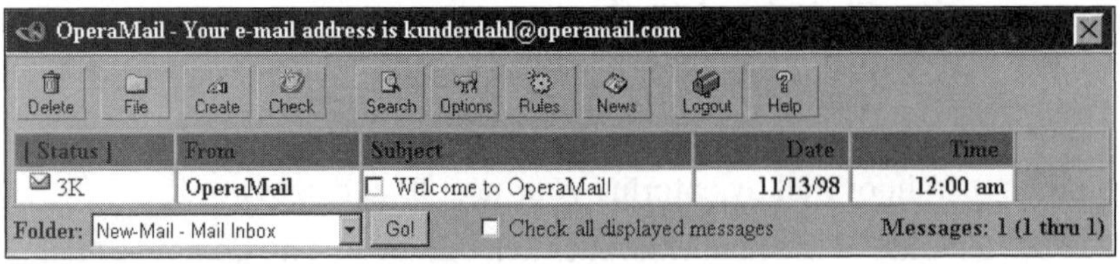

Figure 13-4: OperaMail's interface looks and behaves like a regular e-mail client.

OperaMail offers a number of features that you wouldn't normally associate with free Web-based e-mail. These features include message rules that enable you to reject or move certain types of mail, spam filtering, and even access to newsgroups.

In some ways, you could think of OperaMail as a companion e-mail program to Opera, much as Outlook Express comes with Internet Explorer, and Netscape Communicator includes Messenger. But unlike a standard e-mail client, your OperaMail account can be accessed from any computer, even if it doesn't have Opera installed.

Cross-Reference

To learn more about the Opera Web browser, check out Chapter 11, "Making the Web Sing with Opera."

Juno WebMail

Juno's WebMail (`http://webmail.juno.com`) is a unique e-mail service in that it is *not* Web-based like the other programs discussed in this chapter. WebMail is actually a free e-mail client that you download and install on your computer, just like Eudora or Outlook Express. But WebMail differs from other clients in that it can only be used to access a free Juno e-mail account.

If you're running Windows and have a modem installed, you can use Juno. You simply install their software and use it to dial up the Juno server to both send and receive your mail. The service is free, and the only catch is that you can access your mail only using the Juno program — you'll still have to use another program for your other e-mail accounts.

Getting Juno

It's easy to get the Juno software. The following steps assume you have a Web browser, however. If you don't yet have access to the Internet, Juno says it's perfectly okay to have a friend download the software for you so that you can install it on your system. However, because the software contains some cryptographic capabilities, there are limitations under U.S. law. Juno's Web site has full details, available if you click the link for downloading instructions and export limitations.

To download Juno:

1. Go to the Juno Web site at `http://webmail.juno.com`.

   Click a link that says Get Juno Now! and then click Download Now!

2. This takes you to another page with Juno's licensing agreement and export rules. If you scroll down the page a bit, you will see additional instructions on system requirements and downloading procedures. Note that downloading may take 20 to 30 minutes, and that's assuming that Internet traffic is fairly light. The best time to download software is late at night or early in the morning before everyone else gets to work.

3. Proceed with the download, and take note of where the downloaded program is being stored. The name of the file may vary depending on the software version, but when we performed the download it was a 4.7MB file called `junoinst.exe`.

Installing Juno

Once you download the Juno software, run the self-extracting file to install it on your PC. Here are the steps:

1. Click Start ⇨ Run.

2. When the Run dialog box appears, Browse to `junoinst.exe` and select it.

3. Click OK to begin the installation process. Follow the simple on-screen instructions.

4. When the installation is complete, Juno asks you whether you'd like to start the program now. Click Finish to continue.

Starting Juno

The first question you are asked when you launch Juno for the first time is whether you are starting a new account or restarting an old one. If you already have a Juno account, click Import Account. Otherwise, click Create New Account. This takes you to the first in a series of screens that gather data about you, your computer, your interests, and so on. Click Next to start the process.

The first screen gives you the user agreement — read it carefully. It says such things as "you will provide complete and accurate information and keep it updated and current" and "you may not use a fictitious name or a name other than your own" and "you will be held responsible for anything anyone using your account does with it." If these types of things bother you, spend some time looking closely at the not-so-fine print before you continue.

The next few screens are all about setting up your system to work with Juno. Pretty simple stuff, and default answers are chosen for you. If you don't know the answers to some of the questions, leave the default set the way it is. Juno then gives you the option of choosing an Automatic modem check or a Manual modem check during which time the program determines what kind of modem you are using. Try Automatic first — in most cases Juno identifies your modem type without any trouble. The modem check enables Juno to configure a dial-up connection on computers that don't already have one. This can be handy if you are installing Juno on a portable computer that you don't normally use for getting online.

Note   Juno will not perform this check if you are already connected to the Internet using another dial-up connection.

Finally, you arrive at a screen where you are asked to choose your e-mail account name and a password. Then click Activate Account. Juno automatically dials an 800 number (unless, you already have an Internet connection established).

Once connected, Juno checks your e-mail account name, and, if it finds that the e-mail address you have chosen is already in use, it will prompt you to select another one. When that's done, it will download a list of local access numbers. The next screen asks you for the number you are dialing from and then suggests local numbers you can use to access Juno. You may need to scroll down until you find your area code. Next you'll be prompted to choose specific numbers for using Juno's e-mail and Web service.

The Member Profile is where Juno gets all the information about what type of advertising might work with you as a customer. Be prepared to answer several pages' worth of questions. But when you're done, you are given the option of firing up Juno and checking for new messages. Figure 13-5 shows the first message I received using the service.

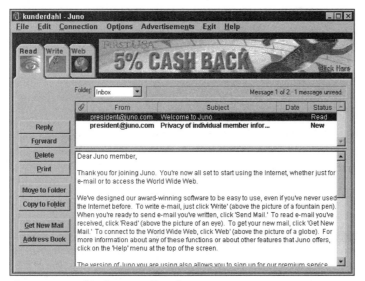

Figure 13-5: This first e-mail welcomes you to Juno.

Using Web-Based E-mail with Outlook Express

Web based e-mail services like those discussed here generally use an HTTP mail server, as opposed to the standard POP or IMAP servers used by traditional e-mail services. Most e-mail clients are not designed to support HTTP servers, so in most cases you will have to access an HTTP mail account using a Web browser. Outlook Express, however, *can* be configured to access mail on an HTTP server.

Setting up an HTTP account in Outlook Express

You configure an HTTP mail account in Outlook Express just as you would any POP or IMAP account. In fact, if you are already using Outlook Express you may have noticed an option to set up a Hotmail account when you configured your regular e-mail account. Microsoft built in the Hotmail option to Outlook Express because they own Hotmail, but you can (in theory at least) configure the program to access any HTTP server. To do so you would need to obtain the HTTP server name from the service that hosts your account. However, many services restrict you to accessing your account from a Web browser, in which case you won't be able to use Outlook Express. Check the Web site of the service for more information; some may provide direct access to their HTTP mail server as an added-cost option.

Before you set up an HTTP mail account, you will need to have the appropriate server name and other account information from the provider. When you have that information ready, follow these steps:

1. Launch Outlook Express if you haven't already. On the menu bar, click Tools ⇨ Accounts.

2. In the Internet Accounts dialog box, click Add ⇨ Mail.

3. The Internet Connection Wizard should open. In the first Wizard screen, type the display name you want to use and click Next.

4. In the next Wizard screen, shown in Figure 13-6, notice that you can select the lower radio button to configure a Hotmail account. But if you are configuring a different HTTP mail account, choose the upper radio button, type the e-mail address provided by the service (this is probably the one you chose when you first signed up for the account), and click Next.

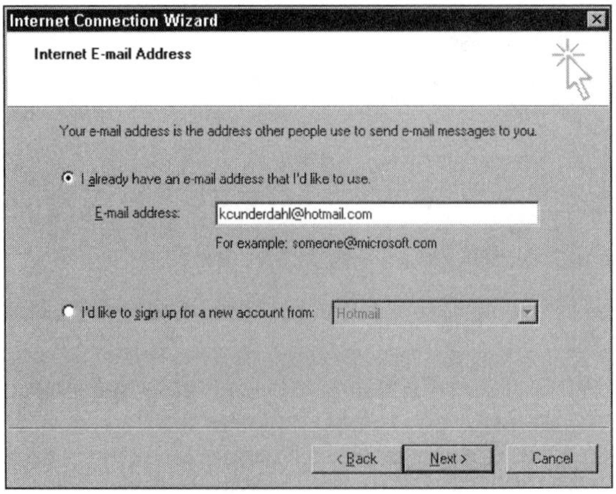

Figure 13-6: Choose the upper radio button to configure other HTTP accounts.

5. Choose HTTP in the upper menu to designate that type of mail server (Figure 13-7). In the second drop-down menu, choose either Hotmail or Other. If you choose Other, type the path for the HTTP mail server in the text box for the incoming mail server. Click Next when you are done.

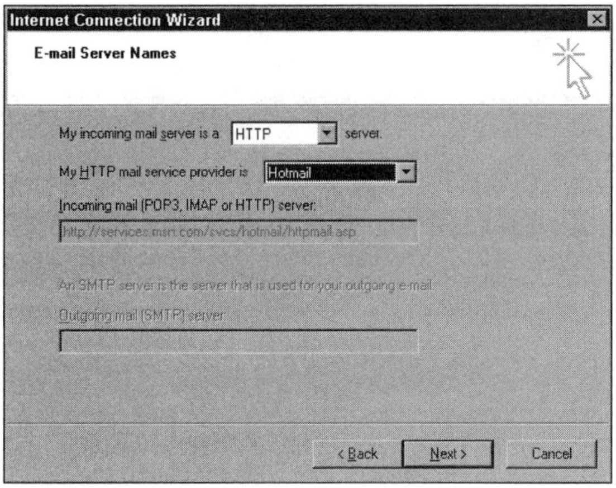

Figure 13-7: Select HTTP for the server type, and enter the server path if necessary. If you choose Hotmail as shown here, the server path is automatically entered for you.

6. In the next dialog box, enter your account name and password, as provided by the mail service.

7. Click Next and then Finish to complete the setup process.

Sending and receiving HTTP mail in Outlook Express

Using Outlook Express to manage your HTTP mail account has many advantages, chief among them the fact that you can use a single program for all of your e-mail. However, Outlook Express does separate it from other mail accounts. As you can see in Figure 13-8, Outlook Express gives HTTP mail, such as Hotmail, a separate Inbox and folders for Sent Items and Deleted Items.

Because the mail from your different e-mail accounts is kept separate, you need to click the Hotmail (or other HTTP account) Inbox to read messages. If you already have a POP mail account, you will notice that an account such as Hotmail works a bit differently. When handling HTTP mail accounts, Outlook Express:

✦ Initially downloads only the message headers. Not until you open a specific message does Outlook Express download the message from the server.

✦ Keeps Sent and Deleted Items folders on the Hotmail server instead of on your local computer. Messages in the Deleted Items folder are automatically deleted when you log off Hotmail.

✦ Cannot create new folders on the HTTP mail server. If you want to save a message locally, you have to save it in a local folder under Local Folders.

✦ Will check your Hotmail account separately, but, for Outlook Express to do so, you must click Tools ⇨ Send and Receive ⇨ Hotmail.

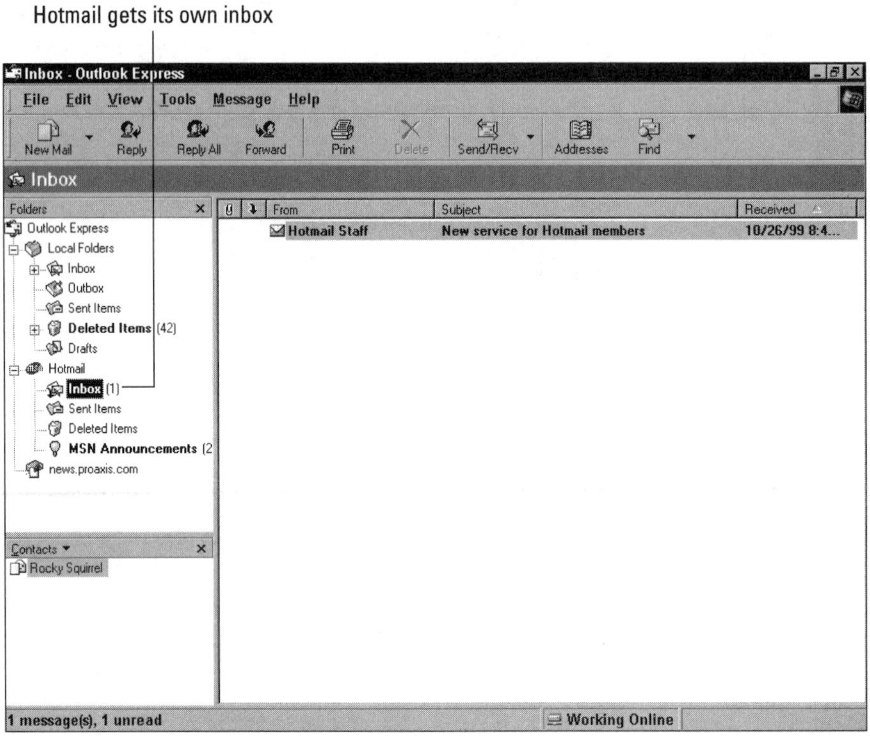

Hotmail gets its own inbox

Figure 13-8: Hotmail gets its own Inbox and associated folders in Outlook Express.

E-mail Forwarding Services

One of the problems with using multiple accounts is that you could spend hours each day just logging on to the various sites and launching mail clients in order to gather and respond to all the messages you receive on each account.

E-mail forwarding funnels all the e-mail into one neat little account. Whether you have one e-mail account or 50, if you have all the accounts assigned to e-mail forwarding, the messages make it to the forwarded account and that's the only one you have to check. No more dialing up CompuServe, your local ISP, and AOL separately. With Web-based e-mail forwarding, if you log on to the Web, you can get your messages. It's that simple.

This section explores several of the most popular free e-mail forwarding services. As you will notice, they are all similar, but have their own quirks and perks.

Bigfoot

Bigfoot (`http://www.bigfoot.com`) offers an e-mail forwarding service with a huge set of additional features, including spam blocking, filtering, and auto-responders. You may already be familiar with Bigfoot because of the Bigfoot people-finder service. This is the people search group that shows interested persons not only your e-mail address, phone number, and street address information, but even draws a map to your house.

Joining Bigfoot

If you have decided you're ready to join Bigfoot:

1. Access the Bigfoot home page at `http://www.bigfoot.com`.

2. Click Join Bigfoot. A screen is displayed asking you to provide your name and e-mail addresses.

3. Click Go.

4. In Step 1, enter the required information. Enter your desired password – twice – and click Next.

5. In Step 2, Bigfoot collects some demographic information from you. Of interest here is the option to choose a display option for your contact information in Bigfoot's directory, as well as the option to receive a free horoscope reading. (What have you got to lose?)

6. In Step 3 you do nothing at all, except click Continue.

7. In Step 1 of the second part of the registration phase, shown in Figure 13-9, you can choose a user ID based on variations of your name and existing e-mail address. Or, if you prefer, you can type your own preference. When you have made a choice, click Next.

8. In addition to forwarding e-mail, Bigfoot gives you a permanent Web link so that other people who link to your Web page won't experience broken links when you move your page. This has the added feature of adding your site to Bigfoot's Web directory. If you want to take advantage of this feature, fill out the required information in Step 2 and click Next.

9. Steps 3 and 4 ask for more demographic data. After you've filled each out, click Next and Finish respectively.

10. Step 5 advises you of Bigfoot's spam policy. Read and heed.

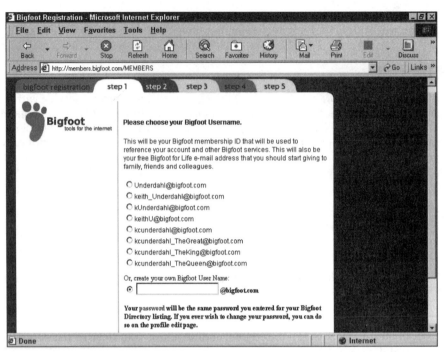

Figure 13-9: Choose a Bigfoot Username. This will be your Bigfoot e-mail address.

Using Bigfoot

After you complete the sign-up procedure, you should end up in the Member's Area. Click Edit your Bigfoot e-mail tools. This will display a list of available services, along with information about associated costs, if any. Forwarding is free.

If you click the link to set up e-mail forwarding, you should see a box similar to Figure 13-10. In the "Forwarding Address" field, make sure that the e-mail address you use for most of your e-mail correspondence is listed. You can always come back and change the Forwarding Address, which means that as long as other people have your Bigfoot e-mail address, any messages they send you will go to the correct place.

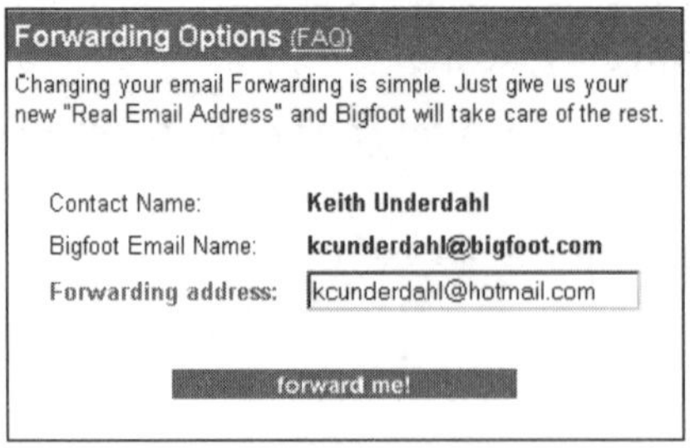

Figure 13-10: Type your regular e-mail address in the Forwarding Address field to forward all Bigfoot mail to that location.

Tip

If you are having business cards made up for yourself, consider using your Bigfoot e-mail address on them. People tend to hang on to those cards for a while, and it would be nice to know that the e-mail address shown on that card will always be valid.

Exiting from Bigfoot

When you are ready to leave Bigfoot, just leave. There's no particular sign-off or exit procedure. You can just point your URL at another location and go on your merry way.

iName

iName is another e-mail forwarding service, available at `http://www.iname.com`. Like GeoMail described earlier, iName offers free e-mail with one of hundreds of vanity domain names. This means you can create an e-mail address like `brianu@ consultant.com` or `brianu@doctor.com`. This enables you to keep your primary e-mail address private and simplify difficult-to-remember or hard-to-use e-mail addresses.

To sign up, simply go to the site, click *Sign Up Here*, and follow the instructions on the screen. The process is pretty straightforward, and you will be asked for the obligatory demographic stuff.

When you are done configuring your account and have arrived at your mailbox, click Options on the left side of the screen and then click Forwarding Address. This will open a screen that enables you to forward mail from your iName account to another account that you may have. The change will go into effect after approximately one minute.

Summary

This chapter has introduced you to a number of free e-mail and forwarding options. Not only are you free to travel the world with your laptop and stay connected through e-mail, now you can travel *without* your computer and still stay in touch with the office, with your family, with your friends. Web-based e-mail provides you with the option of checking your mail from any computer connected to the Web. And e-mail forwarding enables you to have your messages moved to a central location for whatever reason — whether you want privacy for your primary e-mail address or just want to simplify a complicated address.

✦   ✦   ✦

Doing More With E-mail

In the previous two chapters, you've learned about various types of e-mail — how you get it, how you use it, whether or not you have to pay for it. But as you become proficient with sending and receiving e-mail, you will want to do more than simply use it to send text messages quickly. You'll also want to send an Excel worksheet to a coworker, receive a jpeg picture of your grandkids, or submit a proposal to a client.

To send and receive files with your e-mail messages, you need to be able to attach the files to the message. This requires an e-mail client that supports attachments. Outlook Express, Outlook, Netscape Messenger, Eudora, and most Web-based e-mail utilities support attachments — in fact, almost all current e-mailers do. This chapter explores the various issues surrounding e-mail attachments.

We'll also look at special message formatting. Why discuss it here? When you send a specially-formatted e-mail message, the formatting information actually travels in an attachment. Thus, it is important to learn not only how to apply formatting, but also what it means to the recipient and what must be done to read it properly.

Sending and Receiving Files with E-mail

The process of sending and receiving files attached to your e-mail messages varies slightly from e-mail program to e-mail program, but regardless of the type of e-mail program you use, there are a few basic issues you'll need to consider when you send and receive files. You'll learn more about these later in the chapter, but here's a quick list of what you'll need to know:

✦ **Attaching files**. Every program that enables you to send files with your e-mail messages has a procedure for attaching the file. You usually do this with an "attach" or "send file" command.

✦ **Saving files**. When you receive a message that has an attachment, a symbol (usually a paper clip) appears with the header information in your e-mail program. To save the attachment, you need to open the message first.

✦ **Decoding files**. Sometimes attached files arrive encoded. This means that the file has been converted to an encrypted form, enabling more secure transmission. If you receive an encoded file, you need to decode the file before you can open and view it.

✦ **Decompressing files**. Still other attachments will arrive in your Inbox as compressed files. Most of these have a .zip extension, particularly if the sender uses Windows. Most compressed files for Macintosh systems use the .sit extension, and .bin is a common extension for UNIX/Linux compressed files. To decompress those files, you need to have a program specifically designed for that task.

What Do Attachments Look Like?

This section gives you a quick look at the way attachments appear when they first arrive in your e-mail program. We'll go into the specifics of how to send and retrieve file attachments later in this chapter.

In Outlook Express

When you are using Outlook Express and receive a message with a file attachment, you see a paper clip symbol to the left of the message in the Inbox (see Figure 14-1). When you open the file, the attachment icon appears in the header of the message.

In Netscape Messenger

When you are using Netscape Messenger (the mail utility included with Netscape Communicator), you don't get any visible sign from the Inbox that a file is attached to your message. When you open the message, however, a file attachment icon appears beside the header information (see Figure 14-2). When you click the icon, the file icon is displayed in a pop-up window along the bottom of your screen. You can then double-click the file icon to display a dialog box asking whether you want to open or save the file.

Attachment icon

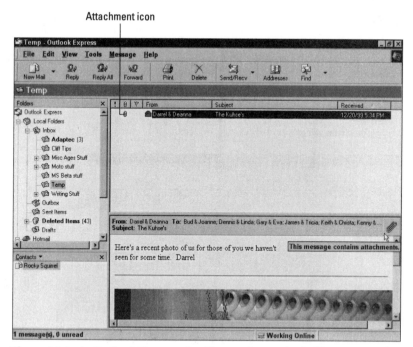

Figure 14-1: In Outlook Express, the file attachment looks like a paper clip.

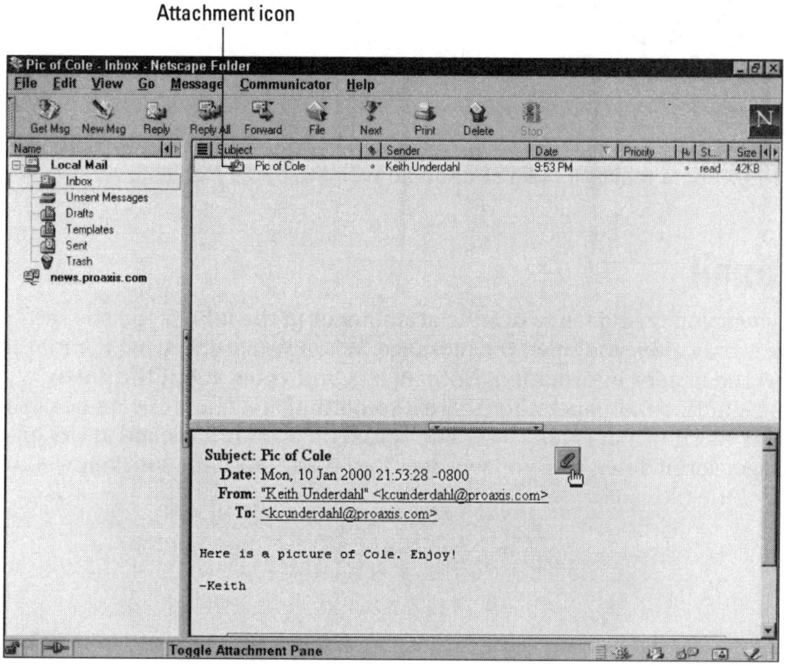

Attachment icon

Figure 14-2: The file attachment isn't visible in Netscape Messenger until you open the message.

In Eudora

In Eudora, messages come in clearly with an attachment showing as a paper clip icon in the left side of the Inbox (see Figure 14-3). The file icon itself appears at the end of the message; you can either click the icon or the linked filename to display your choices for working with the file.

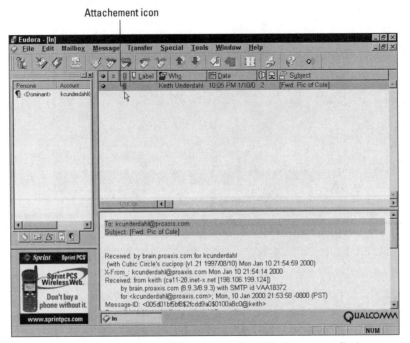

Figure 14-3: Eudora makes it plain and simple with the paper clip icon.

In Hotmail

Hotmail gives you no evidence of a file attachment in the Inbox; you see the attachment only after you open the message. When you are viewing the message, just below the header information, Hotmail lets you know about the file by displaying a horizontal paper clip (there's something new) and the name of the attachment, as shown in Figure 14-4. The actual file icon is attached at the end of the message; scroll down and you will see "Download Attachment" followed by the name of the file.

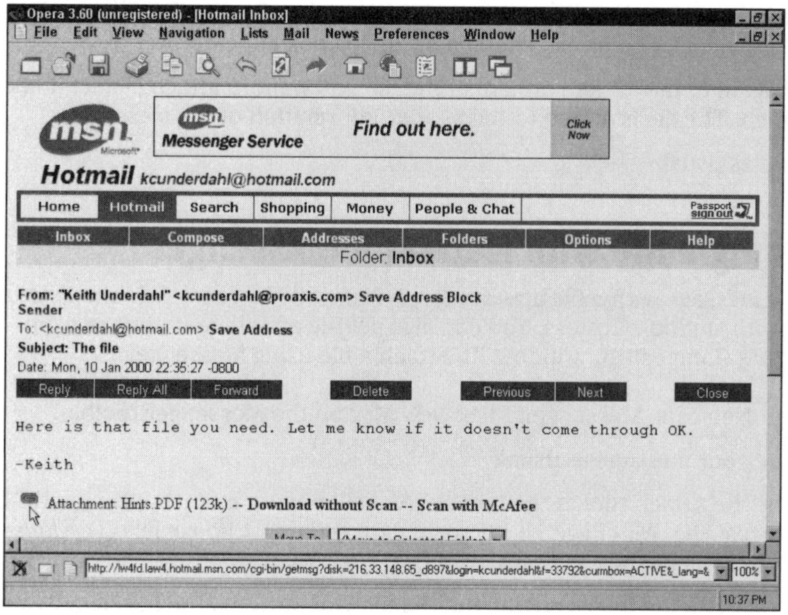

![Screenshot of Opera 3.60 (unregistered) - [Hotmail Inbox] showing a Hotmail message from Keith Underdahl with subject "The file" and an attachment.]

Figure 14-4: Hotmail uses a different strategy to show you the attached file, but it's still pretty obvious.

Note   Some types of attachments — such as jpeg images — will simply appear directly in your message on Hotmail in place of the sideways paperclip icon.

Attaching a File to a Message

Before you attach a file to a message, you may be wondering what type of files you can send. The answer is that anything you can save in a file, you can send as an attachment. Working on a digital recording? Send it along! Just getting finished with next month's newsletter? Attach it to a message to the editor and give her a chance to see it on-screen before she sees it in print.

Attaching a file with Outlook Express

To send a file attachment using Outlook Express:

1. Start Outlook Express.
2. Click the New Mail button.
3. Write your message as usual.

4. Click the Attach button on the toolbar (you can also choose Insert ⇨ File Attachment). The Insert Attachment dialog box appears.

5. Navigate to the folder containing the file you want to attach. Select it and click Attach. The file is added to the header information of the message.

6. Send as usual.

Attaching a file with Netscape Messenger

Sending a message with a file attachment in Netscape Messenger is similar to the process with Outlook Express. You can also set file attachment options from Messenger's Composition window. To attach a file using Messenger:

1. Start Netscape Messenger. Click New Msg on the Messenger toolbar.

2. Type your message as usual.

3. Click the Attach tool in the toolbar. A small pop-up menu appears with three choices: File, Web Page, or Personal card (vCard). Choose File. The *Enter file to attach* dialog box appears.

4. Navigate to the folder containing the file you want to attach, select it, and click Open. The file information is added to the header section of the message.

5. Click Send to send the message with the file attached.

Attaching a file with Eudora

The procedure for attaching a file to a Eudora message is similar to both other mailers discussed here. To attach a file using Eudora:

1. Start Eudora.

2. Click New Message.

3. Compose your message as usual.

4. Click the Attach File button on the toolbar. The Attach File dialog box appears.

5. Locate the directory in which the file you want to attach is saved. Select the file and click Open. The name and path of the file is displayed in the "Attached" line of the header area.

6. Click Send.

A Few File Attachment Tips

✦ Files take much longer to download than messages—send files only when necessary.

✦ If you are working with fairly large files, use a utility such as WinZip to compress them before sending. Or use Zipit, Stuffit, or Compact Pro for Macs.

✦ If you are working with multiple files, compress them into one file using a zip utility instead of sending multiple attached files.

✦ Do not send attachments to mailing lists. This will foul many list operations and probably enrage the other list members.

Receiving an Attached File

When you receive a message with a file attachment, you need to select and save the file independently of the message. This section explains how to retrieve file attachments with three different mail programs.

Caution Some recent computer viruses—such as the well-known Melissa virus and its variants—have propagated themselves as file attachments in e-mail messages. They can even come from people you know, so be cautious. Scan all incoming attachments with antivirus software before you open them, and don't open any files that you weren't expecting. If you use Windows, be especially wary of executable attachments with an .exe extension.

Receiving a file with Outlook Express

To receive a file using Outlook Express:

1. Double-click the message with the file attachment to open the message window.

2. To save the file, click File ➪ Save Attachments. When the Save Attachments dialog box appears, which is shown in Figure 14-5, choose a folder in which you want to store the file and click Save. If you are using Windows or Unix, you can also right-click attachment listings in the message header and choose Save As.

Caution Outlook Express 5 had a security flaw when it was first released that made it susceptible to certain virus-infected file attachments, even if you did not manually open them. If you do not have Internet Explorer 5.01 or later, click Help ➪ Microsoft on the Web ➪ Product News, and look for the free download of the security patch. This patch is integrated in versions 5.01 and later.

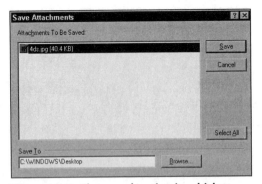

Figure 14-5: Choose a location in which to save the attachments. Here you can see that an attachment is about to be saved to the Windows desktop.

Receiving a File with Netscape Messenger

To receive a file attachment using Netscape Messenger:

1. Display the message with the attachment you want to save.

2. Click the file attachment icon. The file icon is displayed in the bottom of the message area, as shown in Figure 14-6.

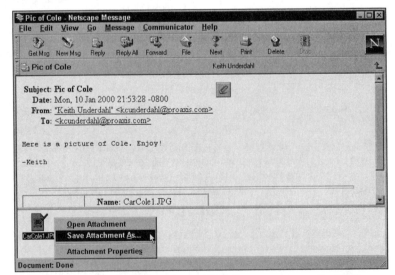

Figure 14-6: Click the file attachment icon in Netscape to display the file icon in the lower portion of the message.

3. Right-click the file icon and click Save Attachment As. If the attachment is a graphic, choose Save Image As.

4. Choose the folder in which you want to save the file and click Save. The file is saved as specified.

Receiving a file with Eudora

In Eudora, to save a file attachment:

1. Open the message with the file attachment you want to save.

2. Scroll to the bottom of the file.

3. Right-click the file icon, choose Save Attachment As and select a location in which you would like the attachment saved.

Note   If you are using Eudora on a Macintosh, e-mail attachments will be stored in System Folder ⇨ Eudora Folder ⇨ Attachments Folder. Drag-and-drop the attachments to another location if you want to save them.

Sending and Receiving Files with a Web-Based Mail Program

In the previous chapter, you learned about a number of Web-based e-mail programs. These programs enable you to send and receive e-mail from any computer on which you can access the World Wide Web. You don't need a separate mail client to use it. Most Web-based e-mail programs — even free e-mail programs such as Hotmail and Yahoo! Mail — also support attached files. This section shows you how to send and retrieve file attachments using Microsoft's Hotmail, located at `http://www.hotmail.com`.

Cross-Reference   For more information about getting and using Hotmail, see Chapter 13, "Using Web-Based E-Mail Services."

Sending file attachments with Hotmail

To send a file using Hotmail:

1. Start Hotmail as usual. Enter your user ID and password to access your account.

2. Click the Compose link near the top of the mail window.

3. When the Compose window appears, click Attachments.

4. When the Attachments screen opens, as shown in Figure 14-7, click Browse and locate the file you want to attach to the message.

5. Select the file and click Attach to Message.

6. Repeat steps 4 and 5 until you have attached all of the files that you would like to send, and then click Done.

7. When you have returned to the Composition window, write your message as usual and click Send when you're done.

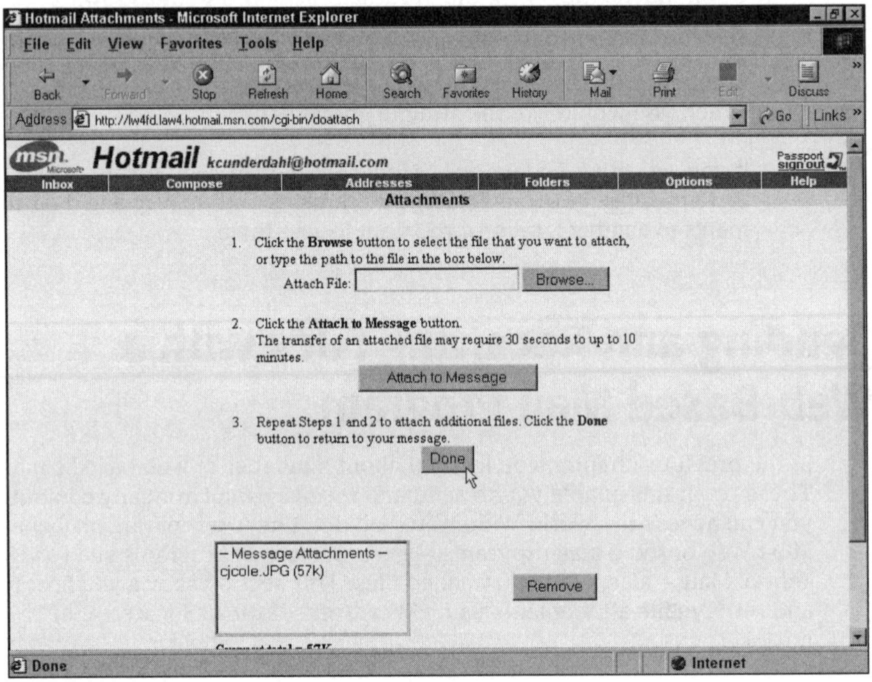

Figure 14-7: Click Browse and locate the file you want to attach to your outgoing Hotmail message.

Receiving file attachments with Hotmail

When you receive a message with a file attachment in Hotmail, it won't be readily apparent when you're looking at the Inbox. When you open the message, however, you'll see the attachment icon at the bottom of the message, like the one shown in Figure 14-8.

To save a file attachment using Hotmail:

1. Scroll down until you see the attachment listing in the message.

2. If you don't have an updated antivirus program installed and operating on your computer, click Scan with McAfee to scan the file for viruses to start the download process. If you do have an antivirus program installed, click the Download without Scan link.

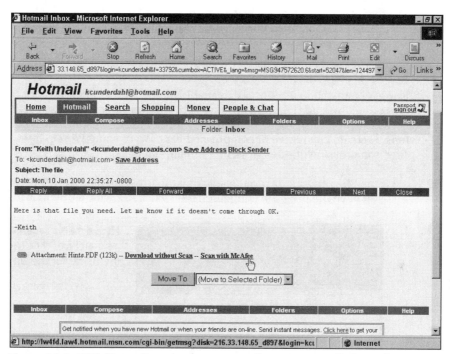

Figure 14-8: With Hotmail, you've got to open the message to find out about attachments.

Dealing With Compressed Attachments

While the ability to send files via e-mail is a convenient and efficient way to do your work, you may be limited by the size of files you can send. Most people still connect to the Internet through relatively slow dial-up connections, and many mail servers won't accept attachments that are larger than 5MB. If you send a file of that size to someone with a slow Internet connection, it could take more than half an hour to download.

To combat this problem, many people use file compression utilities to shrink the size of the files they send. In the Windows world, two of the most popular compression utilities are PKZIP (http://www.pkware.com/) and WinZip (http://www.winzip.com/). By compressing files and making them smaller, you shorten transmission times and can easily group multiple files into a single package.

Note If you use a Macintosh, a popular compression utility is Stuffit Expander from Aladdin Systems (http://www.aladdinsys.com/). Linux users have a dizzying number of options, some of which you can find at Tucows (http://www.tucows.com/), listed under Compression utilities for your OS and interface.

Compressing files

Several compression utilities are available on the Web as shareware or freeware. Once you download the utility, you need to run the self-extracting installation file to access the program. When you've installed the utility, you can follow a few basic steps to create an archive of compressed files. We're using WinZip here, but most other compression utilities work in a similar manner:

1. Start the program by double-clicking the program icon. Depending on how you have the program configured, you will see a window similar to Figure 14-9.

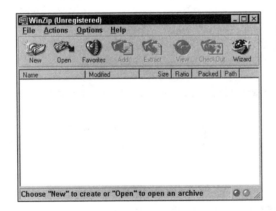

Figure 14-9: When you start a new archive, click New and enter the name for the zip file.

2. Click the New icon. When the New Archive window appears, navigate to the drive and folder in which you want to create the new archive, enter a filename, and click OK. The new file is created.

3. The Add dialog box, which is shown in Figure 14-10, appears automatically. Move to the folder containing the files you want to add, select the files you want to compress, and click Add. The files you selected are added to the zip archive.

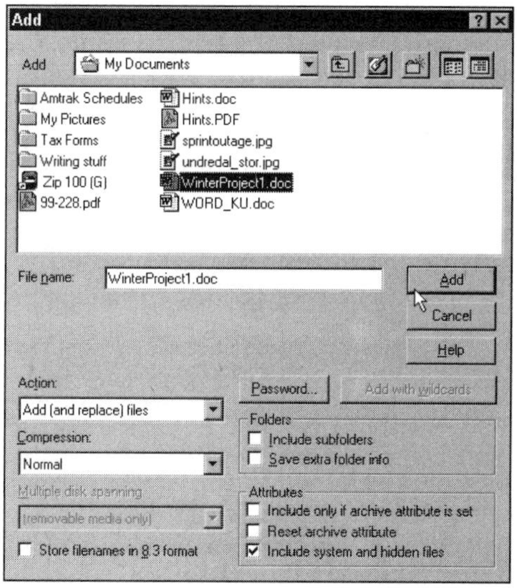

Figure 14-10: Add files to the zip file by moving to the folder containing the files you want to zip, selecting them, and clicking Add.

Note

You can select multiple noncontiguous files by pressing and holding the Ctrl key (in Windows) or the Option key (in Macintosh) while you click the various files. When you click Add, the files are added to the zip file.

When you are done creating the compressed archive, you can open your e-mail program, begin composing your new message, and attach the zipped archive to the message. When you send the message, the zip file will be sent along with it.

Decompressing files

When you receive a compressed file attachment, depending on the type of utility you have (and the version you are using), you can open the file one of two ways:

✦ If you use Windows and you already have a compatible compression utility (such as WinZip) installed, you can open the file by double-clicking the attached file icon in the e-mail message window.

✦ You may need to save the file to disk, start your decompression utility, and then open the file.

If you have saved the compressed file to your hard drive, open your decompression utility and then open the file. If you have WinZip, the procedure is as follows:

1. Start the zip utility as usual.

2. Click the Open button. The Open Archive dialog box appears.

3. Navigate to the folder containing the zipped file you want to open. Select the file and click Open. The files are displayed in the WinZip window, as shown in Figure 14-11.

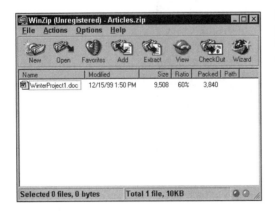

Figure 14-11: The files in the zipped file are shown in the WinZip window after you open the archive.

4. Click Extract. When the Extract dialog box appears, choose a directory in which to store the extracted files and click Extract again.

Keep in mind that when you extract files from a compressed archive, they will be decompressed back into their original format. For instance, if you just extracted a bunch of Microsoft Word documents from a .zip file, the extracted Word documents will have .doc extensions instead of .zip.

Using Special Mail Formatting

When e-mail first came into being it was a text-only medium. But in recent times several standards have appeared that allow for special formatting of messages. These advancements created a problem, however, because some mail programs are still only capable of receiving plain text. Messages with special formatting need to be compatible with lower-tech mailers while still meeting the needs of ever more demanding users. The solution: Place the formatting information in attachments.

The two standards that affect the mail you send and receive are MIME and Uuencode. Both have something to do with the form in which your messages and files are sent and received. But that's about where the similarities end. Let's tackle them one at a time.

What is MIME and do I have to worry about it?

MIME is an acronym for Multipurpose Internet Mail Extensions. MIME is really an industry stab at making dissimilar message formats work together so you can communicate effectively with other people, even though they may use a totally different kind of mailer. If you want to include graphics, sound, or Web pages in your message, MIME helps make sure the recipient receives your transmissions the way you send them.

Most popular mail programs today support MIME. Outlook Express and Outlook 2000 do this transparently; there's no option you need to select in order to start the process. Netscape Communicator and Eudora both include MIME as one of the options you can select for sending files; files you receive in MIME format are ready automatically without any action from you. Older e-mail programs require you to decode MIME messages manually, but as long as you are using a reasonably modern e-mail client, this shouldn't be a problem.

In addition to the acronym MIME, you'll also see S/MIME and PGP/MIME. Both of these MIME formats support different types of security protocols. S/MIME stands for Security MIME and PGP/MIME stands for Pretty-Good-Privacy MIME. Both types are variations on the MIME theme, offering greater security support for the transmission of messages and files. For more information on S/MIME and PGP/MIME, see the Internet Mail Consortium's site at `http://www.imc.org/smime-pgpmime.html`.

Uuencode and Uudecode

While MIME is an industry attempt to standardize a message format so we can communicate seamlessly, Uuencode is an answer to binary files that get boggled by systems that don't handle binary mail. Uuencode converts the files into ASCII text and sends it through the system. When you receive a Uuencoded e-mail, you need to use its partner, Uudecode, to convert the file back into a readable binary form. Virtually all e-mail programs now do this conversion for you, although earlier versions of mail programs didn't do it automatically and left you with cryptic-looking text you were forced to convert yourself before reading. Uuencode is supported by all of the mail clients described in this book.

Note

You may hear other people mention "binary" files when discussing mail attachments. A *binary file* is a file stored in a binary format (ones and zeros) that is only readable by your computer. *Text files*, on the other hand, contain the kind of text that humans are more familiar with. Most mail servers can receive binary attachments, but a few can't. The encoding scheme BinHex addresses this by converting binary data into ASCII text. Learn more about binaries in Chapter 23, "Finding and Using Newsgroups."

What about HTML formatting?

Many e-mail clients now also support HTML formatting. Generally, if you have an e-mail client that enables you to apply special character formatting in your messages, such as boldface text or background colors, it does so by using HTML code. As with MIME and Uuencode, the information for this formatting is actually included in an attachment to the text of the message, and if you send an HTML-formatted message to someone who uses a reader that doesn't support the format, they will only see the text. Depending on how their software renders unrecognizable attachments, they will only see the text and the source code, or they could be treated to lines of unintelligible garbage.

> **Tip**   One thing you definitely should not do is send HTML messages to a mailing list. List servers usually cannot handle these formatting attachments, and the results may be fouled digests and other errors.

Summary

In this chapter, we've covered a lot of ground. From a basic discussion of sending and receiving file attachments to specific procedures in three different programs — Outlook Express, Netscape Messenger, and Eudora — to exploring file compression, MIME, Uuencode, HTML mail formatting, and more, you have learned the ins and outs of file attachments. The next chapter helps you organize the mountains of e-mail that will soon be finding their way to your Inbox.

✦   ✦   ✦

Taking Charge of Your E-mail

I f you've used e-mail for any length of time, you know those messages can begin to pile up. Some messages are important, like the ones from your boss or your best friend. Other messages aren't so important, and some, like unsolicited spam, are just plain annoying.

This chapter takes a look at ways you can hold on to those messages you need to keep around for a while, showing you various methods of saving and preserving important information. It will also discuss what you should do with unwanted e-mail, especially spam. How do you get rid of it? What can you do to avoid getting more of it in the future?

Deciding What You Should Keep

The first question you need to tackle, of course, is which messages you need to keep. If you use e-mail for business purposes, your employer may have some say in the types of correspondence that are most important, such as letters from clients or e-mail about a project.

Note   The federal government passed legislation several years ago (after the Oliver North investigation) prohibiting people from destroying or "shredding" e-mail evidence. The NARA (National Archives and Records Administration) includes e-mail in the Federal Records Act (FRA), and federal agencies must have plans in place for the management of e-mail messages.

Like your other computer files, it's important to organize and back up copies of your e-mail messages. You can do this in several ways:

♦ Sort your messages by placing them in folders with a unique identity, such as a client or project name.

✦ Copy your messages into a word processing file and save them to your hard disk or a floppy disk. If you are connected to a local area network that is backed up frequently, store your messages in a network directory.

✦ Use an e-mail archiving program to store your messages in a format you can search and access later.

✦ Print the e-mail and store it in a traditional file cabinet.

Using Folders

Whether or not you've been using computers for any length of time, chances are that you have used folders — also called directories — for a while now. Folders are used to store files, other folders, and every operating system has tools to help you navigate the file and folder system.

No matter which e-mail program you're using, the program organizes messages by using folders. The folder that stores your incoming messages is called the *Inbox*. The folder that stores your sent messages is usually called the *Sent Items* folder (the exact name will vary depending on which program you are using). Other e-mail programs give you additional folders by default. You may see a *Draft* folder, an *Outbox* folder, and a *Trash* folder.

Note   How many folders can you have? As many as you want to create. Just remember that the folders and the messages they store eat up hard disk space. Create only as many as you need and keep only those you use.

Creating Outlook Express folders

Outlook Express may not have invented the concept of folders, but the program certainly put them to good use. When you first start Outlook Express, you are greeted with the Inbox, Outbox, Drafts, and Sent Items folders. You can create as many additional folders as you need, for as many projects as you've got and as many interests as you've got time for. For example, you could include folders for people, publishers, projects, and more.

The process of creating folders in Outlook Express is a piece of cake. Here's how:

1. In the folder list on the left side of the Outlook Express window, select the folder in which you want to create a new folder. You will probably want to create most of your subfolders within the Inbox folder.

2. Click File ➪ New ➪ Folder. The Create Folder dialog box appears, as Figure 15-1 shows.

3. In the Create Folder dialog box, you tell Outlook Express where you want to create the folder. If the correct location is selected, type a name for your folder and click OK. The new folder is added to the folders list.

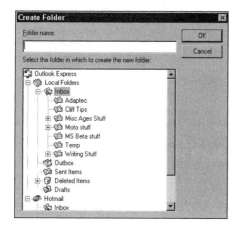

Figure 15-1: You create both folders and subfolders in the Create Folder dialog box of Outlook Express.

Note

Outlook Express provides an easy way for you to move messages to different folders. You can either drag the message from the Inbox window to the folder icon in the left side of the Outlook window or you can open the Edit menu and choose Move to Folder. Navigate to the folder in which you want to store the message and click OK.

Creating new folders with Netscape Messenger

Creating and working with folders in Netscape Messenger makes your job easier and helps you keep track of e-mail messages you will need again and those you want to delete. To create a new folder in Netscape Messenger

1. Open the File menu and choose New Folder. The New Folder dialog box appears, as shown in Figure 15-2.

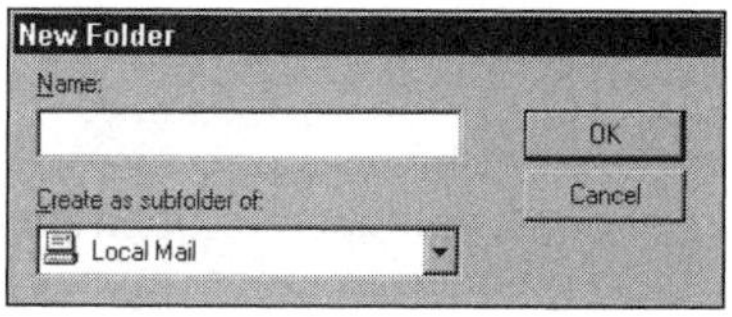

Figure 15-2: Create a new folder to store selected e-mail messages.

2. Type a name for the folder in the Name text box.

3. In the *Create as a subfolder of* box, click the down-arrow and choose the folder in which you want to create the new folder. For example, if you want to create the folder as a subfolder of the Inbox folder, choose Inbox from the drop-down menu.

4. Click OK. The new folder is added to the set of Messenger folders.

Creating folders in Eudora

Eudora starts out with three mailboxes, not folders: In, Out, and Trash. When you decide to add a mailbox, you have the option of adding a mailbox or a folder. In Eudora, a folder is the larger collection of smaller mailboxes. When you add a mailbox, the box name is simply added to the Mailbox menu. When you add a folder, you are prompted first for the folder name and then for the mailbox name.

To add the folders/mailboxes to Eudora:

1. Start Eudora and display the Inbox.

2. Open the Mailbox menu and choose New. The New Mailbox dialog box appears, as shown in Figure 15-3.

3. Type a name for the mailbox. If you want to create a folder instead of a mailbox, click *Make it a folder*.

4. Click OK. Eudora adds the mailbox to the Mailbox menu so you can select it easily later.

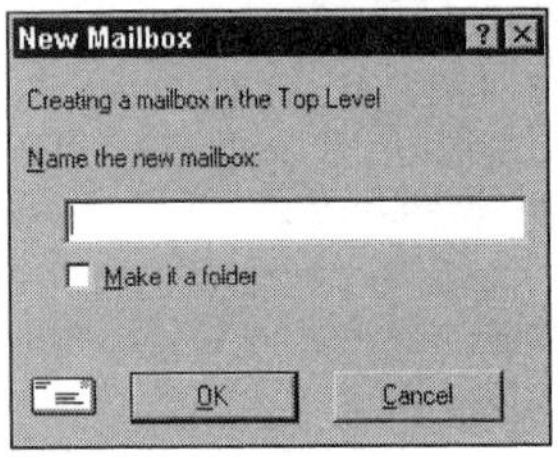

Figure 15-3: Use the New Mailbox dialog box to enter the name for a mailbox or folder you are creating to store your messages.

Managing Messages

What does it take to manage your messages? First, you need to open them, which you learned to do in previous chapters. Then you need to store them in folders related to the projects, topics, or people they regard. Finally, you need to be able to arrange the messages in the order you want, search for messages you need to find, save the messages you want to keep, and delete those you no longer need. Using

Netscape Messenger as an example, this section explores each of these message-management procedures, with various tips about similar procedures in Outlook Express and Eudora.

Arranging messages

You have two options for the way in which you organize your messages: You can move the messages into the folders you want, and you can sort the messages in a particular order once you get them there.

To move messages to a new folder:

1. Select the messages you want to move to the new folder.

2. Open the Message menu and select the Move Message submenu, which is shown in Figure 15-4. Click the folder you want to file the message in. If you are putting it in a subfolder of the Inbox, you may have to click *Inbox* to see the list of subfolders.

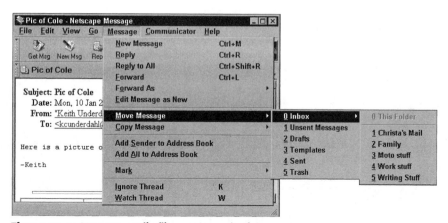

Figure 15-4: You can easily file messages in the Netscape folder of your choice.

To sort the messages in a folder:

1. Display the folder with the files you want to sort.

2. Open the View menu and choose Sort. A pop-up menu appears showing the number of sort options, as shown in Figure 15-5.

3. Choose the method of ordering the messages. The messages are sorted in the order you select. Table 15-1 explains the different sort types.

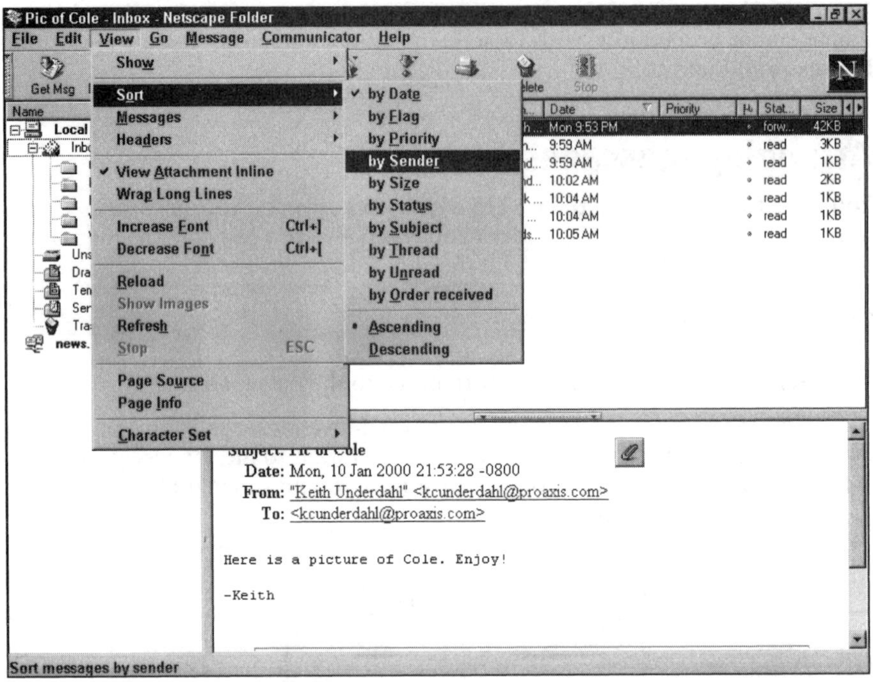

Figure 15-5: You can sort the messages in the Netscape folders in a variety of ways.

Table 15-1
Understanding Netscape's Message Sort Options

Sort Type	Description
by Date	Sorts the messages by the date they were received
by Flag	Sorts according to the flag you assigned to the messages
by Priority	Orders the messages by the priority (low, medium, or high) assigned by the sender
by Sender	Organizes the messages by sender
by Size	Enables you to order the messages according to message size
by Status	Lets you determine sort order based on the status of the message
by Subject	Enables you to organize messages in alphabetical order, grouping similar subjects
by Thread	Keeps all message threads together
by Unread	Groups all unread messages together

Sort Type	Description
by Order received	Sometimes the order in which you receive messages may not correspond to the dates of each one. In practice, however, this will be very similar to sort *by Date*.
Ascending	Displays messages in ascending order, first according to the sort you have selected and then alphabetically by subject.
Descending	Organizes messages in descending order, first by the sort you have selected and then alphabetically in descending order by subject.

Sorting with Outlook Express. To sort messages in Outlook Express, display the folder you want to sort; then open the View menu and choose Sort By. A pop-up menu appears, giving you the option of sorting by Priority, Attachment, From, Subject, Received, Ascending, and Group Messages by Subject. When you click your choice, the messages are sorted according to the field you specified.

Sorting with Eudora. When you want to sort your Eudora messages, display the Mailbox you want to sort, open the Edit menu, and choose Sort. A pop-up menu appears, giving you the option of sorting by various criteria. When you click your choice, the messages are ordered according to the field you selected.

Locating messages

When you have saved a lot of unrelated messages, or the messages you have saved have fairly cryptic names, locating specific message can be difficult. Fortunately, there are easy ways to find what your looking for.

The procedures for Outlook Express, Netscape Messenger, and Eudora are similar. To find a message in Netscape Messenger:

1. Open the Edit menu and choose Search Messages. The Search Messages dialog box appears, as Figure 15-6 shows.

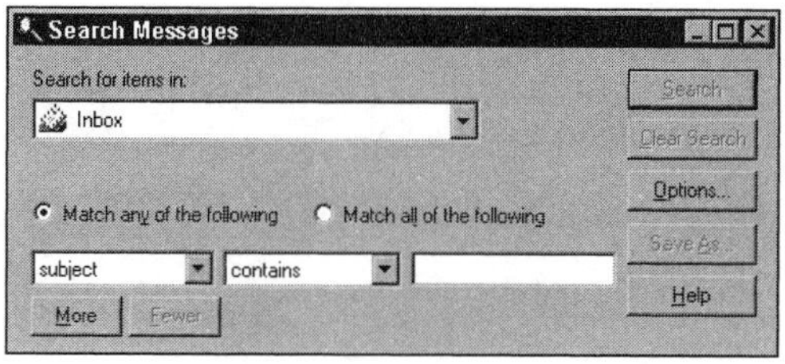

Figure 15-6: The Search Messages dialog box enables you to search for messages in any folder in Messenger.

2. In the *Search for items in* text box, click the down arrow and choose the folder in which you want to search.

3. Click in the criteria boxes and choose first the field (such as *sender*, *subject*, *body*, and so on) in which you want to search and the argument (*contains*, *is*, *isn't*, and so on) for the search.

4. Click in the blank criteria box and enter the text or value you are searching for. For example, if you wanted to search for a message that talks about security issues, you could enter the following criteria:

   Search for items in **Inbox** *where the* **body contains security**

5. Click Search. Netscape begins searching for the text as you specified and displays the results.

Note

If you make a mistake entering the criteria and want to start again, click Clear Search.

Locating Text and Messages in Outlook Express. When using Outlook Express, you'll find the commands for locating text and messages in the Edit menu. To locate text within the current message, use the *Edit ⇨ Find ⇨ Text in this message* command. To search for messages within a particular folder, choose the *Edit ⇨ Find ⇨ Message in this folder* command and choose the folder you want to search in the *Look in* box.

Finding Text in Eudora. When you want to locate text in a message in Eudora, open the Edit menu and choose Find. The Find submenu appears; choose *Find Text* (to search text within message bodies) or *Find Messages* (to find words in message headers). Enter the text for which you want to search and click Find. Eudora begins searching the messages in the Inbox and displays the first message with the text you entered.

Copying messages

Copying messages is easy, no matter which e-mail program you use. You have three options:

✦ You can drag and drop the message from one folder to another.

✦ You can use the Edit menu's Copy and Paste commands to copy and paste the message into another folder or mailbox.

✦ You can use the shortcut keys Ctrl+C and Ctrl+V (on a Macintosh, use the Command button instead of Control) to copy and paste the message in the desired folder.

Saving messages

The process of saving messages involves simply saving the message as a file using the Save command. To save a message using Netscape Messenger:

1. Display the Inbox and select the message you want to save.

2. Click File ➪ Save As ➪ File. In Eudora or Outlook Express simply click File ➪ Save As.

3. In the Save As dialog box, navigate to the disk and folder in which you want to save the file.

4. Enter a filename, choose a file type (if applicable), and click Save.

All three of the e-mail programs described here can save messages in plain text format, which is the default format for Netscape Messenger and Eudora, and an optional format in Outlook Express. Outlook Express' default format is a proprietary format with a .eml extension. Messenger also gives you the option of saving messages in HTML.

Deleting messages

Once you start sending and receiving e-mail, it's only a matter of time until you have quite a collection of messages to manage. To keep things under control, delete the messages you don't need—they take up much-needed resources and clutter up your hard drive. However, some businesses (including federal agencies, as mentioned earlier) have policies regarding what kind of e-mail messages should be kept. Check with your supervisor or system administrator to find out any particulars that affect the messages you should or should not save.

Regardless of the policies at your work place, undoubtedly you'll want to delete a number of e-mail messages. In fact, you will probably delete the majority of e-mail messages you receive, depending on what you use e-mail to do and with whom you correspond. Every e-mail program has a Trash folder or Trash mailbox that is routinely "dumped" according to the frequency you specify. To delete an e-mail message:

1. Select the e-mail message you want to delete.

2. Click the Delete tool on the program's toolbar. The message is placed in the Trash mailbox or Deleted Items folder, depending on which program you use.

To remove all the messages in Netscape Messenger's Trash folder, open the File menu and choose Empty Trash on Local Mail.

To carry out the Outlook Express trash, click Edit ➪ Empty 'Deleted Items' Folder. To take out Eudora's trash, display the Trash mailbox by opening the Mailbox menu and choosing Trash. Then open the Special menu and choose Empty Trash.

Archiving Old Files

Archiving is the process of saving old files you no longer need. Different programs have different means of doing this—many people use backup utilities to save their important files either to tapes, their hard disk, or removable disks they store in another location. Archiving messages is a slightly different process because the messages themselves are accessible only through your e-mailer, unless you save them in a file in another format, such as a word processing file.

Storing e-mail

Because e-mail messages are kept within your e-mailer in a form you cannot easily access by using a file manager in your operating system, it's not a simple matter of dragging and dropping the files to a new location. You *can* archive your e-mail in a number of ways, depending on which type of archive you are most comfortable with. Here are some archiving options:

✦ You can save individual e-mail messages in a word processing file and compress and store the files.

✦ You can print the e-mail messages you want and store them in a hard copy file.

✦ You can use an archival utility to manage and archive old e-mail messages.

Saving e-mail

Earlier in this chapter you learned the procedure for saving your e-mail as a file. Because e-mail is available only within the e-mail program itself, you may need to use the File ⇨ Save As command in your e-mail program to save the e-mail to disk. You might, for example, want to create a disk that stores only messages from a particular client. Label the disk with that client's name, and when the Save As dialog box is displayed, navigate to the disk drive in question. Be sure to save the file in a plain text format (in Windows it will have the .txt extension) so you will be able to import the file as needed into other documents.

E-mail Archiving Tips

✦ Don't save anything you don't need.

✦ Organize your e-mail by folder as soon as you read and act on it.

✦ Don't make archiving harder than it has to be. If printing and filing works for you, do it.

✦ If you use an archiving utility, be sure coworkers or others using your system know how to access archived e-mail if necessary.

Note   Another method of preserving a copy of e-mail you send is to send a copy to yourself. When you address the recipient in the To line, add yourself to the BCC: (blind carbon copy) line. The message comes back to you as an incoming message and then you can store it in the client folder as needed.

Printing e-mail

It may seem outdated but it's still a great way to keep track of those messages you must not misplace: Print your e-mail. The process is simple — just display the message (whether you're using Outlook Express, Messenger, Eudora, or another mailer), open the File menu, and choose Print. Make the necessary selections for printer options, and click Print. After a moment or two (depending on the printer), your e-mail message is printed. File it away to preserve the paper copy.

Filtering Your E-mail

Junk mail is a reality we all deal with, whether we are individuals with mail slots or corporations with mail rooms. Electronic junk mail, usually called *spam*, creates an unusual problem, particularly for large organizations. If you get flooded with "real" mail, what happens? The post office sends over bags and bags of mail, which get stored in the mail room until people can get through the volume. If you receive a flood of e-mail messages, what can happen? Your server can get overwhelmed, business can grind to a standstill, and important communications that must happen don't. Clearly you need to sort the good from the bad. But how? That's where filtering can help.

Filtering enables you to specify which messages you will and won't accept. You can filter mail piece-by-piece by deciding, "Yes, I want to read this one," or "No, I'm going to toss that one out" — or you can have an e-mail program do it for you. Most popular e-mail programs now provide a means to filter — Eudora has a strong filtering feature, as does Netscape Messenger and Outlook Express.

Filtering with Outlook Express

To direct incoming mail with Outlook Express:

1. Open the Tools menu and select Message Rules ➪ Mail.

2. The New Mail Rule window opens, as shown in Figure 15-7, where you can set rules and conditions for various mail-related activities.

Note   If you have already created some rules, you will first see the Message Rules dialog box. This dialog box can be used to delete, activate, and deactivate rules, and if you want to create a new one as shown here, just click New.

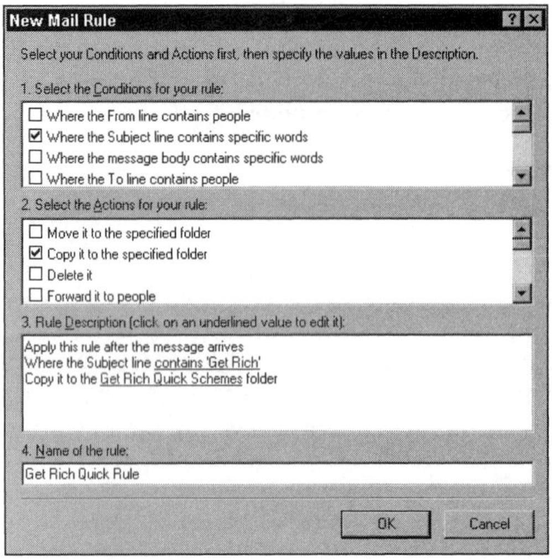

Figure 15-7: You can enter the criteria for sorting and filtering your messages in the New Mail Rule dialog box in Outlook Express.

3. Set a **Condition** in the first box. This tells Outlook Express what you are looking for, be it a specific sender, or words in the subject, in the body, and so on. In Figure 15-8 you can see that we are looking for specific words in the subject.

4. In the second box, select an **Action**. If Outlook Express finds a message that meets your condition, this is what will happen to it. In the example shown in Figure 15-8, a copy of the message is being placed in a specific folder.

5. In the **Rule Description** field, click the blue links to enter any additional information required by your selections in boxes one and two. As you can see, we have specified that all messages containing the phrase "Get Rich" in the subject will automatically be copied to the folder called "Get Rich Quick Schemes."

6. In the fourth box, give the rule a descriptive name. Click OK when you are done.

Filtering newsgroup messages involves the same procedure. Simply click Tools ➪ Message Rules ➪ News and follow the steps listed previously. If you want to block a specific sender, click Tools ➪ Message Rules ➪ Blocked Senders List, and click Add to add people or organizations from whom you do not want to receive mail.

Filtering with Messenger

Netscape Messenger enables you to set up filters to weed out unwanted mail. You can add, edit, or delete filters; you can also deactivate and then activate filters you have created.

To add a filter to Netscape Messenger:

1. When Messenger is displayed, open the Edit menu and choose Message Filters. The Message Filters dialog box appears.

2. Click New. The Filter Rules dialog box appears, as shown in Figure 15-8.

3. Enter a name for the filter in the *Filter name:* box. Enter your criteria in the appropriate text boxes. If you have additional criteria to enter, click the More button to display additional fields. For example, if you want to block messages from Jim Smith regarding a free Florida vacation promotion, you could enter information so the criteria reads like this:

   If the **sender** *of the message* **contains Jim Smith** *and the* **Subject** *of the message* **contains Florida** *then* **Move to folder Trash**.

   If you add multiple criteria for the filter, you also need to decide whether all of the criteria must be met, or only one. Use the radio buttons above the criteria to make this decision.

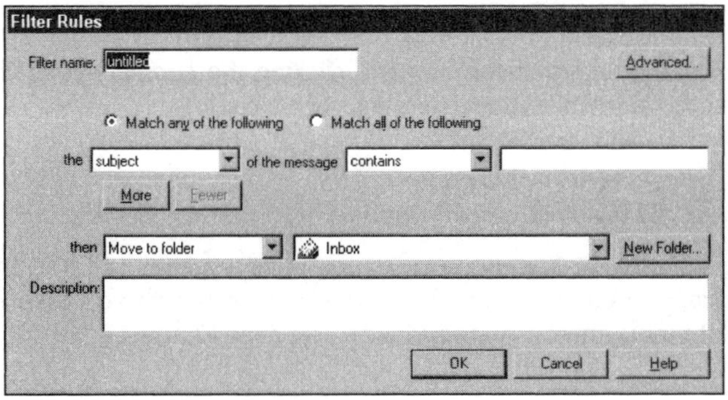

Figure 15-8: The Filter Rules dialog box gives you the means to enter the criteria for filtering.

4. Click OK. Figure 15-9 shows the created filter.

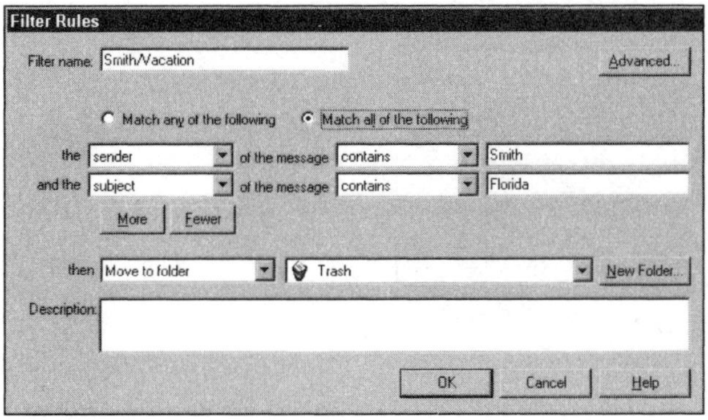

Figure 15-9: A filter in Messenger might have one or more criteria — this one has several.

Note Filter precedence is the order in which filters are used. For example, if you want to filter only those messages from Jim Smith that are about Florida vacations, you would have Messenger locate the messages from Jim Smith and then filter the Florida subject lines. You can change the filter precedence in the Message Filters dialog box. Just click the up-arrow to increase the filter's precedence; click the down-arrow to decrease precedence.

Activating and deactivating filters

To activate or deactivate a filter in Netscape Messenger:

1. Display the Message Filters dialog box.

2. Click the check mark or dot to the right of the filter. If the filter has a check mark next to it, the filter is active. If it has a dot, it is inactive.

Note If you want to delete a filter you have created, display the Message Filters dialog box, click the filter you want to delete, and click Delete.

Tip Want to see what Messenger is filtering out? You can turn on the filter log by displaying the Message Filters dialog box and clicking the *Log Filter Use* check box. When you want to see what you're missing, click View log.

Filtering with Eudora

Like Outlook Express and Messenger, Eudora provides a means of filtering unwanted messages. In Eudora, you use the Make Filter dialog box, which you display by opening the Special menu and choosing Make Filter (see Figure 15-10).

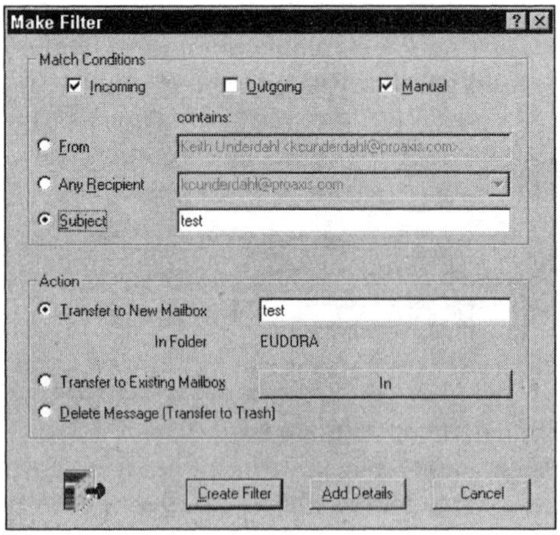

Figure 15-10: Creating filters involves the use of the Make Filter dialog box in Eudora.

To create a filter in Eudora:

1. Display the Make Filters dialog box.

2. Choose the Match Conditions you want to apply: Do you want to filter incoming or outgoing mail? Do you want Eudora to apply the filtering automatically or do you want to do it manually?

3. Specify the filtering criteria. Choose the item you want to enter the criteria for ("From Jim Smith," for example).

4. Choose the action you want Eudora to take when the criteria is met. You can specify the mailbox in which you want the mail to be stored—and remember, you can put the messages in the trash, if you choose, by clicking Delete Message (Transfer to Trash).

5. Click Create Filter. The filter is created and applied so the next time mail arrives with the criteria you specified it will go directly into a folder or the trash can, according to the selections you made.

If you want to do more advanced filtering, you can click the Add Details button in the Make Filter dialog box. The Filters dialog box appears, as Figure 15-11 shows. Here you can enter more specialized information related to the filter you want to create. For example, you can filter out messages with specific text or addresses in the header information or you can have Eudora dump messages from a specific sender in a specific folder (such as Trash). If you want to see a log of what Eudora is filtering out, click the Filter Report tab.

Identifying filtering problems

Even though filtering works and can help you deal with the issue of junk mail on a sender-by-sender basis, people have identified a number of problems as they try to fight the junk-mail movement through filtering:

✦ **Filtering is time consuming**. Entering the necessary information to block a particular sender takes several minutes of your time—maybe longer. You must really be bugged by someone before you'd take the time to block them or funnel their messages directly into the Trash.

✦ **Filtering takes continual updating**. You know how often people change e-mail addresses—how likely is it that you will be able to set a filter to block mail from an individual or a company that will remain viable ad infinitum? Chances are the sender will show up with a new e-mail address in a matter of months—or less. That means you'll be modifying filters or creating new ones on a regular basis.

✦ **Filtering can block needed messages erroneously**. It's all well and good to block spam to avoid the hassle of online solicitation, but what happens when you miss a job offer or a letter from a client because the filter you set up keeps the messages out?

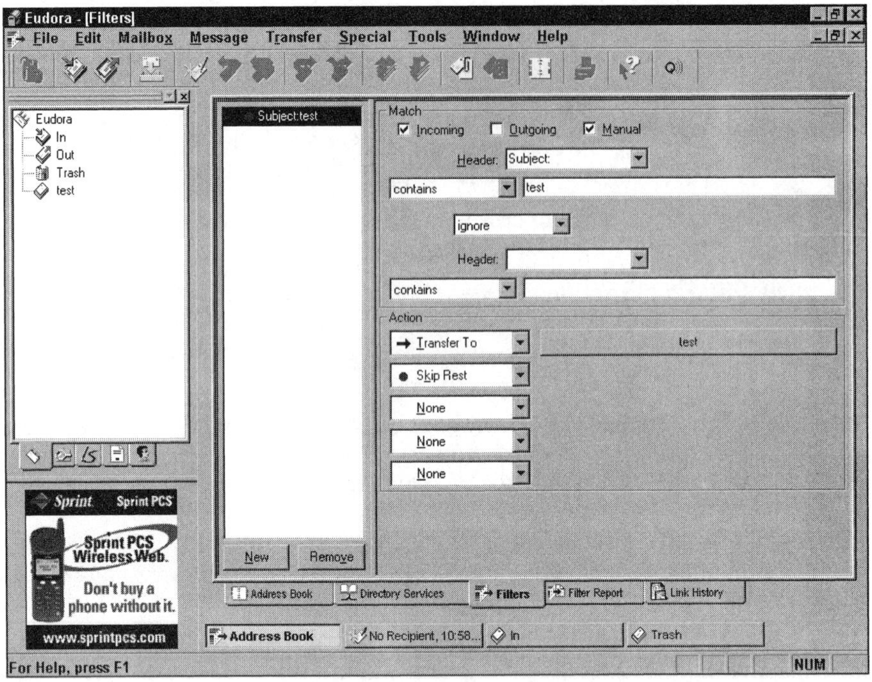

Figure 15-11: The Filters tab in Eudora gives you the option of entering more specialized filtering criteria.

✦ **Filtering can be used in the wrong way**. We don't like to think that our employees or our coworkers might block access because of a hidden agenda, but it could happen. We might be counting on our messages getting to a certain individual in a timely fashion, but a filter may strip us out of the running before our words are even read.

The best answer is still to keep a careful eye on your e-mail system. Know who you want to receive messages from and who you don't; and take the time to keep your filters current and active.

Avoiding Spam

Spam is getting such a bad name one could actually begin to feel sorry for the Hormel meat company. Bad press. Bad feelings. Hard words.

If you are relatively new to the e-mail scene, you may be wondering what spam is and what all the fuss is about. You may be receiving spam and not even recognize it. This section helps you learn what spam is, find out what the issues are, and discover how you can take some action against it.

Defining spam

Spam is junk mail that is sent to you, the user, when you haven't requested anything from the company at all. It's similar to bulk junk mail in that you can open your Inbox and find all sorts of things — phony win-a-trip-to-Florida mailers, music catalogs, movie clubs, multilevel marketing schemes, get-rich-quick promises, chain letters, date-a-rama questionnaires — all competing for your attention.

The reason spam is so hated is that it is even more intrusive than the mail the postal worker stuffs in your mailbox. And you wind up paying for electronic spam in the form of your online time. That makes it not only an annoyance and an intrusion; in some places it makes it illegal.

Cutting through the spam

Explore some of the newsgroups and hang out in a few e-mail forums and you'll find that we are rapidly becoming a spam-sensitive culture. You can feel violated by those annoying and unwanted messages in your Inbox. The biggest argument against spam is that it makes it more difficult to sift through messages to get to the important messages. How can we cut through the spam and make our e-mail time as productive as we can?

✦ **Use a filter**. As you know, Outlook Express, Messenger, and Eudora all have filtering features you can implement to block out messages that you don't want to receive. Filtering takes a lot of resolve — you've got to make it a point to filter out each spammer as you encounter one — but it makes your system cleaner and cuts down on the amount of mail you must sort through.

✦ **Don't send spam**. Be sensitive to what is perceived as spam. Even if you are not sending hundreds of mail messages to unsuspecting people, remember that people have little time and little patience for long files and unnecessary verbiage. And keep in mind that spam isn't limited to advertisements; things like jokes or chain letters that you find humorous may be very annoying to the people you forward them to.

✦ **Be vocal**. When you receive spam, you don't just have to take it. There are a number of groups you can join to enlist with the cause of spam-removal. You also can write to your (or someone else's) congressperson. We've included Web links to some politicians leading spam legislation; you'll find them listed later in this chapter.

✦ **Decide on a course of action or inaction**. You have a number of things you can do when you are being spammed; not everyone agrees on the best course of action. Some people would have you reply to the e-mail and say "No thank you!"; others suggest you flood the spammer with a taste of his or her own medicine; others say do nothing and lay low because when you respond you confirm that you are in fact out there, and they will continue sending messages until you (or they) expire. For more information about possible courses of action, see the next section "Responding to spam."

Responding to spam

Scouring the Web reveals a number of different responses to the spam problem. As you will see, opinions are varied. One thing is apparent: What to do about spam is really up to you. Here are a smattering of responses you may want to try:

✦ **Nothing**. Just let the spam come in and delete it as it happens. Many users caution that if you respond at all, you merely confirm to the spammer that your address is indeed active—that once they know your e-mail address is valid they will continue to spam it. These cautions even apply to spams that say something like, "Respond here to remove yourself from the list."

✦ **Respond to the spammer** (a) aggressively, by flooding the system with e-mail, or (b) politely, by sending a simple "No thank you" and asking to be taken off the list.

✦ **Support the tagging idea**. By adding a tag—a marker that identifies the message as spam—to the header of spam mail, the spammer makes it easier for you to filter out unwanted messages.

✦ **Encourage your ISP to ban spammers**. The online community can agree not to work with ISPs that provide services to spammers.

✦ **Don't use an ISP that sells your information to spammers**. Some ISPs sell your personal information to spammers; check their policies before you sign up.

✦ **Use a key (encryption) system**. Add numeric keys to everyone's e-mail address so only those who have your key could send you e-mail.

Cross-Reference For more about encryption and the ways keys safeguard the transmission of your data, see Chapter 32, "Maintaining Your Online Privacy and Security."

✦ **Change your e-mail address**. If people change their e-mail addresses regularly, spammers would have a hard time tracking them. Spammers' lists would soon be meaningless, and spam would lose its sizzle. But on the other hand, who wants to reprint business cards, letterhead, and miscellaneous identification pieces every time an e-mail address changes? Not you!

✦ **Obtain a separate e-mail address to draw spam**. Often when you register for something on a Web site, you are asked to provide your e-mail address. Unfortunately, this often leads to spam. Consider obtaining a separate e-mail account—such as a free account like those described in Chapter 13—that you only use when you have to provide an e-mail address to a Web site. This will help you keep spam out of your regular e-mail account.

Note When you register for services on Web sites—such as software downloads or free e-mail—you will often be asked something like, "Would you like us to send you additional information?" Almost without fail this option is selected by default, but if you don't want to receive bulk mail from the company, you should deselect the option. If you leave the option checked, you have no one but yourself to blame for the additional mail.

Making spam illegal

Some e-mail users think spam should be made illegal and punishable by law; others think methods of regulation not involving government would be the better way to go. Regardless of the continuing discussion, a number of legislative efforts in the United States and abroad have attempted to stem the growth of unwanted spam throughout the online world.

Thus far antispam legislation in the U.S. Congress has been largely unsuccessful, but some states have been able to pass their own laws. Some laws enable ISPs to sue parties who send out spam in violation of their policies, while others provide for fines and damages against spammers if they send unsolicited commercial e-mail to persons who register with a state "no-spam" registry.

In 1999 the state of Washington enacted just such a law (Chapter 19.190 RCW) that enables individuals to collect damages from individuals and companies that send certain kinds of unsolicited advertisements. If you are a Washington resident, you can learn more about the law by visiting `http://www.wa.gov/wwweb/AGO/junkemail/`. If you live elsewhere, check with your state's attorney general or your legislators to find out what laws may apply in your area.

Another good place to learn about legal issues as they pertain to spam is at the Web site of the Coalition Against Unsolicited Commercial Email, or CAUCE (`http://www.cauce.org/`). CAUCE is an organization formed by *Netizens* who are concerned about the spread of spam. CAUCE also has counterparts in Europe (`http://www.euro.cauce.org/`) and Australia (`http://www.caube.org.au/`).

Regulation Doesn't Always Come From Government

Although some antispam efforts have asked government to step in, many anti-spam efforts have come from within the Internet community and industry. On January 18, 2000, a coalition of Usenet administrators planned to institute a ban on newsgroup postings from all Excite@Home domain names. This came in response to what the administrators called "vast quantities of Usenet spam" from @Home domains, combined with a general unresponsiveness from the Excite@Home Network when they were asked to control the problem.

The administrators planned to institute a "Usenet Death Penalty"—or UDP—that would have effectively cut off all subscribers to the @Home service from posting to Usenet newsgroups. The UDP was outlined in a posting to the newsgroup `news.admin.net-abuse.usenet`.

Fortunately for all parties involved, the UDP was cancelled before it even began when Excite@Home finally responded to the complaints and dramatically reduced the amount of spam flowing from its users. The action served as a vivid example of how some Internet problems can be resolved "in house," without the need for added government regulation.

Finding help from antispamming groups

Here are four antispamming groups and their URLs:

✦ Aristotle, a group working with Cyber Promotions to enable registered users to block up to five e-mail addresses, can be reached at `http://www.aristotle.org`.

✦ Coalition Against Unsolicited Commercial E-mail (CAUCE) can be reached at `http://www.cauce.org`.

✦ The Direct Marketing Association (DMA) allows consumers to register a preference regarding whether they want to receive spam or not at `http://www.e-mps.org/en/`.

✦ The Internet Service Provider Consortium (ISPC) is an ISP trade group that can be reached at `http://www.ispc.org`.

Summary

In this chapter, you've learned various methods of organizing your e-mail messages. Specifically, you've learned to create and work with folders and subfolders; save your e-mail messages; arrange, copy, find, delete, and print messages; and archive old messages you don't need cluttering up your Inbox but may need at some point down the road.

This chapter also introduced you to ways you can control what actually comes into your Inbox, and gives you options for what to do with it when it does. You learned how each of three major e-mail programs uses filters to help you control your e-mail, and you discovered what spam is, what the rage is about, and how you can respond to your own spam attacks.

✦   ✦   ✦

Finding Everything You Need on the Web

◆ ◆ ◆ ◆

Finding stuff on the Web is easy — the problem is that what you find isn't always what you're looking for. This part helps you untangle the Web and gives you the ability to effectively and efficiently find the things you need.

Whether you're looking for software, news, graphics, music, or missing people, this part shows you how to find what you want. You also learn about different ways to communicate online, including chat and newsgroups.

Using Search Engines

◆   ◆   ◆   ◆

The Web, in case you haven't noticed, is a very big place — and getting bigger all the time. Unfortunately, it has no organization to speak of — no equivalent to the Dewey decimal system of your local library. Oh, sure, you know that an address with .edu in it is probably a university, and that .gov is associated with pages from the government, but those are rather broad categories. Just think how hard it would be to find, say, one particular encyclopedia entry if all the pages in all the books in the library had been ripped out and thrown randomly around the building. That's roughly the task you'd face trying to find one page on the World Wide Web if you had to search through it page-by-page. Fortunately, there's help available — and this chapter tells you how to find it and use it.

Defining Search Engines

A search engine is simply a piece of software that searches a database according to some specific criteria. Search engines have existed for years, but they've really come into their own as a way of finding information on the Internet. As a result, numerous Web sites let you provide the criteria by which you wish to search the Web pages contained within that site's database. You're then provided with a list of sites that match your criteria, which you can visit simply by clicking the provided link.

Each search engine hunts through its own database. How that database is gathered depends on the site. Yahoo!'s database, for instance, is created primarily from sites suggested by users. Others, such as Webcrawler and Lycos, use special software that constantly scours the Web, following links and adding each page it comes across to the database.

The differences in the methods used to build the databases mean that no search engine can be counted on to turn up absolutely every single page matching the search criteria, and that no two search engines will ever turn up exactly the same list.

For this reason, it's a good idea to use more than one search engine when trying to dig up information on the Web. A good deal of repetition is possible, but not as much as you might think.

Performing Simple Searches

Suppose you need to find out everything you can about chocolate (to pick a topic more or less at random). Here's how you'd go about it on six popular search engines — and the different results you'd get.

Yahoo!

Let's start with Yahoo!, at www.yahoo.com. Each main category listed on the home page is organized into subcategories, which in turn are organized into subsubcategories and sometimes subsubsubcategories. Eventually you reach a list of links (see Figure 16-1), complete with brief descriptions, and can choose the ones that interest you. Yahoo! pioneered this style of online directory, and although most other search engines now have their own directory, Yahoo!'s is still among the most extensive.

If you want to use the search capabilities at Yahoo!, you will be directed to not only sites whose names or descriptions contain the word or words you're using as your search criteria, but also to directory categories that include the search word, which in turn may lead you to informative sites you might otherwise have missed.

In the case of chocolate, Yahoo! turned up ten category matches and 966 site matches. Because it lists only 20 matches at a time, to minimize the size of the displayed page, you see all ten category matches and only 10 of the site matches. A link at the bottom of the page enables you to call up the next 20 site matches.

Click any link that looks interesting, and away you'll go to that site.

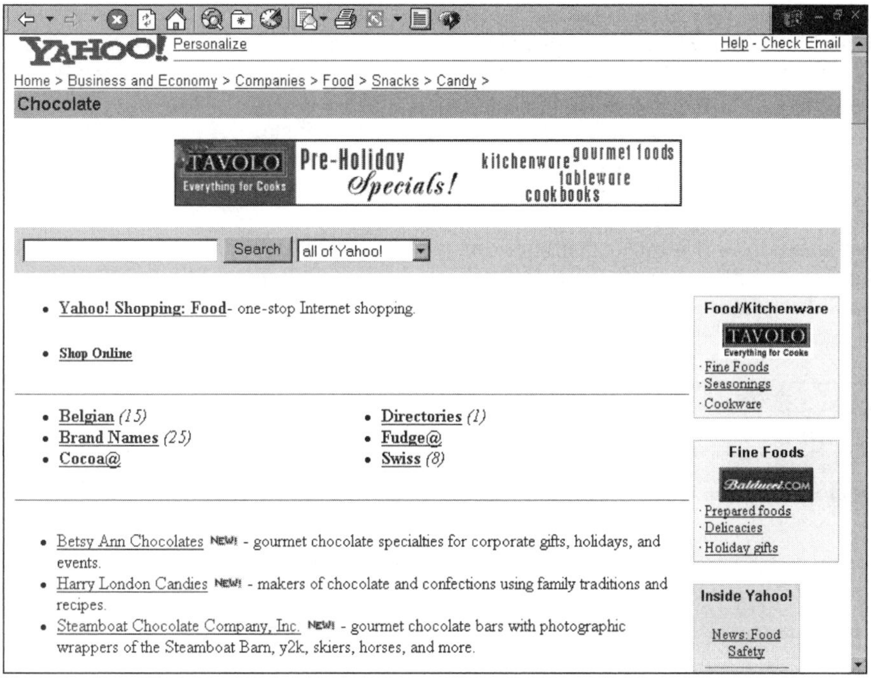

Figure 16-1: Yahoo! offers an extensively categorized directory. Notice that the Chocolate category, shown here, contains subcategories listen in the middle and links to individual Web sites at the bottom.

AltaVista

AltaVista has one of the largest databases of Web pages, most of which are uncovered by its own Web-scouring software. You can access it at www.altavista.com.

Entering the term "chocolate" into AltaVista returns a whopping 613,745 matches, displayed ten at a time.

Because AltaVista indexes individual pages, you'll often find many pages from the same site listed, unlike Yahoo! — which accounts for part of the huge discrepancy in the number of matches. You can, however, link to other pages that AltaVista identifies as belonging to the same site by clicking the "More pages from this site" link at the bottom of many listings.

One of the most interesting new features of AltaVista is a translation service called Babel Fish (see *The Hitchhiker's Guide to the Galaxy* by Douglas Adams). Click the "Translate" link at the bottom of a search result to display the window shown in Figure 16-2. The URL for the site you want to translate should be shown. Select the translation path you wish to use and then click Translate. A new window opens, showing a rough translation. In this example, we want to translate a site about chocolate from German to English.

We should point out that translations performed by Babel Fish are literal and thus subject to various errors and misinterpretations. Still, for a free service, Babel Fish can't be beat.

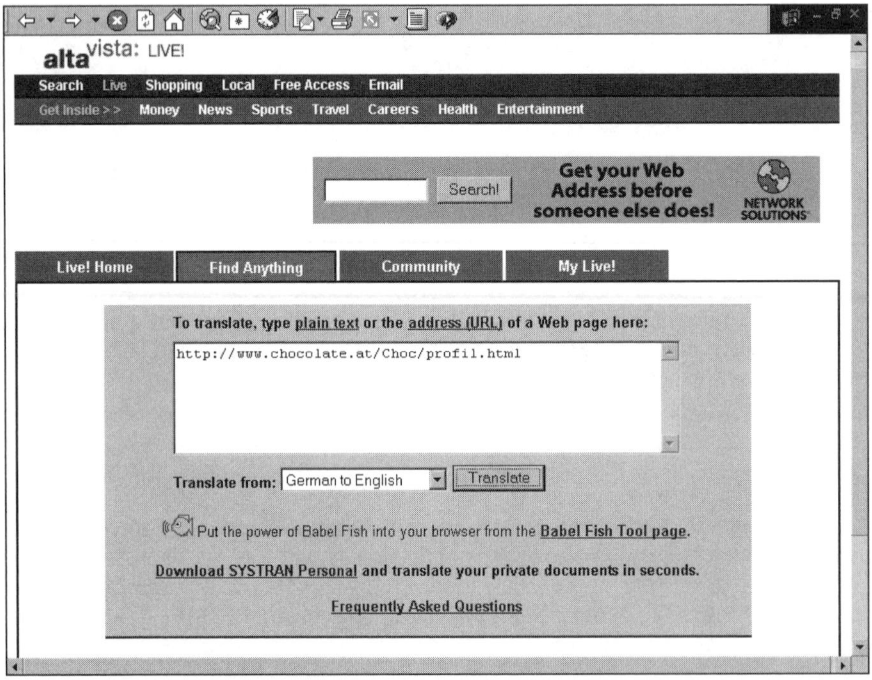

Figure 16-2: Use AltaVista's Babel Fish to translate foreign language Web sites.

Lycos

Lycos, like AltaVista, has an extensive database of Web sites. You can access it at www.lycos.com.

Lycos has features in common with both Yahoo! (its directories are similar to the categories at Yahoo!) and AltaVista (its Web database is constantly being updated by software that searches through the Web's nooks and crannies for sites, and then automatically indexes them).

Lycos returns its matches by categorizing them into a few initial groups. In a search on chocolate, Lycos first lists the four most popular chocolate-related Web sites, based on how often they were chosen by other people who searched on the same topic. Below the four most popular links are the first ten of 141,967 Web site matches. The Web site section also included four links to category listings in Lycos' directory.

In addition to standard Web pages, Lycos searches news articles. In our example, 2,234 articles mentioning chocolate were found, and the first three were shown. Below this is a shopping guide with three (of 1,151 found) product listings, and three shopping categories. This may be useful if you feel like shopping online, but in this case all of the shopping links related to chocolate-colored garments rather than food.

Excite

Another popular search engine is Excite (`www.excite.com`), which is organized very much like Lycos and Yahoo!, but with a greater emphasis on news and shopping links. As such it makes for a pretty good Home Page if you are looking for a good place to start your browsing.

When your results come up, the organization is similar to Lycos but with a slightly cleaner appearance. For chocolate, four relevant Excite categories were listed, followed by 10 Web sites out of 151,621 found. Some news articles are listed next, followed at last by a Discussions section with links to Excite-sponsored message boards. Also listed here are some Usenet newsgroups that discuss chocolate.

If you prefer, you can choose to list results only by title, without any description. This method enables you to see 20 matches at a time, but makes it harder to tell if they're worth following up or not.

If you wish to chase down your topic via the directory, you may have to dig through several layers of categories, much like following a topic through the categories and subcategories of Yahoo!. Along the way you'll pass dozens of tempting Web sites and other interesting features, but eventually you'll see a list of sites that Excite particularly recommends. Again, this gives you at least some assurance that someone has visited the site before you and found it worthwhile.

HotBot

The prize for nicest-looking site among search engines goes to HotBot (`www.hotbot.com`), which probably isn't too surprising, because it's the search engine that the cybermag *Wired* has put in place.

HotBot offers you more immediate choices as to how you want the result to be displayed than most search engines. On the left side of the screen (Figure 16-3) you'll notice a number of choices to help you narrow and control your search somewhat. In the Look for box you can choose whether you want HotBot to find any of the words, an exact phrase, a person, or one of a few other options. You can also specify that only recently modified pages be listed, helpful if you want to avoid the woefully out-of-date information that some people leave online for years at a time. HotBot also lets you specify languages, the number of listings that will be shown per page of results, multimedia enhancements, and how the results are displayed.

Figure 16-3: HotBot makes it easy to customize your searches with the options at left.

Of course, if you want to, you can simply accept the default, and (in the case of searching for chocolate) see full descriptions of the first ten sites HotBot has indexed that contain the word "chocolate," as well as a list of HotBot categories dealing with chocolate. HotBot has long been known as one of the most powerful search engines on the Web. It did not list a specific number of hits for our chocolate quest, stating simply that "more than 100,000" sites were found.

Other search engines

The search engines briefly touched on here are just some of those available on the Web. A good place to find others is on Yahoo!, which, because it sees itself more as an online directory than a search engine, provides direct links to other search engines at the bottom of every page (and to AltaVista, with which it has a partnership, at the top of every page).

Other major search engines include WebCrawler (owned by Excite) at `www.webcrawler.com`, and Infoseek, at `infoseek.go.com` (see Figure 16-4).

Figure 16-4: Infoseek's main page is packed with useful links, yet remains relatively easy to read.

Several other search engines exist, but they aren't as well known. The best way to find search engines? Do a search for "search engine" using another search engine! (Yahoo! has links to dozens of them.)

Executing Advanced Searches

HotBot, as you saw earlier, makes it easy for you to fine-tune your searches through the use of forms. The other search engines don't use forms, but you can still fine-tune your searches.

Suppose, for instance, you're not interested in chocolate per se, but specifically in recipes for hot chocolate. You have several ways you can go about fine-tuning your search to try to uncover any such recipes that might be lurking on the net. What follows are general suggestions; the specific method of accomplishing each may vary slightly from search engine to search engine. Look for a link marked "options" or "advanced search" or something similar near the blank into which you type your search criteria to find out how you can use these advanced search methods with your favorite search engine.

✦ **Use alternative words.** "Chocolate" isn't turning up that perfect recipe for hot chocolate? Try using "cocoa" instead, because that's what many people call it. Try to think of all the different terms that might apply to the topic of your search, and then conduct additional searches using those new terms. You'll be amazed at how much good information you missed when you only used the words that first came to your mind.

✦ **Add search terms.** Another easy way to fine-tune your search is to add more terms to your criteria. In this case, instead of just typing in the term "chocolate," you might type in three words: hot, chocolate, and recipe. The search engines will now search for Web pages that include any of those words, which will naturally increase the number of matches. Generally Web pages that contain all of those words will be listed first, however, and there's a good chance you might find what you're looking for among them. It's kind of hit and miss, though; a better way is to . . .

✦ **Search for an exact phrase.** In most search engines, you can search for an exact phrase by putting quotation marks around it. "Hot chocolate recipe," by way of example, reduces the number of matches AltaVista returns to a very manageable 15.

✦ **Include and exclude specific words.** This is typically done by using plus (+) or minus (–) signs. For example, in a search for a hot chocolate recipe, you could insist that all the pages, in addition to containing the word *chocolate*, must also contain the word *hot*, but must not include the word *instant*. You can do this by typing "chocolate +hot –instant." If you know your primary search term can be used in more than one way, this trick can be very helpful.

✦ **Use Boolean operators: AND, OR, AND NOT.** These little words are the most powerful tools you have for fine-tuning searches, and most search engines support them. (Some support additional ones as well.) Generally, Boolean operators have to be entered in all-capital letters. Here's how they work:

• **AND.** Documents found must contain all the words joined by AND. For example, if you type "Chocolate AND hot AND recipe," the search engine will retrieve, for example, only those documents that contain all of those words. This avoids the problem of conducting multiple words searches and getting matches with Web sites that contain any of them.

- **OR.** Documents found must contain at least one of the words joined by OR. For example, you could search for "chocolate OR cocoa," because hot chocolate is called cocoa by some people.

- **AND NOT.** This means that documents cannot contain the words that follow. "Chocolate AND NOT cocoa" would indicate that you're not interested in the recipes of people who dare to call hot chocolate cocoa.

- Most search engines also let you group Boolean operators together, using parentheses. This can enable you to make very precise searches: ("hot chocolate" OR cocoa) AND (recipe OR formula) AND NOT instant, for example. It looks kind of like algebra, doesn't it?

Using Metasearch Engines

As noted, no one search engine will find everything on the Web related to your search topic: to be thorough, you really need to use several search engines. But doing so can be a long, drawn-out process.

Fortunately, there's an easier way: use a metasearch tool instead. A metasearch tool is a Web site that enables you to enter your search term just once, and then delivers that term to many different search engines and returns the results. You generally see only the top few matches from each search engine, but because all the search engines put their best matches first, chances are you'll find what you're looking for (if it exists) in one of those first few matches.

Just as several different search engines exist, so do several different metasearch tools. Two of the best are MetaCrawler and Dogpile.

MetaCrawler

MetaCrawler, at `www.metacrawler.com` (see Figure 16-5), is one of the oldest metasearch tools on the Internet. It searches AltaVista, Excite, Infoseek, Lycos, Yahoo!, and WebCrawler simultaneously, eliminates duplicates, and then shows you the results in order of relevance.

As with ordinary search engines, you can fine-tune your search, looking for any or all of your terms or an exact phrase. You can also decide how many hits you want reported from each search engine queried (keeping this number small speeds your search) and how long you want MetaCrawler to wait for results from each search engine before giving up (some popular search engines can run very slowly at peak times).

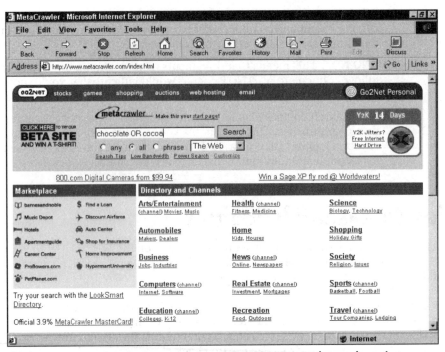

Figure 16-5: MetaCrawler is a quick way to use ten top-notch search engines simultaneously.

Dogpile

MetaCrawler accesses ten search engines. But if even that isn't enough, try Dogpile (www.dogpile.com). Dogpile can access up to 18 search engines, and can also search newswires, Usenet newsgroups, and FTP sites. MetaCrawler is excellent for most searches; Dogpile should be used when you're determined to wring every last bit of information out of the Web.

Dogpile doesn't send your request to every search engine at once; instead, it sends it to three at a time. If it doesn't get at least ten hits from the first three, it automatically moves on to the next three. Once you have ten hits, you click a button to move on to the next group of three search engines.

Dogpile lets you fine-tune your search using many of the advanced search options mentioned earlier, including enclosing exact phrases in quotation marks and using Boolean operators. Your search preferences can be saved so that you can use the same settings again in the future. Click the "Custom Search" link to customize your Dogpile search preferences.

One big advantage of metasearch tools such as this is that you don't have to learn the idiosyncratic methods all the other search engines use for fine-tuning searches; the meta-search tool automatically edits requests so that it doesn't send illegal commands to any of the other engines.

Summary

An enormous amount of valuable information exists on the World Wide Web, but lack of organization makes it difficult to track down. Fortunately, search engines are tirelessly surfing the Web in your stead, finding and indexing pages. All you have to do is phrase your request correctly. Fortunately, there are ways to fine-tune your search. Using alternative words, exact phrases, and Boolean operators can help your zero-in on what you're looking for. In addition, you can save time by using metasearch engines, which search multiple search engines at once, helping you find the information you need.

✦　　✦　　✦

Finding Cool Software on the Web

In This Chapter

Describing shareware and freeware

Finding shareware, updates, patches, and drivers on the Web

Using FTP to upload and download software

Protecting yourself against viruses on the Web

This chapter covers how to find great software and helpful information on the Web, as well as how to avoid viruses. You'll learn how to send and receive files via *File Transfer Protocol* (FTP) and how to download and keep track of software you download. We'll also take a look at viruses and learn how to protect your system from them.

Finding Shareware, Freeware, and Commercial Demos

Let's start by discussing some distinctions between the types of software available on the Web: shareware and freeware. Shareware and commercial demos generally include tutorials that teach you how to use the program. Once you pay for the software and receive a registered copy, you'll usually get additional capabilities — such as sounds, pictures, videos, and the ability to save game levels — that were missing from the unregistered copy of the program. Shareware and demos usually work for a short trial period only, say about 30 days or so.

Freeware, another category of programs you'll find on the Web, is absolutely free. Freeware programs are usually small utilities that enhance an existing program in some way. Icons for Windows applications, programs that play musical notes when a printing job is finished, or that convert pictures to a new format are good examples of freeware. You may be asked to register your freeware, but you'll not have to sit through screens of warnings prompting you for money.

Some freeware programs are actually "light" versions of bigger programs that you must pay for. Eudora Light is a good example, because it is a functional, nonexpiring e-mail client that lacks some of the more advanced features of Eudora Pro. RealNetwork's RealJukebox is another example; the program is free, but if you pay for RealJukebox Plus!, you can get added capabilities.

Defining shareware

Shareware is everywhere on the Web. A good shareware program is a simpler, more focused and less cumbersome version of something you might spend lots of money on at the software store. Shareware — also known as commercial demos — lets you give software a test drive before you spend money on it.

With most shareware, you can download the entire program and put it through its paces, whether the goal is to catalog a thousand invoices or assemble all your favorite programs as single-click icons at the bottom of your desktop. Most shareware programs cost less than 50 dollars to register — indeed, some cost far less. Some shareware can be used indefinitely without being registered, but most do expect you to pony up the registration fee after somewhere between two weeks to a month. Some shareware programs include a registration screen as part of the startup process, so every time you begin the program, you'll be informed how long you've had this puppy on your computer and reminded to send in your 20 dollars. Some shareware programs simply stop working after a specific period of time or number of uses has passed if you haven't paid.

In the past, shareware programs were largely developed by eager computer programmers who would rather go it alone than work for a big firm. Part hobbyist, part entrepreneur, shareware authors often developed ingenious small programs for themselves and distributed them to others almost as an afterthought. Of late, even large software corporations see the distribution of shareware as a way to get one's foot in the door with potential customers.

Hunting for quality shareware

The quality of available shareware is as varied as the day is long. There are definitely some lemons out there, so it's advisable to allow others to pick out the cherries for you. Happily, that's what the myriad of download collection pages are all about. Try to surf for shareware from a reputable collection, from a site in which a dedicated individual or staff has pruned the vines for you. Most of the top sites offer a rating system and a brief description of system requirements, features, length of the trial period, and the cost of registration. For a place to start, take a look at these sites:

```
shareware.cnet.com
www.zdnet.com/downloads/
www.davecentral.com
www.filez.com/zhub.shtml
www.tucows.com
```

You can find additional sites listed in this book's Web Directory under the heading Computers: Software.

Seeking updates and patches for your software

Software publishers never truly kick back after a program is released and wait for the profits to roll in. Software is constantly improved, updated, and refined, and those updates and refinements are often available for download on the Web. Updates could simply be service packs that fix bugs in the original release, or they could be updates to keep the programs current. Antivirus software, for instance, requires constant updates of active virus types, and tax software requires a fresh database of new tax laws to be truly useful.

These types of supportive downloads are usually offered for free. It is a good idea to periodically check the software publishers' Web sites to ensure that your programs are current and in top form.

> **Tip**   To make checking for updates easy, create a category of bookmarks in your Web browser for software updates, and fill it with links to the Web sites of software publishers for programs you use.

Looking for drivers for new computer equipment

The Web is a good place to find the newest drivers for computer equipment you recently purchased, such as a printer, modem, or sound card. Sometimes vendors assume customers have access to the Web and are not always careful to include the most recent drivers with your new equipment.

The best place to look for drivers is on the manufacturer's Web site. Most hardware manufacturers have a driver download section online. To aid your search, make sure you have the model number and any other specifications handy.

Of course, some manufacturers don't provide drivers online, and if the company no longer exists, they certainly won't have a Web site. In these cases, you may still be able to find drivers for your equipment online, even for very old and obsolete devices. Here are a few excellent resources of hardware drivers online:

✦ **The Driver Zone (**www.driverzone.com**).** Drivers are categorized by device type. Each category contains a list of the ten most popular brands at the top, followed by an alphabetical list of manufacturers below.

✦ **Mister Driver (**www.mrdriver.com**).** Provides a searchable database, as well as a forum where you can communicate with others who are searching for device drivers, and an auction area where you can buy or sell hardware.

✦ **Drivers Headquarters (**http://www.driverzone.com/**).** Includes a searchable archive of drivers for computers running Windows.

Finding a Shareware Utility

CNET Shareware.com is one of the best locations for finding good software on the Web. To search for software that enables you to play MP3 files:

1. To reach CNET Shareware.com, type **http://shareware.cnet.com/** in your browser's address box.

2. At the Shareware.com main screen, select your operating system in the Choose From list box.

3. Type the keywords for your search. For this example, type MP3.

4. Click Search to produce a list of programs.

You may have to browse a bit to find something that matches your needs exactly. When we searched for programs relating to MP3s, we found utilities for recording, editing, and playing MP3s, as well as a variety of programs that simply included some sort of MP3 playback. When we conducted a search for MP3 programs for Windows, we found 166 matches. By contrast, just 13 matches for the Macintosh were returned, and we found nothing for Linux.

Search results generally include a variety of useful bits of information, such as:

✦ A brief description of the program's function

✦ The file name of the download

✦ Information about whether the program is freeware or if there is a trial period

✦ The size of the download

✦ Platform requirements

✦ A date when the file was last modified

Using a Mirrored Site

If you are looking for a popular shareware program or a fix for a program you bought, you can bet that thousands of other people are doing the same thing. Popular software sites often set up mirror sites. A mirror site is an exact replication of a site, created at another location. So if you are having a hard time downloading a program because of high traffic, see if there is a mirror available. To log onto a mirror, just click the provided URL. Mirror sites are often identified by their geographic location, so for best results try to pick one that is closest to you.

When you find a program you want to download, click its link. Most software download sites then ask you to choose a mirror site to download from, as shown in Figure 17-1 and Shareware.com is no exception. Click a mirror site link to begin the download. At this point, you'll probably be prompted to choose a location in which to save the download, as described in the next section.

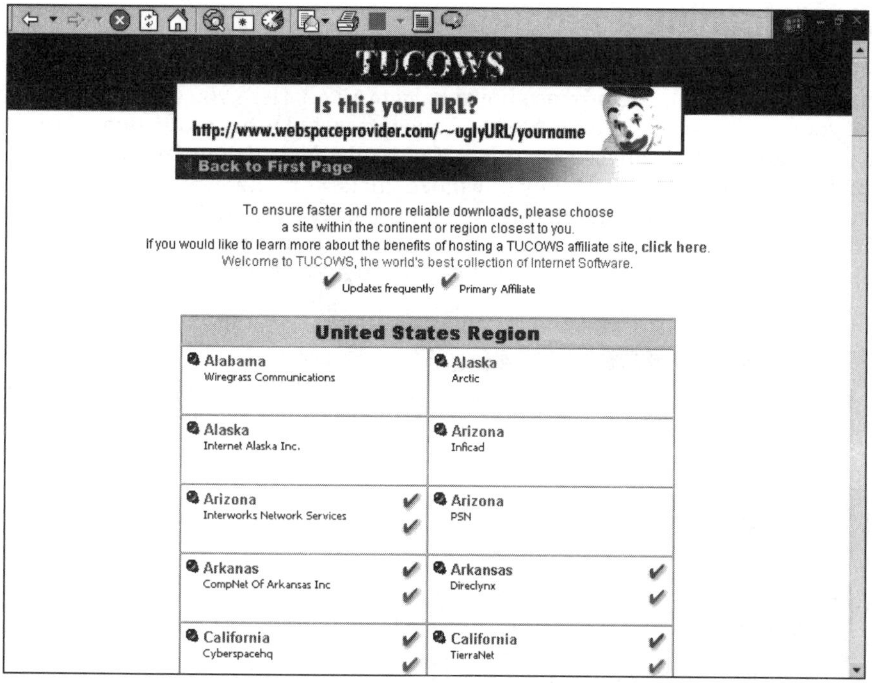

Figure 17-1: Tucows offers a list of mirror sites. Choose one that is close to your geographic location.

Downloading Files and Installing Programs

Once you've located the software you want, you still have a few steps before the program is actually running on your computer. You must identify where you want the file saved and then download the file. After this, you may have to decompress the files, if it arrived as part of a compressed or zipped archive. Then you must locate the file that begins the installation process. The location of the program files after they are installed will be different than the downloaded destination. At the end of the installation process, take note as to how you'll start the program: Is there a new icon in your Start menu or Apple menu? Do you need to run the program from a Linux shell? What folder is the program's startup icon saved in? Is there a new shortcut on your desktop? Check the download site for instructions on installing and launching the new software *before* you log off.

Downloading a program

After locating a file for downloading and clicking its filename or icon to download it, you may see a dialog box, as shown in Figure 17-2. Here you can select a location on your computer to save the file to. In the interest of virus protection, save it to a removable disk (such as a Zip drive) if possible. Also, if your antivirus software enables you to scan files as they download, make sure that feature is enabled before the download begins. Later in this chapter, we'll review antivirus software for the Web and downloaded files. After your security concerns have been met, click the appropriate check box to continue downloading the file to your hard drive.

Figure 17-2: When you are about to download a file, a File Download dialog box like this one will appear in most browsers.

After selecting a folder for your downloaded file, a progress window should appear. This visual aid will tell you how much of the file is downloaded and give you an estimate of the time remaining. You'll also be able to read the name of the folder where your file will end up, and the transfer rate, in KB per second.

Tip   Many downloads are compressed, or "zipped." If you don't have a compression program installed on your system, it should be one of the first programs you download from the Web. WinZip (www.winzip.com) is one of the most popular compression programs for Windows, and Stuffit Expander is used on many Macs.

Installing a program

After completing the download, you need to locate the file on your computer's hard drive. If you had to unzip the file, you may see several different files in the folder where it was downloaded. One of them will usually be a setup file, often called Setup. In Windows, it should have the .exe extension and an icon that looks like a computer. Most Macintosh installation programs have the word "Install" or "Installer" in them. Also look for a "readme" file before installing. If you see one, double-click it to read. This may contain special instructions, such as to restart the computer with extensions off if you are using a Macintosh. Before installing, make sure you have no programs open at this time. Most setup programs also require you to disable antivirus programs before you begin the actual installation process. When you're ready, double-click the executable file icon. Follow the on-screen instructions to complete installation.

 Caution Before you install the program, scan it with antivirus software. See the section on virus protection later in this chapter.

Using File Transfer Protocol

FTP, or *File Transfer Protocol,* is the most efficient way to transfer large files from one computer to another. For many, the Web has become synonymous with the Internet, but the Web is only a part of the Internet. FTP traffic still accounts for a great deal of Internet activity.

Transferring files via FTP is amazingly fast, compared to uploading and downloading through a Web page as shown in the previous section. You won't have to worry about advertising, no chance of a pushed news notice or infomercial applet appearing and drawing bandwidth away from the work at hand. The typical FTP interface is not elegant. You won't find file descriptions or photographs on an FTP site, simply a directory tree structure that branches as you click on a folder. Eventually, you'll find the file you want to download, or a directory that will receive your uploads, whatever you are looking for. Filenames are lowercase, following the UNIX file structure.

Note Although here we are showing you how to access an FTP site with your Web browser, you can also access many FTP servers with a dedicated FTP client such as WS_FTP or Fetch. See the section on using WS_FTP LE later in this chapter to learn more.

Linking between FTP sites and Web pages

Often, on the Web, you are accessing an FTP site even though it doesn't look like one. When offering a file to the public for downloading, Web page designers create links to as many sites as possible for retrieval. One of these is sometimes an FTP site. It helps to be comfortable with traversing the folders and recognizing a bit of the lingo of a typical FTP site.

You can log on to an FTP site with most browsers just by typing in the site name, preceded by `ftp://`, rather than the familiar `http://`. For example, use your browser to access the ciesin.org FTP site by typing `ftp://ftp.ciesin.org/` in the browser's URL address area. Figure 17-3 shows how this site is accessed in Internet Explorer. Documents are located in the folders, which you can open by double-clicking them.

Figure 17-3: An FTP site accessed through a browser. Double-click a folder to open it and see the documents within.

Tip   If you are using Internet Explorer, you can change the way items on the FTP site are displayed by clicking the Views button on the toolbar.

Navigating FTP sites

FTP sites open to the public for downloading are known for their wealth of resources and liberal access privileges. Many contain millions of files. However, categorizing, virus testing, and writing descriptions for all these files is a huge job that often depends on weekend labor. Don't expect much hand-holding when looking for a file on an FTP site.

Major FTP sites are often found at universities, and are repositories for legal and governmental documents, administrative records, academic research, schematics, product specifications, as well as a myriad of drivers, computer games, shareware, and multimedia files. Your company may even have a private FTP site that you need to access once in a while (they should provide you with a password and login information for this).

Locating the /pub directory

Unless you have special privileges at a particular site, most of what's available for you will be found within a folder called pub (and subdirectories therein). Pictured in Figure 17-4 is the Tech Support folder of Logitech's FTP site. Here are FAQs and downloads for many of Logitech's products.

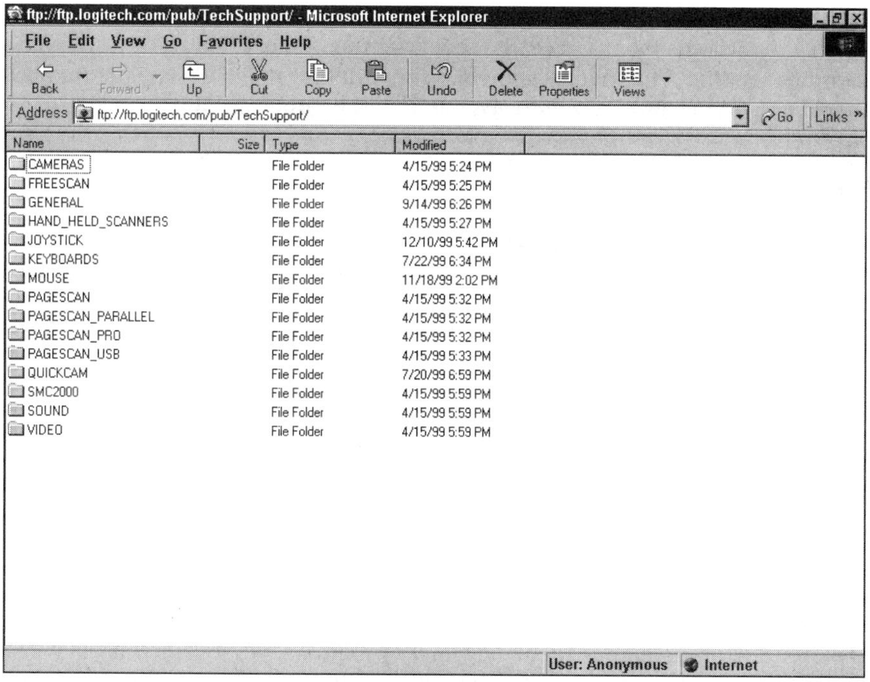

Figure 17-4: The Logitech Tech Support FTP site.

Locating a readme or index file

Because an FTP site's resources are so gargantuan, it's best to look for a FAQ, readme, or index file when you first log on. These files usually contain information you'll need to navigate the site. Even a simple index may be so large that you'll have to download it before viewing it.

Logging on as a guest

While advanced privileges and authorization is often required to upload files to an FTP site, anyone can download from most FTP sites by logging on as Anonymous and using your e-mail address as a password. When your User ID and password are requested, type the word **Anonymous** for your User ID and enter your e-mail address as the password.

Uploading files to an FTP site

Some major FTP sites enable you to upload files, which their administrators will review and then make available to the public. Uploaded files can be anything that is relevant to the content of that particular FTP site and can include text, graphics, sound, or even video files. FTP sites are also useful if you wish to send particularly large files to a friend or work associate. Many businesses that frequently handle large computer files, such as software companies and publishers, have FTP sites where developers and authors can upload their work.

When submitting a file for upload, remember to submit a text description of what it is you're sending. That makes somebody's work that much easier, and increases the chances that your upload will be available to the public soon.

Using WS_FTP LE

A simple way to upload and download files via FTP is to use an FTP client for Windows called WS_FTP. It's published by Ipswitch (www.ipswitch.com) and can be downloaded directly from Ipswitch or from an online download archive such as Tucows. WS_FTP LE is a freeware companion to Ipswitch's WS_FTP Pro. However, the freeware license is only available to students, teachers, government workers, and individuals at home using the client for personal, nonbusiness use.

> **Note**   A popular FTP client among Macintosh users is called Fetch. Fetch was developed by the Dartmouth College Software Development program, and you can learn more by visiting Dartmouth's Web site at http://www.dartmouth.edu/pages/softdev/.

WS_FTP enables your computer to access information on a server. This program weighs in at about a megabyte of hard drive space, and is as easy to use as Windows Explorer and other similar file management programs. WS_FTP installs in seconds, and presents an interface with default settings that will not require much adjustment on your part to get started.

To connect with an FTP site using WS_FTP, do the following:

1. After installing WS_FTP, dial up your ISP.

2. Start WS_FTP by clicking its icon in its folder, or launching the program from the Windows Start menu. When you start the program, you'll see the General tab of the Session Properties dialog box, ready for your input. In the Profile Name box you can select a preset profile, or click New to create a profile for an FTP site that isn't listed.

3. In the Password area, type your e-mail address.

4. In the Host name area, type an FTP site address, unless you are using one of the preset profiles. In Figure 17-5, you can see that we are accessing the FTP site of the U.S. Internal Revenue Service. Fun!

   The Host Name area is like the URL address locator of your browser. It's here that you type the address of the FTP site to which you want to connect.

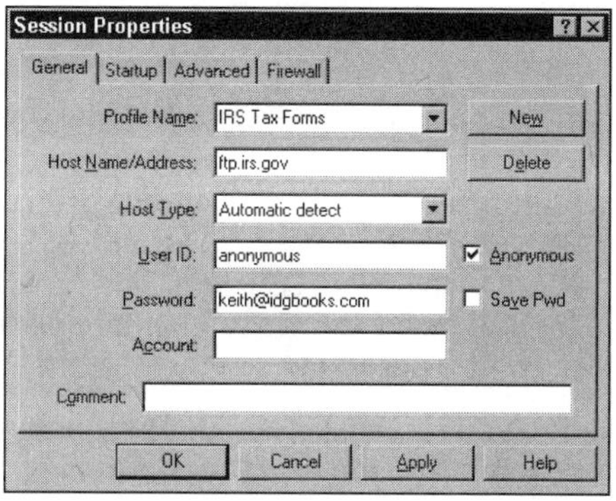

Figure 17-5: In an FTP client, the Host Name is where you type your destination FTP site.

5. Make sure that the Anonymous box is checked and that User ID is anonymous. Typing Anonymous as a User ID and using your e-mail address as a password gives you "roving and downloading" privileges at most public FTP sites. With the exception of your e-mail address instead of mine, your Session screen should look like what is shown in Figure 17-5.

6. If you want to start with a specific folder, such as /pub, click the Startup tab and enter the folder's name and path.

7. If you would like to save the FTP destination and configuration information, click the Save button. That way you won't have to type it again.

8. Click OK. This initiates the connect process. The boxed space right above the buttons on the bottom row of the next screen is the Status area. Use this area to monitor your connect progress. A series of commands and "handshaking" protocol will flicker by in this boxed area. You need not concern yourself with their content. Keep your eye on it for the reassurance that something is indeed happening. When you have successfully logged on, your screen will look something like what's shown in Figure 17-6.

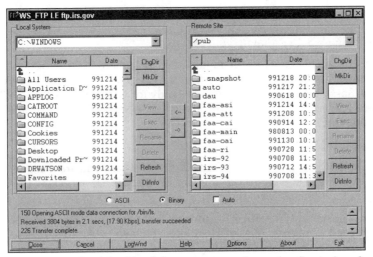

Figure 17-6: The right side of the screen now shows the directories of the FTP site, the host. The left side shows the contents of your hard drive.

Inside the FTP site

Now that you're inside a site, focus your attention on the main WS_FTP screen.

✦ On the left is your computer, where it says Local System. The directory shown is where downloaded files will be saved. You can create your own folder for downloaded FTP files, or just designate an existing one.

✦ To change the active directory on your local system, double-click a folder or click the two dots at the very top of the directory tree. Clicking these dots moves up one directory, or folder, in the tree.

✦ Unless you are sure that you will be downloading only text files, click Binary, rather than ASCII. This check box option is found at the lower middle of the screen.

Make sure that you have the correct folder open on the right side before beginning any downloads.

Working the FTP directory tree

Now let's look at the directory structure of the FTP site, shown over on the right side of the window.

Again, click the two dots to go up the directory tree, and click any directory to log to it. In the rectangle below are the files within that directory. If you aren't sure where the files you need are located, look for a text file called Readme or Index. WS_FTP enables you to preview text files, so once you've located an index file select it and click View. The file is instantly downloaded and opened in your default text reader (probably Notepad).

Downloading and uploading with WS_FTP LE

To download a file from an FTP site using WS_FTP LE:

1. On the FTP site (the Remote Site), locate the file you wish to download and select it. Then click the transfer button in the middle of the window (an arrow pointing to the left).

2. When the file has finished downloading, the file will suddenly appear on the left side of the screen (the Local System). You won't see a confirmation message.

To upload a file to the FTP site using WS_FTP LE:

1. Make sure you are in a folder where uploading is enabled. If you're not sure, read and review the FTP site's readme files, which should provide information about uploading to the site. In many cases, a folder that enables uploading will be called "upload" or "incoming."

2. On the Local System, locate the file you want to upload and select it. Then click the transfer button (the arrow that points to the right). When the file is finished uploading, it will appear on the FTP site. After the file is reviewed by the administrators, it will then be placed where the public can view it and download it.

Because FTP sites need to be accessed by computers with different operating systems, FTP sites will not employ Windows 95 or Macintosh conventions, such as long filenames. Therefor, before uploading files you should make sure that file names have less than eight characters.

When you have finished working with the FTP site, click Close at the bottom left of the main screen.

Starting a new session

To start a new session from the main WS_FTP screen, click Connect. You'll again see the Session Screen, prompting you to type in a Host Name and Remote Host destination directory. You may have to at times reestablish connection with the same site. Remember, if you've saved a site configuration, you don't need to do all that typing again. Just click the Open button on the main WS_FTP LE screen.

> **Tip**
>
> If you have trouble logging on to an FTP site, try placing a minus sign in front of your password. This tells the server to separate the password from other commands.

Working with FTP through your browser

Remember our FTP example with WS_FTP LE? Figure 17-7 shows how accessing `ftp://ftp.irs.gov/`, that same site, looks when viewed through Internet Explorer. To navigate the site, simply click up or down the directory tree, as explained earlier. The interface is a bit more graphic. Please note that, when typing an FTP address into your browser Address bar, you must include the `ftp://` prefix, even though you may be in the habit of leaving off `http://` for Web documents.

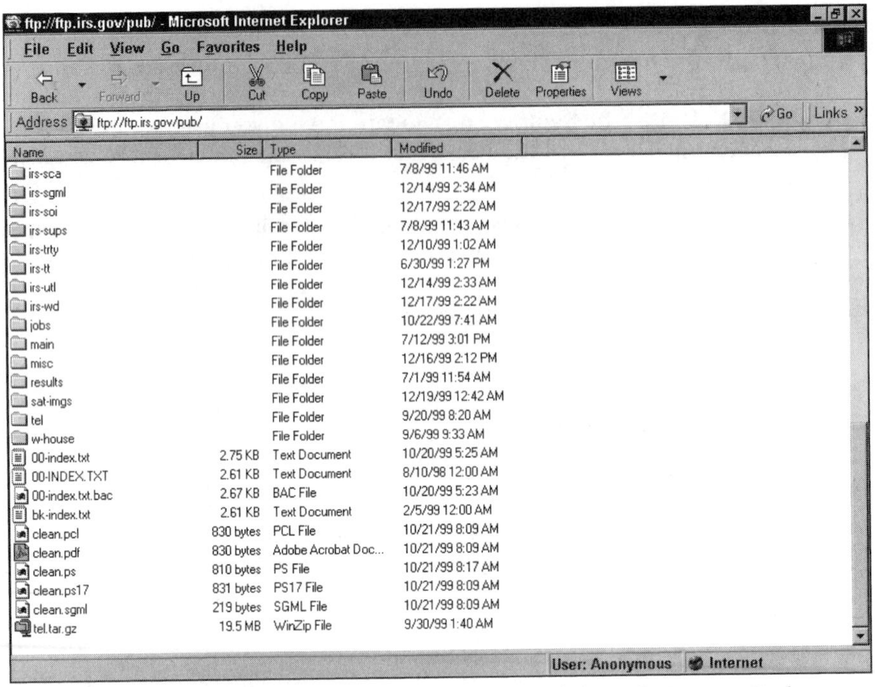

Figure 17-7: How the IRS FTP site looks when viewed through Internet Explorer.

Some FTP sites present files in FTP structure, but also publish their list of files as a Web page, neatly accessible via buttons.

Downloading with your browser

Figure 17-8 shows the process of downloading a file from the Internal Revenue Service's FTP site (`ftp://ftp.irs.gov/pub`) via a Web browser. Downloading can be done using several methods. The simplest method is to drag a file from the FTP site to a folder on your local computer. But if that doesn't work, try using Edit ⇨ Copy, or right-click the file and choose Copy to Folder. This method opens a Browse for Folder dialog as shown in Figure 17-8, where a folder can be selected in which to save the file.

Uploads can be performed in roughly the same manner, but you need to view all readme files and instructions left by the FTP site administrator to ensure that your upload complies with their policies. Don't try to randomly upload files to any directory.

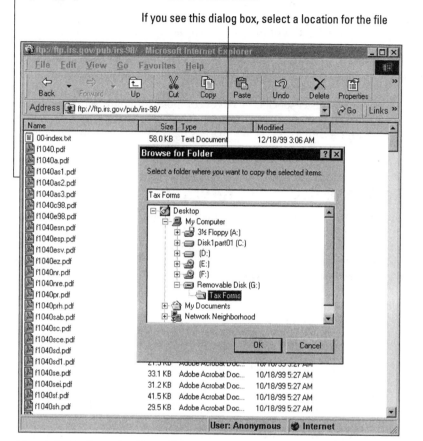

Try dragging a file from the FTP site to a local folder

If you see this dialog box, select a location for the file

Figure 17-8: Downloading a file to your computer

Protecting Your Computer From Viruses

When you download software, you should make sure that the files that you download do not contain viruses. Viruses are usually sneaky, mischievous programs created to disrupt computer systems. Some viruses are virtually harmless, such as ones that merely present a comical message on the screen when booting up. Many viruses, though, are malicious and are programmed to erase data on your hard drive and otherwise foul up your daily work. Like their biological counterpart, viruses contain a message to endlessly replicate themselves, and thus can be transferred from a hard drive to a floppy disk without your intentionally copying the offending file. If a computer is discovered to have a virus, one should assume all floppy disks that have been in contact with it are infected.

Some viruses can lay dormant on your computer until an appointed day, when it will promptly proceed to write damaging data to your hard drive's boot sector, which usually creates a nonrecoverable error. January 5, March 6, and December 25 are dates associated with computer virus attacks. On those dates, you might choose to boot up from a virus-protected floppy disk (see "Creating an emergency boot floppy" later in this chapter). Likewise, if you hear of a virus attacking a friend or associate's computer, you ought to run a virus check on your own machine.

Caution   Although many viruses specifically target computers running Windows, do not fall into a false sense of security if you use another operating system. Macintosh computers, for example, are vulnerable to many of the same macro viruses that infect Windows machines.

Getting a virus from the Internet

Viruses are programs, and they can hide in executable files or macros. You cannot activate a virus by downloading a picture or a sound file. Any file that contains a command to run — to execute a command in some way — could carry a virus. But passive documents like pictures do not. Word processing documents with macros attached can carry viruses, however.

It's important to note that your computer usually won't become infected with a virus by simply downloading an e-mail message or even opening the message. However, be careful when you receive an e-mail with a file attached, especially if the e-mail is from somebody you don't know. Opening a file attached to an e-mail can infect your computer with a virus.

Caution   Although you usually can't be infected by an e-mail attachment unless you manually open it, a notable exception applies to some users of Outlook Express 5 and Internet Explorer 5 for Windows. Early versions of Outlook Express 5 could be fooled by a rare type of virus that disguised itself as an image file, so that simply reading the e-mail message could infect your computer. Microsoft has developed a patch for this security hole, which you can download at `http://www.microsoft.com/Security/Bulletins/MS99-032.asp`. This security patch has been incorporated into Internet Explorer 5.01 and all subsequent versions.

Using antivirus software

Virus protection software does two things: First, it recognizes known viruses and can eliminate these from your computer. It can erase files contaminated with the virus, or, at times, extract the virus from the file itself, leaving the file functional or at least repairable. Besides being able to recognize and nuke all the latest beasties known at the current time, antivirus programs understand the behavior of the executable files on your computer, and will take action if a file appears to be acting like a virus, such as carrying out lots of replicating commands or trying to write information to the boot sector of your hard drive. If an antivirus program thinks something is amiss on your computer, it can lock you out and prevent you from writing any data to your hard drive until the program is satisfied that all is safe and well.

Types of antivirus protection

Antivirus programs protect your computer in two ways. First, they acts as a sentry, preventing viruses from making their way into your computer. These programs stand guard all the time, operating in the background while you work. When a program file is opened, the antivirus software will examine it for viruses. When you boot up or shut down, these programs automatically scan your memory for viruses, and system files as well. Antivirus programs sometimes balk when you try to install software, because you are introducing unknown, executable files to the system. A good antivirus program can be easily disabled and enabled, so that you can install software that you are sure comes from a reputable source.

The other way good antivirus programs protect your computer is by periodically searching for and destroying viruses found on the system. Typically, you can have the antivirus software automatically perform checks at regular intervals, or you can run the check yourself. Virus programs that operate in the background can, at times, conflict with other programs you may also have running in the background.

Tip If you experience a lot of system crashes, try disabling your antivirus program temporarily. Just don't forget to turn the antivirus program back on before you download more files or need to perform a routine check!

Creating an emergency boot floppy

One of the best defenses against viruses is to create an Emergency Boot Floppy Disk. Many virus programs, such as McAfee and Dr. Solomon, include a program to create emergency boot disks. (Dr. Solomon's actually comes with a bootable virus-killer floppy that you can use right out of the box.) An emergency boot disk includes antivirus files with the capability to locate and destroy all known viruses. If you suspect your computer may be infected, boot up from this floppy. The floppy would then search your computer for viruses and destroy them. Once your computer has been checked and cleaned of viruses, you can remove the floppy and boot normally. Having a way to boot up virus-free is important because many viruses attack during the boot process and often have the potential to reduce your hard drive to a barren wasteland.

Updating your antivirus software

A good antivirus program needs to be updateable. You should be able to quickly receive new data files that recognize the most recent viruses. Some antivirus programs facilitate automatic updating, logging on and downloading new lists as they become available from the company's Web site. (Dr. Solomon, and McAfee are good examples of this.) Antivirus data from three years ago is as valuable as tickets to the 1994 World Series.

Preventing viruses by knowing your software sources

One way to protect yourself from a virus is to download software only from reputable and well-known sources, such as established software companies with a reputation to uphold. You can take chances with most graphic, sound, video, or other nonexecutable files, but exert more caution with programs. Also be cautious when downloading files that might include macros, such as word processing documents and spreadsheets. When downloading software, you may to want to read the description to see if it was checked for viruses first. If not, run a virus check on it as soon as you download it. If the downloaded file is zipped, make sure your virus checker is configured to check compressed files as well. The instruction for checking compressed files is often "Read archives." When downloading from the Internet, please remember: There's no such thing as a guaranteed, 100 percent virus-free program.

Surveying antivirus software

Numerous programs are available to protect your computer from virus attack. A 30-day trial version of one such program, Panda Antivirus Platinum for Windows, is included on the *Internet Bible* CD-ROM.

Note We're showing an antivirus program for Windows here, primarily because Windows systems tend to be attacked by viruses more often. This is not necessarily because Windows is less secure than other operating systems, but it does appear to be specifically targeted more frequently. Viruses can attack any computer system, so make sure you are using a reliable antivirus program no matter what type of computer and OS you have.

One of the good things about Panda's Antivirus program is that it doesn't seem to affect overall system operations as much as other antivirus programs. Some programs severely bog down system performance, but Panda's product appears to have minimal impact on the speed and efficiency at which Windows runs.

Panda Antivirus installs quickly; during installation it asks some questions about how you want to configure the program. For instance, it asks if you want the program to search system files for viruses every time you boot up your computer. This will slow the boot-up process somewhat, but it can also protect you from some of the most dangerous types of viruses. You will have to restart your system after Panda Antivirus is done installing.

Note If you are using the trial version of Panda Antivirus from this book's CD, you'll first see some information about the trial copy and an initial window with options to register. Click Start Panda Antivirus in this window to display the window shown in Figure 17-9.

After restarting your computer, Panda Antivirus immediately scans the memory for viruses. Finding none, it will then see display a dialog box like that shown in Figure 17-9. You can select items from the list to scan, including the following:

✦ **Memory**. Many viruses live in memory when the computer is running.

✦ **Removable disk drives**. This can include floppy drives, Zip drives, tape drives, and other rewritable, removable media. Master Boot Record viruses can live on floppy disks and infect your system if you inadvertently reboot while they are in drive A.

✦ **Hard drives**. All local hard drives and partitions should be scanned regularly.

✦ **CD-ROM drives**. Scan all new CDs you obtain to ensure they are clean *before* you install any software from them.

✦ **E-mail**. Many newer viruses live in e-mail messages, especially if you use Microsoft Outlook. When you select this item, all of your e-mail programs should be listed on the right side of the window. Panda scans all messages and attachments.

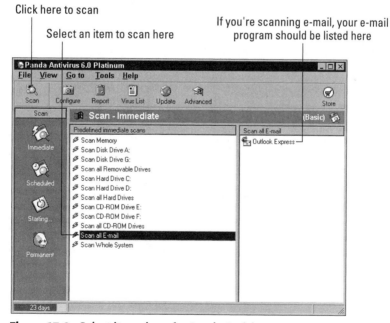

Figure 17-9: Select items here for Panda Antivirus to scan.

Of course, you can initiate a virus scan of your computer any time you want. To start a scan, select an item, such as your hard drive, floppy drive, or memory, and click the Scan button on the toolbar. If a virus is found, Panda can disinfect the source and produce a report. Once scanning finishes, click OK in the Scan dialog box to return to the main Panda window. When you close Panda Antivirus, it remains active on your computer and should automatically identify any known viruses that appear.

Tip Don't forget to update your antivirus program regularly. New viruses are being created all the time, and the only way to protect yourself from them is to regularly update your virus data files. Panda Antivirus includes an Update button on its main toolbar that automatically downloads the most recent antivirus information into your program's virus database.

Other antivirus programs

Panda Antivirus is just one virus-fighting program. Numerous others are available, and you can find many of them at some of the popular download sites mentioned earlier. Some good programs include:

✦ **BugScan**. Mountain Ridge Dataworks (www.mrdataworks.com) offers this antivirus package exclusively for Macintosh systems. BugScan doesn't have as many features as other packages, but it does scan your files for some of the most common types of viruses that infect Macs. It costs just $20, and is available as nonexpiring shareware. Registration gives you access to technical support.

✦ **F-Secure Anti-Virus**. Offered by F-Secure (www.datafellows.com), F-Secure Anti-Virus is available for a variety of operating systems including Windows, DOS, Macintosh, UNIX/Linux, and OS/2. Some versions offer a 90-day trial period; individual copies cost $99.

✦ **McAfee VirusScan**. McAfee (www.mcafee.com) offers one of the most popular antivirus programs for Windows computers. A 30-day trial copy is available for download from their site, as is an online tool that enables you to check your system over the Web. You can purchase the program for just $29.95. A version of McAfee VirusScan also accompanies the Windows 98 Plus! accessory package offered by Microsoft.

✦ **Norton AntiVirus**. Norton AntiVirus from Symantec (www.symantec.com) is another popular antivirus package available for Windows and Macintosh. The program costs $39.95 for the Windows version, and $69.95 for Macs. A 30-day trial is available for Windows.

Summary

In this chapter, you've learned how to find good software on the Web and how to track down what it is you really want. Also, you've found out how to keep track of favorite software sites, as well as the increasing collection of downloads that will accumulate on your hard drive. You've looked at FTP sites, which can be great sources of software and information, and you've seen how to get around in them. Finally, you've learned about computer viruses, what they are, how they can attack your computer, and what you can do to protect your computer from a virus attack.

✦　　✦　　✦

Finding the Best Online Audio and Video Sites

When multimedia first hit the Web and you could listen to music or watch video files delivered via the Internet, the experience, too often, was like listening to a dog sing: what's intriguing is not how well the dog sings but the fact that it sings at all. Today's more sophisticated Web surfer is only interested in audio and video that provides information he or she can't easily get anywhere else. In other words, Web surfers are interested in only the best sites for online audio and video — some of which we've highlighted in this chapter.

Using Various Video and Audio Formats

Two types of audio and video files are available on the Web:

✦ Downloadable files that must be saved to your computer's hard disk before they can be played

✦ Streaming files that play as they are sent to your computer

We'll take a look at both of these file types in more detail.

Playing nonstreaming formats

Nonstreaming, or downloadable, audio and video files are usually accessed through a link somewhere on the Web page. If they're in a format that your browser supports, or if you have the correct plug-in, a video or audio player will usually appear once the file is downloaded. You can then listen to or watch the file as often as you like, stopping, starting, and "rewinding" it as you please—though of course, because everything is digital, there's no actual rewinding going on. Figures 18-1 and 18-2 illustrate audio and video players at work.

Figure 18-1: Listening to downloaded audio files, such as MIDIs from your browser, usually brings up an audio player like this . . .

Figure 18-2: . . . whereas videos are generally shown in a small window like this one. (The size of the video display often depends on the power of your system and the capabilities of the plug-in.)

Audio formats

Sound files come in a number of different formats with a variety of filename extensions, such as .aiff, .au, .wav, .mid, and .mp3. Some browsers can play these formats automatically while others require you to install a plug-in. Of these, MP3 is growing in popularity much more rapidly, with more and more software—and now hardware too—tailored specifically to users of MP3 audio.

Waveform formats

The audio files with the extensions .wav, .au, .aiff, and .mp3 are *waveform* formats. That means the files are created much like a tape recording: A voice or a musical instrument is captured by a microphone attached to a computer, which records the sound digitally.

Some waveform file types were designed for specific types of computers:

✦ **AIFF** stands for Audio Interchange File Format. Developed by Apple for storing high-quality sampled audio and musical instrument information, it's also used by various types of professional audio software. Most AIFF files were created on a Macintosh.

✦ **AU** is the predominant UNIX sound format. It's common on the Internet because many of the machines on which the Internet is based are UNIX.

✦ **WAV** is the Windows standard for waveform recordings, so when you see a .wav file, you can assume it was created on a PC.

✦ **MP3** is more formally known as MPEG Audio Layer Three (for more on MPEG see the following section on video formats). MP3 is not designed with any one computer platform in mind. It's very popular on the Internet because it can compress near-CD-quality sound by a factor of 12 while maintaining the same high fidelity, or even more, while retaining reasonable sound quality. Several companies — such as Diamond Multimedia — now make portable MP3 players to take advantage of this new medium.

Synthetic audio formats

Synthetic audio formats differ from waveform files in that they only contain instructions, rather than an actual recording, which are interpreted by your computer's sound card. In this respect, the synthetic audio file works like a piano roll for a player piano.

✦ **MIDI**, which is short for *Musical Instrument Digital Interface*, is a type of synthetic audio file. MIDIs have one great advantage over waveform files, and one great disadvantage. The advantage is that they are much, much smaller than most waveform files. A high-quality recording of a complete piece of music in waveform format could take hours to download; a MIDI file of the same piece of music could be downloaded very quickly. Even a tiny 5K MIDI file can produce several minutes of music.

The big disadvantage to MIDI files is that they're at the mercy of the equipment receiving them. A synthesizer or a high-quality computer sound card plugged in to a good set of speakers can make a MIDI file of an orchestral work sound like a live recording of the Berlin Philharmonic. An old sound card from just a few years ago, on the other hand, will make that same MIDI file sound like someone batting out a tune on a $20 electronic keyboard.

Video formats

Video files, too, come in a variety of formats:

✦ **AVI**, which stands for Audio/video interleave, is the file format used by Video for Windows.

✦ **MOV**, which is short for movie, is the format used by Apple Computer's QuickTime video system. Although QuickTime was originally developed for Macintosh computers, players are also available for PCs. QuickTime can also be used for sound files or graphics, if you have the appropriate plug-ins.

✦ MPEG, which stands for Moving Pictures Experts Group, is the video equivalent of JPEG. This format compresses sound and movie files to make them easier to move around the Internet.

To learn more about JPEGs and other graphic formats, check out chapter 19, "Finding the Best Graphics on the Web."

Streaming files

The biggest problem with some audio and most video files is that they tend to be large — so large that the average user really, really has to want them before he or she is willing to take the time necessary to download them.

This problem was alleviated somewhat by the development of streaming audio and video. Instead of having to download an entire file before it can be played, streaming audio and video players can play a file while it's still being downloaded. Streaming technology not only makes audio and video playback more accessible, but it even has made possible live radio and video broadcasts over the Internet. Many television and radio networks now broadcast simultaneously over the Internet.

Tip Do you want to find out if your favorite radio station is broadcasting on the Internet? Check out Broadcast.com (`http://broadcast.com/`). It's a good place to find many live streaming programs.

Streaming audio works reasonably well on average systems; streaming video tends to look more like a slide show. Streaming files are also at the mercy of Web traffic; if overall Internet traffic is high, or if many people are trying to access the same streaming file that you are, the signal can be of very poor quality, and may not even work at all. But as more and more people gain high-speed access to the Web, look for increased availability of streaming audio and streaming video.

Just like ordinary audio and video files, streaming audio and video come in more than one format, each of which requires its own plug-in (naturally). We'll talk about three of those plug-ins in the next section.

Playing Multimedia Files

Numerous programs are available to let you play multimedia files that you find online. We'll discuss three of these programs here: RealNetworks' RealPlayer G2, Apple's QuickTime 4, and Microsoft's Windows Media Player 6. Each has its own proprietary format for streaming files, which means there's a good chance you will end up using more than one. For instance, Film.com (www.film.com) requires you to use RealPlayer to view movie trailers on their site, whereas at the Star Wars Web site (www.starwars.com) you must use Apple QuickTime. Still other sites offer streaming files in multiple formats; NASA (www.nasa.gov) offers streaming media in a choice of RealPlayer or Windows Media Player formats.

You can also use each of these programs to play nonstreaming files. These can include the file types described earlier in this chapter, such as MPEG and MP3, or they can be proprietary nonstreaming formats specifically designed for one program or the other. Which one you ultimately use will depend less on your own preference and more on what is required by the sites you like to visit. In fact, if you use multimedia on the Web for very long, you will probably end up with two or all three of these plug-ins installed whether you like it or not.

Listening to RealPlayer

RealPlayer is probably the most popular plug-in for playing streaming video and audio on the Web. That's because more sites use RealPlayer formats than any of the other plug-ins. The RealPlayer also plays other types of popular media, including MP3 files, and is available for Windows and Macintosh.

At the RealPlayer Web site, www.real.com, which is shown in Figure 18-3, you can download the latest version and find dozens of links to sites that use RealPlayer.

Note Netscape Communicator 4.7 comes with RealPlayer, so if you use Netscape 4.7, you probably already have the RealPlayer installed.

The best thing about RealPlayer is that it works in the background; whenever you click a link to a streaming audio or video file, RealPlayer automatically launches. You can open the RealPlayer window at any time by double-clicking its icon in the Windows system tray or selecting it from the Windows Start menu. If you use a Macintosh, you can locate it in a program folder of your hard drive.

When open, the size of the window may vary, depending on what is selected in the View menu of the menu bar. You can change the view by clicking the View menu and selecting or deselecting various options. If desktop space is a concern, you may want to choose the Compact setting.

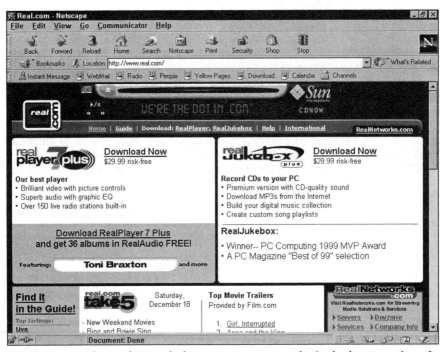

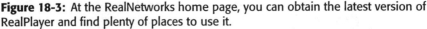

Figure 18-3: At the RealNetworks home page, you can obtain the latest version of RealPlayer and find plenty of places to use it.

In addition to playing streamed audio and video from various Web sites, RealPlayer G2 contains some content of its own. When you open RealPlayer in Normal view, you will notice some buttons on the left side of the window with names of various news and entertainment resources (see Figure 18-4). These are called the destination buttons, which will link you to a variety of online information.

You can also get the slightly more sophisticated RealPlayer Plus, but you have to pay for it. RealPlayer 7 Plus includes enhanced audio and video playback quality and 150 built-in radio stations. At press time there was also a special offer of 36 free albums in RealPlayer format if you purchase RealPlayer. Unfortunately, one of our authors experienced difficulty trying to actually obtain the albums, so we recommend that your buying decision not hinge on such an offer.

Figure 18-4: Listen to and view streaming media using the RealPlayer.

Viewing QuickTime 4

Another popular streaming media player is QuickTime 4, developed by Apple. It's available for Macs (of course) and Windows. If you've bought a new Macintosh recently, QuickTime should already be installed. Otherwise, you can download it at www.apple.com.

Although RealPlayer seems to rule the streaming audio market, QuickTime is more popular among those who offer streaming video. Many movie studios, for instance, offer online movie trailers in QuickTime format. QuickTime is also used by many Web sites that offer virtual reality (VR) elements, such as those discussed later in this chapter.

QuickTime is a full-featured multimedia package. When you install QuickTime 4, you can select from a wide array of features, including:

- ✦ **Internet Extras**. Supports Internet-based VR objects, as discussed later in this chapter.
- ✦ **Still Image**. Provides a viewer for still graphics such as jpeg and gif.
- ✦ **Effects**. Adds support for visual effects.
- ✦ **Music**. Enables QuickTime to support MIDI and other music forms.
- ✦ **Authoring**. Adds tools for creating your own QuickTime content.
- ✦ **Capture**. Captures media, such as still images of a movie.
- ✦ **QuickDraw 3D**. Installs QuickDraw 3D.
- ✦ **QuickTime for Java**. Adds QuickTime Java support.
- ✦ **Diagnostics**. Helps you troubleshoot problems you may encounter with some media in QuickTime.

The Quicktime setup program gives you three installation options: full, minimum, and custom. The full installation will set up everything, of course, but more hard disk space will be required. If you hard disk is cramped for space, you can select the Quicktime components individually by choosing the Custom option. To get the most out of your Web experience, we suggest that at a minimum you install the Internet Extras, Music, and QuickTime components.

As you know, QuickTime can handle many types of media. But its forte is video and virtual reality. Figure 18-5 shows a sample movie being played using QuickTime 4.

Figure 18-5: Apple's QuickTime 4 is a popular player for video media.

Watching Windows Media Player 6

Trust Microsoft to develop its own tool for streaming audio and video. Called Windows Media Player (or WiMP, for short), it has one advantage over RealPlayer and QuickTime: it's built right in to Internet Explorer 5. However, more sites still use RealPlayer and QuickTime than WiMP. And, of course, if you use a Macintosh or Linux you won't be able to use Windows Media Player.

WiMP can play virtually any form of digital audio or video file available online today, but as you can see in Figure 18-6, its interface is plain and features are light. Microsoft is reportedly working on an upgraded version of the Media Player, and among the new features being considered are additional MP3 capabilities such as playlists and library management, which are tools you can use to organize the MP3 files you download or record. But as of this writing, WiMP 6 is the best we get.

Figure 18-6: Windows Media Player can handle virtually any form of media the Web can throw at it.

The main strength of WiMP is that it can handle so many different types of media. And when you encounter a type of audio or video file that the Media Player doesn't know how to play, it automatically downloads a code from Microsoft that enables it to play the file.

Finding Great Online Audio and Video

Because they're the easiest way to add audio and video to a Web site, downloadable audio and video files can be found all over the Web. Some of the most interesting sites are those that provide streaming audio and video, so that's what we'll concentrate on.

The best sources of links to sites using streaming audio and video are the home pages of RealNetworks (http://www.real.com/) and WindowsMedia.com (http://windowsmedia.microsoft.com/). Because RealNetworks and Microsoft are the purveyors of the two best-known players, they are eager to show off their software.

RealNetworks' manages several of the best sites themselves, including the following:

Film.com

One of the favorite uses of video on the Web is to post movie clips or trailers, and this is one of the best sites to find them. Film.com (at www.film.com, of course) includes not only trailers from the latest Hollywood blockbusters in RealVideo format but clips from classic movies.

Film.com is a showcase for both streaming video and streaming audio. Along with reviews, commentary, and movie news and discussion, this site also features movie soundtracks.

MusicNet

If the most common use of streaming video is showing movie trailers and clips, the most common use of streaming audio is playing music. MusicNet (www.musicnet.com) is one of the best-organized and most eclectic of these sites, offering clips in genres ranging from alternative to country, from a variety of new albums (see Figure 18-7).

In addition to current albums, you can access an archive of past albums. More than 1,000 audio clips are available in all. MusicNet also has a growing emphasis on MP3 music.

When you call up a particular album, you'll often see an additional link that takes you to a Web site devoted to that particular artist, composer, or style of music, where you may very well find still more RealAudio or other audio files to enjoy.

Be Careful with Copyright

Audio and video clips found on the World Wide Web may be easy to obtain, but that doesn't mean you can use them any way you want. Many Web users forget that most audio and video files are protected by copyright; it's against the law to use copyrighted material without permission. Viewing or hearing a clip is perfectly acceptable, but putting the clip on your own Web site without permission is not.

How can you tell if material on the Internet is copyrighted or not? Many clips come with a copyright notice. Elsewhere on the site you may find additional copyright information, which may grant you usage rights for specific purposes. If you're still not sure whether a sound or video file is copyrighted, it's best to simply ask. E-mail the Webmaster of the site where you found the material and ask if it's copyrighted, who owns the copyright, and (if the copyright belongs to the Webmaster or site owner) if you can have permission to use it. Be very specific about your plans for the clip; this information helps the copyright owner decide whether or not you can use it.

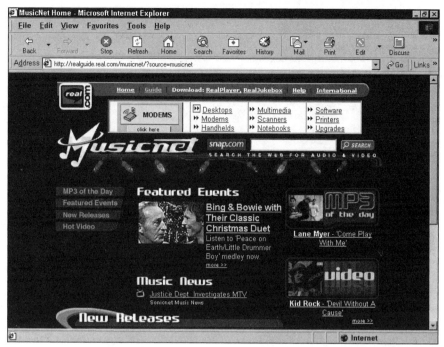

Figure 18-7: No matter what your musical tastes (well, almost), MusicNet offers high-quality stereo cuts from recent albums for you to enjoy.

LiveConcerts

Not all music on the Internet has been previously recorded; increasingly, you can listen to live concerts using streaming audio (and sometimes watch, using streaming video). RealNetworks' LiveConcerts site (http://www.liveconcerts. com) is a good place to find links to upcoming live events (see Figure 18-8).

Better yet, past events are archived, so you can hear that live concert The Derailers gave at the House of Blues in New Orleans in January even though you didn't hear about it until March.

LiveConcerts also includes press conferences, interviews, and other fascinating files drawn from the world of music.

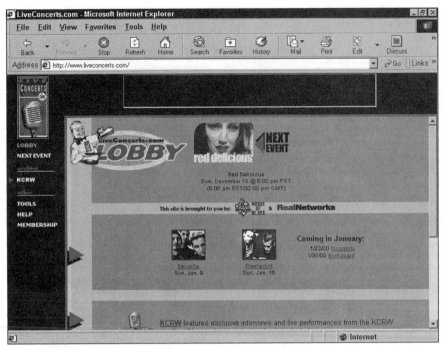

Figure 18-8: You say your favorite band is playing in California and you just can't make it? If you're lucky, and your favorite band is as wired as it ought to be, you'll be able to catch the concert right here on the Web.

Getting Your Favorite MP3 Tunes

If there is any form of media online that can truly be called "Hot," it is MP3. As mentioned earlier, MP3 files offer near-CD-quality playback using a fraction of the storage space. Consider this: When you buy a music CD at the local record store, the music is recorded in a format called *CD Audio*. A single CD can hold just 74 minutes of CD Audio music, tops. But if you record the music in MP3 format, that same disc could hold over *14 hours* of music with little or no discernible loss of quality.

Let's look at it another way. Suppose you want to buy a copy of the song *Brick House* by The Commodores. The song is about three and a half minutes long, and if you download it in MP3, it will use about 4MB. In standard CD audio format, the same song would require roughly 50MB! Few people are willing to download a file that large, but 4MB is pretty reasonable, even if you have a relatively slow 28.8 Kbps connection.

> **Note**
>
> Many audiophiles point out that some sound quality, however imperceptible, is lost in MP3. A more noticeable hit in sound quality also occurs if the MP3 is recorded at a lower rate to minimize storage space. Still, most of the lost quality is beyond the range of human hearing, so this seems like a small price to pay for music that can be exchanged over the Internet so easily.

So, now that you know what MP3 files are, and you have downloaded some songs to your hard drive, what can you do with them? Unless you sit in front of your computer most of the day, music that can play only on your PC isn't very useful. Here are some other things you can do with MP3 files:

✦ **Download them into a portable MP3 player**. Numerous companies now sell portable MP3 players, such as Diamond Multimedia (www.diamondmm.com) and Creative Labs (www.americas.creative.com). See the following section on choosing an MP3 player.

✦ **Record them onto a CD in MP3 format**. A few companies, such as the MamboX MP3 CD player (www.mambox.com) are developing hybrid CD players that can also read MP3 files. Most CD-recording software enables you to record MP3s onto a data CD, and in this format a single disc can hold many hours of music.

✦ **Convert them to CD Audio using an MP3 Decoder**. Some programs, such as Adaptec's (www.adaptec.com) Easy CD Creator 4 Deluxe, include built-in decoders that convert MP3 files into CD Audio format as you burn them onto a recordable CD. This process enables them to be played in any existing CD player, but you also lose the space efficiency of MP3.

Choosing an MP3 player

If you decide to buy an MP3 player, here are some things to keep in mind:

✦ **Size.** MP3 players can be extremely small; just make sure your finger can push those tiny buttons!

✦ **Storage.** This is probably the most important thing to consider. We recommend getting a player with at least 64MB of storage. A definite plus is anything that utilizes a popular form of removable media, such as SmartMedia or CompactFlash cards already used in many digital cameras.

✦ **Interface.** How does it connect to your computer? Does it use a serial port, USB, or Firewire port? Does your computer have an available port of the correct type? If not, you won't be able to download music into the player.

✦ **Software/Compatibility.** Make sure the player works with your operating system and that it has some software to help you configure the player.

MP3.com

Sources for MP3 music are cropping up everywhere, but almost all of them are online.

One of the most popular sources is MP3.com (`www.mp3.com`). MP3.com is an excellent one-stop location for filling many of your MP3 needs. The main screen of the site looks a lot like many popular search engines. The site includes music categories that you can click to brows for available MP3 music.

MP3.com offers quite a bit of free music, mostly from lesser-known independent artists. When you locate a song that looks interesting, you can first listen to a streaming audio version of it to decide if it is something you might be interested in. If you like it, click the Download link to download an MP3 version.

In addition to music, MP3.com includes news and information about MP3 technology, including players and other hardware that might be of interest to you.

Touring the World Through a Virtual Window

Everyone has an idea about what the Internet is. Some people see it as little more than an interactive replacement for television, while others see it as a tool to expand the way they do business in the world. But one of the most common things said about this fabulous medium is that it can be a window that looks out from your home or office upon the rest of the world.

Sounds good, doesn't it? But what exactly does it mean to open a window to the rest of the world? This entire book seeks to answer that question, but for now let's take a very literal approach. How can you use the Internet to *see* things that are far away and otherwise unreachable?

One way is to take virtual reality tours on the Web. *Virtual reality* (VR) refers to an unreal world inside a computer that is meant to mimic the real world as closely as possible. Developers create three-dimensional realms and then publish them for all the world to see and tour. VR tours abound on the Internet. Some are mundane tours of new car cockpits, while others take you to fabulous places that most of us will never see, such as the International Space Station.

Another way to see far-off places through the Internet is via Web cameras or "Web cams." Thousands of people and organizations around the world have connected digital cameras to the Web, and you can see what the cams are pointing at simply by visiting a Web page. Web cams are fun, and, unlike VR tours, don't really require anything spectacular in terms of technology.

The next two sections show you how to tour the world through virtual — and actual — reality.

Experiencing virtual reality on the Web

Virtual reality on the Web is still pretty new, primarily because it usually requires a high level of bandwidth that most people don't have. It is actually most common on the Web sites of auto manufacturers, who use QuickTime 4 to facilitate VR tours of new car interiors.

Another, more advanced way to facilitate virtual reality on the Web is to use a page programmed in Virtual Reality Markup Language (VRML). VRML enables developers to produce a three-dimensional model on the Web. Your browser requires a special plug-in to use it, so if you visit a VRML page, you will probably be prompted to download a VRML 2.0 plug-in.

One of the most interesting virtual reality sites that we've found online is the VR tour of the International Space Station (ISS) offered on NASA's Web site (`http://spaceflight.nasa.gov/station/`). NASA offers two versions of the tour: One is a VR tour of the station's interior, and the other is a 3D VRML tour of the exterior. To take the VRML tour, visit the page listed previously and do the following:

1. Scroll down the page and click the link called Space Station VRML.

2. If this is your first time viewing a VRML site, click the Download plug-in link, and select a plug-in to download.

   If you cannot download a plug-in here, visit the Microsoft or Netscape Web site (depending on which browser you are using) and locate a VRML plug-in there. Sorry, but there are no VRML plug-ins for Opera.

3. In the VRML Models list box, select a model to download. In our example, we are downloading the larger Graphics Enhanced model.

4. The ISS_VRML page should open, as shown in Figure 18-9.

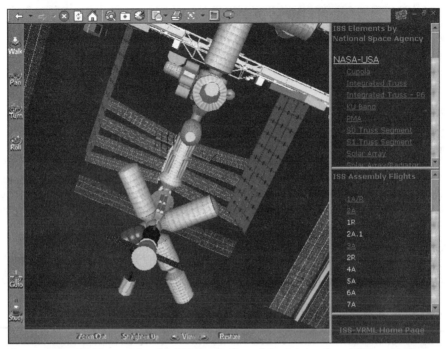

Figure 18-9: NASA provides this VRML 3D tour of the International Space Station on its Web site.

Most VRML sites include controls to help you move around within the model. Experiment with the site a bit, but don't get lost!

Finding and visiting Web cams

Web cameras have many uses. Some record scenic vistas while others broadcast heavy traffic areas during the rush hour. Some show items of scientific interest, while others are, well, more esoteric in nature.

Most Web cams are set to refresh automatically at a specific interval, ranging from once every ten seconds up to once per day. In Figure 18-10 you can see images recorded by the Rat Cam, which is located at the Oregon Museum of Science and Industry (www.omsi.edu). This camera monitors the daily life of some rats living in OMSI's Life Sciences lab.

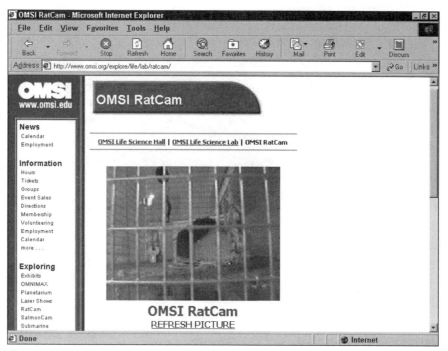

Figure 18-10: The OMSI Rat Cam provides a window to the daily life of rats in a cage.

> **Tip**
>
> If you have Windows 95 or higher and IE4 or higher, you can set a favorite Web cam as a desktop item. Simply right-click anywhere on the cam in Internet Explorer and choose Set as Desktop Item from the menu that appears. Now the cam will appear on your Windows desktop, even when your Web browser is closed. The cam can be refreshed any time your Internet connection is active by right-clicking it and choosing Refresh.

Figure 18-11 shows a camera maintained by the Oregon Department of Transportation (www.odot.state.or.us), which monitors this local mountain pass. Many transportation departments use Web cams to keep tabs on the condition of roads and intersections.

A number of excellent Web cam lists are available. If you're interested in finding Web cams that watch some truly off-beat stuff, visit these sites:

```
http://www.webcamworld.com/
http://www.ewebcamera.com/
http://www.camcity.com/
```

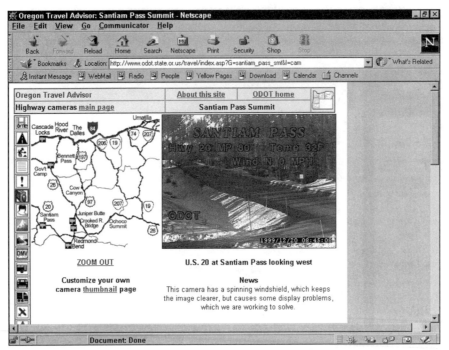

Figure 18-11: This Web cam monitors conditions at a local mountain pass.

Summary

Audio and video add immeasurably to the excitement of the Web—if you've got the bandwidth to enjoy them. Thousands of sites offer files for downloading, and more and more sites are also offering streaming audio and video. If you want to add motion and sound to the existing text and graphics of your Web-surfing space, start by downloading RealPlayer G2, QuickTime, and Windows Media Player—and then explore. For you, the Web will suddenly become an even more exciting place.

✦   ✦   ✦

Finding the Best Graphics on the Web

The most important element of any Web page is its text, because text is what communicates ideas — and if a Web page isn't communicating anything, why waste time looking at it? Some folks, however, would no doubt say that a picture is worth a thousand words — and generations of designers would point out that, no matter how good your text, people won't read it if it looks boring. That's where graphics come in. They spruce up Web pages by illustrating ideas, catching the roving eye of the passing surfer, and in general sprucing up the aesthetic appeal of the Internet. As a result, the Web is awash in graphics of all sorts. Whether you're looking for buttons and backgrounds for your own Web page, or photos and clip art you can use on your computer as wallpaper, add to documents, or print out for your own amusement, you can find them on the World Wide Web.

Understanding Graphic Formats: GIF, JPEG, and PNG

Today's browsers can view a number of graphic formats. By far the most common are GIFs and JPEGs, but a new format designed to be especially Web-friendly, PNG, is gaining ground.

GIF

GIF stands for Graphic Interchange Format. This format for efficiently transmitting images from computer to computer was popularized by CompuServe in the 1980s. Because it was so well-known, it was adopted by the designers of the World Wide Web in the early 1990s and, as a result, many images on the Web are in GIF format.

GIF images are limited to a maximum of 256 colors, or eight bits per pixel. They're best suited for black-and-white line art and text, images with a limited number of distinct colors, graphics with sharp edges, and graphics with text over the top of them. One problem with using GIF images is that the compression method used to make them — LZW — is patented, raising a few legal concerns.

JPEG

The palette limitation of GIFs is one reason that the JPEG (Joint Photographic Experts Group) format has become extremely popular, especially among photographers, artists, and anyone else who wants a high-quality image, with color as close to the original as possible. JPEGs can display 16.7 million colors, or up to 24 bits per pixel.

JPEG files are also often smaller than GIF files, because the JPEG compression system enables you to decide how much you want to compress an image file — although, the smaller you make it, the more you degrade the picture. Still, you can often get acceptable results with a file noticeably smaller than a typical GIF file, which means your Web page will load faster.

JPEG compression is better at dealing with photographs than with diagrams and text: it doesn't always reproduce sharp edges well. As a result, many Web designers use JPEG primarily for photographs and the GIF formats for most other graphic elements, such as the image shown in Figure 19-1.

PNG

PNG (pronounced "ping") stands for Portable Network Graphics. Designed specifically as an improvement on GIF, PNG offers slightly better compression than GIF and can display millions of colors like a JPEG. It also allows for variable transparency of colors, control of image brightness no matter what kind of computer you're using, and a better method of progressive display. (You see the graphic load while it gradually gains resolution. The graphic doesn't really load any faster, but it seems that way because you're not staring at a blank screen.) PNG also offers "lossless" compression, which means it can be compressed and restored and compressed again without any loss of quality, unlike JPEGs.

PNGs combine the benefits of both GIF and JPEG, reproducing images with edges as sharp as GIF and photographs as high-quality as JPEG. Plus, nothing about the format is patented, so licensing is not an issue. PNG has been recommended and approved as a graphic format by the World Wide Web Consortium, and it is supported by Internet Explorer 5 and Netscape Communicator 4.7.

A good place to learn all about the new graphic format, PNG, is at the PNG home page, `http://www.cdrom.com/pub/png/`.

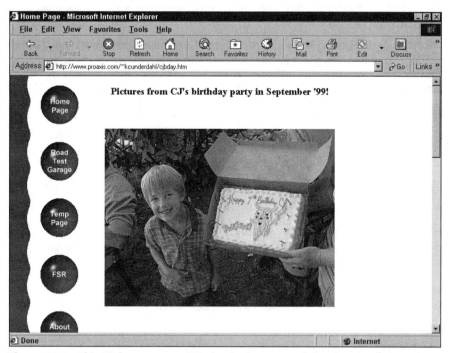

Figure 19-1: This Web page uses GIFs for the buttons at left, whereas the photograph at right is a JPEG.

Displaying and Saving Images

You generally don't have to think twice about displaying an image you find on the Web; your browser does it automatically. Occasionally, however, you may run into an image saved in a format that your browser can't display. In such a case, you may have to install a special plug-in to view the image. Most Web sites that require the use of a plug-in also provide a link to a site where you can obtain that plug-in.

Some popular picture formats that may require you to download a plug-in or special graphics program include .tif, .jpg, .pic, and .bmp.

Digital images are everywhere — but they're not all freely available for you to use on your Web page. Something, too, many Web surfers forget is that most pictures belong to someone — and that someone has to give you permission to use them. It's called "copyright," and using copyrighted material without the permission of the copyright owner is against the law.

Sometimes it's hard to tell if material on the Internet is copyrighted or not (some material is in the public domain). The best way to be sure is simply to ask. If you see an image on someone else's Web site you'd like to use for your own purposes, e-mail the Webmaster of that site and ask if the image is copyrighted. If it is, ask who owns the copyright, and (if the copyright belongs to the Webmaster or whoever owns the site she or he runs) if you can have permission to use it. Explain clearly what you intend to do with it. If you're just saving it on your computer, there's probably no problem, but if you want to reproduce it in a calendar that you're going to sell at $20 each, the copyright owner is definitely going to want a piece of the action.

The process of saving images from the Internet to your computer is easy. In both Netscape and Internet Explorer, right-click the picture you want to save (on a Mac, select the picture and hold the mouse button down until a dialogue box appears); choose Save Image As (in Netscape) or Save Picture As (in Explorer) as shown in Figure 19-2; and then designate the file folder in which you want to save the picture and type in a name to save the picture under in the usual Save As dialog box.

Figure 19-2: Use the shortcut menu to save pictures to a more permanent location.

You can save any graphic file this way, from a photograph to clip art to a button, icon, or line.

Both Netscape and Internet Explorer also give you the opportunity to save an image as your Windows wallpaper. Wallpaper in Windows can be used to decorate the desktop background. You can do this by right-clicking and choosing Set as Wallpaper.

Finding Images to Download

As you know, the World Wide Web is full of images — so full of images that finding the one you want can be difficult.

Fortunately, several sites offer organized collections of images. A good way to find these sites is just to search for "clip art" using your favorite Internet search engine.

Another good way to find graphics related to a specific topic is to search for Web sites related to that topic. Once again, though, remember to ask for permission before copying any graphics to your Web page.

 To learn how to use search engines to find graphics and other goodies on the Internet, take a look at Chapter 16, "Using Search Engines."

Some good sources of graphics

Dozens, if not hundreds, of sites on the Web are devoted to graphics. Many of them are commercial sites that sell collections of clip art, photographs, or other images. However, plenty of other sites also offer graphics free for the personal use of its visitors.

XOOM

ZDNet is a major source of information on everything to do with computers, and its XOOM software library, at `http://zdnet.xoom.com`, is a major source of free graphics.

Just click the type of image you're looking for, and you'll be presented with a list of subjects. Click the subject, and you'll see a catalog of thumbnail-sized images. Click the one that interests you to bring up a full-sized image.

XOOM also boasts a large collection of sound files.

Filez

Filez (yes, that's the way they spell files), at `http://www.filez.com/zhub.shtml`, isn't really a graphics-oriented site — it's a specialized search engine. Whereas the search engines discussed in Chapter 16 seek out Web sites according to the criteria you provide, the Filez search engine, which is shown in Figure 19-3, seeks out files — everything from games to utilities to, yes, graphics. It's different, too, in that it doesn't search the Web, it searches FTP directories.

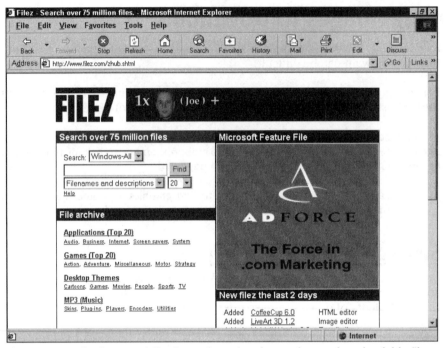

Figure 19-3: Filez is a specialized search engine that seeks out downloadable files instead of Web sites.

To conduct a search for graphics using Filez:

1. To narrow your search, click the Search list box to select the type of category in which you would like to search (such as, things compatible with your operating system, or types of media like graphics, movies, or sound).

2. In the search box, enter the word you want to search for (for example, "mountains").

3. Choose the number of matches you want to list from the final list box.

4. Click Find.

The results appear as shown in Figure 19-4. Filez gives you the name of each file, its size, the date it was last modified, and a description.

Clicking one of these listings brings up another page showing you where you can download the file; clicking the filename again retrieves it and displays it in your browser. From there, it's a simple matter of right-clicking and saving it to store the file permanently on your hard drive.

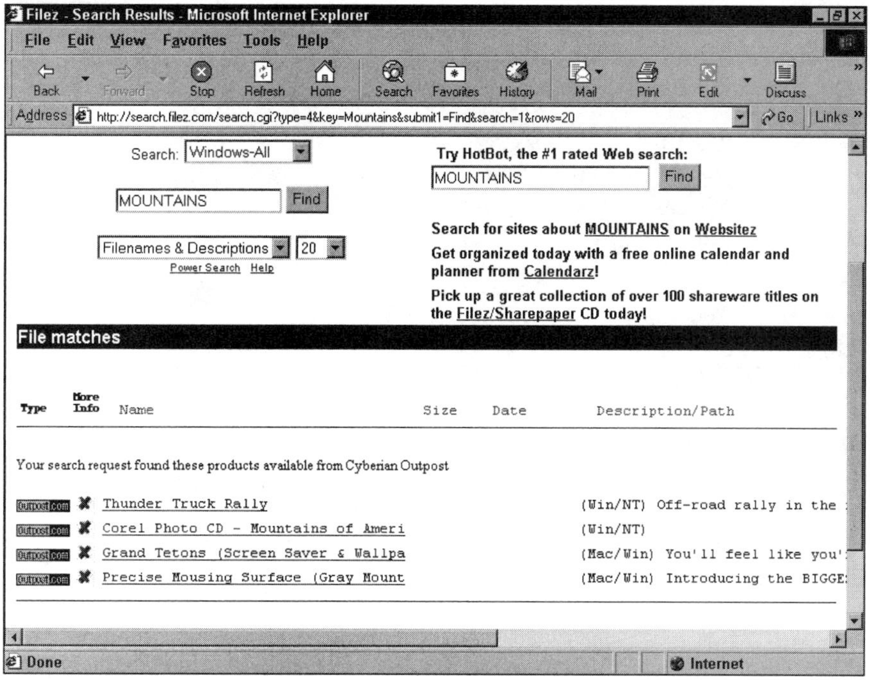

Figure 19-4: Looking for pictures of mountains — or anything else? Filez is a powerful tool for finding them anywhere on the Internet.

Whenever you're looking for an image of a specific sort, you'll find Filez an immensely useful tool.

NASA Photo Gallery

If you're looking for graphics related to space and aviation, then you definitely have to pay a visit to NASA's online photo gallery (http://www.nasa.gov/gallery/photo/), where you can find magnificent astronomical photos — images from manned and unmanned space flights and pictures from decades of aeronautical research, which are freely available, for the most part, without copyright restriction.

In addition, from this site you can access non-NASA sites having space or aeronautical photos, such as the European Space Agency's collections of photos taken by its Earth-observation satellites. From photos of the space shuttle to stunning images of the planets to pictures taken under the sea, the NASA Photo Gallery has them all (see Figure 19-5).

Figure 19-5: This stunning image of astronaut Edwin Aldrin on the surface of the moon is easily accessible online, along with many others, thanks to NASA. Many of them are available in both GIF and JPEG formats.

Elated Button Kits

One of the most common reasons people search for graphics on the Web is to add them to their own Web sites. As a result, many sites are devoted to meeting this need.

Unique buttons are highly prized by Web-site designers, and dozens of terrific designs, both regular and animated, are available for free from Elated Communications Ltd., in the form of button kits (http://www.elated.com/toolbox/buttonkits/). The buttons are organized into themes, which makes it easier to find the ones that might interest you.

Click the theme that interests you and you'll see a display of all the buttons in that kit. Simply right-click each button you want and save it to your hard drive. From there, you can add it to your own Web page.

Elated does ask, if you use their buttons, that you provide a link from your page to theirs. Sounds fair!

The Graphic Station

Another good source of graphics for Web site designers is The Graphic Station, at `http://www.geocities.com/SiliconValley/6603/`, where hundreds of icons, bars, balls, lines and animations are available.

Clip Art Warehouse

Still another giant source of Web graphics is the Clip Art Warehouse, which has buttons, icons, backgrounds, animated GIFs, lines, and more. It's at `http://www.clipart.co.uk/`.

> You should follow an important rule whenever you use a graphic image from one of these sites: Save it to your computer and then add it to your Web site from there. Don't simply insert a link to the graphic. Those types of links will only slow down your Web page and the site you link to, and could eventually force the clip-art site to close down. Most of these sites contain a warning to that effect.

Other sites

Additional (though generally not quite as large) collections of public-domain images can be found at the following sites:

✦ Sunet (`ftp://ftp.sunet.se/pub/pictures/`). As you can tell by the URL, this is an FTP archive, not a Web page, but it boasts a huge collection of images ranging from fractals to fantasy art.

✦ Sunsite (`http://sunsite.doc.ic.ac.uk/media/visual/collections/funet-pics/jpeg/`). Another giant collection of images, divided into categories for easier browsing.

✦ Vol.it Image Archive (`ftp://ftp.volftp.vol.it/collection/gifs/`). Again, this is an FTP archive. It contains thousands of photos, images, and clip art.

Summary

Exciting images can be found all over the Web, and today's browsers make it easy for you to view and copy them to your computer. Just be sure that you have permission from the copyright owner if you plan to do more than just look at them. You can find dozens and dozens of Internet sites where you can obtain graphics, many for free, others for a (generally) low price. Whatever image you're looking for, chances are good you can find it somewhere online. Happy hunting!

✦   ✦   ✦

Finding People on the Internet

◆ ◆ ◆ ◆

In This Chapter

Finding e-mail addresses

Finding phone numbers

Using people search services

◆ ◆ ◆ ◆

Y ou know how it is. You're good friends with someone, and then one of you moves somewhere else. At first you call or write every month, then every few months, then you send the occasional card at Christmas, and then one year the card comes back marked "MOVED: ADDRESS UNKNOWN," and that's it. You've lost track of each other. You feel terrible about it, but what can you do?

Well, thanks to the Internet, you can do quite a lot. Tracking down people — even people who don't have an Internet account themselves — is easier than it has ever been. In this chapter, you'll look at some of the sites on the World Wide Web that can help you track down your long-lost friends . . . or that deadbeat cousin who owes you money.

Finding People

"Finding people" can mean different things to different people. You might consider someone "found" when you locate an e-mail address for him or her, or maybe you don't think someone is found until you've uncovered a phone number or even a street address.

Cross-Reference If you're lucky, the person you're looking for has a Web site or is mentioned on someone else's Web site. In this case, a search of the Web using search engines should turn them up. To learn more about how to use search engines, check out Chapter 16, "Using Search Engines."

Sometimes, however, ordinary searches turn up nothing, in which case you may need to turn to specialized search engines designed specifically to help you find people. Several of these exist on the Web. Most of them, as you might imagine, focus primarily on turning up an e-mail address for the person you're looking for.

It would be great if there were a central directory that contained everyone's e-mail addresses — but, alas, it doesn't exist yet. Instead, you generally have to hope that the person whose e-mail address you're looking for has done one of four things:

✦ Registered his or her e-mail addresses with one of the many "people-finder" search engines you'll look at in this chapter. Some such engines require you to provide your name and e-mail address before they'll even let you search. That helps them build their directory.

✦ Contributed to a Usenet newsgroup or e-mail discussion list. The people-finding search engines add information gleaned from those sources to their directories, too, and regular search engines can also turn them up.

✦ Posted their e-mail address to a Web site. Again, both people-finding search engines and regular Web search engines can locate names and e-mail addresses on Web pages.

✦ Obtained an account with an online service that feeds people search engines, such as America Online or CompuServe. Online services generally provide a way to search their databases for members' e-mail addresses.

Many of these search engines also provide "white pages" information: that is, the same information you could get out of the white pages of local telephone books — a phone number and sometimes even a street address.

Many also provide "yellow pages" information: that is, business listings divided into categories. You probably wouldn't turn to the yellow pages first to look for someone, however, unless you happen to know the name of his or her employer but don't know where the employer is located.

Tip Your search will be much easier if you have at least a general idea of where the person you're trying to find is located — ideally which city, but failing that, at least which state or province or, at the very worst, country. Anything you can do to narrow the search parameters makes it more likely you'll find the right person.

Finding friends and acquaintances has never been easier. There's one more caveat: Your searches may result in multiple instances of a single name, even if you narrow your search by location. So you still may not have found the one person you're looking for. But at least you've narrowed things down.

Note Just for fun, try looking up your own name. You may be surprised at what information about you is out there on the Internet. But don't be alarmed. Most sites offer ways for you to block or limit information.

Great People-Finding Sites

Here are some sites you'll want to try as you launch your search for your long-lost whatever on the Web:

Bigfoot

Bigfoot (http://www.bigfoot.com) boasts that it has the largest database of e-mail and white pages information on the Internet. If you know the name of the person you're searching for, you simply enter it in the Search box on the home page (see Figure 20-1), check the e-mail or white pages box to determine what kind of search you want to conduct, and click Search. Bigfoot's Web page is pretty busy, but it's an excellent resource nonetheless.

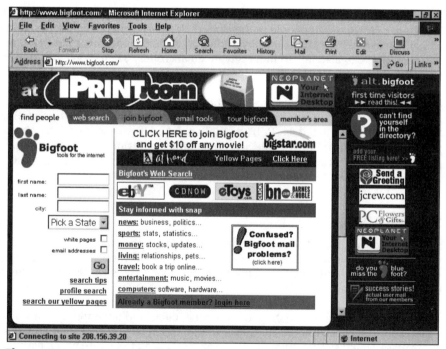

Figure 20-1: Enter a name, click Search, and Bigfoot provides you with a list of e-mail addresses or information from phone book white pages for people with the name you specify.

In addition to offering the e-mail directory and white pages, Bigfoot offers a number of additional services, including:

✦ A Web search engine

✦ Free e-mail accounts

✦ NeoPlanet — a Web software package for Windows users that combines the features of a Web browser, e-mail client, and chat in a compact, simple-to-use package.

Yahoo! People Search

Formerly known as Four11, Yahoo! People Search (`http://people.yahoo.com`) is another powerful directory service that features a refreshingly simple interface. It boasts millions of listings that anyone, registered or not, can make use of.

You can search for an e-mail address or a phone number — although phone number listings are restricted to people in the United States — by entering the first and last name. You can narrow the search by adding a city and/or state for phone number searches. You can also link to more advanced searches, where you can enter more specific information.

One of the more interesting features of the Yahoo! People Search directory is a tool called SmartNames. SmartNames recognizes various nicknames, understanding that "Bob" might also be listed as "Rob" or "Robert." And if you can't find the person you are looking for, Yahoo! People Search includes a section in which you can quickly try your search in another directory called 1800USSEARCH.com. (The 1800USSEARCH.com service costs $39.95 per search.)

Switchboard

Switchboard (`http://www.switchboard.com`) is another top-notch people-finding tool that can help you find people, e-mail addresses, businesses, and Web pages. In addition, Switchboard helps you find directions using Maps On Us, and it offers free e-mail and Web pages.

To search for a white page listing for someone, click Find a Person; to search for an e-mail address, click Find E-mail. Guess what happens if you click Find a Business? In any case, you'll see a similar search form. (As usual, the white pages listings are only for the United States.)

If your search is successful, you will be presented with links to a variety of information, including — if an address was available — links to maps and local items of interest.

WhoWhere?

WhoWhere? (`http://www.whowhere.lycos.com`), founded in 1994 by two Stanford University graduate students, is now part of Lycos. WhoWhere? allows you to perform an initial search of an e-mail directory, phone listings, or the Web.

You can search the personal profiles of people who have registered with WhoWhere? to find people by location, school, personal interests, group affiliations, or more. To do this, you use the Advanced Search by clicking the Advanced link under the e-mail or phone number radio buttons on the main search page.

World Email Directory

A lot of the people-finding search engines on the Web are great for finding addresses in the United States and (sometimes) Canada but don't help much when it comes to searching for people elsewhere in the world.

The World Email Directory (`http://www.worldemail.com`) is much more international in scope. It claims to be the fastest-growing search engine for people, businesses, and organizations on the Web, with access to more than 18 million e-mail addresses worldwide and more than 140 million personal and business phone numbers and street addresses.

The World Email Directory's search form (see Figure 20-2) is quite different from most of the other search engines' forms: It's just a series of four blanks into which you can put whatever information you might have, from a name to a location to a hobby. For example, you might enter a last name in the first blank, a city in the second, a business affiliation in the third, and a personal interest in the fourth, and WED will do its best to find a match.

In addition, WED offers links to other useful people- and business-finding tools from all over the planet, from regional search engines to a list of embassies and consulates worldwide.

InfoSpace

InfoSpace (`http://www.infospace.com`) calls itself "The Brand That's Building the Internet." You'll find directories here for everything, it seems, from lottery results to government officials (see Figure 20-3) — and it includes several good tools for people-finding.

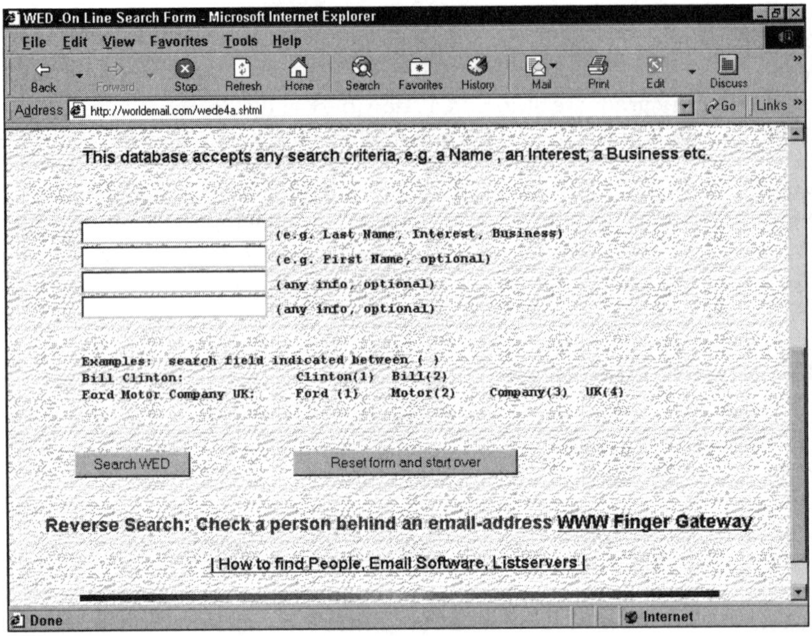

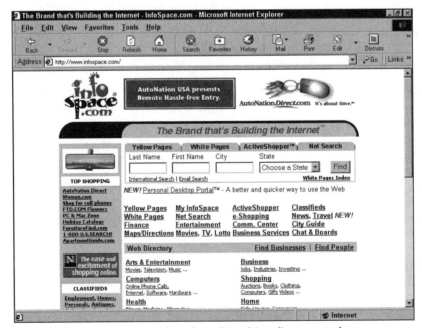

Figure 20-2: The World Email Directory's search form enables you to enter any information you might have as criteria for a search.

Figure 20-3: InfoSpace provides a broad-reaching directory and an easy-to-use search form.

InfoSpace's default search form appears on the main page and asks you for the first and last name of the party for whom you're searching and, optionally, a city and state. All information available on the individual in InfoSpace's directory is listed when the results are displayed; there is no need to search separately for e-mail addresses and phone numbers.

InfoSpace also provides a reverse e-mail address look-up: Enter an e-mail address, and it gives you the name of the person to whom it belongs (if, of course, both the e-mail address and the name are in its database).

Internet Address Finder

The Internet Address Finder (http://www.iaf.net) is an extensive e-mail directory with more than 6.7 million entries. They claim that the database is growing, but we should note that the number hasn't changed since we wrote the first edition of this book back in 1998. Unlike many of the others, IAF concentrates exclusively on e-mail addresses: It doesn't have "white pages" content.

The IAF search form is very straightforward: You must enter a last name, and then you can narrow your search with a first name, organization, and/or domain. Internet Address Finder also provides a reverse e-mail address look-up service.

BigBook

Some of the e-mail directories and white-pages sites listed above offer a yellow pages feature "on the side." There are also sites that specialize in yellow page services. BigBook (http://www.bigbook.com) is one of them. From the home page (see Figure 20-4), you can conduct a quick search among 11 million U.S. businesses by name or by category.

For each business listed, BigBook supplies the business address and phone number. For some businesses, additional information is available, including hours of operation and even maps to the business location.

The detailed search lets you add more features, such as a specific address, and to choose to search only among businesses for which BigBook has certain information — for example, businesses with a Web site.

Besides helping you find specific businesses (obviously), BigBook can also be helpful in a search for an individual — provided you know what sort of business that individual is in.

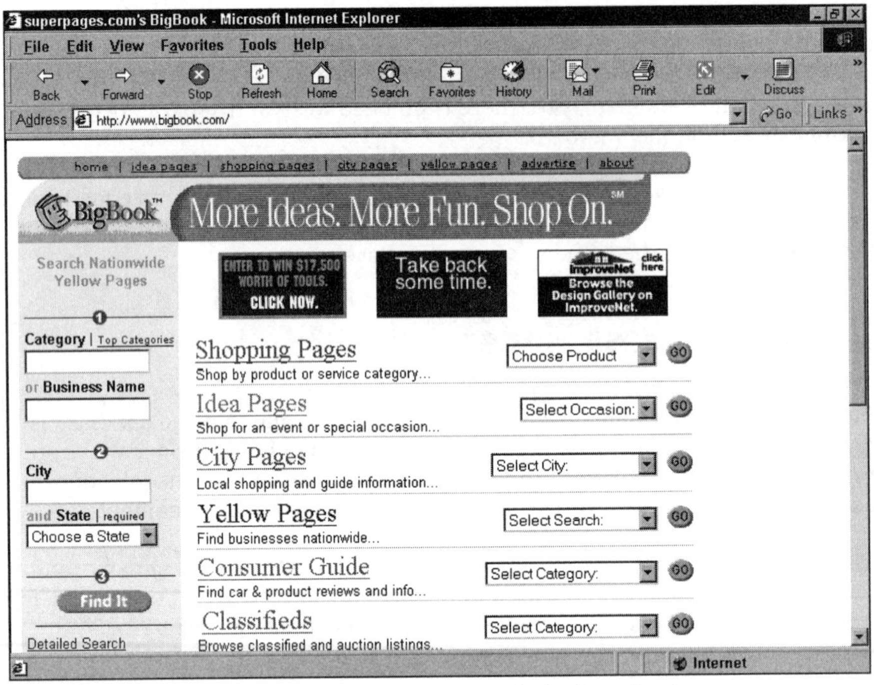

Figure 20-4: BigBook specializes in helping people find U.S. businesses.

BigYellow

BigYellow (http://www.bigyellow.com) is very similar to BigBook in that it provides information about millions of U.S. businesses.

From the basic form, you can search by business name, category, city, or state. With the detailed search form, you can be more specific, adding a metro area, a zip code, or an area code.

Summary

It's a shame to lose track of someone you care about — and now, with the power of the Internet at your fingertips, you may find it easier to prevent. By searching white pages, e-mail databases, and yellow pages on the Web, you've got an excellent chance of uncovering how to contact your long-lost acquaintances. Keeping in touch has never been easier.

✦   ✦   ✦

Doing Online Research

CHAPTER

21

Those of us who do a lot of research in the course of our jobs find it hard to remember those long-ago days (seven years ago? eight?) when we didn't have access to the immense resources of today's Internet. Back then, research depended on things called "books" (remember them?) that were gathered into "libraries." Sometimes we used "the mail" (not to be confused with e-mail) to contact sources; sometimes we used "the telephone."

All right, so we still use those methods. Good libraries, in particular, are still in no danger of being replaced by the Internet for the serious researcher. But the fact remains that the Internet is well on its way to becoming the single most important source of information for people who want to find out something—no matter what that something is. For convenience, speed, and sheer quantity of information, nothing beats the Internet.

Using the Web in School

Personal computers first entered classrooms two decades ago. At first, they were little more than novelties that ran simple quiz programs and perhaps taught the nerdier students how to number lines of Basic code. The main purpose was to make students feel comfortable with using computers, but in reality they did little more than bathe students in their warm cathode rays. Now, thanks to the Internet, computers are invaluable assets in schools. They bring real, unquestionable value to the learning experience by expanding research material and guiding students to new and exciting places. The Web even enables students to attend class without traveling to a campus. We will explore these exciting new trends in the following sections.

Research

Whether you're composing your master's thesis or developing a third-grade recycling project, your work requires some research. In bygone days this meant hours of pacing through the stacks at your local library, and the book you needed was probably checked out or at a different branch anyway. The World Wide Web addresses many of the problems traditionally associated with doing research, if for no other reason than the simple fact that it is much bigger than any conventional library could ever be.

One problem with doing research online is that anyone can publish a Web page. There are no "Web Police" helping to ensure that everyone who claims to be an expert actually is one. It is solely up to the viewer to decide whether a source is credible.

Of course, if you are a teacher this situation can provide an interesting learning experience all its own. For years it's been common to expose students to a wide variety of reference materials, ranging from scientific journals to checkout-stand tabloids. Directly comparing and analyzing such resources bolsters the students' reasoning and decision-making skills, because they must choose what is and is not a reliable source of information. Similar exercises can be conducted using the Internet. Try this with a group:

1. Choose a research topic, such as Thomas Jefferson.

2. Conduct an Internet search on the topic.

3. Locate 10–20 Web sites, and write down the URLs for each.

4. If possible, print or save one article from each Web site. Also, obtain as much information about the author/publisher as possible.

5. Have the group analyze this information and evaluate each one for reliability. Does the author demonstrate expertise? Are references cited? Does the material appear to have been updated recently?

In answering these questions, the students will decide which materials are the best and most reliable. Not only can this be useful in showing students that they must question the source when they read something, but it can also provide a fun and intriguing segue as the class moves on to new subject material. If we were indeed about to begin studying Thomas Jefferson, this would have exposed the students to a wide variety of resources pertaining to the former president and perhaps piqued their interest. Those who are eager to learn more may return to some of those Web sites outside of class time. Figure 21-1 shows one result of a search we did on Thomas Jefferson.

An incredible amount of reference material is available online, but it takes some work to find sources that are both in-depth and credible. Ultimately, it will be up to you and you alone to determine the reliability of any source you read.

#	Relevance	Name: Main Author, Creator, etc.	Full Title	Date
☐ 1	●●●●●		CHP newsletter.	
☐ 2	●●●●●		Thomas Jefferson Research Center. T.J. Pasadena, Calif.	
☐ 3	●●●●●	Budd, Henry, 1849-1921.	St. Mary's Hall lectures, and other papers. By Henry Budd.	1898
☐ 4	●●●●●	Van Ness, William Peter, 1778-1826. [from old catalog]	Speeches at full length of Mr. Van Ness, Mr. Canes, the attorney-general, [Ambrose Spencer] Mr. Harrison, and General Hamilton, in the great cause of the people against Harry Croswell, on an indictment for a libel on Thomas Jefferson ...	1804
☐ 5	●●●●●		Mr. Jefferson's music [Sound recording].	1977
☐ 6	●●●●●	Evans, John. [from old catalog]	Narrative of the proceedings of the religious society of the people called Quakers in Philadelphia, against John Evans ...	1811
☐ 7	●●●●●	Padover, Saul Kussiel, 1905-	Thomas Jefferson and the foundations of American freedom / Saul K. Padover.	1965
☐ 8	●●●●●	Wertenbaker, Thomas Jefferson, 1879-	Old South: the founding of American civilization.	1963
☐ 9	●●●●●	Honeywell, Roy John, 1886-	Educational work of Thomas Jefferson.	1964
☐ 10	●●●●●	Miller, Samuel Jefferson Thomas, 1919-	Cristobal Rojas y Spinola, cameralist and irenicist, 1626-1695 [by] Samuel J. T. Miller and John P. Spielman, Jr.	1962
☐ 11	●●●●●	Thompson, Daniel P. (Daniel Pierce), 1795-1868.	Green Mountain boy at Monticello; a talk with Jefferson in 1822. Introd. by Howard C. Rice, Jr. Drawings by Gillett G. Griffin.	1962
☐ 12	●●●●●	McCormick, John, 1918-	Versions of censorship; an anthology edited by John McCormick and Mairi MacInnes.	1962
☐ 13	●●●●●	Jefferson, Thomas, President, U. S., 1743-1826. [from old catalog]	Handbuch des Parlamentarrechts;	1819
☐ 14	●●●●●	Skeen, Carl Edward. [from	Jefferson and the West, 1798-1802	1960

Figure 21-1: These sites are the results of a search we conducted at the Library of Congress on Thomas Jefferson. Each link leads to documents that pertain to Jefferson.

Virtual field trips

Hyperbole aside, students can virtually travel all over the world using their computer and an Internet connection. This Internet exploration can take the form of visiting informational Web sites; live "Web cams" that show you another part of the world in real time; journeys through online museums and libraries; and conversations with others from all over the world.

One interesting project that puts kids in touch with each other is KIDLINK (http://www.kidlink.org/), a Web site that serves as a link-up point for kids through age 15. Viewers can choose from a number of different languages before entering the site, and once inside kids can communicate using mailing lists, chats, or Web pages. KIDLINK encourages kids to talk with each other in a relatively safe environment about how they would like the world to be in their future. This is a truly international project, and it has some great teacher resources as well.

E-mail interviews

Another way students are using the Internet with increasing regularity is to conduct e-mail interviews. This logical use of the medium allows students to gain first-hand information from experts who might otherwise be inaccessible. This interaction is great, and it positions the Internet as a useful tool for the student. Unfortunately, it is also something that can easily go wrong.

We've interviewed a number of people on various topics, and in general those done via e-mail were the least successful interviews that we have done. A good interview involves more than simply asking a set of prepared questions and jotting down the answers; your questions should serve only as jumping-off points for longer, more fascinating conversations between you and the interviewee. Listen to a one-hour talk show on the radio sometime and count the number of specific questions that are actually asked and you'll see what we mean.

One of the elements that disappears with e-mail is the nonverbal aspect of interviewing. You will miss out on things like gestures, voice inflection, facial expressions, and other things that help keep a good conversation alive. Furthermore, students are often looking for specific information when they conduct interviews, and so their prepared questions are usually very specific. The result? Bland, specific answers.

Let's suppose for a moment that we're working on a research paper about the Big Bang Theory. We have some questions for Professor Hubble of State University, so we arrange for an e-mail interview. One of the things we want to learn more about is Cosmic Background Radiation:

✦ "Was the discovery of the Cosmic Background Radiation significant?"

✦ Prof. Hubble's response: "Yes."

"Yes" isn't the kind of quotable material that we are looking for. The main problem here is that we asked a yes/no question. Think of this as the Golden Rule of e-mail interviews: if your question can possibly be answered in only one or two words, throw it out. Here is a better question:

✦ "Why was the discovery of the Cosmic Background Radiation significant?"

✦ Prof. Hubble: "The discovery of the CBR gave us a clearer understanding of . . ."

What a difference—if that question doesn't get a cosmologist going, nothing will! Remember, you chose your interviewee precisely because he or she is an expert, so don't be afraid to make them talk. E-mail can be an incredibly useful tool for students, not only because it broadens access to experts, but also because it greatly reduces the risk of misquoting. Ask the right questions, and e-mail can be your ticket to better school success!

Online classes

A growing number of institutions now offer distance education via the Internet. Classes that involve at least some Internet "facetime" are common, and some classes are conducted entirely online. A few accredited institutions offer nothing but online classes. The concept offers a number of significant advantages:

✦ It helps students who can't attend classes on a physical campus obtain an education.

✦ Students who might be too shy to participate meaningfully face-to-face have been shown to be much more active in online classes.

✦ Online classes can be more interactive than other forms of distance education, such as correspondence courses and telecourses.

✦ Class discussions are recorded in the form of e-mail messages and Web page forums. This allows students to refer to things said in class and reflect on them more effectively.

✦ Some student costs are reduced, such as transportation, text books, and other reference materials.

✦ Students rest better because they don't have as many nightmares about showing up in class naked.

Of course, with these advantages come some new problems that traditional classroom learning has not had to cope with:

✦ Students and schools must purchase expensive hardware and software to conduct and support these classes.

✦ Simple technical difficulties like poor phone connections, high Internet traffic, or malfunctioning computers can severely hamper the learning process.

✦ Coordinating a large number of students to get together at the same time for online chats can be difficult.

✦ Many instructors still find that online classes only happen as a result of their personal efforts. Little support from their institutions means that many online classes do not last more than one or two terms.

All of these problems are important and need to be dealt with if this form of education is to be successful. The last one is particularly diabolical because most online instructors also have traditional classes they must teach.

Because their colleagues do not "see" everything that is going on with the online class, the instructor may be expected to carry a full load of regular classes and conduct the online training on his or her own time. This situation is unfortunate, but as online classes grow in popularity it will hopefully become less of a problem.

Investigating Sources of Information Online

The biggest problem with the Internet is that it lacks organization. As one writer put it, "the Internet is an enormous library in which someone has turned out the lights and tipped the index cards all over the floor." This means that finding information on the Internet takes work. When you do find it, however, it can be saved in an easily usable form on your computer, and it's often — but not always — more up-to-date than what you can find in the world of printed information.

Cross-Reference   Search engines are one way to find information online. To learn more about how to use search engines, turn back to Chapter 16, "Using Search Engines."

The basic tool of online research is the search engine, but search engines are certainly not the only way to mine useful information from the Internet's cyberspatial depths. Here are some others:

✦ **Usenet newsgroups**. Currently more than 24,000 newsgroups exist, covering just about every topic. By posting to a newsgroup where the topic you're interested in is discussed, you can track down knowledgeable experts in just about any field of endeavor, many of whom will be happy to answer your questions. You can find newsgroups with the search engine Deja.com (`http://www.deja.com`).

Note   Some newsgroups are pickier than others about strangers jumping in to their discussions. It's a good idea to "lurk" for a while (read messages without posting) to get a feel for how the newsgroup is likely to respond to your request for information.

✦ **Mailing lists**. Mailing lists are similar to newsgroups, except you receive all the postings to the list (or, in some cases, a digest of them) by e-mail. Some mailing lists restrict their membership to members of a certain organization or profession, but others can be freely subscribed to by anyone. You can usually find information about mailing lists at Web sites relating to your field of study, or you can search one of several mailing list directories.

Tip   Two excellent mailing list directories are Liszt at `http://www.liszt.com/`, and ONElist at `http://www.onelist.com/`.

✦ **Webrings**. Webrings are a relatively new innovation on the Web. They're essentially group sites with similar subjects, linked into continuous loops: Each member links to the next member until the last member links with the first member, closing the loop. More than 80,000 Webrings exist, according to Webring.org, the organization that invented them. Visitors can either travel the ring by moving consecutively from site to site, or can jump at random to other sites in the ring. Find a Webring related to the topic you're researching, and you'll find site after site that may provide useful information — without having to go the sometimes frustrating and time-consuming search-engine route. Visit `http://www.webring.org` to search for a Webring that interests you.

✦ **Virtual libraries**. You'll find many virtual libraries on the Internet, some general-reference and some subject-specific. Lots of topics don't have virtual libraries devoted to them, but if the subject you're interested in does, you'll find it a valuable source of information. One of the best general-reference virtual libraries is the Internet Public Library (`http://www.ipl.org`) that provides access to books and other texts available over the Internet. You can browse, or search by author, title, or Dewey subject—just like in a real library.

✦ **Electronic journals and magazines**. Many printed magazines, journals, newspapers, TV stations, and other more traditional forms of information media are now publishing electronic versions. Most contain only some of the content included in the regular version of the magazine or program; however, they almost always also include additional information not included in the regular version of the magazine or program. Thousands of magazines and journals—on every topic imaginable—exist only on the Internet. In fact, because it is so easy for anyone with Internet access to publish online, the line between a magazine and a personal Web site is becoming very blurred.

Visiting Great Sites for Research

Hundreds of great sources of information on every conceivable topic are available on the World Wide Web; discussing them all would fill a book this size and probably a couple more. The best sites for research (aside from search engines, online directories, and virtual libraries) probably depends on what your topic is. Someone researching the burial customs of ninth-century Afghanistan is hardly going to see eye-to-eye with someone researching the clothing customs of twentieth-century snowboarders when it comes to the best sites for information on the Web.

So, like a good researcher using an Internet search engine, let's narrow our terms of reference for this chapter. The sites that follow are some of the best in three specific areas: education, government, and business.

Educational references

A well-rounded education should include reading, writing, and arithmetic (the three R's), plus science, geography, and the arts. The following are some outstanding reference sites—together they cover all these categories.

Reading: The WWWebster Dictionary

Don't have a dictionary or a thesaurus handy? Well, now you do! Just go to the WWWebster Dictionary (`http://www.m-w.com/netdict.htm`), enter the word you want defined, and click Search. Back comes the answer from *Merriam-Webster's Collegiate Dictionary, Tenth Edition*, as shown in Figure 21-2.

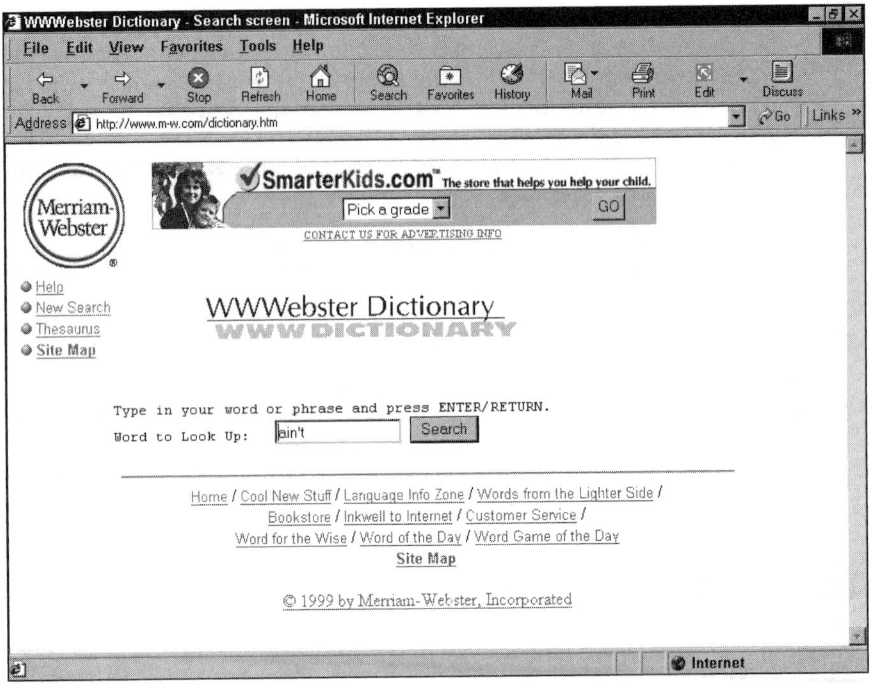

Figure 21-2: Enter your search term in the WWWebster Dictionary, and back comes the answer, sometimes complete with illustration. You can also click the Thesaurus button to find synonyms of the word.

The Merriam-Webster site also includes other valuable (and sometimes just plain fun!) information about words and language, including guides to new words just entering the language, a fascinating look back 150 years at Noah Webster's Third (dictionary, that is), a brief history of the English language, word games, a guide to business communication, and more.

Writing: Creative Writing for Kids

You'll find dozens, if not hundreds, of sites on the World Wide Web devoted to writing, but most of them are aimed at adults. Creative Writing for Kids (`http://kidswriting.about.com`) is different. It was developed by Diane Dobbs, who specializes in reading and writing development for children of all ages. She brings her knowledge as a teacher and the perspective of a mother to the process of helping children develop their creative writing skills. Her site, which is completely searchable, offers links to many other good writing sites, categorized into beginner, intermediate, and advanced writing levels, as well as links to other resources related to everything from grammar to plots.

Diane updates the site weekly, highlighting useful Web sites and providing Internet, vocabulary, grammar, spelling, and punctuation tips. Most of the site is aimed at young authors, but Diane also includes a section in each feature article aimed at the grown-ups who help children learn.

Arithmetic: Mega-Mathematics

If you're looking for mathematics information, an excellent resource is Mega-Mathematics (`http://www.c3.lanl.gov/mega-math/`), hosted by Los Alamos National Laboratory. Mega-Mathematics offers resources, activities, and information for students, teachers, and mathematicians.

Mega-Mathematics places special emphasis on the fact that math is a living science, with research ongoing. Thus, the site becomes an excellent resource, especially if you are a teacher and want to keep your students up-to-date with the latest in mathematics.

Science: ScienceDaily

No one can keep up with everything that's happening in the world of science — but some of us like to try. One of the best sites for getting some sense of the latest scientific findings from around the planet is ScienceDaily (`http://www.sciencedaily.com`), "Your link to the latest research news," which is shown in Figure 21-3.

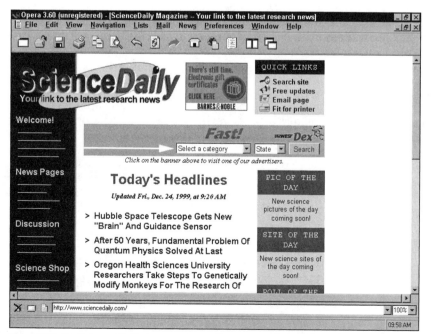

Figure 21-3: ScienceDaily is an outstanding research tool if you're interested in the most up-to-date information about scientific research around the world.

ScienceDaily is a free, advertising-supported online magazine that supplies breaking news from every scientific field from astronomy to zoology. The articles it presents are news releases submitted by leading universities and other research organizations around the world, posted in their original form, with a contact name and link to the organization's home page.

ScienceDaily also offers links to other sources of science news on the Internet, as well as links to interesting science-related sites and more than 200 science newsgroups. Free weekly e-mail bulletins summarizing the top news stories of the past week are also available.

Geography: The Perry-Castañeda Library Map Collection

The Perry-Castañeda Library Map Collection at the University of Texas at Austin contains more than 230,000 maps covering all areas of the world. The Library has about 2,100 maps online, which can be seen at the Library's Web site at `http://www.lib.utexas.edu/Libs/PCL/Map_collection`. The maps that are online are in the public domain, so they can be used freely by anyone who accesses them. The main page for the collection provides links to maps of current interest, so it's easy to follow current world events.

Because the maps are in the public domain, this collection is an excellent resource for educators. You won't have to worry about obtaining special permission before reproducing them for class.

Many other map- and geography-related sites populate the World Wide Web, and the Perry-Castañeda Library Map Collection Web site includes links to most of them. If you need a map for a particular location, this is the place to start.

The Arts: Internet ArtResources

Internet ArtResources (`http://artresources.com`) is an online magazine that aims to be in the forefront of art resources on the Web — and appears to have succeeded. It includes feature articles, reviews, news from galleries, news about artists, an image catalogue, and more.

One of the most impressive parts of Internet ArtResources is the Image Catalogue, which currently offers over 2,000 images online. If you're looking for a gallery showing a particular artist, or want to know more about galleries in a particular city, or want to know more about a museum, fair, event, or art school, this site can help.

Internet ArtResources is worth visiting to see the beautiful images it presents on its front page alone; but you'll find so much useful information here that, if you're at all interested in the visual arts, you'll want to come back again and again.

Business resources

It wasn't all that long ago that businesses were few and far between on the Web, and information about and for business was even scarcer. Today, though, every business worth its salt has a Web page, and business people all over the world turn to the Web on a regular basis for the news and information they need to compete effectively in the global economy.

Business Wire

Lots of news services on the Web cover business news, but most of them are general news services with a business section. Business Wire (`http://www.businesswire.com`) concentrates just on providing you with the most thorough coverage of business news, updated hourly, that you can find anywhere on the Internet.

You can browse the day's news by industry (for example, high tech, entertainment, sports) or by company (including a large collection of corporate profiles). Business Wire also has an area called Vcall that hosts online video conferencing for a number of member corporations, and there is an exhaustive collection of links to other business sites on the Web.

CBS Marketwatch

If it's the latest market news you're after, then CBS Marketwatch (`http://cbs.marketwatch.com`), a joint venture of CBS and Data Broadcasting Corporation (DBC), provides you with just what you need.

For example, you can look up stocks, mutual funds, money market funds, and indexes on four continents. Market summaries, leaders, gainers and losers, industry groupings, and international stocks by country are also available, as are free charts and portfolios.

Bloomberg

Bloomberg (`http://www.bloomberg.com`) provides real-time figures and extensive data about the financial world to major investors who use their proprietary terminals. The full power of those terminals naturally isn't available on the Web, but a ton of other information is: business news headlines from around the world, market news, company profiles, and more (see Figure 21-4).

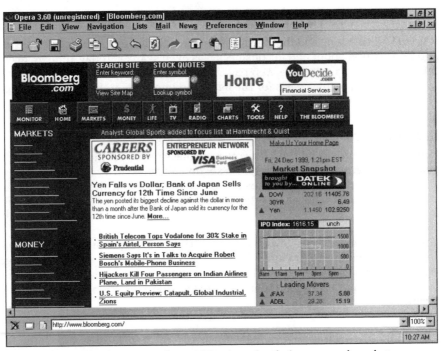

Figure 21-4: Major investors rely on Bloomberg for their news and market quotes; now you can get a taste of what Bloomberg has to offer at its site on the World Wide Web.

Government resources: FedWorld

There's no question that one of the largest creators of Web sites on the planet is the U.S. government. Every department, related agency, and facility seems to have its own Web site. How do you find them all?

You need to know really only one site to access government resources: FedWorld, located online at `http://www.fedworld.gov`. FedWorld is hosted by the U.S. Department of Commerce, but provides links to virtually all online federal government resources.

FedWorld is fully searchable: just type a keyword to search the FedWorld Information Network. You can also search for Government reports or browse from a list of specific FedWorld information resources. Or, if you prefer, you can access federal agencies through the Federal Quick Jumps (provided you know the agency's acronym) or browse through each branch of the government, plus government agencies and corporations and selected additional links related to the government in some way. Without a doubt, FedWorld is an excellent research tool for digging into the workings of the federal government.

Citing Online Resources

You probably already know that when you conduct research for a paper or other similar project, proper citation of the resource is important. In fact, if your writing project is for a class, citation is one of the things that you'll be graded on. Today, the two most common citation standards are those developed by the American Psychological Association (APA), and the Modern Language Association (MLA). Both standards have long been used for citing books, periodicals, journals, brochures, interviews, speeches, and other traditional resources. Fortunately, both standards can easily be adapted to cite electronic resources such as Web pages, e-mail messages, and newsgroup postings.

Proper citation is important, and electronic resources on the Internet present some unique challenges that must be take into account when you do research online. Foremost among your concerns should be the fact that something like a Web page can be quickly and easily changed, unlike a printed resource that, once committed to paper, is pretty static. You might quote a Web page, but then tomorrow the Webmaster changes — or even deletes — the page so that your quote is no longer available. For this reason, it is extremely important that you cite not only the exact URL of any electronic resource you use, but also the date that you accessed it.

Tip
We strongly suggest that you print any online resource you plan to use. A printed copy will be easier to work from and will serve as evidence of your source should it ever be questioned in the future.

Ultimately, the information shown here is only a basic guide to citing online resources. If you are working on a project for a class, make sure that you get specific information from the teacher about how they want citations formatted. He or she may request additional information — such as the time of access — that is not mentioned here.

Using the APA format

The basic syntax of an APA-style citation for an online resource is as follows:

> Author/editor. (Year). *Title* (edition), [Type of medium]. Producer. Available: Exact URL [Access date].

To see this method in action, here is a citation for our resource on this section, a Web page published by Nancy Crane of the University of Vermont:

> Crane, N. (1997). *Electronic Sources: APA Style of Citation*, [Online]. University of Vermont. Available: http://www.uvm.edu/~ncrane/estyles/apa.html [1999, December 24].

The producer in this case is the University of Vermont, but that information may not always be available. If a piece of information cannot be located, leave it out. If you are citing a different type of online resource, such as a newsgroup posting or e-mail message, some modification to this format will be necessary. In these cases you will generally add the e-mail address of the sender after their name, replace the URL at the end of the citation with the e-mail address of the recipient or address for the newsgroup. The date of the resource listed after the author should include the month and day in addition to the year, and the *Title* should be replaced with the subject of the message. Again, consult your instructor if there is any doubt as to the exact format you should use.

Using the MLA format

The MLA format is similar to APA, but not exactly the same. If you are using MLA citations, use the following format:

> Author/editor. *Title*. Edition or date (if available). *Title of Electronic Work*. Medium. Publisher. URL. Access date.

This format is a bit simpler than APA because there is not as much punctuation to remember. Here is an example:

> Crane, Nancy. *Electronic Resources: MLA Style of Citation*. 1997. Online. University of Vermont. http://www.uvm.edu/~ncrane/estyles/mla.html. 24 December 1999.

If the resource was an online version of an article that was originally published in print form, additional information might be necessary. And, of course, in the case of e-mail and newsgroup postings, you should replace the *Title* with the message subject, add the sender's e-mail address to the author section, and replace the URL with the newsgroup address or recipient's e-mail address. For a full breakdown of MLA citation issues, the best place to visit is the MLA Web site at `http://www.mla.org/`.

Researching Genealogy Online

The Internet has been a powerful research tool since its inception, and one of the fastest growing uses for it today is among people who wish to research their family history online. Not only is a wealth of information available through your portal to the online world, you can also use it to contact distant relatives that yesterday you didn't even know you had.

One of the most powerful new tools for online genealogical research is FamilySearch (`http://www.familysearch.org`), maintained by the Church of Jesus Christ of the Latter-Day Saints (LDS). The LDS Church is based in Utah, and for decades has been one of the most valuable resources for genealogy researchers all over the world.

What makes FamilySearch so valuable is the fact that it provides not only a vast database of historical information that you can quickly search, it also provides thousands of links to useful Web sites all over the world. These sites include

✦ **Libraries**. These can be public or private archives of genealogy data.

✦ **Personal family sites**. Individuals can register their own genealogy Web site with FamilySearch, thereby adding it to the collection.

✦ **Government offices**. These include archives of public records, voting registries, emigration/immigration data, and military records.

Genealogy resources

FamilySearch provides links to thousands of excellent resources to help you research your family's history. But it isn't the only resource available online. The following is a list of some other sites you may want to try.

Ancestry.com

Boasting a searchable database of 500 million names, Ancestry.com (`http://www.ancestry.com`) is another excellent place to begin your research. The site's main page is organized like many online news sites, with a variety of useful links available in an easy-to-use format. The page also features a list of new databases.

Ancestry.com is not a free service, but they have frequent specials that are worth checking out. For instance, when we checked the site on December 24th, they were offering free access for the Christmas holiday. If you wish to join Ancestry.com, the fee is just $5 per month.

Coats of Arms – Designs of Wonder

If your family had a traditional coat of arms, you may be able to find a color image of it online at Coats of Arms – Designs of Wonder (`http://www.designsofwonder.com/`). They boast of having over 3,500 coats of arms from around the world, and the quality of the coats we viewed was impressive. The images are copyrighted, but the site owner grants individuals the right to download up to ten images for use on their personal genealogy Web sites.

The Genealogy Home Page

The Genealogy Home Page (`http://www.genhomepage.com/`) doesn't have as fancy an interface as some of the other sites mentioned here, but it does have an easy-to-navigate directory of links to various genealogy resources. If you're new to genealogy, we suggest that you check their listing for Genealogy Help and Guides. There is more to the process than sitting around listening to Grandpa tell his old stories (although, admittedly, that is the *funnest* part of genealogy research), and the sites listed here can answer a lot of your questions.

GenForum

Computer databases are nice, but sometimes your best tool is other genealogy researchers just like yourself. GenForum (`http://genforum.genealogy.com/`) is a site that puts genealogy researchers in touch with each other in a variety of forums. Of particular interest are the surname forums, where you can post questions and read information on a specific surname. And if you don't find a forum for a specific name, you can request that one be created. Look for an Add Forum link near the bottom of each forum page.

Vital Records Information for United States

Government vital records offices are among the best resources for genealogy resources. This Web site, at `http://www.vitalrec.com`, provides links to information about vital records depositories in U.S. states and territories. Listings generally include mailing addresses, as well as information about fees for obtaining records from the various departments listed. Where available, Web links to relevant government departments are also provided.

Summary

The sheer volume of information available on the Internet is mind-boggling — and trying to track down the particular bit of information you need can seem mind-boggling, too. But by exploring all the options available, you should be able to turn up what you need, whether it be weather data, business news, or the names of your ancestors. And your task is being made easier all the time by top-notch, content-laden research resources on the Web, such as those we visited in this chapter.

✦   ✦   ✦

Taking Time to Chat

As you know, the Internet has revolutionized communi-
cation. You can learn from and be entertained by sites
on the World Wide Web, correspond via e-mail, and share
information in newsgroups. But what about live, person-to-
person communication? Where can people go on the Internet
to converse in real time?

The best answer to that question lies in thousands of "chat
rooms" across the Internet. In these virtual rooms people
gather to discuss, argue, make friends, "flame" each other, and
even get technical support. The phenomenon of chat has been
popular since the early days of the Internet and continues to
be so today. But there have been many changes along the way,
most of them making chatting easier and more user-friendly.
This chapter discusses some basic chat concepts and then
moves on to describe how to use several different types of
chat technologies that are available to you.

Visiting Chat Rooms

The term *chat room* is really a euphemism for a computer
(called a chat server) that allows multiple persons to log on
at the same time. The people who are logged on can type
messages, which everyone else immediately sees. In spirit,
conversations are held in the chat room as if the participants
were all standing in a room together, perhaps at a party or
meeting. In fact, many of the conventions used in chat room
communication are intended to directly simulate an actual
gathering.

Most chat room communication is done in the form of typed
text, but some Web-based chat software allows you to add
graphics, sound, and even video to your chat room messages.

The software you use for chatting is called a *chat client*, and there are many different clients available. A chat client gives you access to chat rooms, just as a browser (Netscape Navigator or Internet Explorer, for example) gives you access to Web pages and an e-mail client (such as Outlook Express or Eudora) enables you to read e-mail. Generally speaking, chat rooms have specific topics of discussion. For instance, chat room topics can range from discussions about the "X-Files" to parenting to Linux user support. Some chat rooms are purely social while others provide help and advice. Some companies periodically host live chat to help answer customers' questions and provide technical support.

Describing types of chat

Chat exists in several distinct forms. Each is unique and has its own advantages and disadvantages. Table 22-1 shows the three basic types of online chat.

Table 22-1 Types of Chat			
Chat Type	**Description**	**Advantages**	**Disadvantages**
Internet Relay Chat (IRC)	A live, text-based chat protocol that uses the Internet to relay messages between the server and users.	Efficient, true real-time communication.	IRC commands can be difficult to master; text only.
Web-based chat	Uses HTML or Java-based clients to provide chat in WWW sites; this is common at many online communities.	Easy to find and use; you can often paste graphic and sound files into your messages.	Tends to be much slower than IRC; some of the "real-time" feeling can be lost in the waiting.
Instant messaging	Clients that enable you to communicate with specific people using a "closed" channel rather than a public room.	Operates independently of your Web browser, letting you surf while you chat. It is also more private.	Most are not real time, and many people try to use instant messaging in place of e-mail.

It's important to know what type of chat you are using, but consciously choosing one type or the other may be irrelevant. In fact, you may use IRC or Web-based chat in addition to an instant messaging program, depending on whom you want to communicate with. If you're going to use IRC or Web chat, you've got to find a chat room with a topic that interests you, as discussed next.

Finding a chat room

Most chat rooms have a subject of interest or focus and draw visitors with similar interests. For instance, golfers join golf-related chats in order to meet fellow golf enthusiasts and discuss the finer points of the game. Likewise, "X-Files" fans meet to chat about their favorite television show; parents use parenting chat rooms to share experiences and share advice on the challenges of raising children; and a Windows 2000 chat room might be a good place for Windows users to discuss tips and tricks with Windows experts.

Literally thousands of chat rooms exist across the Internet, and finding one that suits your exact needs or interests may seem futile. But fear not! It may not be as difficult as you think to find that perfect chat room. There are a number of good places to start looking. You can begin at a Web site that serves as an online magazine or other popular destination for your desired topic. For instance, suppose you're planning a vacation to the Caribbean (lucky you!). A good place to start looking for information is at the Microsoft Expedia Web site (`http://expedia.msn.com/`). Notice that the Latin America & Caribbean Community shown in Figure 22-1 provides a link to the MSN Chat home page. Although not specifically geared toward chat about the Caribbean, or even travel, you should still be able to find a chat room that is relevant.

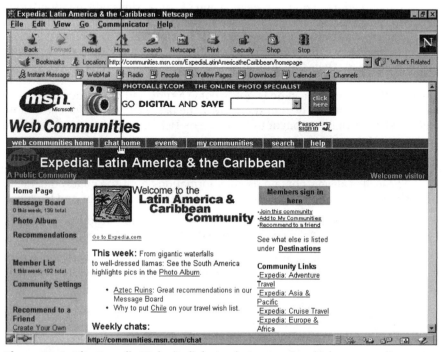

Figure 22-1: The Expedia Web site links to chat rooms in which you can discuss travel.

This is just one example of how many Web sites link you to chat rooms. Another easy way to find active chat rooms is to look on the Web site of an online community or your Internet service provider. Many online communities host a wide variety of chat rooms, which are usually grouped into the neighborhood or community area that they correspond to.

Finally, you might want to try a good, old-fashioned Web search with one of the Internet search engines. Look for Web sites that provide links to various chat rooms, such as the sites listed by Yahoo! at `http://dir.yahoo.com/Computers_ and_Internet/Internet/Chats_and_Forums/`. You'll probably have some dead links to contend with, but many of these Web sites can be excellent starting points for finding good chat rooms.

Practicing good chatiquette

When you walk into a room full of people and strike up a conversation, there are some rules of conduct that you usually follow. First, there are the basic things that Mom taught you, such as not interrupting, remembering to say "please" and "thank you," and not running with scissors. But there are other rules as well. For instance, it would be inappropriate to insult the hors d'oeuvres or shout obscenities during a church social.

Unfortunately, some people have the mistaken impression that civil behavior is unnecessary in the world of online conversation. Spend enough time in cyberspace and you'll find yourself on the receiving end of some truly rude and obnoxious behavior. Such messages are referred to in Net jargon as "flames" or "flame mail," due to their inflammatory nature. What can we say? There are some rude people out there, and they will try to hide behind the anonymity of their online identities to compensate for their tiny little lives.

The best thing that you can do is not become a rude and obnoxious person yourself. This is easy to do, but there are some basic guidelines for acceptable online behavior that you ought to be aware of. Here are some general things to keep in mind:

✦ Read the Rules of Conduct or FAQ for a chat room before you actually enter. These files always contain useful information about the chat room, including specific rules about what is and is not acceptable behavior and language.

✦ When you first log on to a chat room, go ahead and introduce yourself. Usually a simple "hi everybody" will do it.

✦ Don't say something in a chat room that you would not say to everyone's face if they were really there. Most people in chat rooms are not interested in bravado.

✦ Watch the language! If you're not sure what kind of language is and isn't okay, log off and read the FAQ or Rules of Conduct.

✦ If you have something private to say, say it privately. This is especially important if you're having an animated disagreement (also known as an argument). This not only saves you and the other person from embarrassment, but it also protects others in the chat room who don't want to hear it.

✦ Respect the opinions of others, even if they conflict with your own. Sometimes the best strategy is simply to agree to disagree.

✦ Read the Rules of Conduct or FAQ for a chat room *before* you actually . . . oh wait, we already said that. Well, you get the idea.

What can happen if a person doesn't follow the rules? Again, that depends on the room. At the very least, one might get counter-flamed by others and be urged to go away. If problems persist, most chat moderators have ways to ban offending chatters from entering chat rooms in the future.

Once you've learned to be a responsible chatter, you need to learn some of the unique language and characters used in live chat. Most of this unique language comes in the form of acronyms for common phrases, a noble effort to decrease bandwidth and provide relief to overworked typing fingers. The other major group of special characters is known collectively as emoticons or smileys, and they lend a more personal feel to this otherwise cold medium. Table 22-2 lists a few of the more common acronyms and emoticons used in chat rooms. These little gems can also be used in e-mail and other forms of communication!

Table 22-2
Common Acronyms and Emoticons Used in Chat Rooms

ACRONYM	Definition	EMOTICON	Meaning
AFAIK	As Far As I Know	:-)	Happy
AFK	Away From Keyboard	:-(	Sad
BCNU	Be Seeing You	:-|	Knowing Look
BG or <BG>	Big Grin	;-)	Sly Wink
BTW	By The Way	:-D	Laughing
CYA	See Ya!	X-(	Brain dead
FOAF	Friend Of A Friend	>:-(	Mad
FWIW	For What It's Worth	$:-(	Bad hair day
FYI	For Your Information	<:-|	Dunce
G or <G>	Grin	~:-)	Alfalfa
GD&R	Grinning, Ducking, and Running	:-o	Oh my goodness!

Continued

Table 22-2 *(continued)*

ACRONYM	Definition	EMOTICON	Meaning
GMTA	Great Minds Think Alike	:-#	Lips are sealed
IIRC	If I Remember Correctly	\o/	Praise the Lord!
IMHO	In My Humble Opinion	:-@	Screaming
L8R	Later	:-P	Sticking tongue out
LOL	Laughing Out Loud	o:-)	Angel
ROFLMHO	Rolling On Floor Laughing My Head Off	:-[	Vampire
SO	Significant Other	:-*	Kiss
TFTT	Thanks For The Tip	B-)	Sunglasses
TTFN	Ta Ta For Now	+<:-)	Pope
VBG	Very Big Grin	@->-;------	A rose for you
YMMV	Your Mileage May Vary	:-\	Undecided

Of course, Table 22-2 provides only a short list of acronyms and emoticons that you can use. Part of the fun of being a part of the chat community is that you can invent your own cute little keystroke savers; just don't forget to make sure that other people know what they mean!

Live chat is a fun way to talk to and get to know others who share your interests. However, you must take care to avoid alienating yourself and others in this potentially volatile online world. Following some basic rules of courtesy and common sense will help you to not only stay online with various chat servers, but it will also open up a whole new world of communication for you. And who knows: You might even make some new friends!

Caution

Remember, absolutely anyone can log on to a chat room, and some of those people are not necessarily trustworthy. Furthermore, most chat servers are not terribly secure, meaning that a message you send to only one person may not be as private as you think. Because of this, you should avoid sharing personal information in a chat room. Some people even hide their own age and sex to avoid being harassed.

Furthermore, if someone reveals details about his or her personal life, don't trust them implicitly. A 14-year-old girl could just as easily be a 65-year-old man behind the nickname, and vice versa. Finally, be extremely wary about meeting a fellow chatter in person. If you do wish to meet with someone, choose a public place with other people around, and always be on your guard.

Using Internet Relay Chat

Chatting on computers is nothing new. Indeed, our own first "live chat" session took place over 20 years ago, between our TRS-80 and a friend's Apple II across town. And geeks, er, computer professionals, were tapping away at each other long before that. But these older, rudimentary chat sessions differed from the chat rooms of today in one very important aspect: They only involved two people. That's right: Decades of chat sessions were solely one-on-one affairs.

But in 1988, a Finn named Jarkko Oikarinen coded a program called *Internet Relay Chat* (IRC), which was revolutionary in two respects. First, it was more user-friendly than terminal and other communication programs that came before. Second, and more important, it allowed more than two computers to be logged on to the server at once. Thus, a chat room was no longer limited to just two chatters, and because of this, live chat exploded in popularity. The possibilities of this new medium began to shine through.

In the traditional sense, IRC works independently of the World Wide Web. It is its own entity, like e-mail or Usenet. Nevertheless, many popular IRC chat rooms are now accessible from Web pages.

Note   IRC chat rooms are referred to as channels, and their names are always preceded by a pound sign (#). So a chat room for fans of a pioneering German techno-band is called #kraftwerk, and one dedicated to battered, deep-fried tofu might be called #batteredtofu.

Installing mIRC

One of the most popular IRC clients is mIRC. This program is available as shareware from the mIRC home page, located at http://www.mirc.co.uk/. Or, you can download it from Tucows (http://www.tucows.com/). It only takes a few minutes to download, and installation is a snap.

Note   IRC clients are available for all major operating systems used today. We located a number of clients for Macintosh, Linux, and BeOS at Tucows (www.tucows.com) so if you don't have something already installed this is an excellent place to start.

Once the download is complete, you need to install the program. To install mIRC, close all open programs and perform the following:

1. Click the Windows Start button and choose Run.
2. Click Browse and navigate to the folder in which you saved the mIRC installation file.
3. Click Open and OK to begin installation.
4. Read the onscreen instructions and click Install.

Just like that, mIRC is installed. You can launch the program by clicking Start ⇨ Programs ⇨ mIRC ⇨ mIRC32. The first time you launch mIRC, you see an introductory dialog box similar to Figure 22-2, reminding you about the author (nice mug, huh?) and the fact that this is shareware. Remember, if you plan to continue using mIRC, you must register the program. For now, just click the close (X) button of the introduction window.

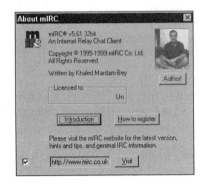

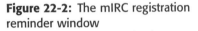

Figure 22-2: The mIRC registration reminder window

Using mIRC

After the introduction, you are asked to set up mIRC for its first use. Here you need to input some basic information about yourself and your preferences. Check the information on the first screen of the setup window. Near the top you need to choose an IRC server to use; if you aren't sure what to do here just accept the default for now. Also enter your identification information, but choose carefully; this is how you will be identified to other chat room members.

You can check other options by selecting items in the list on the left side of the window. But again, for now you may just want to accept the defaults. After you've checked your setup options, click Connect to IRC Server. With any luck, that should get you logged on to the server that you chose on the IRC Servers tab.

Note   Servers are actually computers located around the Internet that host connections to the network of IRC chat channels. Each server hosts the same channels so you should try to choose a server that appears to be close to your physical location. If you have trouble connecting, try choosing a different server.

Now that you've successfully connected to the IRC server, you're ready to join a chat room. Click the Channels Folder button on the toolbar. In the Channels Folder dialog box, shown below in Figure 22-3, you'll find a list of chat rooms. Scroll through the list until you find something that looks interesting. Select a channel and click Join.

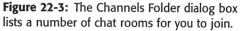
Figure 22-3: The Channels Folder dialog box lists a number of chat rooms for you to join.

If you're not satisfied with what you find in the list of chat rooms, choose OK to close this window and click the List Channels button on the toolbar. This opens the List Channels dialog box, in which you can search for a channel that interests you. To see a full list, leave the Match text box blank and click Get List! You'll eventually see a list of several thousand chat rooms for you to search through.

Tip   Trouble staying connected? Try logging on to a different server. You are not restricted to choosing an IRC server that is close to your geographic location — after all, you're just using your existing Internet connection — although closer servers usually provide a more reliable connection.

Double-click a channel name to join it. In no time flat you'll be logged on to the channel you selected, and folks will be greeting you. A window similar to Figure 22-4 will open, listing other members of the chat and the current status of the conversation.

Even compared to previous versions of IRC software, mIRC is very user-friendly. It doesn't require that you learn a lot of cryptic commands and keystrokes to perform many tasks, and the Windows-style arrangement of menus and a toolbar makes it that much simpler. And of course, you'll probably find that IRC servers tend to be measurably faster than their Web-based counterparts.

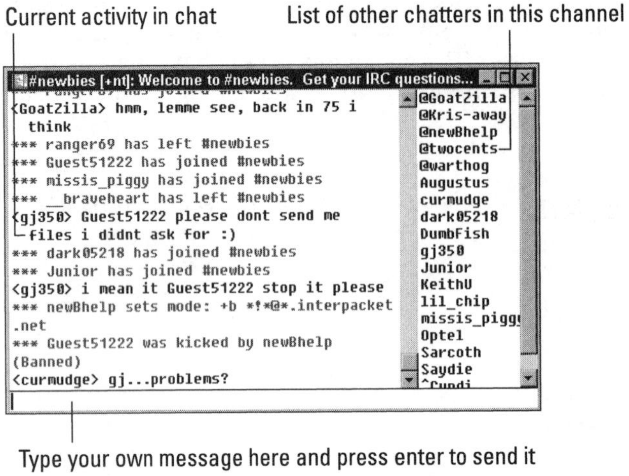

Current activity in chat   List of other chatters in this channel

Type your own message here and press enter to send it

Figure 22-4: We have encountered a large group in the #newbies chat channel.

Exploiting Web-Based Chat

IRC dominated the world of live chat in the late '80s and early '90s, but in the realm of online communication, IRC has lost ground to Web-based chat clients, which use HTML or Java software to carry messages through the Web browser. Web-based chat clients are easy to use, but because they rely on the already high-trafficked Web, they tend to be a little slower than their IRC counterparts.

As long as you use a semi-modern Web browser, the difference between using an HTML- or Java-based client is unimportant. Newer versions of Internet Explorer and Netscape Navigator present few if any problems. Your chat session actually works through an applet or plug-in to the browser, and if you don't have the right one, that's no problem. In fact, if this is your first time at a given chat site, there's a good chance that you won't. Fortunately, if you have a Java-capable Web browser (such as Internet Explorer or Netscape) the applet will launch automatically. If another type of plug-in is required, you may have to follow some specific instructions at the site to download and install it.

Caution   As with any other executable software that you download, there is a remote possibility that a virus might accompany the next chat client you download.

Your Web browser should warn you about this before beginning the download, and if you don't trust the source completely you might want to consider finding a different chat site. Scan all new software with a virus-checking program if you have one.

Entering a Web-based chat room

Once you've found a chat room you would like to visit (see the section "Finding a chat room" earlier in this chapter), entering it is a snap. Look for a link that says Chat or something equally obvious. Such a link usually takes you to a log on screen, like the one used by Talk City, which is shown in Figure 22-5. Depending on the policies at the host site, you may need to register before you can enter a chat room.

Tip   If you can't find a room right now, visit Geocities (www.geocities.com) or Talk City (www.talkcity.com) so that you can follow along with the example shown here.

While some chat rooms won't give you a choice of chat clients to use, other sites such as Talk City might offer a selection of clients, ranging from light-featured "basic" clients to larger clients with more options and features. Usually, your choice will depend on how long you want to wait for the download.

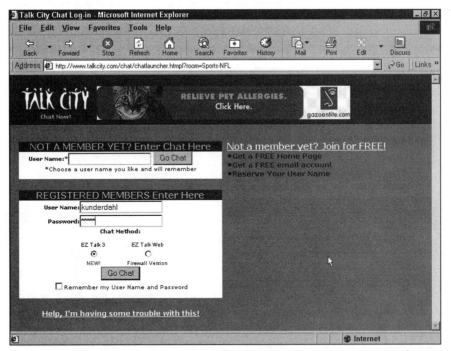

Figure 22-5: The Talk City logon screen allows you to choose between two chat clients, EZ Talk 3 or EZ Talk Web.

If you are given the opportunity, pick a nickname before you enter the chat room. This is the name that others in the room will see, so choose carefully. Be creative and pick something that other people are not likely to have. This will help you to build your own identity online and it will help others to recognize you later. You may also consider choosing a gender-neutral name, especially if you want to avoid unsolicited flirtations. Some sites ask for your real name or e-mail address, but this information is usually not broadcast to the rest of the chat room. If you're not sure about any of the choices, look for a Help link to learn more.

Using the chat client

Chat clients abound on the World Wide Web, and each one is a little different. Nevertheless, there are some basic principles that you can follow when participating in a chat room. First of all, most chat clients contain the same basic elements in their user interface. Figure 22-6 illustrates those elements as they appear in the Talk City Java chat client.

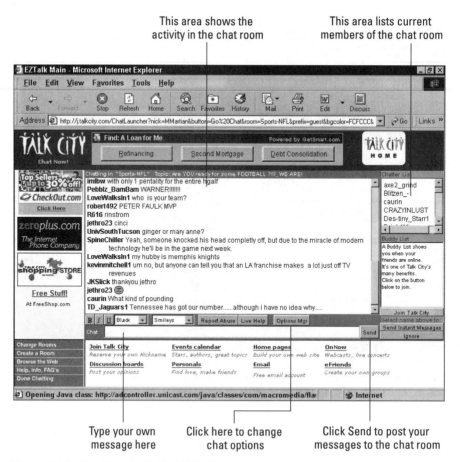

Figure 22-6: Chatting football at Talk City

Once you're in, you'll probably feel that finding and joining the chat room was the easy part. It may be all you can do just to keep your head above the virtual flames!

Most chat clients offer some useful options to help you tailor your chatting experience. Most let you change how often the activity window is refreshed (every 15 seconds is a common default), and you can usually insert a few basic graphics to spice up your messages as well. Look for a link in the chat client for graphics or other multimedia elements.

> **Tip** If you plan to use images a lot, you may want to print out the instructions for inserting them so that they're handy when you need them.

Exiting the chat room

When you are ready to leave a chat room, look for a button somewhere on the chat client interface that says "Leave chat" or "Log off chat" or something to that effect. If there doesn't appear to be such a button, click the Options button and choose Exit.

You may be tempted to leave a chat room by clicking the Back button on your browser's toolbar. However, this is not the best way to exit a chat room and it can actually cause you some problems. Clicking the Back button or typing a new URL into the Address bar will indeed take you out of the chat window, but your entity does not truly leave the chat. You—or at least your nickname—will remain logged on to the chat room for an indefinite period of time. As a result:

✦ Other people in the chat room will think you are still there, even when you're not. They might try to send messages to you or hold a conversation, and then you will appear rude for ignoring them.

✦ If you want to reenter the chat room in the near future, the server will not let you use the same nickname. Why? Because someone else in the chat room is already using that name.

Communicating with Instant Messaging Programs

As the number of people connected to the Internet has grown, communication habits and needs have changed as well. For some people, e-mail is simply not immediate enough, live chat is too transitory in nature to relay important information, and online conferencing is too complicated and slow. Enter instant messaging programs such as AOL Instant Messenger, Mirabilis ICQ, Yahoo! Messenger, MSN Messenger, and others.

Instant messaging programs differ from IRC, Web-based chat, and e-mail in several ways:

✦ Discussions generally take place as one-on-one affairs, rather than in more public forums such as a chat room.

✦ Each client uses its own proprietary network that it communicates over. Thus, the people you communicate with must use the same client.

✦ A status window tells you if your contacts are currently online or not.

✦ Instant messaging programs are stand-alone applications, meaning that you don't have to leave your Web browser or e-mail program open to use them (although they do require an active Internet connection).

We'll briefly discuss four of the more popular hybrid chat-clients in the following sections.

AOL Instant Messenger

You might already have America Online's Instant Messenger installed on your system and not even know it. The program accompanies some newer versions of popular software, such as Netscape Communicator and Navigator. Usually you will be asked if you want to install Instant Messenger when you run the setup program for the software it came with.

AOL claims that 37 million people use AOL Instant Messenger, but we suspect that this is actually just the number of people to whom it has been distributed via Communicator and other packages. A large number of the people who have received a copy of Instant Messenger probably aren't actually using it. Still, the program's wide proliferation means that there's a pretty good chance that many of the people you want to contact already have it.

If you don't have it, you can easily download Instant Messenger from AOL at http://www.aol.com/aim/. The software is free, and you don't have to be an AOL member to use it. Versions are available for both Windows and Macintosh. The idea behind Instant Messenger is that when you log on to the Instant Messenger network, friends and associates will be able to see that you are online. The software normally logs you on automatically every time you connect to the Internet, making it a virtual no-brainer.

To use Instant Messenger for the first time, open it by clicking Start ⇨ Programs ⇨ Netscape Communicator ⇨ AOL Instant Messenger. You will be prompted to log on, but if you haven't registered yet, it won't work. Click the Sign on button, and when an error message is displayed click More Info. Here you will find a link to let you register with the service.

Why not just use e-mail?

You may be wondering if it's really worth the trouble to use an instant messaging program instead of plain old e-mail, chat, or conferencing software. It's a good thing to wonder about, and depending on your needs an instant messaging program may or may not be worth your time.

The primary advantage this software has over e-mail is timeliness. When you send an e-mail, it usually takes at least several minutes before the other person actually receives the message. Assuming the recipient checks his mail and gets your message in a timely manner, whatever response he sends will then take several more minutes to get back to you. Thus, with a minimum five to ten minute lag time, holding a true conversation via e-mail can be frustrating.

On the other hand, live chat is a little too quick for some people. Messages scroll by in chat rooms pretty fast, and if the other person gets up to refill her coffee, she might completely miss your post. Besides, chat rooms are not even remotely private. This leaves us with conferencing software such as Microsoft NetMeeting and Netscape Conference. While these are both versatile and well suited to the heavy business user, their servers can be ghastly slow and the interfaces complicated to understand.

The instant messengers provide a nice compromise. They are quicker than e-mail, messages won't disappear after two or three minutes and, for the most part, they are easier to use. They provide an excellent way to keep in touch with friends, family, or business associates in real time, without demanding too much from your system or Internet connection. Telecommuters will find them especially handy because keeping in touch with the home office is a snap and instant messengers don't rack up long distance phone charges.

Problems? Yes, there are some. First of all, anyone you want to contact with one of these clients must also have the same client. This requires some coordination on your part, and getting a large group (like your entire family) to agree on one client can be a challenge. Also, be careful not to let one of these clients completely replace your other communication methods, particularly e-mail.

Tip
We were amazed at the number of screen names that are already being used by someone else. If the user names you try to choose keep getting rejected, try adding a number or two to the end.

The Instant Messenger interface will appear, similar to Figure 22-7.

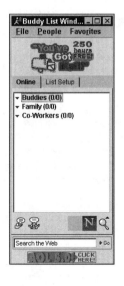

Figure 22-7: The AOL Instant Messenger user interface enables you to easily determine who is online.

Other features of Instant Messenger include:

✦ The capability to add other users of Instant Messenger to your buddy list.

✦ A user interface that lets you know who on your buddy list is currently online.

✦ Communications via live chat or in an e-mail style format.

✦ A "ticker," which can be placed onscreen to scroll a list of news headlines, as shown in Figure 22-8. Click a headline to link to that story.

Figure 22-8: A ticker window offers scrolling links to news headlines. Click the Close (X) button if you don't want the ticker to be displayed.

Chatting or composing messages with Instant Messenger is easy. Click a name on your buddy list to open the Instant Message window and begin typing your message. The window offers some options for formatting your text, making it easier to spice up your words a bit. Click Send when you are done typing. AOL Instant Messenger is simple to use, and the number of people who use its network is impressive. And it's simplicity will no doubt win more than a few hearts.

Mirabilis ICQ

Mirabilis (http://www.mirabilis.com/) offers ICQ, a program similar to AOL's Instant Messenger but with more features. Besides being able to see when your friends and associates are online, you can also integrate ICQ with Microsoft NetMeeting or Netscape Conference to facilitate video and audio conferencing. Despite competition from much larger companies, ICQ remains extremely popular and is considered the standard by which other instant messaging programs are measured. Numerous versions of ICQ are available for virtually every operating system in use today, including handheld devices such as PalmPilot and computers running Windows CE. Visit Tucows (www.tucows.com) or virtually any other major software site for current downloads.

Once you have downloaded and installed ICQ, you have the option of choosing between Simple Mode and Advanced Mode, but for the greatest versatility we suggest that you stick with the Advanced Mode. Advanced Mode allows you to forward Web site URLs and file attachments, and to take advantage of many other options.

As long as the ICQ window is open, it will remain on top of all other windows (although some Macintosh versions do not do this).

Most people either love this feature or hate it, but it's easy to change; you can do so in the Options menu, or just minimize the ICQ window to the taskbar.

As you can see in Figure 22-9, ICQ provides you with the current online status of other people in your contact list. To add people to your contact list, click Add Users near the bottom of the window. Depending on a person's security settings, you may have to request authorization before adding someone to your list. Fortunately, the onscreen instructions provided by ICQ are pretty easy to follow.

When a message is incoming, ICQ issues an audible "Uh-oh!" warning and flashes a notecard icon in the system tray. If the ICQ window is open, the flashing notecard will appear next to the name of the person who is sending it. To read the message, simply double-click the notecard icon. To compose and send a message to someone in your contacts list, double-click a name. A message composition window opens, similar to Figure 22-10. All you have to do is type your message and click Send. If the other user is online, he will receive a notification of the message instantly.

Tip   There is, unfortunately, a lot of spam (much of it "adult" oriented) sent randomly to ICQ users. If you don't want to receive unsolicited spam and Web page announcements from people who are not on your contact list, click ICQ ⇨ Security and Privacy. On the Security tab, select the option "My authorization is required." On the Ignore List tab, select the desired options to block others from spamming your ICQ account. Click Save and then Done when you are finished making changes.

This number identifies your account

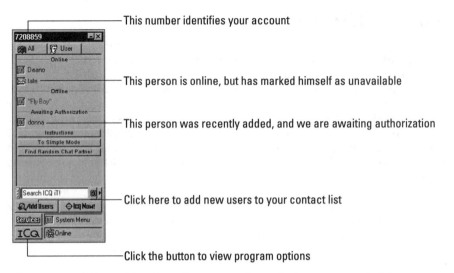

This person is online, but has marked himself as unavailable

This person was recently added, and we are awaiting authorization

Click here to add new users to your contact list

Click the button to view program options

Figure 22-9: ICQ provides the online status of people in your contacts list.

Figure 22-10: A message is about to be sent to an ICQ contact.

Another nice feature of ICQ is the ability to manually modify your online status with the ICQ network. In the ICQ window, click the Online button at the bottom of the window and choose a different status from the list. If you have Windows 95 or higher, you can right-click the ICQ icon in the system tray, choose Status from the menu that appears, and select a new status.

ICQ is an easy way to keep in touch with others, assuming they also have ICQ. It provides a more timely method of communication than e-mail and combines some useful features from both chat clients and conferencing software. Download it for yourself and see what other features you might be able to take advantage of.

Yahoo! Messenger

Yahoo! has also entered the instant messaging fray with its own program called Yahoo! Messenger (`http://messenger.yahoo.com/`). Formerly known as Yahoo! Pager, Messenger is packed with features such as voice chat and rich Web content. Versions of Yahoo! Messenger are available for Windows, Macintosh, Windows CE, and Palm OS. A Java version is also available and should run on virtually any Java-capable system.

The Messenger interface is extremely simple. Click the Add button to add friends to your contact list, and double-click a name to begin composing a new message. If you don't know the Yahoo! ID of a person you want to link up with, click Add ⇨ Help ⇨ Adding New Friends to search the Yahoo! Directory.

As you might expect from the Internet's premier Web directory, Yahoo! Messenger is also a good source of up-to-the-minute news. The program has several tabs, as shown in Figure 12-11 below, which provide different kinds of information at a glance. The tabs are:

✦ **Friends.** This is your communication center where you can chat with your contacts.

✦ **Stocks.** Business news is updated every few minutes when the markets are open.

✦ **News.** News from Yahoo!'s Web site is piped right into your computer (as long as your Internet connection is active) and you can check it by simply clicking this tab. This is handy if you like to stay on top of the headlines but don't feel like opening your browser all the time.

✦ **Sports.** Current scores and links to related stories are provided here.

✦ **Overview.** This tab can serve as a control center where you can manage your Yahoo! Messenger account. A tree-like structure lets you customize options for the various components of Messenger.

Yahoo! Messenger is an excellent program, especially if you appreciate the added Web content that it provides. Yahoo!'s network doesn't have as many members as AOL's or ICQ's, but it is growing and should win new converts in the future.

Click the News tab to view current headlines

Figure 22-11: Current headlines are always available on the Yahoo! Messenger News tab.

MSN Messenger

Because MSN Messenger did not enter the market until 1999, Microsoft was late joining the instant messaging wars. Perhaps this explains why MSN Messenger has been slow to catch on. People looking for an instant messaging program want one that is connected to a network with many users, and when MSN Messenger was first released it had, naturally, the smallest network. You can download MSN Messenger for Windows or Macintosh at `http://messenger.msn.com/`.

Note

> MSN Messenger requires you obtain an MSN Passport in order to use it. If you have a Hotmail account, you already have one. If not, see Chapter 13 to learn how to obtain one.

Most instant messaging programs are simple little applications, and MSN Messenger is perhaps the simplest of them all. This is quite surprising considering who produced it, but as you can see in Figure 22-12, the controls are few and intuitive.

MSN Messenger is closely tied to your Hotmail account. In fact, if you click the Mail button on the Messenger toolbar, your browser opens to your Hotmail Inbox. Unfortunately, if you use an e-mail program such as Outlook Express to read your Hotmail account, there is no way to configure Messenger to automatically open that program instead of your browser.

One thing that *is* nice about MSN Messenger is that, like ICQ, it is very easy to change your online status. Simply click the Status button on the toolbar and choose a new status that will be displayed to other users.

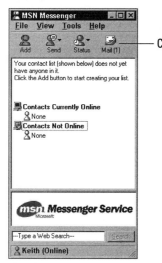 ———— Click here to check your Hotmail Inbox

Figure 22-12: The MSN Messenger program window is about as simple as they come.

Summary

Live chat on the Internet is not a new concept, but it is one that has gained a significant following during the last couple of years. It allows real-time (or almost real-time) conversation between an unlimited number of netizens on almost any topic. But before you can chat effectively, there are some important things you need to know. Not only should you understand the basic concepts behind live chat, but you must also be mindful of proper chatiquette and know how to use the different kinds of chat clients and where to find the best chat rooms. Once you've mastered this, a whole new online world awaits. Happy chatting!

✦   ✦   ✦

Finding and Using Newsgroups

✦ ✦ ✦ ✦

In This Chapter

Investigating
newsgroup basics

Using a news client

✦ ✦ ✦ ✦

Newsgroups have been around for many years, beginning as a forum for Unix users to communicate with each other in the late 1970s. Newsgroups increased in popularity soon after the National Science Foundation set up the original 56 Kbps network connecting five supercomputer centers in 1985, when universities and other institutions started creating newsgroups on the network in large numbers. Despite these early beginnings, newsgroups have avoided falling into obscurity, as gophers and BBS's have.

Note   For the sake of clarity, it is important to note that the terms "newsgroup" and "Usenet" are used interchangeably here and throughout the online world. Usenet is generally used to refer to the vast network of news servers, but that does not mean there is any organization that oversees or sets standards for Usenet.

The newsgroup concept is simple. Groups are usually arranged by specific topics or interests, and messages posted to the group are put into a list that anyone can read. When you open a message, it's downloaded from the news server, and you read it much like you would read an e-mail message. You can also reply to or forward messages or compose and post new messages to the group using the same techniques you would use for e-mail. This chapter describes newsgroups and discusses how to install and use a newsgroup client.

Investigating Newsgroup Basics

To better understand the concepts at work here, try to think of newsgroups as a kind of virtual round table. Anyone can post a message to a newsgroup, and anyone else can read that message. But besides simple text, people can share images and other files with the newsgroup by simply attaching them to messages.

Newsgroups are usually organized for some common interest. For instance, if you like Mexican food, then you might want to join the newsgroup called `alt.food.mexican-cooking`. In that group, you and others who share an interest in Mexican foods can post instructions on how to make tamales, cooking tips and tricks, pictures of enchiladas, request a recipe for molé, and anything else that comes to mind (hungry, yet?). The following are some basic concepts that apply to newsgroups:

✦ To join a newsgroup, you first have to know its name. The news server at your ISP will contain a list of newsgroup names (perhaps as many as 90,000) that you must download.

✦ After you search through the list and find a group you want to join, you must subscribe to it. Subscribing doesn't cost anything, nor does it require you to send any information about yourself. It's just a simple click of a button, and that button is usually called Subscribe.

✦ If you're a business owner, newsgroups can be a great way for you to obtain feedback on your products or services. If you find a group that your customers frequent, you can monitor what they say about you! But don't spam the list; this might alienate more customers than it attracts!

✦ Having trouble with some new software or hardware? Look for a newsgroup that contains fellow users of that item for support and discussion. These can be great alternative sources of information if the official company tech support isn't being very helpful.

✦ Reading, replying, and posting to newsgroups usually works like e-mail. If you are using Microsoft Outlook Express, pine, or Netscape Communicator, learn their respective e-mail functions first.

Caution　Do not say or do anything in a newsgroup that you would not like the entire world to see. Never post personal information in newsgroups, such as your address or phone number. You may also want to use a separate e-mail screen name just for newsgroup posts.

An excellent place to learn more about newsgroups is at Deja.com (`http://www.deja.com/`). Deja.com is a Web site dedicated to the Usenet community. Although it is not actually a news server, Deja.com does allow you to search news archives at the site. As you can see in Figure 23-1, Deja.com strives for a community atmosphere, and is worth checking out if you like meeting people and having discussions about various things. Deja.com does an excellent job of identifying current hot topics, and can point you in the direction of related discussions in Usenet. We particularly enjoy the ratings feature, where viewers can rate various subjects and then view what others have had to say about it.

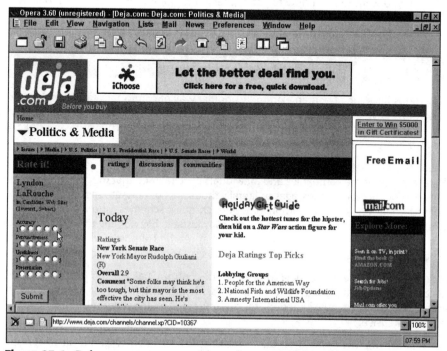

Figure 23-1: Deja.com serves as a guide to the wonderful world of Usenet.

Newsgroups can be a great way of keeping in touch with others who share your interests or concerns, especially if you don't have time for other things such as live chat. But as with anything in the online world, some level of caution must be exercised. The following sections tell you more about how to find and participate in newsgroups.

Using News Clients

Most news clients are remarkably similar to e-mail clients. In fact, Microsoft's Outlook Express, Netscape's Messenger, and pine all function as combination e-mail/news clients. This section describes how to use these three news clients.

We assume that you have an Internet account with a provider that offers a news server. If you're not sure, contact your ISP to find out if they provide one, and if so, ask them what the server name is. We will also assume that you have already configured your dial-up connection.

Cross-Reference   If you want to learn how to get connected to the Internet fast, take a look at Chapter 1, "Getting Connected Fast!"

The Changing Role of Newsgroups

Newsgroups have long been an extremely popular way of communicating among netizens. Newsgroups have been used for socializing, complaining, assisting, and anything else that people can think of to talk about. Unfortunately, because newsgroups are so public, they have also been subjected to a wide range of abuses.

Perhaps the greatest problem surrounding newsgroups today involves spam, or unwanted advertisements. Some companies and individuals have learned that they can post advertisements or other unwanted messages to literally thousands of newsgroups at virtually no cost. The most common types of spam involve get-rich-quick schemes, phony vacation package offers, and adult Web sites. The spam, by the way, usually has nothing to do with the newsgroups they are posted to. The volume of spam has reached almost epidemic proportions, to the point where the content of some newsgroups is more than 50 percent spam!

Furthermore, because it is almost impossible to control what goes into newsgroups, and also because it's relatively easy to hide one's identity when posting, newsgroups have become a hotbed (no pun intended) for pornographic material and other things that you may find offensive.

One response to these problems is that some people have left newsgroups in favor of e-mail lists. Mailing lists work somewhat like a newsgroup, in that they usually concentrate on a specific issue or interest. However, when you subscribe to a mailing list, the messages are sent directly to your inbox as e-mails. If you send a message to the list, other subscribers see it, but the general public does not. Such lists offer a good alternative to newsgroups, primarily because it is easier to control spam, and administrators can remove list members that regularly post objectionable or inappropriate materials to the list. Unfortunately, high-volume lists can also clog your e-mail inbox with dozens or even hundreds of messages a day that you may or may not have time to read.

Another response is that many *moderated* newsgroups have appeared. These groups have a person (or group) who oversees content and removes messages that are deemed inappropriate. Many moderated groups actually have the word "moderated" in their name, but it should also be mentioned in the newsgroup's FAQ.

Despite porn and spam, newsgroups can still be a useful tool for communicating on the Internet. You will have to decide for yourself if the advantages outweigh the potential problems.

Avoiding Spam in Newsgroups

It's not bad enough that most newsgroups contain a lot of spam; simply posting a message to a group could expose you to a flood of unwanted spam in your e-mail account. The main reason for this is that a number of unscrupulous organizations have created programs called spambots. Spambots comb newsgroup postings looking for e-mail addresses. If you post something to a group, your e-mail address will appear in the header information and will inevitably be vacuumed up by a spambot. Likewise, if your e-mail address appears in the body of a posting, the spambot can find it there too.

Fortunately, spambots are pretty dumb, so you can easily avoid them by exercising some care. First of all, if you post to a newsgroup, modify the "reply to" e-mail address in your news client using an antispam countermeasure. The most common thing to do is to place the words "nospam" or "die-spam-die" in the middle of your address. When human beings want to respond to your post, they can easily identify this tactic, especially if you create a signature that says something like, "To reply, remove 'die-spam-die' from my e-mail address." Thus, legitimate responses can still be sent, but the nonintelligent spambots will simply identify an invalid address.

Outlook Express 5

Outlook Express 5 is an e-mail and news client that is available for Windows and Macintosh. If you have Windows, Outlook Express 5 comes bundled with Internet Explorer 5. Browsing newsgroups with this program is simple if you are already familiar with its e-mail services.

Cross-Reference

If you haven't yet familiarized yourself with Outlook Express, see Chapter 12, "Choosing an E-mail Client and Using E-mail."

Setting up Outlook Express to read the news

Before you can use Outlook Express to read the news, you need to install it and set it up. For now we'll assume that you've already installed it, and that you are ready to use it for browsing newsgroups. To begin browsing with Outlook Express, perform the following:

1. Launch Outlook Express by double-clicking its icon on the desktop. You may also find it on the Windows Quick Launch toolbar next to the Start button.

2. Make sure that you have established a connection to the Internet.

3. On the menu bar click Tools ➪ Accounts.

4. Select the News tab in the Internet Accounts dialog box and click Add ➪ News.

5. When the Internet Connection Wizard appears, follow the instructions. When you come to the dialog box shown in Figure 23-2, enter the News Server domain name in the News (NNTP) server box. This information should be provided by your ISP.

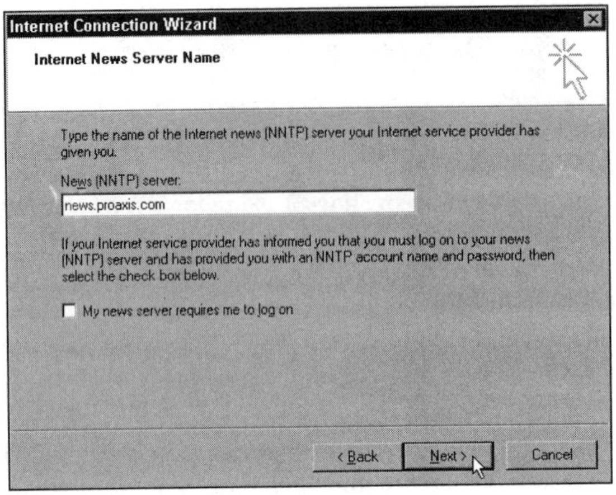

Figure 23-2: Enter the news server domain name in this wizard box.

6. When you get to the last wizard screen, click Finish. Then click Close to close the Internet Accounts window.

7. You should now see a listing for your news server in the Folder list on the left side of the Outlook Express window. Click that listing to begin browsing newsgroups.

The first time you access the news server, you must download a list of newsgroups. Most news servers list more than 30,000 groups (and possibly three times that many), so even with a relatively fast modem this will take a few minutes. Rest assured, you will only have to do this once; go get a cup of coffee while the list downloads.

Searching and subscribing with Outlook Express

After the list of newsgroups has been downloaded, you can scroll through the list to find a group that interests you. But because there are so many, scrolling can be quite futile. Fortunately, Outlook Express makes searching through the newsgroup names very simple. To begin searching, try this:

1. In the "Display newsgroups which contain" box, type a word that closely describes a subject in which you are interested. The list of newsgroups shrinks to only those groups that contain the letters or words that you typed.

2. If you find a group you want to join, select it and click Subscribe.

3. Click Go To. The group list disappears, and a list of message headers is downloaded. By default, only the first 300 message headers in that group will be downloaded. Figure 23-3 shows a list of headers being displayed by Outlook Express.

4. Read messages just as you would a regular e-mail.

One thing you may notice as you browse the newsgroups is that some messages are part of *threads*. A thread begins when someone posts a response to a message. Others may post additional responses, and even respond to the responders. Thus, all of these messages become part of an online conversation, and collectively they are referred to as a thread. Outlook Express indicates when a message is part of a thread by placing a plus sign next to the message, as shown in Figure 23-3. If you click the plus sign, the list expands to show other messages in that thread. This helps you keep track of a conversation you are interested in or may want to be a part of. Any time you respond to a message, your post becomes part of the thread.

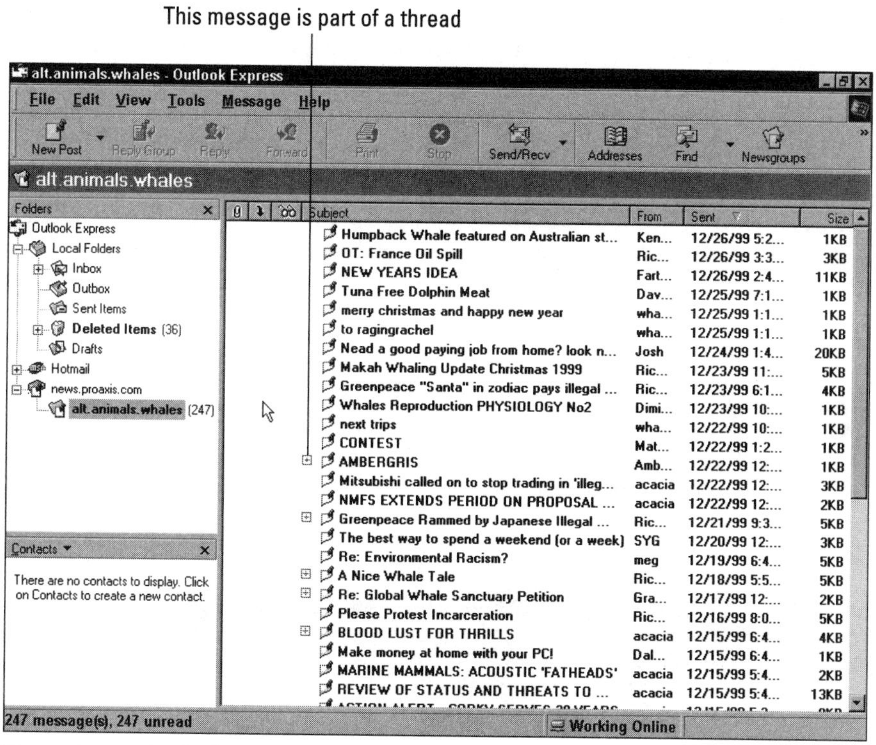

This message is part of a thread

Figure 23-3: Outlook Express peruses a newsgroup.

Being part of the news with Outlook Express

Because, Outlook Express acts as both an e-mail and newsgroup client, reading and composing newsgroup messages is very simple. When reading newsgroup messages with Outlook Express, the following are helpful concepts to remember:

✦ By default, Outlook Express downloads only the first 300 message headers in a group. To download additional headers, click Tools ➪ Get Next 300 Headers in the menu bar.

✦ Unread messages will be shown in boldface in the header list.

✦ Double-click a message header to read that message. Because only the headers are downloaded initially, it may take a few seconds or even minutes for large messages to download. Look at the Size column in the header list to determine approximately how long the download will take.

✦ If you want to read messages offline, you will need to download the actual message bodies first. To download more than one message, hold down the Ctrl key or Shift key and click the messages. Then choose Tools ➪ Mark for Offline ➪ Download Message Later on the menu bar. Finally, click Tools ➪ Synchronize All. When you've completed these steps, the icons in the subject field of each downloaded message will become a full sheet of paper (rather than the torn half sheet of non-downloaded messages). When the synchronization is finished, you can disconnect your Internet connection.

After you have been reading the newsgroup for a while, you may be ready to participate yourself. To compose and post a message to a newsgroup, do the following:

1. Open Outlook Express and click the newsgroup in which you want to participate. You may have to expand the folder list by clicking the plus sign next to the name of your news server.

2. Click New Post in the Outlook Express toolbar. The New Message window opens, and the address of the newsgroup is automatically entered in the To field.

3. Compose your newsgroup posting just as you would an e-mail message, as shown in Figure 23-4. Be sure to enter a subject in the Subject field, and address any carbon copies you want to send.

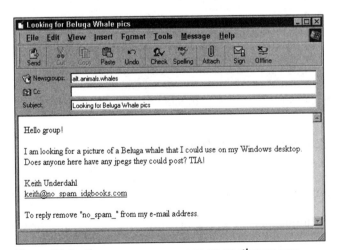

Figure 23-4: Compose your newsgroup posting as you would an e-mail message.

4. When you're done, click Send. The message is posted to the newsgroup.

Replying to a message is just as easy. But before you reply, consider exactly who you want to reply to. You have two options:

✦ **Reply Group.** This option sends your reply to the newsgroup, where anyone can read it.

✦ **Reply.** This sends your reply to only the original author of the message. If your reply is of a private nature, or perhaps is off the newsgroup topic, use this option.

Of course, you can also forward the message to someone else via e-mail. Simply click the Forward button. Whichever option you select, choose wisely! Public postings of private messages have caused many embarrassments over the relatively short history of the Internet.

Reading multi-part attachments with Outlook Express

Many people use newsgroups to exchange files such as movies, pictures, and music. These files are usually very large, so large that they are often posted in several parts rather than in a single, huge message.

There are several good reasons for this *multipart* posting. First of all, many servers place a limit on the size of individual postings. If a server limits a post to 500KB, then an MP3 file that is 5MB will simply be too big for a single message. Furthermore, smaller messages are more likely to be downloaded successfully.

People who post multipart attachments usually label them appropriately in the subject. For instance, if an MP3 is posted in 12 parts, the first part will probably be labeled 1/12, the second part will be 2/12, the third 3/12, and so on.

If you download a single message in a multipart series, it will display as thousands of lines of unintelligible code when you try to open it. Fortunately, Outlook Express helps you handle these multipart postings. In this respect it is superior to Netscape Messenger, because Messenger does not have provisions for handling these types of attachments. To download a multipart attachment, do the following:

1. Locate and select each part of the attachment.

   Hold down the Ctrl key as you click on each part. Make sure that only messages in the multipart series are selected.

2. On the Outlook Express menu bar, click Message ➪ Combine and Decode.

3. In the Order for Decoding window (Figure 23-5) place the attachments in numeric order, starting with part 1.

   You can move a part up or down in the list by selecting it and clicking the Move Up or Move Down buttons. Continue this procedure until they are in the correct order. You may need to use the scroll bars to see the numbering scheme for the series.

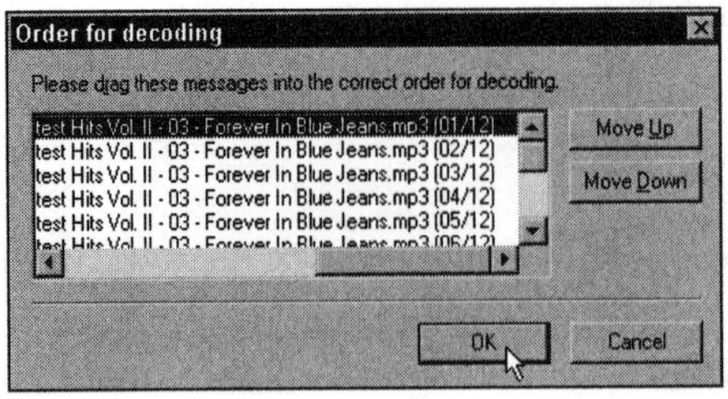

Figure 23-5: Make sure the attachments are listed in the correct order before you combine and decode them.

4. Click OK to begin the process.

Depending on the speed of your connection, it will probably take a while to download, combine, and decode all of the attachment parts. Keep in mind that you won't be able to use Outlook Express for anything else until the process is complete. When it is finished, a single message window will open and the attachment will be listed.

> **Caution**   Don't forget to check any attachments you receive from newsgroups with an antivirus program before opening them!

Unsubscribing from newsgroups using Outlook Express

If you find yourself losing interest in a particular newsgroup, unsubscribing from it couldn't be easier. In the Outlook Express folder, right-click the newsgroup you want to leave and choose Unsubscribe from the shortcut menu, which is shown in Figure 23-6. If you no longer subscribe to any newsgroups, Outlook Express will say so and ask you if you want to view a list of newsgroups, presumably so that you can join something new. Click Yes or No as desired.

Netscape Messenger 4.7

If you have the full version of Netscape Communicator 4.7 (and not just the stand-alone Navigator Web browser), you can use the Messenger component for your newsgroup activities. Messenger is also Netscape's e-mail client and is available for Windows, Macintosh, and Unix variants (such as Linux). If you don't have a copy of Netscape Messenger 4.7, versions of Netscape Communicator for Windows and PowerPCs (Macs) can be found on the *Internet Bible* CD-ROM.

> **Cross-Reference**   To learn more about how to configure and use Netscape Messenger, read Chapter 12, "Choosing an E-Mail Client and Using E-Mail."

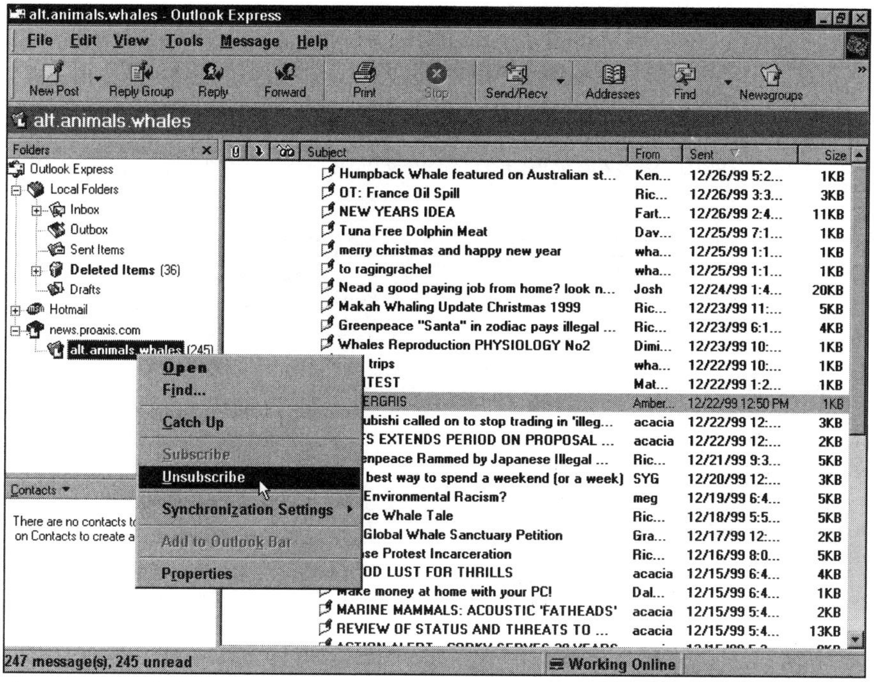

Figure 23-6: Click here to unsubscribe from the newsgroup.

Setting up Messenger

As with any other news client, Messenger has a few simple setup procedures that need to be carried out before you can read newsgroups. To get Messenger ready, perform the following:

1. If Navigator is already open, click the Read Newsgroups button on the Component bar, or choose Communicator ➪ Newsgroups.

2. If this is the first time you have used Netscape's news or mail capabilities, you will need to set up a new user profile. Follow the instructions in the profile wizard.

3. Make sure you enter the correct news server name when the wizard asks for it. If you're not sure what that name should be, check with your ISP.

4. When you're done, the main Messenger window appears. Click the name of your news server in the folder list on the left side of the screen. You may be prompted to connect to the Internet (otherwise, establish your Internet connection manually if necessary).

5. The Subscribe to Discussion Groups window appears. If this is your first time, Messenger will need to download the list of newsgroups first. Because there could be as many as 90,000 different newsgroups, this may take a few minutes. Fortunately, you only have to download the whole list once. When it's done, you'll see the beginning of a long list, similar to Figure 23-7. Now you're ready to begin your adventures in newsgroup land!

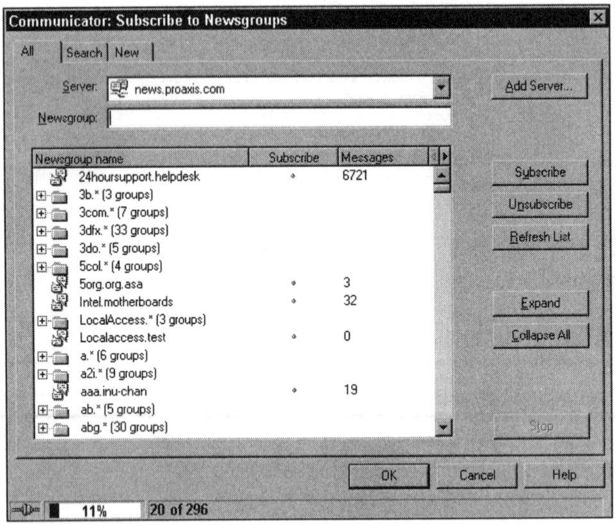

Figure 23-7: The list is downloaded, ready for you to browse!

> **Note**   If you set up your news account earlier and need to download the newsgroup list from within Messenger, select the server in the folder list and click File ⇨ Subscribe. The download process will begin automatically.

Locating and joining newsgroups with Messenger

Now that you have a list of newsgroups staring you in the face, it's time to read some news. As you can see in Figure 23-7, the Subscribe to Newsgroups window is quite different from the newsgroup list presented by Outlook Express. For one thing, you'll see that the groups are organized into submenus, rather than in one, giant list. You can navigate through this list using the same techniques you would use to browse your hard drive using a program like Windows Explorer.

Finding a newsgroup using the All tab of this window can be a little frustrating. To search more efficiently, try the following:

1. In the Subscribe to Newsgroups window, click the Search tab to bring it to the front.

2. Type a word, such as **astronomy**, in the Search for box.

3. Click Search Now.

4. To subscribe to the group, highlight the group and click Subscribe. A check mark appears in the Subscribe column of the group list. As you can see in Figure 23-8 below, we subscribed to a newsgroup called `gac.physics.astronomy`.

5. Click OK.

The Message Center window displays the newsgroup you subscribed to under the name of your news server. Now you're ready to start reading and participating.

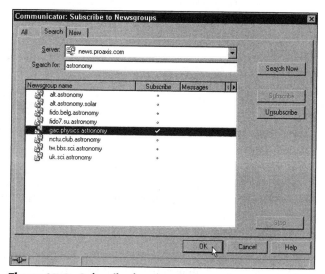

Figure 23-8: Subscribed and ready to read some news!

Reading and participating in newsgroups with Messenger

Viewing the contents of a newsgroup with Messenger is similar to using Netscape Messenger for e-mail. When you are ready to start reading newsgroups with Messenger, consider the following:

✦ To read a newsgroup, click its name in the folder list on the left side of the window. A list of headers for messages in that group will be downloaded.

✦ If the newsgroup you are trying to read is large, you may see a dialog box asking you if you want to download all headers, or just the first 500. You can also specify a different number of headers to download, if you wish.

✦ The Netscape Newsgroup window is divided into two panes, as shown in Figure 23-9. The upper pane lists message headers, and the lower pane shows the contents of a message. Click a header in the upper pane to download it, and then read the message in the lower pane.

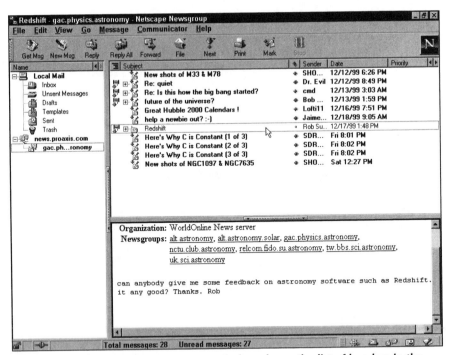

Figure 23-9: The Netscape Newsgroup window shows the list of headers in the upper pane and message contents in the lower.

✦ Double-click a message header to view it in its own window. This is especially desirable when the message contains images that might be hard to see in the small lower pane of the Newsgroup window.

When you want to reply to a message in a newsgroup, click and hold the Reply button on the toolbar and choose one of these options:

✦ **to Sender Only.** This option sends your reply only to the person who wrote the original message. Choosing this method is best if what you have to say is of a private nature.

✦ **to Newsgroup.** This option is the default method if you simply click the Reply button once. Your reply will be posted directly to the newsgroup.

Alternatively, click and hold the Reply All button and choose one of these:

✦ **to Sender and All Recipients.** This option sends your reply to the original author and anyone else who might have gotten a copy of it, but the reply does not go to the entire newsgroup.

✦ **to Sender and Newsgroup.** Use this method if you want to reply to the group and the original author, but you're not sure if he or she is still subscribed to the group.

Choosing the correct method of reply is extremely important. You do not want to shoulder the embarrassment of having posted a private message out where all the world can see it! Once you've chosen your reply method, compose and send your message just like you would if you were composing the message from scratch. You can also send new messages to a newsgroup in hopes of starting a new discussion thread. To create and post a message to a group, try this:

1. Click New Msg on the Netscape Newsgroup toolbar.

2. The message composition window opens with the newsgroup URL automatically entered in the Group field. Enter any additional addresses as needed.

3. Type your message, as shown in Figure 23-10.

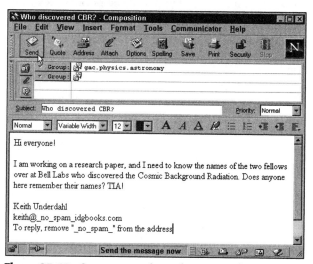

Figure 23-10: Our message is ready to go to the newsgroup, complete with an antispam e-mail address.

4. When you are done, click Send on the toolbar. Your message is sent to the newsgroup and automatically posted.

Unsubscribing from newsgroups with Messenger

Unsubscribing from newsgroups you no longer read is always a good idea. It keeps your folder list from becoming too cluttered, and, because Netscape checks for new messages every time you log on, it cuts down on bandwidth. To unsubscribe:

1. If you are currently in the Newsgroup window for the newsgroup, click the close (X) button in the upper right corner of that window.

2. In the folder list, right-click the newsgroup that you're tired of reading and select Remove Newsgroup from the shortcut menu. Alternatively, click it once to select it and press Del on your keyboard.

3. When you are asked to confirm that you really want to leave the group, click OK.

As with Outlook Express, many of Messenger's newsgroup functions work a lot like e-mail. Using Messenger is simple and relatively straightforward, even for people who are new to computers.

Summary

Newsgroups can provide a wealth of information. And thanks to some of the excellent news clients available today, finding, reading, and participating in newsgroups is easier than ever. In this chapter we discussed what to expect from newsgroups, and we also introduced you to three popular news clients.

✦   ✦   ✦

Web Directory

As wonderful as the Internet has become, an old fashioned book can still be easier to use. So, in that spirit, we offer the following Web Directory as a way to help you get started on some new Web—surfing adventures. Listed in this directory are nearly one thousand Web sites, divided into about 140 different categories based on subject matter or general content.

Using the Web Directory is easy. If you are searching for something specific, try to think of where you might find that item in your telephone company's yellow pages. We have organized Web sites using a similar logic here, although the categories are tailored specifically to the Internet. To go to a site that looks like it will have what you're looking for, type the URL for that site into the address bar of your Web browser. The URL appears below each Web site name, and usually starts with something like `http://www`. See Appendix A of the *Internet Bible* to learn more about URLs than you ever cared to know.

The Web Directory is included on this book's CD-ROM as an HTML document. This means you can click any URL in the HTML version and be instantly transported to the sites you choose. What could be easier? See Appendix C, "Using the Internet Bible CD-ROM," for more on how to use the CD-ROM.

In addition to Web sites, we also include numerous newsgroups in this directory where we felt they were both appropriate and valuable. See Chapter 23, "Finding and Using Newsgroups," for more information on how to use a news client.

One caveat we will mention is that the ever changing nature of the Internet means that some URLs in this directory may no longer be active when you read this. If you find that a Web site address listed here has changed, try searching for it at one of the Web sites listed under "Search Engines."

However you choose to take advantage of it, this directory should prove to be both valuable and entertaining as you journey across the World Wide Web. Happy Surfing!

A
B
C
D
E
F
G
H
I
J
K
L
M
N
O
P
Q
R
S
T
U
V
W
X
Y
Z

Acting

See also: Celebrities, Movies & Film, Radio,
Television, Theater

Acting Workshop On-Line

http://www.execpc.com/~blankda/
acting2.html

AWOL, Acting Workshop On-Line, is an
excellent resource for actors of both stage
and screen. The site has how-to articles,
useful links, and more.

American Federation of Television and Radio Artists

http://www.aftra.org/

The American Federation of Television and
Radio Artists is an AFL-CIO affiliated union
for persons in news and broadcasting,
entertainment, the recording business,
commercials, and industrial media.

Le Centre Du Silence

http://www.indranet.com/lcds.html

Interested in mime? Check out Le Centre
Du Silence, a Web site devoted to the art
of mime, including information about
training.

Screen Actors Guild

http://www.sag.com/

Wanna be in pictures? Better check out
the Screen Actors Guild, a union for film
actors.

news:alt.acting

This site offers interesting discussion
regarding acting, with an emphasis on
theater. The site seems reasonably free
of spam.

Agriculture

See also: Farming, Environment, Forestry, Gardening,
Plants

U.S. Department of Agriculture

http://www.usda.gov/

Check here to learn more about the U.S.
Department of Agriculture. Includes agriculture news, disaster assistance information, links, and agency information.

UC Sustainable Agriculture Research and Education Program

http://www.sarep.ucdavis.edu/

Learn all about sustainable agriculture
through the Sustainable Agriculture
Research and Education Program at the
University of California.

news:alt.sustainable.agriculture

This newsgroup covers sustainable agriculture, and there is also quite a bit of discussion on organic farming as well.

AIDS

See also: Health

The American Foundation for AIDS Research

http://www.amfar.org/

The American Foundation for AIDS
Research is a leading nonprofit organization that supports AIDS research. Check
here for news and conference and event
schedules, or learn how to make a
donation.

Celebrity AIDS Benefit Inc.

http://www.cab.org/

Celebrity AIDS Benefit Inc. is dedicated to fund-raising efforts for fighting the AIDS virus.

Community Programs for Clinical Research on AIDS

http://www.cpcra.org/

The Community Programs for Clinical Research on AIDS Web site is a great place to learn about research happening in your community. The site contains research papers and other data and links to community programs in your area.

Critical Path AIDS Project

http://www.critpath.org/

The Critical Path AIDS Project is an outstanding resource for people who are doing research into this disease or are looking for other information. The Web site is low on high-tech frills, but high on real, usable information.

The Magic Johnson Foundation

http://www.magicjohnson.org/

The Magic Johnson Foundation is committed to raising money for AIDS education, prevention, and care, primarily for young people.

Pets Are Wonderful Support

http://www.pawssf.org/

Pets Are Wonderful Support is an organization that helps persons with AIDS stay with and care for their pets. Learn more about the organization here.

news:sci.med.aids

This group is very heavy on the scientific content for AIDS-related medicine and practice.

Alcohol

See also: Cooking, Health

Alcoholics Anonymous

http://www.alcoholics-anonymous.org/

The Alcoholics Anonymous Web site is a starting place to learn more about this organization. The site is available in English, Spanish, or French.

Beershots: Microscopic Views of Beers From Around the World

http://micro.magnet.fsu.edu/beershots/

Beershots: Microscopic Views of Beers From Around the World is one of those great, geeky sites done by engineers with too much time and electronics equipment on their hands. Someone had a lot of fun putting this Web site together!

Stainless In Seattle

http://www.beeronline.com/

Stainless In Seattle offers a complete range of supplies for the home brewer.

Virtual Vineyards

http://www.virtualvin.com/

Can't find just the right wine? Try Virtual Vineyards, a place to buy wine, food, gifts, or just learn more about wines. Check out their Wine and Food Trivia!

The Webtender: An On-Line Bartender

http://www.webtender.com/

Can't remember how to mix that special drink? Try The Webtender: An On-Line Bartender, which has a searchable database of hundreds of drinks.

news:alt.food.wine

This group has some good discussions about wine and is light on the spam content.

news:rec.food.drink.beer

Do you like beer? Find some interesting conversations about it here, as well as a number of anecdotes and impressions of past and present brews.

Animals

See also: Agriculture, Environment, Science

Allpets.com

http://www.allpets.com/

Allpets.com is an excellent online magazine and encyclopedia providing information about living with and caring for pets of all shapes and sizes. This is a great learning resource if you want to learn more about a given animal or breed.

The Aviary

http://theaviary.com/

The Aviary is the ultimate online destination for lovers of birds.

Dinosauria On-Line

http://www.dinosauria.com/

Dinosaria On-Line is your window into the Mesozoic Period. This site is dedicated to presenting a current and accurate overview of dinosaurs.

The Humane Society of the United States

http://www.hsus.org/

The Humane Society of the United States is a great resource for learning more about how you can share the world with animals. The site also contains links to regional offices across the USA.

Jelly Cam

http://www.aquarium.org/jellies/index.htm

Check out the Jelly Cam to see live images (via spy cam) of jellyfish at the Oregon Coast Aquarium. The picture updates every 30 seconds.

The OMSI Rat Cam

http://www.omsi.edu/sln/rat/cam/home.html

The OMSI Rat Cam is one of those live spy cams, this one imaging "rodentry" from the Oregon Museum of Science and Industry.

People for the Ethical Treatment of Animals

http://www.peta-online.org/

Serious about animal rights? Maybe you should check out an organization like People for the Ethical Treatment of Animals (PETA).

Wolf Haven International

http://www.wolfhaven.org/

Some people love them, and some people fear them, but almost everyone seems fascinated by the wolf. Learn more about wolves and their lives at Wolf Haven International.

World Wildlife Fund Global Network

http://www.panda.org/

If you're interested in learning more about how you can help preserve the world and its wildlife, check out the World Wildlife Fund Global Network page.

Worm World

http://www.nj.com/yucky/worm/

Worm World is guaranteed to contain more than you ever wanted to know about worms. Learn about the different types of worms, body parts, how they can help as recyclers, and more fun stuff.

Yahoo!

http://www.yahoo.com/Science/Biology/
Zoology/Animals__Insects__and_Pets/
Organizations/Humane_and_Rescue_
Societies/

This page in the Yahoo! directory serves as a quick link to animal humane organizations across the world, although most of the listings appear to be in the USA and Canada.

news:alt.binaries.pictures.animals

This newsgroup always has some spectacular animal photos posted. Definitely worth a look!

Anthropology & Archaeology

See also: Science

American Anthropological Association Homepage

http://www.ameranthassn.org/

If your work or research involves anthropology, you might want to check out the American Anthropological Association Homepage. The page covers information about the association, as well as ethics issues and other policies.

ArchNet

http://spirit.lib.uconn.edu/ArchNet/

ArchNet is a product of the University of Connecticut, and serves as a sort of "virtual library" for archaeology on the Internet. A great place to start your research.

The Bureau of Applied Research in Anthropology

http://w3fp.arizona.edu/bara/

The Bureau of Applied Research in Anthropology is an excellent place to learn about research, brought to you by the University of Arizona. The site also lists student opportunities in anthropological research.

Internet Archaeology

http://intarch.ac.uk/

Internet Archaeology serves as an online journal for archaeological science. This is a good place to go for full-text, in-depth papers and articles.

Worldwide Email Directory of Anthropologists

http://wings.buffalo.edu/academic/
department/anthropology/WEDA/

WEDA is the Worldwide Email Directory of Anthropologists, a searchable database of contact information. This is a great resource if you need to talk to experts about your research.

news:alt.archaeology

Alt.archaeology usually has some interesting reading on the subject of archaeology. Most of it is even spelled correctly! The group has a medium spam content.

news:sci.anthropology

This group carries a great deal of current discussion on anthropology and the issues surrounding it. Like alt.archaeology, sci.anthropology gets a medium amount of spam.

Archery

See also: Guns

Archery Information Service

http://www.archery-info.com/

The Archery Information Service is a great online resource. The site contains links, tournament information, and other services.

Archery Mall

http://www.archerymall.com/

Want to shop online for archery products? Try the Archery Mall, which links to various manufacturers and businesses.

Bow-Pro Archery Equipment

http://bow-pro-archery.com/index.html

Bow-Pro Archery Equipment manufactures a variety of archery-related accessories.

International Archery Federation

http://www.archery.org/

FITA is the International Archery Federation, the world-governing body for this sport. The Web site has news about the Federation and sport, articles about events, and listings of current world records.

news:alt.archery

The alt.archery newsgroup is full of great discussion on archery-related topics and is quite spam-free to boot!

news:rec.sport.archery

This newsgroup is also an excellent discussion venue, and, like alt.archery, it doesn't have a huge spam problem.

Architecture

See also: Art, Real Estate

Architectural Slide Library

http://www.lib.berkeley.edu/ARCH/

UC Berkeley maintains the Architectural Slide Library. The Web site includes SPIRO, an online visual database of architectural slides from a wide variety of periods and genres. You can search by name, location, period, or topic, and view images with brief descriptions.

Architecture Through the Ages

http://library.advanced.org/10098/

Architecture Through the Ages offers an online tour of architecture in various bygone cultures. Categories include Aztec, Cathedrals, Chinese, Classical, Egyptian, Greek, Mayan, and Roman.

Barn Again

http://www.agriculture.com/ba/ba!home.html

Do you love barns? Who doesn't? Check out Barn Again, an organization that is helping to preserve and restore historic farm buildings. The Web site contains news, "Barn Talk," and a picture gallery.

Castles of the World

http://www.castles.org/

Castles of the World has lots of pictures, links, and such.

Frank Lloyd Wright Building Conservancy

http://www.swcp.com/FLW/flw.html

Surf to the Frank Lloyd Wright Building Conservancy to learn about the buildings of this master and about efforts to preserve those that still remain.

The Homepage of Lighthouses

http://www.worldlights.com/world/

The Homepage of Lighthouses is an excellent place to surf if you are at all interested in these illuminating structures. The site includes information about lighthouses around the world, a children's lighthouse coloring book, and more.

news:alt.architecture

Alt.architecture offers discussion on architecture from both a professional and layman's point of view.

Art

See also: Architecture, Graffiti, Photography

Aesthetics On-Line

http://www.aesthetics-online.org/

Learn about the philosophy of art, art criticism, and aesthetics at Aesthetics On-Line.

Eyes on Art

http://www.kn.pacbell.com/wired/art2/

Pacific Bell (yes, the phone company) has a fascinating Web site devoted to art, called Eyes on Art. In addition to exhibiting various works, the site also suggests activities for you to explore.

Words of Art

http://www.arts.ouc.bc.ca/fiar/glossary/gloshome.html

Words of Art serves as an online glossary for the visual arts. This is a great place to learn, especially if you are just beginning to study art.

The World Wide Web Virtual Library: Museums

http://www.comlab.ox.ac.uk/archive/other/museums.html

The World Wide Web Virtual Library: Museums provides a comprehensive collection of links to online museums throughout the world. The site is low-tech, but that just means you won't fall asleep waiting for it to load!

news:alt.binaries.pictures.fine-art

This newsgroup usually contains hundreds of fine art images, free for you to download!

Astrology

See also: Psychics, Unexplained Phenomenon

Asian Astrology

http://users.deltanet.com/~wcassidy/astro/astroindex.html

Learn about Asian Astrology here. The site also includes an Asian astrology bookstore.

Astrology Atlas Database

http://www.astro.ch/atlas/

If you are an astrologer, check out the Astrology Atlas Database, available in English, French, and German.

Astrology Spot

http://www.astrologyspot.com/

Check your daily horoscope online at the Astrology Spot!

fourthdimension.net

http://www.fourthdimension.net/

Have an online Tarot reading at fourthdimension.net.

Jonathan Cainer's Zodiac Forecasts

http://stars.metawire.com/index.html

Jonathan Cainer's Zodiac Forecasts is a great place to check your horoscope. Daily and weekly horoscopes are available.

news:alt.astrology

Alt.astrology has a lot of conversation about astrology and just enough spam to make things interesting.

Astronomy

See also: Science, Space

Arp's Catalog of Peculiar Galaxies

http://members.aol.com/arpgalaxy/index.html

Tired of seeing the same old boring galaxies day in and day out? Surf on over to Arp's Catalog of Peculiar Galaxies, an excellent place to get information for research or casual browsing.

The Astronomy Café

http://www2.ari.net/home/odenwald/cafe.html

The Astronomy Café is another excellent Web site if you're doing research. The site's author, Dr. Stan Odenwald, touts it as "The Web site for the astronomically disadvantaged." Includes a Q&A feature to help answer your astronomy and cosmology questions, too.

Astronomy Freeware and Shareware

http://www.cvc.org/astronomy/freeware.htm

Astronomy Freeware and Shareware is just that. Get software to help you map the sky, learn more about a star's characteristics

with the Hertzprung-Russell calculator, and more.

Star Journey

http://www.nationalgeographic.com/features/97/stars/

Star Journey from *National Geographic* is a fun and educational way to explore the stars. Includes a lot of images and data from the Hubble Space Telescope.

news:sci.astro

Here is a very active newsgroup, full of astronomy and cosmology discussion. It's also a good place to ask your tough questions.

Autos

See also: Maps, Travel

AAA/CAA

http://www.aaa.com/

At the Web site of the AAA/CAA you can learn about auto club benefits and services and link to regional offices throughout the USA and Canada.

The Antique Automobile Club of America

http://www.aaca.org/

The Antique Automobile Club of America claims to be the oldest and largest automobile historical society in the world. Learn about club events and activities, link to local clubs, and get other information.

Art Cars in Cyberspace

http://www.artcars.com/cover.html

Art Cars in Cyberspace pretty much speaks for itself. Check out the cars, schedule of events, and roadside attractions.

Auto Race Museum

http://www.autoracemuseum.com/

The Auto Race Museum in Bedford, Indiana boasts over 100 cars. Go in person and see retired Indy 500 cars, sprint cars and NASCAR cars, or take a virtual tour at the Web site.

Autoweb.com

http://www.autoweb.com/

Autoweb.com has classifieds, the Kelly Blue Book guide to used car values, auto recall information, and a good buyers guide to new cars. The classifieds are not as extensive as Trader Online, but the rest of this site's content is very good.

Carpoint

http://carpoint.msn.com/

Carpoint is part of the Microsoft Network, but you need not be an MSN member to take advantage of this huge resource. Find extensive auto-related information here.

Cars & Culture

http://www.carsandculture.com/

Cars have become more than simple transportation devices. That phenomenon is celebrated and documented here at Cars & Culture.

ClassicNet

http://www.primenet.com/~komet/classic/clascars.html

ClassicNet has some nice photos and links to a wide array of other auto sites.

Cosmic Ray Art Cars

http://www.geocities.com/SunsetStrip/1485/artcar.html

Can't get enough of those wacky art cars? Well, surf on over to Cosmic Ray Art Cars.

This site also has an extensive collection of art car links.

Edmund's

http://www.edmunds.com/

Check used car values or research a new car at the information-packed Edmund's site.

Kelly Blue Book

http://www.kbb.com/

The Kelly Blue Book is considered the authority on auto pricing information in the auto sales industry. Visit their online site to find the retail or trade-in value of your car today.

National Motorists Association

http://www.motorists.com/

The National Motorists Association helps you fight for your motorist rights. This organization was instrumental in toppling the 55 mph speed limit on USA highways. At this site you can learn about the Association, and get information about legislative and legal issues.

Race Rock

http://racerock.net/racerock/index.html

Located in Orlando, FL, Race Rock is the ultimate restaurant for a racing enthusiast. If you enjoy high-performance machinery and great food, this is the place to be.

The Speedtrap Registry

http://www.speedtrap.com/

One of the most famous Web sites of recent years has been this one, The Speedtrap Registry. Before your next journey, check here to find out where the traps are.

A
B
C
D
E
F
G
H
I
J
K
L
M
N
O
P
Q
R
S
T
U
V
W
X
Y
Z

Trader Online

http://www.traderonline.com/

Trader Online has a large, easy-to-use database of vehicles for sale. Includes cars, trucks, motorcycles, boats, aircraft, RVs, and heavy equipment.

Veggie Van

http://www.veggievan.org/

Interested in alternative-fueled cars? Check out the Web site of the Veggie Van, a van powered by vegetable oil that has toured the USA from coast to coast.

news:alt.autos

There are literally hundreds of automobile-related newsgroups, but this one is as good a place to start as any. Also, some of the other "general interest" auto groups seem to break down into brand-bashing and flame-war venues as often as not.

Aviation

See also: Skydiving, Travel

■ Aviation: Aircraft

The Aircraft Gallery

http://www.geocities.com/
CapeCanaveral/8585/

The Aircraft Gallery contains photos, specs, and news on American and foreign military aircraft. There is even a chat room here!

Biplanes and Aviation

http://www.inlink.com/~skywolf/

Do you like biplanes? If so, you'll probably also like the Biplanes and Aviation Web site!

Gregg's Common Commercial Aircraft Spotters Guide

http://www.geocities.com/
CapeCanaveral/1273/spotting.html

Gregg's Common Commercial Aircraft Spotters Guide is an excellent resource for commercial airplane buffs.

National Air and Space Museum

http://www.nasm.si.edu/

For a thorough source of information on aviation history, check out the Web page of the National Air and Space Museum, a part of the Smithsonian Institution.

Pegasus Fear of Flying Foundation

http://www.pegasus-fear-fly.com/
index.html

According to Pegasus, one out of ten Americans are afraid to fly. For those afflicted millions, Pegasus Fear of Flying Foundation provides support and training to help overcome "aerophobia."

Ryan Kirk's Ultimate Skunk Works Site

http://www.geocities.com/
CapeCanaveral/Lab/3993/

Are you interested in the world's top secret spy planes? You'll find lots of great photos and information on such exotic aircraft as the SR-71, U-2, and the F-117 Stealth Fighter at Ryan Kirk's Ultimate Skunk Works Site.

■ Aviation: Air Freight

Airborne Express

http://www.airborne-express.com/

Check out the Web site of Airborne Express, where you can track shipments and learn more about the company and its services.

DHL
http://www.dhl.com/

Ship quickly all over the world with DHL. You can track shipments on the Web site, and they also provide a number of service bulletins for the countries it serves.

Federal Express
http://www.fedex.com/

This is the official Federal Express Web site, where you can track packages, find the nearest drop box, or learn how to set up an account.

Guaranteed Mail Service
http://members.aol.com/agms/
jmexprs.htm

Need to send a letter to Russia or another country in the Commonwealth of Independent States? Check out Guaranteed Mail Service, which offers low cost mail and courier services to these locations.

TransAfrica
http://www.transafrica.com/

Do you need a shipping company that specializes in service to Africa? Try TransAfrica, which claims to be the world's largest wholesale provider of air courier service to Africa.

■ Aviation: Airlines

American Airlines
http://www.americanair.com/

American Airlines is one of the easier to use airline Web sites, which you'll appreciate if you need to check fare prices in a hurry.

Continental Airlines
http://www.flycontinental.com/

Check out the home page of Continental Airlines to learn about fares or book a flight. The site also has quite a few articles and travel tips.

Delta Air Lines
http://www.delta-air.com/

Check the Web site of Delta Air Lines and Delta SkyLinks for trip planning help, ticket fares, and information about the frequent flier program.

Northwest Airlines
http://www.nwa.com/

Northwest Airlines has a nice looking Web site, and like most of the others, it offers online fare prices and online booking.

Southwest Airlines
http://www.iflyswa.com/

If you're looking for a low air fare, you might want to check the Southwest Airlines Web site. This is especially important because some travel agents' computers do not check with Southwest when they search for fares.

TWA
http://www.twa.com/

Check out the latest from TWA, and keep your eyes peeled for special offers on air fares here.

United Airlines
http://www.ual.com/

The United Airlines Web page lets you plan and reserve your flights and learn more about the company.

US Airways

http://www.usairways.com/

The US Airways Web site offers travel and frequent flyer program information, but you will not be able to check fare prices or reserve flights online.

Virgin Atlantic Airways

http://www.virginatlantic.com/

Virgin Atlantic Airways has a home page that makes checking fares and other travel information simple.

■ Aviation: Airports

The Airport Search Engine

http://www.uni-karlsruhe.de/~un9v/atm/ase.html

The Airport Search Engine is a great way to find information on airports throughout the world. You can search for airports by city, country, or the three-letter code assigned to most airports. Results return quickly, and then you can link to specific information about that airport, including ground transportation, lodging, a map of the terminal, and even an airport yellow pages.

Yahoo!

http://www.yahoo.com/Business_and_Economy/Companies/Travel/Airports/

Most major airports now have Web sites that list information about flight schedules, weather, ground transport and other services, and parking information. Check Yahoo!'s list of airports to find the one you're headed to.

Banking

See also: Business, Finance

Bank Rate Monitor

http://www.bankrate.com/

Check the Bank Rate Monitor for the latest in mortgage, credit cards, loans, savings, and other interest rates offered by banks.

BankSite

http://www.banksite.com/

BankSite is an online banking directory for consumers. It provides information about banking in general and links to specific bank Web sites throughout the world. The site also has a "One Minute Loan Test," where you can figure out what kind of a loan you are probably eligible for.

FDIC

http://www.fdic.gov/consumers/consumer/index.html

FDIC, the government agency that insures many bank deposits, has a consumer information page located here. This site is packed with valuable information for anyone who has or uses money.

Federal Reserve Bank

http://www.bog.frb.fed.us/otherfrb.htm

Link from the Federal Reserve Bank to one of the 12 districts throughout the USA.

MasterCard/Cirrus ATM locator

http://www.mastercard.com/atm/

A large ATM locator is the MasterCard/Cirrus ATM locator from MasterCard. You can also link to other MasterCard business and consumer resources from this site.

Online Banking Report
http://www.onlinebankingreport.com/
fullserv.html

Are you considering online banking? Read the Online Banking Report to find out which banks provide what services, and then link to those banks. This site also has some useful tips and tricks for successful online banking.

Bed & Breakfasts

See also: Travel

The Border to Border Bed & Breakfast Directory
http://www.moriah.com/inns/

The Border to Border Bed & Breakfast Directory lists B&Bs throughout California, Oregon, and Washington. Includes descriptive entries, links, and contact information.

Go Native!
http://www.go-native.com/

Go Native! is one of the largest online databases for finding a bed and breakfast that I have seen. The listings generally only give you contact information, but there are over 8,000 listings.

Triple One Travel Directory
http://www.triple1.com/

Triple One Travel Directory lists a number of B&Bs, vacation rentals, adventure tour operators, and other travel services.

Women.com Inn Finder
http://www.women.com/travel/places/
innfinder/

The Inn Finder will search for inns all over the USA and Canada.

Bicycles

See also: Outdoors, Parks

The BikePlan Source
http://www.bikeplan.com/

The BikePlan Source is a place to learn about the efforts of this advocacy group, and what you can do to be a part of it.

East Coast Greenway
http://www.greenway.org/

Surf to the East Coast Greenway to learn about this trail that lets you ride from Maine to Florida.

Exploratorium's Science of Cycling
http://www.exploratorium.edu/cycling/

Want to learn more about the science of cycling? You'll appreciate the Exploratorium's Science of Cycling page, which is nicely designed and full of great information.

GearHead
http://www.gearhead.com/

GearHead is a "Mountain Bike Cyberzine" with news, product news and reviews, and sports.

The International Mountain Bicycling Association
http://www.outdoorlink.com/imba/

The Web site for The International Mountain Bicycling Association is a good place to find news and club information.

Stolen Bike Registry

http://www.telalink.net/~cycling/
stolen.html

Lost yer bike? Let someone know about it at the Stolen Bike Registry. Even the site owners acknowledge that the likelihood of ever seeing a stolen bike again is slim, but this is a good idea nonetheless, and it's a free service.

Boats

See also: Outdoors

American Sailing Association

http://www.american-sailing.com/

The American Sailing Association (ASA) concentrates its efforts on sailing education, and provides training throughout North American and the Caribbean.

By-The-Sea

http://www.by-the-sea.com/

By-The-Sea is an online boating magazine, and, I might add, has an excellent name! The site contains numerous articles, a lot of product information, and other reader services.

Hobie Cat

http://www.hobiecat.com/

Hobie Cat has been around since the 1960s, but the technology used is changing. How high-tech can a light sailboat get? How about a tri-hulled, two-masted, foil-borne, 35+ mph wind-powered boat with better turning ability than most cars?

Ice Flyer

http://www.iceflyer.com/

Have you ever had one of those days when you wanted to go sailing but your favorite lake was frozen solid and the weather forecast called for a cold and windy day? With Ice Flyer, those are optimum sailing conditions! Using windsurfer sails and a triskate layout, you don't need to stop sailing just because of Mother Nature. Wheels are also available for use on land.

The Internet Waterway

http://www.iwol.com/

The Internet Waterway is a thorough resource for boating and watersports information on the Internet. The site contains links to information about almost every aspect of being on or around the water.

Personal Watercraft Illustrated Online

http://www.watercraft.com/

Personal Watercraft Illustrated Online is a full Web version of this watercraft magazine.

Steamboating Magazine

http://www.steamboating.com/

The Steamboating Magazine celebrates the era of steamboats with information for owners and enthusiasts of steam-powered watercraft.

news:rec.boats

This newsgroup discusses everything from personal watercraft to the Titanic. Very little if any spam.

Books

See also: Art, Science Fiction, Shopping

Amazon.com

http://www.amazon.com/

Amazon.com is one of the Internet's great success stories. Amazon started as the world's first online bookstore, but has expanded it's catalog to include a wide variety of products, such as music, software, electronics, and toys.

Banned Books Online

http://digital.library.upenn.edu/books/banned-books.html

Surf to Banned Books Online to learn about banned books in USA and world history. Some of the listings might surprise you!

Barnes and Noble

http://www.barnesandnoble.com/

This is the online version of the famous Barnes and Noble bookstores. The site has regular specials, a book search, and author information.

Bonfire of Liberties

http://www.humanities-interactive.org/bonfireindex.html

Bonfire of Liberties is a fascinating site that talks about book burning in history and the many faces of censorship.

The History of Printing

http://communication.ucsd.edu/bjones/Books/booktext.html

The History of Printing is low-tech but contains an excellent historical account. Learn about all the events that have culminated in this book that you now hold in your hands!

IDG Books Online

http://www.idgbooks.com/

Surf on over to our own Web site at IDG Books Online! See what's new from the leading publisher of computer books in the land!

Ingram Book Group

http://www.ingrambook.com/

Ingram Book Group is a large book wholesaler. Check out their A-list to see which titles are selling the fastest!

The Libyrinth

http://rpg.net/quail/libyrinth/

The Libyrinth is a fascinating site for the lover of literature. Worship the words online here!

news:rec.arts.books

As with many other topics, literally hundreds of newsgroups exist to discuss various aspects of books, from specific authors to whole genres. This group usually has some stimulating conversation about various works, but has a moderate spam content.

Bowling

BallGuide.com

http://www.ballguide.com/

Ballguide.com serves as an information resource for anyone who is preparing to buy a bowling ball. Check here to learn all about your new ball before you buy.

Bowling Tournaments, The Official Page of Amateur Bowling

http://www.bowling300.com/

Bowling Tournaments, The Official Page of Amateur Bowling is an invaluable resource for bowlers looking for tournaments to enter. The site also lists a number of useful links and sponsors a weekly bowling chat.

PBA Tour

http://www.pbatour.com/

PBA Tour is a sanctioning body of professional bowling in the USA. This site lists information about their tournaments and events, TV schedules, and membership information.

news:alt.sport.bowling

Find lots of in-depth discussion among bowlers in this low-spam newsgroup.

Business

See also: Banking, Finance

Business Resource Center

http://www.morebusiness.com/

The Business Resource Center is a great source for the small business owner or self-employed person. The site has a heavy emphasis on legislative issues and some useful articles to help you get started.

Business Wire

http://www.businesswire.com/

Business Wire is a wire service for business news, which means that you might hear it here first!

EPA's Energy Star Program

http://www.epa.gov/energystar/

Surf here to learn about the EPA's Energy Star Program for small businesses. Includes a variety of other useful resources.

Home Office Association of America

http://www.hoaa.com/

The Home Office Association of America is dedicated to people who work at home full time or telecommute. The site includes their newsletter, ideas, and links to other useful sites.

Small Business Administration

http://www.sbaonline.sba.gov/

The Small Business Administration is an arm of the US government working to help America's small businesses. Look here for more information on what they can do, including legislative information and disaster relief.

Camping

See also: Outdoors

Benz's Campground Directory

http://personal.cfw.com/~benz/camp.htm

Benz's Campground Directory is low tech but easy to use and full of useful information. Includes listings for thousands of campgrounds in the USA, Canada, and Mexico.

Camping-USA!

http://www.camping-usa.com/

Camping-USA! offers a searchable database of various campgrounds.

KOA Home Page

http://www.koakampgrounds.com/

The KOA Home Page is the official site of Kampgrounds of America. Find a campground and learn how to make your reservation right away!

National Forest Service Campgrounds

http://www.gorp.com/dow/

Here's a guide to National Forest Service Campgrounds throughout the USA, courtesy of GORP (The Great Outdoor Recreational Pages).

Songs for Scouts

http://www.macscouter.com/Songs/

What to do late at night, sitting by the campfire? Why, sing a campfire song from the Songs for Scouts Web page! I much prefer the "Gross Songs."

Candy

See also: Cooking

Bean Tasting

http://www.meddybemps.com/3.3.html

No one laughs at wine connoisseurs, so why should we laugh at jelly bean connoisseurs? Find out about this fine art at Bean Tasting, a Web site devoted to the "Ritual & Romance" surrounding this tasty activity.

The International PEZ Collectors Association

http://www.pez.org/

You knew someone had to do it, and they did. The International PEZ Collectors Association supports this Web page, which pays homage to these fun little candy dispensers.

The Page of Bad Candy

http://www.videogamenews.net/badcandy/

The Page of Bad Candy is a small but entertaining site. Protect yourself from vile confections!

Peepmania!

http://www.critpath.org/~tracy/new.html

If Peepmania! is not proof positive that there are Web pages devoted to anything and everything, than I don't know what is. This page is dedicated to the ubiquitous Marshmallow Peep, a brightly colored, sugar-coated blob of marshmallow that plagues mankind every Easter.

Celebrities

See also: Acting, Movies & Film

Celebrity Web

http://www.celebrityweb.com/

Celebrity Web has some truly outstanding quality photos in its collection.

The Internet Movie Database

http://us.imdb.com/search.html

The Internet Movie Database enables you to search their database for actors, actresses, directors, and crew.

The Kink

http://www.castboy.com/

The Kink is Castboy's Gateway to Hollywood. This site contains strange and bad photos of various celebrities. Formerly known as The Couch.

news:alt.gossip.celebrities

This newsgroup can actually be a fun place to participate in celeb gossip, and it doesn't have quite as much spam as most of the other celebrity newsgroups do.

Cellular Communication

Airtouch Communications

http://www.airtouch.com/

Airtouch Communications is a major provider of cellular services. Their home page contains information about the company and its services, as well as employment opportunities.

American One

http://www.america1.com/

American One provides affordable cellular phones and service in various states across the USA.

Cellular One

http://www.cellularone.com/

Check with Cellular One for nationwide cellular service. The site also allows you to link to regional operations of the company.

GTE

http://www.gte.com/

GTE offers a wide variety of communications services, including cellular services.

Motorola

http://www.mot.com/

Motorola is a leader in cellular communication (and modems, too), and their Web site helps you learn more about their products and services. You might even find your next job here!

Chat

Café Utne

http://www.utne.com/cafe/

Café Utne celebrates the fine art of conversation. There is almost always some stimulating conversation happening here.

Chatter's Jargon Dictionary

http://www.stevegrossman.com/jargpge.htm

Confused by all the jargon and weird speech happening in chat rooms? Check out the Chatter's Jargon Dictionary, a useful Web site with a huge listing of words, phrases, and abbreviations.

GeoCities — Chat

http://www.geocities.com/cgi-bin/chat/chat_entry

GeoCities — Chat forum has dozens of chat rooms to choose from, covering a wide range of interests.

Parent City

http://www.parentcity.com/

Parent City offers chat rooms for parents, which includes discussions with experts and fellow parents.

Talk City

http://www.talkcity.com/

Talk City has one of the largest selections of chat rooms on the Internet. A nice feature is the fact that their home page lists the chat rooms, and by each listing is a number indicating the number of people currently logged on to each chat.

Women's Wire

http://www.womenswire.com/

Women's Wire is part of Women.com, an online community for women. Women's Wire offers a number of fascinating chat rooms to choose from.

Children

See also: Education, Family, Schools, Toys

CyberKids

http://www.cyberkids.com/

CyberKids is very cool! This online magazine is by and for kids, but grown-ups will enjoy it too!

KIDLINK

http://www.kidlink.org/

KIDLINK is a useful site that links kids (up to age 15) from around the world in online dialog. Communication is facilitated through mailing lists, chats, and art exhibition sites.

KidNews

http://www.kidnews.com/

Surf to KidNews to check news and article by and for (you guessed it) kids!

Kidsworld-online

http://www.kidsworld-online.com/

Kidsworld-online is full of entertaining and educational activities.

Mr. Edible Starchy Tuber Head

http://winnie.acsu.buffalo.edu/potatoe/index.html

Mr. Edible Starchy Tuber Head looks suspiciously like a popular toy patterned after a potato, and acts like him too. Create your own unique Starchy Tuber Head online here!

Nye Labs Online

http://nyelabs.kcts.org/

Check out the coolest Science Guy on the planet, Bill Nye, at Nye Labs Online! We can't imagine a funner way to learn about science than with Bill Nye, the Science Guy.

Yahooligans!

http://www.yahooligans.com/

Yahooligans! Is a spin-off of Yahoo!, designed specifically with younger cyber-surfers in mind. But best of all, it's not just for kids!

Christmas

Christmas.com

http://www.christmas.com/

Christmas.com has a wide variety of information about Christmas around the world.

The Christmas Corner

http://www.chebucto.ns.ca/~ai251/xmaspag.html

The Christmas Corner has stories, recipes, games, carols, and more to keep you and your family entertained during this holiday.

Christmas Haiku

http://www.scifaiku.com/xmas/

Read any good Christmas Haiku lately? Check out Christmas Haiku at the Haiku Habitat for many great poems.

Stormfax

http://www.stormfax.com/whtexmas.htm

Will there be a white Christmas this year? Find out how likely it will be at Stormfax, which lists the likelihood of a white Christmas for numerous cities across the USA.

Clip Art

See also: Computers: Internet, Desktop Publishing

Barry's Clip Art Server

http://www.barrysclipart.com/

Barry's Clip Art Server has hundreds of free clip art images for you to download.

ClipArtConnection.com

http://www.ist.net/clipart/index.html

ClipArtConnection.com offers a huge selection of free clipart. Items are arranged in alphabetical categories, and the site also contains some links.

TuDogs

http://www.tudogs.com/

TuDogs is one of the largest sources of free clip art and other graphics on the Internet.

news:alt.binaries.clip-art

This newsgroup always has some nice clip art for you to download free, and you can also use the group to request special images.

Clothing

See also: Shopping

Joe Boxer

http://www.joeboxer.com/

The Joe Boxer Web site has the interesting distinction of being the first marketing-type Web site on the Internet. It is, well, interesting, and is sure to either severely entertain or severely frustrate you.

Levi Straus & Co

http://www.levi.com/

If you like jeans (and who doesn't?) you know Levi Straus & Co. Their official Web site includes company history and product information. Replace those worn out dungarees!

L.L. Bean

http://www.llbean.com/

L.L. Bean offers shopping online at their Web site, with overnight shipping available.

The Ultimate Outlet Home Page

http://www.spiegel.com/spiegel/shopping/ultimate/

The Ultimate Outlet Home Page features some great deals on clothing and accessories from the Spiegel catalog.

Coffee

Extreme Coffee, Inc.

http://www.extremecoffee.com/

Extreme Coffee, Inc., offers "hyper-caffeinated" coffees, because sleep is over-rated. If you don't have time to pour a cup of coffee, you can buy the candy-coated beans. Learn more or buy online!

Starbucks

http://www.starbucks.com

Learn more about the world-famous Starbucks here. You can get information about the company, sponsored events, and even buy Starbucks accessories on the web. There is also a store locator if you need a familiar cup of coffee in an unfamiliar place.

Trojan Room Coffee Machine

http://www.cl.cam.ac.uk/coffee/coffee.html

Truly a classic of the Web, the Trojan Room Coffee Machine is a spy cam that let's you see the Trojan Room's coffeepot. Rumor has it that this site was developed so that people here could check to see if there was coffee in the pot before they got up from their computers.

Collectibles

See also: Hobbies, Toys

H.O. Slotcar Collector's Web Site

http://members.aol.com/hifisapien/slotcars.htm

Can't get enough of those great little electric slot cars you got for Christmas? Surf on over to the H.O. Slotcar Collector's Web Site to find out more about collecting and racing these exciting models.

The M & L Collectors Exchange Market

http://www.mlcem.com/

The M & L Collectors Exchange Market is a good place to buy, sell, and trade a wide variety of collectibles. For-sale items are separated into some useful categories that are generally easy to use.

The Toymart

http://www.toy-mart.com/

The Toymart has a pretty low-tech Web site, but they have some really neat stuff for sale. Find lots of automotive collectibles, Barbie stuff, and trains.

Comics

See also: Hobbies, Humor

The Comic Zone

http://www.unitedmedia.com/comics/

The Comic Zone features a number of comic strips for your enjoyment, including Peanuts, Dilbert, Robotman, and others.

Happy Shadows Press

http://www.happyshadows.com/

Happy Shadows Press offers comics with strange and often dark humor.

WebComics

http://www.webcomics.com/

WebComics features over 40 online daily and weekly comic strips.

news:rec.arts.comics.strips

This group includes discussion about various comic strips and has very little spam.

A
B
C
D
E
F
G
H
I
J
K
L
M
N
O
P
Q
R
S
T
U
V
W
X
Y
Z

Communities

See also: Chat, Cultures, Relationships, Religion, Science Fiction

Angelfire
http://www.angelfire.com/

Angelfire is a newer entry into the online community world. They offer free Web page space, and a number of other resources to help you develop your Web page.

Café Utne
http://cafe.utne.com

Café Utne celebrates the fine art of conversation. There is a heavy emphasis on chat and forums here.

GeoCities
http://www.geocities.com/

GeoCities offers free Web page space, free e-mail services, chat, community areas, and more. This is one of the largest online communities in existence.

Parent Soup
http://www.parentsoup.com/

Parent Soup is an online community dedicated to parents of kids of all ages. Consult with experts, chat with others, or show off pictures of your kids!

Talk City
http://www.talkcity.com/

Talk City is mainly chat oriented. If you feel like talking, this is the community for you!

Tripod
http://www.tripod.com/

Another great online community to join is Tripod, which offers free Web page space and other services. Find your own place in one of their "Pods."

The Well
http://www.well.com/

The Well is one of the oldest online communities on the net. Chat, conference, or even get Internet access from the Well.

Women.com
http://www.women.com/

Women.com is a community specifically aimed at women. Check out Women's Wire, Beatrice's Web Guide, and Healthy Ideas!

Computers

■ Computers: E-mail

Bigfoot
http://www.bigfoot.com/

Bigfoot is both a free e-mail site and a people search engine. But sorry, there is no Sasquatch here!

Eudora
http://www.eudora.com/

This is the Web site for Eudora, a stand-alone e-mail client. On the main page of the site, you can learn about the client or connect to another page where you can download the version of Eudora you want.

Hotmail
http://www.hotmail.com/

Hotmail offers free Web-based e-mail services. Surf to their Web site to learn how you can sign up.

Juno

http://www.juno.com/index.html

Find out how to get free e-mail from Juno here! It's a very popular service.

MailCity

http://www.mailcity.com/

MailCity is another excellent Web-based free e-mail service. Access it from any Internet connection!

Net@ddress

http://www.netaddress.com/

Get free e-mail via Net@ddress. Check your mail from any Internet connection.

RocketMail

http://www.rocketmail.com/

Yahoo! has its own free e-mail service called RocketMail.

Vivian Neou's List of Lists

http://catalog.com/vivian/

Vivian Neou's Web site is a no-frills affair, but it contains the "List of Lists," a catalog of tens of thousands of e-mail lists, searchable by subject and content. Here's a great place to find a list that you're interested in.

■ Computers: Hardware

56K.COM

http://www.56k.com/

Has all the confusion about 56 Kbps modems got you spinning? Don't feel like the Lone Ranger. A good place to learn more about this modem technology is here at 56K.COM. The site offers news, buyer's guides, and some exhaustive primers to help you sort it all out.

AMD

http://www.amd.com/

The AMD Web site is the place to start if you want to learn more about their CPUs. These chips can be an affordable alternative to Intel CPUs.

Byte Runner Technologies

http://www.byterunner.com/

Byte Runner Technologies builds high speed I/O serial cards for PCs. Their products can be a quick way to expand the number of peripherals you can hook up to your computer.

Crucial Technology

http://www.crucial.com/

Crucial Technology specializes in PC memory. Buy SIMMs and DIMMs online, learn how the chips are made, and even find some volume discounts!

Dell Computer

http://www.dell.com/

Surf to Dell Computer to find your next PC, check the price, and buy it!

Egghead Computer

http://www.egghead.com/

Egghead Computer is a complete source for buying hardware and software on the Web!

Epson

http://www.epson.com/

The Epson Web site is the place to learn about Epson printers, imaging products, storage devices, and handheld PCs.

A B C D E F G H I J K L M N O P Q R S T U V W X Y Z

Evergreen Technologies
http://www.evertech.com/

So you say your old computer is too slow, but you can't afford to deep-six the whole thing and buy a new system? Well, surf on over to Evergreen Technologies and check out their CPU upgrade packages that make speeding up an old PC easy!

Gateway 2000
http://www.gw2k.com/

The Gateway 2000 Web site is another great place to find your next PC. You can also find online tech support for the Gateway PC you already bought!

Global Village Communications
http://www.globalvillage.com/

Global Village Communications offers a variety of communications products for computers, including modems. Learn more about their products here.

Hewlett-Packard
http://www.hp.com/

Hewlett-Packard is renowned for its outstanding printers, imaging devices, and computers. Surf here for product information, find technical support, or learn more about the company in general.

Hitachi
http://www.hitachi.com/

Surf to Hitachi's Web site to learn about their monitors, imaging devices, and laptops. This Web site does not offer online sales, but it does have quite a bit of product information.

IBM
http://www.ibm.com/

IBM almost single-handedly created the PC revolution. Surf to their Web site to find out what they're doing now!

Intel
http://www.intel.com/

The Intel home page is a good place to find information about Intel's latest products. The site contains numerous links to technical documents that you can download.

Iomegazine
http://www.iomega.com/

Iomegazine is the Web site of Iomega, makers of mass storage devices. Check here to learn more about Jaz, Zip, and Ditto disk drives.

Lexmark
http://www.lexmark.com/

Lexmark specializes in printers for business applications. Check here to learn more about what they have to offer, and even get online technical support.

Micron
http://www.micronpc.com/

Micron offers a huge assortment of PCs, from powerful servers to compact notebooks. Check here to see what's available, order online, or obtain technical support.

Microtek
http://www.mteklab.com/

Need more information or tech support for Microtek scanners? Check out their Web site, which also contains some interesting stories and testimonials from people actually using Microtek scanners in the field.

NEC
http://www.nec.com/

NEC produces a dizzying array of communications products, as well as monitors, printers, fax machines, and more.

Sun Microsystems
http://www.sun.com/

Get support, product, and consulting information, and learn about Java and more at the Web site of Sun Microsystems.

UMAX
http://www.umax.com/

Surf here to learn about UMAX products such as scanners, digital cameras, network adapters, memory, and even whole computers.

■ Computers: Internet

See also: Chat, Communities, Search Engines, Security, Shopping, Web Page Design

BrowserWatch
http://browserwatch.internet.com/

BrowserWatch provides the latest information and news pertaining to the world of Web browsers, including Active-X controls, plug-ins, and other emerging technologies.

Cisco Systems
http://www.cisco.com/

Cisco Systems offers a wide variety of products and services to solve tough Internet networking issues.

Developer.com
http://www.developer.com/

Developer.com is a source of information for professional Web developers. It includes a reference library, news, useful links, and more.

Electric Minds
http://www.minds.com/

Electric Minds is a fascinating site that explores and celebrates the art of conversation on the Internet.

The FCC Access Charge Reform Page
http://www.fcc.gov/isp.html

The FCC Access Charge Reform Page is the place to look for information on government activities as they pertain to Internet Service Providers.

HotWired!
http://www.hotwired.com/

HotWired! is an online version of Wired! magazine. The site has a high-tech look (with terrible color choices), yet loads in a reasonable amount of time. Find the cutting edge of the Internet covered here!

HTML Station
http://www.december.com/html/

Have a question about Web publishing? Surf to the HTML Station, an excellent resource for HTML authors. Full specifications and many useful tips make this site invaluable.

Intel WebOutfitter Service
http://intelweboutfitter.com/content/cie/us/preview.htm

The Intel WebOutfitter Service is a new Internet service that delivers cutting-edge content, tools, tips, and Web sites developed to maximize the Internet experience of Pentium III processor-based PC users. When you register, Intel will also send you a CD loaded with handy utilities and browser plug-ins.

MIT Media Lab

http://www.media.mit.edu/

The MIT Media Lab is always working on some Internet-related research project.

NetLingo

http://www.netlingo.com/

Are you getting lost in this mess of jargon and scuttlebutt that is the language of the Internet? Bring your questions to the NetLingo site, where you can search for a term and read its definition. NetLingo keeps a list of new terms on its main page, making it easier to keep up with new terms as they surface.

Netscape

http://www.netscape.com/

Surf to the Netscape home page to learn about the popular Internet browser.

The Palace

http://www.thepalace.com/

The Palace offers Web-based communications clients that can be used for chat, conferencing, and other methods of live conversation. The Palace puts special emphasis on ways that its products can be used for commerce.

Stroud's Consummate Winsock Applications

http://cws.internet.com/

Need the ultimate resource for Internet Winsock software? Surf to Stroud's Consummate Winsock Applications (Stroud's CWS).

W3C

http://www.w3.org/

A question we sometimes forget to ask is, "Who is responsible for making the Web what it is today?" W3C, the World Wide Web Consortium, is it. This is the place to learn about standards and tools used on the Web.

Your Own Personal Net

http://www.ypn.com/

What exactly is Your Own Personal Net? Well, it's part search engine, part news service, and part directory. Find a lot of site reviews and live event listings here, and the articles are chock-full of relevant links.

■ Computers: News and Reference

CNET.COM

http://www.cnet.com/

CNET.COM is easily one of the largest news and information sources about computers on the Web. Get the latest technology news or browse through the many CNET services. This is a good place to come if you need to learn more about PC hardware and software.

SERVICE 911.COM

http://www.service911.com/

Are the manuals for your new hardware or software not exactly forthcoming with information on where to get help? We're not surprised. Fortunately, SERVICE 911.COM contains a database of support addresses and phone numbers for literally thousands of vendors in the industry.

The USB Home Page

http://www.usb.org/

The USB Home Page is the best place to start if you need to find technical information on the Universal Serial Bus and connecting hardware.

Webopaedia

http://www.webopaedia.com/

The Webopaedia is a great place to go if there is some term or concept related to computers that you don't understand. Each definition also includes links to related Web sites.

ZDNet

http://www.zdnet.com/

Ziff-Davis is a powerhouse for computer magazine publishing, and ZDNet is their official Web site. Find the latest in technology news and product reviews here.

■ Computers: Software

Corel

http://www.corel.com/

Learn about software from Corel here, such as WordPerfect, Paradox, CorelDRAW, Quattro Pro, and even some freebies!

DaveCentral.com

http://www.davecentral.com/

DaveCentral has a long reputation as being a great site for Windows downloads, and a Linux section has recently been added.

Filez

http://www.filez.com/zhub.shtml

Filez claims to have over 75 million downloadable files. To help you find what you want, they also have a nice search engine.

Galt Shareware Zone

http://www.galttech.com/

Surf to the Galt Shareware Zone for thousands of downloadable files. Check out the Software Spotlight!

Intuit, Inc

http://www.intuit.com/

Surf to the Web site of Intuit, Inc. to learn about their products like TurboTax, Quicken, Quick Books, and more.

JIAN

http://www.jianusa.com/

JIAN offers a variety of useful software for small businesses and entrepreneurs. Their Web site offers secure online ordering, product information, and technical support.

Microsoft

http://www.microsoft.com/

Microsoft produces a variety of software such as word processors, spreadsheets, games, operating systems — perhaps you've heard of them? The Web site contains a great deal of software and utilities that you can download for free, as well as helpful information for Windows and other Microsoft products.

Shareware.com

http://shareware.cnet.com/

Software doesn't need to be expensive to get the job done. Sometimes all you need is a simple utility to make your life a little easier. If that is what you are looking for, CNET's shareware.com is a good place to start your search.

Slaughterhouse

http://www.slaughterhouse.com/

Slaughterhouse is a very useful site for downloading shareware, freeware, and demonstration software. When you search for a specific title here, you'll find that other, similar programs are displayed as well, enabling you to compare and test a variety of programs without having to know the exact name of all of them.

Superkids Educational Software Review

http://www.superkids.com/

Superkids Educational Software Review provides information and reviews of popular educational software. This is a comprehensive source to help you find the right educational software before you spend your money.

TUCOWS

http://www.tucows.com/

TUCOWS is one of the largest sites for Internet software. Find it all here!

Tuneup.com

http://www.tuneup.com/

Tuneup.com has thousands of updated drivers and other utilities designed to make your PC run better.

WinSite

http://www.winsite.com/

WinSite claims to be the planet's largest archive of Windows software. Find games, utilities, and other useful applications.

WinZip

http://www.winzip.com/

WinZip is indispensable if you plan to download or exchange files over the Internet. Find out about this classic file compression utility or download it here!

ZDNet.com

http://www.zdnet.com/downloads/

ZDNet.com is another great place to look for downloadable applications and files. I particularly like the browser section which has numerous plug-ins for your favorite browser and the OS section where you can find modules to customize the behavior of your operating system.

Cooking

See also: Dieting, Restaurants

Epicurious

http://www.epicurious.com/

Looking for an outstanding collection of recipes? Try Epicurious, with over 6,500 recipes from the pages of *Bon Appétit* and *Gourmet* magazines.

Lawrence Wheeler's Favorite Mexican Recipes

http://www.geocities.com/
TheTropics/9632/mexican.html

Lawrence Wheeler's Favorite Mexican Recipes Web page has some truly hideous color choices in its layout, but the recipes are great!

Non-Alcoholic Recipes

http://www.drmike-hypnosis.com/
recipe.html

Would you be interested in some creative, nonalcoholic drink recipes? Surf to Non-Alcoholic Recipes for a nice selection of easy-to-assemble concoctions.

Recipe Archive Index

http://www.cs.cmu.edu/~mjw/recipes/

The Recipe Archive Index serves as an archive for recipes posted to the rec.food.recipes newsgroup. This site is absolutely no-frills, technology-wise, but has a huge archive of tasty dishes.

Searchable Online Archive of Recipes

http://soar.berkeley.edu/recipes/

SOAR is a Searchable Online Archive of Recipes. The site has almost 40,000 recipes cataloged, and you can either search for a specific dish or browse through their easy-to-use directory.

Virtual Vittles

http://www.netmegs.com/~vittles/

Tired of the same old thing, week in and week out? Surf on over to Virtual Vittles, which posts new recipes every week!

news:rec.food.recipes

Rec.food.recipes is a great place to pick up new ideas, ask questions, or post your own favorites. This newsgroup has little or no spam.

Crafts

See also: Art, Hobbies

BeadNet

http://www.mcs.net/~simone/
beadnet.html

BeadNet is an amazing resource for anything you've ever wanted to know about beading. The site includes discussion, project ideas, links, history, tips, and more.

Ceramica on line

http://www.dinamica.it/col/english/
homei.htm

Ceramica on line is devoted to the many aspects of working with ceramics. Lots of good information here!

Fremlin's Forgery

http://www.fremlinsforgery.com/

Fremlin's Forgery contains tutorials, images, and links related to the art of blacksmithing. Download anvil sounds, too!

International Internet Leathercrafter's Guild

http://iilg.org/

The International Internet Leathercrafter's Guild has a wealth of information regarding the art of working leather. Check it out!

The Knapper's Corner

http://www.eskimo.com/~knapper/

The Knapper's Corner is dedicated to the art of flint knapping. Surf here to learn how to make your own arrowheads and other tools, as well as get information about various "knap-ins" and other events related to this art.

National Quilting Association

http://nqa.society.webjump.com/

If you want information about quilting, check out the National Quilting Association Web site.

Online Origami

http://members.aol.com/stamm/
index.html

If you've ever gotten a thrill out of folding paper, then you ought to check out Online Origami. The site has links, information about various organizations, and patterns for making your own Origami designs.

Stampcity

http://members.delphi.com/
stampcity1/index.html

The art of rubber stamping is growing rapidly, and you can learn more about it at Stampcity. Contains tips, techniques, links, and more!

Credit

See also: Banking, Business, Finance

American Express
http://www.americanexpress.com/

American Express offers credit-related information on its Web site, as well as a large online travel service, business services, and financial services.

Credit Chequers
http://www.credcheq.com/

Credit Chequers offers online consumer credit reports and other credit-related services.

Debt Counselors of America
http://www.dca.org/

Debt Counselors of America is a nonprofit organization dedicated to helping consumers deal with debt. Includes counseling information as well as reports about credit fraud and scams.

Equifax
http://www.equifax.com/

Equifax is a large credit reporting bureau for businesses. Consumers can also order their own credit report online.

Master Card International
http://www.mastercard.com/

Learn more about these credit cards, get personal and business financial information, locate ATMs, and more at the Master Card International home page.

Trans Union Corporation
http://www.tuc.com/

Trans Union Corporation is another credit reporting bureau. Consumers can learn about and order credit reports online, and there is a full range of business services offered as well.

Visa International
http://www.visa.com/

Surf to the official Visa International Web site to find product and service information, news about Visa-sponsored events (which is almost everything), and some valuable consumer tips. There is even a helpful ATM locator!

Cultures

See also: Art, Communities, Museums, Religion

American Association of Baby Boomers
http://www.babyboomers.com/

Were you born between the years 1946 and 1964? You might want to check out the American Association of Baby Boomers. Their Web site includes baby boomer news, interesting facts about the year you were born, and information about the association.

Asian Studies WWW Virtual Library
http://coombs.anu.edu.au/WWWVLAsian/VLAbout.html

The Asian Studies WWW Virtual Library provides cultural and country information, links, and a variety of other resources.

Boom!
http://www.tiac.net/users/edufax/BOOM!/frontpage.html

Boom! calls itself a "light e-zine for baby boomers." The site contains feature articles, a horoscope, and more.

The Burning Man Project

http://www.burningman.com/

Burning Man has become something of a counterculture revolution, and you can learn more about it (including upcoming events) at The Burning Man Project.

Central & Eastern European Languages

http://www.cusd.claremont.edu/
~tkroll/EastEur/index.html

Are you heading to Eastern Europe any time soon? Pick up some basic phrases in 14 different languages at the Central & Eastern European Languages Web site.

Encyclopedia of Cajun Culture

http://www.cajunculture.com/

The Encyclopedia of Cajun Culture is just that. Surf here to learn about the history, food, music, and traditions of this fascinating culture.

Journal X

http://www.journalx.com/

Journal X always includes some humorous bits and discussion for anyone who feels like they are part of the Generation X culture.

Native American Resources

http://www.cowboy.net/native/

Native American culture is too diverse to cover in a single Web site, but the Native American Resources Web page has an excellent collection of links to various tribal home pages, Native American organizations, government and educational resources, and information pertaining to art and culture.

NativeWeb

http://www.nativeweb.org/

NativeWeb is dedicated to native peoples around the world. Includes many links, job listings, event schedules, and more.

NetNoir

http://www.netnoir.com/

NetNoir is the "Black Network," and provides information on entertainment, news, people, business, politics, and more.

NomadNet

http://www.netnomad.com

NomadNet contains links to a variety of African resources and Web sites. Find links to the African culture that you're studying.

Polynesian Cultural Center

http://www.polynesia.com/

The Polynesian Cultural Center is a source for information on Polynesian cultures, along with a bit of tourist information for Hawaii and other Pacific islands.

Dance

See also: Acting, Art, Music

The Ballet Archive

http://www.kuwayama.com/
balletarchive/

The Ballet Archive provides a database of ballet abstracts and summaries.

DancePages.com

http://www.dancepages.com

DancePages.com offers a multitude of resources for dance instructors and students alike.

A
B
C
D
E
F
G
H
I
J
K
L
M
N
O
P
Q
R
S
T
U
V
W
X
Y
Z

A
B
C
D
E
F
G
H
I
J
K
L
M
N
O
P
Q
R
S
T
U
V
W
X
Y
Z

Dancer's Delight

http://www.msu.edu/user/okumurak/

Break dancing lives! . . . at Dancer's Delight! You can also learn more about hip-hop, popping, house, and Japanese rap (?!) here.

The Worldwide DancePages Directory

http://www.newdance.com

The Worldwide DancePages Directory links to sites all over the world specializing in modern dance. Learn about choreographers, dance companies, and arts festivals here.

Darts

See also: Hobbies

Blowpipe home page

http://echigo.hits.ad.jp/~dhiguchi/index_e.html

Although it's not what everyone thinks about when you say darts, the Blowpipe home page is interesting nonetheless. Learn about this Japanese sport here.

Bulls Eye Online

http://www.bullsinet.com/

Bulls Eye Online is "at the center of it all" in the world of darts. The site has news and information about this sport.

news:alt.sport.darts

Discuss or learn more about darts in this newsgroup. The group has a low spam count.

Dating

See also: Marriage, Relationships

Brenda's Dating Advice for Geeks

http://www.geekcheck.com/

Brenda's Dating Advice for Geeks is designed specifically for the, ahem, computer industry. Very cool and entertaining site, with personals!

The Dating Patterns Analyzer

http://www.cam.org/~jmauld/English/dateanal.html

The Dating Patterns Analyzer lets you fill out a survey, and then analyzes your dating habits and determines what makes you happy.

Match.Com

http://www.match.com/

Match.Com offers a complete online matchmaking and dating service for just $9.95, with thousands of new people signing in every week!

Mix 'n Match

http://www.mixnmatch.com/

Mix 'n Match is another online dating resource, with personals, chat rooms, polls, articles, and more.

Swoon

http://www.swoon.com/

Swoon is not a dating service (although there are personals). Instead, think of it as a news service that covers "Dating, Mating, and Relating" as they put it. Swoon includes some celebrity gossip as well.

Yahoo! Classifieds

http://classifieds.yahoo.com/
personals.html

Yahoo! Classifieds offers a free place for you to post and view personals. The database is searchable by city or state, and you can even look at nationwide ads!

Death & Dying

The End of Life

http://www.npr.org/programs/death/

National Public Radio produced a documentary on the end of life, and that program is chronicled here. Includes transcripts and other resources.

Invincible Summer

http://www.drizzle.com/~hall/invsum/

Invincible Summer offers support for people who have lost their only child or all their children.

The Preplanning Network

http://www.preplannet.com/

The Preplanning Network helps you prepare ahead of time for the inevitable. Lots of useful information.

Suicide @ rochford.org

http://www.rochford.org/suicide/

Suicide @ rochford.org is a valuable resource for information about suicide prevention and education. Check the Web site to find out about emergency help.

Willowgreen

http://www.opn.com/willowgreen/

Willowgreen provides information pertaining to bereavement, grief, coping with loss, and personal inspiration in times of sorrow.

Desktop Publishing

See also: Clip art

Adobe Territory

http://dtphelp.com/adobe/index.html

Adobe Territory is the place to go with your questions or help needs for the popular Adobe publishing products.

The Corel Room

http://dtphelp.com/corel/

The Corel Room is an excellent resource if you use Corel software to do your desktop publishing.

The Desktop Publishers Journal

http://www.dtpjournal.com/

The Desktop Publishers Journal is an online version of this print magazine. The site contains selected articles and some useful links, but the full content of the magazine is not available online.

Ideabook

http://www.ideabook.com/

Ideabook is another great online source of images, artwork, ideas, and news. Worth a look!

Julian Foster's Printing Tips Page

http://www3.teleplex.net/jr/

Julian Foster's Printing Tips Page provides pages and pages of helpful tips that help you output your documents to outside printers more effectively. The site has not been updated for a while, but the information is still extremely useful and valid.

Paper Direct

http://www.paperdirect.com

Need some cool paper? Of course you do, especially if you plan to do any desktop publishing. Check out Paper Direct to see some of the neat things they have to offer.

news:comp.text.desktop

This group is a little quiet compared to some others, but what you will find there is very useful.

Dieting

See also: Cooking, Fitness, Health

Ask the Dietitian

http://www.dietitian.com/

Ask the Dietitian is a Web site where you can get answers to a variety of nutrition questions.

The Calorie Control Council

http://www.caloriecontrol.org/

The Calorie Control Council is an industry group for businesses that help people with dieting needs. Their Web site also contains a lot of educational material regarding health and dieting.

Diettalk

http://www.diettalk.com/

Diettalk offers many useful resources, but perhaps the most interesting are the chat rooms they host, where you can talk live with others about dieting issues.

Low Fat Living

http://www.xe.net/lowfat/

Low Fat Living has recipes and other information designed to help you reduce fat and live healthier!

news:alt.support.diet

This newsgroup is an excellent source to discuss dieting issues and find out what others have to say.

Disabled Services

See also: Health

The Disabilities Awareness Webring Network

http://www.deanjoyce.com/dawn_webring.htm

The Disabilities Awareness Webring Network is a ring of Web sites that promote disability awareness. Includes support groups, companies, organizations, and personal Web pages.

Independent Living USA

http://www.ilusa.com/

Independent Living USA helps disabled persons live independently through a variety of advocacy and educational roles. The Web site contains links and other useful information.

Outdoor Resources for People with Disabilities

http://www.gorp.com/gorp/eclectic/disabled.htm

Gorp (Great Outdoor Recreational Pages) hosts the Outdoor Resources for People with Disabilities page. This site has a host of information about how and where to enjoy the great outdoors.

The Tools For Life Assistive Technology Center

http://www2.gasou.edu/tools/tools.htm

The Tools For Life Assistive Technology Center is committed to raising awareness about assistive technology. The site includes information about the Center, as well as assistive and adaptive technologies.

Trace Research and Development Center

http://trace.wisc.edu/

Trace Research and Development Center works toward helping disabled persons achieve their goals by making computers and communications technology more accessible. Selected documents are available online.

news:misc.handicap

This newsgroup offers widely varying topics of discussion, and a little bit of spam for good measure.

Diving

See also: Outdoors

DiveBuddy White Pages

http://www.divebuddy.com/

If you dive, you know it's not a good idea to dive alone. Find your next partner at the DiveBuddy White Pages. This site is a registry of sorts, where you can register yourself or hook up with others so that you will always have a dive buddy!

Divernet

http://www.divernet.com/

Divernet is an online diving magazine, with articles, travel information and tips, Q & A forums, and more. You can also learn about various products here and link to other useful scuba sites.

Divers Outlet

http://www.diversoutlet.com/

Divers Outlet is a large retailer of scuba gear, and they also do online sales at their Web site. Find the link for the "Online Catalog" to begin shopping.

Dive Travel

http://www.divetravel.net/

Plan your next diving adventure with Dive Travel. This is an online travel agency designed to help you plan diving travels.

Scuba Central

http://scubacentral.com/

Scuba Central is another great online magazine. The site hosts, among other things, scuba humor, a chat room, and a nice photo gallery.

The Scuba Depot

http://www.scubacatalog.com/

The Scuba Depot is an online catalog. The site is low tech, but you might find some good deals here!

news:rec.scuba

Rec.scuba always has some stimulating conversation about diving.

Divorce

See also: Family, Marriage, Relationships

Divorce Central

http://www.divorcecentral.com/

Divorce Central serves as a resource for "the divorced and the divorcing." They offer support and discussion on the various issues surrounding divorce.

Divorce Source

http://www.divorcesource.com/

Divorce Source is another comprehensive information source. The site hosts chat rooms, offers links to legal information, and supplies a complete set of links to local resources throughout the USA and Canada.

Flying Solo

http://www.flyingsolo.com/

Flying Solo offers "Life Management Resources" for persons dealing with divorce and separation. The site also offers information for the disabled and the elderly.

Single Parent Resource Center

http://singleparentresources.com/

The Single Parent Resource Center offers tips, links, and other information in support of single parents and their children.

news:alt.support.divorce

This newsgroup is usually supportive, although there have been flame wars here from time to time.

Drugs

See also: Health

D.A.R.E.

http://www.dare-america.com/

The Web site of the popular D.A.R.E. (Drug Abuse Resistance Education) program has a number of resources and activities for kids, parents, and educators. It's a nice, easy-to-use site.

Drug Watch International

http://www.drugwatch.org/

Drug Watch International works to create a drug-free culture and opposes drug legalization efforts. Their Web site has some links and online resources available.

Media Awareness Project

http://www.mapinc.org/

The purpose of the Media Awareness Project (MAP) is to encourage moderation and reform in drug policy. Find out more about the organization here.

The National Drug Strategy Network

http://www.ndsn.org/

The National Drug Strategy Network Web site contains numerous links to information about policy reform, news, treatment, government activities, and more.

Recovery Related Resources

http://members.aol.com/powerless/RRR.htm

If you're looking for recovery-related resources, check out the Recovery Related Resources Web page. Many, many links take you to regional sites throughout the USA and Canada.

Street Terms Database

http://www.drugs.indiana.edu/slang/
home.html

Don't know the meaning of some new slang terms? Indiana University has created the Street Terms Database, which enables you to search for a slang term from over 3,000 selections.

Economics

See also: Banking, Business, Finance

Economist Jokes

http://paul.merton.ox.ac.uk/work/
economists.html

Been studying economics too long? Well, you could use a good laugh. Surf to Economist Jokes, which even Adam Smith would enjoy.

Federal Reserve System Beige Book

http://www.bog.frb.fed.us/fomc/
BeigeBook/default.cfm

Read reports about the state of the economy from the Federal Reserve System Beige Book, available online.

Morgan Stanley Dean Witter

http://www.msdw.com/

The Morgan Stanley Dean Witter Web site is an excellent place to learn about current happenings in this field, including investing tips and online forums.

The Nobel Prize Internet Archive

http://nobelprizes.com/nobel/
economics/economics.html

The Nobel Prize Internet Archive provides a listing of Nobel Prize Winners in Economic Science from 1969 through the present on this page. Check here to answer your research questions!

U.S. Census Bureau

http://www.census.gov/econ/www/

Economists are always quoting U.S. Census Bureau statistics, so maybe you would benefit from a visit to the Census Bureau's Web page yourself. The site includes a lot of news and statistics as they relate to the national and global economy.

The WWW Capitalism Web Site

http://www.capitalism.org/

The WWW Capitalism Web Site celebrates and defends the capitalist system. Find essays, a library, links, and more. Some of the material here feels like propaganda, but it is interesting nonetheless.

news:sci.econ

Sci.econ is full of in-depth discussion about the current state of the economy.

Education

See also: Children, Schools

Education Free Forum

http://www.edforum.com/

Education Free Forum is not, despite the name, working to free our society of the burden of education. Nay, it is actually an online webzine that offers links to free offers for educators, parents, and students.

Global Schoolhouse

http://www.gsh.org/

Global Schoolhouse provides a wealth of online resources for educators. Among the many resources offered is assistance in creating a Web page for your class or school. This Web site is sponsored by Microsoft.

Integrating the Internet

http://www.indirect.com/www/dhixson/

Integrating the Internet is about (surprise) integrating the Internet into daily school activities. This site includes a weekly newsletter and a variety of good ideas for teachers.

Junior Achievement

http://www.ja.org/

Interested in helping students learn about business and economics? Surf to the Web page of Junior Achievement to learn how you can get involved with this organization that promotes learning in these areas.

KIDLINK

http://www.kidlink.org/

KIDLINK serves to link kids through age 15 from around the world in online dialog. Communication is facilitated through mailing lists, chats, and art exhibition sites.

NASA's Online Educational Resources

http://quest.arc.nasa.gov/OER/

NASA provides Online Educational Resources, which is a collection of links to sites that promote or provide information about computers and network technologies used to enhance learning in schools.

School Search Engine

http://www.schools.com/tabs/tabs.search.html

The School Search Engine enables you to search through an online database to find Web sites of thousands of independent schools, and then link to them.

SLOW

http://www.stanford.edu/group/SLOW/

SLOW (their name, not ours) is the Stanford Learning Organization Web, and is hosted by Stanford University to provide resources into the nature and development of educational organizations.

Teaching & Learning on the World Wide Web

http://www.mcli.dist.maricopa.edu/tl/

Interested in learning more about how the Internet can be used in education? Surf to Teaching & Learning on the World Wide Web, a comprehensive online study and resource on this topic.

Teachnet.com

http://www.teachnet.com/

Teachnet.com is the home of Teachers Edition Online, an online magazine with news, articles, and lesson ideas for teachers.

TENET

http://www.tenet.edu/

TENET, the Texas Education Network, is devoted to bringing resource material free of charge to teachers in Texas.

University Top Links

http://www.university.toplinks.com/

Students can link to numerous useful resources on careers, research, activism, entertainment, and more at University Top Links.

The Welcome Web Teacher's Lounge

http://edu-ss10.educ.queensu.ca/~hudsonp/

The Welcome Web Teacher's Lounge offers a place for teachers new to the Internet to learn more about how to use this technology.

news:misc.education

This newsgroup offers a range of education-related discussion, although there seems to be a slight emphasis on the politics of schooling.

Electricity & Electronics

See also: Computers

Consumer Direct Warehouse

http://www.consumer-direct.com/

Consumer Direct Warehouse offers a huge variety of electronics and appliances, complete with online shopping!

Electrical Fun

http://www.voltnet.com/

Who says electricity has to be boring? Surf to the Electrical Fun Web site and be jolted out of your doldrums.

The Institute of Electrical and Electronics Engineers

http://www.ieee.org/

The Institute of Electrical and Electronics Engineers (IEEE) serves persons in this business and also provides standards for a variety of devices.

JVC America

http://www.jvc-america.com/

JVC America is the place to go to learn more about their wide array of consumer and professional electronics. The site also links to retailers of JVC products.

Kenwood

http://www.kenwoodcorp.com/

Kenwood specializes in home and car stereo products. Surf here to learn more and link to regional sites.

The National Electrical Code Internet Connection

http://www.mikeholt.com/

The National Electrical Code Internet Connection helps you learn more and to prepare for the code exam.

Panasonic Online USA

http://www.panasonic.com/

The Panasonic Online USA Web site enables you to obtain product information, get customer service, or find out where to buy products.

RCA

http://www.rca-electronics.com/

Learn more about RCA electronics at their Web site.

ReplayTV

http://www.replaytv.com/home

Are you tired of having to record shows to watch them at a convenient time? With ReplayTV, you can take control of your television. Record shows, pause live TV broadcasts, set up special channels for your favorite programs, and integrate your satellite, cable, and broadcast sources into one easy-to-use package, with no more video tapes.

Sanyo

http://www.sanyo.com/

Sanyo offers information about its products and even lets you buy online!

Sony

http://www.sony.com/

Sony makes some consumer electronics devices (perhaps you've heard of them?). Learn about all their latest offerings right here on their Web site.

Employment

See also: Business, Veterans

America's Job Bank

http://www.ajb.dni.us/

America's Job Bank is an outstanding source for finding job information online.

Career Resource Center

http://www.careers.org/

The Career Resource Center has a number of great items to help you with your career, including job search tips, employer listings, and job postings. You can also link to regional information from this site.

JobOptions

http://www.joboptions.com/

JobOptions is an excellent resource for online job search and career information, for both job seekers and employers.

Monster Board

http://www.monsterboard.com/

Despite the unlikely name, the Monster Board is a great place for job seekers and employers alike. Their site includes thousands of job listings, as well as tips on resume writing, relocating, interviewing, and more.

Employer & Employee.com

http://www.employer-employee.com/

Employer & Employee.com is a comprehensive resource for articles and information pertaining to the workplace. The site has a strong emphasis on improving employee-employer communication.

Rebecca Smith's eResumes and Resources

http://www.eresumes.com/

Rebecca Smith's eResumes and Resources is an excellent place to learn more about preparing an effective resume.

news:

Newsgroups are a good place to look for job listings in your local area. Search for newsgroups with "jobs" in their name, and then locate one that pertains to your local area.

Entertainment

See also: Celebrities, Communities, Magazines, Movies & Film, Radio, Science Fiction, Television, Theater

Discovery Channel Online

http://www.discovery.com/

Delve deeper into your favorite subjects here at Discovery Channel Online. You can also find programming guides and companion articles for shows on the Discovery Channel cable TV network.

eDrive

http://www.edrive.com/

eDrive is a great place to surf for articles and Web guides for current entertainment news and pop culture.

E! Online

http://www.eonline.com/

E! Online has entertainment content similar to the E! cable network. Participate in one of their online polls!

Hollywood Online

http://www.hollywood.com/

Hollywood Online is all about entertainment news, dirt, and what have you. You'll really like the downloadable soundtrack clips and celebrity sound bites!

Mr. Showbiz

http://www.mrshowbiz.com/

Mr. Showbiz is all about "showbiz" and nothing else. No TV tie-ins, no pop culture examinations, just news, reviews, and interviews connected with entertainment.

Playbill On-Line

http://www1.playbill.com/playbill/

Playbill On-Line offers entertainment news, but perhaps their best feature is the stage show listings for shows across the country. Search for a show, and then link to information on places to eat and stay in the local area.

Rogue Market

http://www.roguemarket.com/

Rogue Market has an unusual concept: At this Web site you can "invest" in various celebrities, and then watch your investment rise or fall based on the successes of that person's career. This is a fun, entertaining way to get in touch with your fellow students of pop culture.

Environment

See also: Animals, Forestry, Outdoors, Parks, Plants, Recycling, Science

Ecology Communications

http://www.ecology.com/

Ecology Communications has a well-presented site containing information about ecology and the environment.

Ecomart

http://www.ecomart.com/

Ecomart is the "paper free" online shopping guide to ecofriendly products.

Environmental Organization Web Directory

http://www.webdirectory.com/

The Environmental Organization Web Directory is a huge catalog of environmental organizations and Web sites. The site works like many other Internet search engines; you can either perform a keyword search or browse through their directory tree.

Environmental Protection Agency

http://www.epa.gov/

Visit the Web site of the U.S. Environmental Protection Agency to see what the American government is doing to protect the environment.

E/The Environmental Magazine

http://www.emagazine.com/

E/The Environmental Magazine covers various environmental issues, such as sustainable agriculture and air pollution. The Web site contains selected articles from the magazine.

Greenpeace International

http://www.greenpeace.org/

Browse the Greenpeace International home page to learn about the organization, current activities, resources, news, and more.

The Nature Conservancy

http://www.tnc.org/

Surf to The Nature Conservancy Web site to learn more about this organization. The Web site details their current activities and lets you know how you can get involved. The site also hosts a "Nature Chat" room.

Population Ecology

http://www.ento.vt.edu/~sharov/popechome/

The Population Ecology Web site is run by the Department of Entomology at the Virginia Tech. This is a great place to find information about how population impacts the planet.

The World Society for the Protection of Animals

http://www.wspa.org.uk/index.html

The World Society for the Protection of Animals is dedicated to (surprise) protecting animals. Check here for news or to find out what the organization is currently working on.

news:sci.environment

Sci.environment contains diverse and often heated discussion about various environmental topics.

Facsimile Services

See also: Computers: E-mail

Faxaway

http://www.faxaway.com/

If you routinely send faxes while you're traveling, here's a service that will interest you. Faxaway offers a service that will fax your documents for you. All you have to do is e-mail Faxaway the document and they'll do the rest. There is a fee, but if you routinely need to fax while on the road, it is worth it.

GFIFax

http://www.gfifax.com/

GFIFax offers fax server software for Microsoft Exchange as well as stand-alone software for Windows and intranets.

Premier Document Distribution

http://www.xpedite.com/

Premier Document Distribution offers a wide variety of fax services, including e-mail broadcasting and international service.

Family

See also: Children, Divorce, Education, Relationships, Religion, Travel

The Adoption Links Page

http://home.ptd.net/~jgbur/

The Adoption Links Page contains a wealth of resources for learning more about adoption.

Facts For Families
http://www.aacap.org/web/aacap/publications/factsfam/index.htm

Facts For Families offers information on dealing with psychiatric disorders that affect children and adolescents. The site is sponsored by AACAP, the American Academy of Child and Adolescent Psychiatry.

Families Under Construction
http://www.famucon.com/

Families Under Construction is a great Web site with a wide variety of resources. Perform a "marriage check-up," learn about parenting issues, and find out about the challenges of keeping your family together in the 90s.

Family.com
http://family.go.com/

Family.com is a fun and useful Web site containing resources for families. The site contains a great deal of information about events and also has links to local information about parenting and activities. Check out the family travel section!

Family Internet
http://www.familyinternet.com/

Family Internet contains resources on finance, entertainment, health, education, and more.

Family Service
http://www.familyservice.org/

Family Service offers numerous programs that concentrate on strengthening and supporting families and communities.

MetLife Online
http://www.metlife.com/

Check out MetLife Online for helpful information on marriage, children, and many other family issues.

Parent Soup
http://www.parentsoup.com/

Parent Soup is an online community for parents. The site contains a wealth of information for expecting parents all the way through parents of adults.

Farming

See also: Agriculture, Animals, Architecture, Environment, Plants

American Farm Bureau
http://www.fb.com/

Find out about and link to local and state farm bureaus from the American Farm Bureau Web site. The site also contains *Voice of Agriculture*, a news service and webzine covering issues surrounding farming.

Christmas Tree USA
http://www.christmas-tree.com/real/

Christmas Tree USA provides links and information on Christmas tree farms across the USA.

Future Farmers of America
http://www.ffa.org/

Future Farmers of America hosts a collection of agricultural education Web sites. Surf here to find important and useful links.

Old Farmer's Almanac

http://www.almanac.com/

Remember the Old Farmer's Almanac? You know, that book your Grandpa used to decide when to reap, when to sow, and how to know which way the wind blows? Well, here it is on the Internet, and not a second too soon, I might add!

United Farm Workers

http://www.ufw.org/

The United Farm Workers is an AFL-CIO affiliated farm workers union. Surf to their official Web site to read news and other information that concern farm workers in the United States.

news:gov.us.topic.agri.farms

This newsgroup contains regular postings of government activities, as well as weekly crop reports.

Finance

See also: Business, Economics, Money, Real Estate, Retirement, Taxes

Ameritrade

http://www.ameritrade.com/

Ameritrade is the cheapest place we have seen for online stock trading. They advertise an $8 fee for most trades!

Datek.com

http://www.datek.com/

Datek.com is another excellent online broker. They offer $9.99 trades online.

E*TRADE Securities, Inc.

http://www.etrade.com/

"Someday, we'll all trade this way." So says the E*TRADE Securities, Inc. Web site. Trade online, get financial news, and more at this exhaustive site.

Fidelity Investment

http://www300.fidelity.com/

Fidelity Investment offers, among other things, online trading. Several people I know use the service and claim it is accurate and easy to use.

FinanCenter

http://www.financenter.com/

FinanCenter is directed towards helping people with their personal finances. The site includes tips on budgeting, home and car buying, credit, insurance, and more.

Microsoft Investor

http://moneycentral.msn.com/home.asp

Microsoft Investor is another good place to check on your investments online.

New York Stock Exchange

http://www.nyse.com/

Get the latest stock market information at the official Web site of the New York Stock Exchange. What better place to learn about investing your money?

PC Quote Online

http://www.pcquote.com/

To check current quotes and get market information at a glance, take a look at PC Quote Online.

Quote.com, Inc.

http://quote.lycos.com/index.html

Quote.com, Inc. offers a 30-day free trial of their online trading services. They are also an extensive source for researching your investments, and they even have a gift shop (?!).

Silicon Investor

http://www.techstocks.com/

Surf to Silicon Investor for news and discussion on the world of finance in high technology. This site contains a huge base of postings from members, which can be a great source of information.

StockMaster

http://www.stockmaster.com/

StockMaster offers a quick reference to what is happening in the major stock markets of the world. This site makes a great desktop wallpaper if you have Windows 98!

TD Waterhouse

http://www.waterhouse.com/

TD Waterhouse is another excellent trading company, with a flat $12 fee for transactions of less than 5000 shares.

news:misc.invest

Misc.invest contains postings about news items, investments for sale, and scam alerts; the site has some spam.

Fire

The Fire Museum Network

http://firemuseumnetwork.org/

The Fire Museum Network links together nearly 300 fire museums across the USA and Canada.

The Fire Station

http://www.flash.net/~jturner/

The Fire Station contains links to fire departments and agencies around the country. Other features include job listings, hazardous material information, and, of course, recipes.

Kids Fire Safety Tips

http://members.cruzio.com/~hoax1950/KidsFireSafetyTips.html

Kids Fire Safety Tips provides children and parents with fun ways to learn about fire safety and prevention.

Operation Safe Home

http://www.smokedetector.org/

Operation Safe Home provides detailed information regarding smoke detectors. Includes installation instructions, and fire preparation tips.

Western States Fire Information Resource

http://www.wsfire.com/

The Western States Fire Information Resource provides numerous links, information, and other resources about fire safety and control.

First Aid

See also: Health

Active First Aid Online

http://www.parasolemt.com.au/afa/

Active First Aid Online serves as an interactive directory of first aid information.

Kaiser Permanente

http://www.scl.ncal.kaiperm.org/
healthinfo/cpr/

Kaiser Permanente offers online information about Cardiopulmonary Resuscitation (CPR). It includes instructions as well as information on where to get CPR training.

Fishing

See also: Boats, Outdoors

Anglers On Line

http://www.streamside.com/index.html

Anglers On Line (not to be confused with the *other* AOL) is a fun and informative place to visit if you love fishing. The site includes news, a "trading post," and chat rooms.

Carp Net

http://www.carp.net/

Carp Net is devoted to carp fishing (no surprises here). Includes tactics, tackle, an e-mail list, links, goodies, and much more.

Fishing Broadcast Network

http://www.fbnonline.com/

The Fishing Broadcast Network serves as an online guide to all things fishy. Check out the online fishing games!

The Fishing Network

http://www.the-fishing-network.com/

The Fishing Network is another great resource for fishing enthusiasts all over the world.

The Fish Net

http://www.thefishnet.com/

The Fish Net has tips, a bookstore, and more—all on the world of fishing. And no, you will not find any jokes about tacky lingerie here.

Fly Angler's OnLine Magazine

http://flyanglersonline.com/

Fly Angler's OnLine Magazine contains news, tips, chat, and more covering the world of fly fishing.

news:alt.fishing

Alt.fishing offers fishing reports, tournament information, and general fishing discussion.

Fitness

See also: Dieting, Health, Martial Arts

The Fitness Jumpsite

http://primusweb.com/fitnesspartner/

The Fitness Jumpsite works like a search engine for fitness, nutrition, and health-related sites. It's easy to use, comprehensive, and nicely laid out to boot!

Fitness Online

http://www.fitnessonline.com/

Fitness Online offers chat, celebrity fitness information, nutrition, training tips, and more.

Runner's Web

http://www.runnersweb.com

Race on over to Runner's Web if you love running. Check here for race results, health information, news, trivia, and more!

Timages

http://www.timages.com/

Timages offers an online Yoga class to help you learn more about keeping both your body and spirit in shape.

The Worldguide Health & Fitness Forum

http://www.worldguide.com/Fitness/hf.html

The Worldguide Health & Fitness Forum contains in-depth fitness information. Includes resources about your anatomy and why you need to take care of it.

www.turnstep.com

http://www.turnstep.com/

Learn all about aerobics at www.turnstep.com, also known as the "Aerobics Page." The site contains a great deal of information about aerobics, including a library of aerobics patterns.

news:misc.fitness

Misc.fitness contains general-interest fitness discussion and a medium amount of spam.

news:misc.fitness.aerobic

For detailed discussion about aerobics, diet, and more, check out this newsgroup.

Flowers

See also: Gifts

1-800-FLOWERS

http://www.1800flowers.com/

Order flowers online for that special someone right here at 1-800-FLOWERS. Check out some of the other great gifts they have to offer, as well!

1-888-888-ROSE

http://www.888-888-rose.com/

1-888-888-ROSE is another excellent place to order and send flowers online.

Virtual Flower Company

http://www.virtualflower.com/

Short on cash but full of love? Send virtual flowers from the Virtual Flower Company, free! Real flowers also available.

Forestry

See also: Agriculture, Environment, Outdoors, Parks

The National Arbor Day Foundation

http://www.arborday.org/

The National Arbor Day Foundation offers workshops, conferences, and other educational resources that help people plant and care for trees.

forestry.com

http://www.forestry.com/

Forestry.com serves as a place for discussion and information-sharing in the field of forestry. Check on events, look for a job, download information, and more.

Gaia's Forest Conservation Archives & Portal

http://forests.org/

Learn about forest conversation efforts all over the world at the Gaia's Forest Conservation Archives & Portal. The site does an excellent job of maintaining a world view of important conservation issues.

SmartForest

http://www.imlab.uiuc.edu/smartforest/

SmartForest is an interesting tool for people studying forest management. It serves as an interactive simulation of a forest, and you can check data and watch progress and changes over a 25-year period.

Society of American Foresters

http://www.safnet.org/index.html

The Society of American Foresters serves professionals in forestry professions. Learn more about this organization and forestry in general here.

Steve Shook's Directory of Forest Products, Wood Science, and Marketing

http://www.forestdirectory.com/

Steve Shook's Directory of Forest Products, Wood Science, and Marketing is a Web directory of 1700+ sites dealing with these issues. It's another great place to do research.

U.S. Forest Service

http://www.fs.fed.us/

The U.S. Forest Service Web site is a comprehensive source of forestry information. It's an excellent place to start your research or link to National Forest sites on the Internet.

news:bionet.agroforestry

This newsgroup contains forestry discussion and normally has some vastly divergent views on controversial issues.

Furniture

See also: Home Improvement

Air Tech

http://www.airtech.net/

Air Tech (Air Technologies Corporation) offers chairs and other ergonomically designed products, primarily for computer users. Order online using their secure server or just learn more about these products.

Anthro Corporation

http://www.anthro.com/

Anthro Corporation offers sturdy, well-designed furniture for using with and around your computer operations.

Bean Bag Store & More

http://www.bhome.com/about.htm

Who doesn't love bean bag chairs? Check out the Bean Bag Store & More for chairs of varying sizes, all the way up to the "Family Lounger," which accommodates multiple sitters.

BeHOME

http://www.behome.com/

BeHOME is both an online magazine about home design and furnishings and a place to shop for fine furniture online!

Classic Director Chair Company

http://members.tripod.com/rockinmag7/directorschair.html

You're really nobody until you have a director's chair with your name embroidered on it. So, why not order one for yourself from the Classic Director Chair Company, which offers several sizes and options to choose from.

Henry Hall Office Products

http://www.henryhall.com/

Henry Hall specializes in high-tech furniture for demanding office and computer settings.

Vitra

http://www.vitra.com/

Vitra offers furniture designs that can only be described as art. Find out about their intriguing designs here or visit their online museum of fine furniture designs. And to top it all off, the Vitra Web site has some fascinating design elements to it as well.

The World of Leather

http://worldofleather.com/

The World of Leather offers a number of leather furniture designs. For best results, wear shiny leather or vinyl when seated in leather furniture.

Gambling

See also: Games

Biff479's Picks

http://members.aol.com/Biff479/

Biff479's Picks offers free handicapping information on upcoming sports events. This site is low tech but updated regularly.

Casino CoCo

http://www.casinococo.com/

Casino CoCo is an online casino based on Saint Martin in the Caribbean. The site contains some games that are "for fun" and some that are for real money.

The Casino Network

http://www.casino-network.com/

The Casino Network helps you plan a gambling trip by enabling you to reserve hotel rooms, search for casinos, and link to a variety of gambling-related Web sites around the Web.

Fabulous Vegas

http://www.netcore.ca/~billk/
vegas_casino.html

Surf to Fabulous Vegas for tips on how to play various casino games for fun and manage your money effectively.

Gamblers Anonymous

http://www.gamblersanonymous.org/

Gamblers Anonymous works to help compulsive gamblers regain control of their lives. Learn more here.

Internet Video Poker

http://www.sancho.com/poker/

Internet Video Poker enables you to play poker online for free. Accrue points when you win a hand, but be careful, it's addictive!

The United States Gambling Research Institute

http://www.usgri.org/

The United States Gambling Research Institute conducts research into legalized gambling in the USA.

The Virtual Slot Machine

http://www.pacificnet.net/~sonic/
vslot.html

The Virtual Slot Machine enables you to play the slots online with fake money!

The Wizard of Odds

http://www.thewizardofodds.com

The Wizard of Odds provides a nice no-frill site listing rules for most popular casino games.

Games

See also: Gambling

Funny Bunny Trail

http://usacitylink.com/easter/

The Funny Bunny Trail has, among other things, an annual online Easter Egg Hunt. Search the Web to find Easter Eggs!

GamePen.Com

http://www.gamepen.com/

GamePen.Com in an online video gaming magazine, offering reviews, strategies, demos, cheats, and more.

Happy Puppy Game Site

http://happypuppy.com/

Games, free demos, and playing tips are what you'll find at the Happy Puppy Game Site. Plus, the site has some truly outstanding graphics. Happy Puppy covers not only PC games, but Nintendo, Playstation, and more!

Internet Park

http://www.amo.qc.ca/

Play word games such as Jumbled, Ready Mix, and Anagram online at Internet Park. The site offers a 20-day free trial, and if you continue playing the fee is $3.50 (US) per month.

Microprose

http://www.hasbrointeractive.com/microprose/index.cfm/

Microprose is one of the veteran computer game companies, and is still making innovative and challenging games. Whether you are interested in starting a railroad empire in the late 1800s or a space-faring empire in the far future, racing a vintage Formula car or a brand new Grand Prix machine, Microprose has a reputation for building the best simulation games.

Red Storm Entertainment

http://www.redstorm.com/

If you like Tom Clancy's books, you'll probably enjoy the games from Red Storm Entertainment. This game company is focused on creating realistic and intellectually challenging games.

Tic-Tac-Toe

http://netpressence.com/npcgi/ttt

Play Tic-Tac-Toe at this site hosted by Jeff Boulter. You can set the board up to 7 by 7, and the computer is tough!

The Wargamer

http://www.wargamer.com

The Wargamer is one of the most comprehensive sites for armchair generals, focusing on the most realistic simulations available. It features reviews, demos, scenarios, and tips for a variety of tactical, operational, and strategic wargames.

The War Page

http://aylic.com/War/war.html

Shall we play a game? Check out the links to various war games at The War Page.

World Wide Web Scavenger Hunt

http://deil.lang.uiuc.edu/web.pages/
www.scavengerhunt.html

Want to test your skills as a Web surfer? Give the World Wide Web Scavenger Hunt a try, where you search through the Web to answer challenging questions.

Zarf's List of Interactive Games on the Web

http://www.leftfoot.com/games.html

Zarf's List of Interactive Games on the Web is a list of interactive games on . . . well, you get the idea. The site provides links to dozens of games that you can play online.

Gardening

See also: Agriculture, Farming

Aggie Horticulture

http://aggie-horticulture.tamu.edu/
tamuhort.html

Aggie Horticulture (hosted by Texas A & M University, natch) is packed full of information for green thumbs everywhere.

Better Homes and Gardens Gardening Home Page

http://www.bhglive.com/gardening/
index.html

Surf to the Better Homes and Gardens Web site to see online information from this popular magazine.

GardenWeb

http://www.gardenweb.com/

Find fascinating articles, discussion forums, event schedules, online catalogs, and more at GardenWeb.

Gothic Gardening

http://www.gothic.net/~malice/

Explore the "darker side" of gardening with Gothic Gardener. The motto says it all: "Something Wicked This Way Grows!"

The (no) Problem Garden

http://www.netusa1.net/~lindley/

The (no) Problem Garden operates on the principle that there is no such thing as a problem garden. View art, read tips, and learn how to deal with common problems.

Organic Gardener's Web

http://www.geocities.com/RainForest/
8810/ogweb.html

The Organic Gardener's Web is a place for organic gardeners to get together for discussion and information sharing.

Sherry's Greenhouse

http://www.teleport.com/~earth/

Sherry's Greenhouse has a variety of material related to greenhouse growing and gardening, updated daily! Ask Sherry your questions and have them answered online!

news:rec.gardens

Rec.gardens has discussion of a wide variety of gardening topics.

Gay, Lesbian, & Bisexual

See also: Communities, Cultures

All Out Arts

http://www.users.interport.net/~clgri/

All Out Arts works in educating the gay and lesbian community in the various arts. Surf here to find out about their latest programs.

Data Lounge

http://www.datalounge.com/

For daily news, a calendar of events, and an online dating service, surf to Data Lounge.

PlanetOut

http://www.planetout.com/

PlanetOut is an online community for gay, lesbian, bisexual, and transgender people. Find news, books and videos, humor, politics, chat, and more!

Pride Net

http://www.pridenet.com/

Pride Net serves as an online resource for the gay, lesbian, bisexual, and transgender community around the world. This site has some great info to help you plan your travels!

Queer Arts Resource Home Page

http://www.queer-arts.org/

The Queer Arts Resource Home Page is hosted by this organization, which promotes and celebrates the contributions of gays and lesbians to art throughout history.

Stonewall Revisited

http://www.stonewallrevisited.com/index.html

Learn about one of the most pivotal events in the gay rights movement at Stonewall Revisited. Includes personal stories and articles about current issues.

Genealogy

See also: Family, History, Libraries

Ancestry.com — The Genealogy Research HomeTown

http://www.ancestry.com/

Ancestry.com — The Genealogy Research HomeTown is an excellent place to do your research online. The site has a large cache of databases for you to search through and find your ancestors.

Cool Site of the Month for Genealogists

http://www.cogensoc.org/cgs/cgs-cool.htm

The Colorado Genealogical Society sponsors Cool Site of the Month for Genealogists. The site contains useful links to great genealogical resources.

Family Tree Maker

http://www.familytreemaker.com/

The Family Tree Maker Web site offers much more than simple product information. There is also a lot of helpful information to aid your genealogical research, and you can even post classifieds to request information on the site!

The Genealogy Home Page

http://www.genhomepage.com/

Find an extensive set of links to online resources at the Genealogy Home Page.

National Genealogical Society

http://www.ngsgenealogy.org/

Learn about genealogy at the Web site of the National Genealogical Society or just find out what the society is doing now. This site has numerous articles and other resources to help you conduct effective research.

U.S. Census Bureau

http://www.census.gov/ftp/pub/

Visit the home page of the U.S. Census Bureau for online access to some of their records.

news:alt.genealogy

Check out this newsgroup for discussion and questions from genealogy researchers. Post your own questions, too!

Geography

See also: Geology, Maps, Regions, Science

Geo-Globe

http://library.advanced.org/10157/

Play interactive online games at Geo-Globe that help you test and refine your knowledge of geography.

The Global Statistics

http://www.stats.demon.nl/

The Global Statistics site is a simple, easy-to-use resource of basic demographic data for many countries of the world. It includes population, cultural, and economic data.

How far is it?

http://www.indo.com/distance/

How far is it? A good question, and you can probably find out here. A no-frills Web site, you simply enter two locations and voila! the air distance is calculated based on latitude and longitude. Some lesser-known places aren't recognized (it knows where Mexico City is, but not Oaxaca), but it is useful nonetheless.

Map Machine

http://www.nationalgeographic.com/resources/ngo/maps/

Download some stunning maps from the Map Machine from *National Geographic*. The site offers political and physical maps in numerous varieties.

Mike's GIS Home Page

http://fox.nstn.ca/~mkostiuk/gispage.html

If you're looking for online Geographic Information System Resources, check out Mike's GIS Home Page. This site is absolutely "no frills," but the numerous links are truly useful.

TerraServer

http://www.terraserver.microsoft.com/

Microsoft's TerraServer is touted as the world's largest online database. The site includes satellite images of many parts of the world, down to disturbing detail.

U.S. Gazetteer

http://www.census.gov/cgi-bin/gazetteer

The Census Bureau offers the U.S. Gazetteer, a searchable resource for population data and maps.

Geology

See also: Geography, Science, Seismology

Donald Blanchard's Earth Sciences Web Site

http://webspinners.com/dlblanc/

Learn about plate tectonics and other geological wonders at Donald Blanchard's Earth Sciences Web Site. This site offers an easy-to-understand explanation of these geological theories.

Geology Link

http://www.geologylink.com/

Geology Link is an outstanding resource for geology information. The site includes educational forums, daily news about geological events, images, and much more.

National Park Service Park Geology

http://www.aqd.nps.gov/grd/

The National Park Service has its own geology resource located online at the NPS Park Geology page. The Park Service also hires many geologists to work in the park system, and has job listings online.

The U.S. Geological Survey

http://www.usgs.gov/

The U.S. Geological Survey offers an indispensable source of information on Biology, Geology, and other science topics. This is a dependable resource for that research paper you're working on!

Volcano World

http://volcano.und.edu/

Volcano World has lots of information on Volcanoes on Earth and elsewhere. This project has been put together by the University of North Dakota using data from NASA and other sources.

Gifts

See also: Flowers, Jewelry, Marriage, Shopping

All American Gift Directory & Catalog

http://www.aagift.com/

Surf to the All American Gift Directory and Catalog for links and gift catalogs online.

American Greetings

http://www.americangreetings.com/

Here's a good idea: create a Web site where cybersurfers can create, purchase, and send their own custom greeting cards without leaving the comfort of their desks. Sound good? Well, that's exactly what American Greetings has done. Check it out!

Cardmaster

http://www.cardmaster.com/

Cardmaster lets you send virtual gifts and greetings via e-mail. Free services include horoscopes, poems, flowers, invitations, and much, much more!

The Original Horse Turd in a Box

http://home.earthlink.net/~inabox/turd.html

Need the perfect "gift" for that someone special? Why not send them The Original Horse Turd in a Box? Here is an idea whose time has come. Accept no substitutes!

Perfect Present Picker

http://presentpicker.com/ppp/

So you say you need to gift someone, but you're all out of ideas? You should check out the Perfect Present Picker, a Web site that helps you with gift ideas by taking you through a "gift wizard." At the end of the wizard, you will be presented with a list of items from various companies, and you can link to them to make a purchase!

Go Karts

See also: Hobbies

The Karting Web Site

http://www.muller.net/karting/

Surf to The Karting Web Site for news, photos, links, calendars, classifieds, and more. The site serves as an online magazine for this sport, and is comprehensive.

National Kart News

http://www.nkn.com/

National Kart News is the online version of this karting magazine. The site contains a monthly feature article, a chat room, tech info, and more.

Vintage Karts

http://www.vintagekarts.com/

Check out the karts of yesteryear at Vintage Karts. This Web site also includes a minibike section.

news:alt.autos.karting

Discuss karting in this newsgroup, and read some spam for good measure!

Golf

See also: Sports

GOLF ONLINE.COM.

http://www.golfonline.com/

GOLD ONLINE.COM focuses on the players of this sport, including news and interviews. You'll also find an online pro-shop, golfing tips, and a whole lot more.

GolfWeb

http://www.golfweb.com/

Get golfing news, tips, or shop online with GolfWeb. The site also contains a number of discussion group forums, classifieds, and travel information!

Saint Duffer

http://www.st-duffer.com/duffer.html

Receive a blessing on your golf game from Saint Duffer, the patron saint of golf. Learn all about the saint at this humorous Web site.

XGolf

http://www.xgolf.com/

XGolf is about the sport of golf with an attitude. Surf here for alternative views on the current and future state of the sport.

news:rec.sport.golf

Discuss golf and read gossip on the rec.sport.golf newsgroup. Most of the spam here is golf related.

Government

See also: Education, Geography, Geology, Law, Libraries, Military, Regions, Space, Taxes, Veterans

Center for Intelligent Information Retrieval

http://cobar.cs.umass.edu/

The United States government hosts hundreds of Web sites, and searching through them all can be quite frustrating. The Center for Intelligent Information Retrieval (formerly known as *GovBot*) offers a solution by serving as a search engine for government-owned online resources. Search using keywords to find just what you're looking for.

A
B
C
D
E
F
G
H
I
J
K
L
M
N
O
P
Q
R
S
T
U
V
W
X
Y
Z

EUROPARL
http://www.europarl.eu.int/

EUROPARL is the Web site of the European Parliament, available in numerous languages. Learn about current news and activities here.

Federal Times Online
http://www.federaltimes.com/

Federal Times Online is the Web site of this weekly newspaper serving federal employees.

FedWorld Information Network
http://www.fedworld.gov/

Search through hundreds of government Web pages at the FedWorld Information Network, a government-run search engine for its numerous online resources.

Global Computing, Inc. U.S. State Home Pages
http://www.globalcomputing.com/states.html

Link to the Web sites of U.S. states from the Global Computing, Inc. list of U.S. state home pages.

The Jefferson Project
http://solstice.stardot.com/jefferson/

For a truly outstanding list of online political resources, government and otherwise, surf to The Jefferson Project.

Organization of American States
http://www.oas.org/

The Organization of American States serves and represents the many nations of North and South America.

THOMAS
http://thomas.loc.gov/

THOMAS provides online information on the United States Congress. Surf here to check activity on the floor, search the congressional record, read pending bills, or just learn more about the legislative process.

United Nations
http://www.un.org/

Browse the Web site of the United Nations to learn about current activities, news, international law, and other geopolitical information.

Graffiti

See also: Art

Art Crimes
http://www.graffiti.org/

Surf to Art Crimes to learn more about urban graffiti art. The site contains some outstanding images of art from various cities throughout the world.

TheHead.com
http://home.earthlink.net/~thehead/

Check out this Web site called TheHead.com, devoted to the words and images of bathroom walls throughout America. Fascinating, but not for the squeamish.

The JazePages
http://www.jaze.com/graffiti/index.html

Read some fascinating articles about graffiti at The JazePages.

National Graffiti Information Network

http://infowest.com/NGIN/

The National Graffiti Information Network is devoted to efforts to stop graffiti. The information is a little old but can be useful nonetheless.

Guns

See also: Archery, Military, Outdoors, Sports

Gungear.com

http://www.gungear.com/

Purchase shooting accessories and other goods online at Gungear.com.

Guns Unlimited

http://www.guns-unlimited.com/

Guns Unlimited promotes itself as a virtual gun show, where you can buy, sell, and trade guns and accessories online.

GunWeb

http://www.gunweb.com/

Check out the online firearms magazine GunWeb for news, articles, links, and more.

National Rifle Association

http://www.nra.org/

Visit the Web site of the National Rifle Association to learn more about this large organization promoting gun owners' rights.

NoRust Bags

http://hometown.aol.com/norustbags/index.htm

NoRust Bags protect your guns or anything else that can corrode for up to five years.

Second Amendment Foundation

http://www.saf.org/

At the Second Amendment Foundation's site, you can learn more about an organization that is working hard to protect the rights of gun owners through America's courtrooms and through education initiatives.

Violence Policy Center

http://www.vpc.org/

The Violence Policy Center is devoted to educational efforts to reduce violence. Surf here to learn more about the Center and its efforts.

Gymnastics

See also: Fitness, Sports

GYMN

http://www.gymn-forum.com/

GYMN is an online gymnastics forum, with event info, links, photos, trivia, and more.

Gymnastics, Acrobatics & Trampoline Page

http://www.thewere.com/gymnastics/gym.html

Check out a wide variety of links, stories, poems, and other information at the Gymnastics, Acrobatics & Trampoline Page. The site has a special emphasis on Olympic competitions.

USA Gymnastics

http://www.usa-gymnastics.org/

USA Gymnastics is the governing body of gymnastics competition in the USA. Check here for event information, athlete's profiles, gym club links, and more!

A
B
C
D
E
F
G
H
I
J
K
L
M
N
O
P
Q
R
S
T
U
V
W
X
Y
Z

Health

See also: AIDS, Alcohol, Dieting, Disabled Services, Drugs, First Aid, Fitness, Mental Health, Science, Tobacco

The Alternative Medicine Homepage
http://www.pitt.edu/~cbw/altm.html

Locate resources and information for alternative medicine at the Alternative Medicine Homepage.

Centers for Disease Control and Prevention
http://www.cdc.gov/

Worried about disease outbreaks around the world? Have your anxieties soothed (or justified) at the Web site of the Centers for Disease Control and Prevention.

Combined Health Information Database
http://chid.nih.gov/

The Combined Health Information Database is an excellent place to visit if you are conducting health-related research. Search the database to find abstracts and titles of various resources on your topic.

Healthfinder
http://www.healthfinder.gov/

Locate health resources online at Healthfinder. The site contains links, news, and other information for your health research.

Healthy Ideas
http://www.healthyideas.com/

Healthy Ideas is brought to you by Women's Wire and *Prevention* magazine. This is a great place to learn more about current women's health issues.

Internet Health Library
http://www.health-library.com/

Get health and medical information and tips online at the Internet Health Library. The site works like an Internet search engine, with keyword or directory searches available.

WebDoctor
http://www.gretmar.com/webdoctor/home.html

Practicing physicians have their own online resource at WebDoctor. Link to chats, news, journals, and other important information to assist you in your work.

WebMD
http://www.webmd.com

WebMD is a useful resource for medical professionals and other people concerned with health and health care in general.

History

See also: Education, Genealogy, Libraries

History
http://www.corvinia.org/history/history.html

History is a set of links related to (are you ready for this?) history. Sites are arranged into themes based on period, dating from the present all the way back to prehistoric times.

The History Channel
http://www.historychannel.com/

Surf to The History Channel Online for a wide variety of history-related information. Check out message boards, travel information, daily historical events, and much more.

History Timelines on the Web

```
http://www.search-beat.com/
history.htm
```

Timelines are an extremely useful tool when studying or teaching history, and you'll find a huge selection of them at History Timelines on the Web. Clicking timeline titles on this Web site links to other sites that actually contain the timelines.

Rulers

```
http://www.geocities.com/Athens/
1058/rulers.html
```

Need information about world rulers past and present? Check out Rulers, an index of those people who have shaped the world. The site also contains current news as it applies to world leaders.

Scholar's Guide to WWW

```
http://members.aol.com/DAnn01/
webguide.html
```

Teachers and historians can find links to a wealth of information at the Scholar's Guide to WWW. The site is maintained by Richard Jensen, Professor Emeritus of History at the University of Illinois Chicago.

news:alt.history

Discuss a variety of historical issues and topics at alt.history.

news:alt.history.what-if

Who says learning and discussing history can't be fun? Check out the interesting conversations going on at alt.history.what-if, where participants as the "What if?" question about various historical events and people.

Hobbies

See also: Collectibles, Comics, Crafts, Darts, Go-Karts, Toys, Railroads

Coin Universe

```
http://www.coin-universe.com/
index.html
```

Coin collectors will enjoy spending time at Coin Universe. View the price guide, check out the collector's auction, and link to other coin sites!

eHobbies

```
http://www.ehobbies.com
```

eHobbies is more than a Web-based store for hobby-related equipment, supplies, and material. This site also includes an online community and magazine devoted to (you guessed it) hobbies.

The Emerald City Modeler's Home Page

```
http://www.feist.com/~downen/
```

Learn about all things modeled at the Emerald City Modeler's Home Page by Troy Downen. You name it, it's here.

Firewalk Extreme

```
http://www.mastery.net/firewalk/
index.html
```

Is firewalking a hobby? Sure! Learn all about it at Firewalk Extreme, complete with some very hot animation!

Juggling Information Service

```
http://www.juggling.org/
```

Surf to the Juggling Information Service, if you think you can handle it.

National & International Railroad Junction

http://www.rrjunction.com/

Check out the National & International Railroad Junction for links to various railroad modeling Web sites around the world.

National Model Car Builders' Museum

http://www.xmission.com/~msgs1/nmcbm/

The National Model Car Builders' Museum is dedicated to preserving the history of car models and model building.

Paper Airplanes

http://www.geocities.com/
CapeCanaveral/1817/

Learn the finer points of paper airplane construction and flight from former world record holder Ken Blackburn at his paper airplane Web site.

Ship Modelers Association

http://www.ship-modelers-assn.org/

If you enjoy modeling ships, then you should check out the Ship Modelers Association.

Sport Rocketry Magazine

http://www.nar.org/SPR/

Learn all about the sport of model rocketry at Sport Rocketry Magazine.

Train Shack

http://www.trainshack.com/

If you like model or toy trains, check out the Train Shack to see what they have to offer. Items for sale include Z through G model trains, as well as Brio and Thomas the Tank Engine wooden trains.

Home Improvement

See also: Architecture, Furniture

Better Homes and Gardens Home Improvement Encyclopedia

http://www.bhglive.com/homeimp/

The Better Homes and Gardens Home Improvement Encyclopedia offers tips, ideas, and instructions for performing home projects in a variety of subject areas.

Home Ideas

http://www.homeideas.com/

Get some great ideas for home projects at Home Ideas. The site includes product information, discussion areas, links, an online store, and more.

Home Time

http://www.hometime.com/

Visit the Web site of Home Time, a weekly TV show devoted to various home improvement projects. Get detailed information about the projects you see on the show.

MasterPlumber.com's

http://www.masterplumbers.com/

Plumbing can be one of the scariest aspects of home improvement and repair. Link to MasterPlumber.com's to take the mystery out of plumbing.

Reader's Digest World

http://www.rdathome.com/

You can find almost anything at Reader's Digest World, including some great home improvement tips!

Surfin' StrawBale

http://www.moxvox.com/surfsolo.html

Straw bale construction is affordable and makes a lot of sense. Learn more about it at Surfin' StrawBale. Includes numerous useful links.

That Home Site!

http://www.thathomesite.com/

That Home Site! is a humorous site dedicated to less than perfect homes. The site includes home upkeep, recipes, information about home offices, pets, and more.

This Old House

http://www.pbs.org/wgbh/thisoldhouse/

Surf to the Web site of This Old House, the popular TV show on appreciating and restoring historic homes. The Web site contains information on recent house projects.

Toiletology 101

http://www.toiletology.com/index.shtml

Learn everything you need to know to keep your potty running smoothly at Toiletology 101. Plunge in!

Yurt Quest

http://user.aol.com/VirtualMu/YurtQuest/index.html

Learn how to build the traditional Mongolian structure at Yurt Quest: In Search of a Ger. And if you don't even know what it is, learn that here too!

Humor

See also: Comics, Communities

Bad Air and Space Museum

http://www.badairandspace.com/

The Bad Air and Space Museum has a multitude of exhibits demonstrating potential problems when current, worldly socio-economic problems extend into space. "Will work for food/air."

Comedy Central Online

http://www.comedycentral.com/

Visit Comedy Central Online for program information, daily news about comedy, daily comedy about the news, and more.

Comedy.com

http://www.comedy.com/

Comedy.com lets you search for comedy clubs and comedians or view their "Joke of the Day."

Hardware Wars

http://www.mwp.com/mwp/Hardwars.html

The Farce is Back when you order the short film classic Hardware Wars! The film is "A Space Saga of Romance, Rebellion, and Household Appliances." Order it online here!

Hitchhiker's Guide to the Galaxy

http://www.h2g2.com/

If you ever need any helpful tips to get the most out of life or answers to difficult questions, you can probably find them here. Don't panic, always bring a towel, and check out the Earth Edition of the Hitchhiker's Guide to the Galaxy.

I Hate Computers

`http://extlab1.entnem.ufl.edu/`
`IH8PCs/index.html`

I Hate Computers contains numerous articles and other humorous bits. Can you guess what the authors don't like?

Looney Links

`http://www.lunaticlounge.com/`
`looneylinks/`

Looney Links is a strong candidate for best compendium of weird sites on the Web. A subpage of the Lunatic Lounge, a great humor site, Looney Links offers an astonishing variety of just plain weirdness.

the ONION

`http://www.theonion.com/`

Bend back those tulips of the Internet and find the ONION, an outstanding source of satire and wit online. Don't laugh at your computer, laugh with it!

Pun of the Day

`http://www.punoftheday.com/`

Find a groaner at Pun of the Day. Updated weekly.

PythOnline

`http://www.pythonline.com/`

Your visit to cyberspace simply isn't complete until you've visited one of the Monty Python-inspired Web sites like PythOnline. Join the Spam Club and learn more about the origins of this bit of Internet jargon.

Scott Pakin's automatic complaint-letter generator

`http://www-csag.cs.uiuc.edu/`
`individual/pakin/complaint`

Do you have a serious problem with someone else's behavior? Take your complaints to Scott Pakin's automatic complaint-letter generator.

The Useless Pages

`http://www.go2net.com/internet/`
`useless/`

The Useless Pages is the granddaddy of time-wasting metasites. Through the Useless Pages you'll find a virtually unlimited melange of strange, wonderful, stupid, offensive, and/or hilarious Web sites for your endless distraction.

Wonders of the Web

`http://web.wt.net/~psherr/wow/`
`wow.htm`

This site features a vast host of wacky, weird, or just plain silly sites ranging from the Anti-cheese Hamster Liberation Alliance to the World Wide Web Ouija.

Inventing

See also: Marketing

The Internet Invention Store

`http://www.catalog.com/impulse/`
`invent.htm`

Check out new inventions at The Internet Invention Store. You can also link to various inventing resources or learn how to get your own inventions listed on the Web site.

Inventors Assistance League

`http://www.inventions.org/`

Learn how to protect and use your inventions at the Inventors Assistance League.

National Congress of Inventor Organizations

http://www.inventionconvention.com/ncio/ncio.index.html

The National Congress of Inventor Organizations offers free online assistance and resources for inventors, including scam alerts, government information, and more.

Jewelry

See also: Gifts, Shopping

Collectible Costume Jewelry

http://www.costumejewelry.com/

Browse and order antique and collectible costume jewelry at Collectible Costume Jewelry.

Jewelry Mall

http://www.jewelrymall.com/

Link to jewelry information and online shopping at A Jewelry Mall. The site also contains jewelry jokes and schedules of gem shows.

JewelryNet

http://www.jewelrynet.com/

JewelryNet is another excellent online resource for finding jewelry resellers and other information online.

Watchnet

http://watchnet.com/

Buy, sell, trade, or just talk about watches at Watchnet. The site hosts a chat room, dealer links, and much more.

news:rec.crafts.jewelry

This newsgroup is an excellent place to talk about jewelry, or even make trades, purchases, and sales!

Language

See also: Cultures, Education

Babel Fish

http://babelfish.altavista.com/

Named for the fabulous creature of literary fame, AltaVista's Babel Fish can be used to translate words or phrases to or from English, German, Italian, Spanish, French, or Portuguese.

Communication Connections

http://www.widomaker.com/~ldprice/

Find an extensive collection of links to various language learning sites around the Internet at Communication Connections.

ESL Home Page

http://www.lang.uiuc.edu/r-li5/esl/

Learn English with one of the resources listed at the ESL (English as a Second Language) Home Page.

International Language Schools

http://www.edunet.com/lsindex.html

Search for a language school at International Language Schools. The site enables you to search worldwide resources, or you can choose to search only in the UK or USA.

news:misc.education.language

Check out discussions about language in the misc.education.language newsgroup. Also, check out the questions people are asking to see if you can help!

Law

See also: Government, Security

The Consumer Law Page
http://consumerlawpage.com/

Research consumer law, including occupational injuries, at The Consumer Law Page.

ExpertLaw's Lawyer and Legal Humor
http://www.expertlaw.com/humor/

What's wrong with lawyer jokes? Lawyers don't think they are funny, and nobody else thinks they are jokes. Find the best and the worst of legal humor at ExpertLaw.

FindLaw
http://www.findlaw.com/

FindLaw is a search engine of law resources on the Internet. The user interface looks almost exactly like the Yahoo! search engine, with keyword or directory searches and common links at the top and bottom of the main page.

Law.Net
http://www.law.net/

Law.Net serves as a resource for legal information on the Internet. Their information is directed primarily at lay persons rather than other lawyers, so it is easier to make sense out of.

Legal Pad Junior
http://www.legalpadjr.com/

Legal Pad Junior contains law and legal information for kids. It's an excellent resource, with information for kids and teachers.

The World Wide Web Virtual Library
http://www.law.indiana.edu/law/
v-lib/lawschools.html

Locate law schools and libraries around the world at The World Wide Web Virtual Library.

WWLIA Home Page
http://www.wwlia.org/

Search for worldwide legal information at the WWLIA (World Wide Legal Information Association) Home Page. The site includes hundreds of links, including links to new resources on the front page.

news:misc.legal.moderated

The moderated misc.legal newsgroup maintains a good mix of legal discussion, without breaking down into conjecture and current event rants.

Libraries

See also: Education, Genealogy, Government, History, Schools

American Library Association
http://www.ala.org/

Surf to the Web site of the American Library Association for news, events, information about the organization, and links to library resources.

Library of Congress
http://lcweb2.loc.gov/

Visit the Library of Congress Web site for a wealth of information about American history. The archives contain valuable personal accounts of historical events, important documents, and a huge number of great photographs.

National Archives and Records Administration

http://www.nara.gov/

Find out what the National Archives and Records Administration can offer for your research into genealogy, the Kennedy assassination, and other federal records at this Web site.

Smithsonian Institution Libraries

http://www.sil.si.edu/

The Smithsonian Institution Libraries hold some of the largest resources of historical information in the world. Surf to their Web site to find out how you can access that information.

webCATS

http://library.usask.ca/hywebcat/

Check out webCATS for a list of links to libraries with online catalogs of information.

Magazines

See also: Entertainment, News

Atlantic Unbound

http://www.theatlantic.com/

Atlantic Unbound is an online spin-off of the *Atlantic Monthly*, although the publishers state that this is actually an evolving publication all its own. Unbound deals with politics, society, the arts, and culture.

Beat Generation

http://members.aol.com/beatgeninc/
beatgen/beatgen.html

Beat Generation borrows an old label and pastes it onto this e-zine for persons in "Generation X." Sorry, no Kerouac or Ginsberg here!

Electronic Newstand

http://www.enews.com/

The Electronic Newstand is a magazine that discusses and links to other magazines. A great place to start if you're not sure where to look.

e-zine-list

http://www.meer.net/~johnl/
e-zine-list/

Search through lists of online magazines at John Labovitz's e-zine list.

Jam!

http://www.canoe.ca/Jam/

Check out entertainment news and commentary at Jam! Music, TV, movies, books, theater — it's all here!

On The Wire

http://www.catsail.com/

For catamaran sailors, On The Wire features tech tips, reviews, humor, places to sail, and much more.

People Online

http://pathfinder.com/people/

If you enjoy *People Magazine*, then you'll want to check out People Online. The site includes daily news and gossip on people in the media.

Salon Magazine

http://www.salon1999.com/

The online version of Salon Magazine has many fascinating articles online. Check here for a different, less-sanitized view of news and life in our times.

Maps

See also: Autos, Geography, Libraries, Regions, Travel

DeLorme: CyberRouter

http://route.delorme.com/

The DeLorme: CyberRouter is an easy-to-use Web site, thanks in large part to the fact that the Web page does without unneeded fluff. After the trip is routed, the site makes some maps available to you with the intended route highlighted.

Green Map System

http://www.greenmap.com/index.html

Get maps of ecologically significant cities and sites at the Green Map System.

MapQuest

http://www.mapquest.com/

MapQuest is perhaps the most interactive mapping site on the Internet. It includes complete trip routing services and easily customized maps.

Maps On Us

http://www.mapsonus.com/

Maps On Us is another easy to use an interactive mapping system that provides free map routing on its Web site.

PCL Map Collection

http://www.lib.utexas.edu/Libs/PCL/
Map_collection/Map_collection.html

Find maps of nearly every area of the world online at the PCL (Perry-Castañeda Library) Map Collection.

TerraServer

http://www.terraserver.microsoft.com/

Microsoft's TerraServer is said to be the world's largest online database. The site includes satellite images of many parts of the world, detailed enough to display the lawn furniture in your own back yard.

The Xerox PARC Map Viewer

http://pubweb.parc.xerox.com/map/

The Xerox PARC Map Viewer is the epitome of a no-frills Web site, but it provides an extremely accurate map of the world. Sorry, no trip routing services here!

Yahoo! Maps

http://maps.yahoo.com/yahoo/

Need to find an address quickly? At Yahoo! Maps, you just enter a street address and the site displays a map showing your location. There aren't many options here, but it serves its intended purpose well.

Marketing

See also: Business, Economics, Inventing

American Marketing Association

http://www.ama.org/

The American Marketing Association serves marketing professionals and educators in the USA. Surf here to learn more about the Association.

Characteristics of a Telemarketing Fraud Scheme

http://www.usps.gov/websites/
depart/inspect/fonetact.htm

The United States Postal Service has some tips to help you recognize scams at Characteristics of a Telemarketing Fraud Scheme.

International Facts and Statistics

http://www.mightymall.com/sevenseas/facts.html

If you need GNP and other economic information about various countries around the world, check out International Facts and Statistics.

MouseTracks

http://nsns.com/MouseTracks/

Find Internet-related marketing tips and information at MouseTracks.

The Museum of Public Relations

http://www.prmuseum.com/

It is well known that we can learn a lot from the past, and that is certainly true at The Museum of Public Relations. This site studies successful public relations efforts to help marketers decide on good future strategies.

news:misc.business.marketing.moderated

Check out this newsgroup for discussion and marketing ideas. Ironically, this newsgroup has virtually no spam.

Marriage

See also: Children, Cultures, Divorce, Family, Relationships, Religion

African Wedding Guide

http://melanet.com/awg/

Learn about African wedding traditions and adaptations at the African Wedding Guide.

Bridal Planner

http://www.bridalplanner.com/

Get comprehensive wedding planning information at the Bridal Planner. Includes expert advice, worksheets, a bookstore, chat room, superstitions, and more!

The Bride's Online Guide

http://www.westworld.com/~reina/bride.html

Check out wedding-related links or "Ask the Bride" at The Bride's Online Guide.

Way Cool Weddings

http://www.waycoolweddings.com/

Way Cool Weddings is a webzine of real wedding Web sites, with a new wedding featured every week!

Wedding Circle

http://www.weddingcircle.com/

Locate planning resources, view announcements, learn customs and traditions from various cultures, or plan your honeymoon at Wedding Circle.

news:alt.wedding

Alt.wedding contains discussion about various wedding and family issues.

Martial Arts

See also: Fitness, Sports

American Center for Chinese Studies

http://www.kungfu.org/

Learn about Shao-lin Kung Fu at the Web site of the American Center for Chinese Studies. The site lists events, links to schools, and more.

Barrel's Martial Arts Links

http://www.barrel.net/martial-arts

Barrel's Martial Arts Links lists hundreds of links to martial arts Web sites. The listings are categorized by style.

Kun Tao

http://www.worldkungfu.com/

View weekly physical and mental exercises, or get other information about Huc Chung Kun Tao at Kun Tao, produced by the World Kung Fu Federation.

The Martial Arts Network

http://www.martial-arts-network.com/

The Martial Arts Network provides information on a variety of martial arts issues and styles online.

news:rec.martial.ats

Rec.martial.arts contains discussion on all styles of martial arts. The site is used by people speaking many different languages, so don't be surprised if you can't understand everything in the group.

Mental Health

See also: Drugs, Health

Behavior OnLine

http://www.behavior.net/

Behavior OnLine is designed specifically as a resource for mental health and applied behavioral science professionals.

Internet Mental Health

http://www.mentalhealth.com/

Internet Mental Health provides information and assistance for various mental health issues. This site is a great resource for your research, or even for mental health professionals.

Mental Health Net

http://www.cmhc.com/

Read daily news and information at Mental Health Net or link to one of thousands of mental health Web sites listed here.

Psych Central

http://psychcentral.com/

Check in with Dr. John Grohol to find information about psychology, mental health, and weekly live chats with the doctor at Psych Central. This site includes information on how to beat that nasty Internet addiction.

news:alt.society.mental-health

Read or participate in mental health and behavioral science discussion, although you will have to tolerate a little spam along the way.

Military

See also: Government, Guns, Veterans

11th Armored Cavalry Regiment

http://www.irwin.army.mil/11acr/

The 11th ACR "Blackhorse" is undoubtedly the best cavalry unit in the world today. The Blackhorse operates as the much-feared OPFOR (OPposing FORce) and the mission is simple: train America's Army. During the Cold War, a Russian general said that the best Russian tank battalion wasn't Russian, it is the 11th Armored Cavalry Regiment at Ft. Irwin, CA.

Air Force Link

http://www.af.mil/

Air Force Link is the official Web site of the United States Air Force, and is a great place to start if you want to learn more about the service or its operations.

Anderson AFB Typhoon Update Center

http://www.andersen.af.mil/

The official Anderson AFB Web site from Guam is very nice and has some truly useful info. Among other things, the site includes a Typhoon Update Center and Space-A travel information.

Armed Forces.Com

http://www.armedforces.com/

Armed Forces.Com contains hundreds of links to Web sites from, for, and about the United States military.

DefenseLINK

http://www.defenselink.mil/

Search through military and government Web sites for specific keywords or topics at DefenseLINK, a service of the United States Defense Department.

The Great War

http://www.thegreatwar.com

It's fairly easy to find good reference material on World War II, but with the advent of tanks, machine guns, aircraft, and chemical warfare, World War I marked the beginning of a bloody new era of warfare. At The Great War you can learn more about the people, the battles, the technology, and the tactics that changed the way we see warfare.

International Military Sales Plus

http://www.imsplus.com/ims.html

International Military Sales Plus is an excellent online store with thousands of military surplus items.

MarineLINK

http://www.usmc.mil/

Start your journey with the United States Marine Corps at MarineLINK, the official Web site of the Corps.

Rongstad's Worldwide Military Links Index

http://members.aol.com/rhrongstad/
private/milinksr.htm

Link to Web sites of military forces and organizations around the world, including citizen militias and related groups, from Rongstad's Worldwide Military Links Index.

The U.S. Navy Welcome Aboard

http://www.navy.mil/

The U.S. Navy Welcome Aboard page is a good jumping-off point with lots of links and public affairs stuff. One of the neatest things here is the ability to send e-mail to sailors aboard ship. "All I need is a tall ship, a wind to sail her by, and a laptop to read my e-mail."

Missing Persons

See also: Search Engines

BirthNet

http://www.birthnet.com/

BirthNet is a "Worldwide Family Registry" which helps parents avoid potential tragedy by retaining critical identification information on kids.

A
B
C
D
E
F
G
H
I
J
K
L
M
N
O
P
Q
R
S
T
U
V
W
X
Y
Z

Child Alert Foundation

http://www.childalert.org/

The Child Alert Foundation offers resources for finding missing children, abducted children, and runaways.

Child CyberSEARCH Canada

http://www.childcybersearch.org/

Search for missing kids in Canada online at Child CyberSEARCH Canada.

Child Quest International

http://www.childquest.org/

Find a wealth of missing child resources at the Child Quest International Web site. The site contains children's listings, prevention resources, and more.

Missing Persons Pages

http://missing.inthe.net/index.asp

Check out this free service offered by Missing Persons Pages to help you find someone who's missing.

The Reunion Network

http://reunion.com/

Locate missing persons or long lost friends at The Reunion Network. The site contains classifieds, reunion announcements, and many other useful links.

news:alt.binaries.missing-adults

Search or help others search for missing or estranged adults in this newsgroup.

news:alt.binaries.missing-kids

This newsgroup enables people to share information about missing children, but there is some spam here to contend with.

Money

See also: Banking, Business, Credit, Finance, Taxes

Euro 2002

http://euro.pearl-online.com/

Surf to the Euro 2002 Web site to learn about the European single currency project. Available in German, French, and English.

History of Money from Ancient Times to the Present Day

http://www.ex.ac.uk/~RDavies/arian/llyfr.html

Learn about the background of money and currency at History of Money from Ancient Times to the Present Day by Glyn Davies.

United States Treasury Currency Information

http://www.treas.gov/currency/

Learn about UNITED STATES currency, including how it is made and the concepts of its use, at the United States Treasury Currency Information Page. Do you know who's face was on the $100,000 bill? Find out here!

Universal Currency Converter

http://www.xe.net/currency/

Need to convert your cash? Check exchange rates quickly and easily at the Universal Currency Converter Web site!

Motorcycles

See also: Autos, Maps, Outdoors, Travel

American Motorcyclist Association

http://www.ama-cycle.org/

Learn about the American Motorcyclist Association at its official Web site. Get racing news, membership information, and the latest news on the AMA's legislative activities.

BikeNet

http://www.bikenet.com/

BikeNet is an excellent online magazine from England. They usually have a very good news service, along with road tests, touring articles, and more.

Corbin Motorcycle Saddles

http://www.corbin.com/

Corbin Motorcycle Saddles has a good place to do some online shopping and find that special seat for your bike.

Cybercycle Magazine

http://www.cybercyclemag.com/

Cybercycle Magazine is another, relatively new online magazine devoted to motorcycling. I thought I saw an emphasis on European motorcycles when I visited the site, but they do not advertise that this is their bread and butter.

Independent Biker

http://www.independentbiker.com/

Independent Biker is put together by the same people who make *Street Bike*, but IB is geared toward the Harley-Davidson enthusiast. "Cycle Lords of the High Truth" is a must read!

Interactive Motorcycle

http://www.activebike.com/

Interactive Motorcycle is a truly unique webzine. This site has some serious, well-crafted writing and is definitely worth a look.

The Iron Butt Association

http://www.ironbutt.com/

The Iron Butt Association home page is something interesting and unusual in the world of motorcycling.

Motorcycle Online

http://www.motorcycle.com/

Motorcycle Online is an exclusively online motorcycle magazine. You can find road tests, product reviews, classifieds, and more. As a bonus, the Web site even loads quickly!

Motorcycle-USA

http://www.motorcycle-usa.com/

Motorcycle-USA has the biggest collection of moto-related links I have seen. The site also contains news, chat rooms, and a "Fantasy Racing" game.

Motorworld

http://www.motorworld.com/

Motorworld is based in San Francisco; it usually contains some fascinating and cheeky articles.

Street Bike Magazine

http://www.streetbike.com/

This is the online version of Street Bike Magazine, a west-coast publication for motorcycle enthusiasts.

news:rec.motorcycles

Rec.motorcycles is usually quite active with motorcycle-related discussion, and has a little bit of spam for good measure.

Mountain Climbing

See also: Geology, Outdoors, Parks, Sports

ClimbOnline
`http://www.climbonline.com/`

Visit ClimbOnline for news, chat, climbing tips, links, and more relating to the world of climbing.

Hikenet
`http://members.aol.com/hikenet/index.html`

Hikenet is another excellent online resource for climbing information, stories, and chat.

Rock 'N Road
`http://www.rocknroad.com/`

Surf to Rock 'N Road for a complete list of climbing areas in North America. The comprehensive site includes information about thousands of sites, including descriptions, access information, directions, and more.

news:rec.climbing

The people in the rec.climbing newsgroup discuss a variety of climbing issues, including gear, tips, and more.

Movies & Film

See also: Acting, Celebrities, Entertainment, Science Fiction, Television

Film.com
`http://www.film.com/Default.htm`

Film.com is another excellent movie site, but with a greater emphasis on reviews, film festivals, and even some downloadable film clips.

Film Scouts
`http://www.filmscouts.com/`

Check out Film Scouts for all the latest on new films. This site also has an emphasis on independent films.

Hollywood Online
`http://www.hollywood.com/`

Hollywood Online has news, reviews, movie guides, and more. A must for the movie buff.

The Internet Movie Database
`http://www.imdb.com/`

The Internet Movie Database has over 120,000 movies on file in a searchable database.

MovieLink
`http://www.777film.com/`

MovieLink online offers reviews, a movie search feature, and downloadable trailers!

Mr. Cranky
`http://www.mrcranky.com/`

If movie critics are supposed to hate everything, then the glass is always half empty with Mr. Cranky. Check out this excellent movie guide, where films are rated depending on how bad they are, not how good they are.

Reel
`http://www.reel.com/`

Reel claims to be the planet's biggest movie store. The site includes trailers, movie news, 85,000 movies for sale, and 35,000 movies for rent.

The Screenscribe

http://www.rt66.com/cedge/

Fancy yourself a screen writer? Surf to The Screenscribe, which includes some links that might be of interest to you.

Ultimate Movies

http://www.ultimatemovies.com/

Most new movies now have their own Web site, sometimes many months before the intended release date. Ultimate Movies catalogs and links to new movie Web sites and is continually updated.

news:alt.movies

Alt.movies contains movie discussion of a more general nature, including a lot of talk about new releases.

news:alt.cult-movies

Alt.cult-movies contains discussion from fans of cult movies, and there also appear to be a lot of folks here who like to argue about the "Worst Movie Ever Made."

Museums

See also: Art, Cultures, History, Libraries, Railroads, Science

Art Museum Network

http://www.amn.org/

Link to art museums around the world at the Art Museum Network.

California State Railroad Museum

http://www.csrmf.org/

The California State Railroad Museum is devoted to preserving railroading history, including 21 diesel-electric and steam locomotives.

Exploratorium

http://www.exploratorium.edu/

The Exploratorium, a science museum in San Francisco, always has an array of online exhibits at its Web site.

The Louvre

http://mistral.culture.fr/louvre/louvrea.htm

Visit the online presence of the world's most famous art museum, the Louvre in Paris, France. The Web site is simply outstanding!

Portola Railroad Museum

http://www.oz.net/~samh/frrs/

Have you ever dreamed of operating a 125-ton locomotive? At the Portola Railroad Museum in California, there are six engines available for rent, and instruction is free. The museum also features over 30 engines on display, including a steam engine built by the Baldwin Locomotive Works in 1887!

United State Holocaust Memorial Museum

http://www.ushmm.org/

Dedicated to the memory of the millions who suffered under Nazis persecution, the United States Holocaust Memorial Museum provides a number of exhibits, teaching resources, and research materials about the Holocaust and genocide.

The World Wide Web Virtual Library: Museums

http://www.comlab.ox.ac.uk/archive/other/museums.html

Visit The World Wide Web Virtual Library: Museums page to find links to online museums around the world.

Music

See also: Dance, Entertainment, Shopping

CDnow

http://www.cdnow.com/

CDnow calls itself the world's largest music store. You can find a wealth of information about music recordings (and movies, too!), and the prices are very reasonable. There is also a RealAudio feature where you can hear samples of some tracks, but I was not able to get this feature to work.

Columbia House

http://www.columbiahouse.com/

You've seen the Columbia House ads in magazines and mailboxes for years, and now they're on the Web! Purchase music, movies, and CD-ROMs for pennies on the dollar!

Harmony Central

http://www.harmony-central.com/MIDI/

MIDI enthusiasts and artists will find a huge resource of information, news, links, and more at Harmony Central.

myLAUNCH

http://www.mylaunch.com/

Read music news or participate in chats at myLAUNCH. Membership is free and gives you full access to the many features available here.

Tunes.com

http://www.tunes.com/

Tunes.com is another great place to shop online and sample complete tracks using RealAudio!

Yamaha

http://www.yamaha.com/

Check out the official Yamaha Web site for information about their many music-related products, including instruments, electronics, and educational programs. This is one of the most information-packed corporate Web sites that I have seen.

news:alt.music

There are hundreds of music-related news-groups, but this one might be a good place for you to start. Find general discussion on music topics, although the group has a slant more toward fans and collectors rather than the musicians themselves.

News

See also: Communities, Magazines, Sports, Television, Weather

ABCNEWS.com

http://www.abcnews.com/

ABCNEWS.com offers up-to-the-minute news on current events. The site also contains links for local news and has a non-Java site for the bandwidth-challenged.

CNN Interactive

http://www.cnn.com/

CNN is a major cable TV network providing round-the-clock news. Perhaps you've heard of it? Check out CNN Interactive, their complete news Web site.

The Electronic Telegraph

http://www.telegraph.co.uk/

The Electronic Telegraph is a great news source. This UK site has a thorough emphasis on international news.

Los Angeles Times

http://www.latimes.com/

More up-to-the-minute news stories, this time direct from the Los Angeles Times. Despite the fact that this is a local newspaper, there is significant national and international news coverage.

MSNBC

http://www.msnbc.com/

MSNBC is a collaboration between Microsoft and the TV network NBC. It provides complete national and international news, but the first time you go there you will have to go through a "setup" procedure that takes several minutes.

The NACEC

http://www.nacec.org/

The NACEC (North American Center For Emergency Communications) offers emergency communication services in times of disaster or crisis. They also provide a good means of emergency communication between military members and their families.

The Nando Times

http://www.nandotimes.com/

Want still more international news? Try The Nando Times. The site is heavy on frames and tends to load a little slowly, depending on the Internet connection.

New York Times

http://www.nytimes.com/

The Web site of the New York Times has a unique look in that it is designed to actually look like a newspaper. That is, if newspapers had high-resolution GIFs and Java applets!

Pathfinder

http://www.pathfinder.com/

Time-Warner's Pathfinder is a guide to the many Time-Warner services and also a thorough news source.

The Red Herring

http://www.redherring.com/

This Web site is the online version of *The Red Herring*, a magazine that covers, as they put it, "the business of technology." There seems to be a heavy emphasis on computer and Internet technology issues discussed here.

Salon Magazine

http://www.salonmagazine.com/

Salon Magazine offers news with a definite twist. This is not the usual, sanitized stuff from the "official" news agencies. Salon reporters have some strong voices that really come out in the articles.

U.S. News & World Report Online

http://www.usnews.com/

At U.S. News & World Report Online, you can link to the *U.S. News* site or .EDU, a news site devoted to college ratings and career information. *U.S. News* concentrates more on in-depth reporting rather than up-to-the-minute coverage.

The Wall Street Journal Interactive Edition

http://www.wsj.com/

The Wall Street Journal Interactive Edition is like its hard-copy cousin, in that it focuses on the financial world.

washingtonpost.com

http://www.washingtonpost.com/

Surf to washingtonpost.com for news from this sometimes controversial but oft-quoted Washington D.C. newspaper.

Outdoors

See also: Bicycling, Boats, Camping, Diving, Environment, Fishing, Forestry, Motorcycles, Mountain Climbing, Parks, Skateboarding, Skiing & Snowboarding, Snowmobiles, Sports, Surfing, Travel

Adventure Sports Online

http://www.adventuresports.com/

Link to information about adventurous travel and recreation at Adventure Sports Online.

America's Roof

http://www.americasroof.com/

If you like feeling on top of the world, you'll enjoy America's Roof. The site catalogs the highest points in each of the 50 states in the USA. Each state contains links to Web sites relating to outdoor adventures in that area.

GORP Great Outdoor Recreation Pages

http://www.gorp.com/

If you can't find it at GORP Great Outdoor Recreation Pages, it probably can't be done outside. Link to a huge variety of topic-specific sites within the GORP network, check out news and weather reports, and find travel information at this outstanding Web site.

Outdoor Resources Online

http://www.azstarnet.com/~goclimb/

Check out the Web site of Outdoor Resources Online, which lists more than 1500 outdoor- related Web sites, listed by category.

Outdoors OnLine

http://outdoorsonline.rivals.com/ Outdoors

Outdoors OnLine is a webzine for the outdoors and hunting enthusiast. You'll find a lot of interesting things here, ranging from hunting news to wild game recipes.

Outside Expeditions

http://www.getoutside.com/

Outside Expeditions offers some unique kayaking, biking, and walking adventures along Canada's East Coast!

Wilderness Resource List

http://www.geosmith.com/wilderness/

The Wilderness Resource List links to various Web sites to help you learn about traveling and surviving in the wilderness.

Parks

See also: Bicycles, Environment, Forestry, Mountain Climbing, Outdoors

Grand Canyon National Park Foundation

http://www.grandcanyonfund.org/

The Grand Canyon National Park Foundation is an organization working to preserve the world's biggest nonsubmerged hole.

Jobs in National Parks, Preserves, Monuments & Wilderness Areas

http://www.coolworks.com/showme/ natprk.htm

How would you like the world to be your office? Find out how at Jobs in National Parks, Preserves, Monuments & Wilderness Areas.

National Park Service
http://www.nps.gov/

The Web site of the National Park Service is a good starting point for information on national parks in the USA. Includes links to information on specific parks across the country.

National Parks Worldwide
http://hum.amu.edu.pl/~zbzw/ph/pnp/swiat.htm

Link to information about thousands of national parks around the world at National Parks Worldwide. This Web site is hosted by Polish National Parks, and lists parks by country.

The Pacific Crest Trail Association
http://www.pcta.org/

The Pacific Crest Trail Association provides useful information for those who want to hike along this legendary trail.

State Parks Online
http://www.mindspring.com/~wxrnot/parks.html

Link to information and Web sites for state parks in all 50 states at State Parks Online.

The Total Yellowstone Page
http://www.yellowstone-natl-park.com/

The Total Yellowstone Page is a celebration of America's greatest and oldest national park. Lots of good, detailed information and links.

Yosemite.com
http://www.yosemite.org/

Learn more about one of the USA's most visited national parks at Yosemite.com. The site offers a complete resource for information about the park, travel advisories, planning information, and more.

news:rec.parks
Rec.parks is a low-volume list, but it sticks to discussion related to parks, and has little in the way of spam.

Photography

See also: Art

The Aperture Gallery
http://www.tssphoto.com/gallery/

The Aperture Gallery has some truly fine images on display and for sale. Check for periodic news about their awards!

Casio
http://www.casio.com/

Can't decide if you're ready to shell out the big bucks for a digital camera? Check out some product information first at the Casio home page. This site focuses on Casio digital cameras.

Eastman Kodak
http://www.kodak.com/

The Eastman Kodak Web site is the place to go to learn about their many photographic products. Don't forget to check out their digital cameras and other PC products!

Focus on Photography
http://www.goldcanyon.com/photography/index.html

Read introductory material to the art of photography, and then link to various Web sites around the Internet at Focus on Photography.

A B C D E F G H I J K L M N O **P** Q R S T U V W X Y Z

Photographers on the 'Net

http://www.photographersonthenet.org

Search through listings and link to photographers with Web sites around the Internet from Photographers on the 'Net. Artists are listed by geographical location and specialty.

The Photo Page

http://www.generation.net/~gjones/

Link to hundreds of photography-related Web sites from The Photo Page, an extensive collection of links.

Photoshopper

http://www.photoshopper.com/

Buy, sell, or trade used and collectible camera equipment online at Photoshopper.

Shutterbug

http://www.shutterbug.net/

Check out the online version of *Shutterbug*, a print magazine devoted to photography. The Web site contains classifieds, featured articles, product reviews, and more.

news:rec.photo

Discuss techniques and equipment at rec.photo. This site sticks to photography, with occasional spam.

Plants

See also: Agriculture, Environment, Farming, Science

Carnivorous Plant Database

http://www.hpl.hp.com/bot/cp_home

Learn everything you've ever wanted to know about those wacky carnivorous plants at the Carnivorous Plant Database.

Center for Aquatic Plants

http://aquat1.ifas.ufl.edu/

Satisfy your growing interest in aquatic plants at the Center for Aquatic Plants. This site has some great resources for research projects!

Chia Pet Zoo

http://www.accessone.com/~jonathin/

Do you love Chia Pets? If so, surf to the Chia Pet Zoo, which includes an online "zoo" as well as Chia Pet tech support (?!).

Medicinal and Poisonous Plant Database

http://www.wam.umd.edu/~mct/Plants/index.html

Learn the medicinal and poisonous properties of various plants at the Medicinal and Poisonous Plant Database.

Plants Database

http://plants.usda.gov/

The Plants Database is an excellent Web site with lots of information on various plants. The Web site is hosted by the U.S. Department of Agriculture Natural Resources Conservation Service.

Wildflower Center

http://www.wildflower.org/

Find out how to get in touch with local native plant resources at the Wildflower Center.

news:bionet.plants

Check out discussion of botany and plant issues from botanists and lay persons alike in this newsgroup.

Poetry

The Academy of American Poets

http://www.poets.org/

For anyone interested in poetry, this site is a great place to start. The Academy of American Poets sponsors the National Poetry Month every April—find out about it online.

Haiku Society of America

http://www.octet.com/~hsa/

Want to learn about haiku? The Haiku Society of America is a nonprofit organization founded in New York in 1968 to promote the writing and appreciation of haiku in English. You can learn about the society's publications, contests, and regional events at this site.

Poets & Writers

http://www.pw.org/

Poets & Writers is a nonprofit organization that provides support and exposure to poets and writers by assisting them in their search for career-related information, outlets for their work, opportunities for professional advancement, and community with other writers. This site gets you connected!

news:rec.arts.poems

A newsgroup dedicated to the sharing and discussion of (you guessed it) poetry. Some spam here, but some fine discussion, too.

Psychics

See also: Astrology, Unexplained Phenomenon

The Cyber Psychic

http://www.hollys.com/cyber-psychic/

Have your past, present, and future read online at the Cyber Psychic. The site features a weekly live chat and more!

New Vision Psychic Services

http://www.newvision-psychic.com/index.html

Read articles and other information in New Vision Psychic Services, an online magazine for the psychic community.

Psychic Chicken Network

http://www.ruprecht.com/

Is the Psychic Chicken Network really psychic, or just psychotic? You be the judge at this site where the chicken answers all of life's questions for you. But be careful, you might not always like the answer!

Radio

See also: Acting, Entertainment, Television

AudioNet

http://www.audionet.com/

AudioNet is the Broadcast Network on the Internet. The site enables you to listen to broadcasts from more than 260 radio and television stations, thousands of sporting events, and other broadcast services. They even have an online juke box of CDs for users with ISDN or better connections!

Federal Communications Commission

http://www.fcc.gov/

If you want to have anything to do with radio broadcasting in the USA, you'll have to learn a thing or two about the Federal Communications Commission (FCC).

National Public Radio

http://www.npr.org/

Get the latest news or find out what's happening on National Public Radio at this Web site. You can also hear live audio of current news on the hour, link to member stations, or search through some of the outstanding special programs NPR has hosted.

Radio 411

http://radio411.com/

Find links to Web sites that contain information about almost anything that has to do with radio at Radio 411.

Virtual Radio

http://www.virtualradio.com/vr.html/

Download songs or leave messages about music subjects at Virtual Radio, which serves as a virtual radio station.

Railroads

See also: Hobbies, Museums, Travel

Amtrak

http://www.amtrak.com/

Amtrak is the major passenger rail service in the USA. The Web site contains train and route information, as well as an online reservation system.

California State Railroad Museum

http://www.csrmf.org/

The California State Railroad Museum is devoted to preserving railroading history, including 21 diesel-electric and steam locomotives.

The European Railway Server

http://mercurio.iet.unipi.it/home.html/

Visit the European Railway Server for information on railroads in Europe. The information here is arranged for both train hobbyists and travelers alike.

Portola Railroad Museum

http://www.oz.net/~samh/frrs/

Have you ever dreamed of operating a 125-ton locomotive? At the Portola Railroad Museum in California, there are six engines available for rent, and instruction is free. The museum also features over 30 engines on display, including a steam engine built by the Baldwin Locomotive Works in 1887!

The Railway Exchange

http://www.railwayex.com/

Professionals in the railroad business and laypersons alike can find useful information at The Railway Exchange. The site includes many business-related links, a railroad dictionary, and commercial product information.

Side Tracked

http://www.railroad.net/side_track/

Side Tracked lists Web sites that are dedicated to one particular railroad. By each listing, the sites are identified as having come from a corporate source, historical society, or a person interested in that road.

A
B
C
D
E
F
G
H
I
J
K
L
M
N
O
P
Q
R
S
T
U
V
W
X
Y
Z

The Subway Page

http://www.reed.edu/~reyn/
transport.html

Link to subway information in major cities throughout the world from The Subway Page. Download maps of systems to help you know where you're going in strange cities!

Real Estate

See also: Architecture, Finance

Acreage.com

http://www.acreage.com/

View online listings of acreage properties around the USA at Acreage.com.

Consumer Information Catalog

http://www.gsa.gov/staff/pa/cic/
housing.htm

The U.S. Government's General Services Administration (GSA) offers a number of free and low-cost booklets to help prospective homebuyers prepare for their purchase. View a selection of these publications online at the Consumer Information Catalog.

HomeScout

http://www.homescout.com/

Frustrated with real estate searches on the Internet? I recommend the HomeScout, which provides a thorough, unified database of properties for sale. After you perform a search, you can usually link to the Web sites of local agents for further property information.

International Real Estate Digest

http://www.ired.com/

IRED (International Real Estate Digest) provides worldwide real estate information, including consumer help, professional sites, mortgage news and information, and more.

New Homes Search

http://www.newhomesearch.com/

Find just the right home and builder for your new dream home at New Homes Search, a database of new home builders and services across the USA.

propertyline.com

http://www.propertyline.com/

Search for and view commercial property listings online at Propertyline.com. The site also contains news and a directory with links to various resources in the commercial real estate market.

Rent.Net

http://rent.net/

Rent.Net is an online rental guide, with thousands of listings for the USA, Canada, and some overseas locations.

Recycling

See also: Environment

The Compost Resource Page

http://www.oldgrowth.org/compost/

Learn all about composting and link to other useful sites at The Compost Resource Page.

The Environmental Hotline
http://www.1800cleanup.org/

Get recycling tips or link to local recycling centers and resources at The Environmental Hotline.

Operation Landfill Elimination
http://www.geocities.com/RainForest/5002/index.html

Operation Landfill Elimination lists some truly creative uses of seemingly useless items, in an effort to help you reuse worn out items rather than throw them away.

Recycle City
http://www.epa.gov/recyclecity/

The U.S. Environmental Protection Agency hosts Recycle City, a site with interactive recycling-related activities to help people learn about recycling. This is an especially good site to teach kids the importance of reducing, reusing, and recycling.

Recycler's World
http://www.recycle.net/recycle/

Surf to Recycler's World for a complete selection of links to recycling companies and other related Web sites. Links are divided into categories based on materials.

news, happenings, and links to entertainment and other relevant information.

National Pages
http://info.fuw.edu.pl/national.html

National Pages is a simple page which links to the national pages of several countries of the world.

Small Islands Information Network
http://www.upei.ca/~siin/

Link to information about small islands of the world at the Small Islands Information Network.

Virtual Tourist
http://www.vtourist.com/

The Virtual Tourist catalogs World Wide Web servers throughout the world by geographical location.

The World Fact Book
http://www.odci.gov/cia/publications/factbook/index.html

Our nosey friends at the CIA have prepared The World Fact Book, which is actually an excellent online resource for cultural, political, economic, and geographic information on the nations of the world.

Regions

See also: Geography, Government, Maps, News, Restaurants, Search Engines, Theater, Travel

CitySearch
http://www.citysearch.com/

CitySearch is a jumping-off point for various city-specific pages in the USA, Canada, and Australia. Each city page lists local

Relationships

See also: Communities, Dating, Divorce, Family, Marriage

Blender of Love
http://www.loveblender.com/

Read poems and stories about romance at the Blender of Love.

Breakup Girl

http://www.breakupgirl.com/

The very cool Breakup Girl Web site offers discussion, support, and various articles designed for people (mainly women) involved in breakups.

Flirt Online

http://www.flirt.com/cgi-bin/
frontdoor.cgi

Flirt Online hosts ongoing live chat, with a five-day free trial period. Guess what the topic of discussion is in the chat room?

Mark's Apology Note Generator

http://net.indra.com/~karma/
formletter.html

Can't find the right words to say, "I'm sorry?" Get a nudge in the right direction from Mark's Apology Note Generator. The site now has a female version, as well!

Relationship Growth Online

http://www.relationship-growth.com/

Get information about how to improve your relationships at Relationship Growth Online.

Spouses and Partners

http://www.nolo.com/encyclopedia/
mlt_ency.html

Nolo's Legal Encyclopedia offers Spouses and Partners, a Web site that offers information about the legal aspects of marriage and relationships.

news:alt.romance

One of the best ways to learn about relationships is to talk to others that are involved in them. Alt.romance is a newsgroup with romance and relationship discussion on a wide variety of topics and issues.

Religion

See also: Communities, Cultures, Family, Marriage

Ages Software

http://www.ageslibrary.com/

Ages Software provides hundreds of important Bible commentaries and historical documents affordably by publishing them on CD-ROM.

Comparative Religion & Religious Studies

http://www.academicinfo.net/
religindex.html

Search for and link to Web sites containing academic information on most major religions of the world at Comparative Religion & Religious Studies.

The Highway

http://www.gospelcom.net/thehighway/

The Highway offers spiritual guidance and information. Includes articles, a chat room, youth information, gospel MIDIs, and more.

Hinduism's Electronic Ashram

http://www.hinduismtoday.kauai.hi.us/
ashram/

Visit Hinduism's Electronic Ashram for news, cultural, and spiritual information for Hindus.

Nida'ul Islam

http://www.islam.org.au/

Read about Islam and Islamic issues at Nida'ul Islam, a bimonthly magazine for the Islamic faith.

Ontario Consultants on Religious Tolerance

http://www.religioustolerance.org/

Learn about various religions and tolerance at the Web site of Ontario Consultants on Religious Tolerance.

Religion and Philosophy Resources on the Internet

http://www.bu.edu/sth/sthlib/library.htm

Link to numerous religious and philosophical resources at Religion and Philosophical Resources on the Internet.

Shambhala Sun

http://www.shambhalasun.com/

The *Shambhala Sun* is an alternative print magazine for Buddhists. The Web site contains featured articles from back issues and information about the current issue.

Shoot the Messenger

http://www.shootthemessenger.com.au/

View popular culture and news from a Christian point of view at the webzine Shoot the Messenger.

United in Christ

http://members.aol.com/pendletonw/

Find research information or boost spiritual awareness at United in Christ, sponsored by the United in Christ Music Ministries.

news:alt.religion

The alt.religion newsgroup contains diverse discussion on many religious issues.

Restaurants

See also: Cooking, Regions, Travel

Chef Smiler's Restaurant Resources

http://www.poky.srv.net/~smiler/rest.html

Persons in the restaurant business are sure to find something of interest at Chef Smiler's Restaurant Resources.

Dine.com

http://www.dine.com/

Dine.com offers restaurant listings for many major USA cities. Readers have submitted most of the entries.

Eric's Idiosyncratic Restaurant and Food Guide

http://www.mapville.com/riback/eats.htm

Locate eateries that are out of the ordinary or otherwise unique at Eric's Idiosyncratic Restaurant and Food Guide.

Fodor's Restaurant Index

http://www.fodors.com/ri.cgi

Search for restaurants by city and read recommendations at Fodor's Restaurant Index.

Food Finder

http://www.olen.com/food/

Do you really want to know what's in that burger? Use the Food Finder to search for nutritional facts about those fast foods you love to eat.

National Restaurant Register's Menu-OnLine

http://www.onlinemenus.com/

Are you new to town and looking for a good place to eat? Check out this site. You can do a nationwide search of restaurants to find the right food, the right price, at the right location.

Restaurant Home Pages

http://www.restaurant-pages.com/

Check out the Restaurant Home Pages for a great selection of links to, well, restaurant home pages. You can search by name, food type, or location.

The Zagat Restaurant Survey

http://www.zagatsurvey.com/

The Zagat Restaurant Survey lets you search through its listings of thousands of eateries throughout the USA and gives impressions of each.

news:alt.restaurants

Discuss restaurants, ask about an area you are traveling to, or even find restaurants for sale at the alt.restaurants newsgroup.

Retirement

See also: Finance

LivOn

http://www.livon.com/

LivOn is the Senior Living Online Network; it helps you search for senior housing and retirement communities across the USA.

The Retire Early Home Page

http://www.geocities.com/WallStreet/8257/reindex.html

Retiring early is everyone's dream, and at The Retire Early Home Page you can learn how to make that dream a reality.

Rodeo

See also: Sports

CyberRodeo

http://cyberrodeo.com/guysgals/

CyberRodeo is devoted to cowboys and cowgirls in the sport of rodeo, famous and otherwise.

National Barrel Horse Association

http://www.nbha.com/

If you're a barrel-horse aficionado, this is the place to go. The National Barrel Horse Association's Web site contains news, events schedules, links, and a whole lot more.

Roughstock

http://www.roughstock.com/roughstock/

Visit Roughstock for rodeo news, event information, entertainment, and more.

Schools

See also: Children, Education, Libraries

All About Grad School

http://www.allaboutgradschool.com/

It doesn't take a PhD to figure out what the All About Grad School Web site is about! Chat with others and get other helpful information for your post-grad work.

American School Directory

http://www.asd.com/

Link to Web sites and information about 106,000 K-12 schools throughout the USA at the American School Directory.

Education Programs in Technology Transfer

http://www.nalusda.gov/ttic/
test1.htm

The Education Programs in Technology Transfer Web site provides links and information on degree and nondegree technology programs.

Internet Resources for Institutional Research

http://www.airweb.org/links

The Internet Resources for Institutional Research provides a host of links, news, and even live chat on issues of higher education and research.

NewPromise.com

http://www.caso.com/home/home.phtml
NewPromise.com is a guide to thousands of courses offered online by accredited colleges and universities.

Petersons.com

http://www.petersons.com/

Petersons.com provides information about educational institutions of all types, including universities, distance learning programs, summer camps, studies abroad, and private schools. The site is hosted by Peterson's, publisher of college guides and other related materials.

School Search Engine

http://www.schools.com/tabs/
tabs.search.html

Need to find the Web site of a specific school? Try the School Search Engine, which enables you to search through Web sites of thousands of independent schools, and then link to them.

Study in the USA

http://www.studyusa.com/

International students wishing to study in the USA can get useful information, tips, and links at the Study in the USA Web site.

The Web66 Home Page

http://web66.coled.umn.edu/

The Web66 Home Page is a project of the University of Minnesota; it provides links to thousands of schools that have Web sites or are otherwise online. This is also a great resource to help teachers get the most out of the Internet.

TheWorld Lecture Hall

http://www.utexas.edu/world/lecture/

Want to find out if anyone offers a specific college course on the Web? Look no further than TheWorld Lecture Hall, which serves as a link to thousands of online courses.

Science

See also: Animals, Anthropology & Archaeology, Astronomy, Environment, Geography, Geology, Heath, Museums, Plants, Seismology, Space

Ask Dr. Science

http://www.ducksbreath.com/

Ask Dr. Science. Why? Because he knows more than you do! Read daily questions or submit your own!

The National Science Foundation

http://www.nsf.gov/

The National Science Foundation, largely responsible for what we now know as the Internet, has a vast array of online scientific resources. Start here to begin your research.

The NeoScience Institute

http://www.necrobones.com/neosci/

Mad scientists have their own home on the Web at The NeoScience Institute. "No theory too absurd to explore, no safety hazard too large to overlook, no result too bizarre to discount, no cost too high (unless it costs money)." From brain transplant kits to spirit calls and multidimensional shower heads, this site has it all. Check it out!

The Proceedings of the National Academy of Sciences

http://www.pnas.org/

View articles from a variety of disciplines in The Proceedings of the National Academy of Sciences, an online journal of this organization.

Science News Online

http://www.sciencenews.org/

Science News Online is an outstanding source for research information because many articles from 1994 to the present can be found online.

Science Online

http://www.sciencemag.org/

Science Online has many full-text articles available online, making it a good place to conduct your research.

Scientific American

http://www.sciam.com/

Visit the online version of *Scientific American* to view feature articles, ask questions, and read the latest science news.

Science Fiction

See also: Books, Communities, Entertainment, Movies & Film, Space, Television, Unexplained Phenomenon

Alan's Kaiju Page

http://www.parlorcity.com/awinterrowd/kaiju/

Godzilla is attacking the Web! Read more about this terrible lizard at Alan's Kaiju Page.

Art Bell

http://www.artbell.com/

Visit Art Bell's Web site. Art is a radio talk show host, whose main interest is in science fiction, UFOs, and the like!

Bad Air and Space Museum

http://www.badairandspace.com/

The Bad Air and Space Museum has a multitude of exhibits demonstrating potential problems when current, worldly socioeconomic problems extend into space. "Will work for food/air."

Borg Collective

http://www.geocities.com/Area51/
Cavern/9452/collective.html

Be assimilated into the Borg Collective. The *Star Trek*–related site contains images, a history of the Borg, and a nifty screen saver!

The I Hate Star Trek Page

http://members.tripod.com/~Desslok/
dietrek/trkstink.htm

Less than enamoured by *Star Trek*? Maybe you'll find something of interest at The I Hate Star Trek Page. The parodies are sure to make you LOL.

The Klingon Language Institute

http://www.kli.org/

The Klingon Language Institute is dedicated to bringing the Klingon language to us earthlings. Hold conversations, ask for a bathroom, or insult someone's honor in this obscure yet firm dialect.

The Official Star Wars Web Site

http://www.starwars.com/

The Official Star Wars Web Site is as good a place as any to begin looking for stuff about these Sci-Fi classics. There are literally thousands of sites on the Web related to *Star Wars*, so consider this a first step!

Planet of the Apes

http://www.spleenworld.com/apes/

Journey to the Planet of the Apes to learn about these 1970s classics, not to mention a proposed new movie. Ceasar, Dr. Zaius, Nova; they're all here!

Science Fiction Tales Online

http://www.fantasyrealms.simplenet.com/

Read stories or post your own at the Science Fiction Tales Online site.

The Starfleet Headquarters Experience

http://members.aol.com/wwwgeo/
trek.htm

Interested in *Star Trek*, but just don't know where to start? Try The Starfleet Headquarters Experience.

Search Engines

See also: Computers: Internet, Missing Persons, Yellow Pages

About.com

http://www.about.com/

About.com is a network sites that include over 650 "environments," each overseen by an expert guide. In this user-friendly place, you can find just about anything.

Alta Vista

http://www.altavista.digital.com/

Alta Vista is run by the Digital Equipment Corporation and offers a nice, easy-to-use search interface.

Beatrice's Web Guide

http://www.bguide.com/

Beatrice's Web Guide is actually the result of a collaboration between Women's Wire and Yahoo!. It is nicely laid out, but because of the high content emphasis, power users may prefer one of the more traditional search engines.

Bigfoot

http://www.bigfoot.com/

Can't find that long-lost special someone? Try looking for them with the resources available at Bigfoot! The site also has information about the new Web browser NeoPlanet.

Deja News

http://www.dejanews.com/

Deja News specializes in newsgroup searches. This is a good way to find out what people are saying about your company or find discussion groups for your favorite topics.

Excite

http://www.excite.com/

Excite has one of the more attractive interfaces, and an outstanding system of channels.

Fast Search

http://www.alltheweb.com/

Some people just want to find what they are looking for and find it quickly. Being impatient myself, I use Fast Search. Searches are very fast, and the pages are displayed without advertising banners, so the results are displayed quickly.

Hitchhiker's Guide to the Galaxy

http://www.h2g2.com/

If you ever need any helpful tips to get the most out of life or answers to difficult questions, you can probably find them here. Don't panic, always bring a towel, and check out the Earth Edition of the Hitchhiker's Guide to the Galaxy.

HotBot

http://www.hotbot.com/

HotBot is renowned for having one of the most accurate and thorough keyword search engines, and fine-tuning your search is a piece of cake. The price for all this searching power is a ho-hum directory, but the payoff is worth it!

Infoseek

http://guide.infoseek.com/

Infoseek has a good search feature, and a user-friendly system of channels. Each channel contains links to related sites as well as special content related to the channel's subject.

InfoSpace

http://www.infospace.com/

Find almost everything, including people, businesses, Web sites, classifieds, and more at InfoSpace. This site would make an excellent home page from which to begin your browsing every day!

LookSmart

http://www.looksmart.com/

LookSmart contains an easy-to-use directory system as well as keyword searches and current new items on its front page.

Lycos

http://www.lycos.com/

Lycos offers customizable keyword searches along with a system of Web Guides that are similar in concept to Infoseek's channels.

Nerd World

http://www.nerdworld.com/

Nerd World is the place for hardcore searches. Some people will really appreciate what you can do here, and some, well, won't.

Northern Light Search

http://www.nlsearch.com/

Northern Light Search is a newer search engine, and it contains a number of features to help you customize your search a bit more effectively.

Search Engine Watch

http://www.searchenginewatch.com/

Search Engine Watch is not a search engine. But it is an excellent place to go if you need to understand search engines better. Are you a Web surfer who wants to know how to make your searches more effective? Or are you a Web master who can't figure out why your site isn't listed by some search engines? Look here for answers.

Search Spaniel

http://www.searchspaniel.com/

Search Spaniel is a "power search" site that uses a variety of other search engines to perform your keyword search.

Switchboard

http://www.switchboard.com/

Switchboard is primarily an online yellow pages, but also contains extensive people-search capabilities and Web searching.

Webcrawler

http://webcrawler.com/

Webcrawler is actually owned by Excite, but offers a unique interface. This site is very news intensive, making it a good stop if you want to find out what is going on in the world.

WhoWhere?!

http://www.whowhere.lycos.com/

Need to find someone in a flash, without a lot of extraneous content? Check WhoWhere?! and begin your search.

Yahoo!

http://www.yahoo.com/

Yahoo! is lauded as the world's most frequently visited Web site. It offers keyword searches and the most extensive directory on the net.

Yahooligans!

http://www.yahooligans.com/

Yahooligans! is a spinoff of Yahoo!, designed specifically with younger cyber-surfers in mind. But best of all, it's not just for kids!

Security

See also: Computers: Internet, Law, Shopping

BelSign NV-SA

http://www.belsign.be/en/dcc/user/index.html

The BelSign NV-SA specializes in authenticating procedures and digital IDs. You sign up online and choose the level of certification you want.

InfoWar.com

http://www.infowar.com/

InfoWar.com is a comprehensive Web site that discusses all aspects of information security, including cryptography, viruses, Internet security, terrorism, and more.

RSA Data Security, Inc.

http://www.rsa.com/

RSA Data Security, Inc. offers a complete range of cryptography and authentication technologies. They also have an informative FAQ to help you learn more about online security.

Verisign

http://digitalid.verisign.com/

Verisign specializes in digital IDs, helping you to prove to other Net users that you are who you say you are by adding a digital ID to your e-mail messages. Microsoft includes a link to Verisign on their own Web site, although you can use other vendors for digital IDs if you prefer.

news:alt.security

The alt.security newsgroup primarily discusses computer-related security issues, although there will inevitably be discussions of pepper spray and locksmithing, as well.

Seismology

See also: Geology, Science

Big Trouble in Earthquake Country

http://www.lhs.berkeley.edu/SII/SII-eqcountry/5eqcountry.homepage.html

Students in grades 9 through 12 can learn about earthquakes and associated hazards to communities at Big Trouble in Earthquake Country.

Earthquake Information from the USGS

http://quake.wr.usgs.gov/

Want a comprehensive, reliable source of information on earthquakes? Try Earthquake Information from the USGS. Among other things, find out when and where the latest earthquakes have occurred or link to other data collection sites.

The Strong Motion Database

http://smdb.crustal.ucsb.edu/

Research using records of hundreds of earthquakes filed in The Strong Motion Database.

news:sci.geo.earthquakes

Discuss earthquakes and various seismology issues in the sci.geo.earthquakes newsgroup.

Shopping

See also: Books, Clothing, Computers, Gifts, Jewelry, Music, Security

Bloomingdales

http://www.bloomingdales.com/

Shop Bloomingdales online at their Web site. The site also has store and other company information.

Classifieds2000

http://www.classifieds2000.com/

Classifieds2000 has thousands of ads for almost everything under the sun, including cars, employment, general merchandise, personals, and even roommates.

Disney.com

http://www.disney.com/shop/

The Disney.com shopping page is a place to buy all of your favorite Disney goodies online. Check here for some great gift ideas.

JCPenney

http://www.jcpenney.com/

Shopping from the JCPenney catalog is a time-honored American tradition, and the department and catalog store now brings that tradition into cyberspace with its new home page.

MotherMall.com

http://www.mothermall.com/

This is truly one Mother of a Mall! Shop online in the many stores, which are divided up on nine different "floors."

NetGrocer

http://www.netgrocer.com/

NetGrocer has an interesting idea: buy your groceries online! Actually, most of their items are dry goods and other general supplies, but it's an interesting concept nonetheless!

ONSALE

http://www.onsale.com/

ONSALE calls itself the Online Auction Supersite, and we can't argue. Keep an eye on this site for super deals on computer products, sports and leisure equipment, and consumer electronics.

QVC

http://www.qvc.com/

QVC, the popular cable TV shopping channel, has a very good Web site that lists basically everything they sell.

ShopNow.com

http://www.shopnow.com/

ShopNow.com claims to be the largest online shopping mall in the world. "Stores" are categorized into topic areas similar to a directory tree used at some Internet search engines. This makes the online mall easy to use.

Web Warehouse

http://webwarehouse.com/

Link to various consumer goods stores online at the Web Warehouse.

Skateboarding

See also: Outdoors, Sports

Concussion

http://www.etheria.com/concussion/

Concussion is a very cool Web site devoted to skateboarding, as well as surfing and rock 'n roll.

IASC Blueprints

http://www.tumyeto.com/tydu/skatebrd/ organizations/iascblue.html

Download printable blueprints to build your own ramp at IASC Blueprints.

SkateTalk

http://www.skatetalk.com/index.html

SkateTalk specializes in live chat, with several rooms to choose from.

Skateworld

http://home.thezone.net/~troy/

Check out event information, music, ramp plans, pictures, and more at Skateworld.

Tumyeto.com

http://www.tumyeto.com/

Roll into Tumyeto.com for news, images, events, a Skate Park Index, and much more.

news:alt.skate-board

This newsgroup (make sure you include the hyphen) pretty much sticks to skateboard talk, without wasting too much time on fashion and other unrelated items.

Skiing & Snowboarding

See also: Outdoors, Sports

Board the World

http://www.boardtheworld.com.au/

Follow a team of snowboarders as they travel the world in search of the best boarding locations at Board the World.

Colorado Ski Museum

http://www.vailsoft.com/museum/

Learn about skiing history and the Ski Hall of Fame at the Colorado Ski Museum.

Cyberspace Snow and Avalanche Center

http://www.csac.org/

Find out the latest information on avalanche conditions and weather at the Cyberspace Snow and Avalanche Center.

The Mountain Zone

http://www.mountainzone.com/

The Mountain Zone is an online magazine for skiing, snowboarding, mountain biking, and more. Find lots of information here, including weather and expedition reports.

Resort Sports Network

http://www.rsn.com/

Check on weather conditions and "Resort Cams" for ski resorts around the world at the Resort Sports Network.

SkiNet

http://www.skinet.com/

SkiNet indexes links to sites with information about travel, gear, snow reports, technique, magazines, and classifieds.

TWSNOW.COM

http://www.twsnow.com/

Read news and snow info designed specifically for snowboarders at TWSNOW.COM (TransWorld Snow).

news:rec.skiing

Discuss general skiing topics at rec.skiing, and endure just a little bit of spam.

news:rec.sport.snowboarding

Rec.sport.snowboarding covers various snowboarding topics, from snow reports and travel tips to equipment-for-sale ads.

Skydiving

See also: Aviation, Sports

Adventure Living

http://www.adventureliving.com/

Adventure Living is devoted to numerous adventure sports, including skydiving. The site includes skydiving stories, photos, and tips. One goal of this site is to share information with people who are interested in skydiving but haven't necessarily tried it yet.

Skydive WWW

http://www.skydivewww.com/

Skydive WWW contains information on drop zones around the world, stolen gear listings, weather, articles, and more!

United States Parachute Association

http://www.uspa.org/

The United States Parachute Association is the official voice for skydiving enthusiasts in the USA. Learn more about this organization and the sport in general at this Web site.

news:rec.skydiving

This newsgroup discusses the sport of skydiving, with many stories and items for sale.

Snowmobiles

See also: Outdoors, Sports

American Snowmobiling OnLine

http://www.amsnow.com/

Surf to American Snowmobiling OnLine for racing info, riding tips, reviews, classifieds, and more.

Snowmobile Online

http://www.off-road.com/snowmobile/

Off-Road.com hosts Snowmobile Online, a webzine for snowmobile enthusiasts. Read about new sleds, product reviews, news, and anything else that has to do with the sport.

Snowstuff

http://www.geocities.com/MotorCity/Downs/2503/

Snowstuff focuses on snowmobiles from Arctic Cat, Polaris, Ski-Doo, and Yamaha, with photos and specifications of various models.

news:rec.sport.snowmobile

Discuss trail conditions, sled maintenance, riding, and more in this newsgroup.

Space

See also: Astronomy, Government, Science, Science Fiction

NASA

http://www.nasa.gov/

What better way is there to travel into space than with NASA? Their home page has lots of cool images, information about upcoming projects and missions, and more.

Nasa Human Space Flight

http://spaceflight.nasa.gov/index-m.html

See what's happening with the International Space Station, the Space Shuttle, and even plans to send humans to Mars. The future is now.

National Space Society

http://www.nss.org/

Visit the National Space Society to learn more about life in space, astronauts, space travel, and more.

Space Today Online

http://www.tui.edu/STO/STO.html

Space Today Online is another excellent news source, including info on present and future USA, ESA, and Russian space flight projects.

Views of the Solar System

http://www.hawastsoc.org/solar/homepage.htm

Views of the Solar System is truly one of the gems of the Internet. The site contains information about the planets and other objects in our solar system, including stunning images of each planet, physical data, links, and complete descriptions.

Windows to the Universe

http://www.windows.umich.edu/

Windows to the Universe is a graphically oriented learning project designed to let the public learn more about the universe we live in.

Sports

See also: Golf, Guns, Gymnastics, Martial Arts, Mountain Climbing, News, Outdoors, Rodeo, Skateboarding, Skiing & Snowboarding, Skydiving, Snowmobiles, Surfing

The Clubhouse

http://www.netspace.org/users/david/sports.html

The Clubhouse contains an extensive list of links to various sports-related Web sites. Listings are categorized by sport and include many fan, team, and news sites.

CNN/SI

http://www.cnnsi.com/

CNN/SI is a collaborative effort of CNN and Sports Illustrated. The site provides extensive sporting news and commentary.

ESPN SportsZone

http://espnet.sportszone.com/

Looking for total sports news? You can't go wrong at the ESPN SportsZone, which contains outstanding coverage of sporting events, articles, stats, and scores.

Interactive Internet Sports

http://www.iis-sports.com/

Test your sports trivia knowledge, make predictions, or "mouth off" to your favorite (or least favorite) team at Interactive Internet Sports.

NFL.COM

http://www.nfl.com/

Get your football fix at NFL.COM, the official site of the National Football League. Follow the road to the Superbowl right here!

The Official Site of the National Basketball Association

http://www.nba.com/

Basketball buffs will feel right at home at The Official Site of the National Basketball Association. Includes daily live chats with your favorite stars!

SportsZine UK

http://www.sportszineuk.co.uk/

SportsZine UK contains links, chat, and news for sports in the U.K.

Surfing

See also: Outdoors, Sports

Adventure Surf Unlimited
http://www.adventuresurf.com/

Adventure Surf Unlimited provides information about taking a surfing adventure all over the world. The site provides surf maps, a World Review, board information, and more.

Crazy Joe's Surf Lounge
http://www.thegrid.net/fleming/

View daily sunset images of California beach and world surf reports at Crazy Joe's Surf Lounge.

OceanBlue
http://www.oceanblue.com/

Ocean Blue is dedicated to beaches, surfing, and ocean sports. Find the best beaches here!

Taxes

See also: Finance, Government, Money

1040.com
http://www.1040.com/

Get tax preparation and legal information at 1040.com. The site also enables you to download common U.S. federal and state tax forms.

The Digital Daily
http://www.irs.ustreas.gov/prod/cover.html

The U.S. Internal Revenue Service produces The Digital Daily, a daily news

webzine covering various tax-related issues.

Tax Analysts
http://www.tax.org/default.htm

Tax Analysts provides news and other services related to US, State, and International tax law.

Tax Help Online
http://www.taxhelponline.com/

Tax Help Online helps you deal with audits and tax collection problems, and even provides some tips to let you lower your taxes as much as possible.

Tax Problems
http://www.nolo.com/ChunkTAX/TAX.index.html

Learn how to deal with your Tax Problems more effectively at this site, sponsored by Nolo.

news:misc.taxes

Read questions about taxes or ask your own in the misc.taxes newsgroup.

Television

See also: Acting, Entertainment, Movies & Film, News, Radio

PBS
http://www.pbs.org/

Check out program guides, see previews, and obtain useful companion material for shows on PBS here. You can also link to other affiliates with Web sites from the PBS home page.

Television on the Web
http://www.geocities.com/Tokyo/
1264/tv.htm

Television on the Web provides links to the Web sites of TV stations and networks across the USA.

TV-Free America
http://www.essential.org/orgs/tvfa/

Learn about National TV-Turnoff Week, and other anti-television efforts at TV-Free America.

TV Guide
http://www.tvguide.com/

This Web site is an online version of TV Guide. Link to TV listings for your area or just read up on entertainment news.

Ultimate TV
http://www.ultimatetv.com/

Check out TV news, reviews, and ratings online at Ultimate TV.

Theater

See also: Acting, Entertainment, Regions

Acting Workshop OnLine
http://www.execpc.com/~blankda/
acting1.html

Link to hundreds of Web sites with resources for actors and actresses from AWOL — Acting Workshop Online.

Jam! Theater
http://www.canoe.ca/Theatre/

Jam! Theater is a complete guide to theater and stage performance in Canada.

Playbill On-Line
http://www1.playbill.com/

Playbill On-Line has complete news and information about theater, including both the people and the performances. The site also hosts live chat!

Shakespeare and the Globe
http://www.rdg.ac.uk./globe/

Learn about William Shakespeare, his theater, and the reconstruction of the Globe at Shakespeare and the Globe.

news:rec.arts.theater

The rec.arts.theater newsgroup discusses theater, but much of the content is geared toward acting professionals who are looking for work or have other questions.

Tobacco

See also: Health

The American Cancer Society
http://www.cancer.org/

The American Cancer Society has posted a wealth of information about tobacco and the potential health risks on its Web site.

CDC's Tips: Tobacco Information and Prevention Source
http://www.cdc.gov/tobacco/

The Center for Disease Control hosts CDC's Tips: Tobacco Information and Prevention Source, for providing health and research information on tobacco products.

Cigar Friendly.com
http://www.cigarfriendly.com/

Cigar enthusiasts will enjoy Cigar Friendly.com, with events, travel information, reviews, and more.

The Master Anti-Smoking Page
http://www.smokefreekids.com/smoke.htm

The Master Anti-Smoking Page links to various anti-smoking resources, including tips on how to quit, research information, and more.

Smokers.com
http://www.smokers.com/

Smoking is always welcome at Smokers.com, a Web site devoted to communication and community between avid smokers.

Toys

See also: Children, Collectibles, Hobbies

Dr. Toy's Guide
http://www.drtoy.com/

Find out the best toys for your kids at Dr. Toy's Guide. The site rates toys based on their suitability for various age groups.

F.A.O. Schwartz
http://www.faoschwarz.com/

So you don't live anywhere near an F.A.O. Schwartz store? I'm truly sorry, but now there is less reason to despair: The World of Toys is on the Web! I recommend the cool daily factoids.

Fibblesnork
http://www.fibblesnork.com/

Fibblesnork is the ultimate online guide to all things Lego. The site includes a kit guide, Site of the Week, and numerous links.

The Official Lego Page
http://www.lego.com/

The Official Lego Page is a good jumping-off point for the serious plastic brick-building maniac!

Raving Toy Maniac
http://www.toymania.com/

If you love action figures and other great toys, you'll go bonkers over the Raving Toy Maniac.

The Toy Link Internet Connection
http://pages.prodigy.com/ttlic/main.htm

Link to hundreds of Web sites for toy collectors and enthusiasts at The Toy Link Internet Connection.

Trouble in Toyland
http://www.pirg.org/pirg/consumer/products/toy/97/index.htm

Trouble in Toyland surveys dangerous toys and posts warnings on its Web site. Learn more about the organization and the toys it says are dangerous.

news:rec.toys
Discuss your love of toys or find neat stuff for sale on the rec.toys newsgroup.

Travel

See also: Autos, Aviation: Airlines, Bed and Breakfasts, Family, Maps, Motorcycles, Outdoors, Railroads, Regions, Restaurants, Weather

American Express Travel

http://www.americanexpress.com/travel/

American Express Travel can serve as a kind of virtual travel agent, while it lets you reserve flights, hotels, and rental cars, and gather vacation tips.

Amtrak

http://www.amtrak.com/

Ride the American rails with Amtrak. The Web site contains complete travel planning services and information about the trains and routes.

Atevo! Travel

http://www.atevo.com/

Atevo! Travel is a great place to plan your next holiday or business trip. In addition to traditional travel agency-like services, Atevo! also contains some intriguing travel articles and photos of exotic destinations.

Biztravel

http://www.biztravel.com/

Biztravel offers trip-planning information tailored to the business traveler. It's also a great place to learn more about the next city that you're traveling to, and you can also check to see if your flight is on time before you even get to the airport!

Epicurious

http://www.epicurious.com/

Epicurious has a great collection of travel information, including *The Condé Nast Traveler*.

Excite Travel

http://city.net/

Excite Travel from City.Net provides a host of travel services, including air, hotel, and rental car reservations and air fare tracking. You can also browse through the site to find out more about your destination. Find out where to eat, what to see, and how to act.

Flifo

http://www.flifo.com/

Flifo is an online travel service oriented towards business travelers. Look for low air fares, check to see if your flight is on time, or reserve rental cars and hotel rooms.

Global Online Travel

http://www.got.com/

Global Online Travel enables you to make all your reservations online, without making you wait for a lot of other fluff to download.

Greyhound Bus Lines

http://www.greyhound.com/

The Web site of Greyhound Bus Lines has information about the company, discounts, fares, and bus schedules. Some links on this site do not always function properly, but it is a useful tool when everything works right.

The Hotel Guide

http://www.hotelguide.com/

Check The Hotel Guide for a comprehensive database of hotel information. The search feature is easy to use and helpful if you don't know exactly where to stay.

The Internet Travel Network

http://www.itn.net/

The Internet Travel Network offers a well-rounded selection of travel information and services. Besides the basic reservation abilities, you can get driving directions, check weather, participate in travel-related discussions, and find out which frequent flier program is the best.

Kids Travel

http://pathfinder.com/travel/klutz/

Kids Travel helps you and your kids learn how to enjoy traveling. Includes information about getting around and on traveling in the USA and abroad.

Microsoft Expedia

http://www.expedia.msn.com/daily/home/default.hts

The folks in Redmond have their own travel information service, and they call it Microsoft Expedia. Find special deals and use the online travel agent to plan your trip.

Mungo Park

http://www.mungopark.com/

Mungo Park shares monthly adventures with their readers by travelling to places all over the world. This site, which enables you to "virtually" travel around the globe with their celebrity correspondents, introduces you to exciting new places and fascinating people. A new adventure every month.

Preview Travel

http://www.previewtravel.com/

Another online travel agency, Preview Travel offers a number of useful business and vacation travel planning services.

Tackiest Place in America

http://www.thepoint.net/~usul/text/tacky.html

A Web site devoted to finding the Tackiest Place in America? You'll find it here, with many excellent photos of the defiled destinations. The site calls itself a "contest," although I am not sure we want to know what the "prize" would actually be.

The Travel Channel

http://www.travelchannel.com/

The Travel Channel is an online version of that cable television network, and has some fascinating travel articles, photography, and travel spotlights. The site has a number of links to other travel-related Web pages as well.

Travelocity

http://www.travelocity.com/

Want to plan your trip all in one place? Try Travelocity, which has information on vacations and cruises, destination guides, reservation services, and last minute deals. You can also check for the lowest air fares here.

Uniglobe

http://www.uniglobe.com/

Uniglobe offers travel reservation and planning services, and also has a number of travel articles that tell you about a destination and how to plan your own trip there.

U.S. State Department
http://travel.state.gov/

If your travel will take you out of the USA, check out the Web site of the U.S. State Department. The site tells you what documents you will need. Don't forget to check any travel advisories the department might have issued for Americans traveling abroad.

U.S. Submarines, Inc
http://www.ussubs.com/

It's happened to all of us. You suddenly find you have more money than you know what to do with. The friendly people at U.S. Submarines, Inc might be able to help. They can provide you with your own "Personal Luxury Submarine," displacing up to 1500 tons, with 5,000 square feet of interior space arranged on four decks and easily capable of transoceanic voyages. As for a destination, perhaps you'd like an underwater habitat to retreat to when the pressures of land-based life seem too much.

Unexplained Phenomenon

See also: Astronomy, Psychics, Science Fiction

Art Bell
http://www.artbell.com/

Art Bell is a late night radio talk show host, whose main interest is in science fiction, UFOs, and unexplained stuff. This Web site has a lot of cool things; my favorite is the Chupacabra photo gallery!

The Legend of Nessie
http://www.nessie.co.uk/index.html

The Legend of Nessie is an information resource for the Loch Ness Monster, as well as tourist information for the highland country of Scotland! Best viewed with Nesscape (yuk, yuk).

Northwest Mysteries
http://www.nwmyst.com/

Northwest Mysteries has some fascinating Bigfoot, UFO, and other related stories.

Paranormal Parlor
http://www2.clearlight.com/
~oddsend/paranorm.htm

Link to all things unexplainable at the Paranormal Parlor. Lots of great links here!

Veterans

See also: Employment, Government, Military

Defense POW Personnel Office
http://www.dtic.mil/dpmo/

The Defense POW Personnel Office serves as a starting point for information on POW/MIA personnel of the U.S. Department of Defense.

Department of Veterans Affairs
http://www.va.gov/

Surf to the Department of Veterans Affairs Web site to learn about news and veterans programs offered by the department.

Veteran.Net
http://veteran.net/

Veteran.Net provides a complete source of job search information to help US military veterans plan their careers and keep them on track. The site also includes links to state and local government resources.

The Veteran's Observer

http://www.theveteransobserver.com/

The Veteran's Observer serves veterans across the USA with news, memorial information, and more.

Vietnam Veterans of America

http://www.vva.org/

Visit Vietnam Veterans of America for information, services, and support for Vietnam War veterans.

news:soc.veterans

Soc.veterans is a newsgroup to discuss veteran's issues, although there also appears to be a lot of political discussion as well.

Weather

See also: News, Travel

Intellicast

http://www.intellicast.com/

Intellicast has the look and feel of a large news service, but it specializes in world and national weather. Special features include travel information, ski reports, and health information.

National Weather Service

http://www.nws.noaa.gov/

The official Web site of the National Weather Service has current weather, climatic data, and an extensive listing of storm and foul weather conditions.

The Weather Channel

http://www.weather.com/

The Weather Channel is a great source for weather and travel news. Included are forecasts, satellite weather maps, travel conditions, and more!

WeatherNet

http://cirrus.sprl.umich.edu/wxnet/

WeatherNet is a comprehensive source for linking to weather information worldwide. Includes links to forecasts, satellite images, weather cams, and more.

World Weather Links

http://www.geocities.com/
SiliconValley/3452/weather1.html

Find the latest satellite images at World Weather Links. Includes numerous weather-related links.

Web Page Design

See also: Computers: Internet

The Bandwidth Conservation Society

http://www.infohiway.com/faster/
index.html

Learn how you too can prevent monotony at The Bandwidth Conservation Society. The site contains tips and information on how to reduce bandwidth use on your Web pages.

HTML Hut

http://www.jwp.bc.ca/saulm/html/

Link to resources of free graphics, script advice, animations, and more from the HTML Hut.

Java

http://www.developer.com/
directories/pages/dir.java.html

Need to learn Java? This is the best place I can think of to start. The site has a reference section and also offers numerous Java applets for use in your own Web site.

MediaBuilder
http://www.mediabuilder.com/

MediBuilder offers free images, animations, and links to other resources to help you beautify your Web site.

Mega Web Tools
http://protect.simplenet.com/
tools.htm

Another great source for free images, animations, and backgrounds is Mega Web Tools.

Web Pages That Suck
http://www.webpagesthatsuck.com/

Web Pages That Suck is still the best resource for learning effective (and defective) Web page design. Learn what not to do before it's too late!

WebReference.com
http://www.webreference.com/

WebReference.com is a great resource for answering those tough questions you have as a Webmaster.

Yale C/AIM Web Style Guide
http://info.med.yale.edu/caim/manual/

See what the folks at Yale have to say about nice Web pages at the Yale C/AIM Web Style Guide.

Yellow Pages

See also: Search Engines

BigBook
http://www.bigbook.com/

BigBook is an extensive, easy-to-use directory of millions of U.S. businesses. The site also includes links to maps and driving directions, a useful feature once you find a business in BigBook that you want to visit.

BigYellow
http://www.bigyellow.com/

BigYellow is another excellent online yellow pages that contains listings for both businesses and individuals.

The Global Yellow Pages
http://www.globalyp.com/world.htm

Link to phone book listings all over the world at The Global Yellow Pages.

Switchboard
http://www.switchboard.com/

Switchboard helps you find phone numbers and e-mail addresses for individuals, listings for businesses, and Web sites.

Creating Your Own Web Content

U sing the Web as your stage, the World can be your audience. If you plan to open your own e-business or you simply want to use the Web to show off baby pictures to your family across the country, this is the place to start.

In this part, you learn how to create really great Web sites. We take you from the basics all the way through advanced Web-site building topics. You also learn how to host files on your computer that other people can access, and how to create Web content using office productivity software, such as Microsoft Office and Corel WordPerfect.

Doing Basic Web Design

Depending on your goals and how much time you feel like spending learning the process, there are many ways to make a Web page. Do you want to launch your Web page as soon as possible, or take the time to get under the hood and find out what makes it tick? If you understand a bit of how HTML (HyperText Markup Language, the language of Web page design) works, you'll be able to troubleshoot your creations and make them more flexible in various browser environments.

For now, we'll concentrate on creating Web pages the old fashioned way: by typing and editing "raw" HTML code. This will help you gain a basic understanding of HTML and how it works, an important skill even if you later choose to create your Web pages with a graphical editor.

Tip If you absolutely don't want to learn a single HTML tag, you can jump ahead to Chapters 27, "Using Web Design Tools for Windows," and 28, "Using Web Design Tools for Macintosh and Linux." Or if you want to learn about creating a basic page fast, check out Chapter 4, "Creating a Web Page in Ten Minutes."

Defining a Web Page

The main component of a Web page is a small HTML document that, when opened, contains the text of the Web page as well as instructions that display graphics and other files comprising that page in a browser. If the page consists entirely of text, the HTML file will include all of the content for the Web page. Otherwise the HTML page will serve as a simple frame for a variety of other components. An HTML file can contain headlines, bulleted lists, and body text, but the magic of this short HTML page is its capability to call upon other larger files, such as pictures, graphs, and even videos and sounds. The HTML language provides a simple system to create links with other files, wherever they may be: on your own computer, another server, or someplace on the Web.

A Web page tells a graphic to open, how large that picture should be, and where it should be positioned on the page. The same page contains links to other pages in that same Web site and links to other Web sites of interest to your visitors. Your page can also contain sounds, tables, updateable graphs, animations, and videos.

Distinguishing a Web site from a Web page

As we mentioned in Chapter 4, a Web page is not the same as a Web site. A Web site is a group of pages created to present your company, your ideas, or your services in a thorough, interactive manner. (For example, "Click here to learn about our product line. Click here to read reviews about our software. Click here to download a demo.") In a way, a Web site is kind of like a magazine, and each Web page is an article in that magazine.

Connecting Web pages to the Web

After you've created your Web page or Web site—by typing text, creating links, inserting graphics, and arranging the rest of the content just the way you like it—you'll have to upload those files to a server. Until all your Web-related files are on a server, the world cannot visit your Web site. That's why most ISPs provide members with space for storing Web page files. You'll learn how to publish your site on a Web server later in this chapter. For now, please remember that all the files related to each Web page should reside in the same folder.

Planning Your Web Site

Planning is the key to success, whether you're starting a business, preparing for your retirement, storming the beach at Normandy, or creating a Web site. A little bit of foresight now could save a lot of time and heartache later on. Before you dive into the process of actually producing the HTML for your site, ask yourself a few basic questions:

✦ **Who will view this site?** Is this a personal site that you are creating for the benefit of your friends and family, or will your visitors be the customers of your business? Or, are you creating the official Web site of your bird club? Your audience should determine the ultimate focus of the site.

✦ **How much time do you have?** The most popular, dynamic sites on the Web employ full-time Webmasters. You probably don't have that much time available for creating a Web page, but you have to determine how much time you *do* have. If you put up an "Under Construction" banner and then ignore the site for several months, no one will be interested in viewing it.

✦ **How much server space is available?** Many ISPs provide 5–10MB of server space, and if this is all you plan to use then you will have to make sure that all of your Web pages, pictures, and other related files fit within the available space. Otherwise, you will have to obtain additional server space.

Once you've answered these basic questions, you can work on planning the physical layout of the site. Most Web sites begin with a main page that acts as an index, or table of contents, for the rest of the site. A good main page usually follows these guidelines:

✦ The file name should be *index.html* or *home.html*. If you name it something else, Web browsers won't be able to find it when visitors try to view your site.

✦ Try to fit the most important content on a single, 640 × 480 pixel screen, although an 800 × 600 pixel screen area will suffice for most users if you absolutely need more space. If visitors to your site have to scroll down a lot on the first page, they will probably lose interest.

✦ Keep pictures to a minimum. Because graphics tend to be large, they can slow down the rate at which your Web pages load. A few small graphics and logos are okay, but try to design the page so it loads relatively quickly, especially because most Internet users still connect at speeds slower than 50 Kbps.

✦ Include links to all major pages, designing a list of links as you would a table of contents in a book. Viewers won't want to dig through many different pages just to find your contact information.

Selecting development tools

Besides planning the actual content of your site, you need to decide what kind of software you will use to create it. It's possible to create and publish your site with nothing more than a text editor and a command line FTP program. But why make life hard on yourself? Choose tools that meet your needs and make your work more efficient.

What follows is a list of basic tools that you should have to create a typical small Web site. Obviously, there are many other tools that you can use, which we will discuss later, but for now you should have programs that meet all of the following needs.

Text editor

This is probably the single most important piece of software. You can use the text editor that came with your operating system, such as Notepad (Windows), vi (Linux), or SimpleText (Macintosh). If you want additional features such as Find and Replace and the ability to open larger documents, you can use a more advanced editor, such as Textpad (`www.textpad.com`) or BBEdit (`www.barebones.com`). You can even use a word processor, but you have to make sure that it saves your HTML documents in the correct format.

Tip   In Windows, you can force a word processor to save HTML without text formatting by choosing *Plain text* from the Save As Type list box, and then surround the file name in quotes like this: "`index.html`."

Web page editor

Many people find it easiest to do most HTML creating and editing in a graphical Web page editor, such as Adobe PageMill, Microsoft FrontPage, Microvision WebExpress, or Netscape Composer. Modern word processors, such as Microsoft Word 2000 and Corel WordPerfect 8 enable you to create HTML pages, as do desktop publishing programs like Deneba's Canvas and Microsoft's Publisher. But for reliable daily editing, a dedicated Web page editor is best.

Cross-Reference   To compare available Web page editors, check out Chapters 27, "Using Web Design Tools for Windows," and Chapter 28, "Using Web Design Tools for Macintosh and Linux."

Graphics editor

Graphics are a major part of most Web sites today. If you plan to use pictures or other graphics, you should obtain a program that enables you to edit and retouch them. If you have a digital camera or scanner, you may have received a program like Adobe PhotoDeluxe as part of the deal. Other, more advanced graphics editors include Adobe Photoshop and Illustrator, Deneba's Canvas, GIMP, and Microsoft PhotoDraw.

FTP client

Some Web site editors provide a wizard that makes it easy to transfer files to your Web server. But you should still have and know how to use a good FTP client, such as WS_FTP or Fetch. This will give you greater control over the files you have on the server.

Creating Your First Web Page

A simple home page or a page introducing a product or service should have the following components:

- ✦ A page title
- ✦ A main headline
- ✦ Body text

The page should include many other things, of course, but let's start simply by explaining each of these elements.

The page title

The page title, which appears in your browser's title bar, is not the same as the filename of your HTML document. The title should be an accurate (but brief) description of your page. Search engines use the title to determine your page's relevancy to their search results.

The main headline

This headline is different from the page title (in the browser's title bar) or the filename. It appears at the top of the HTML page and can be either artistic or simply a level one heading directly typed into your document. This heading tells the visitor what your page is all about. It should be clear and to the point.

Body text

Body text is where you describe yourself, your page, and your offerings to the world. Two or three paragraphs of introductory text is always enough. Part of this introduction is to tell visitors where to click if they want to learn more. Think of your home page (or introductory page) as a business card. It's a doorway. Use the body text and your links to point them to the appropriate door.

Applying Basic HTML Tags

Now that you know what the basic elements are, you can begin creating your first Web page. HTML operates by using a standard set of tags to mark the elements discussed here, as well as many others for formatting and other uses. An HTML tag is enclosed in brackets, as in <BODY>. This tag would then be followed by the text, links, images, and other elements that will appear on your Web page, followed by a closing tag that looks like </BODY>.

To see HTML in action, let's create a simple page using the most basic elements of a Web page. Begin by opening a basic text editor, such as Notepad or vi. For this example you should not use a word processor such as Word or WordPerfect. Now, type in the following tags and text:

```
<HTML>
<HEAD>
<TITLE>A Very Short Page</TITLE>
</HEAD>
<BODY>
This is my first Web page in HTML.
</BODY>
</HTML>
```

When you're done, the result should look something like Figure 24-1. Be sure to save your work, and give it a simple name such as **mypage.html**.

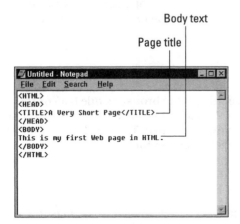

Figure 24-1: A few lines of HTML have been typed into a text editor.

 When you save the file, make sure that you save it as an HTML document. This will mean adding the .htm or .html extension (either one will do) to the end of the file name, even if you aren't using Windows. If you do not add this extension, most browsers will not be able to open it.

Once you have saved the file as an HTML document, try opening it in a Web browser to make sure it turned out okay. Open your browser, click File ⇨ Open, and navigate to the file on your hard drive. It should look something like Figure 24-2.

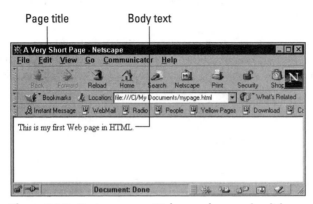

Figure 24-2: Test your new Web page by opening it in a Web browser.

Note
Notice that whatever you typed between the `<TITLE>` tags appears in the title bar at the top of the Web browser window. The title of your page should be descriptive, even though it may not appear within the body of the page itself.

Congratulations! You're on your way to becoming a Webmaster. But . . . you're not there yet. For now, let's take a closer look at some tags. As we mentioned earlier, HTML tags usually have two parts; one tag serves as an opening, the other a closing. In the simple page you just created, you used tags to open and close the title (`<TITLE> </TITLE>`), the header information for the document (`<HEAD> </HEAD>`), the body text (`<BODY> </BODY>`), and even the HTML itself.

Tags can also be used to apply formatting. For instance, if you want a block of text to be centered on the page, you would surround it with `<CENTER>` and `</CENTER>`. Or if you want some text to be italicized, surround it with the tags `<I>` and `</I>`. And if the body contains more than one paragraph (it usually will), each paragraph will begin with `<P>` and end with `</P>`.

Some tags do not require a closing tag. For instance, if you want to insert a graphic file called `kids.jpg`, the tag for that might look like `<IMG SRC="kids.jpg">`. A line break in the middle of a paragraph (`<BR>`) is another tag that works alone.

Understanding HTML headings

HTML has six levels of headings that you can use within the body. These headings are predefined styles in the HTML standard, and all modern browsers interpret them the same way. Headings come in handy because you don't need to waste time entering a bunch of formatting tags to make your headings stand out the way they should.

The tag `<H1> </H1>` creates a level one heading. Using that simple Web page you created earlier, turn the phrase "This is my first Web page in HTML" into a heading. Position the cursor before the word "This" and type `<H1>`. Now position the cursor at the end of the sentence and type `</H1>`. You've just created the largest heading. If you view your document in a browser, the type appears bold and much larger than before.

To create a smaller heading, surround your phrase with `<H2> </H2>`. To make yet a smaller heading, use the `<H3> </H3>` tag. This system of HTML tags creates six levels of headings, as shown in Figure 24-3.

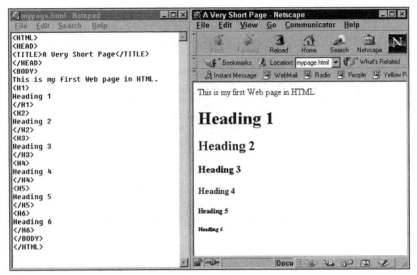

Figure 24-3: <H> tags make it easy to create headings in your Web pages.

Adding Other Web Page Components with HTML

Your Web page can contain many other components, which generally fall into a few basic categories:

✦ Eye and ear candy, such as graphics, background images, pictures, buttons, animated GIFs, videos, and sounds.

✦ <META> tags that add important information to the headers of Web pages.

✦ Small and handy utilities such as page hit counters, visitor guest books, and ticker tape messages that run at the bottom of your page.

✦ Bigger and more practical odds and ends, such as forms and surveys, graphs that display updateable data, and tables that facilitate financial transactions.

✦ Multimedia capability, such as audio files and animations that require special plug-ins.

✦ Scripts that enable visitors to run search engines or even check stocks right from your page.

✦ "Push technology" components, such as setting aside a segment of your Web page screen that provides late-breaking news relevant to your page's content.

Working with hyperlinks

You can easily designate a portion of text as a hyperlink. Simply surround it with the <A> </A> tag. The following statement creates a link to the IDG Books Web site. The link is the text phrase "Visit IDG Books Online" and appears as follows:

```
<A HREF="http://www.idgbooks.com">
Visit IDG Books Online</A>
```

Let's look closer at the <A HREF> tag:

✦ The A means that this tag will be a type of anchor. An anchor is either the start of a link (where you click to go to another location) or the destination of a link.

✦ The HREF means that text inside the tag will be an active link. If you click the link, it will take you to a new location.

✦ The destination referred to in your link (in this case, the IDG Web site) must be inside quotation marks.

Now, if a visitor clicks the phrase on your Web page, they'll move to the IDG Web site. The final </A> closes the hyperlink tag. Everything before the </A> and in quotation marks is considered to be part of the link, or *clickable*.

Inserting your e-mail address

You want people to e-mail you for the two following reasons: First, to express interest in what you are doing, and second, to let you know if something on your page is amiss. You should always encourage visitors to report problems. Their input tells you what you need to fix . . . and there is always something to fix.

Creating a link that allows people to quickly send you e-mail is much like creating a hyperlink. You simply enter the tags for a hyperlink as described previously, except that you replace the destination URL with your e-mail address. It will look something like this:

```
<A HREF="mailto:keith@idgbooks.com">
Click here to send Keith an e-mail.</A>
```

Notice that the *mailto:* protocol is included in the address. Although you usually leave this part of an e-mail address off when you are composing mail in your e-mail program, it is important to include it here. This will help the reader's computer identify it as an e-mail link, and it should cause their e-mail program to launch automatically.

Tip   You can create links to newsgroups just as you would to an e-mail address. Simply replace *mailto:* with *news:* and type the newsgroup address in place of the e-mail address. A typical news link would look like `<A HREF="news:rec.snowboarding">`.

Positioning graphics

Let's examine a few more HTML examples. Remember, an HTML document is a set of instructions to the visiting browser. The following example displays a small graphic on a Web page. On a new line, type:

```
<IMG SRC="logo.gif" HEIGHT=160 WIDTH=110. ALIGN=LEFT>
```

This command tells the visiting browser to display a .GIF image called "logo." The image should appear 160 pixels tall and 110 pixels wide. Also, it should be aligned to the left side of the page. The browser then searches the server folder for an image called logo.gif and displays it at the size specified.

One thing you always need to be mindful of here is the directory structure of your Web site. The above tag links to a file called *logo.gif* that is located in the same directory as the page itself. But what if you store your images in a separate folder? You can do that, but the tag must list the correct path. For instance, if you keep graphics in a folder called *images*, the above tag would have to be entered like this:

```
<IMG SRC="images/logo.gif" HEIGHT=160 WIDTH=110. ALIGN=LEFT>
```

This tells the browser to get the image logo.gif from the images subdirectory. If the correct path isn't listed in the tag, an error will occur in the page, and the graphic won't display.

Tip   When you specify the height and width of a graphic (especially jpegs) in an HTML tag, the graphic sometimes displays improperly and looks *pixelated*, or blocky. Thus, it is often more desirable to use a graphics editing program to make the image the desired size, and then use it on the Web page in its "native" size.

Specifying a background

You can specify that the background of your page be a certain color or image. If the image is smaller than the page itself, it will be tiled continuously. To specify a black background color, use the following code:

```
<BODY BGCOLOR="#000000">
```

Insert the background color specification right after the body tag. HTML uses this number code, called hexadecimal, for creating colors. Every color you use on your

Web page has a unique hexadecimal value. If you are using a style sheet, you can also specify colors by RGB value or name, but for now we'll stick to hexadecimal values. If you use an HTML editor, you won't need to worry about it; most editors enable you to choose a color from a palate, and then the editor automatically inserts the correct value in the HTML document.

Cross-Reference To learn more about creating and using style sheets, take a look at Chapter 26, "Working with Advanced Web Page Components."

The W3C Web site's guide to styling HTML documents (`http://www.w3.org/MarkUp/Guide/Style.html`) provides a list of hexadecimal values for the most common colors in a Web page. As you can see in Figure 24-4, it lists values for 16 basic colors. Because all modern browsers recognize these standard colors, it is a good idea to stick with these. Besides your page's background, these colors can also be used for fonts and various other elements.

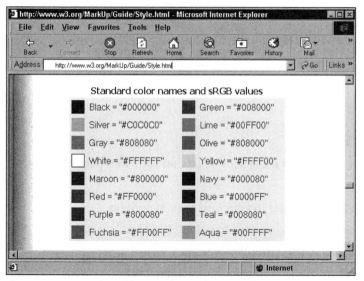

Figure 24-4: W3C's guide to HTML styles provides a useful list of hexadecimal values for the most common colors used on Web pages.

To specify that your background should be a image, type a tag like this:

```
<BODY BACKGROUND="clouds.gif">
```

This tag tells the browser to use the image *clouds.gif* as the background, and if the graphic is smaller than the open window it will automatically be tiled.

Tip — Remember, the larger the image, the longer it will take to load. This can be especially problematic if you are using light-colored text over a dark background image. If the text loads first, it may be virtually invisible until the background image finishes loading. Also, be mindful of the fact that some background images make text very difficult to read.

Adding alternate text

When adding a graphic to a Web page, make sure to include text for those visitors whose graphics capabilities are turned off. Some people still surf the Web in a text-only environment. You can easily type something for people to read if they can't see your picture with the <ALT> tag, as shown in the following statement.

```
<A HREF="progear.htm"><IMG SRC="progear.gif"
ALT="Click here for the best prices in all pro gear"
ALIGN="top"></A>
```

In the preceding example, an image called "progear.gif" is displayed (<IMG SRC= "progear.gif"). Clicking it takes the visitor to a Web page called "progear.htm" (<A HREF="progear.htm">). The alternative text that graphics-disabled visitors see is "Click here for the best prices in all pro gear" (ALT="Click here for the best prices in all pro gear"). Notice the </A> tag closes the entry because the .GIF is a link.

Creating lists

Chances are, you will end up using a lot of lists on your Web pages. Lists have countless uses. You can

- ✦ Provide an index of pages in your site, with hyperlinks
- ✦ List ingredients or steps needed to complete a task
- ✦ Organize hyperlinks to other Web sites in a logical order
- ✦ Create your own David Letterman–style top ten list
- ✦ Lay out important points in your book about using the Internet

HTML provides some simple tags that enable you to easily create bulleted, numbered, or definition lists. A bulleted list is similar to that just used, and looks like this:

```
<UL>
   <LI>Item one</LI>
   <LI>Item two</LI>
   <LI>Item three</LI>
</UL>
```

Notice that the list starts and ends with the <UL> and </UL> tags, and that each item starts with <LI> and ends with </LI>. If you like abbreviations, you can think of LI as standing for *List Item*, and UL representing *Unordered List*. If you want to create an *Ordered List*, a.k.a. a numbered list, it will look something like this:

```
<OL>
   <LI>Step one</LI>
   <LI>Step two</LI>
   <LI>Step three</LI>
</OL>
```

A *Definitions List* is a bit different, because rather than having a bullet or number in front of each list item, it has a word. You specify the word as part of each list item. It will look like this:

```
<DL>
   <DT>Term one</DT>
   <DD>Definition of term</DD>
   <DT>Term two</DT>
   <DD>Definition of term</DD>
   <DT>Term three</DT>
   <DD>Definition of term</DD>
</DL>
```

The item enclosed in the <DT> tags is the Definition Term, and the <DD> item is the *Definition Definition* (we couldn't make this up). A Definitions list is handy if you want to provide a list of links with descriptions. The Definition term could be the name of the page that the link leads to, and the definition could be a short description of that page. In this case, it will look best if only the term is hyperlinked.

Publishing Your Web Site

As we mentioned earlier, if you want other people to access your Web site, it will have to be published on a Web server. If it remains on your local computer, only users of your computer — and perhaps your local network — will be able to view it.

The exact method you use to publish your site will depend largely on the server you are publishing it to. This will often be the Web server provided by your ISP, or it could be a server that offers free space on the Web. If you are using a Web site editor like those described elsewhere, it may provide a wizard or other similar tool to help you transfer your Web page to the server. Otherwise, you'll use an FTP client such as WS_FTP to transfer the files.

When you do publish your site, make sure that you transfer all of the following elements to the Web server:

✦ HTML files

✦ Graphics, including all jpegs and gifs

✦ Sound or other multimedia files used by the page

✦ The directory/folder structure used by your site

Before publishing your site, you also need to find out if the Web server uses case-sensitive file names. Most do, especially those running a UNIX-based operating system. In general, you should make sure that file names and file name references in your HTML use the same case. Many Webmasters simply use all lower case letters in file names, and that is a good strategy to follow.

Using an FTP client

For now let's assume that you will use an FTP client to transfer Web site files to your Web server. Chapter 17, "Finding Cool Software on the Web," describes the basics for using WS_FTP LE, a client offered for free by Ipswitch (www.ipswitch. com) for home and private users. However, if you are developing Web sites professionally you will have to purchase WS-FTP Pro, or use another client. Many other FTP clients are available (such as Fetch for Macs), so check some of the software sites described in Chapter 17 to see what is available.

Like most good FTP clients, WS_FTP enables you to perform many functions that will be important to you as you publish your Web site to a Web server. Figure 24-5 shows some of the tools that you will find useful.

After you've transferred your files to the Web server, close the FTP client and test the Web page in a browser. If some of the files don't display properly — pay particular attention to graphics — you may need to rename them or change the case of the filename. In WS_FTP, select a file on your Web server and click Rename to modify the filename, as shown in Figure 24-6.

Using a free Web server

Numerous Web sites now offer free server space for your Web pages. Usually the right to use this free space is contingent upon your willingness to let the site place advertising banners or pop-up windows on your site, but you may decide that this is a small price to pay (especially if your ISP doesn't provide Web server space for you).

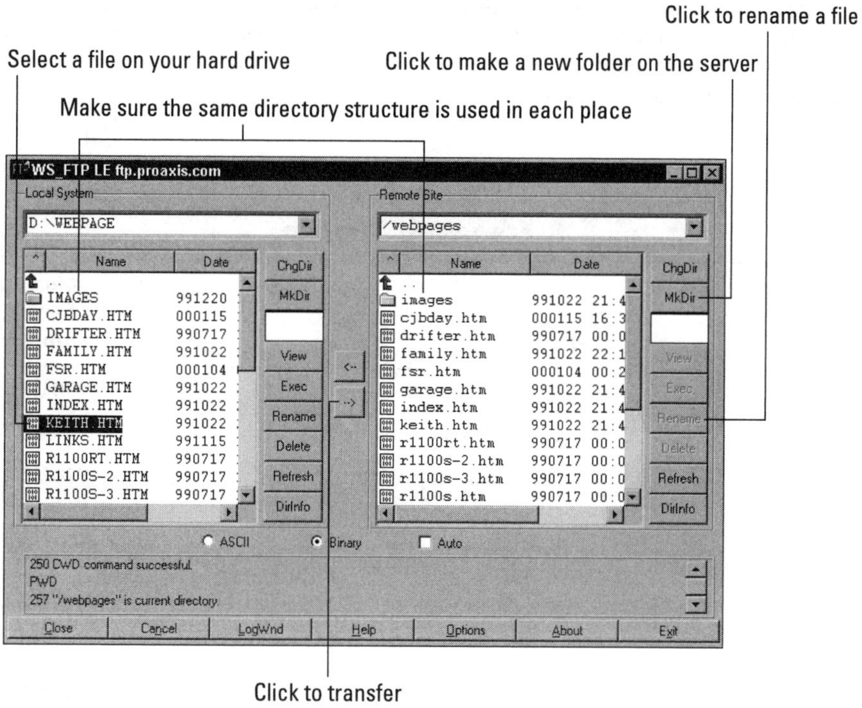

Click to rename a file

Select a file on your hard drive   Click to make a new folder on the server

Make sure the same directory structure is used in each place

Click to transfer

Figure 24-5: WS_FTP is a powerful tool to help you manage your Web site files.

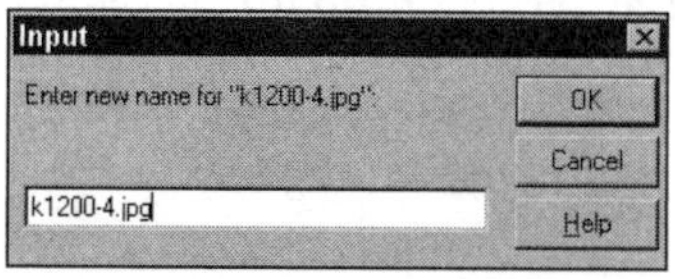

Figure 24-6: Most Web servers are case-sensitive with file names.

When you search for "free" Web server space, research offers carefully to make sure you know what you're getting. Some sites say that you can set up a free Web page, even though in reality you are allowed only a single page, and the content is limited to the answers you provide to a few basic questions asked by their site creation wizard. You should also make sure that you review the server's policy on content. Are there certain kinds of content they won't allow? Does the site insist that your site contain a specific kind of content? Are you allowed to sell items on your pages? Is there an additional charge if your site has high traffic?

Table 24-1 lists some servers that offer free space for your Web pages, along with the maximum amount of space they provide. All of the sites listed here place ad banners on member sites, although in most cases you can eliminate the ads by paying a monthly subscription fee.

Table 24-1 Free Web Servers		
Server	**URL**	**Maximum free space provided**
50MEGS.COM	`http://www.50megs.com/`	50MB
Angelfire	`http://angelfire.lycos.com/`	30MB
Freeservers	`http://www.freeservers.com/`	20MB
Homestead	`http://www.homestead.com/`	16MB
MSN Home Pages	`http://msnhomepages.talkcity.com/`	12MB
Nettaxi	`http://www.nettaxi.com/`	25MB
Tripod	`http://www.tripod.lycos.com/`	11MB
XOOM.COM	`http://xoom.com/`	Unlimited
Yahoo! Geocities	`http://geocities.yahoo.com/`	15MB

This list is not all-inclusive, of course, and new free servers crop up almost daily. Even the sites listed here may change their policies or the amount of space they provide, so do a little research before you sign up. The servers listed here can give you an excellent starting point, especially if you don't have enough space (or any space at all) on your ISP's Web server.

Employing Web Page Design Tips

If you understand your limitations and don't attempt anything too complex, your site can be just as rich in content as those made with lots of expertise and a big budget. If you've never created a Web page, the following tips are worth keeping in mind:

✦ **Pay attention to good-looking sites**. Surf around and notice what works. When you stumble on a page you like, take a minute to determine why you like it. Pay special attention to economical use of space, simple design, and clever ways of getting one's message across. A novice can easily emulate good style.

✦ **Remember the average user**. High-speed Internet connections are a hot topic now, but most people still connect to the Web through dial-up connections that are slower than 50 Kbps. Also, most people don't have 21-inch monitors, so try to design your Web site with 640 × 480 or 800 × 600 resolution in mind.

✦ **Learn a little HTML**. If you know enough to interpret the background machinery of your page, you'll be more apt to troubleshoot minor problems and not be entirely at the mercy of whatever Web design software package you ultimately decide to use. Just as it is wise for a car owner to know a bit about what's under the hood for his own safety, it's good for you to understand enough HTML so you are not stumped at an important moment.

✦ **Test your site**. Ideally, try testing it with more than one browser. The most common browsers are Internet Explorer and Netscape Navigator, but it may also be worthwhile to test it in Opera, NeoPlanet, or another browser alternative.

Summary

This chapter introduced you to some basic Web design concepts; you should now know just enough to be dangerous. Even if you ultimately decide to create your site using a Web page editor like those described in Chapters 27 and 28, having a basic grasp of HTML concepts will be important as you develop and test ever more advanced pages. In the next couple of chapters we'll delve deeper into Web design and show you how to use some tools that will help you develop a top-quality site.

✦   ✦   ✦

Applying Intermediate Web Design Features

In the previous chapter, you learned some HTML basics
and how to put them to use. You even created your own
page, producing the basic headers and tags required to format
an HTML document, programming hyperlinks, applying colors,
generating lists, and inserting images.

With those basic skills you can get by for a while, creating
the kind of Web pages that populated the Web five or six years
ago. But soon you will be ready to move on and learn more
about Web publishing. This chapter takes you to the next
level. Now you'll learn more about working with graphics;
tracking how many people visit your site; promoting your
site; and even adding a search engine.

But first, you'll learn how to work with tables on your Web
pages. Many Web developers use tables to control the layout
of items on a page, and you'll learn how to do this here.

Using Tables on a Web Page

When discussing tables, the first thing that probably comes
to mind is rows and rows of numbers with identifying labels
off to the side. In this chapter, though, we use tables as a Web
design aid. If you've ever been frustrated while trying to place
two graphics side by side "just so" on a Web page or line up
a paragraph of text right next to a picture, you'll appreciate

tables. HTML documents tend to favor the placement of objects one on top of the other, not side by side. So if you've ever looked at a Web page featuring a nice row of three pictures, each with identifying captions beneath them, and remembered that when you tried to do the same thing, all you got was grief, the answer is: Use a table. Graphics you insert into table cells will center easily, the cells growing or shrinking to accommodate the size of your placed object. Likewise, text inserted into a table cell constrains itself much more predictably than paragraph text on a standard HTML page.

To illustrate this design principle, let's start by looking at the Kelley Blue Book Web page (`http://www.kbb.com`), a great site for pricing new, used, and trade-in vehicles. The page, shown in Figure 25-1, makes obvious use of tables.

Figure 25-1: The Kelley Blue Book Web page

Take a look at the layout of this page. Notice how elements are organized on the main portion of the page; notice how an item like "Used car values" includes a graphic, heading, and text, and they are aligned together. Other items, such as "Buying & Selling" and "More Research" are similarly laid out. Although you can't see it, the site uses an invisible table to organize elements so nicely.

Building a table

Creating a table of your own requires a bit more typing than other HTML elements you've created up to now, but it is straightforward nonetheless. Here is what the HTML looks like for a table that is three cells wide and three cells tall:

```
<TABLE BORDER="1" CELLPADDING="2">
  <TR><TH>Heading 1</TH><TH>Heading 2</TH><TH>Heading 3</TH>
  <TR><TD>Item 1</TD><TD>Item 2</TD><TD>Item 3</TD></TR>
  <TR><TD>Item 1</TD><TD>Item 2</TD><TD>Item 3</TD></TR>
</TABLE>
```

To begin a table, you start with the opening Table tag, and specify the border width and cell padding (`<TABLE BORDER="1" CELLPADDING="2">`). `BORDER="1"` means that the table will have a border that is one pixel wide, and `CELLPADDING="2"` means that there must always be 2 pixels of blank space between the cell borders and any picture or text inside it. The Table tag will be closed (`</TABLE>`) at the end of the table.

Two other table attributes that aren't shown here are `CELLSPACING` and `WIDTH`. `CELLSPACING` is used in the same way as `BORDER` and `CELLPADDING`, and adds space between each cell. `WIDTH` enables you to specify the width of a table, but rather than specifying a pixel width, you express it in a percentage of window width. For instance, if you want the table to span 75 percent of the window's width, you would specify `WIDTH="75%"`.

> **Note**
>
> If you want the table to be a certain width no matter how wide the browser window is, you can leave off the percent (%) sign and enter a value in pixels. So if you want the table to be 400 pixels wide, you would specify `WIDTH="400"`. Just keep in mind that if the table is wider than your visitors' windows, they will have to scroll left and right to view the whole thing.

HTML commands for tables are set up row by row. The following command (when used within a table) creates a single row of table cells, divided into three columns:

```
<TR><TD>Column 1 data</TD><TD>Column 2 data</TD><TD>Column 3
data</TD></TR>
```

The Table Row tag begins a row (`<TR>`), and the Table Data tags (`<TD>`) specify data cells within the row. Notice that in the first sample of table code, the cells in the top row use Table Head tags (`<TH>`) instead of Table Data. This creates headings in the row, which includes the kind of formatting you would expect for a heading.

Finally, the closing Table Row tag closes each row (`</TR>`). The table would look like what is shown in Figure 25-2. (I added the text for easier identification.)

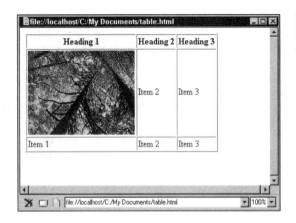

Figure 25-2: This table was created with the code listed in this chapter. Notice the table headings in the first row.

Tip You can also specify custom sizes for individual cells by adding a WIDTH= or HEIGHT= tag to the <TD> tag. So if you want a cell to measure 50 × 50 pixels, make the opening tag <TD WIDTH="50" HEIGHT="50">. These size adjustments will affect other cells in the same row or column as the cell you are customizing.

Placing objects inside a table cell

To place text or a picture inside any cell, just type between the <TD></TD> tag. For example, to put a picture of some trees called trees.jpg inside a cell, you'd type <TD><IMG SRC="trees.jpg"></TD>.

You could also specify width and height, as well. For example:

```
<TD><IMG SRC="trees.jpg" WIDTH="95" HEIGHT="125"></TD>
```

And now, here is the magic fact about HTML tables, why everybody uses them to make Web pages: A table cell will automatically shrink or expand to accommodate its contents. Figure 25-3 shows the table we created earlier, but with a graphic inserted in a cell.

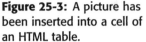

Figure 25-3: A picture has been inserted into a cell of an HTML table.

Creating a table-based page

As we showed you earlier, many Web designers use invisible tables to control the layout of a page. The Kelley Blue Book site uses them, and so does the page shown in Figure 25-4. In fact, the page shown there uses one giant table that holds all of the content on the page.

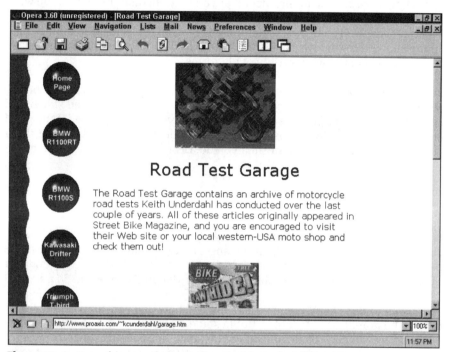

Figure 25-4: Everything on this page lives inside an invisible table.

Perhaps the most important thing you may notice about the table on this page is that you don't notice it; the table itself is invisible. This is done by specifying a BORDER value of zero. The TABLE tag looks like this:

```
<TABLE BORDER="0">
```

Here and in many other Web sites, the table is used to control the alignment of text and images. Without a table, the graphic buttons on the left side of the page would never be able to align alongside other graphics and paragraphs of text as they do here.

Table pitfalls

A few problems can crop up as a result of your use of tables in a Web page. First of all, the early generations of Web browsers, such as Mosaic, may not interpret the table properly. This is much less of a concern now, because people using such an old browser have more to worry about than not being able to view your site.

The other, more significant problem that you may encounter involves the width of your tables. If your table contains nothing but text, page width isn't a major concern because Web browsers automatically wrap text and shrink tables based on the size of the window. That is the beauty of HMTL, its flexible nature enabling it to be read across a wide variety of platforms.

But if you insert a number of graphics into the table, you can thwart the browser's ability to make it fit automatically. A couple of wide graphics placed side by side in cells of a table can easily cause the table to run off the screen. Even if the graphics are contained within the edges of your own screen, be mindful of the fact that many viewers have a smaller monitor than you do. Design your tables accordingly.

Working with Graphics

In Chapter 24 you learned how to insert graphics into a document, and how to control their size. You learned, for instance, that you can specify the width and height of a graphic using codes like `WIDTH="100" HEIGHT="80"`. This code tells the browser to display the graphic so that it is 100 pixels wide and 80 pixels tall.

Moving on to this chapter, you've also learned how you can control the alignment of text and graphics using tables. But in some cases this is not always the most desirable way to control alignment. For instance, suppose you are writing an article that includes a few pictures for illustration. You may want the text to flow smoothly around the pictures as they appear throughout the article, but doing this with tables is tricky and causes almost as many problems as it solves.

The better solution is to specify an alignment for a picture within a paragraph. You do this by adding the `ALIGN` attribute to the image tag. So, if you align a graphic on the right side of the page, text will wrap around the left side of the image as shown in Figure 25-5. The tag looks something like this:

```
<P><IMG SRC="trees.jpg" WIDTH="200" ALIGN="RIGHT">This image
has been...</P>
```

This exact tag is used in the HTML file shown in Figure 25-5. Notice that we have specified a width for the graphic, even though it is not important to the alignment issue we are discussing here.

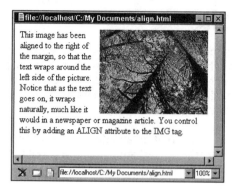

Figure 25-5: The picture in this HTML document has been aligned so that the text wraps around it.

Using the `ALIGN` attribute, you can align a picture at the right or left side of a paragraph. In some cases, the graphic may be big enough that it actually causes subsequent paragraphs to flow around it as well, as shown in Figure 25-6.

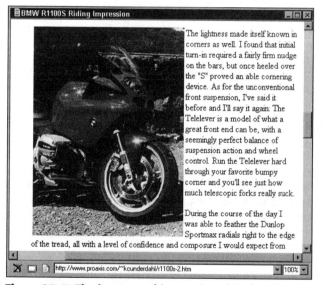

Figure 25-6: The image on this page is so big that the subsequent paragraph must wrap around it as well.

Tip   Sometimes you may notice that the wrapping text is too close to the image. If this is a problem, add some padding between the words and image by adding the attribute `HSPACE="3"` to the image's tag. This inserts three pixels of space along the horizontal edge of the graphic.

Tracking Visits To Your Site

Professional Webmasters could write volumes about methods of and uses for tracking how many people visit a given Web page, who they are, where else they've been, how often they return, and a grocery list of other items that can be gathered every time a Web user surfs to your site. Why collect all this information? "Marketing!" is the obvious answer, but if you're not selling anything why should you care?

Well, maybe you don't. But even if you are only creating an informal Web site for sharing pictures and information with your friends and family, you're probably more than a little interested to see how many people visit your site. You can do this fairly easily, with a simple hit counter.

Setting up a hit counter

The first step to popularizing your site is to make sure you can measure the results of your efforts. You'll need a hit counter and a guest book. A hit counter counts the number of times your site is visited. In its simplest form, it's a small row of numbers that increases each time someone logs on to your site. The most simple hit counter records the same value whether 20 people visit your site or if the same person visits 20 times. The reason why this segment is not called "Creating a Hit Counter" is because most often you merely borrow a hit counter from a company, an advertiser with an agenda of its own, or someone who offers advanced Web services at a price and is willing to provide a free hit counter simply to get you in the door.

Linking, not downloading

Figure 25-7 shows examples of free counters from the Beseen Web site (http://www.beseen.com/), and, because every counter available from their site also happens to display their name, they get something tangible out of the arrangement as well. (Clicking the counter takes you to their page. BeSeen also offers free services such as putting a chat room or message board on your Web page. These are paid for by advertisers who put their banner ads on your screen while the chat room or message board is being used.)

To use these Web counter examples, just select the counter you want to use and complete the registration information. The necessary HTML code for the counter is e-mailed to you, and all you need to do is copy and paste the code into your HTML document. The code links to a graphic and a script that resides on their server, which means you don't need to download a picture from their site or copy the CGI code.

Registering for a hit counter

One nice way to set up a counter is to use FastCounter (http://www.bcentral.com/fastcounter/). You can register for this service in a short time, and they merely ask that you place a link to FastCounter (a Microsoft product) on your home page. The FastCounter Web page offers free counters and it's connected with Link Exchange, which is one of the most helpful all-purpose Web promotion sites around.

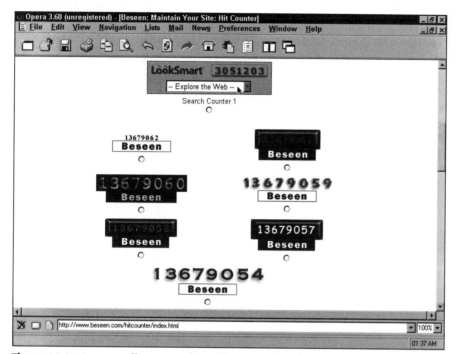

Figure 25-7: Beseen offers a number of free counters that you can use on your Web site.

On the FastCounter page, you specify a password for unlocking your counter's statistics, pick a counter type, choose a starting number, and specify how often you want the Web statistics e-mailed to you. After signing up, you receive an e-mail message with the HTML code for the link you must place on the page as part of your agreement. Figure 25-8 shows the HTML you copy to your document, with its reference to both the CGI that controls the counter as well as the graphic.

Counter caveats

Sometimes using a hit counter hosted on another server can slow down your own page's performance. If many other people are accessing this server at the same time, your page can be slow to load. Also, if the server decides to quit the business or changes their URL, your hit counter stops working.

One other point to consider when using a hit counter is that the information given might not be all that flattering. To have the world know that only 26 people have logged on to your Web site might be counterproductive, especially if you are hoping to sell advertising.

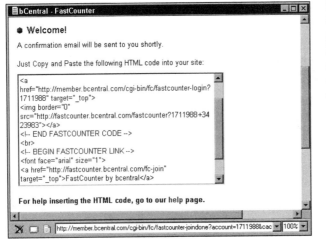

Figure 25-8: FastCounter will provide you the HTML code you will copy to set up a counter on your own site.

Tip   If your counter shows that your page has only been visited 26 times, you have to ask yourself how many of those hits were from you. If you don't want your own visits skewing the statistics, disable page hit counting in your Web browser. In Internet Explorer you can find this option on the Advanced tab of the Internet Options dialog box; alas, Navigator and Opera do not enable you to disable this function.

Installing a Guest Book

One other way to track your Web site's visitors is to install a guest book. A guest book enables people to let you know they dropped by. A good guest book helps visitors remember your site. A guest book is a form which people can use to give you feedback on what they think of your site. Most guest books also have a feature that enables other visitors to see the comments and names left at your site. Most guest books are CGI-driven as well and require some sort of cooperation from your ISP. Many ISPs provide you with instructions for installing one, as long as you do it their way, and don't try to install your own CGI-bin folder. You can also find Java-driven guest book software online.

Creating your own guest book

Check with your ISP to see if they offer a guest book as part of their package of Web development tools available to members. Chances are, if they offer Web server space for your Web pages, they also have a guest book function. The exact steps will vary depending on the provider, because when you set up the guest book you will actually be using CGI scripts and other tools that reside on their server.

What is CGI?

CGI stands for *Common Gateway Interface*, a standard for programs that are used on Web servers to transfer information between the server and a user. CGI programs are written in a variety of programming languages, including Java, Perl, C, and others.

CGI programs — also called *scripts* — have many uses. For example, CGI scripts may be used to collect customer feedback, take online orders, or conduct surveys. Web servers usually have a specific directory in which they hold CGI programs used by Web sites on that server, and that directory is almost always called *cgi-bin*.

Generally speaking, if you want to create your own CGI programs to be used with your Web site, you will have to make special arrangements with the host of the Web server that you use. More likely, you will want to take advantage of some of the CGI programs that are already available for your use. Contact your server host (probably your ISP) to see what kind of CGI programs are available.

If the ISP or Web server offers a guest book feature, it will usually require you to give your guest book page a specific name, such as `guest.html`. You may have to enter a set of specific commands, which may begin with a line like this:

```
<form method=POST action="/cgi-bin/guest.cgi">
```

This HTML tag tells the browser that this is the beginning of a form command. A form is a specific type feature used in HTML, like a table or heading. The `action` in this code refers to a `guest.cgi` script in the server's cgi-bin directory. The name and path for the script must be provided by the Web server.

Note CGI commands on Web servers are usually case-sensitive, so make sure that you type all HTML tags in the appropriate case as specified by the server.

Next you will be asked to input a few lines of code that ask for specific input from the reader. The syntax and names of these tags will vary depending on the server. Figure 25-9 shows the code required to create a guest book on the Web server of our ISP, ProAxis (`www.proaxis.com`).

Notice that we ask several questions in the form portion of the page, such as "Who are you?" and "Your E-mail address:". Each is followed by a tag that refers to a specific type of form `input` — in this case `text`, because the readers will by typing words — a value name, and a `size` for the text box that will be used. The `name` of each value is set by the Web server, but we can adjust the `size` of each box all we want.

At the end of the form you see the following tag:

```
<input type=submit>
```

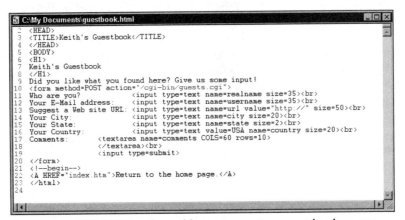

Figure 25-9: This HTML code enables us to create a guest book on our Web server.

This tag tells the server to insert the Submit button, which users can click when they're done filling out the guest book. The form is then closed (`</form>`) and a tag is inserted to tell the server to begin inserting user inputs (`<!--begin-->`). This is a standard HTML tag, and should be identical with virtually all CGI-based guest books. Every time someone fills out the form and clicks Submit, the things they typed will be added where the `<!--begin-->` tag sits. The end result, once published on the server, should look like Figure 25-10.

As you can see, it's pretty simple. Just make sure that you check with your ISP (or whoever hosts your Web site) to obtain the following pieces of information:

✦ Is a CGI script for a guest book available? If so, what is the path to that script?

✦ What should the filename of the guest book be? Where should the file be stored?

✦ What are the names of the form fields that can be used?

Finding more guest books on the Web

If your Web server does not provide CGI-scripts for a guest book, fret not. Numerous sites across the Web host free guest book features that you can link to from your own Web site. This means that when someone clicks the link for your guest book, their input will be recorded by the server of the Web site that hosts your guest book.

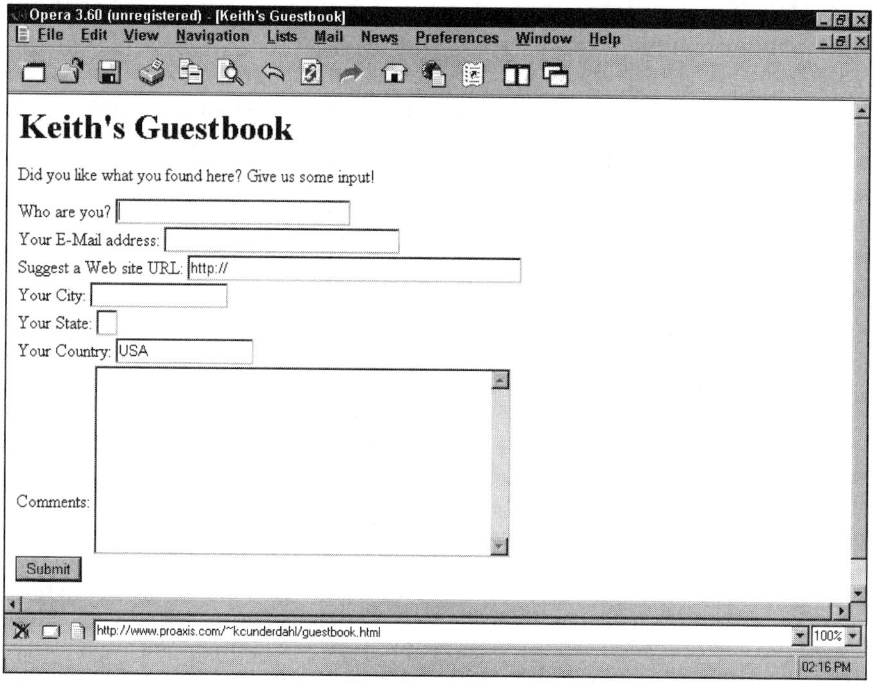

Figure 25-10: This guest book resulted from the HTML code shown in Figure 25-9.

Most of the guest books are free, supported by advertising banners that (surprise) appear on your guest book when people read it. As with free Web servers, free e-mail, and other "free" services around the 'net, you will have to decide if accepting advertising is worth having the use of free guest book space.

Here is a list of a few sites that offer free guest books:

✦ **Guestbook4free.com.** (http://www.guestbook4free.com/) This site offers free guest books, and can be configured to send you an e-mail every time someone signs your guest book. You can also set up a ratings form that enables viewers to vote on a topic you choose. Elvis or The Beatles? Mary Ann or Ginger? Faith or good works? U.S.S. Enterprise or Battlestar Gallactica? Whatever you want to feature, giving your readers a chance to ponder one of life's great questions certainly adds a fascinating element to your guest book.

✦ **Guestcities.** (http://www.guestcities.com/) The free guest books offered by Guestcities enables you to block certain kinds of content from your guest book, such as HTML code or offensive language.

✦ **GlobalGuest.** (`http://globalguest.com/`) Free guest books here can be customized with colorful wallpaper; you can add MIDI music to the guest book and take advantage of longer guest books pages.

✦ **GuestWorld.** (`http://www.guestworld.com/`) Owned by Lycos (of search engine fame), GuestWorld offers you a customizable look and e-mail notification whenever a visitor signs the guest book. You can also filter out objectionable images, language, and unwanted html that unsavory visitors might enter.

Creating an Anchor

In Chapter 24, "Doing Basic Web Design," you learned how to create hyperlinks using the `A HREF=` tag. You can use hyperlinks to jump to other Web sites, or to other pages within your site. But did you know that you can also link to other locations within the same Web page? Yes! You can!

Imagine that this book, *Internet Bible*, is a Web site. Each chapter—including this one—is a separate page in the site. If we refer you to a discussion of hyperlinks in Chapter 24, we may link that text so that if you click on it, you jump instantly to Chapter 24. But what if we refer to another section in that chapter? For instance, if we ask you to consider what was said in the section "Publishing Your Web Site," it would make sense to provide a hyperlink that enables you to jump back to that section.

But how do we tell the browser to refer the reader to a specific portion of this chapter? Take a look at this hyperlink:

```
<A HREF="http://www.idgbooks.com/IB/chapter25.html"> See "Using
Tables on a Web Page" earlier in this chapter.</A>
```

If you click on this link, it would simply return you to the top of the page. The problem, as you can see, is that you need to be able to specify locations within HTML documents, rather than just identify the files themselves. You do this by creating *anchors* at specific locations in HTML documents. You can then create a hyperlink that points to that anchor. An anchor looks like this:

```
<A NAME="tables"></A>
```

You add this tag at the location in the document where you want to create the anchor. So in the case of our mock `chapter25.html`, we would put this anchor at or near the heading for the section that described tables. You can place as many anchors throughout your HTML documents as you wish, but each one must have a unique name.

Caution Don't forget to include the closing </A> tag when you insert an anchor in an HTML document. This element is important, even though you will normally insert it immediately after the opening tag.

To link to the anchor shown previously, we would type this:

```
<A HREF="#tables"> See "Using Tables in a Web Page" earlier in
this chapter.</A>
```

We simply place the name of the anchor (preceded by the # symbol) in the HREF tag where the target is identified. Because this link points to an anchor in the same HTML file, thus making it an *internal link*, a filename is not necessary. But if we link to that location from another file, the tag would read:

```
<A HREF="http://www.idgbooks.com/IB/chapter25.html#tables">
See "Using Tables in a Web Page" in chapter 25.</A>
```

Although this example shows that you can link to anchors using external links, this is usually not very safe. Why? Web pages change frequently, and you may not remember to update all links if an anchor is changed or deleted. The most common use of anchors is to facilitate internal links within a single Web page.

Note We use the term *anchor* here, but they are also sometimes called *bookmarks* or *jump points*. Whatever the name, the function remains the same.

Using Meta Tags to Promote Your Site

When you view the source code of a commercially developed Web page, you'll notice that there are a lot of tags that we have not yet described here. Visit various Web sites and use the View ➪ Source feature in your Web browser to see what we mean.

One general category of tags that you will see near the top of many sites are <META> tags. Meta tags provide various bits of information that usually don't directly affect the way a page is displayed in the browser. *Meta data*, the information included in Meta tags, often provides information to search engines and other Web sites about what kind of Web page you have.

For instance, if you are creating a Web site for your bird club, you can include words like bird, birds, parrot, finch, sparrow, birdcages, and such in a Meta tag. These words near the beginning of the HTML document serve as flags to search engines, and your page will get a higher rating when someone does a Web search using one or more of those words. You include words like this in a *keyword* Meta tag that looks something like this:

```
<META NAME="keywords" CONTENT="bird, birds, parrot, finch,
sparrow, birdcages">
```

Another type of Meta tag used by many search engines is a *description* tag. Many search engines look for a description Meta tag, and will display it with the search results. A good description tag might look like this:

```
<META NAME="description" CONTENT="The Official Bird Club of the
Umpqua River Valley">
```

These tags should appear in the header area of an HTML file (that is, between the `<head>` and `</head>` tags, the same place the title is entered). For best results, make the keyword Meta tag the first one, placing it directly below the Web page title. Type as many keywords as you wish, and try to think of words that people might search on if they are interested in a site like yours. Put it all together, and the header of your bird club page might look like this:

```
<HTML><HEAD><TITLE>UMPQUA BIRD CLUB ONLINE</TITLE>
<META NAME="keywords" CONTENT="bird, birds, parrot, finch,
sparrow, birdcages">
<META NAME="description" CONTENT="The Official Bird Club of the
Umpqua River Valley"></HEAD>
```

These simple tags take only a few minutes to create, but will have a significant impact on the number of people who visit your site. If you are interested in attracting more visitors to your site, this is the easiest, cheapest, and quickest way to do it.

Adding a Search Engine to Your Web Page

Some search engines let you place code on your own Web page that links to their engine. This is usually done with a banner and HTML code that they provide through an affiliate program. Having a search engine on your site can add an extra level of functionality to your Web pages, particularly if you have a page that consists of nothing but links anyway.

In addition to search engines, some online retailers also enable you to place banners on your site that search the retailer's database for various products. Barnes & Noble (`www.barnesandnoble.com`), for instance, enables you to place a banner on your site where your viewers can quickly search for books, music, software, or any other product that Barnes & Noble sells. If someone buys an item through the link on your site, you receive a payment equal to five to seven percent (depending on the product) of the purchase price.

Caution   Many search engines and online retailers welcome the opportunity to spread their fame, and would have no problem with you adding them to your page. But you should check the site's policy on this matter before you copy or link to anything.

Using a corporate search engine

In the case of Barnes & Noble, you have many options for linking to their site. For instance, you can create a list of specific books, create links to various sections of the Barnes & Noble site, or just provide a general link. They also offer a variety of banners that you can use.

Every site that enables you to place search engines and links on your Web pages has a specific procedure you must follow, but for the sake of example we'll take you through the process with Barnes & Noble here. Follow these steps:

1. Visit the Barnes & Noble Web site (`www.barnesandnoble.com`) and click the link called Affiliate Network, which can be found under bn.com Services.

2. On the page that describes the affiliate program, click the "Join Now" button, and complete the application form that appears. You must be prepared to provide accurate information about yourself, including your address and phone number.

3. When you have submitted your application, you should receive an automatic confirmation via e-mail very quickly.

4. Click the link to visit affiliate.net (`http://www.affiliate.net/affnet/`). This is the site that provides the actual instructions you must follow to set up the link. A "Getting Started" link helps get you, well, started. Follow the instructions to create links from your site to Barnes & Noble.

Based on the type of link you choose to create, the site will give you specific instructions for adding the link to your own pages. Eventually you should come to a button that says "Make my code" which you must click to generate the necessary HTML to add to your site. The code will be generated, and you can copy and paste it into your HTML documents. The end result should look similar to Figure 25-11.

Checking your links frequently

Now a problem could arise with your search engine should the document you are referring to (in this case, the Barnes and Noble page) become altered in some way. Perhaps the Web administrator or page designer has rearranged the Web site, and the URL you are calling up in your site is no longer valid. That's why, if you power your own site by referencing many sources outside it, you must take extra care to check your links frequently.

When someone clicks this link and buys a book, we earn money

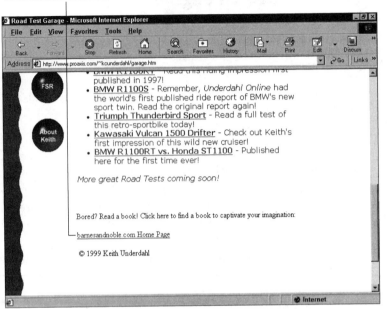

Figure 25-11: A Barnes and Noble search engine has been added to this Web page.

Summary

As you build your HTML skills, you put yourself on the path to becoming a true Webmaster. This chapter showed you how to take better control of your Web pages with the use of frames and additional graphics tools. You also learned to add a few elements to make your pages more interesting, such as guest books and search engines. In the next chapter we'll cover even more advanced topics, like frames, forms, Java applets, and style sheets.

✦   ✦   ✦

Working with Advanced Web Page Components

How interested are you in designing Web sites? If you're like many users, you may quickly find (or have already found) that the cryptic skills required to program Web pages in HTML can become a new and exciting way to express your creativity. The previous two chapters have introduced you to some of the possibilities of HTML, but no matter how much you learn there will always be that question in the back of your mind: What else is there?

To some extent, this chapter tries to answer that question. No, you won't learn the meaning of life here, nor will you learn everything there is to know about publishing online. But you will learn how to use some of HTML's most advanced capabilities and how to do things that most nonprofessional Web site creators never even try. You'll learn how to divide your Web pages into separate frames, and you'll create your own forms. Then you will tackle Java, a programming language that enables your Web pages to execute commands on readers' computers, and we'll show you how to simplify a lot of your HTML with style sheets. Finally, we'll discuss how you can accommodate users with older Web browsers, enabling them to enjoy the complexities of your site rather than leaving them in the virtual dust.

Working with Frames

Frames enable you to separate a single Web page into several unique segments. In all of the pages you created in previous chapters, if you move down the screen the whole page scrolls up. But what if you have organized a row of buttons along one side of the screen that you want to keep in view at all times? Or, what if you have an advertisement banner across the top of the page that you want to remain in view even as the user scrolls down? By separating the browser window into separate sections, frames enable you to do these things.

Before you start slicing up your Web pages into frames, you should be aware of some drawbacks. Frames were controversial right from the start because older Web browsers don't support them. Most people now use a browser that supports frames, but that hasn't made frames any more popular. For one thing, frames significantly slow down the speed of a Web site, and, because most people still use relatively slow dial-up connections, they often find that framed pages are unpleasant to view. Finally, every bit of screen space you consume with additional frames leaves less space for the actual content that your viewers want to see. Keep in mind that many viewers use small, 14- or 15-inch monitors, and most laptop monitors are even smaller.

Creating a page with frames

In spite of it all, frames can be useful. DaimlerChrysler's various Web pages, notably `www.chrysler.com` and `www.jeepunpaved.com` make effective use of frames with pages that are both easy to view and reasonably quick to load.

Try creating frames yourself by doing the following exercise, which will create a two-frame Web site.

Determining the Web page layout

Your first step to creating a Web page with frames is to determine what you want your page to look like. Consider the overall site, and decide if all of your content will work if you trim some of the main window off to create a frame along the left side, the top, or the bottom. Keep in mind that clicking a link in one frame can alter what the other frame displays. You can even get totally carried away and treat frame boundaries as if they were the outlines of each of your page's main components. Most often, though, two or three frames per page are sufficient. In this example, you'll create a two-frame frameset that will display two Web pages side by side: a table of contents (`Toc.htm`) and Welcome page (`Welcome.htm`).

Producing a frameset

The second step is to create your frameset. Almost every HTML editor has a Frame Wizard or some sort of help dialog for setting up frames. But if you're creating your HTML the "old fashioned" way, the code for a simple frame might look like this:

```
<HTML>
<HEAD>
<TITLE>My Framed Page</TITLE>
</HEAD>
<FRAMESET COLS="25%,75%">
    <FRAME SRC="TOC.htm" NAME="Side">
    <FRAME SRC="Welcome.htm" NAME="Main">
</FRAMESET>
</HTML>
```

The command `<FRAMESET COLS="25%,75%">` instructs the browser to create a frame based on columns (rather than rows), the first column taking up 25 percent of the screen, and the second column 75 percent. Notice that the `<FRAMESET>` tags appear after the `<HEAD>` for the HTML document, right where the `<BODY>` would normally go.

Creating the frames themselves

Nested inside the FRAMESET command are the commands that create the frames themselves. `<FRAME SRC="TOC.htm" NAME="Side">` creates a frame called *Side*, in which will be displayed a Web page called `Toc.htm`. The second frame, `<FRAME SRC="Welcome.htm" NAME="Main">`, will be named *Main* and will display a Web page called `Welcome.htm`. This is important because what we've created so far is not a Web page, but rather, a set of two frames in which Web pages will be placed.

Including the NOFRAMES command

At the bottom of a frameset page, you should include a `<NOFRAMES> </NOFRAMES>` tag. This is where you type text for people whose browsers cannot display frames. It's a good idea to create an alternate page for such visitors to your site. Text that you type in between the `<NOFRAMES>` tag will appear only in older frameless browsers, but will be ignored by others. When you're done, your NOFRAMES script should look something like this:

```
<NOFRAMES>
Your Browser does not support frames. Click <A
HREF="Normal.htm">here </A>for a frame-free page.
</NOFRAMES>
```

Saving your frameset and displaying the contents

This frameset just shown should be saved as an HTML document, (perhaps `Frameset.htm`) but if you open it in a browser, it will not display anything, until you create those two other Web pages (`Toc.htm` and `Welcome.htm`). If those two pages are present in the folder, then they'll be displayed when you load `Frameset.htm`, as shown in Figure 26-1.

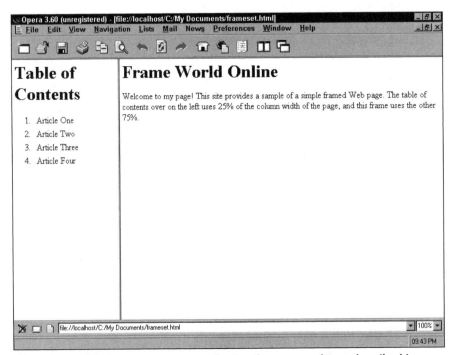

Figure 26-1: This frame set was created using the same code we described in this section.

When the user clicks the phrase *Article One*, we want that article to open in the main frame of the window. To do this, we need to employ the use of frame targets.

Creating frame targets

Targets are very useful when you want to link to pages located inside of frames. Take a look at the HTML of the Table of Contents Web page (`TOC.htm`), which is shown in Figure 26-1 on the left side of the screen. You'll see how frame targets are used to load an article into the main frame window:

```
<H1>Table of Contents</H1>
<OL><LI><A HREF="Article1.html" TARGET="Main">Article One</A>
<LI><A HREF="Article2.html" TARGET="Main">Article Two</A>
```

```
<LI><A HREF="Article3.html" TARGET="Main">Article Three</A>
<LI><A HREF="Article4.html" TARGET="Main">Article Four</A></OL>
```

First of all, we see that the phrase "Table of Contents" is displayed as a level-one heading (`<H1></H1>`). Then we see the command to create a numbered list (`<OL></OL>`, "ordered list"), and inside the list commands for each list item (`<LI></LI>`).

The phrase "Article One" is clickable (`<A HREF="Article1.html">`). Click it and it opens a Web page called *Article1.html*. But where does it open it? In a new window? No. It opens in the frame called *Main*, which we created earlier. The command `TARGET="Main"` when included as part of the `<A>` tag tells the browser to open this new Web page inside the frame, as shown in Figure 26-2. Remember that the code used in `Frameset.htm` that we described earlier assigned a name to each frame, and *Main* is the name we assigned to the main window.

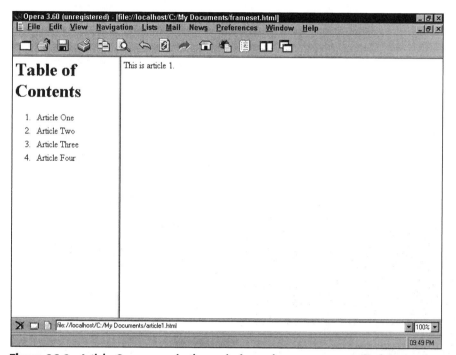

Figure 26-2: Article One opens in the main frame because we specified that action in the `<A>` tag.

When typing the `<A>`command, don't forget the quotation marks, or the closing `</A>` tag, which is easy to leave out if you're not careful. Also, `TARGET` names are case-sensitive. For example, if you've typed `TARGET="MAIN"` instead of `TARGET="Main"`, the page will not open in a frame. It will open in its own new browser window.

Remember, because every file used by the frameset is actually a separate HTML page, you can place any item in a frame page that you would in any other page. Just pay special attention to the layout; items that fit nicely on a normal Web page may be too large to fit inside a frame.

Using Forms

Including a form on your page enables visitors to give you feedback. You create "fields" in your forms. A form field can be a space where someone can type their name, a check box for specifying an option, or an area where someone can sound off for an entire paragraph or more. In fact, if you followed along with the section on adding a guest book to your Web site in Chapter 25, you've already created a simple form.

Forms can have many uses. Figure 26-3 shows the HotBot search engine, which includes a form for visitors to specify various options to customize their searches. As the Web page designer, you can decide what fields a form should include. If you've ever visited a Web site that asks for your e-mail address, the forms used in such cases are usually as simple as the type we are discussing here.

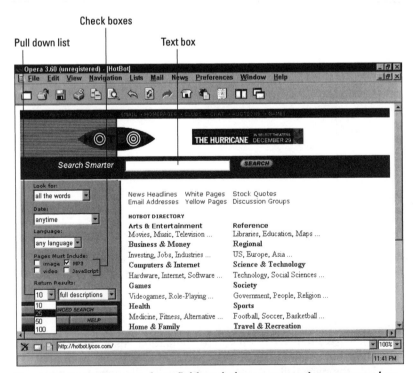

Figure 26-3: HotBot uses form fields to help you customize your searches by providing some choices on the left side of the screen.

Creating a form

First, let's talk about a form's necessary features. A form tag (`<FORM></FORM>`) must have a METHOD and an ACTION. These commands are part of the FORM tag and determine how the form will communicate with the server. For form METHOD, you will use the word POST or GET. The POST method tells your form to feed the server its information line by line. Unless directed otherwise by your ISP administrator, type POST, rather than GET.

In the ACTION area, type in the CGI (Common Gateway Interface) script that makes your form active. Without it, the form data will simply sit on the page. Your ISP will have specific guidelines about the type and location of CGI scripting allowed on their server. CGI is a universal way to execute programs on the Web. CGI scripts are written in computer languages such as C++ or Perl, and most Web site designers simply utilize an existing script, rather than create their own. Consider this line of HTML code from the guest book example we used in the previous chapter:

```
<form method=POST action="/cgi-bin/guests.cgi">
```

In the ACTION area, we are referring to an existing script, identifying its location. Referred to correctly, this CGI script is what powers your form. From this location, the CGI script brings your form to life, giving you the feedback your visitors provided. You need not write a script yourself, but its location on your server must be specified exactly in this ACTION area. To truly take advantage of the power of the CGI script you need to obtain instructions from your ISP administrator before finishing your form.

Understanding form fields

Between the `<FORM>` and `</FORM>` tags are the form fields. Each form field has a name, a few adjustable parameters, such as its maximum size, and the ability to specify if the field should either display some information or be blank. A form field might look something like this:

```
<INPUT type=text name="username" size=15>
```

The `<INPUT>` tag is used to show that input will be called for from the user. It does not require a closing tag, but you do have to specify the TYPE of input that is expected, a NAME for the input, and other attributes as necessary. In this example, because we are presenting a text box where users can type in information, we have specified that the form field where the username is will be entered should be 15 characters long. Input types include:

✦ **text** — The user types text into the field.

✦ **password** — The user types a password into the field, as is done in a text box, but to keep the password secure, the text appears as asterisks.

✦ **radio** — A user can click a button to select a single item from a list.

✦ **check box** — When the user clicks on the box, a check mark appears.

✦ **submit** — When the user clicks the submit button, the contents of the form are sent to the server.

✦ **reset** — When clicked by the user, the reset button clears the form.

✦ **file** — The user can select from a pull-down list of options.

After you specify the `type` of the form field, you must then specify a `name` for the CGI script that the field will use. The exceptions to this are the `submit` and `reset` data types, which do not require a CGI script to function. Finally, you may specify a value, size, or other variable depending on the `INPUT` type. For instance, in the case of a `text` or `password` input type, you can specify how big you want the text box to be by entering `size="30"`. This command will create a text box that is 30 characters long. If you don't specify a size, the default value is 20.

If the input type is a radio button or a check box, you will use a `value`. It might look like this:

```
Which artist/group do you prefer:
<form method=POST action="/cgi-bin/choose.cgi">
<P>
<INPUT type=radio name="band" value="Elvis"> Elvis<BR>
<INPUT type=radio name="band" value="Beatles"> The Beatles<BR>
</P>
</FORM>
```

This form asks people to vote on a preference, and it presents two radio buttons to facilitate the vote. `"Elvis"` is the value for the first radio button, and `"Beatles"` is the value of the second. As with any CGI-based form, this assumes that the CGI script `choose.cgi` understands those values and knows what to do with them. For instance, in this case we could assume that the field name `band` serves as a counter, and that is why we are using it here. You will have to obtain that information from whomever is providing the CGI scripts that you use.

Customizing your buttons

A form can include other elements such as drop-down menus, radio buttons, and *text areas*. But one final element you must never leave out of your form is the submit button. Most browsers know how to create a basic button, and you can specify what it will say using a `value`. For instance, if you want your submit button to say "Vote," you can simply write an input field like this:

```
<INPUT type=submit value="Vote">
```

In Figure 26-4, you can see we created a hypothetical form that uses `value="Vote"` for the submit button, and `value="Clear Form"` for the reset button.

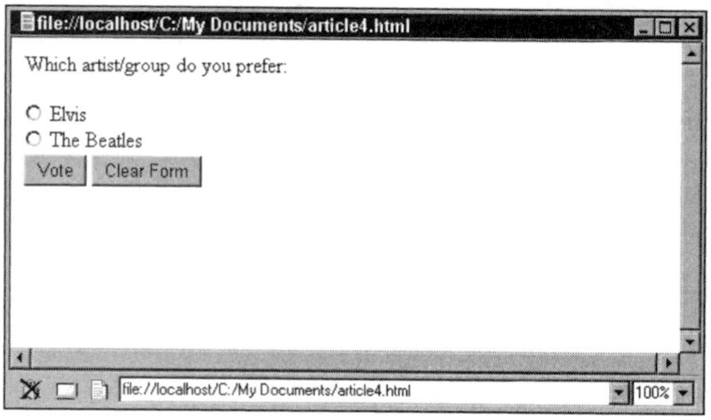

Figure 26-4: In this form, the wording used on the submit and reset buttons has been customized using a value tag.

While we're looking at this form, take a look at the overall layout. Here is the exact code used to create it:

```
<HTML>
<BODY>
Which artist/group do you prefer:
<form method=POST action="/cgi-bin/choose.cgi">
<P>
<INPUT type=radio name="band" value="Elvis"> Elvis<BR>
<INPUT type=radio name="band" value="Beatles"> The Beatles<BR>
<INPUT type=submit value="Vote"> <INPUT type=reset value="Clear
Form">
</P>
</FORM>
</BODY>
</HTML>
```

Notice that Elvis and The Beatles are on separate lines. This is because, as you can see in the code, they are separated by a line break tag (<BR>). Another <BR> tag separates the choices from the buttons at the bottom of the form. But the "Vote" and "Clear Form" buttons are on the same line, separated only by a space. Can you think of ways to improve the layout of this form? Try this:

✦ Place an additional <BR> or <P> between the second radio button and the submit buttons so that there is more space.

✦ Place the entire form in the cell of an invisible table, and then give that cell a different background color. You can do that by placing a bgcolor tag in the <TD> tag at the beginning of that cell. For instance, if you wanted to color the cell silver, the tag would be <td bgcolor="#C0C0C0"> You can replace the hexadecimal color value with another value if you wish. This will make the form look separate from the rest of the screen's content.

✦ Make the words "Elvis" and "The Beatles" hyperlinked to other pages that contain more information about the item. That way, if someone isn't exactly sure who Elvis is (maybe they think you mean Elvis Presley rather than Elvis Costello), they can click on the name to get clarification.

CGI-free forms

Neatly arranging the form elements around your page is only half the battle. The form has to deliver your information. As mentioned earlier, using a CGI script to deliver and organize data from your form can be complex and requires the cooperation of your ISP administrator. If you want to create forms and have no taste for such intricacy, you have three other choices available. You can create a form with the following:

✦ An automatic e-mail response

✦ A Java applet

✦ A Web design product with special technology for activating forms and databases

Each of these options is discussed in the sections that follow.

Creating an e-mail form

You can specify that data from your form be sent to you as a simple e-mail message. The data would not be in a table or categorized. Rather, the results would appear as plain text in the body of an e-mail message sent to you after a visitor filled out your form and pressed Submit. To create a simple e-mail-based form, for the ACTION attribute, type mailto: followed by your e-mail address. Unfortunately, some older Web browsers don't support this method of retrieving form data. The HTML for a form submitted via e-mail might look like this:

```
Which artist/group do you prefer:
<form method=POST action="mailto:keith@idgbooks.com">
<P>
<INPUT type=radio name="band" value="Elvis"> Elvis<BR>
<INPUT type=radio name="band" value="Beatles"> The Beatles<BR>
<INPUT type=submit value="Vote"> <INPUT type=reset value="Clear
Form">
</P>
</FORM>
```

When users click Submit, their e-mail program will automatically launch and, without any other interaction on their part, the results of their submission are e-mailed to you as an attachment. In the case of the previous form, if someone votes for Elvis, the e-mail attachment you receive will contain the following text in the body:

```
band=Elvis
```

Creating a Java applet form

Another method for creating a form on your page without using a CGI script is to create a form with a Java applet. Web designers use Java applets to create programs that can be run on the Web. In the case of creating a form, you could use a Java applet to compile and submit data to you, rather than employing a CGI script. Java-run forms can take a while to load, and, of course, not every Web browser supports Java. Nonetheless, a growing number of Web sites include Java-based forms. More about adding Java elements to your Web page is discussed later in this chapter.

Creating a form with Q & D's WebForms

Q & D Software offers a program called WebForms, downloadable at `http://www.q-d.com`. WebForms helps you create both CGI and non-CGI based forms. If you choose to create a non-CGI form, the results of each submission are e-mailed to you as an attachment that can then be processed with the WebForms Response Reader. The WebForms Forms Generator provides a list of tabs with information for you to enter. When you are done with all of the tabs, go to the Completion tab and click Complete. If there is any additional information you must enter, a dialog box will tell you what still needs to be done.

The program is fairly straightforward, as long as you have a basic understanding of how forms work. Fortunately, you've been reading along up until now (you have been, right?), so it should go quickly. If everything is okay when you click Complete, the program generates an HTML file. It is a 16-bit application, so take note of the fact that it assigns the extension `.htm` to the file rather than `.html`. The generated HTML file can then be transferred to your Web server. Figure 26-5 shows a form that was created by WebForms.

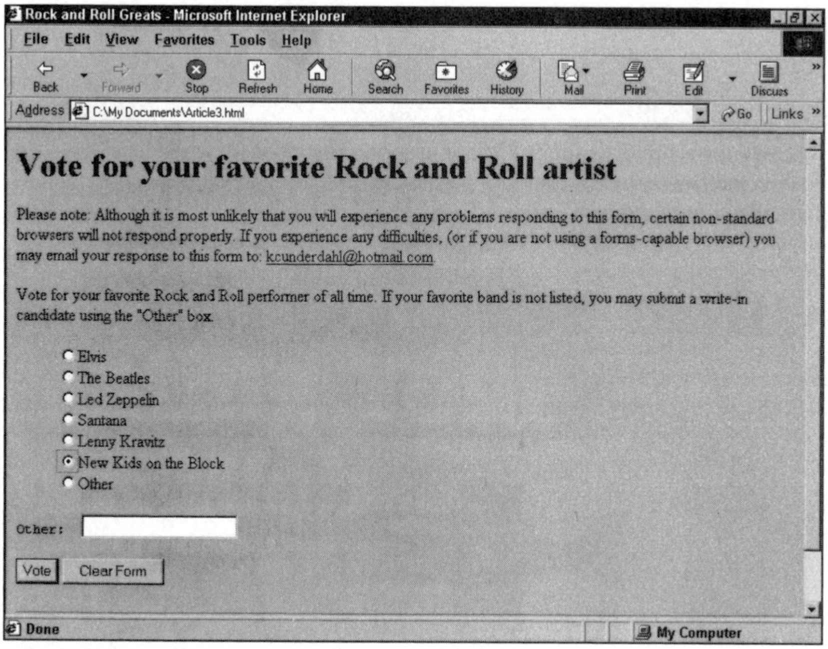

Figure 26-5: This form was created using WebForms.

When a user submits a response to the form you created, it is e-mailed to you as an attachment (the body of the e-mail will be blank). Save this attachment to disk as a text file, and then import it into WebForm's Response Reader using the File ⇨ Responses ⇨ Import menu command. Figure 26-6 shows a display of some of our voting results after we clicked the View Responses button in WebForms.

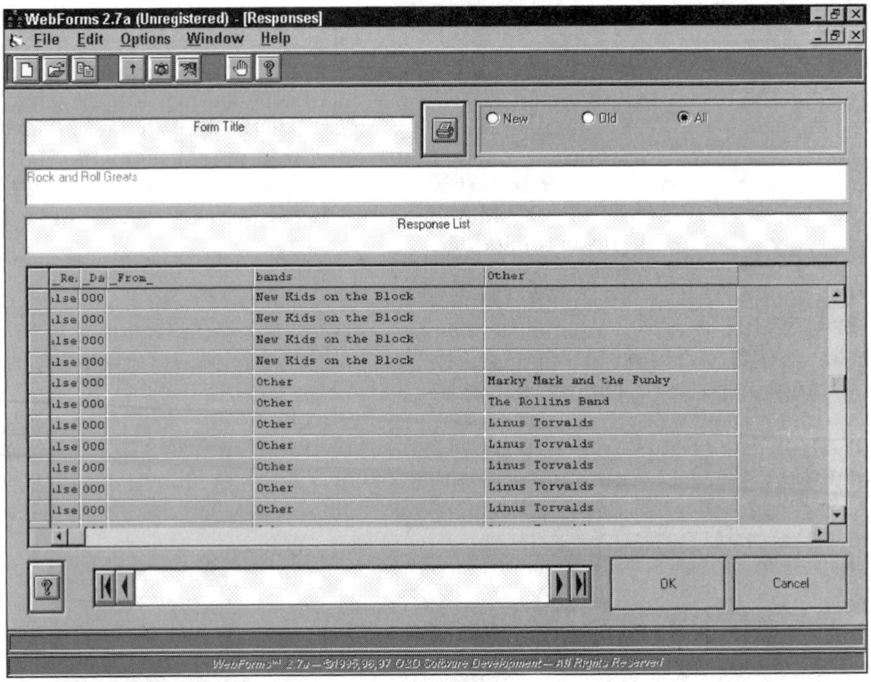

Figure 26-6: WebForm's Response Reader reports responses to your form. If you allow Internet users to vote in a poll you create, be prepared for some unconventional responses.

Adding Java Elements to Your Site

This section covers some basics about Java. We discuss the difference between the Java language and JavaScript, and explain how you can use Java applets to enhance your pages. For those who want to dig deeper, we point the way to excellent tutorials and source material on the topic.

What is Java?

Java is a computer language that frees Web designers from having to create complex CGI scripts, the type of scripting that requires lots of cooperation from your Web server. Its uniqueness lies in the fact that you can create programs by dragging objects around your screen rather than writing complex code "by hand," so to speak. Java is similar to, though less complicated than the popular and powerful standard language, C++. Java enables programmers to create small stand-alone programs that can be incorporated easily into a Web page. These programs can be extremely simple, such as on-screen animations or mouse rollover effects. Java can also create forms and work with complex databases, without requiring the form designer to know how to program.

Finally, the greatest strength of Java is its cross-platform capability. Java scripts can run on virtually any type of computer in use today, including those running Macintosh, Linux, UNIX, and Windows. And the relative simplicity of Java makes it ideally suited for use on the Web.

Using Java applets

You can work with Java applets simply by knowing how to insert them into a Web page. Most often, the way to get started is simply a matter of specifying parameters for an applet creator, who will build the program you'd like to include on your page. The applet creator makes an HTML document for you to copy and edit further. You then copy the contents of that HTML document to your own Web page, thereby copying any source files included with the applet to your Web page directory.

Most Web design software enables you to insert Java applets easily. Java applets are created to enable you to alter them somewhat, whether you want to create a border around the entire Java applet, adjust the speed of a text animation, or determine what text the Java applet should work with. You can adjust the parameters of a Java applet by viewing the document's HTML source code and simply typing in new values. This can be done in any text or HTML editor. Or you can use any one of the dozens of friendly applet creation tools that simply prompt you for changes you want to make (Do you want the animation to blink? Spin around? How long should your cartoon remain on the screen?), and then the program will do the math for you.

What can you create with Java?

One ought not think that Java is only fit for creating cartoons on Web pages. It can run corporate-sized databases, updating information quickly and making changes available on a corporate intranet or to the WWW at large. You can also design Java-based hit counters and guest books, music tools, and slide show programs. The advantage to Java programming is the fact that your product will run on virtually any system.

Whose Java?

Controversy arises because the Java language and related, supportive software are actually proprietary products of Sun Microsystems. Some Web designers hesitate to push Java to its limits because incorporating so much of one company's technology into your work makes you rather dependent on the marketing and business decisions of that company. Netscape developed JavaScript a few years ago, not as a challenge to Java, but to create a link between existing technology and the new standards. Microsoft has offered it's own implementation called Jscript. Because the Java language creates platform-independent Web pages and page components, Microsoft originally saw Java code as a threat to its hegemony. But Java is now fully supported by Internet Explorer 5, so apparently Microsoft has chosen to accept change rather than resist it.

Running Java applets

For Java applets to run, the visitor must have a Java-powered browser. Most Java applets will not run in Navigator or Internet Explorer Versions 2 or older, nor will they run in Opera as delivered. However, you can download Sun's Java plug-in for Netscape to enable Java in Opera. Visit the Opera Software home page (www.opera.com) and click the plug-ins link to learn more.

In this book, we limit ourselves to looking at software that facilitates the quick creation of Java applets, and how to adjust them and make them work for you. Except to point the way towards some marvelous tutorials on the subject, we don't delve into the specifics of Java code, other than to recognize and work with the Applet tag and some other basics. As with HTML, if you understand a little of how a Java applet looks in code, you can recognize and correct simple problems of syntax and such.

Creating Java applets

Applet builders help you create online slide shows and multimedia presentations. For example, McWeb Software's (www.mcwebsoftware.com) J-Perk creates a variety of special effects for your Web pages, utilizing Java code to implement the effects. You can use J-Perk to create slide shows with a series of images, buttons that change when the mouse hovers over them, animations, and more. You can find J-Perk and many similar Java creation utilities at popular software Web sites such as ZDNet (www.zdnet.com) and Tucows (www.tucows.com).

J-Perk provides a variety of wizards that vary depending on the type of Java applet you are trying to create. In Figure 26-7 you see the wizard that helps you create animations and slideshows.

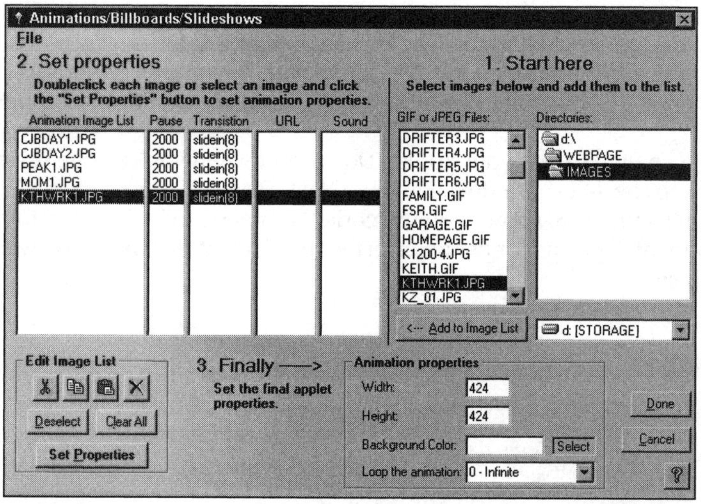

Figure 26-7: J-Perk makes it easy to create slideshows with your image collections.

Here we are creating a slideshow using five different pictures. Each image is listed here, and we can change various aspects of the images by selecting each and clicking Set Properties. The wizard enables us to customize various aspects of the slideshow, including:

✦ **Image order.** Click and drag items up and down in the Image List to change the order in which they will be displayed.

✦ **Pause.** Set the length of the delay between images. J-Perks expresses the delay in milliseconds.

✦ **Transition.** Specify a way in which images appear or disappear on the screen. For example, the images can slide in from the side, scroll up from the bottom, shrink into nothing, and so on.

✦ **URL.** You can create a hyperlink to a different URL for each image. For example, if you create a slideshow that features various products, you can link the product images to pages that contain information about the products.

✦ **Sound.** If you want a particular sound file to play with a specific image you can also specify that here.

Finally, you need to review any other available options for the applet. You should specify the size, for instance, as well as a background color and an option for how many times the animation should be looped. The background color is important because some images may not fill the entire applet window, and this is the color that will show in the uncovered space. If you want the slideshow to continue looping forever, choose *infinite* for the looping option.

When you are done, click Done. You should see a message that tells you which files you will need for the applet to run properly. Make a note of what this window tells you; if you don't copy the appropriate `.class` files along with the images, sounds, HTML files, and whatever else is associated with the applet, it simply won't work properly.

Next you'll have a chance to test your applet. Do so, and when you're done reviewing it switch back to the J-Perk window and click Next. Step 2 of the Preview Wizard, which is shown in Figure 26-8, shows you the code that needs to be inserted into your HTML document. The code must be inserted in the location where you want the applet to appear.

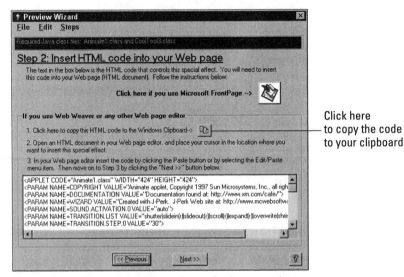

Click here to copy the code to your clipboard

Figure 26-8: This screen shows the code that must be copied into your HTML document.

Finding Applets Around the Web

Many sources online offer free applets that you can download and use. These usually consist of the necessary `.class` files, as well as some sample HTML files that contain all of the code that you will need. One of these is CodeBrain.com (`http://www.codebrain.com/`). CodeBrain offers many such sample applets, and when you download one it will generally come as a fully functional Web page, including HTML files, `.class` files, and any other required sample files, including images and sounds.

To use these for your own purposes, simply open the HTML file in a text editor and replace targets and any other information to make it suit your needs. Then, simply copy the part of the HTML that actually controls the Java applet into your own HTML pages, and voila!, instant Java. If you're not sure what to look for in a Java applet's associated HTML, read on.

In Step 3 of the wizard you "publish" all required files to your local hard drive. When you are done, you will have to copy the appropriate `.class` files into the folder where your Web page files are stored if you want to test it on your local computer. On our Windows system we were able to copy the required files — in this case `Animate1.class` and `CoolTool3.class` from the folder `C:\Program Files\J-Perk 5.01`.

Fine tuning your applets

Whether you create your Java applets with J-Perk, another applet creator, or obtain a free applet from somewhere on the Web, chances are you will want to fine-tune the HTML a bit. For instance, when we created our slideshow in J-Perk, we simply picked a bunch of images from our hard drive, but the path we specified isn't necessarily the same path that the applet will encounter on the Web. Consider this code from the HTML that J-Perk generated, and that we copied into our HTML file:

```
<PARAM NAME=IMAGE.0 VALUE="CJBDAY1.JPG">
<PARAM NAME=IMAGE.1 VALUE="CJBDAY2.JPG">
<PARAM NAME=IMAGE.2 VALUE="PEAK1.JPG">
<PARAM NAME=IMAGE.3 VALUE="MOM1.JPG">
<PARAM NAME=IMAGE.4 VALUE="KTHWRK1.JPG">
```

These five lines identify the images that will be used by the slideshow, but if we publish this on our Web server right now it won't work. Why? We store our graphics in a subfolder called *images*, and most HTML files remain in the root directory. This code will look for the images in the root directory, but won't find them. Thus, we need to modify this code to show the correct path to the images. Furthermore, our Web server specifies case-sensitive file names, so we need to double-check that the cases of the file names shown are correct.

The corrected code looks like this:

```
<PARAM NAME=IMAGE.0 VALUE="images/Cjbday1.jpg">
<PARAM NAME=IMAGE.1 VALUE="images/Cjbday2.jpg">
<PARAM NAME=IMAGE.2 VALUE="images/Peak1.jpg">
<PARAM NAME=IMAGE.3 VALUE="images/Mom1.jpg">
<PARAM NAME=IMAGE.4 VALUE="images/Kthwrk1.jpg">
```

Now let's look at some more code from the applet's HTML:

```
<PARAM NAME=PAUSE.0 VALUE="2000">
<PARAM NAME=PAUSE.1 VALUE="2000">
<PARAM NAME=PAUSE.2 VALUE="2000">
<PARAM NAME=PAUSE.3 VALUE="2000">
<PARAM NAME=PAUSE.4 VALUE="2000">
```

Here you can see some parameters listed for each image in the slideshow. We can tell that each parameter corresponds to a specific image because of the number listed after the decimal in each parameter name. So, the parameter PAUSE.2 applies to IMAGE.2, which we know is called Peak1.jpg. This parameter obviously applies to the pause between each image, and Java applets use milliseconds as their standard unit for time measurement. Because there are 1,000 milliseconds in a second, we can see that each image will display for two seconds before the next one replaces it. If you want to change the interval, modify the value shown here. And remember, there is no rule that says each image in a slideshow has to be displayed for the same amount of time!

Take a look at the code for the applet itself:

```
<APPLET CODE="Animate1.class" WIDTH="424" HEIGHT="424">
```

The CODE item in the <APPLET> tag should correspond to a .class file that you copied to your Web server. Here again, notice the path. If you place the .class files in a separate folder, correct the path of the CODE shown here. You can also usually modify attributes of the applet, such as the WIDTH and HEIGHT attributes shown here. Measures of size for Java applets are expressed in pixels.

And, of course, the applet should close with the </APPLET> tag. All of the code surrounded by the <APPLET> and </APPLET> tags should pertain only to the applet, so be sure not to enter any other code into that space.

Working with free cut-and-paste applets

As we mentioned, you can find many applets online that are of the cut-and-paste variety. Basically, you download an HTML file or two, maybe some sample images, and some .class files. Usually you will get all of these files in a ZIP archive or something similar. These applets are usually very small, which means you will spend more time melding them to fit your needs than you will waiting for a download.

CodeBrain.com (www.codebrain.com) is one of the best places to find free Java applets, including the fireplace applet shown in Figure 26-9. The download of the kit for this applet was just 34K.

After you download the applet, you will probably have to decompress it with a program such as WinZip for Windows, or Stuffit Expander or UnZip for Macs. To ensure you don't lose any of the components, create a new folder specifically for the applet files and extract them to that location. Then open the HTML file in a text editor. Figure 26-10 shows the HTML code for the fireplace applet.

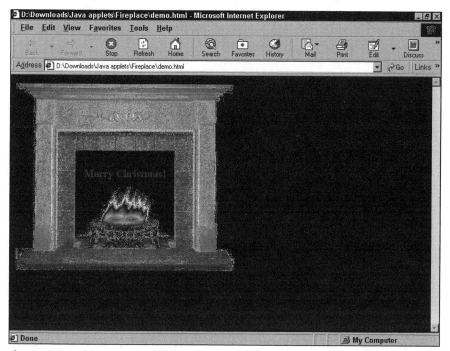

Figure 26-9: This animated fireplace is a Java applet we got for free from CodeBrain.com.

Inevitably, there will be some code in the sample HTML file that you don't want to copy into your own files. For instance, notice that the body of the code in Figure 26-10 begins with `<BODY bgcolor="#000000">`. This means that the background color of the page will be black, and this has nothing to do with the actual Java. If you wanted to change the background color, or apply no color at all, you would not affect the functionality of the applet. Of course, the color may have been selected to match the colors used by the applet itself, but color choice is something you can look at and judge for yourself.

Other than that, virtually all of the code shown in Figure 26-10 would have to be copied into your own HTML files if you want to use the applet. Take a close look at these lines of code:

```
<PARAM NAME = "Image1"          VALUE="fire_001.jpg">
<PARAM NAME = "Image2"          VALUE="fire_002.jpg">
<PARAM NAME = "Image3"          VALUE="fire_003.jpg">
<PARAM NAME = "Image4"          VALUE="fire_004.jpg">
<PARAM NAME = "Image5"          VALUE="fire_005.jpg">
```

```
TextPad - [D:\Downloads\Java applets\Fireplace\demo.html]                        _ 8 X
File   Edit   Search   View   Tools   Macros   Configure   Window   Help          _ 8 X

 1  <HTML>
 2
 3  <BODY bgcolor="#000000">
 4
 5  <table border="0" cellpadding="0" cellspacing="0">
 6  <tr>
 7  <td colspan="3"><img border="0" src="Fireplace000_top.jpg" width="405" height="120"></td>
 8  </tr>
 9  <tr>
10  <td><img border="0" src="Fireplace000_left.jpg" width="111" height="175"></td>
11  <td><APPLET CODE = "CodeBrainYak.class" WIDTH=182 HEIGHT=175>
12    <PARAM NAME = "Notice"            VALUE="Applet by www.CodeBrain.com">
13    <PARAM NAME = "BackgroundColor"   VALUE="0,0,0">
14    <PARAM NAME = "FontName"          VALUE="TimesRoman">
15    <PARAM NAME = "FontSize"          VALUE="20">
16    <PARAM NAME = "FontStyle"         VALUE="bold">
17    <PARAM NAME = "Text"              VALUE="Merry Christmas!">
18    <PARAM NAME = "TextXY"            VALUE="16,47">
19    <PARAM NAME = "TextShiftXY"       VALUE="1,1">
20    <PARAM NAME = "TextColor"         VALUE="255,11,11">
21    <PARAM NAME = "TextHotColor"      VALUE="22,255,22">
22    <PARAM NAME = "StatusBarText"     VALUE="Happy Holidays!">
23    <PARAM NAME = "Image1"            VALUE="fire_001.jpg">
24    <PARAM NAME = "Image2"            VALUE="fire_002.jpg">
25    <PARAM NAME = "Image3"            VALUE="fire_003.jpg">
26    <PARAM NAME = "Image4"            VALUE="fire_004.jpg">
27    <PARAM NAME = "Image5"            VALUE="fire_005.jpg">
28    <PARAM NAME = "AnimateMode"       VALUE="3">
29    <PARAM NAME = "Link"              VALUE="http://www.codebrain.com">
30    <PARAM NAME = "Dwell"             VALUE="100">
31  </APPLET></td>
32  <td><img border="0" src="Fireplace000_right.jpg" width="112" height="175"></td>
33  </tr>
34  <tr>
35  <td colspan="3"><img border="0" src="Fireplace000_bottom.jpg" width="405" height="39"></td>
36  </tr>
37  </table>
38

                                            1    1    Read Ovr Block Sync Rec Caps
```

Figure 26-10: This HTML code can be copied into your own Web pages if you wish.

This series of five images flashes by so quickly that it gives the illusion of a flickering fire in the fireplace. If you are using a cut-and-paste applet that also uses images, you could replace these images with your own, if you wish. For instance, we saw one applet that showed a moonscape with several spaceships hovering about. You could replace the spaceship graphics in the applet code with, say, Snoopy's dog house, and it would look like the Sopwith Camel was hovering over the moon instead of nasty gray aliens. The possibilities are endless, but only if you are willing to look carefully at the HTML and customize it as only you know how.

From cj: Keith, there was some discussion about Snoopy and the Red Baron,

But back to the fireplace. This applet came with a collection of graphics, and if we want the fireplace applet to function properly, not only do we have to copy the HTML code into our own Web page, but we must also copy the following items to our Web server:

✦ The HTML files

✦ Any images, sounds, or other files referred to in the HTML code

✦ The .class file(s) that came with the applet.

These must reside on the Web server in order for the applet to work.

Creating a Java-based drop-down menu

J-Perk (and many other applet creators) also gives you the ability to quickly create Java-based *drop-down* (also called *pull-down*) menus on your Web pages. Drop-down menus enable users to choose items from a drop-down list, similar to the drop-down lists you see in many of the other programs you use. This is handy because it enables your users to choose from a long list of items, without you having to use up valuable screen real estate with a long, boring list.

You begin by launching J-Perk and choosing the Pulldown Menu wizard from the Other Special Effects tab, as shown in Figure 26-11.

Click here to begin the Pulldown menu wizard

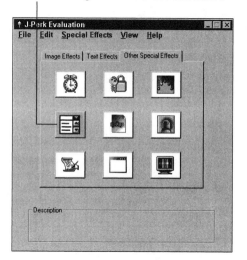

Figure 26-11: Choose the Pulldown Menu wizard to begin creating a Java-based drop-down list.

The first screen of the wizard, shown in Figure 26-12, is fairly straightforward. You create a new menu item by clicking Insert Menu item, and you can specify that each menu item links to a specific URL. As shown in the figure, we are creating a drop-down list that links to four pages at our Road Test Garage Web site.

Depending on the features you enable, there may or may not be any special files — such as .class files — that you need to copy. In the case of the list we were making, all that was needed was to copy the script into our HTML file. In general, when you are creating a Java-based pull-down menu, the code will have two parts. The first part of ours looks like this:

```
<SCRIPT LANGUAGE="JavaScript">
function JumpTo(form) {
    i = form.elements[0].selectedIndex;
```

```
        window.parent.frames['self'].location =
form.elements[0].options[i].value;
        }
//-->
</SCRIPT>
```

Choose whether you want a drop-down menu or a list box

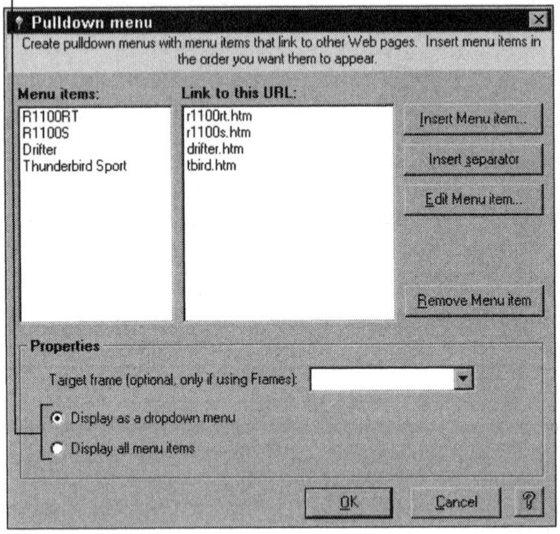

Figure 26-12: Answer the questions to create a Java-based pull-down menu.

This script should appear in the body of your HTML, but it does not have to be right near the actual form code. Basically, this JavaScript (remember, JavaScript is Netscape's free variation of Java) takes the place of the CGI script that would usually be necessary for the form in the second half of the code, as shown here:

```
<FORM METHOD=POST ACTION="#" onSubmit="return false">
    <SELECT>
        <OPTION VALUE="r1100rt.htm">R1100RT
        <OPTION VALUE="r1100s.htm">R1100S
        <OPTION VALUE="drifter.htm">Drifter
        <OPTION VALUE="tbird.htm">Thunderbird Sport
    </SELECT>
  <INPUT TYPE=Submit NAME="Submit" VALUE="Go to"
onClick="JumpTo(this.form)">
</FORM>
```

Looks familiar, doesn't it? You can see that this is similar to what you created when you learned about forms earlier in the chapter. But rather than referring to a CGI script on your ISP's Web server, it simply relies on the JavaScript that you pasted into the HTML file at the same time. Looking at this code, you can see how easy it would be to update the list items if we add or delete pages. The code shown here creates the pull-down list shown in Figure 26-13.

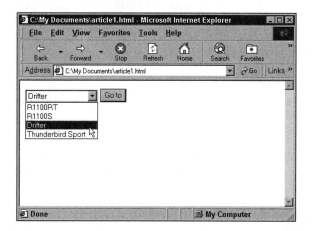

Figure 26-13: A Java-based pull-down menu

And of course, notice that the words "Go to" on the submit button come right from the VALUE= in the last <INPUT> tag for the form. Change the VALUE= and the words on the button will change.

Using Style Sheets

The most common way to compose HTML is the traditional way; code is inserted as it is needed. If you need to apply a certain background color to a table, or format some text a certain way, the most obvious solution is to insert tags that apply that formatting. But what if you decide later on that you want to change the look of all your headings? If you don't want to use the default formatting for <H2> headings, for instance, you can make your own definition for the formatting and style of <H2> headings with *cascading style sheets*.

Not only do style sheets let you change the look of individual pages more efficiently, but you can also use them to control the overall appearance of your entire Web site. Web pages can share a single style sheet, which means that if you change, say, the body background color in the style sheet, all of your Web pages will instantly change to match.

Style sheets live at the beginning of your HTML documents, in the <HEAD>. They are written in the Cascading Style Sheet (CSS) language developed by the World Wide Web Consortium, the same people who propose and oversee standards for HTML. You can learn more about CSS on their Web site, located at www.w3.org.

Creating styles in HTML

For now, the easiest way to use styles in your HTML documents is to begin creating them in individual documents. You can do this using the <STYLE> </STYLE> tags in the <HEAD> element of your page. Styles must be defined in the <HEAD>, because you apply them generally to the <BODY> of the page. Consider this <STYLE> tag:

```
<style type="text/css">
body { color: black; background: white; font-family: Verdana,
sans-serif; }
h1,h2 { color: navy; font-family: Arial, Times New Roman,
serif; }
</style>
```

First, notice that everything is enclosed by the <STYLE> and </STYLE> tags. The opening tag includes a TYPE= definition, which will almost always be text/css as shown here.

After that, things start to get interesting. The second line begins assigning styles to the BODY element. BODY, in this case, refers generally to the body of the page, and specifically to default body text. But notice that we see different syntax than has been used before in HTML; rather than the traditional < > brackets, the actual style definitions are enclosed in { } brackets. Furthermore, the colors are expressed in plain-English text rather than hexadecimal values. The standard color names defined in the HTML 4.0 standard are:

aqua	black	blue	fuchsia
gray	green	lime	maroon
navy	olive	purple	red
silver	teal	white	yellow

These colors can be used when you define styles in CSS for backgrounds, font colors, and anything else that can be colored.

One more thing should be observed about the syntax of the CSS definitions: Each definition ends with a semicolon. In the BODY definition you'll see that the color for body text has been specified as black, and the background color is white. They may not be the most exciting colors, but they are the easiest to read. The final definition involves the font-family used for body text:

```
font-family: Verdana, sans-serif;
```

Because the fonts you prefer may not be installed on the computer of every person who views your Web page, it is important to provide some options. Fonts are listed in order of preference, so the preferred font here is Verdana. But if Verdana is not installed on the user's machine, the browser is instructed to use the default sans serif font instead. Every browser has a default sans serif (and, for that matter, a default serif) font installed, or they wouldn't be able to read anything.

The next definition group is for <H1> and <H2> headings.

```
h1,h2 { color: navy; font-family: Arial, Times New Roman, serif; }
```

These definitions will apply to all text defined as H1 or H2, but nothing else. The color is navy, and three font choices are specified. If Arial isn't available, the browser will defer to Times New Roman, and if Times New Roman isn't available (not likely) then the default serif font will be called into duty.

The beauty of styles and style sheets is that if you decide you don't like the font you chose for the headings, you don't have to go back through the document and change numerous tags that specify the font. Simply scroll up to the style in the document head, change it once, and recheck the appearance. It's just that easy.

Styling page layout

You've seen how to create styles for text formatting and background color. Now let's look at some of the things you can do to control how paragraphs and text are laid out on the page. First let's define some margins for the page:

```
body { margin-left: 10%; margin-right: 10%; }
h1 { margin-left: -5%;}
```

This tag specifies a margin of 10 percent of the screen width on each side of the page for body text. Likewise, headings that use the <H1> tag will begin in the blank space created by that margin, because we have defined a negative margin (-5%) for H1 elements. Without this specification, headings would simply use the same left and right margins as body text.

Creating your own styling groups

All this is well and good if you just use standard tags such as <H1>, <H2>, <P>, and so on, in your HTML documents. But what if you want to create your own paragraph types? Suppose you have a lot of pictures on your Web pages, and they all have captions. You make all of your captions a little small, and they are all italicized. Rather than adding in all the tags to style those captions individually, create a paragraph *class*.

Creating your own class requires two things:

1. You need to define the class in the <STYLE> tag in your document header.

2. You need to specify the class at the beginning of each appropriate paragraph.

Let's start in the body by creating a paragraph class called caption. At the beginning of the text for the image caption, type this code:

```
<P class="caption">Pictured left to right: Jesse Ventura,
Richard Dawson, and Arnold Schwartzenegger.</P>
```

This paragraph is based on a body text <P> paragraph. But we'll change it by adding the following line to the <STYLE> tag in the <HEAD> portion of the HTML document:

```
body.caption { font-style: italic; font-size: 75%; }
```

Notice that we added .caption after body in the definition to specify that the rules listed here only apply to those paragraphs defined in the body as P class="caption".

Linking to other style sheets

As we mentioned at the beginning of this section, you can create a separate style sheet for all of your Web pages, thereby controlling your entire site with just a few quick edits in a single file.

To facilitate this procedure, add a tag to your HTML document header that looks like this:

```
<link rel="stylesheet" href="style.css">
```

The rel="stylesheet" defines the type of link to the Web browser, and href="style.css" provides the actual path to the style sheet file. This example obviously assumes that the style sheet called style.css is in the same directory as your Web pages. If not, correct the path accordingly.

The stylesheet itself is another text file, similar to an HTML file. But it will only contain the header information for the styles; in fact, it only needs to contain everything that you would normally place inside the <STYLE> and </STYLE> tags. You must give it the .css file extension (.css is an abbreviation for *cascading style sheet*) in order for it to work properly, even if you are developing your Web site on a Macintosh. And when you transfer your Web page files to the Web server, the .css file must go as well.

The trouble with style sheets

Style Sheets are a relatively recent addition to the world of HTML, and they are fully supported only by Netscape Communicator or Internet Explorer Versions 4 or higher. Most people now use one of these browsers, but there are still a few stragglers out there holding on to their older browsers. This problem is not catastrophic; they'll still be able to read your words, but they will not see the fancy styling you created with your CSS definitions. Instead they'll be treated to default colors. You can still control styling with standard HTML tags for these people, but going to that much trouble kind of defeats the purpose of using style sheets in the first place, now doesn't it?

Accommodating Older Browsers

Earlier we mentioned providing people without frames a way to visit your Web site, by providing them with their own frameless page, perhaps with mostly text. We used the NOFRAMES tag. Problems for older browsers also occur when you employ Java applets or any other advanced feature. Users with older browsers or browsers that don't support the features you are trying to use can't enjoy the show. You may want to create a *prepage*, a simple page that announces two paths to your site, one for the Java-enabled site, and another for people who can't or don't want to deal with it all. The prepage would be the first page they'd see, and it would contain only those two links.

Otherwise, there is only so much you can do. Time marches on, and so does the beat of Internet technology.

Summary

As we said before, this book cannot possibly tell you everything there is to know about publishing content in the online world. But it is our hope that this chapter has introduced you to some of the more advanced aspects of Web site development that you might be interested in giving a try. Just remember not to use technology for technology's sake. All of the things listed here, such as frames, Java, and style sheets, have their place, and with any luck they may fit into your plans nicely.

✦　　✦　　✦

Using Web Design Tools for Windows

Hypertext Markup Language (HTML) can be difficult to use—it can be hard to remember the tags and syntax, let alone imagine what the Web page will look like by just reading the code. Fortunately, there are HTML editors that are designed to give you a view of your pages that is closer to what Web site visitors will actually see. Many people refer to these HTML editors as *WYSIWYG* (What You See Is What You Get), although this term can be misleading because the appearance of a given Web page varies from browser to browser. Still, you can apply formatting, control layout, insert graphics and hyperlinks, create tables, and insert applets without ever typing a single HTML tag. Because of this, HTML editors present a much simpler way to create Web pages.

HTML editors do have their drawbacks. As we said, they can be somewhat misleading because, although they appear to be WYSIWYG, they are not. HTML is by design flexible, so that one page can look quite different on two different machines, or in different browsers. Furthermore, some editors don't let you manually edit the HTML code, an important capability for many people. Some Web developers also feel that the HTML code produced by editors is bloated and not very clean. But with the relatively small size of even a "bloated" HTML document we don't believe this should be your overriding concern.

In spite of the possible disadvantages, you may well decide that using an HTML editor is the right thing for you. If this is the strategy you have chosen for your Web pages, it is still a good idea to have an understanding of HTML code and how it works. Armed with these tools, you will be set to produce high-quality Web content, whether you produce your HTML the "old fashioned" way or you use one of the easy-to-use yet powerful editors described here.

Because most Web design packages are platform-specific, this chapter looks specifically at software that was designed to be used with Microsoft Windows. If you use Macintosh or Linux, see Chapter 28, "Using Web Design Tools for Macintosh and Linux."

Evaluating HTML Editors

We start by pointing out features you should look for when checking out Web design software. You can choose from many products, and no two products are alike; thus, we run through the most essential features. The reason why you'd even be interested in Web design software is to simplify and somewhat automate the processing of making a Web page or site. Some HTML editors will do this better than others. The features outlined next really will have you "creating your page in no time," rather than scratching your head in bewilderment. Consider the sections that follow to be your essential wish list.

Ease of Use

Most HTML editors are designed to simply make it easier to get your Web page finished and out the door on time. Some programs are better than others at streamlining the process of Web page design. Before buying a product, look it over with the following considerations in mind.

A WYSIWYG interface

Unless you are planning to learn HTML thoroughly, your Web design package should have some sort of WYSIWYG interface. It's not enough to just see the HTML, make an adjustment, and then launch an external browser such as Netscape. It's much more satisfying (especially for a beginner) to see the effect of your change immediately. For example, if you need to adjust the position of a graphic on a page, you'd do that by adding a number of pixels of blank space around your image. This involves a bit of fine-tuning. If you have to keep launching Netscape each time you make an adjustment, you'll run out of patience quite soon. Some products like Sausage Software's HotDog let you divide the screen between HTML viewing and Page viewing. Others provide a workspace that looks exactly like what you'll see online.

Editing quickly and easily

You will sometimes just want to make a fast Web page, and not get bogged down into designing a complex Web site, chock full of all the latest applets and widgets. Some of the most elaborate HTML editors truly give you the moon and the stars, but it may not necessarily make it easier to create a simple Web page. The program you choose should make it easy to edit your page components. For example, if you want to add a table caption, change the name of a frame, or redefine a picture's URL, you should not have to hunt through several menus to find the right option. You want a clearly labeled menu or tab, right-click options, or a toolbar that knows what component you selected, and changes to offer editing features for that component. A dialog box enabling you to adjust the most common parameters for each component should be readily available. It's not enough to enable you to quickly create frames; they should be easy to edit, as well.

Using wizards and templates

When designing a Web component like a form, Java applet, or frameset, certain parameters must be specified. The best Web software comes with wizards, helping you make sure the goodies you add to your page behave the way you think they will. Wizards help you create fully functioning Web components in a step-by-step manner, prompting you for necessary information to make sure all the essential bases are covered.

Because it's important to be able to give your entire site a degree of uniformity — a color scheme, complementary text styles, and a layout sensibility that doesn't change much from page to page — a template can be a useful tool. If a program doesn't come with templates, then look for features such as a "master page" or "style sheet maker." These features provide layout and color sensibilities that repeat throughout the site, enabling you to type in text and add graphics without creating a jarring change in style.

Finding assistance from a clear help system

It's not necessary for Web design software to come with tutorials, but a clear explanation of the program's features and how to use them is essential. Figure 27-1 shows a help file from FrontPage. Each toolbar and dialog box is presented this way, and clicking any feature reveals a quick but descriptive pop-up definition. This feature is provided along with a thorough help file with a good index and table of contents. Help files are especially important for information about procedures that need the cooperation of your ISP Webmaster, such as setting up CGI scripts.

By the way, don't expect much in the way of telephone technical support from a program you've downloaded on a trial basis. Until you register (pay), you are at the mercy of the FAQs, fax-back services, online users' forums, and help files provided with the program.

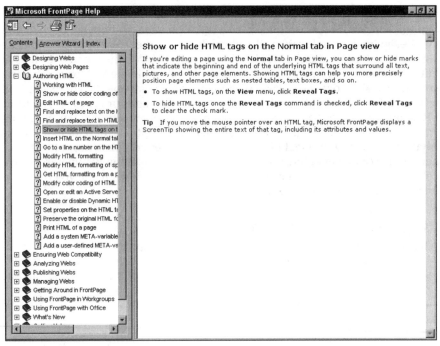

Figure 27-1: FrontPage help files are particularly clear and useful.

Dragging and dropping

It's nice to be able to open a folder on your computer, drag a picture onto your Web page, and then not have to worry any more about it. If this appeals to you, Adobe PageMill 3 is more or less the king of drag-and-drop Web page creation. If you drag and drop a sound file or text document onto a Web page, it appears as a link. Afterwards, upon saving, PageMill resolves all potential broken links.

Designing with flexibility

After you've created a page or two, you'll develop some preferences, your own style of creation; and you'll look for fast ways to add variety to your basic set of tricks. When evaluating a Web design package, make sure they've made it easy to design a page just the way you want it.

Positioning and repositioning page components

Have you ever tried to design a Web page and found that a particular headline and graphic won't fit on the same line together, even though it appears they should? Have you placed two pictures side by side on your page, only to find that they keep jumping apart? Traditional Web documents are quite picky about how objects are aligned.

Some of the newer Web design programs make it easier to move page objects around anywhere you like. Some, like Deneba's Canvas, do so by letting you create layers. Text resides in frames that can be repositioned anywhere on a page, even overlapping a graphic or another text frame. Others let you position objects any-where you like, and then, when saving, construct an elaborate system of tables to facilitate your chosen positions. So if you find that you have lots of nontradi-tional ideas about what a Web page should look like, make sure you get a package that enables easy repositioning of your components.

Optimizing the color and layout

It's important to deploy every possible trick for reducing page load time. If people have to wait too long to view a page, even the cleverest Web sites won't be visited. The best Web design programs come with an optimization feature that can help you reduce page load time. Some will look at all the graphics in your site and find ways to reduce redundant color ranges (the fewer colors an image has, the less time it takes to load). Others check your site for layout problems or HTML commands that don't make any sense. Most good programs will check your entire site for broken links, pointing out where a URL was incorrectly typed, or pointing to a page that does not exist.

> **Note**
>
> Most HTML editors will check for broken links with one caveat: The entire site must have been created with that program in the first place. Some programs, such as WebExpress, check and repair links every time you open your Web site files in the editor.

Using a flexible tree view

When a Web site grows into a number of pages, it's helpful to view the whole site at a glance. This feature is facilitated by a "tree view" or a map view, a Windows Explorer-like interface that enables you to see individual pages as icons, with each page resource (pictures, tables, headings) branching off from each page. Tree views do more than simply inform you where all your site components are. Most programs that offer extended site views let you use the tree to drag components from one page to another. A tree also helps you visualize which pages have yet to be linked together. Figure 27-2 shows a WebExpress' window, which includes a tree view of your entire Web site on the left side of the screen.

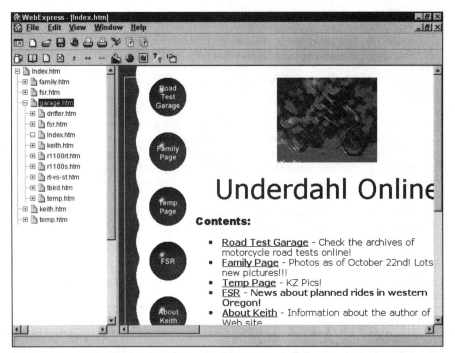

Figure 27-2: WebExpress provides a directory-tree of all the pages in your site on the left side of the screen.

Inserting a comment

Another convenient feature is the ability to insert a comment in your page. A comment is a text entry for informational value only. For example, comments are often used to identify who created a particular applet, or whose code was used for a script, as well as when the page was created and updated. Even though comments are inserted directly in the HTML, Web browsers ignore them so they won't appear on-screen when people visit your site.

Indenting

A program that enables you to indent text can give you a greater ability to align text and graphics. Without it, paragraphs of text and graphics can appear bunched together. The closest thing to an indent command that HTML appears to offer is the `<BLOCKQUOTE>` tag.

Cascading style sheets and Dynamic HTML

Even though the ability to use Dynamic HTML or cascading style sheets might seem a thousand years ahead of your current skill level, it's good to have Web creation software that provides these features. Dynamic HTML helps you design a page that won't leave anyone out. Pages with Dynamic HTML automatically display content that you've created for each type of visitor, according to their level of interest or browser version. Cascading style sheets let you quickly change the look and feel of your entire Web site with just a few quick edits.

 To learn more about cascading style sheets, check out Chapter 26, "Working with Advanced Web Page Components."

Updating page properties easily

Any good Web design product should make it easy for you to edit your basic Web page properties. Controls for changing the color of link text, visited link text, background colors, and bitmaps, should be readily apparent. Also, tools for adding a page description, keywords, and other meta information should be easy to find.

Adding new technology

Make sure you get a program that enables you to add Java applets, ActiveX controls, Java Script, tables, forms, sound files, and videos. If these features don't seem important to you at the moment, they may later. With each new software release, adding such components to your page gets easier and easier. Don't lock yourself out of the future by settling for a program that can't run with the bigger guys, unless you are quite sure you'll never want one.

Under-the-hood editing

Some program features might not make your page look that different, but are important behind the scenes. Keep an eye out for some of these when evaluating a Web design product.

Opening HTML files

One would think this a no-brainer. What Web design program would not enable you to import or open HTML files? Well, there are some packages that create full-featured Web sites with animations, slide show effects, and forms. Trouble is, all pages must be built in their program, applying their own proprietary code and technology. These programs build full-fledged sites, rather than simple pages. You'd be surprised how many programs with this level of sophistication are available for free trial on the Web. The downfall is that you can't import a page you've already started elsewhere. How can you find out if a program has such a limitation? Click File ➪ Open or File ➪ Import. Are one of the file type options HTM or HTML? If not, then that program has more up its sleeve than regular HTML pages, and you must determine if you can live with that limitation.

Updating and managing your Web site files

The best Web design products will gather all your Web-related files and upload them to your ISP. Some software enables you to make changes and update your site, uploading the new or updated files while leaving the rest untouched by the update.

Because it's imperative that all files related to a particular Web project be located in the same directory, a helpful program responds appropriately when you try to link a file outside that folder with a page. Some software simply copies those files to the right folder without further ado. Others give you a warning. This pertains to creating Java applets, as well, when copying certain .CLASS files to the same folder as the Java code itself is all-important. Many programs we look at here do not merely create files for your site, but assist you in uploading, managing, and updating them online. It's also helpful to use a program that will easily update the relevant files if you change your ISP server, password, or personal information. This also includes e-mail addresses and any other profile information that gets regularly included in your pages.

Finding important "extras"

While they may not make a huge difference, here are some extras that you might look for when deciding on a Web page editor:

✦ **A spell checker**. Nothing can ruin the show like an obvious typo when you're trying to sound clever.

✦ **Personal bookmarks**. You can easily lose your place when creating a complex site. Bookmarks can help you keep track of where you are in a project.

✦ **Copy and paste function**. Some Web page design programs let you copy text or pictures to the Windows Clipboard and let you paste it right onto your page.

✦ **Find and replace**. Many Web editors provide a find-and-replace-text feature, enabling you to locate and edit a particular text string within your site.

✦ **Document Weight**. Some editors evaluate your site for loading time and point out where the fat is. Some design software even provides a pie chart showing which components are dragging down performance.

Creating Pages with Web Editors

It's not possible to mention every worthy Web editor on the market today. For starters, we're sticking to software you can download from the Internet and try out for free, or software that's included on the CD-ROM that comes with this book. I mention a handful of the best WYSIWYG editors, a couple full-featured HTML-based programs, and one that does much more than produce HTML. These glimpses and projects we undertake in this section are not meant to be thorough explorations of each product — we're only highlighting here.

Adobe PageMill

Adobe offers PageMill 3, which you can download for free from the Adobe Web site (www.adobe.com). The trial period lasts 15 days after you install the software, after which it costs $79 to register. Adobe has not revised PageMill for a couple of years, but it remains a powerful Web editor that supports most current Web technologies. PageMill excels at letting you drag and drop objects and links right onto your page, and automates lots of under-the-hood chores to maximize your creative time

Getting Started

When you start PageMill, select Site ➪ New, and identify where you want the files stored on your hard drive (specify a folder in the Locations area; PageMill will also create a folder for you, if you have not yet set one aside) and the site's name. The site name is not a filename, so it can be longer than eight.

PageMill's tree view

Click the Settings button, type in your host name, and specify the folders where your Web files should be stored, as shown in Figure 27-3. If you haven't chosen an ISP yet, you can come back to this dialog box later and fill it out. Finally, click OK, and then Create. You'll find yourself back again on the New Site dialog box.

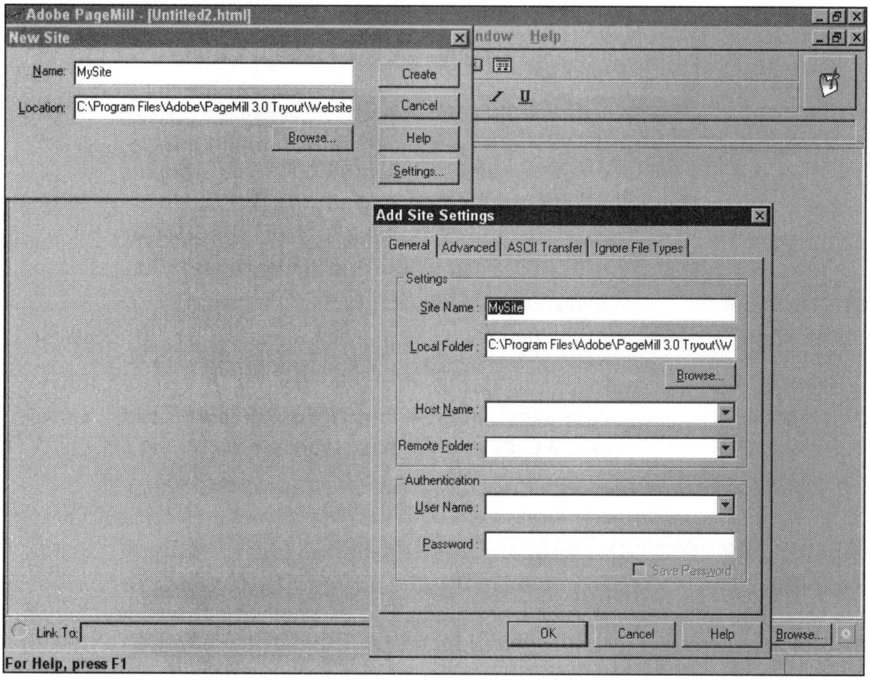

Figure 27-3: Creating a new site with Adobe PageMill

On the left side of the screen, you'll see an Explorer-like icon of your new page. Create content on the page itself, displayed in the work screen on the right, and your changes will be reflected in this Explorer-like Site Overview, which you can see in Figure 27-4. The right side of the screen is an adjustable view, displaying your work screen view, where true page editing takes place. A File List view is also shown on the upper right. If you lose this List view, right-click the Index icon at the far left of the screen and select Show Details. In the Site Overview area, add pages to your new site by right-clicking the site folder and choosing New Blank Page. Minimize the Site overview area by clicking the left-facing arrow at the upper left of the screen.

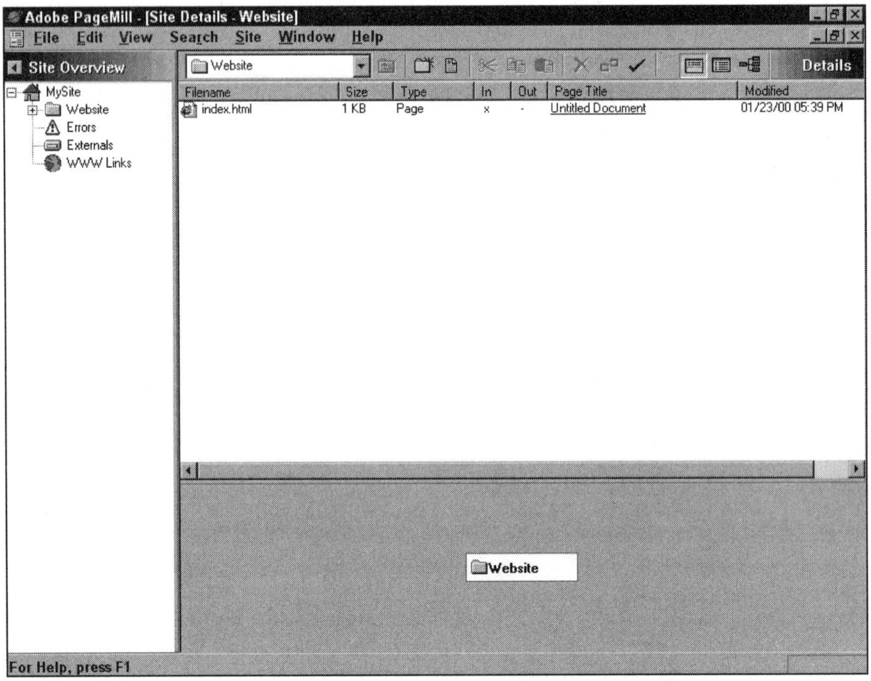

Figure 27-4: The Site Overview panel

Tip

To load a page or set of pages into the Tree View, click Site ⇨ Load ⇨ Browse, and locate your site. To load a page into the page work screen on the right, click File ⇨ Open Page.

Maximizing your workspace

Most often, you'd want to minimize this file list view by dragging the bar toward the top, thus maximizing your workspace. But as your site grows, you may find it helpful to see your HTML files listed by name. You can see a tree-like view of the pages in your site by right-clicking any page's icon (on the left side of the screen) and clicking Show Details. Return to the main work screen, where editing takes place, either by clicking the page title in the File List view or double-clicking the icon on the left side of the screen.

Keeping track of links

Adobe lets you create links to external files (files outside your main Web folder), and will resolve them when you upload or close your page (or, you can click Site ⇨ Gather Externals).

In this Site Overview area, on the left side of the screen, you'll see several icons representing the types of links you'll be building into your page. Click the WWW Links icon to view links you've made on your current page. (These links will not be visible until you've saved your page.) Right-click any link to view it in a new window, verify it, or change its local name. This link checking will not be that important until you have developed a site with several pages, each with links to each other, as well as to sites on the Web.

Click the Externals icon in the Site Overview area to view links you've created on your hard drive to files outside of your Web page folder. Again, right-click these links to reveal opening and editing options, including Gather Links, which copies this file to your Web directory.

Clicking the Errors icon opens a list of all files with links that are not verifiable or links to files that no longer exist or have been relocated.

Adding content to your page

To add content to your PageMill page, use any of the menus or toolbars, or drag a file from any Windows folder right onto your page. If you drag a JPG or GIF file, it will appear in your page. Dragging any other type of file results in a link appearing on your page.

Context-sensitive menu

One of PageMill's nicest features is its Inspector, shown in Figure 27-5, which is like a floating feature menu with tabs that change depending on what page element you are selecting. For example, if you are selecting a picture, you'll see options to change the picture's height and width, and add alternate text. One tab of the Inspector always shows basic page attributes, such as background color, text color, and such. These are editable at any time. The tabs appear to change in anticipation of what feature you may require next.

Figure 27-5: The Attribute Inspector makes it easy to modify objects on your page.

Creating frames in PageMill 3

PageMill creates framed pages in a way that is different from most other Web editors. Click Edit ⇨ Frame, and then click Split Frame Horizontally or Split Frame Vertically (see Figure 27-6). Your page will instantly be divided into two frames along your chosen axis. Any prior content your page had will now be constrained to one of those two frames. Click inside either frame to add content to a page that will, by default, be created inside that frame. You may continue to create more frames by again selecting Edit ⇨ Frame, and then choosing an axis. To save your frames, their associated pages within them, as well as the frameset, click File ⇨ Frameset, and choose an option. You can also choose File ⇨ Frameset to create a new page in any frame.

PageMill 3 "extras"

Other remarkable PageMill features are its ability to import Adobe Acrobat (PDF) files as part of your page. Use the PageMill Pasteboard (View ⇨ Pasteboard) to drag any file from your desktop — it could be a group of links, a GIF, or anything you may need handy for your page. Then, any time you want to include items from this pasteboard on your page, just drag them. The pasteboard has eight tabs, and is a great way to store frequent links, or any Web content you're likely to use on the fly.

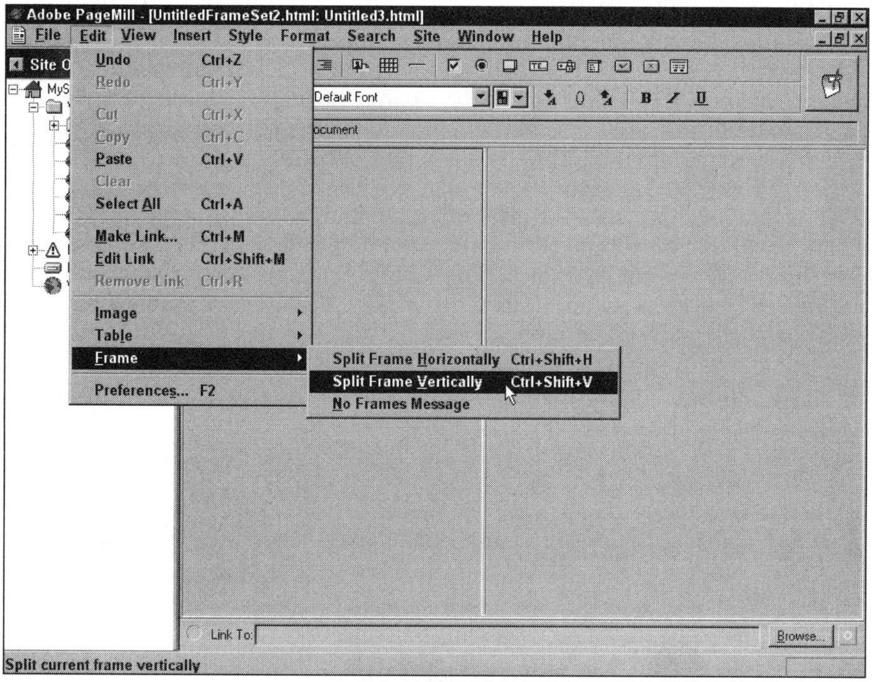

Figure 27-6: Creating frames is easy in PageMill 3.

Deneba Canvas 7

Canvas 7 from Deneba (www.deneba.com) is one of those programs we warned you about earlier in the chapter that cannot import and open HTML files. In fact, it isn't even a true HTML editor. So, why include it here? Canvas is a powerful desktop publishing package that includes a wide variety of capabilities:

✦ **Prepress publishing.** Canvas enables you to publish almost any kind of document, including brochures, newsletters, magazines, posters, and virtually any other kind of printed media. It creates electronic prepress documents that can then be taken to a commercial printer for production.

✦ **Image editing.** You can edit existing images, much like the photo manipulation software described in Chapter 29.

✦ **Illustration.** Canvas enables you to create new illustrations from scratch, such as buttons and other graphics that you may want to use online.

✦ **HTML exporting.** Canvas can export any document you create in the program as an HTML document. It utilizes a complex series of tables and other elements to create a Web page that looks exactly like the master document. It cannot edit HTML, but you can save your documents in the proprietary Canvas format, edit it as you see fit, and simply re-export it when you are ready to update the HTML files on your Web server.

The advantage of Canvas 7 is that it replaces many other types of programs, enabling you to consolidate your work into one program. You don't have to switch from your HTML editor to PhotoDeluxe to retouch an image, or Illustrator to create buttons, or QuarkXpress or Publisher to produce printed materials. Canvas 7 does it all in a single package.

Figure 27-7 shows The Canvas 7 screen as it is used to produce a Web page. We are actually creating a Canvas document, which can then be printed, output to a commercial printing service, or saved as an HTML document.

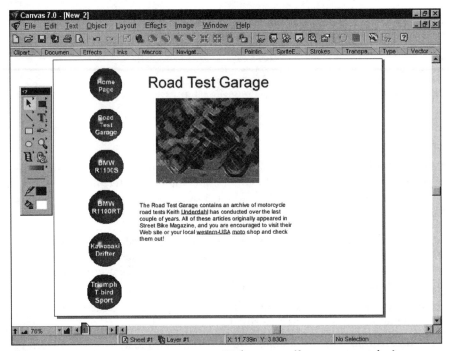

Figure 27-7: In Canvas 7 you create your Web page as if you were producing a prepress document for hard copy publication.

When you save a Canvas document as HTML, you lose much of the document's layout accuracy. For this reason and because this program is far more complex than most other HTML editors, we don't recommend using something like Canvas to produce most of your Web documents. Still, the interesting thing about Canvas is that you can take existing documents such as newsletters and brochures that you created using Canvas and quickly publish them in HTML format. For instance, if you use Canvas to create a company catalog, which is then printed and mailed to customers, in a matter of minutes you can take the same file used to produce the printed catalog to make an online version for your company's main Web site.

When you want to output a Canvas document as HTML, click File ⇨ Save As, and then choose HTML from the Save As Type dialog box. You will see a warning about lost formatting, and then you'll be presented with the HTML Options dialog box shown in Figure 27-8. Here you can set important options for the document. We recommend that you create a new folder in which to store the documents. You can also set some options that affect the graphics on the page.

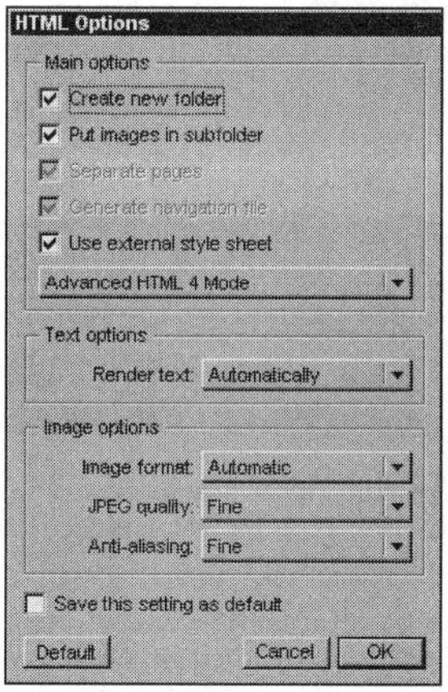

Figure 27-8: Use the HTML Options dialog box to set important options when saving a Canvas document as HTML.

When you save a Canvas document as HTML, the program actually produces many separate files for a given page. Canvas automatically outputs the HTML files, of course, and it also extracts any images and saves them as GIFs or JPEGs as appropriate. The program determines names for the files automatically, so don't expect to recognize all of the file names when the whole page is output. By the way, this is also why it is so important to output the document into its own folder; this is the only way to know for sure which files are part of the document. A style sheet file (.css) is also produced.

As we said, Canvas is not a true HTML editor, and you should not expect to use it as such. But it is an excellent desktop publishing package that incorporates image editing and illustration features, and also happens to produce HTML if you need it. If you're looking for a single package that can handle many different types of publishing needs besides Web publishing, Canvas 7 is a good choice.

HotDog Junior

HotDog Junior is a smaller version of the popular HotDog Professional Web editor that has been on the scene for years. HotDog Junior is unique among this group in that it was designed specifically with the beginning Web developer in mind. In fact, the producers of HotDog, Sausage Software (www.sausage.com), recommend HotDog Junior as an excellent tool that kids can use to produce their first Web pages. You can download a free trial version of HotDog Junior from the Sausage Software Web site, and although the trial period is unlimited, you should pay the $39.95 registration fee if you decide to use it.

Note　HotDog Junior is definitely designed for the beginner, and lacks many of the advanced capabilities that professionals demand. If this is you, HotDog Professional may be your best option. Visit Sausage Software's Web site (www.sausage.com) to learn more about it.

Looking around for the first time

When you first launch HotDog Junior, you will be taken through a series of registration screens (if you haven't already registered). As you can see in Figure 27-9, the HotDog Web creation wizard is pretty hard to miss. The visual cues are what makes this program so well suited to kids.

Click OK and read the information in the next screen, then click OK again. Now you should see a screen that gives you the choice of opening a template or a Web page. If you've already created a Web page and now want to edit it, click the Web pages folder. Otherwise, click the plus sign next to Templates to view a list of templates that you can use to create your page. When you select a template, a preview is shown on the right side of the window, as shown in Figure 27-10.

When you have chosen a template (if you think the templates that are offered are too cutesy, just choose the Blank template), double-click its name on the left side of the screen. You'll hear a sound and be taken to the step that helps you build your page. This stage is where you will spend most of your time. To view a WYSIWYG display of your page at any time, click the View Your Page button at the top of the window.

Tip　Eventually you will get tired of that cute green dog appearing every time you click something in HotDog Junior. If you don't want him to appear anymore, just place a check mark next to "Don't show me this stuff again" the next time he appears.

Figure 27-9: HotDog Junior's friendly interface makes it easy for beginners to get comfortable with the program.

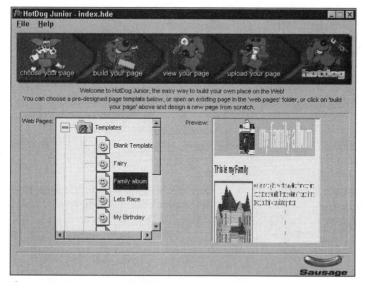

Figure 27-10: Preview the Web page templates and choose the one that looks right for you.

Filling in Web blocks in HotDog Junior

HotDog Junior divides your page into Web blocks, and you can change the contents of each block by clicking on it in lists of blocks that are currently part of your page. You can move existing blocks by clicking and dragging them up and down in the list, or add new blocks by dragging them in from the list of "extra" blocks on the left. To edit the contents of a block, click it and change the information about that block that appears to the right, as shown in Figure 27-11.

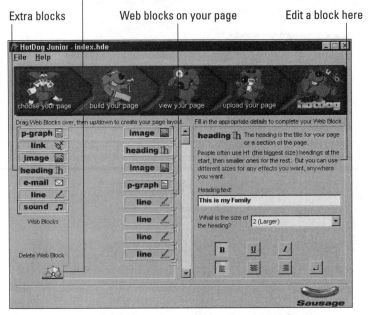

Figure 27-11: Each block represents part of your Web page.

The exact editing options that appear on the right will vary depending on the type of block you are editing. For instance, an image block will let you select a different image file, change the size and alignment of the image, and specify alternative text by typing a title in the Text description box. Likewise, Web blocks that contain paragraphs (*p-graphs*) of text and headings include a lot of options for formatting the words that appear, as well as places to type the actual words that you want to appear.

If you want to get rid of a block that the template automatically inserted, you can drag it from the list over to the Delete Web Block icon in the lower left corner of the program window. Deleting blocks is fun because the spinning saw icon turns them to sawdust whenever you drag the blocks there.

Creating links using HotDog Junior

HotDog Junior's overriding design priority is that it be simple. Part of that simplicity means that it's not as flexible as most other HTML editors. You really begin to notice this when you try to create hyperlinks. You cannot, unfortunately, simply create a hyperlink in the middle of a paragraph of text. You have to create a separate block for the link. There are, however, three easy ways to create links in HotDog Junior:

✦ **Link Images.** Click an image block. Notice that the last item you can edit enables you to apply a hyperlink to the image. This way, if someone clicks on the image, they jump to the new location.

✦ **Add a Link block to your site.** The link block, as shown in Figure 27-12, enables you to specify some text to appear before, during, and after the link. You can then enter the URL for the link in the bottom. The link block will appear as a line of text on your page. If the block is placed right after a paragraph, it will look like part of the paragraph.

✦ **Add an e-mail block to the page.** The e-mail block enables you to insert an e-mail link into your page. It is very similar to a link block.

Previewing your page

Previewing your page is an important step. When you click the View Your Page button at the top of the HotDog Junior screen, the editor automatically builds your page and opens it in a preview window. If the window is too small to preview it effectively, click the Maximize link near the bottom of the screen. Figure 27-12 shows our page being previewed in the Maximized mode. When you are done previewing, simply click the Build Your Page button again to return to the section that enables you to edit the Web blocks.

Tip

You should also preview the page in your Web browser. Click the Browser Preview button to open the page in your default Web browser. When you're ready to move on, click the Minimize button to restore the normal HotDog Junior view.

The preview window also enables you to make some changes to the overall design and style of your site. For instance, try choosing a different style form the Styles drop-down menu in the lower left corner of the preview window. The appearance changes instantly to reflect the style you select.

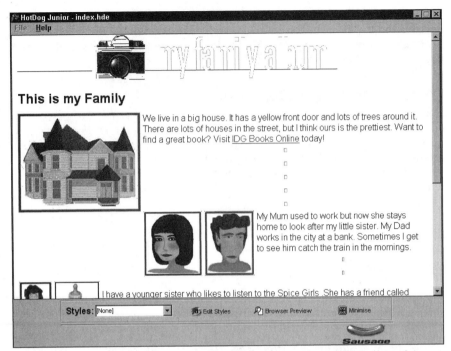

Figure 27-12: To get a good look at your Web page, use the Maximized mode.

Publishing your page

When you are ready to publish your page online, click the Upload Your Page button at the top of the screen. You may be prompted to save the changes you made. If this is the first time you are publishing your page with HotDog, you will be asked to enter some information about your ISP's server. Follow the instructions on-screen and enter the required information. When you have configured your ISP information, you should see the screen shown in Figure 27-13. Make sure that all of the files you need to upload are listed, and then click Publish Your Page.

Adding pages to your site

Chances are, a single Web page just isn't going to cut if for you. You can begin creating a new page from scratch by clicking File ⇨ New on the HotDog Junior menu bar. This will open an empty page layout, and it will be up to you to add the Web blocks you want to use with the page. If you would rather add a page using one of HotDog Junior's templates, click Choose Your Page instead and start from the beginning.

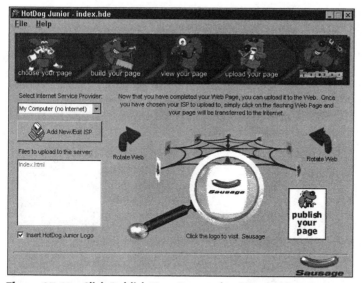

Figure 27-13: Click Publish Your Page to begin uploading your files to the Web server.

Microsoft FrontPage

Microsoft produces a popular Web page editor called FrontPage. FrontPage is available as a stand-alone product, or you may obtain it as part of the Office 2000 package (FrontPage is included only with the Premium and Developer editions of Office). Purchased by itself, FrontPage costs $149, or if you are upgrading from a previous version, the upgrade price is $59.95. Academic discounts are also available, which you can learn more about from Microsoft or your local college's bookstore. A 30-day trial version can be downloaded from Microsoft's Web site.

Note   As of this writing, Microsoft offers a $40 rebate on the new user price through the end of 2001.

Touring FrontPage

FrontPage's interface will make users of Microsoft Office products, such as Word and Excel, feel immediately at home.

FrontPage organizes your Web pages into *Webs*. A Web generally consists of all of the pages in your Web site. For instance, in Figure 27-14 you can see that a Web has been opened, and the pages in that Web are shown in the Folder list. We can open any one of these pages by double-clicking it in the folder list.

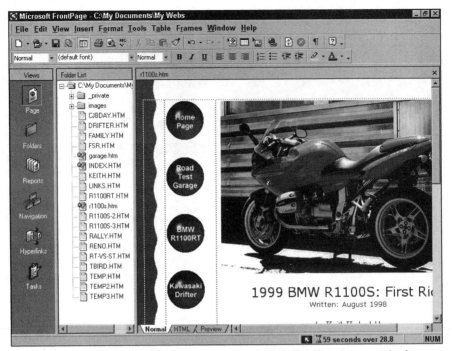

Figure 27-14: FrontPage's interface will seem instantly familiar to users of other Microsoft Office products.

The fascinating thing about FrontPage is the variety of tools that it provides. For instance, if you click the Reports button in the Views toolbar (at the left edge of the screen) a report about your site will be generated. The report will tell you:

✦ The number of files that are part of your site and the amount of disk space they consume

✦ The number of pictures used in your site and the space they consume

✦ Information about links in your site

✦ The number of pages that are estimated to take longer than 30 seconds to load

✦ The number of errors and broken links, if any

The Hyperlinks view is another interesting tool, because it gives you a graphical representation of how your pages are linked together. Figure 27-15 shows one such view of our Web site.

Click a plus sign to expand the view of links

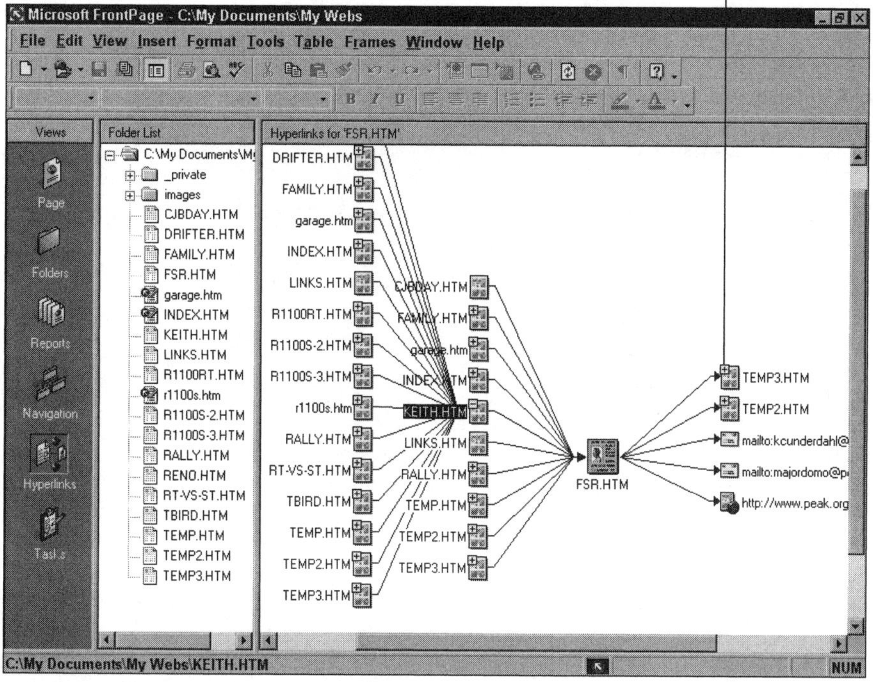

Figure 27-15: FrontPage provides this graphical representation of the links that hold your site together.

As with most Microsoft Office products, the display of FrontPage is very flexible. For instance, if you don't find the items in the Views bar useful, click View ➪ Views Bar to hide it from view. The Folder list can be hidden using the same method, but it is useful enough that we recommend keeping it on-screen most of the time. You can also shrink each bar by clicking and dragging the borders.

Creating a page in FrontPage

FrontPage offers a number of templates to help you begin creating Web pages. Launch the program by clicking Start ➪ Programs ➪ Microsoft FrontPage. Now, click File ➪ New ➪ Page. The New dialog opens as shown in Figure 27-16. Click a template to see a preview in the lower right corner.

A new document window opens, with a layout generated by the template you chose. Most templates also include some sample pictures and text, but you will probably want to get rid of all that stuff and enter your own content. Doing so is fairly straightforward, especially if you have used a Word processor before.

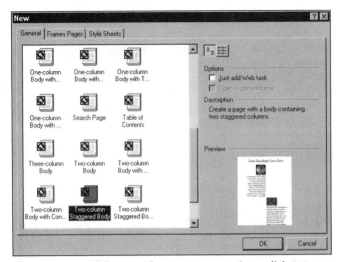

Figure 27-16: Click a template to see a preview. Click OK
when you have chosen the template you want to use.

Note   FrontPage automatically checks the spelling of your documents. If you see red
squiggly lines under some words, FrontPage thinks that they are spelled incorrectly.

Notice that, if you chose a template that makes use of tables to control page layout,
the table borders are shown as dotted lines throughout the page. These lines will
not appear in a Web browser, but they help you better manage the overall page
layout. You can adjust the size of columns and rows in the tables by holding your
mouse pointer over the dotted lines and dragging them to a new size (Figure 27-17).

Creating Web elements, such as hyperlinks, tables, or headings, or inserting
graphics is straightforward. Simply place the cursor in the desired location (or
make a selection) and click the appropriate toolbar button. FrontPage includes
buttons for hyperlinks, inserting tables and graphics, and for inserting components.
The Insert Components button enables you to insert a variety of interesting
components with a single mouse click, including JavaScript items (but, strangely,
not Jscript), such as Web counters and hover buttons.

Tip   Although FrontPage won't show you the actual HTML tags that are used to create
the page, you can see exactly where each code is positioned by clicking View ⇨
Reveal Tags. This reveals the location of most HTML tags and resembles the Reveal
Codes feature in Corel WordPerfect.

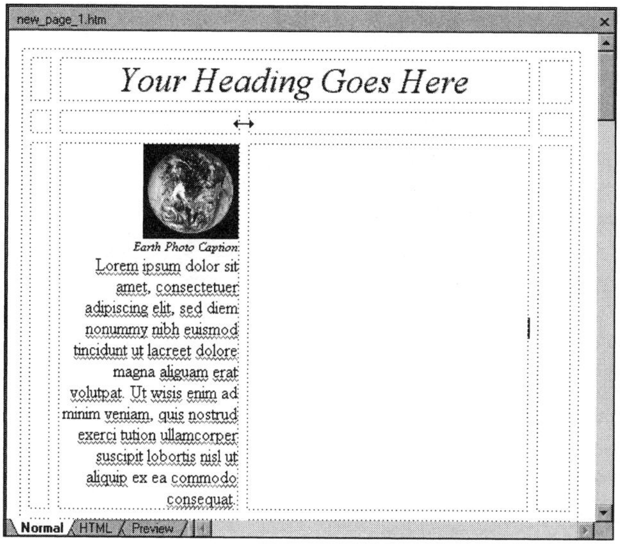

new_page_1.htm   ×

Your Heading Goes Here

↔

Earth Photo Caption
Lorem ipsum dolor sit
amet, consectetuer
adipiscing elit, sed diem
nonummy nibh euismod
tincidunt ut lacreet dolore
magna aliguam erat
volutpat. Ut wisis enim ad
minim veniam, quis nostrud
exerci tution ullamcorper
suscipit lobortis nisl ut
aliquip ex ea commodo
consequat.

Normal / HTML / Preview /

Figure 27-17: Invisible tables are shown as dotted lines.
Click and drag the borders to resize them.

Adding meta data to your FrontPage documents

FrontPage enables you to add <META> tags to your Web pages, but the method for
doing so is not immediately apparent. To add meta data to your page, follow these
steps:

1. Open the page you want to assign a <META> tag to. Right-click anywhere on
   the page and choose Page Properties from the menu that appears.

2. In the Page Properties dialog, click the Custom tab to bring it to the front.

3. Under User variables, click Add.

4. Enter a name and value for the meta variable in the dialog box that appears
   (Figure 27-18).

5. Click OK in each dialog box when you are done.

Notice that the name and value match the NAME and VALUE components of the META
tags. Using these dialogs you can create virtually any kind of META tag you need.

Cross-Reference   To learn more about META tags, see Chapter 25, "Applying Intermediate Web
Design Features."

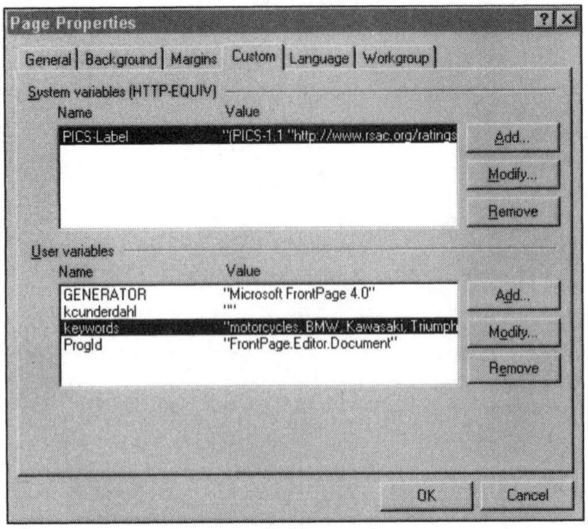

Figure 27-18: Enter Meta variables into the header of your Web pages here.

Creating style sheets in FrontPage

FrontPage makes it easy to create new style sheets. To do so, click File ➪ New ➪ Page. In the New dialog box, click the style sheets tab, and choose a style sheet template that you want to use. After you click OK, you should see the .css code for the style sheet open in the program window, as shown in Figure 27-19. Here you can edit style sheet definitions.

Cross-Reference If you want to know more about style sheets, read Chapter 26, "Working with Advanced Web Page Components."

To attach a style sheet you created to a page, click Format ➪ Style Sheet Links. In the Link Style Sheets dialog box, click Add and select your style sheet. When you click OK, it will be applied to your page.

Publishing your Web site using FrontPage

When you are ready to publish your Web site with FrontPage, save all of your work and click File ➪ Publish Web to open the Publish Web dialog box. This command will publish all of the files associated with your Web site. Click the Options button to specify whether you want to publish all pages or just those that have been updated. Click Publish to complete the transfer.

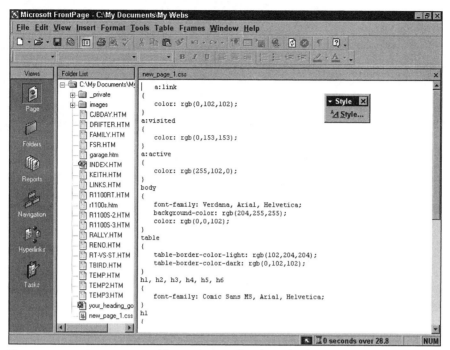

Figure 27-19: FrontPage enables you to easily edit style sheets.

MicroVision WebExpress

MicroVision publishes an excellent HTML editor called WebExpress. WebExpress provides a variety of welcome features in a package that is deceptively simple to operate. We use the term "deceptive" because, although the simplicity of the interface suggests an entry-level program, WebExpress does support leading-edge Web technologies. Perhaps the best endorsement we could provide for this program is to say that it is what we choose to use for our Web publishing needs when we aren't writing about other software.

You can download "Lite" or "Full" trial versions from MicroVision's Web site at www.mvd.com. The Lite version does not include the image gallery and Web site samples, making it a faster download. The program offers a 30-day trial, and if you choose to continue using it the purchase price is $69.95.

Taking the grand tour of WebExpress

You've already seen the WebExpress, interface (Figure 27-2), but here it is again in Figure 27-20. When you first launch the program, you will be taken through some steps to help you create a new Web site. WebExpress' wizard generally creates a full site, with several common pages, rather than a single page. If you don't like a page that WebExpress created for you, click it once in the table of contents on the left side of the screen and click the Remove Page button. Notice that when you click once on one of the pages listed in the table of contents, the toolbars change so that only tools for managing the pages are shown.

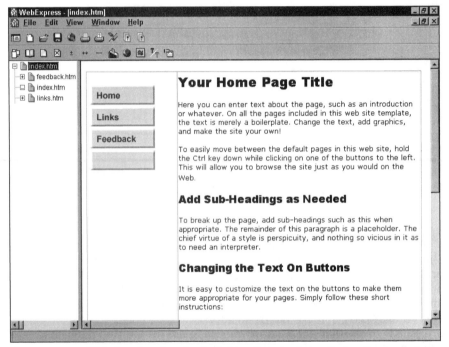

Figure 27-20: Click the plus-signs in the table of contents to display the pages in your site.

As you can see, WebExpress also makes heavy use of tables to control the layout of your site. The table borders are shown in a color that should contrast with the background, but they will not appear on-screen when the site is published and viewed in a Web browser. If you're not sure, preview it yourself by choosing your Web browser from the View menu.

Modifying buttons with WebExpress

Most of the Web site templates that WebExpress uses to help you create your site include buttons. To easily change the text or appearance of these buttons:

1. Click once on the button you want to change so that it has a border line around it.

2. Right-click the selected button image and choose Image Text Properties from the shortcut menu. The Image Text dialog box opens, as shown in figure 27-21.

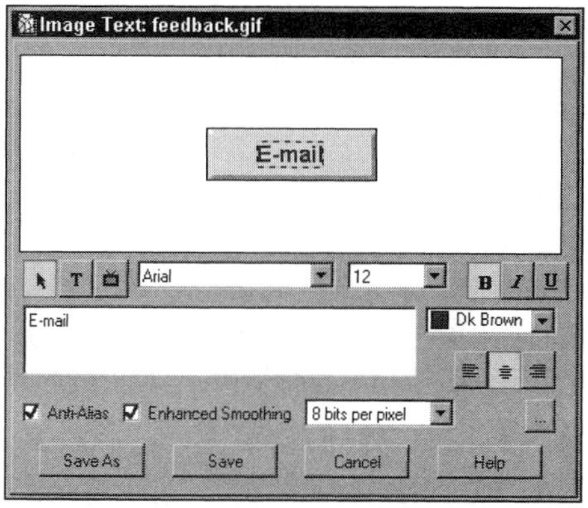

Figure 27-21: Modify the text on your buttons here.

3. If you wish to add text to the button, type the text in the lower section of the dialog box. The text will appear in the button sample in the top half.

4. You can reposition the text by clicking the text and dragging it to a new spot on the button.

5. Make any other changes you want to the text, such as changing the font, color, formatting, or alignment within the text box. Click Save when you are done.

Tip

To create a new button, copy and paste an existing button in the document window, then open the Image Text dialog as described here. After you have assigned a new name to the button, click Save As rather than Save. You can then save the button GIF as a new file. To avoid confusion, try to name the buttons in a way that reflects what they actually say.

Creating hyperlinks using WebExpress

The default buttons that WebExpress creates will usually already be linked to their corresponding pages. If you want to change a button's hyperlink or create a hyperlink for any selected image, text, or object, select it and click the Insert/Edit Hyperlink button on the WebExpress toolbar (it looks like a linked chain). This opens the Create/Edit Hyperlink dialog box. The dialog box has three tabs:

✦ **Local Page** — This tab lists pages that are part of your Web site. If you want to link to one of those, choose it from the list and click OK. If you want to link to a file, click the File button instead of choosing a page from the list.

✦ **WWW URL** — If you are creating an external link — one that leads to another Web site — you can enter it here. WebExpress remembers other URLs you have entered and maintains a list of them here.

✦ **E-Mail Address** — If you want to create a mailto link, do so on this tab. You can also create news links on this tab.

Working with style sheets in WebExpress

WebExpress supports style sheets. The Web site templates include style sheets, which you can import by clicking Format ➪ Import Style Sheets. To edit the style sheet attached to the current Web site, click Format ➪ Edit Style Sheets. Open the Edit Style Sheet dialog box. Here you can choose from the styles that are already defined, and modify them by clicking Edit. Making modifications to the appearance of your Web site through the style sheet rather than individually on each page enables you to standardize the appearance of your pages and change them more efficiently.

Publishing your site with WebExpress

To publish your site from WebExpress, click in the table of contents area on the left side of the window. Then click File ➪ Publish Web Pages. Make sure that all of your server information is correct and click OK.

Note   If you do not see the Publish Web Pages option in the File menu, make sure that you have clicked in the table of contents area on the left side of the program window.

Summary

Manually editing HTML is fine, but there are times when an HTML editor like those discussed here works better for you. They can save time, help you do things that would be too challenging with raw code, and provide overall management functions for your site.

Using Web Design Tools For Macintosh and Linux

In the beginning, there was NotePad, SimpleText, and vi. And it was good, because these applications produced plain text (ASCII) files and were built into their respective operating systems. Plus, HTML coding was very, very simple.

Over time, however, Web developers asked for more, and software developers answered. From simple editors that included easy access to HTML tags to more visual-based design tools — a host of freeware, shareware, and commercial products hit the market. An early graphical tool was the integration of HTML editing into Netscape Communicator, a baby step toward the interactive Web envisioned by Tim Berners-Lee when he was a lone voice advocating for what was to become the World Wide Web.

Web development is more than just the HTML code, however. Today it means graphics — both static and dynamic. And once the site has been created, posting it to the Web server relies on tools that predate the WWW — those that enable FTP. This chapter explores tools for Macintosh and Linux — the premier desktop publishing platform and the end-of-the-century upstart.

Using Web Design Tools For Macintosh

The Macintosh is the premier desktop publishing platform and is a favorite among students and creative professionals. The mix of Web development tools available for the platform is varied, but the focus has been on "front-end" tools, which reflects the platform's strengths in easily creating memorable designs. This section examines HTML editors, image tools, and FTP clients.

Creating Web pages with Macintosh HTML editors

An HTML document is, at its heart, an ASCII document; therefore, any word processing program that can save text as ASCII could be considered an HTML editor. On the continuum of Web authoring tools, on one end are text editors such as SimpleText and BBEdit (Bare Bones Software), which require a basic understanding of HTML. At the other extreme are applications like Microsoft FrontPage and Macromedia's Dreamweaver; these graphical tools are often mis-dubbed WYSIWYG editors because the WWW, unlike desktop publishing, is not WYSIWYG.

The advantage of the text editor is the control that the author exerts over the final code; the application may have shortcuts, wizards, or palettes to provide easy access to some or all of the HTML tags, but its soul is the plain text editor. Thus a disadvantage of the text editor is that the fledgling author must learn some basic HTML before publishing a Web site. Even though HTML is not a difficult language to learn, and there are hundreds of online tutorials, this is more work than many individuals want to undertake.

Graphical tools require only that the author learn the software interface; there is no need to learn HTML, because the editor generates the code behind the scenes. However, graphical editors try to "read the developer's mind" when creating code; as a consequence, they often generate messy code that is not to specification. For a personal Web site, this shortcoming is not (usually) fatal — after all, the site is not fulfilling a business need, and if it "breaks" some browsers, no goodwill or business is lost.

This section examines the most popular text and graphic editors for the Macintosh: BBEdit (commercial version) and Dreamweaver.

BBEdit

BBEdit (currently version 5.1.1) is a full-featured, Macintosh-only text editor that can be used to create HTML pages as well as to write software applications. Consistently voted a "must have" application by Mac Web developers and critics, BBEdit comes in full-strength (commercial) and light (freeware) versions.

Despite the company name, this is not a bare bones product. BBEdit features a complete set of palette-based HTML tools for quick, easy, to-specification HTML creation. And of course, it also enables the experienced HTML developer to type the code by hand. BBEdit is simple enough for the new user to create HTML documents and yet powerful enough to be the professional's editor of choice.

Creating Web pages in the BBEdit environment

The BBEdit desktop, shown in Figure 28-1, includes a document in an editing window, a window showing all open BBEdit files, and a pick-and-choose tag maker. For authors who prefer drop-down menus, the HTML tags are also accessible from the Markup menu. All HTML 4.0 tags and attributes are supported in these two environments, making reliance on memory a thing of the past.

Web-Safe Color Palette   HTML Tools Palette

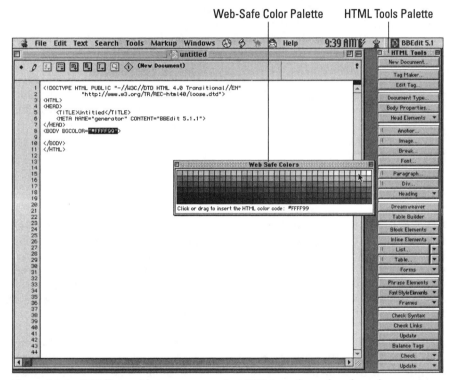

Figure 28-1: BBEdit provides easy access to HTML tags through a drop-down menu or through an HTML Tools Palette. For browser-safe color, drag colors from the Web-safe color palette onto the HTML document, and BBEdit inserts their hex values.

An early lesson Web developers learn is that to make their colors cross-platform, they must use the 216-color browser-safe (or Web-safe) palette. Otherwise, it's possible that a color that looks great on a Mac will not look the same on a PC (or vice versa). BBEdit has a floating palette that enables drag-and-drop or click-and-insert specification of hex colors. No more reliance on (nonsafe) color names because it's too much trouble to look up the palette!

The latest version of BBEdit has an intelligent tag maker. Simply place the cursor anywhere in your HTML document, select TagMaker from the Markup menu, and a list of all legal tags appears. If you place the cursor inside an HTML tag, the TagMaker provides you with tag attributes instead. No more relying on memory to answer the question — is this an HTML 4.0 attribute or one only supported by Microsoft Internet Explorer?

Don't like the standard keyboard shortcuts? Want a shortcut that BBEdit hasn't provided? Under the Edit menu, use the menu command Set Menu Keys, shown in Figure 28-2, to assign a keyboard shortcut to any menu item, whether or not there is a preassigned shortcut. The system will warn you if you have selected a preexisting shortcut; you can overwrite the default or chose another shortcut.

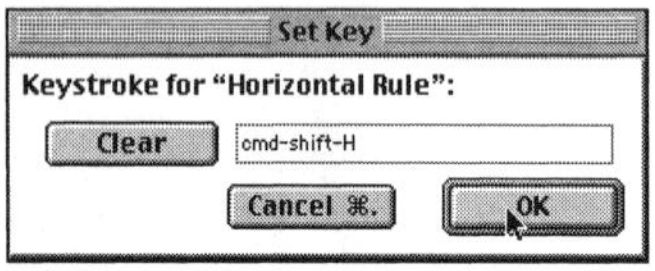

Figure 28-2: BBEdit's Set Menu Keys command enables you to customize keyboard shortcuts for greater productivity and efficiency.

Inserting images with BBEdit

To insert an image into a BBEdit document, place the cursor at the point on the HTML page where you want the image code to appear, you can use the image builder palette to insert the graphic into the page. You can also insert an image by typing the code or dragging-and-dropping the image file into the BBEdit page. When you chose the drag-and-drop method, the image builder palette appears, prefilled with image source and height and width tags. A text field for ALT text is in the palette; should you not complete the information at this step, BBEdit leaves a blank tag as a memory jog: alt="".

An indispensable feature is BBEdit's powerful search-and-replace function. Not only does it have an intuitive interface, but you can also quickly apply search criteria to an entire directory (including subdirectories) without actually opening the affected files.

Tip   Designers often use server-side includes (SSI) to insert common elements, such as navigation footers or headers, into their HTML pages; thus, if a change is needed, it means editing only one file. However, because the server has to do a bit more processing before delivering the requested HTML page, this convenience comes at a cost.

BBEdit enables you to harness this time-saver without having to rely on the server to build the page. To do this, build your documents using a variant of SSI commands: #bbinclude. When it's time to publish the site, use the BBEdit Update Document command to replace each #bbinclude instance with the text of the referenced file. This circumvents all server issues associated with SSI, while letting the developer easily update files.

Specifications and system requirements

✦ Current software version: 5.2.2.

✦ Demo available: Yes, full version.

✦ Freeware available: Yes, BBEdit Lite x.1 (no phone or e-mail tech support).

✦ Purchasing options: Available by Web order from Barebones Software or available from most Macintosh software resellers. Integrated into Dreamweaver, Macintosh version. Price ranges from $39 (upgrade) to $119 (initial commercial purchase).

✦ System requirements: MacOS System 7.0 or later (7.5 or later recommended); 1.2MB RAM; CD-ROM for standard software installation; 20MB hard-drive space.

✦ Technical support: Free, unlimited lifetime support for commercial products. Support is available via the BBEdit Web site, `http://Web.barebones.com/support/support.html`, via e-mail or by phone or fax.

✦ Web site: `http://www.barebones.com/`.

Dreamweaver

With its trademarked Roundtrip HTM, Macromedia provided a much-needed shot in the arm for Web developers when it released Dreamweaver (now Version 3.0). Early graphical editors produced extraneous (or even weird) code. If a developer cleaned up the file in a text editor, all too often the graphical editor overwrote those corrections the next time it was used to open the modified document. It was the epitome of "I know better than you" software engineering.

With Dreamweaver, Macromedia broke out of the pack, combining the ease of use offered by a graphical environment with the power to permanently correct code written by the application. The latest version offers an unprecedented mixture of graphical tools and easy access (to view or tweak) the underlying HTML code.

Using the Dreamweaver desktop

Upon launch, the Dreamweaver desktop, which is shown in Figure 28-3, contains a floating Object palette to the left of the visual document window. The user preferences setting can change the palette view from icons-and-text to icons-only or text-only. To the right, a floating Tools palette launches windows and tools, such as the integrated HTML editor (BBEdit for the Macintosh and HomeSite for the PC). Toward the bottom of the desktop appears the Properties toolbar and the History window.

If the interface appears complex, the site developer can minimize or close windows, depending upon the size of the monitor and desktop, and then open the window when needed. Keep in mind that the visual document window is like any document window — just place the cursor on the page and begin typing!

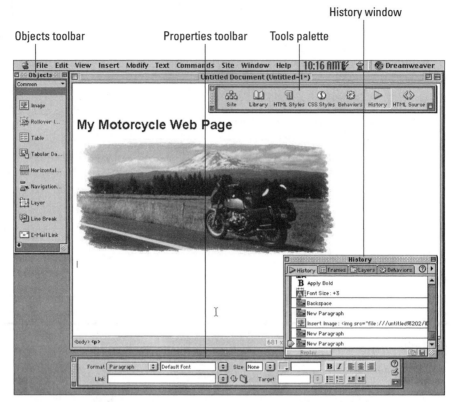

Figure 28-3: Dreamweaver provides a visual editing environment, but preserves the formatting of any code that is imported into the tool, a rare feature of visual editors.

Inserting graphics with Dreamweaver

To insert an image into a Dreamweaver document, place the cursor at the point on the page where you want the image to appear. Then you have three options: select Insert ⇨ Image from the menu bar, click on the Image button in the Object palette, or use the keyboard shortcut. The image is immediately visible in the document window. The underlying code contains the image source and height and width tags; to make the code fully accessible, you have to add the content for the ALT tag. If you want your image to support more than one "hot spot" or link, there is also an integrated image-mapping tool.

New Feature

Continuing to stay one step ahead of the competition, Macromedia has added a Quick Tag Editor to the latest version of the software. This feature enables you to view and edit the underlying HTML code for any object—without having to leave the graphical editing environment (no more toggling back and forth!). Dreamweaver even has a drop-down tag list to help add HTML directly into the document.

Applying Dreamweaver's advanced features

Dreamweaver supports Dynamic HTML development through its graphical interface, or you can add scripting by hand or use the Macromedia Director-like, time-line feature. It also supports stylesheets through a well-organized interface that enables you to specify font family, size, color, and weight and other attributes such as positioning. You can also create custom classes.

Developers often use JavaScript to add interactivity to their sites. For example, when a site visitor places the mouse cursor over an image, cursor will often change — providing instant feedback to the visitor that this is a special image — usually one that is "hot" or that links to another document. This effect is called a *mouseover* or a *rollover*.

For the developer who wants to use image mouseovers on a Web site, but who has absolutely no desire to learn JavaScript, Dreamweaver is a lifesaver. Using wizards accessed from the left-hand object bar, Dreamweaver walks you through the creation of mouseover code, as seen in Figure 28-4. It even includes browser-detect information so that the page does not break older browsers and will preload the images so that there is no delay between mousing over and having the new image appear on the Web page.

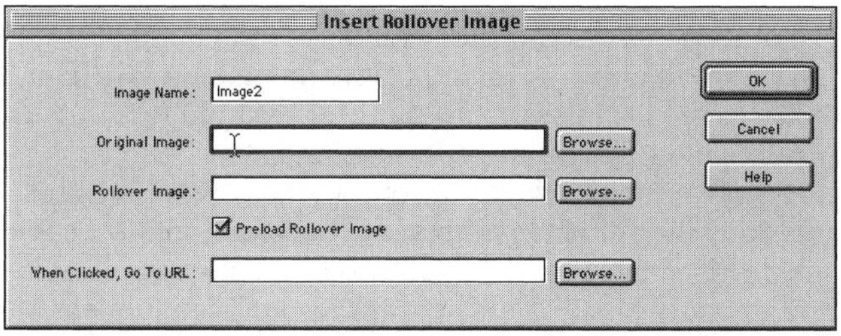

Figure 28-4: Dreamweaver makes creating JavaScript image rollovers a snap.

In addition, Dreamweaver has a powerful site management system, which enables you to FTP an entire Web site, in one step, from your hard drive to your Web server. Dreamweaver will make link corrections if you add or rearrange folder structure. It can also do a UNIX-like comparison and tell you which file is the newest — the one on the Web server or the one on your hard drive. This is especially important when more than one person is developing or maintaining a Web site.

Specifications and system requirements

✦ Current software version: 3.0.

✦ Demo available: Yes, full version, 30-day trial.

✦ Freeware available: No.

✦ Purchasing options: Available by Web from Macromedia Software (`http://www.macromedia.com/`) or available from most Macintosh software resellers. Price ranges from $129 (upgrade) to $299 (initial commercial purchase).

✦ System requirements: MacOS System 7.0 or later (7.5 or later recommended); 1.2MB RAM; CD-ROM for standard software installation.

✦ Web site: `http://www.macromedia.com/`.

Downloading and uploading with Macintosh FTP software

Although FTP (File Transfer Protocol) services are being coupled with other programs these days, sometimes the fastest download (or upload) will be through a dedicated FTP client. Macintosh FTP applications often have graphical interfaces to set commands that would normally be executed in a text, command-line mode, such as changing permissions on directories and files.

Fetch

Fetch (now Version 3.03) was written in the summer of 1989 to provide a file transfer solution for Macs talking to Dartmouth University's various operating systems and to take advantage of Dartmouth's newly acquired Internet connection. Boasting a simple drag-and-drop interface, which can be seen in Figure 28-5, Fetch enables file transfer over a TCP/IP network to and from any machine with an FTP server, including the ability to set permissions to directories and files.

Fetch comes preconfigured with bookmarks for popular Macintosh FTP sites, such as Apple.com, Dartmouth.edu, and Info-Mac archives. The latest version can restart interrupted transfers, making it unnecessary to redownload data that has already been transferred. Fetch is the only Mac FTP client with Apple Event Object Model support; this feature enables powerful scripting with languages such as AppleScript or Frontier. Fetch is also "recordable," so writing a simple script can be as simple as hitting the Record button in your script editor.

Specifications and system requirements

✦ Current software version: 3.0.3.

✦ Purchasing options: Shareware and free to user affiliated with an educational institution or charitable nonprofit organization. Other users should purchase a license; a single user license is $25.

✦ System requirements: MacOS System 7.0 or later.

✦ Web site: `http://www.dartmouth.edu/pages/softdev/fetch.html`.

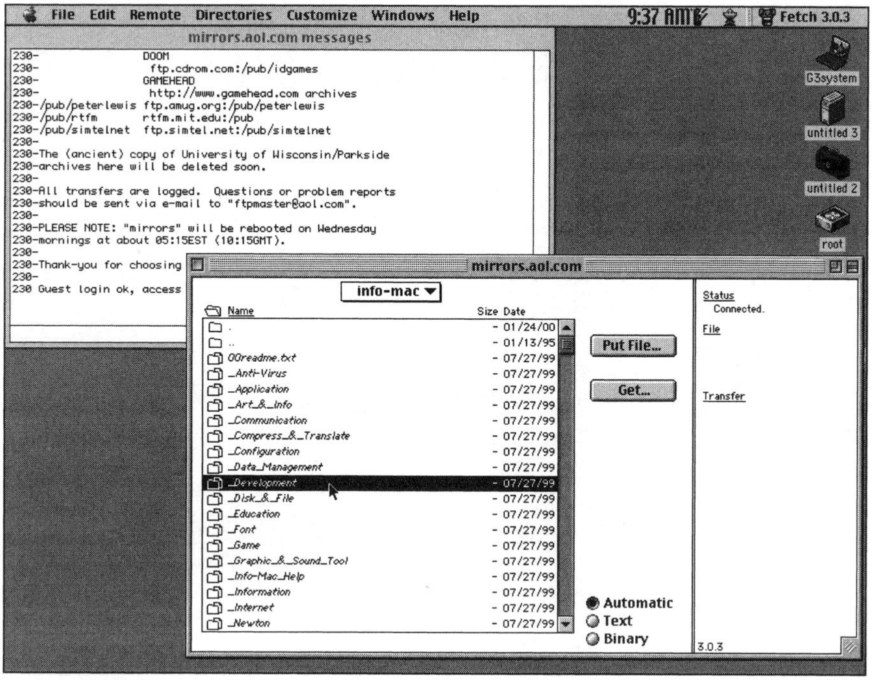

Figure 28-5: Fetch provides a clean drag-and-drop interface for transferring files to Web servers.

Anarchie

Some people prefer Anarchie, which is shown in Figure 28-6, to Fetch. Evolving over a 10-year period, Anarchie was nominated for Macworld's 1999 Editors Choice award for Best Internet Client Software. The current version utilizes features of Apple's OS 9, including the keychain technology for password management and extensive use of Sherlock 2.

More full-featured than Fetch, Anarchie can check to see which files on your local drive differ from those on the server, and it will then upload only the changed files. This version also includes a Watch menu, Traceroute and Ping features, and TCP testing. These tools are useful for troubleshooting. Traceroute, which is shown in Figure 28-6, enables you to see the route your request for an HTML file takes to get to the Web server; you can also see delays along the way. Ping enables to you send a test packet to see if a server is active; this is useful if you're getting no response when you request a Web page.

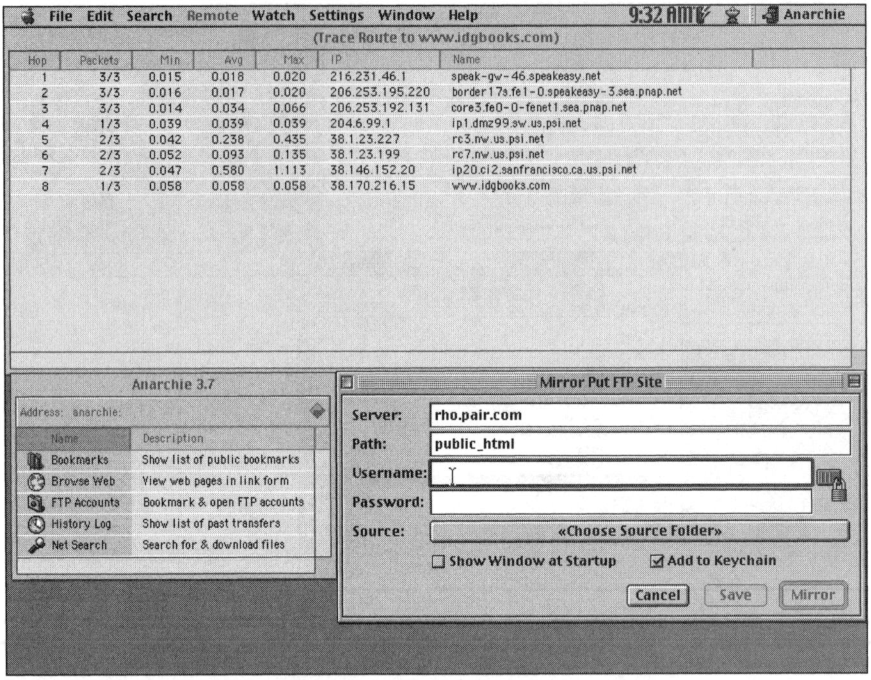

Figure 28-6: Anarchie is more than a simple FTP tool; it can also run a traceroute from a graphical interface (instead of a UNIX command-line).

Specifications and system requirements

    ✦ Current software version: 3.7.

    ✦ Purchasing options: Shareware; a single license is $35.

    ✦ System requirements: MacOS System 7.0 or later.

    ✦ Web site: http://www.stairways.com/.

Visualizing with Macintosh image tools

The most popular commercial image creation and editing tools for the Macintosh are Adobe Photoshop (Version 5.5 is bundled with Adobe ImageReady) and Macromedia Fireworks. Both products enable the developer to create Web-ready art. Fireworks is unique because its native file type is PNG (Portable Network Graphics), the "new kid on the block" for Web graphic formats. The two most supported graphic file formats on the Web are GIF (Graphics Interchange Format) and JPEG (Joint Photographic Experts Group). PNG was developed by an internet group and is expressly patent-free; it is supported by the latest version of major browsers and is expected to, in time, replace the GIF format, which is owned by CompuServe.

GraphicConverter

GraphicConverter, shown in Figure 28-7, is a full-featured image editor that can crop, convert, scale, view, or edit images, and it is one of the best shareware programs ever created for the Macintosh. For Web developers, the magic is that this compact (and affordable) program can open and save images in just about any graphics format — import about 120 graphic file formats and export about 40 formats. It can easily create transparent GIFs, and even includes a batch processing mode.

Figure 28-7: GraphicConverter is an inexpensive but powerful editing tool — enabling Web designers to easily save graphic images in native Web formats.

Tip If you want your graphic to blend into the background of your Web page, then you want a transparent GIF. (JPEGs cannot be made transparent.) What this means is that the background color of your GIF is matched to the background color you have selected for the Web page. When the image appears, it seems to float on the page. No hard edges!

Specifications and system requirements

✦ Current software version: 3.7.2.

✦ Purchasing options: Shareware; single license, $35.

✦ System requirements: MacOS System 7.0 or later and a PowerPC Macintosh.

✦ Web site: http://www.lemkesoft.de/.

ImageMapper

Often you may want to use an image as a navigation tool, but don't want to cut the image into pieces and reassemble using HTML tables. To link the image to more than one HTML file, you have to know the coordinates of the *hot spot* (where the end user will click). If you have ever tried to determine these coordinates manually, you know the hassle involved and why having a tool to define hot spots makes life so much smoother.

ImageMapper does have the ability to pinpoint hotspots for you. It uses a simple, object-oriented interface to define areas of any image that you wish to serve as hypertext links. It also makes it easy to map the image area to the URL associated with the link. ImageMapper also supports JavaScript and creates HTML 4.0–compliant code by prompting users to add ALT tags to their links; this prompt occurs if you have specified that your imagemap should be Lynx-compatible.

To create an imagemap, first open the image in ImageMapper. The floating tool palette provides the tools you need to draw your hotspots directly onto the image. Hotspots can be circles, rectangles, or polygons—or you may draw a freehand shape to fit. When the shapes are complete, just click the Generate button. ImageMapper will pop open a window that contains the code needed for that map. Save the code as a file or copy the relevant sections into your in-work Web document.

Specifications and system requirements

✦ Current software version: 3.0.

✦ Purchasing options: Shareware; single license, $15.

✦ System requirements: MacOS System 7.0.

✦ Web site: `http://www.dcs.gla.ac.uk/~snaddosg/Creations/ImageMapper/`.

Using Web Design Tools For Linux

Linux is a UNIX-like operating system, designed to be a free, open-source alternative to Windows and Macintosh operating systems. Linux is the poster child for alternative operating systems, evidenced by IBM's January 2000 announcement that it plans to make Linux a centerpiece of its computer hardware strategy. Despite this move towards mainstream markets, if you are using Linux as your development environment, you are probably as interested in back-end processes as HTML and design.

Many of the applications available for Linux are downloadable from the Web. Some are freeware, some are shareware, and some are commercial applications. All honor the ethic of the open-source movement. This section provides an overview of editors, imaging programs, and development tools.

Why Open-Source Software is Good for You

Open-source software is *source code* that is available for anyone to use or modify — with no fee. But what is source code? It is code that a programmer can read; this code can then be transformed into something that a computer can understand (commonly called a program or an application).

An analogy might be a recipe; the recipe (for chocolate chip cookies, for example) is the source code. The cook reads the code (ingredients and instructions). Assembling and cooking the ingredients is a similar transformation process. The result is a snack to be consumed by the cook's friends.

The open-source movement is important because software can evolve faster when anyone can read, redistribute, or modify the code. It is philosophically grounded in open *standards*. Standards, for example, make it possible for you to buy a hairdryer in Atlanta and successfully use it (with no modifications) in San Jose (unlike what would happen if you were travelling in Europe or Asia).

When you send e-mail or use the Web, you are relying on open-source software. That's because the foundation of the Internet (its mail transports, Web servers, and FTP servers) are almost all open-source software.

There is more to being open-source than being free, however. For more information on what makes software open-source, see `http://www.opensource.org/osd.html`.

Creating Web pages with Linux HTML editors

You will find three commonly used Unix text editors — pico, emacs, and vi. RedHat Linux ships with emacs and viM (pronounced "vee-eye-em" for vi improved). emacs is accessed from the GNOME desktop; viM is accessed from the UNIX shell (just type **:vi**). All three editors are small, fast, extremely powerful, and keyboard-based.

Gnotepad

However, RedHat also ships with a GUI-based text editor called Gnotepad, which is shown in Figure 28-8. This application is more comfortable for the user who is migrating to Linux from the Macintosh or Windows world — and who has not spent a lot of time working in DOS. It also is more powerful than the simple editors shipped with those platforms; for example, it contains a search-and-replace function. Unlike Windows NotePad (but like SimpleText for the Mac), it enables multiple windows for multiple documents. It also enables HTML viewing using the gtk-xmhtml widget. Gnotepad is bundled with GNOME, the "windows" or graphical interface that ships with RedHat. For more information, see `http://rpmfind.net/linux/RPM/suse/6.1/i386/suse/gnm3/gnotepad-1.1.2-11.i386.html`.

Figure 28-8: Gnotepad is more powerful than simple editors bundled with Mac or Windows systems.

AsWedit

HTML-specific editors are also available for Linux systems. AsWedit, published by AdvaSoft Ltd of London, England, is an easy-to-use HTML and text editor for X-Windows System. It offers a text editing mode as well as two context-sensitive, validating modes for authoring HTML; the two HTML modes are HTML 4.0 Transitional and HTML 4.0 Frameset. AsWedit is a free version available for students and those affiliated with an educational institution. A commercial version of AsWedit is available for $149 per machine. For more information, see http://www.advasoft.com/.

Morphon

Morphon is an XML editor for Linux, which enables you to create documents based on a DTD (Document Type Definition). In addition to supporting a variety of languages, it enables a preview of the document being processed by an XSL stylesheet. For more information, see http://www2.lunatech.com/products/morphon-xml-editor/.

Looking at Linux image tools

Several good image tools have been developed for the Linux platform. If you are a user of Adobe's Photoshop, however, you may not be happy to learn that Adobe has yet to develop a version of Photoshop for Linux. However, an alternative called The GIMP (GNU Image Manipulation Program) is available.

GIMP

One critical aspect of The GIMP is that it is free software: It was released under the General Public License of the Free Software Foundation. Thus, it is a freely distributed software application and is included with RedHat and other Linux systems.

The GIMP, which is shown in Figure 28-9, can be used as a simple paint program, a photo retouching program, or an image converter (creating Web-native file types such as GIF, JPEG and PNG). It has an excellent batch processing system, reflecting its roots as an application written by developers for developers.

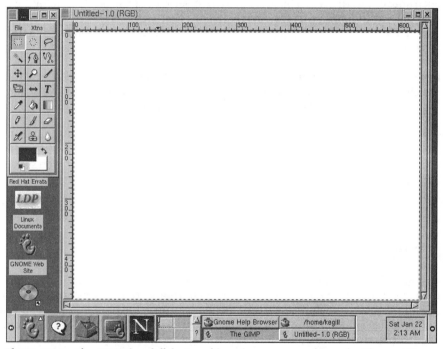

Figure 28-9: The GIMP is a full-featured imaging program shipped with most Linux systems; it is a versatile tool that can create Web-native image files.

For more information on The Gimp, see "An Introduction to The Gimp, `http://www.acm.org/crossroads/xrds3-4/gimp.html`; A Quick Start Guide to The Gimp; `http://www.ssc.com/lj/issue43/2388.html`; or `http://www.gimp.org/`.

Other Linux image tools

Other Linux image tools include GIF-X.Plugin, which creates animated GIFs; GILT, which is a vector drawing program; GyrosCoPe, which is an HTML color picker; Image Magick, which can read, write, and manipulate an image in image formats such as GIF, JPEG, PNG, PDF, and Photo CD; and imaptool, which creates client-size imagemaps. For additional Linux image applications, see `http://www.linuxstart.com/applications/multimedia/graphics.html`.

Surveying Linux development tools

For Web developers interested in creating database-to-Web applications, PHP is a script language and interpreter similar to JavaScript and Microsoft's VBScript. It is freely available and used primarily with Linux Web servers. PHP (the initials come from the earliest version of the program, called Personal Home Page tools) is a free, open-source alternative to Microsoft's Active Server Page (ASP) technology, which runs only on Windows servers. An HTML page that includes a PHP script is typically given a file name suffix of .php, .php3, or .phtml. The latest version is PHP3.0.x; for more information, see `http://www.php.net/`.

Development tools that are often incorporated into most Linux releases include Apache Web server, Java development kit and runtime environment, Netscape Communicator and Navigator, Lynx, mySQL, Perl, and PHP.

For a comprehensive set of tools, check out Linux Web Tools from Walnut Creek CD-ROM. It includes the previous list of tools, as well as browser plug-ins, HTML editors, CGI scripts and tools, graphics editors, Java programs, and Web server administration tools. For more information, see `http://www.cdrom.com/titles/linux/linWeb.phtml`.

Summary

Macintosh and Linux enthusiasts will find a wealth of Web development tools for both systems. Either platform provides an alternative to the Windows operating system. The Macintosh remains an excellent platform for front-end work such as design and graphics. Linux is an excellent host platform and provides programmers with an opportunity to create new applications to meet user demand as the market for Linux desktop systems escalates.

✦   ✦   ✦

Creating Graphics

◆   ◆   ◆   ◆

In This Chapter

Understanding digital images

Evaluating digital cameras

Manipulating photographs with photo manipulation software

Charting Web sites with image maps

Creating animated GIFs, buttons, and other special effects

◆   ◆   ◆   ◆

There's nothing quite so boring as a Web site that's all text and no graphics. Digital images — photos — can change all of that and add some real excitement to your Web site. In this chapter, you learn how to create and use digital images. You also see how you can change images either simply to improve their quality or to make them into something quite outrageous! You'll also learn about creating and using other types of graphics on your Web pages for use as link buttons and other purposes.

Picturing Digital Images

A digital image is really just a special type of photograph — one that's stored electronically rather than chemically. Normal photographs (ones taken with a camera that uses film) store images as chemical changes on film.

Generally, the chemical mix on film is a combination of tiny silver grains, dyes, and other items that bind the whole mixture together and make it stick to the thin plastic backing. This chemical composition produces some pretty incredible results. For example, the quick snapshot you take with a $10 throwaway film camera still has more detail than today's best several-thousand-dollar digital camera. Your new digital camera may be sexy, but it has a way to go to match the quality of a good film-based camera. That gap has been closed somewhat in recent years with the advent of megapixel cameras, but the gap still exists nonetheless.

Visualizing resolution and color

Digital images can be produced directly using a digital camera or indirectly by scanning a photo taken with a film camera. Either way, the end result is the same. The digital image is an electronic representation of the physical object. The *resolution* of a digital image is measured in pixels. Each *pixel*—picture element—is the smallest bit of detail in the image. Thus, a digital image in VGA resolution, 640×480 pixels, has no more than 640 tiny pieces of detail across the width of the image, and no more than 480 pieces across the height of the image. That's 307,200 discrete points in the image. Megapixel cameras produce images with more than a million points of detail, with maximum resolutions equal to or greater than 1152×872.

In addition to resolution, digital images also store information about the colors in the photograph. Color information is generally stored as levels of red, green, and blue (RGB), although some color models use cyan, magenta, yellow, and black (CMYK). Storing additional color information greatly increases the size of the digital image file. Table 29-1 shows typical file sizes for a 640×480 digital image at different color depths.

Table 29-1		
File Sizes of a 640×480 Digital Image at Different Color Depths		
# of Colors	*File Size*	*Bits of Color Data*
256	300K	8
65,536	600K	16
16,777,216	900K	24

Although the 16 million colors possible in a 24-bit image may seem like a lot, remember that good old-fashioned photo film has a virtually unlimited color range (in addition to much higher resolution).

Dots Per Inch vs. Pixels

As we've said, the resolution and size of a digital image is determined by the number of pixels in the image. But let's consider "analog" pictures for a moment, like those taken with a film camera and printed on slides, negatives, or photo paper. When you want to convert analog pictures into digital images to use on your Web site, you have to scan them.

Some scanners are better at picking up detail from your pictures than others. That detail is expressed in *dots per inch* (dpi). Each dot is a grain of detail on the image, so the more dots per inch that your scanner is capable of identifying, the sharper the resolution of the scan.

Higher dpi resolution is nice, but those "dots" are inevitably much smaller than the pixels that will eventually make up your digital images. Modern computer monitors aren't capable of showing more than 72dpi, so even a typical $50 scanner capable of 300 dpi scans is sufficient if you only plan to use it for scanning Web images. Most of those extra dots will be "lost" to the electronic abyss when you save the picture as a JPEG or GIF anyway.

Focusing on output devices

When you take a photograph with a standard film camera, you probably take the film to be processed and printed. If a few of the pictures are quite special, you might have them enlarged. If you really want to get fancy, you might have a small portion of one of the photos enlarged into a big poster-sized print. Throughout the whole process, you expect that all of the photo prints will look pretty good—even the extreme enlargements.

Although you may print your digital images, it's far more likely you'll view them on-screen—in Web pages, for example. Depending on the size of your monitor and the color settings of your display adapter, additional resolution and color depth may not even show up. For example, if your screen is set to display 256 colors, the 16-million-plus colors of a 24-bit color image will mostly be wasted.

Compressing image files

When you're preparing digital images for use on Web sites, you need to remember the effect of larger file sizes on the length of time it takes to load a Web page over the typical modem connection. A lot of excess color information simply makes your Web page too slow to load.

Raw, uncompressed images take a lot of space. Quite a few years ago, people realized that image files (which generally contain a lot of redundant information) could be reduced in size—*compressed*—without significantly reducing the quality of the image. Compressed files require less storage space and are much quicker to transmit over a modem.

There's just one complication in using compressed image files—there are quite a few different file formats and they're not interchangeable. To name a few, there's PCX, TIFF, JPEG, GIF, TGA, and several more. To make matters worse, some file formats have more than one variation. TIFF files, for example, have different file structures depending on whether a Windows or Macintosh system is used. They can also be displayed in compressed or uncompressed modes; if compressed, they might be in any one of several compression formats. All this creates an alphabet soup of graphics formats that would be too much for Web browsers to support.

Fortunately, graphics on the Web have mostly settled on three file formats, and every modern Web browser supports them. The first format, GIF—*Graphics Interchange Format*—was originally developed by CompuServe to permit the exchange of images on the CompuServe network. JPEG—*Joint Photographic Experts Group*—was designed by an independent group as a means of creating standards for compressing images. PNG—*Portable Network Graphics*—is a newer standard designed to replace GIF. Of these standards, JPEG is far more flexible, allowing images to have any color depth and also enabling the image creator to specify different levels of compression. GIF and PNG graphics have less flexibility, but they do have one advantage over JPEG—GIF and PNG images can have transparent areas, which allows the element underneath the image to show through. Still, JPEG images contain the best color characteristics and the smallest file sizes.

Note
The biggest disadvantage of GIF images is that the format is covered by a patent held by CompuServe, and thus software developers (such as Adobe) that create software capable of producing GIFs must pay licensing fees. JPEGs and PNGs have no such licensing requirements.

Just how much can you compress an image file and still expect the image to look good? The answer depends on your needs. Figures 29-1 and 29-2 show two images taken with a digital camera and saved at two different levels of JPEG compression. Figure 29-1 was saved using a higher color mode with the resulting image file size of 105K. Figure 29-2 was saved using a lower quality mode that shrunk the file to 32K.

It's pretty hard to tell the difference between the two images, isn't it? If you look closely, Figure 29-1 has slightly higher quality, but Figure 29-2 is only one-fourth the file size of Figure 29-1. If you're planning on using images on your Web site, keeping the size down is far more important than the small difference in quality.

Figure 29-1: This 105K image was saved using a higher-quality setting.

Figure 29-2: This 32K version of the same image uses a more economical setting.

Tip   If it's really important for your Web site visitors to see the highest quality versions of your images, include a link to a larger copy of the image file. That link enables visitors to load your Web site more quickly and click the link if they want to see the high-quality image.

Using Digital Cameras

Digital cameras are different from ordinary cameras in one very important way. Rather than storing images on film, digital cameras use an electronic sensor called a Charged Coupled Device (CCD) to create an electronic representation of the image. This electronic representation is then stored in the camera's memory until it can be downloaded to your computer.

Storing images electronically makes it easy to use those images as part of a Web site. In fact, if you want to use film images on a Web site, you first have to convert them to electronic images. Clearly, digital cameras offer a large advantage to the Web site builder who wants to include images — there's no need to go through a conversion process before you can use digital images.

The next few sections discuss important features that can make a big difference in how a digital camera might suit your needs.

Measuring photo storage capacity

Unless you're buying one of those single-use cameras, you probably don't worry about how many pictures a camera can store with a film camera. When you're done with one roll of film, you just pop it out and put in another roll. Essentially, film cameras have unlimited picture storage since the pictures are stored on removable film packs. New film is cheap, so if you want to take more pictures, you just buy more film.

Digital cameras have to store their pictures in memory. Virtually all digital cameras on the market today have removable memory cards, but these cards are far more expensive than a roll of film. Sony digital cameras store pictures on standard 3.5" diskettes, but that's an exception to the way most digital cameras store images.

When your digital camera's memory is full, you have several options. You can stop taking pictures, download the pictures to your PC, delete pictures to make room for more, or in some cases you can swap in a new memory card. Unfortunately, extra memory cards are expensive; a 32MB memory card can cost as much as $100 and (with the latest high-resolution cameras) may not hold many more pictures than a $5 roll of film.

The number of pictures a digital camera can store and its ability to transfer those images to your PC is determined by several factors:

✦ **Built-in memory.** We recommend that you buy a camera that has built-in memory to allow faster image caching. This reduces the delay caused as you wait for the camera to write an image to storage before you can take another picture. On-board memory allows the camera to take "rapid-fire" images in a series. Also, you should buy a camera that includes a removable storage media, such as a floppy disk or memory card.

✦ **Image compression.** Some cameras do a better job of compressing images than others. Look for the number of images a camera can store at each of its image quality settings.

✦ **Removable memory.** If a camera uses removable memory cards, make certain it uses a *standard media format*. The two main standards today are CompactFlash and SmartMedia. That way you'll be able to buy larger capacity memory cards than are offered by the camera manufacturer (and probably for less money, too).

✦ **Image download.** Make sure your camera has the ability to download images into your computer. In most cases, digital cameras that use 3.5" floppy disks won't present a problem. Just take the disk out of the camera and pop it into your computer's disk drive. Some cameras can connect to your computer with either a USB or serial cable. If your camera uses CompactFlash and SmartMedia cards for storage, you can also purchase special external drives that you connect to your computer in order to read them.

Gauging digital camera power supply

You may be surprised by the amount of power a digital camera uses. You can go for years without changing the battery in a film camera. Generally, the battery in a film camera simply provides power for adjusting the exposure. Digital cameras use batteries for every operation and accordingly tend to use a lot of them.

One reason digital cameras use a lot of power compared to film cameras is that digital cameras often have an active matrix LCD screen in place of a viewfinder. This screen needs a backlight and is used as more than just a viewfinder. The LCD screen also shows you the pictures you've already taken so you can choose to keep or erase images.

Some cameras, such as those made by Olympus, have optical viewfinders, just like film cameras. This means they typically get more life out of a set of batteries because you do not need to use the LCD screen every time you want to take a picture.

Rechargeable batteries are clearly the best choice for use in digital cameras. When the batteries run down, pop them in the charger and in a few hours they'll be ready to go again. If you take a lot of pictures with your digital camera, a battery charger will pay for itself in no time.

As economical as rechargeable batteries may be, they're not always the handiest solution. If you're traveling, for example, you may find it difficult to recharge a set of batteries. That's why you want to make certain the camera can also use a standard battery, such as AA cells. That way you can use rechargeable AA cells when they're available and alkaline AA cells in an emergency when you can't recharge a set of batteries.

Tip   When you're buying a digital camera, avoid models that do not use removable batteries or use proprietary batteries. If a camera uses standard removable batteries you can get a fresh set of batteries almost anywhere.

Perceiving image resolution

Digital cameras still don't match the resolution and sharpness of a film camera. The image sensors in digital cameras simply can't produce the same resolution that the chemical molecules in film can. Still, for many uses that really doesn't matter very much.

When you place an image on a Web site, you should remember that people visiting a Web site probably have their screen resolution set to 640×480 or 800×600. (A few visitors use a higher setting such as 1024×768, but it's best to plan for 800×600 maximum.) Therefore, images should be created with a resolution smaller than 640×480, which is as large as you'd ever want to use on a Web site.

That's not to say that the higher resolution images produced by some digital cameras is wasted. It's always possible to *crop* an image to cut down the size. In fact, it's often quite handy to be able to use just a small portion of an image — especially if you weren't able to get physically close enough to your subject to fill the screen.

Ultimately, the resolution you get will probably depend on how much money you are willing to spend. The cheapest cameras on the market today produce 640×480 resolution and typically cost less than $200. This may be more than enough, especially if you only plan to use images on the Web. But if you plan to print any of your pictures, you should try to get something with higher resolution. Many people consider megapixel cameras to offer the bare minimum of acceptable quality today, but if you want megapixel resolution you can expect to pay $400 or more. Consumer digital cameras typically top out at about $1500 for the latest state-of-the-art model, but if you are willing to wait a little while, you can save a lot of money as digital cameras become less expensive.

Reflecting on other digital camera issues

Some issues in choosing a digital camera aren't quite so easy to pin down. For example, you might find that one camera just doesn't feel right, or you might find another one a bit awkward in use. The weight and shape of the camera are important factors, but you should decide by picking up a unit and giving it a try.

Some digital cameras use a *fixed focus* lens, while others have a zoom lens. A zoom lens may be quite handy, but it may take some getting used to — especially when you're trying to compose photos on the LCD screen.

One digital camera feature that's handier than you may think is the capability to display the images directly on a TV screen through a built-in video output port. Not only can you view your pictures on any TV, but you can also record the images on your VCR. In addition, the video output port generally works as a real-time video monitor, which means your digital camera can also function as a video camera. Some cameras, such as Sony Mavicas, even let you record MPEG video, and they have microphones for audio recording as well.

Also consider the software that the camera uses. All digital cameras should come with driver software that will work with your operating system (pay special attention to this if you use Linux or Macintosh operating systems). Most also have a utility program that enables you to manage your camera and images with the computer. Figure 29-3 shows the Olympus camera utility for Olympus cameras. Finally, many cameras come with some photo manipulation software as part of the package. One of the most common packaged programs is Adobe PhotoDeluxe, which is discussed later in this chapter.

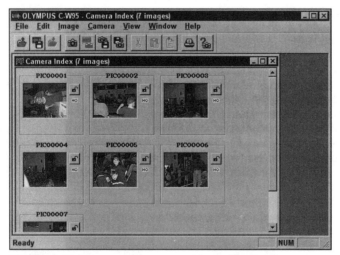

Figure 29-3: Most cameras come with a utility that lets you manage your camera's functions from your computer.

Scanning Photos

Digital cameras aren't the only solution for getting photos into your PC. If you already have a good film camera, or if you intend to work with a lot of old photos, you may want to consider using a scanner rather than a digital camera.

Scanners are a good alternative to digital cameras — as long as you can wait for the original photos to be developed and printed. In fact, you may want both a scanner and a digital camera.

If you use a scanner to produce digital images, you'll find there's one slight complication in comparison with a digital camera. Scanners often have variable resolution settings, and you must choose the appropriate resolution for each scan. To do this, you must first determine the size in pixels you want for the finished image, then set the scanning area, and finally adjust the scanner resolution to produce the desired result. None of these steps are particularly difficult, but they do require some advance planning to achieve your intended result.

In choosing a scanner for creating images for your Web site, you'll want to consider the following factors:

✦ **Twain compliant.** Be certain that any scanner you choose is twain compliant. This means that the scanner meets certain standards to work with a broad range of PC applications.

✦ **Resolution.** You don't need an extremely fancy scanner for Web site work. In most cases you'll want to keep the size of the image files as small as possible, and therefore you won't need a large number of colors or high resolution. Even a 300 dpi (dots-per-inch), 24-bit (color depth) scanner is fine for creating Web site images. Scanners capable of this quality are widely available for as little as $50.

✦ **Scanning software.** Scanners generally include basic scanning software. In most cases, this software is similar to the photo manipulation software discussed in the next section, although the feature set may be minimal. Once you've scanned an image, however, you can use that image in any photo manipulation software as though you had taken the photo with a digital camera.

✦ **Scanning services.** If your scanning needs are minimal, check to see if your local library, college campus, or office service center offers scanning services. Of course, since many simple color scanners are available for under $100, the convenience of having your own scanner may be worth the minimal cost.

Using Photo Manipulation Software

Do you take perfect photographs every time, or are you like the rest of us who could use a little help? Almost any photograph has some area where it could use some improvement, and today's digital photographer has a real advantage over the traditional film photographer in this area.

The available photo manipulation software ranges from the simplest of software packages that often come with digital cameras to high-end products like Adobe Photoshop. Some of the well-known commercial photo manipulation software names include Adobe PhotoDeluxe, MGI PhotoSuite, and Microsoft PhotoDraw.

Employing photo manipulation basics

Virtually all photo manipulation software packages include certain common functions. The following list of functions addresses problems you typically encounter in using digital camera or scanned photographs on your computer or a Web site:

✦ **Red-eye reduction.** This function removes the red spot that often appears in the eyes of people in a flash photograph. The red spot occurs when the camera's flash reflects off the inside of someone's eye.

✦ **Brightness and contrast adjustment.** Photos often benefit from changing the brightness or the contrast in the image, especially when the original exposure wasn't quite perfect or lighting conditions made the photo appear dull and lifeless.

✦ **Color balance adjustment.** Digital cameras often produce photos in which the colors don't look real. By adjusting the color balance you can remove some of the excessive blue, green, or red cast to make the photo look more lifelike.

✦ **Cropping.** It's not unusual to discover that the real subject of your photo only fills a small part of the frame. By cutting the unwanted edges off the photo — *cropping* the photo — you can make your subject stand out and take center stage in the resulting image.

Limited to the preceding tasks, photo manipulation software greatly improves your digital photography. In most cases, however, these tasks are just the beginning.

Using Adobe PhotoDeluxe

Many digital cameras and scanners come with photo manipulation software to help you manage and improve the images you create. Adobe PhotoDeluxe is one of the most popular of those programs. PhotoDeluxe is a "lite" version of Adobe's Photoshop, considered by many to be the industry standard for photo retouching. Photoshop is used by many publishing professionals to prepare images for inclusion in books, magazines, and Web sites. PhotoShop is good, but at $649 ($199 for the upgrade) it is also expensive.

To begin editing an image in PhotoDeluxe, first open the program, and then click File ⇨ Open. The image will open in the PhotoDeluxe window as shown in Figure 29-4.

Figure 29-4: An image has been opened in PhotoDeluxe, and the Touch Up tab is open.

The program has several tabs that hold the various functions of PhotoDeluxe. Notice that the Touch Up tab has several tools that you can use to touch up various aspects of the image:

✦ **Instant Fix.** This tool automatically adjusts the contrast levels for the image and alters some colors. You may or may not be happy with the result, but if you don't like it you can just click the Undo button at the top of the image window.

✦ **Size Orientation.** This tool activates a three-step wizard. The first step enables you to rotate the image. The second enables you to crop the image. Click once on the image and use the handles in each corner and at the sides to crop. The third step enables you to change the size of the image without trimming any of it off. Click the fourth tab when you are done.

✦ **Fix Color.** This tool presents variations on the coloration of your image, as shown in Figure 29-5. Click the Variations button on the variations tab and review the variations that are presented. Click on one of the variations to adjust the colors. You can continue to click on the variations to add more of the color indicated, and press OK to accept your changes (or press Cancel to go back to the original coloration).

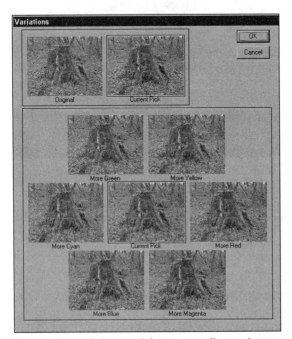

Figure 29-5: Click one of the surrounding variants to adjust color levels.

✦ **Remove Red Eye.** Click this button to remove red eye in portraits. Select tab one of the Red Eye wizard and then click the Select Rectangle button. Then draw a small rectangle around the red eyes you want to fix. Now move to the Remove tab and click Remove Red Eye. Finally, click Done.

✦ **Color Eyes.** You can radically change the appearance of subjects in your photos by adding color to their eyes. The four-step wizard lets you zoom in on the eyes, select an area with the color wand, and then color or paint the selected eye area.

Using special effects in PhotoDeluxe

PhotoDeluxe makes it easy to apply special effects to your images. We can't possibly show them all to you here, but we'll give you a few highlights. Note that when you begin to apply most effects, PhotoDeluxe will ask you to save a copy of the image as a .PDD document.

✦ **Black & White.** To convert your image to black and white, click the Old Fashioned button on the Art tab. Next, click the To B&W tab, and then click the Color to B&W button. This change can have a remarkable effect on your images, especially if you want to show a lot of detail.

✦ **Posterize.** Also on the Art tab, click Posterize. This step applies a special colorized effect to your image, which you can adjust by changing the level shown in the Posterize dialog box

✦ **Colored Pencil.** The Colored Pencil effect on the "Cooler" tab applies to the effect shown in Figure 29-6. Again, the actual effect can be adjusted based on several parameters.

✦ **Note Paper.** Create a two-toned ghost image, as shown in Figure 29-7, with the note paper tool, also on the "Cooler" tab.

Figure 29-6: The picture is given the colored pencil treatment.

Figure 29-7: And here it is with the Note Paper effect.

The possibilities are virtually endless. Again, we cannot possibly show you all of the things you can do with images in PhotoDeluxe, but this can certainly help you get started.

Saving your PhotoDeluxe pictures

When you are done and want to use your newly edited graphic on the Web, you need to save and output it. When you save it, the program saves it in a proprietary PhotoDeluxe (PDD) file format, which you can't use in your Web pages. To save it as a JPEG (or GIF), click File ⇨ Send to ⇨ File Format. In the Save As window, choose the file format in which you want to save it. If you plan to use it online, JPEG is the best choice for color photographs. When you click Save, you will see a message asking if you wish to continue; before you click OK, click the Options button to open the dialog shown in Figure 29-8. This option enables you to adjust the final quality of the colors in the JPEG. The higher quality you choose with the slider, the bigger the file will be.

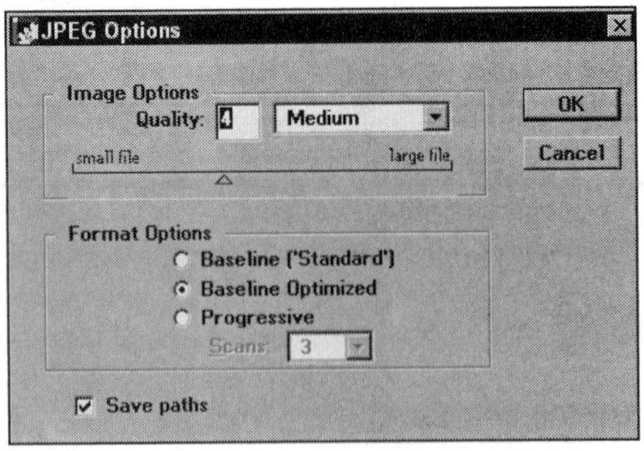

Figure 29-8: Move the slider to adjust the quality of the JPEG you are about to export.

Using Microsoft PhotoDraw

Microsoft offers a popular image editing program called PhotoDraw. PhotoDraw comes with the Premium and Developer Editions of Microsoft Office 2000, and it is also sold separately. Besides modifying existing images, PhotoDraw can also function as an illustration program to let you create new graphics from your own imagination.

Editing images with PhotoDraw

Some of the most common image editing tasks are the simplest. For instance, consider the picture shown in Figure 29-9. Notice anything wrong? The image was taken with a digital camera held in portrait orientation rather than landscape, so as we look at it here the picture is laying on its side. This can be fixed by clicking Arrange ⇨ Rotate ⇨ Rotate Right (or Rotate Left, as the case may dictate). After you rotate the picture, you will have to fix the shape of the canvas area, which you can do by clicking View ⇨ Fit Picture Area to Selection.

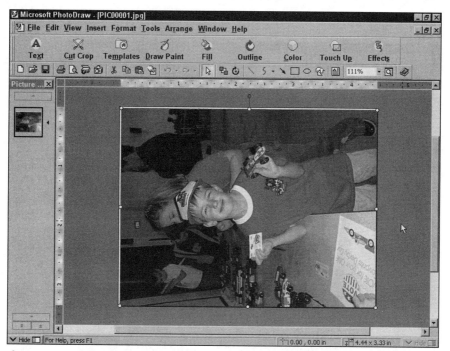

Figure 29-9: This image can be rotated using the Rotate options in the Arrange menu.

To crop the image to a specific area, open an image you want to trim and do the following:

1. Click the Cut Crop button on the PhotoDraw toolbar, and choose Crop from the small submenu that appears.

2. The Crop tool window appears on the right side of the screen. Choose a shape for the cropped item. In most cases, you will choose the square shown at the top of the list.

3. Drag the selection handles until the crop marks surround the area that you want to crop the image to, and click Finish on the floating Crop toolbar. Figure 29-10 shows our cropped image.

Tip

If you are having a hard time cropping because some of the graphic runs off the screen, change the zoom level on the toolbar. Depending on the size of your picture and the screen area, you may need to reduce it to 75 percent of normal size or less.

Choose a shape before cropping

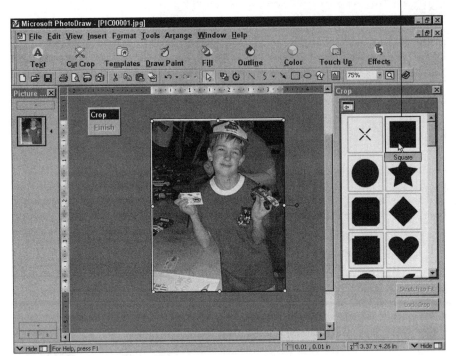

Figure 29-10: This image has been cropped so that the subject fills more of the image.

Touching up portraits

PhotoDraw includes tools to fix many common image problems. For instance, you can fix red eye by clicking Format ➪ Touch Up ➪ Fix Red Eye, which opens a toolbar as shown in Figure 29-11. Here we will click on the eye with the pointer, and then click Fix on the Red Eye toolbar to automatically reduce the red eye effect.

Figure 29-11: Use the Fix Red Eye touch up tool to reduce red eye problems.

Other touch-up effects include

✦ **Special effects.** You can blur or sharpen an image, apply a shadow, or lighten the image with a transparency effect. Blur and sharpen can help reduce a lot of image quality problems produced by low resolution digital camera images.

✦ **Colors.** Adjust color levels, tints and hues, color saturation, or even convert the photo to a negative image.

✦ **Fixes.** You can touch-up picture problems like dust and scratches. This is especially handy if you are scanning older pictures that have slid around inside one too many photo albums.

✦ **Text.** Use the Text tool to insert text into an image. If you are concerned about people copying your pictures, consider placing a tiny copyright notice in the lower corner of your images.

Saving images

When you are done editing graphics in PhotoDraw, you should first save them in the proprietary .mix format, and then save them in JPEG. When you save it as a JPEG, click the Options button in the Save As dialog box to adjust color settings and the compression level. Note that you must select JPEG from the Save As Type menu before these options become available.

Using The GIMP for Linux

If you use Linux, neither PhotoDeluxe nor PhotoDraw is an option for you. Fortunately, you do have an excellent option for graphics editing open to you in a program called The GIMP. GIMP stands for *Graphic Image Manipulation Program* and comes with most installations of Linux. You should be able to find it in your programs menu under graphics programs.

To open a graphic in The GIMP, click File ⇨ Open on The GIMP's floating toolbar shown in Figure 29-12. Navigate to the file's location and open it.

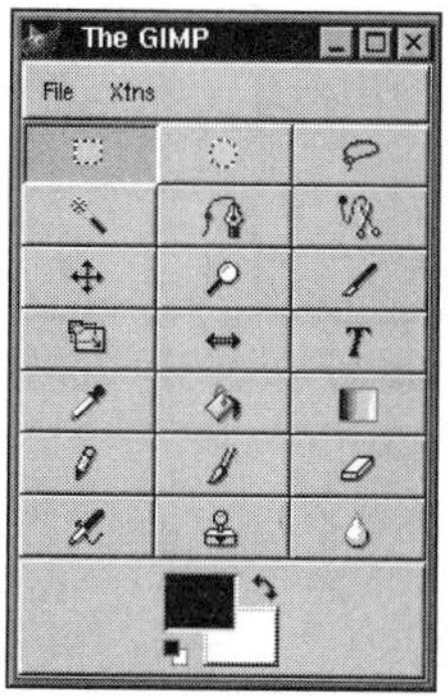

Figure 29-12: The GIMP's floating toolbar provides a variety of tools to help you manipulate your graphics.

When the program is open, you can perform many of the same actions as you would in the other programs discussed here. You may find that the right-click menus are particularly useful. To crop, for example, simply right-click the image and chose Tools ⇨ Crop from the right-click menu. Next use the mouse to click and drag over the area you want to crop the image to. Other useful editing tools include:

✦ Posterizing, recoloring, and other effects can be applied to the image.

✦ Images can be rotated using options in the Image ⇨ Transforms menu.

✦ Script-Fu offers a wide variety of special effects tools such as items that remove every other row of the graphic, add décor effects, apply animated rippling and wave effects, fade and brush effects, and more.

✦ Filters help you retouch images, fix problems, add distortions, and apply special lighting effects.

Really, there are literally hundreds of options available to help you customize your images with The GIMP. In Figure 29-13 we have applied a sparkle effect to make the office look squeaky clean.

Figure 29-13: Your author hard at work. Note the sparkling effect.

When you are done editing, right-click the graphic and choose File ⇨ Save As. You can control the file format simply by adding the appropriate extension — such as .jpg — to the end of the file name.

Using Image Maps

You don't have to spend much time online before you realize how much Web developers have come to rely on graphics in their sites. Many sites use a single, large graphic as a navigation guide to the site. For instance, imagine that a Web site provides links to stores in various states. The Web page shows a map of the United States, and when you click on a state you link directly to a list of stores in that state. How does this happen?

This type of linked image, where different regions of the image link to different pages, is called an *image map*. These links are often referred to as *hotspots*. The HTML code behind image maps is fairly complicated, because it requires you to specify coordinates and shapes for each hotspot. Thus, it is easier to create image maps with WYSIWYG (What You See Is What You Get) software. Numerous programs exist that help you create image maps, but you may find it easier to create them from within your HTML editor if it has the capability. FrontPage is one such HTML editor.

To create hotspots on graphics using FrontPage:

1. Open the page containing the graphic on which you want to create hotspots. If the image has not already been inserted and positioned, do so now.
2. Click the graphic once to select it.
3. Click the hotspot tool you want to use on the Pictures toolbar. Notice that there are three possible shapes: Rectangular, Circular, and Polygonal.
4. Use the mouse pointer to click and drag a hotspot on the picture.
5. When you are done creating the shape with the mouse, the Create Hyperlink dialog box opens. Choose the page you want to link to and click OK. When you are done, the outline of your hotspot should appear on the image, as shown in Figure 29-14.

Hotspot   Polygonal Hotspot   Hotspot

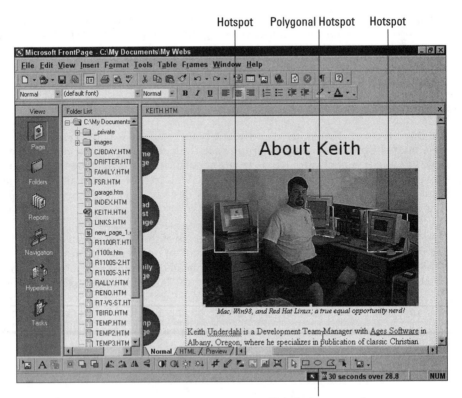

Click the hotspot tools

Figure 29-14: A hotspot has been created around each computer. Notice that a polygonal hotspot has been used to draw the hotspot around the seated individual.

Creating Buttons and Tiles in PhotoDraw

Here are some tips and tricks for making Web images, such as buttons, horizontal lines, and background tiles, in PhotoDraw. The techniques we explore here are applicable to a number of graphic design programs, including PhotoShop and The GIMP.

To make a beveled button using PhotoDraw:

1. Start with a new image and click File ➪ Picture Setup to change the size of the canvas area. For a button, a good size would by 100 pixels by 100 pixels.

2. Click the Draw Paint button and choose the Use the draw circle tool (called an oval tool in some programs) to make a circle. Pressing Shift while drawing will constrain the outline to a circle. You may need to adjust the line color and width to get the edge of the circle looking right.

3. On the right side of the screen, click Fill and choose Two-Color Gradient from the list of fill styles. You can adjust the Start and End colors for the gradient (in our example we used white as the start color), modify the shape of the gradient, adjust the angle (we used 45 degrees), and move the center of the gradient effect. The finished result should look similar to Figure 29-15.

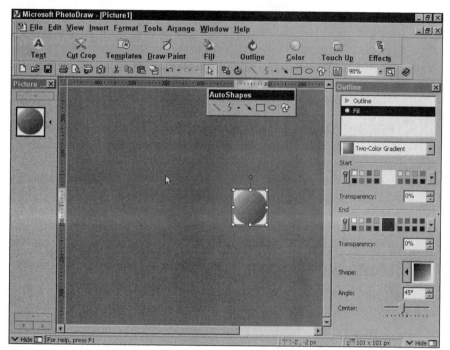

Figure 29-15: Use the Gradient fill style in PhotoDraw to style your buttons.

4. Use the circle tool again to make a circle inside your first one, just a few pixels smaller. Apply the same gradient effects and colors, but turn the gradient pattern around. Since we used 45 degrees as the angle for the first circle, we rotated the second one an additional 180 degrees for a total angle of 225 degrees. The result appears in Figure 29-16.

Figure 29-16: The three-dimensional effect of this button was created by placing a small circle atop a larger one.

5. Use the text tool to type any words you want right onto the button. Use a color that strongly contrasts your gradient colors. If you can already tell that you're going to have to end up shrinking this button, then shrink it first, before you add the text. Nothing looks worse than text that has been substantially resized in a graphic editing program. If you can't find a color that provides enough contrast, type your text, and then save it to the clipboard. Import the clipboard, color the text black. Now import the text again, and position it over the black text, ever so slightly above and to the right. This type of close shadowing adds definition to the text.

6. Save the image in a format you can use on your Web pages, such as .GIF. This format will flatten the image, so make sure you first save the graphic in the graphics program's proprietary format before saving it as a .GIF.

Creating other useful Web shapes

A variety of buttons can be created with the rectangle tool, using the same technique described above. Buttons can be created by drawing "shapes within shapes," and filling each with colors slightly different than the shape beneath it. Simply resize an existing selection and fill it again with a new color, shade, or gradient. To create horizontal lines for Web use, create a long thin rectangle and fill it with a gradient or an image fill that you like.

Making a background in PhotoDraw

You can create your own backgrounds for your Web pages; in fact, it is much easier than creating buttons. Keep in mind that Web browsers tile background images, which means you don't have to create a huge graphic that fills the entire screen. Consider the graphic shown in Figure 29-17; it is relatively narrow, but when used as a GIF background for a Web page, it will be stacked endlessly on top of itself to give the appearance of a full background graphic.

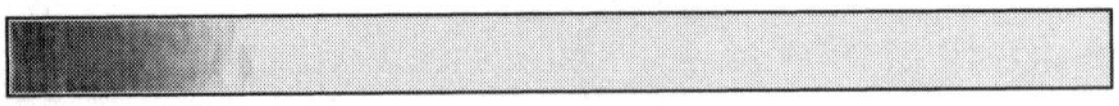

Figure 29-17: This graphic is narrow, but will be tiled in a Web browser.

Creating Animated GIFs

In this section, we look at several products that help you build *animated GIFs*, and explore a few ideas for using them effectively. Animated GIFs are a relatively easy way to spice up your Web page, providing an edge over less dynamic Web sites.

One big advantage of animated GIFs over more sophisticated multimedia elements, such as those requiring Java applets, is that it's just a simple graphic. You don't need to worry about inserting any special code in your HTML to make them work.

Defining animated GIFs

An animated GIF is a collection of pictures — several individual GIF images — arranged in a short movie. Most animated GIFs you're likely to see on the Web are five to ten frames (five to ten pictures sequenced as a movie). They are small in appearance; some animated GIFs are buttons, no larger than, say, 50 × 50 pixels. These animations might display as a rainbow of colors or a rolling ball, for example. You can use any image to create an animated GIF, but you need to convert the image to a GIF file before doing so.

Although this chapter shows you how to create animated GIFs, you can actually download them by the bucketful from the Web. There are many excellent sites for finding all kinds of Web-related artwork. Most of it is free to creators of noncommercial Web pages. If you are building a Web page and use some of this kind of artwork for your site, many Web artists will allow you to use their work so long as you mention them and provide a link to their page. Always double check the "terms of use" for any art or software you download from the Web.

Creating animated GIFs with animation software

Most animated GIF programs work similarly. They provide a wizard, asking you to identify sequentially all the single GIFs you want to compile for your animation. They'll ask you if you want to specify a background color or image behind your animation. Most even allow you to add audio that plays when the GIF animation loads up on the Web page. You'll be prompted to specify if the animation should begin moving when the page is loaded or when the visitor clicks on some element of the Web page. You must also let the program know how fast you want the animation to move, and if it should repeat once, a few times, or go on and on forever. Most good animated GIF programs allow you to view your GIF before you save it, either in a Web browser or in an internal viewer.

When you save your animated GIF, it will appear on your hard drive as a simple GIF file, except it will be larger in file size than most others. We advise against creating an animated GIF larger than 150 × 150 pixels, and we like to point out that most are in the neighborhood of 50 × 50 pixels or smaller. Please keep in mind that it takes a browser quite a while to load an animated GIF. If you try to stuff a single Web page with more than one or two, you'll probably be losing some visitors because of the extended loading time.

Ulead's GIF Animator

Let's start our survey of GIF animators by looking at Ulead's GIF Animator, offered by Ulead Systems (www.webutilities.com). We'll create a GIF that shows lightning coming out of the sky, where each frame shows the lightning moving closer to striking the ground (actually just the bottom of the GIF). Figure 29-18 shows all five frames of this animation grouped together. The GIF began as a picture of lightening striking the ground. That picture was reproduced five times. Adobe Photoshop was used to remove a little more lightening from each picture, until by the fifth frame, only a hint of lightning remained at the top. We then exported each image as a GIF.

Please note that all a GIF animation program is going to do is compile the GIFs in a particular sequence and perhaps add some lettering and transitional effects. You must have already created a set of attractive single images before you begin the animation process.

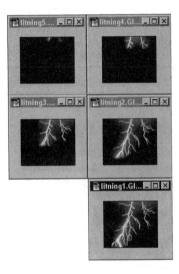

Figure 29-18: These five images will be shown in quick succession to become a GIF animation.

Note
The original picture of this lightning strike was obtained from the image library of the National Oceanic and Atmospheric Administration's (NOAA) Web site at www.noaa.gov. The site offers a wide selection of art that is in the public domain, which means you can use much of it on your own Web site.

Ulead's GIF Animator then compiles the lighting GIFs in the animation wizard. You can also add video—some GIF animation programs enable you to convert an existing .AVI movie or other video format into an animated GIF. When you select the GIFs in Ulead's animation wizard, you can set the delay time between each graphic. But if you decide the lightning needs to move a little faster, for example, you can edit it by selecting each image on the Compose or Edit tab and changing the value for the delay. Ulead uses time increments of 1/100ths of a second, so if you use a delay value of 100, each frame will display for an entire second. After some experimentation with our lightning GIF, we settled on a delay of just 1 because we wanted the lightning to move fast. Figure 29-19 shows the Ulead GIF Animator program window as we edit our lightning GIF.

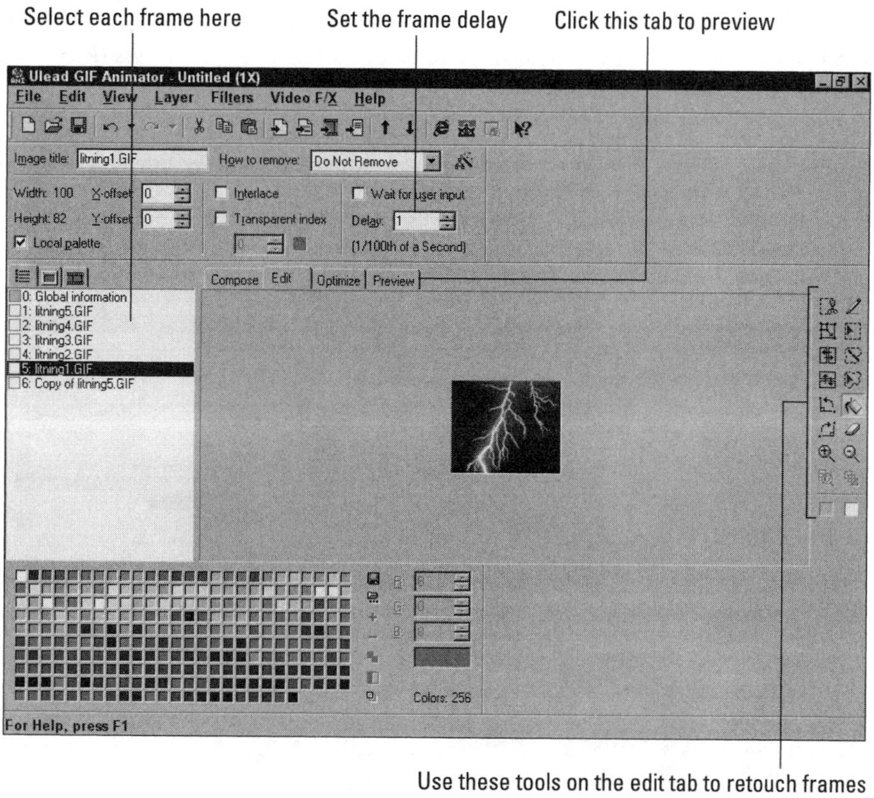

Select each frame here   Set the frame delay   Click this tab to preview

Use these tools on the edit tab to retouch frames

Figure 29-19: GIF Animator makes it easy to edit your GIF animations.

Another setting you should check is Looping. When you click on Global Information in the frame list, the Delay setting area changes to the Looping area. The default setting is infinite, which means your GIF animation will run forever. If you only want it to run once or a few times, remove the check mark next to Infinite and choose another value.

When you are done editing your animated GIF, click File ⇨ Save to save the file. Ulead GIF Animator automatically optimizes the GIF so that it takes up less space. Our lightning GIF measured 100 × 82 pixels, had six frames (one was a blank frame), and used 26K of storage space.

CoffeeCup GIF Animator

CoffeeCup GIF Animator by CoffeeCup Software (http://www.coffeecup.com/) is an excellent GIF animator. CoffeeCup offers a variety of tools that any Web site developer will find useful. A 15-day trial version of CoffeeCup GIF Animator is available, and if you decide you like it you can purchase the program for $30.

The CoffeeCup Gif Animator interface is somewhat busier than Ulead's GIF Animator, but it also provides a bit more information. CoffeeCup also comes with a selection of some very nice free button GIFs that you can use. Figure 29-20 shows the CoffeeCup interface, editing out lightning GIF.

Figure 29-20: The interface for Coffee Cup's GIF Animator provides extensive information about your animation.

One thing that CoffeeCup's program can't do that Ulead's can is retouch graphics. That's really not a big deal, but you need to make sure that you get your GIFs looking just right in a graphics editor *before* you use CoffeeCup to turn them into an animated GIF.

We really like CoffeeCup's Frame Inspector. It is a hovering window that provides a great deal of information about each frame of your GIF. You can adjust virtually any aspect of a frame — such as size or frame delay — by simply clicking in one of the fields and changing the value. Just don't forget to keep values such as the image dimensions and frame delays uniform for each frame. You can select the properties sheet for each frame by choosing a frame from the drop-down menu at the top of the Inspector.

To preview your animated GIF, click the Play button at the right end of the main program toolbar. And of course, don't forget to save your animation when you're through. The full version of CoffeeCup GIF Animator enables you to optimize animations by clicking the Optimize tool on the toolbar (it is next to the play button), but that feature is disabled in the trial version.

The GIF Construction Set

Next, we look at Alchemy Mindworks' GIF Construction Set, available online at www.mindworkshop.com/alchemy/. This program is one of the oldest and most popular Animated GIF creation tools. Although you can accept default settings and thoroughly automate the process, GIF Construction Set allows you to change speeds for each frame in your animation. You can also change overall animation speed without having to go back and recompile from scratch.

Figure 29-21 shows the GIF Construction Set window as we create yet another animated lightning strike. As you can see, the interface is much simpler than the other programs you've seen here, which is part of the strength of this program. The Animation Wizard, found in the File menu, will have you creating and previewing your animation in about five minutes. When selecting images from the browse menu, you can speed things up by "group-selecting" pictures by clicking the image at the top of your list, pressing Ctrl, and then clicking the image at the bottom. GIF Construction Set will load all the images in that list at once, rather than you having to go back and select them one by one.

After specifying which images to use, GIF Construction Set opens an editing screen as shown in the figure. Many of the most important commands in this program can be found in the Block menu. It contains commands that let you reverse the order in which the GIFs are displayed, change the size of the animation, flip or rotate the GIF, and more.

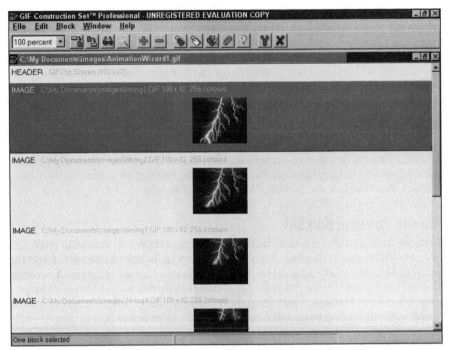

Figure 29-21: The GIF Construction Set organizes our lightning animation.

Creating Cool Effects with Text and Images

Besides creating moving objects with animated GIFs, you may also want to apply special effects to some of your text. You may, for instance, want to create some text that flashes, wiggles, spins, or twists on the screen.

You may also want to create buttons for your Web pages that move or change color when your visitors hover their mouse pointer over them or click them. Buttons like this add a dynamic look to your Web site, yet are subtle enough that they won't detract from the rest of the site.

Making special text effects with Ozzini Texter

Ozzini Software (www.ozzino.com) provides a tool called Text Effects that creates special text effects using Java applets. These effects include flashing text, letters that jitter and jump all over the page, scrolling banners, and more. The window for Ozzini Texter is small and simple, allowing you to create your text and get on with things.

You begin by selecting a tool from the Text Controls window, as shown in Figure 29-22. Here we have chosen the Jitter tool, which makes the letters jump all over the screen. Next, you click in the text area in the Texter window and type your words. To test the effect, click Start. Click Stop when you've seen enough. Unfortunately, to apply other effects you need to clear the text are and start over.

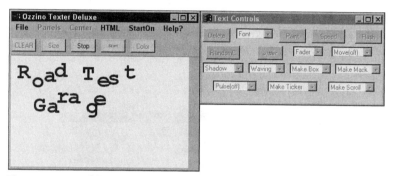

Figure 29-22: This text utilizes the Jitter effect.

When you have some text that you are happy with, click File ⇨ Save (this function only works in the registered version). This saves the applet code to an HTML file. If you want to use the applet that Texter creates in another HTML file, you must open the HTML file and copy and paste the code.

Cross-Reference

To learn more about adding Java elements to your site, check out Chapter 26, "Working with Advanced Web Components."

Creating cool buttons with 1 Cool Button

An excellent tool for creating buttons with mouse rollover effects is 1 Cool Button from Formula Software (www.buttontool.com). This program enables you to make three-position buttons almost instantly.

The 1 Cool Button interface offers three tabs. The first tab provides information that applies generally to the button applet you are creating, and the second tab allows you to change settings for the actual button. There is also a preview window that shows the applet. To test it, click the Play button in the upper right corner of the 1 Cool Button window.

Changing applet properties with 1 Cool Button

The first thing you need to do is click the Applet properties tab and define the size of both the applet and the button. In this example, we have created an applet that is 130 × 50 pixels, holding a button that is 120 × 40 pixels.

> **Note**   To "refresh" the button preview, click the Build Applet tab. This builds the applet based on your current settings, and changes the preview window accordingly.

Changing button properties with 1 Cool Button

Now switch to the Button Properties tab. This tab, which is shown in Figure 29-23, enables you to change the text and appearance of the button, as well as the style of button that is used. You can also add a link URL that the button will lead to when the user clicks it. To reposition the text on the button in any meaningful way, click the More Options button and adjust the start position for the text next to Pos:. Note that the position is expressed in terms of X and Y coordinates on the button itself, regardless of the size of the applet.

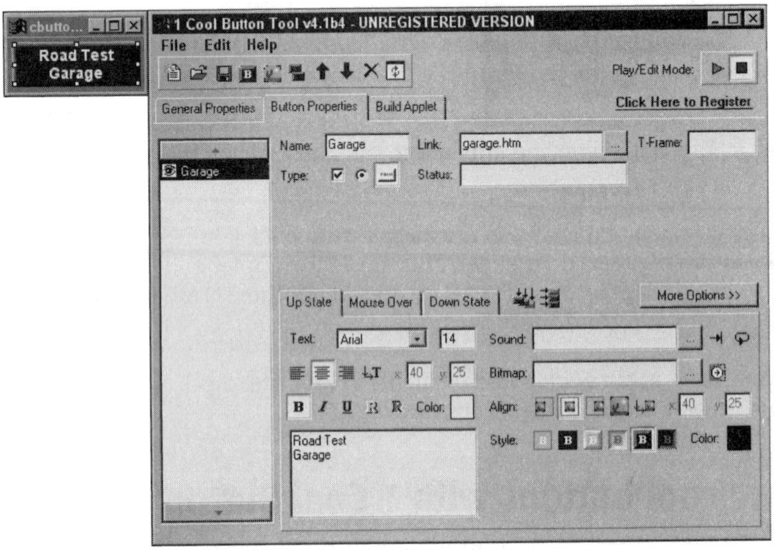

Figure 29-23: Modify the button properties here.

Also note that in Figure 29-23, the text information for the button is shown. You can change the text, text formatting, the color of the button, or even add a sound to it.

Altering the three button conditions with 1 Cool Button

The Button Properties tab is where you set actions for each of the three button states: the Up State, which is the default appearance; the Mouse Over State, which is how the button looks and performs when the visitor passes the mouse over the button; and finally, the Down State, which governs how the button performs when clicked. Of course, you can only assign one hyperlink to each button, not to each button state. The link is only activated when you click the button, not when you pass over it.

Use the three State tabs, which are shown in Figure 29-24, to control the text, bitmap, and action of each button state. When done, each button will exhibit a different appearance and behavior when passed over and when clicked. To preview your button and click it to see how it works, press the green "Play" button at the upper right of the work area, across from the toolbar.

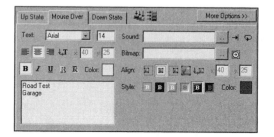

Figure 29-24: The Up State, Mouse Over State, and Down State tabs control the appearance and behavior of a button when the mouse is passed over it and clicked.

Saving your 1 Cool Button

When you save your button, the program automatically creates a folder beneath the 1 Cool Button folder that stores all files related to your button group, including sounds, GIFs, Java .CLASS files, and the HTML you'll need to paste into your Web page to place the buttons appropriately. Remember to copy all files in this folder to the folder set aside for your current Web page project.

Summary

Digital images can be a lot of fun. In this chapter, you learned how to create and modify digital images to use on your Web site or send as e-mail. You also learned a few pointers about choosing a digital camera. Finally, you learned about special images such as animated GIFs that add a high-tech look to your site with very little impact on bandwidth.

✦   ✦   ✦

Hosting a Personal Web Server

If you want to use your Web site to take orders from customers, provide links to other Web sites, or generate feedback such as receipts or personalized messages, you're going to need a Web server. A Web server can be your gateway to the Web. It not only allows people to visit Web pages on your own server (as opposed to pages that you transferred to your ISP's host computer), but it gives you the ability to interact with the visitors to your site. And even if you do normally connect to and use the Web through an ISP, a personal Web server can allow you to temporarily host large files or other types of material that you may not otherwise be able to upload to the ISP's Web server.

It turns out that, without much ado, you can turn your computer into a Web server. In this chapter, we'll look at some of the software that makes it possible. After setting up the software packages we examine here, you can publish Web pages right from your computer, over a LAN, an intranet, or on the Web.

Defining a Personal Web Server

As its name implies, a Web Server "serves" the content of your Web site to the rest of the Internet, making it available to anyone who types in your Web site's URL.

As a result, a Web page you host on your computer will be just as visible as any other page on the Web.

In simple terms, a Web server provides a folder in which you store all the files — HTML files, graphic files, and so on — that make up your Web site. The Web server software then creates a path from the Internet to your computer. When someone enters the URL address of your site into their browser, she is directed down the path to the file that serves as the home page for your site. For example, let's say your Web site's home page (the file is typically called *index.htm*) is located in the following directory on your computer's hard drive:

```
C:\computer_name\mysite\index.htm.
```

The Web address that the Web surfing public sees would probably be:

```
http://computername/mysite.index.htm
```

At the same time, the Web server also provides the ability to link your site to other Web content, collect information using CGI-script applications, such as Forms, and provide other ways for users to interact with your Web site.

Benefits of personal Web servers

One nice feature of having your own Web server is that you can use log files to keep track of information about site traffic, visitor data, and the performance of your Web site.

Another benefit to using a personal Web server is that you can set up your computer as an FTP site. This enables you to employ customized options for how your files are displayed. For example, rather than display your work as a series of Web pages, you can use *directory-style browsing,* which enables visitors to see your site as a series of folders, which they can open and peruse at will. This method is usually faster than Web browsing, and is highly suitable for pages in which information needs to be moved between hands quickly.

Limitations of personal Web servers

The programs we examine here are only meant for low-volume or peer-to-peer publishing, not for managing sites where huge amounts of traffic are expected. Most personal Web servers are capable of serving only about five to nine visitors simultaneously. This means that, if business starts booming, you have to move up to heftier equipment.

Tip
If you plan to keep your personal Web server running indefinitely, you should set it up on a machine that you don't use for anything else. Traffic on the server will use up processor and memory resources, making it difficult for you to use that computer for other work.

Another major problem you may encounter involves addressing and your physical connection to the Internet. Even though a personal Web server allows you to host Web pages on a local computer, you still have to connect that computer to the Internet somehow, usually through your ISP or your company's network.

Assuming you have a connection to the Internet, you also need to have an address assigned to your personal Web server. Whenever you connect to the Internet through an ISP or other server, your computer is identified by a unique IP address. An IP address is a series of numbers that may look something like this:

```
209.26.147.56
```

Numeric IP addresses are behind every Web server on the Internet, even though the only addresses you ever see are the more common URLs. Whenever you connect to your ISP to get online, the ISP assigns you a temporary IP address. You may have one IP address now, but if you disconnect and then reconnect, the ISP's *domain name server* (DNS) will probably assign you a new number. ISPs are given a block of IP addresses they can use, and these addresses are assigned pretty much randomly by the DNS.

Why is this a problem? If you want your computer to act as a server for other Internet users, it must be identified by a permanent IP address. Users may access your computer now, but if you disconnect temporarily and your IP address gets reassigned by the ISP, links created to your original IP address won't work anymore.

If your ISP assigns you a different IP address every time you connect, your best solution is to see about obtaining a static IP address. Many ISPs offer this service, but it usually costs more. You may have to purchase the service as part of a Web hosting package, so review your options carefully.

Choosing the Right Server for You

Personal Web servers run a huge price span. You can pay hundreds of dollars for one that will handle large volumes of traffic, but many are available for low cost or as freeware. The freeware ones usually have very limited features and traffic-handling capability, but for lighter uses they will probably still suit your needs. Those are the servers we will concentrate on here.

24Link

A simple server program, 24Link (`www.24link.com`), sets up a Web site contained in a folder on your local computer. Setup takes just a few minutes and, when installed, it automatically establishes a connection with the 24Link Web site, where you can set up a free account that will allow people to access your Web site. You still have to maintain an Internet connection through your ISP in order for people to visit your site, but as long as the connection is active, your site can be viewed by anyone. 24Link is free and available for Windows platforms.

24Link automatically checks to see if your computer is behind a proxy or firewall, network security features that would otherwise block access to your site. You are then given a URL address for your site, which is based on the user name you submit when you sign up. For instance, if you sign up using the name *crazyfred*, your URL will be:

```
http://www.24link.net/crazyfred
```

24Link is successful because it resolves many of the addressing problems that you may encounter using other Web server programs. Every time you connect to the Internet using your ISP, all you have to do is activate 24Link and the software automatically establishes a connection between your local Web pages and the 24Link Web site. This works even if your ISP assigns you a different IP address every time you connect; 24Link automatically determines the current IP address assigned to your site and updates the link from the 24Link server as needed.

The 24Link window, shown in Figure 30-1, provides a number of useful information items, such as server status and how many "hits" your site receives.

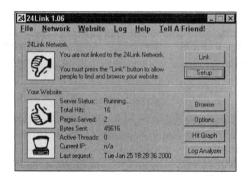

Figure 30-1: 24Link provides some basic tools to let you serve Web pages directly from your computer.

When you want to close access to your site, right-click the 24Link icon in the Windows system tray (next to the clock) and choose Exit 24Link. Without this program running, visitors cannot access your site. Obviously, closing your Internet connection will also break the link. Your site will be unlinked automatically because the 24Link server performs routine checks every 15 minutes.

24Link can be useful even if you aren't going to use the program to host Web pages on your local computer. Using 24Link you can conduct a "final" test of your site before you publish it to your ISP's Web server or whichever server you will eventually use. Before you can access the site on your local computer, you have to specify the local folder where all the Web site files are stored by clicking Website ⇨ Options and changing the folder listed on the General tab. Disabling the option "Allow other computers to browse your Website" on the Authorization tab will prevent others from accessing your local files over your Internet connection while you test the site. You access the local site using the URL http://localhost/ in your Web browser.

24Link provides some useful features to help you manage your site. For example, a Hit Graph, which is show in Figure 30-2, allows you to monitor traffic at your site. Click the Hit Graph button in the 24Link window to view it.

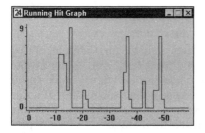

Figure 30-2: This Hit Graph provides usage information on your site.

AnalogX SimpleServer:WWW

SimpleServer:WWW from AnalogX (www.analogx.com), lives up to its name; it is simple. Figure 30-3 shows the SimpleServer program window, which as you can see has just four buttons. The button across the top of the window shows the IP address that is currently assigned to your Internet connection. If you disconnect from the Internet and reconnect later, this number may change. Still, it's important to know, because others can enter this number in the address bar of their Web browser to visit your site.

SimpleServer:WWW is best suited to temporary Web hosting needs. For instance, if you want to temporarily make some large files available for download, SimpleServer:WWW is an excellent option. Simply provide the current IP address (shown at the top of the SimpleServer:WWW window) to the people you want to share the files with.

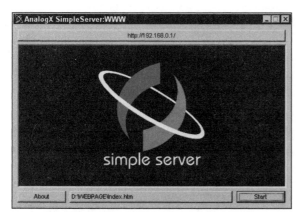

Figure 30-3: SimpleServer is one of the simplest programs you will ever use.

When you are ready to begin serving your Web pages to the world, click Start. If you have some specific people in mind that you want to visit your site, provide them with the IP address shown at the top of the window.

Caution   If you have Internet Connection Sharing installed and configured on your computer, SimpleServer may not detect your IP address correctly. In this case, you will have to either uninstall ICS or use some other software.

vqServer

A common theme that we see in the documentation that comes with all of these simple Web servers is that each claims to be the "simplest" Web server available. Comparing them, you can see why. vqServer is another excellent simple server that can run in Windows, Macintosh, or Linux. It runs as a lone executable program, meaning you don't have to install it, and, as a result, you avoid DLLs (*Dynamic Link Libraries*, large files used by many Windows programs) and other bits and pieces of the program being scattered all over your hard drive.

vqServer, available via download at `http://www.vqsoft.com/vq/server/index.html`, comes as a compressed archive. Before you decompress it, create a new folder and call it something you'll remember, like *Myweb*. This folder will become your Web site folder that will be hosted by vqServer. After you have decompressed the archive, run the executable program. In Windows, the executable file is called *vqServer.exe*.

vqServer creates a folder structure, like the one shown in Figure 30-4, in your Web folder that mimics those used by most full-time Web servers. You should copy your Web site files and folders into the *public* folder.

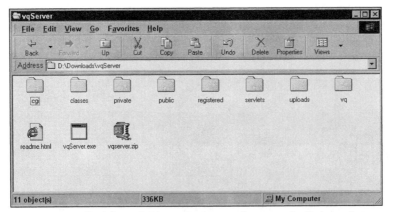

Figure 30-4: All of these folders were created automatically by vqServer. Store your Web site files in the Public folder.

The program, when running, acts as your server. It runs in a window that provides a continuous display of activity on your server. When you are ready to shut the server down, simply click File ⇨ Shutdown in the vqServer window.

Xitami

Xitami by Imatix (www.imatix.com) runs on Windows systems as well as OS/2 and all UNIX variants. There are several versions of Xitami offered, so make sure you download the right one for your operating system. When you run the installation program for Xitami, the Windows version takes you through a fairly standard setup wizard. You will be asked to create a user name and password.

Note   We can't show every version of Xitami, so for this example we are using the full version of Xitami for Windows. There is a console version available as well, but if you're just learning how to run your own Web server we suggest using the full version instead.

Xitami gives you the option to run it automatically whenever you log on to Windows, but we recommend that you run it manually, only when you choose to do so.

When setup is complete, run the program. In Windows it adds an icon to the system tray (next to the clock) when it is running. Right-click this icon and click Setup. Doing so opens an HTML-based administration program, as shown in Figure 30-5.

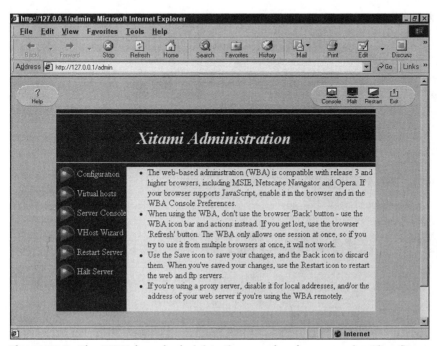

Figure 30-5: The HTML-based administration panel makes managing Xitami easy.

To specify important information about the way the server software is configured, click Configure. This will allow you to identify the location of your Web page directories, your CGI scripts (if applicable), the default pages used by the server, and more.

If other people are having trouble accessing your server, try changing the IP address that the server uses. Scroll down in the configuration window to the Advanced settings and change the Server IP address as shown in Figure 30-6. This important capability is missing in some of the simpler server programs that you can use. Just don't forget to provide the new IP address to the people you want to visit your site.

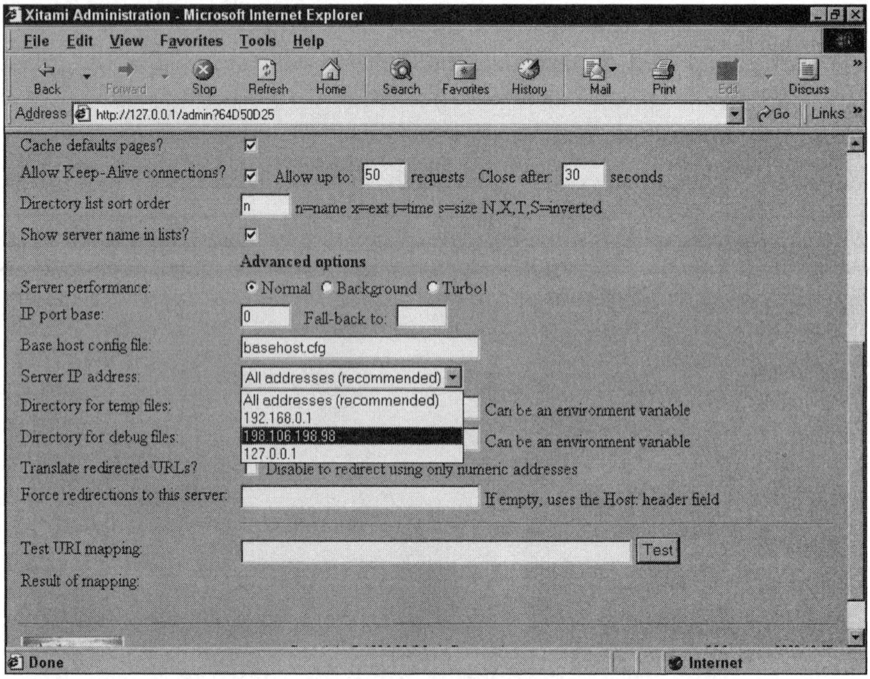

Figure 30-6: You may need to configure a different IP address to make your server visible to others.

Finding More Powerful Web Servers

If it turns out your traffic is too high and you need a more robust server setup, check out one of the Microsoft BackOffice products at `http://www.microsoft.com/backoffice/`. Microsoft strives to provide various levels of server software to support a site's growing presence on the Web. Because they are robust and well supported, Microsoft's server products are used by many Web and network administrators.

If you get really serious, you could set up a separate system running Linux that works exclusively as your server. Linux was specifically designed with this kind of operation in mind, and contains a number of tools to help you manage a server that gets a lot of traffic. Numerous options exist, and as your needs grow you may want to seek them out. An excellent online resource on the subject is ServerWatch, hosted by internet.com at `http://serverwatch.internet.com`.

Summary

In this chapter, you learned how to easily and inexpensively convert your personal computer into a personal Web server, thereby giving you the ability to make a local Web site accessible to the rest of the Internet. Using some of the personal Web servers surveyed in this chapter, you can set forms to collect information from visitors to your site, create links to other Web sites on the Internet, host files that might be too large for your ISP Web server account, and provide a host of other exciting interactive features on your site. Finally, you considered some of the limitations of personal Web servers and learned where you can go to find more powerful Web servers.

In the next chapter, you'll learn how you can efficiently publish simple Web pages using office software that's probably already installed on your computer.

✦   ✦   ✦

Publishing Web Content With Office Software

CHAPTER

31

Throughout this part of the *Internet Bible*, you have learned various ways to publish content online. First you learned how to compose and publish HTML documents starting with lines of code in a text editor, and then you learned how to use some Web page editing software to compose pages more easily.

What if neither of these options appeals to you? Perhaps you're too busy to learn about HTML. Maybe you don't want to install new software on your computer that you'll use only once in a while. Yet, you still want the ability to create a simple Web page every now and then. What do you do?

Consider using the software that you probably already have on your computer. Modern word processors, such as Microsoft Word 2000 and Corel WordPerfect 8, can double as fairly decent Web page editors if you need them, and all of Microsoft's Office 2000 products now integrate Web technologies that make it easier than ever to place your existing documents online. Microsoft Office 97 for Windows and Word 98 for Macintosh have some rudimentary Web publishing capabilities, but they are not as advanced as Office 2000.

This chapter describes first how to create a Web page using Microsoft Word 2000 as your Web page editor. Next you'll learn how to publish Microsoft Excel worksheets and PowerPoint presentations online. Microsoft Publisher can also be used to create attractive Web pages, so we'll cover that here too. And finally, we'll show you how to use Corel's WordPerfect 8 as a Web page editor, and just for kicks we'll do it on a machine running Linux.

Using Microsoft Office 2000 to Create Web Content

One of the most important new features of Microsoft Office 2000 (released in 1999) was a greater emphasis on features that catered to online users. Microsoft saw that the Internet was being used more and more for business-to-business and person-to-person communications, so Office 2000 was designed so that virtually any document you create in any Office program can be published online with only a few mouse clicks.

Creating basic Web pages with Word 2000

Microsoft Word 2000 was designed so that you could create a Web document as easily as you create any other word processing document. In fact, you can take any existing Word document and simply choose File ➪ Save as Web page and voila!, instant Web page.

Considering Word 2000?

Before you decide that Word 2000 is the full-time Web page editor for you, you need to understand that it has many serious drawbacks when compared to dedicated Web editors such as WebExpress or Microsoft's own FrontPage. These drawbacks include:

✦ The HTML code really *is* bloated. It makes heavy use of cascading style sheets, which by itself isn't bad, but it assigns styles to *everything*. The code itself is not very clean and may be difficult to modify in a text editor. For instance, simply inserting a picture generates five full lines of HTML code!

✦ Older Web browsers cannot be accommodated.

✦ Word attempts to preserve all of your formatting. You may expect that Word will save all text using the Normal style as default body text. However, it instead preserves all of the additional formatting you may have applied to the Normal text style, such as bold face, underline, italics, and the size or type of the font.

✦ Word's interface is misleading because, although it provides a WYSIWYG (What You See Is What You Get) view of normal word processing documents, its view of documents you save as HTML is usually way off. Expect HTML documents saved in Word to look much different once they are opened in a Web browser.

✦ You can't insert meta data, image maps, or external elements, such as Java applets.

We could go on. Suffice to say, there are better Web editors available. But if you already use Word 2000 for your regular day-to-day work, it is good to know that it can also produce a reasonably decent Web page when you need it.

Using the Web Page Wizard

The easiest way to create a new Web page with Word 2000 is to use the Web Page Wizard:

1. Launch Word and click File ⇨ New to open the New dialog.

2. Click the Web Pages tab, as shown in Figure 31-1. Notice that several Web page templates are available. For now, double-click on Web Page Wizard.

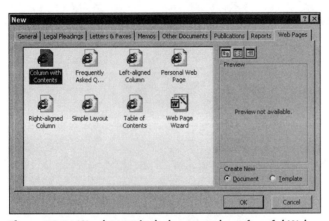

Figure 31-1: Word 2000 includes a number of useful Web page templates as well as a wizard.

3. Follow the instructions on-screen and enter the requested information. You are given the opportunity to create pages with or without frames, choose how many pages your site will have, and even choose a visual theme (or no theme at all).

When you finish the wizard, Word will automatically generate pages based on your input to the wizard. Individual pages will be created as separate Word documents. However, only the main page will remain open; the auxiliary pages will be created but then closed. You can open them using File ⇨ Open.

Adding pictures to your site

Your Web page will be far more interesting if it has graphics. You may want to insert a company logo, a diagram, or an illustrative picture. Inserting a graphic into a Web page you are creating in Word is simple. Click Insert ➪ Picture ➪ From File, and then navigate to the location of the graphic. Once you've inserted it, you can resize the graphic by clicking it once and using the manipulation handles in the corners and at the sides. You can also center the graphic, as shown in Figure 31-2.

Caution Remember, if you resize a graphic in Word, the image quality could be negatively affected. For best results, change the size of your pictures in a graphics editor, such as PhotoDraw or PhotoDeluxe, before inserting them into the HTML documents you create in Word.

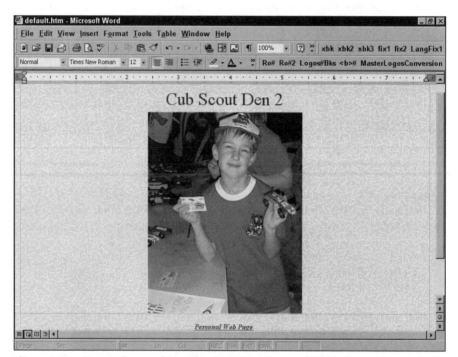

Figure 31-2: Center the graphic using the Center button on the formatting toolbar.

One thing that is important to realize is that the code behind the pictures you insert is complex, but ultimately makes your life easier. For instance, you can insert a picture from any location, without worrying if the path to the file will be correct in the code. This is because Word imports your graphic, and then exports it to its own separate file. The new copy of the graphic is saved in a subfolder where your Web page files are stored and assigned a name that matches the HTML tag by Word. Consider this line of code from the file shown in Figure 31-2:

```
<v:imagedata src="./default_files/image002.jpg"
o:title="PIC00006"/>
```

This is the tag that identifies the picture shown in the figure, and the original filename was `PIC00006.jpg`. You can see that this name is used in the `title=` field, but the actual filename for the image is something new. This image name, along with the folder that it is stored in, was generated automatically by Word. When you copy this Web page to your Web server, make sure that you copy all files and folders into the folder where your Web page files are stored. Remember that if you created the Web site using the wizard, Word created a new folder to store the pages in, so you should be able to copy all of the files and folders shown there and avoid leaving anything behind.

Creating hyperlinks

Word 2000 lets you create hyperlinks, which can be handy in any document that will be viewed by others electronically, even memos and letters. If your boss is reading your memo on the need for ergonomically correct furniture, you can recommend a company that makes good chairs in the memo and make the name of the company a hyperlink to that business's Web site. Your boss clicks on the name and is taken instantly to a Web site with more information.

The procedure for inserting a hyperlink into a Word 2000 document is the same for all the other Office 2000 programs:

1. Select some text or a graphic that you want to link, and click the Insert Hyperlink tool, which can be found on the Standard toolbar. Alternately, you can choose Insert ➪ Hyperlink.

2. When the Insert Hyperlink window opens, as shown in Figure 31-3, select the Web site or document to which you want to link. As you can see, this can be done several ways: You can type in the URL of a Web page to which you want to link, choose an address from the list of recently visited Web pages, select a file you've worked on recently, or create an e-mail link.

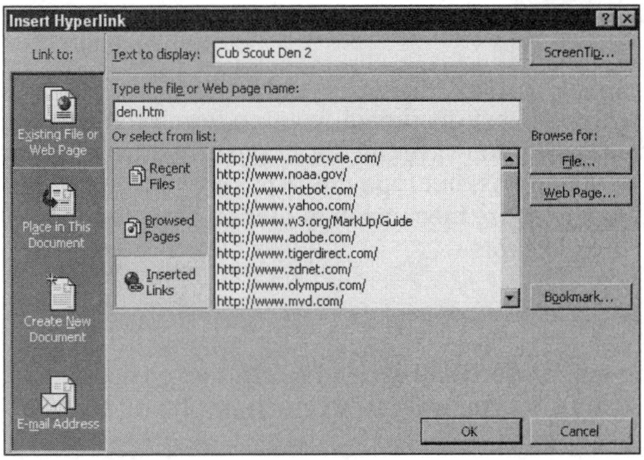

Figure 31-3: Create a hyperlink here.

Editing HTML code in Word 2000

Contrary to popular belief, you *can* use Word 2000 to edit raw HTML code. Normally, Word doesn't show you the code because it converts files from HTML into the standard Word document format when they are opened. If you created the HTML in another program or from scratch, you can expect Word to seriously mess up your code during this conversion process.

To edit HTML code, you need to stop Word from automatically converting the file when it's opened:

1. Open Word 2000 (but don't open your HTML file) and click Tools ⇨ Options.

2. On the General tab of the Options dialog, place a check mark next to *Confirm conversion at Open* and click OK.

3. Now open your HTML document. You should see a dialog box that looks like Figure 31-4, asking you to confirm that you do indeed want the file converted. Click on Text Only and click OK.

Caution   When opening an HTML file, Word automatically highlights the HTML option in the Convert File dialog box. Before clicking OK, double check to make sure the Text Only option is selected. If you convert the file with the HTML option selected, Word will mess up your HTML code.

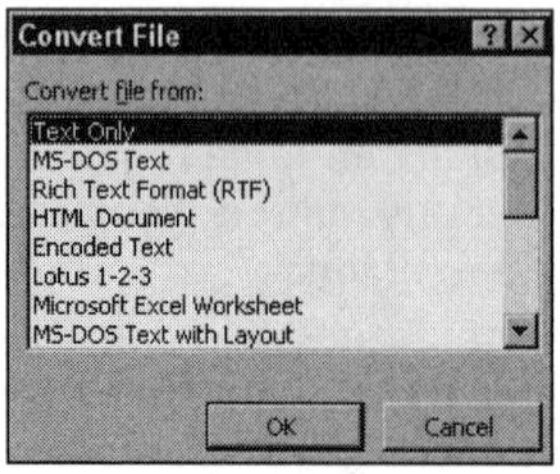

Figure 31-4: Do not let Word convert the file from HTML if you want to edit the raw code.

If you open the HTML file as a text document, your code will remain unmolested by Word 2000's converters. When you save the file, choose Text Only from the Save as Type menu in the Save dialog box, but type the .htm or .html extension on the end of the filename. Enclose the entire filename in quotation marks to make it a full expression. It should look like this:

```
"index.html"
```

Without the quotation marks Word will append a .txt extension onto the filename, right after the .html extension you went to so much trouble to include.

Publishing Excel 2000 worksheets in HTML

Excel 2000 enables you to publish worksheets in HTML, which gives others the ability to easily view them over the Internet or your company's intranet. As with Word, you simply choose File ⇨ Save As Web page to save an Excel worksheet as a Web page. Figure 31-5 shows an invoice created in Excel 2000. Notice that hyperlinks have been created for several cells, such as the name of the employee and the descriptions of the work he did. Each hyperlink leads to a document that provides additional information about the item specified.

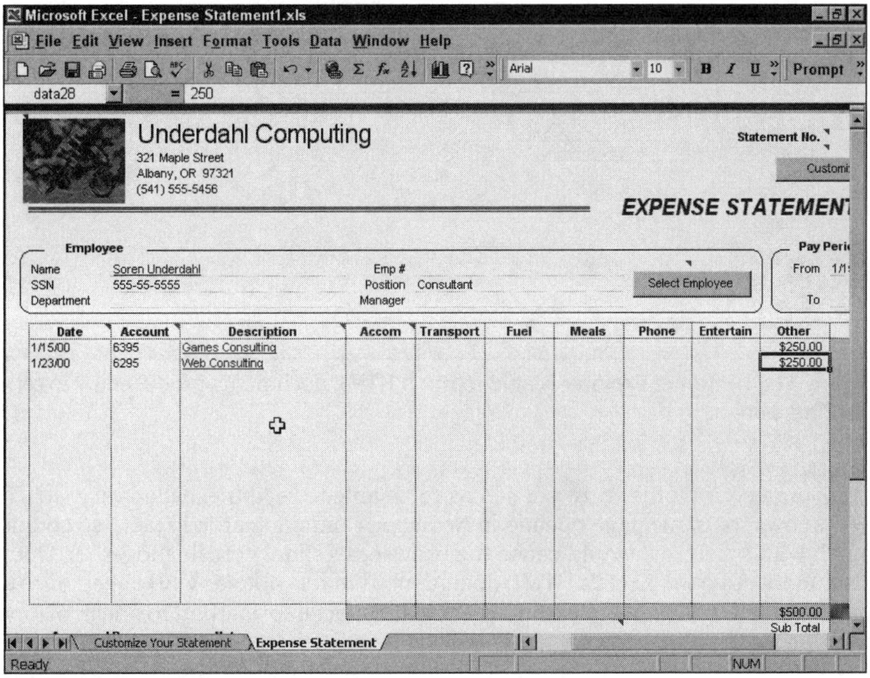

Figure 31-5: This worksheet has several hyperlinks and is about to be saved as a Web page.

The code that is produced by Excel is extremely complex. A simple, single-sheet worksheet that has data in just 7 cells produced a 6KB HTML file, and the code (when opened in a text editor) was difficult to comprehend. The code for the worksheet shown in Figure 31-5 was downright frightening. But it produces a document that can be viewed in Internet Explorer just fine, as you can see in Figure 31-6. The hyperlinks work fine, and footnotes are automatically generated for several items.

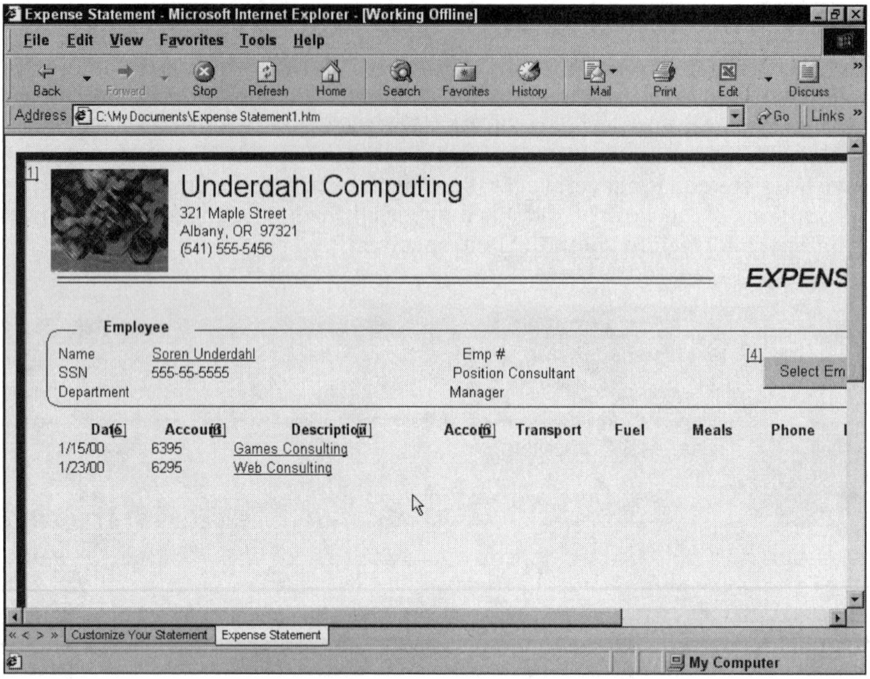

Figure 31-6: Internet Explorer is able to open HTML documents produced by Excel just fine, but . . .

Unfortunately, no other browser seems to be able to read these files very well. Figure 31-7 shows the same page opened in Netscape Communicator. In fact, we couldn't do much with it before it would cause the browser to simply crash altogether. Opera was also unable to open Excel's HTML document. A much simpler worksheet, one that only contained data in a few rows and had no special formatting to speak of, opened just fine.

This situation does not suggest any inferiority on the part of Opera or Netscape; in fact, if anything it illustrates that some types of documents simply aren't ready for online publication. Excel worksheets are a prime example. If you don't know for a fact that your readers are also using Internet Explorer 5, don't try to share an Excel 2000 worksheet in HTML.

One alternative you may be considering is to embed small, simple worksheets into your Web documents. You could produce an HTML document with Excel, and then open the file in a text editor and copy-and-paste the code into your other Web pages. But why? Why use six kilobytes of Excel-generated code what could just as easily be created with just a few lines of code in a standard HTML table?

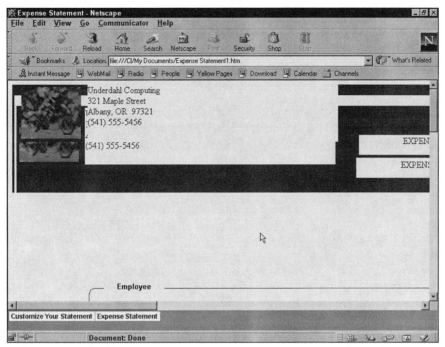

Figure 31-7: . . . other browsers can't handle them as effectively.

Using PowerPoint to publish an online presentation

Now that we've talked you out of publishing HTML documents with Excel 2000, let's move on to PowerPoint. Actually, PowerPoint 2000 is somewhat more effective at producing Web content. It is a program designed for making visual presentations, after all, and what is the Web but a place where people present things visually? But rather than outputting the presentation to transparencies and slides, you can simply output it as a Web page instead.

When you use one of PowerPoint's wizards to create a presentation, you are given the option of producing a Web presentation. If that is how this presentation will primarily be viewed, this is the best choice. If PowerPoint is already open, click File ⇨ New to open the New Presentation dialog box. On the General tab, choose the AutoContent Wizard, and select the Web presentation option when the wizard begins.

When you are done, choose File ⇨ Save As Web page. Presentations that are saved as Web pages are produced using a frames format. The left-side frame provides links to each slide in the presentation, as shown in Figure 31-8.

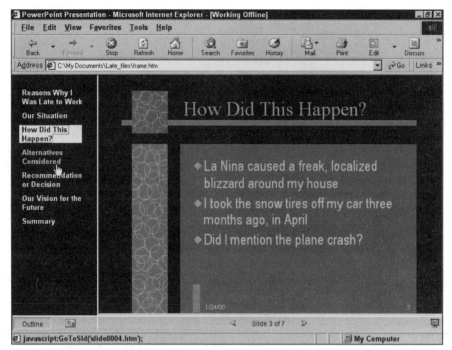

Figure 31-8: This PowerPoint presentation was output as a Web page. Click a link at left to move to another slide.

Alas, as with Excel documents, we found the HTML documents produced with PowerPoint don't work in browsers other than Internet Explorer. If the people who are going to view the presentation are also using Internet Explorer 5, then you have no problem. But if they use something else, you will have to break out the transparency film.

Presenting a Web site in PowerPoint

Rather than publishing PowerPoint presentations online, let's turn things around and use a PowerPoint slideshow to present online content to a room full of people. Suppose you want to present a Web site to a gathered group, but the only equipment that you will be able to use is an overhead projector. Try this:

1. Open PowerPoint and create a new, blank presentation. In the AutoLayout dialog, choose the blank slide.

2. You should now see a blank slide. Click File ➪ Open, and navigate to the Web page you want to open. If the page is located online, you can type the URL in the file name box.

3. The Web page will open in a new slide, as shown in Figure 31-9.

You may need to reposition some items slightly, or even delete some content if it runs off the screen. Just make sure that the key points you want to show in your presentation are visible.

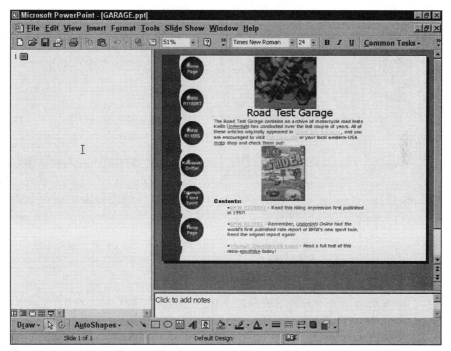

Figure 31-9: This Web page has been turned into a slide in a PowerPoint presentation.

4. After you have the slide looking the way you want it, save it as a presentation. Click File ⇨ Save As, navigate to the location you want to save it, and choose .PPT from the Save As Type box.

5. If you want to add more Web pages to your presentation, click File ⇨ Open and repeat steps 1-4 for each page. Then, return to the original presentation and click Insert ⇨ Slide from Files.

6. In the Slide Finder shown in Figure 31-10, click Browse and locate the presentation files for the other pages you saved. Select the slide and click Insert.

When you have inserted all of the pages you want, you can output the slides as you would any other presentation. Now you have an excellent, efficient way to present a Web site to a large group without a lot of expensive equipment!

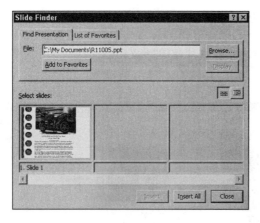

Figure 31-10: Insert slides from the other Web pages you opened to create a single presentation for all the pages.

Using Publisher 2000 to create online content

Microsoft Publisher 2000, which is a desktop publishing program, does a pretty good imitation of a Web page editor, far better than the other Office 2000 programs (except, perhaps, FrontPage). In fact, the Publication Wizard has a wide selection of Web site templates that you can use to quickly create your site. When you first launch Publisher, click Web Sites in the list of wizard categories, and then browse through the list of the *four dozen* wizards that are available. Select the one you want and click Start Wizard.

The wizard presents you with a series of dialogs that ask you a few questions about yourself, your business, your organization, and your desires for the site. This information is used to automatically set up many aspects of the site.

Keep your eye on the Wizard screen on the left side of the window. The screen shown in Figure 31-11 enables you to choose from a variety of color schemes for your site.

Continue clicking Next to move to different screens of the wizard. You can click Finish at any time to close the wizard and edit the page yourself. When you are done editing the page, click File ➪ Save As Web Page. When you choose this option in Publisher, you do not save individual pages. Publisher treats your entire site as a single document, asking for only the folder in which you want it saved. The files are saved, and each individual page and graphic is automatically assigned a filename by the program.

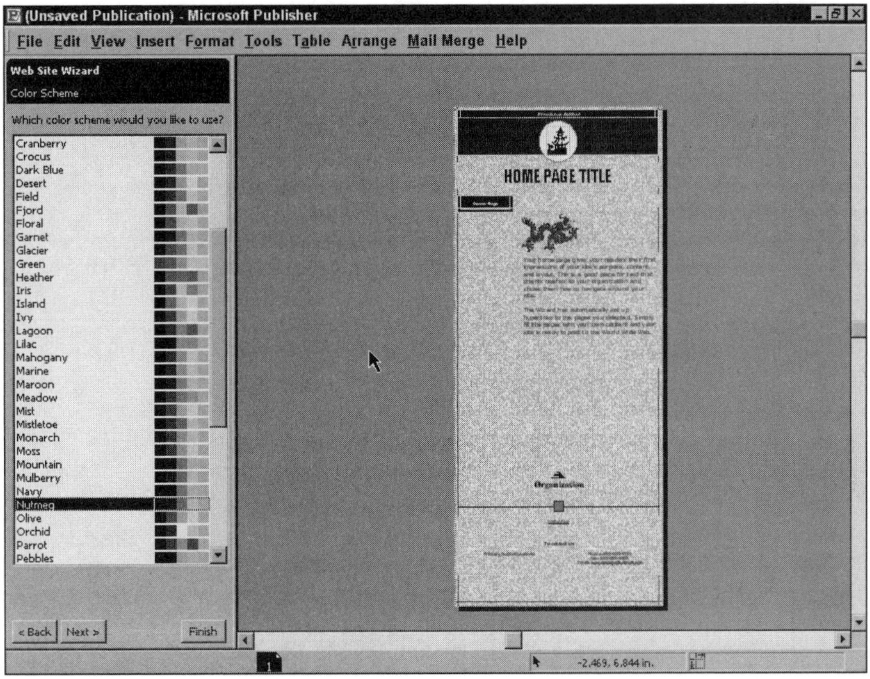

Figure 31-11: Use the Wizard to choose a color scheme for your site.

Unlike Excel, PowerPoint, and even Word, Web pages produced with Publisher 2000 actually work pretty well in any Web browser. Figure 31-12 shows the Web site we created in Publisher open in Opera.

To ensure maximum control over the future of your Web site, make sure you save your Web site as a Publisher file (.pub) before you close it. This will make the Web site easier to edit in Publisher later on. As with Deneba's Canvas desktop publishing program described in Chapter 27, think of Publisher as actually exporting HTML files rather than editing them. Just make the export your last step when you're ready to publish, and you should be fine.

Figure 31-12: Publisher produces Web pages that can be viewed in any browser.

Using Corel WordPerfect 8 to Publish Web Content

Microsoft isn't the only company that adds Web-based features to its office productivity software. Corel has jumped into the fray by giving WordPerfect 8 the ability to publish HTML documents in much the same way that Microsoft Word does. As with Word, WordPerfect is not the most advanced or best-suited Web page editor that is available, but if you use WordPerfect 8 you can use it to produce Web pages in a snap.

> **Note**
> In the examples shown here we are using WordPerfect 8 in Linux. However, this procedure works the same no matter which operating system you happen to be running WordPerfect 8 on.

Begin by creating a normal word processing document in WordPerfect. You can even begin with a document you created earlier. Enter any additional information you wish, and make the layout look the way you want it. For instance, if you want to insert a graphic, click Insert ➪ Graphics ➪ From File, and navigate to the image's location.

To create a hyperlink in WordPerfect:

1. Select the text or graphic that you want to link.

2. Click the Create or Edit a Hyperlink tool on the formatting toolbar. Alternatively, choose Tools ➪ Hyperlink.

3. In the Create Hypertext Link dialog box shown in Figure 31-13, type the URL of the link's destination in the Go To Other Document field.

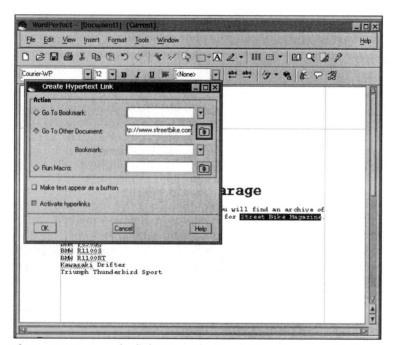

Figure 31-13: Type the link URL in the Go To Other Document field.

4. Click OK when you're done creating the hyperlink.

Publishing your WordPerfect documents in HTML

When you are ready to publish your WordPerfect documents in Web format, click File ➪ Internet Publisher. The Internet Publisher, which is shown in Figure 31-14, makes it easy to create new Web documents or save existing ones as HTML. Since that's the option we want, click Publish to HTML.

After you click Publish HTML, you will be asked to provide a location to publish Web pages to. Click the folder icon to the right of the text box, find a location on your hard drive in which to save it, and name the file.

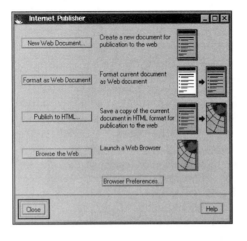

Figure 31-14: The Internet Publisher helps guide you through the process of creating Web documents in WordPerfect.

One thing worth noting about creating Web pages in WordPerfect is the fact that the code produced by WordPerfect is extraordinarily clean and easy to understand when viewed in a text editor. Consider this tag, which refers to an image we inserted in our WordPerfect document:

```
<P ALIGN="CENTER"><img src="garage.html.htg/k1200-4.jpg"
width="113" height="93" align="left" ></P>
```

We could have just as well typed that tag in ourselves if we were creating the HTML in the text editor. This clean-code feature makes modifying WordPerfect's HTML documents later very easy, something that cannot be said about Microsoft Word's HTML documents.

Caution   Although WordPerfect's code is clean, it can still contain some glitches. The most common is the program's tendency to insert a space before the closing bracket (>) of many tags. If an HTML document that you created with WordPerfect doesn't look right when you view it in a browser, check the code in a text editor for this problem.

Summary

Publishing HTML files with office productivity software is becoming increasingly common, probably because everybody uses word processors and many of the other programs that come with these suites. In this chapter you learned not only how to create Web documents with Microsoft Office 2000 and Corel WordPerfect 8, but you also were given a chance to evaluate whether creating Web documents with these programs is always the best course of action.

Living in Cyberspace

◆ ◆ ◆ ◆

Many of the things you enjoy in the real word—
such as family, privacy, money, security, and
entertainment—you can also enjoy in the virtual world of
the Internet. Yet as in the real world, there are also dangers.
Knowing how to benefit from the Internet's many rewards,
while guarding against its hazards, is an important skill
to learn.

In this part, you learn how to live in cyberspace, benefit from
all that it has to offer, and protect yourself from the darker
shadows of the online world.

◆ ◆ ◆ ◆

Maintaining Your Online Privacy and Security

◆ ◆ ◆ ◆

In This Chapter

Making a distinction between privacy and security

Guarding your privacy

Maintaining your security

Using encryption and digital IDs

◆ ◆ ◆ ◆

It's a common mistake many of us make. You download and read your e-mail. You browse a few Web sites. You check out today's headlines on *USA Today*. You believe you're minding your own business — with no major consequence to anyone else. Lots of us out here using the Internet believe that.

But do you know who's watching and even recording your online activities?

In the next few pages you'll learn about privacy and security issues on the Internet: the difference between privacy and security, surfing the Web safely and privately, safeguarding important data, and controlling who receives your personal information. This chapter looks into all these different issues and helps you take steps to make your data transmissions on the Internet more secure.

Distinguishing the Difference Between Privacy and Security

When it comes to data protection, privacy and security are two different matters. They're two sides of the same coin, perhaps, but different enough to tackle separately. Privacy is your right to *not* share all your personal information — name, address, city, state, social security number, income, and so on. It's your own private business how many children you have, what kind of car you drive, even what type of computer you own. Your personal communications — sent via e-mail or snail mail — are your private business. No doubt you wouldn't want certain details of your life projected on the giant screen in Times Square. Similarly, these are data items you want to keep private, and it's your right to do so.

Security, on the other hand, is all about protecting data and information and keeping it out of the less-than-well-intentioned hands of hackers and credit card hijackers. Individuals and businesses are concerned about the transmission of sensitive data such as credit card numbers, income data, health information, and more. They are also concerned about securing important data against all kinds of potential cybercriminals — those people who would seek to do mischief and find a back door into a program and those who would steal, corrupt, or crash systems.

Guarding Your Privacy

Before the advent of the Internet, few of us gave a second thought to the possibility of other people viewing our work files. If you were accustomed to working on a network that was backed up routinely, you may have been sensitive to the idea that you shouldn't save anything to the network drives you wouldn't want to see published in the company newsletter. Many of us have had a humbling experience or two that reminded us that what we thought was private data wasn't so private after all.

The Internet turns that reminder up a few notches and blasts it at us with all the subtlety of an air-raid siren. Today businesses and people can find information about us without our even giving it to them. We get unsolicited e-mails about the graphics board we have in our PCs — how did they know? We hear about a new software upgrade only days after we installed the original program. Somehow the company knew how to contact us without our having contacted them. Connectivity is a great thing when trying to locate someone or something. Connectivity is eerie when someone or something finds you and you don't want to be found.

Discovering where they get your data

It may sound unlikely, but it's true: Every time you do something on the Internet — whether it's browse a Web site, send in a registration card, or search for a favorite topic, someone or something sees what you are doing. Just based on how you use the Internet, what you search for, what groups you talk to, and where you visit, companies can deduce your likes and dislikes and make some preliminary marketing decisions about you. Here's how companies can learn about you:

> ✦ **Browsing the Internet**. Every time you click a link, your visit to a new Web site is logged somewhere on the Web. Some sites and services do nothing but review the ocean of data that comes rolling in from Internet use; they in turn sell the information to companies in the form of lists used for marketing products and services. Your junk e-mail — called *spam* — most likely comes from a company that purchased a list of users who searched for a specific topic or visited a particular type of site.

When you visit a Web site, the information is recorded in a file called a cookie and stored on your hard drive. Some sites use this information to find out more about you. Cookies are described in more detail later in this chapter.

✦ **Mailing Lists**. There's no such thing as one mailing list. Similar to mass mailings done through snail mail, e-mail mailing lists send you unsolicited mail about upcoming upgrades, new products, online events, and more. The mailings lists are kept and sold, much like the mailing lists in our traditional marketing-mail system.

✦ **Your Web page**. Do you talk about your kids, your hobbies, and your job on your Web page? The idea of having a personal Web page is to introduce yourself to the world, right? But personal Web pages are also a source information that can be used by companies to find out how to market directly to you. Consider carefully just how much sharing you want to do with the entire cybercommunity at large.

✦ **Newsgroups**. Any time you participate in a newsgroup, you leave behind information about yourself. Your interests, you curiosities, and more are recorded for an unspecified period in a newsgroup file. If you put your name, e-mail address, and contact information at the end of your newsgroup postings, that information is available to anyone who ever reads the postings you've left.

✦ **Phone books**. Some data comes right out of the phone book — scanned in and ready to use on the Web. Several people-finders exist on the Internet, just waiting for you to think of someone you want to locate. The information that is available can be as benign as e-mail addresses, up to and including phone numbers, your address, and even directions to your house! Take a look at some of the people search engines and see what kind of information is available about you.

To learn more about Web-based people finders, read Chapter 20, "Finding People on the Internet."

Requesting privacy

Bigfoot and the other search services didn't become as popular as they are by upsetting their patrons. If you do find your personal information listed by these services, and you are concerned about your privacy, you can usually request that your information be made private. To do this, you first need to review the policies of the site in question to find out what recourse you have. Look for a link called "Privacy Policy" or something like that (it's usually located in the fine print at the bottom of the page) and click it to learn what options you have, and what you can do about privacy.

Looking for cookies

Many Web sites now track visitors using tools called *cookies*. A cookie is actually a small text file that Web sites use to record personal information about you. Placed on your hard drive when you access some Web sites, cookies do not pose a virus hazard, but the information they gather can include:

✦ What Web sites you have visited

✦ How often you visit them

✦ How long you spent there

✦ Which links you clicked

✦ Personal information such as account names, passwords, and data you fill in on Web forms

Allowing a Web site to write and later reaccess cookies on your hard drive is invasive, but your Web browser does have the ability to prevent cookies from invading your system. The procedure is simple:

✦ **Internet Explorer 5**—Click Tools ➪ Internet Options. On the Security tab, click Custom Level, scroll down the list of security settings, and choose either Prompt (which will generate a warning message that gives you the option to allow or disallow a cookie) or Disable (which will automatically block all cookies).

✦ **Netscape Communicator 4.7**—Click Edit ➪ Preferences, and select the Advanced category on the left side of the window. Under Advanced preferences choose to disable cookies or prompt when one is present.

✦ **Opera 3.6**—Click Preferences ➪ Advanced. Under Logging, remove the check mark next to "Enable Cookies" to disable them.

Unfortunately, the fact that you *can* disable cookies does not necessarily mean that you *should*. If you have disabled cookies or set the browser to prompt you before saving one, you should see a warning message every time a Web site tries to write a cookie. But many Web sites have become so reliant on cookies that their pages can become impossible to view efficiently because you are constantly dealing with these cookie warning messages. It still may be worth a try to disable them, but you may find that it is easier (on the mouse, if not your conscience) to simply leave cookies enabled.

Defending your PC at home

Privacy, as they say, begins at home. Your journeys on the Web can be tracked, and there's only so much you can do about that. You can request to be taken off the people search engines. You can be careful about the Web sites you frequent. You can set up your Web browser to alert you if sites are dumping cookies on your hard drive. You can watch the newsgroups you participate in and limit how much information you put on your Web page.

Pentium IIIs and Online Identification

When Intel announced the Pentium III processor in 1999, one of its new features caused not a small amount of controversy. Each Pentium III has a unique serial number embedded in the unit, with the idea being that you would be able to positively identify yourself when conducting online transactions. A serial number embedded in the chip would — in theory at least — be much harder to forge than a digital certificate or other software identification method.

But the possibility of secure Internet shopping and communication was accompanied by new concerns about online privacy. If your computer positively identifies you to each Web site you visit, it is far easier to track your browsing habits. Some industry observers have also expressed concern that future Webmasters could require you to use such an ID feature in order to access their site.

Fortunately, the serial number feature can be disabled. Intel currently delivers Pentium III processors with the feature disabled, but the first few Pentium IIIs that were manufactured had the serial numbers enabled. Also, some computer resellers may enable the serial numbers before you buy the PC. They can be enabled or disabled using a processor serial number utility developed by Intel. You should be able to access the utility through your Windows Start menu (as of this writing, the utility is only available for systems running Windows 95 or higher). If you don't have the utility, visit Intel's Web site (http://www.intel.com/design/pentiumiii/psover.htm) to download it.

But you have other issues to think about in terms of privacy — even right there at home, on your own personal or work PC. What you do is recorded, right there. The Web sites you visit are stored in your history file. The images you viewed last night are still part of the cache. And those sensitive e-mail messages — even though you encrypted them — are still saved in your Sent folder and ready to be deciphered by anyone with the key and a few spare moments.

Defending your PC at work

Knowing that someone is looking over your shoulder at work is not a particularly new sensation if you have been working on a network for a while. Shared data is in. Conferencing is simple. Files are backed up. No big surprise there.

What may surprise you is that some employers are going a step farther and tracking how their employees use their computers. In fact, programs exist now to help them do just that. Communications tracking programs, for example, track phone and internet use, and can record not only how often you call but who. Ostensibly, this is done to help businesses figure out their communications expenses, but it's not hard to imagine that it could be used for less benign purposes as well. Part of the problem with gathering this type of online information — how many e-mail messages are sent and to whom, which Web sites are visited and how often — is that you can be giving, and getting, more information than you bargain for.

Cleaning up the evidence

If you've been frequenting sites you aren't sure you want your boss or your spouse to know about (not suggesting that you're playing with porn—perhaps you're hanging in a chat room discussing the latest episode of *Star Trek* when you should be researching), you can clean up the Web trail and ensure your privacy in a few simple ways.

Getting rid of cookie crumbs

You may not think you leave much of a trail when you wander across the Web, but think again. Cookie crumbs are scattered everywhere. Cookie files—as described earlier—are stored in your browser's cache of temporary Internet files and are giving other people a pretty keen look into what you do all day.

If you are using Internet Explorer, check out what's in your temporary Internet file folder by following these steps:

1. With Internet Explorer running, choose Tools ➪ Internet Options.

2. Click the General tab. In the Temporary Internet Files area, click Settings. The Settings dialog box appears.

3. Click View Files. A window opens on your screen showing you all the temporary files that are stored, right now, related to your Internet foraging. On our system, this was sobering—a huge number of files, as you'll see in Figure 32-1.

4. Close the window by clicking the Close box. Click OK to return to the Internet Options dialog box.

5. Delete the temporary Internet files by clicking Delete Files; then click OK to close the box.

If you are using Netscape Communicator, you can locate your temporary files— including cookies—by clicking Edit ➪ Preferences, and then choosing the Cache category under Advanced in the category list. The Disk Cache Folder will list the current location of your temporary files, but if you want to view them you will have to browse this folder from your operating system.

With Opera, you will need to locate your disk cache manually. On our system running Windows 98, we found it in `C:\Program Files\Opera\CACHE`.

Changing history with Internet Explorer

Deleting your browsing footprints is really important because IE saves the histories of Web searches for up to several weeks, and each item is pinpointed to the exact day and time, and is accessible instantly, without a password. Netscape doesn't save the histories for a fraction of this time and doesn't organize them for offline presentation like this.

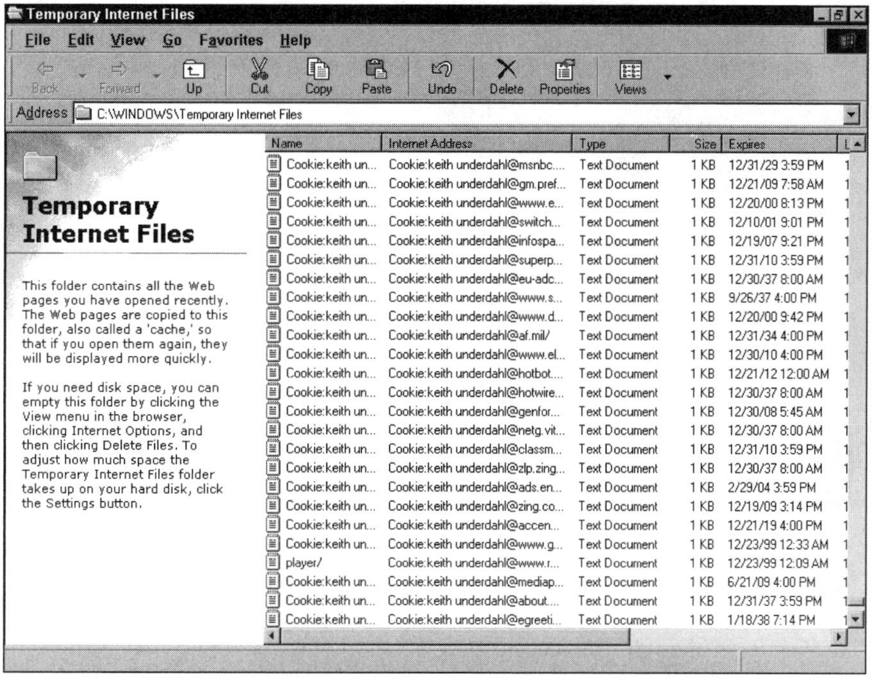

Figure 32-1: Somebody could write a book about you after looking at the leftovers in your temporary Internet files folder.

If you are using Internet Explorer, follow these steps to clear out your history folder:

1. With Internet Explorer open on your screen, choose Tools ⇨ Internet Options. The Internet Options dialog box appears, as shown in Figure 32-2.

2. If the General tab is not displayed, click it.

3. Click the Clear History button. Internet Explorer asks whether you want to delete all files from your History folder.

Tip

To the left of the Clear History button is a setting that controls the number of days the history is kept. You can change this number to a lower (or higher) number of days and have Internet Explorer clean out your history folder more frequently.

4. Click Yes. The history is cleared and the Web sites are wiped away — as if you'd never been there (except for the cookies, of course).

Note

When you clean out the history folder, you are removing the links to sites you have visited recently. If you routinely add sites you want to return to in your Favorites folders, you shouldn't need the history items, anyway. The favorites remain saved as long as you want them — removing the history entries does not affect them in any way.

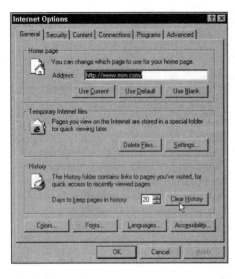

Figure 32-2: You can delete your Web trail by wiping out your history in Internet Explorer.

Clearing the Netscape cache

Netscape Communicator has two caches — a memory cache and a disk cache — that track your most frequently accessed documents. This feature was designed to cut down on the time it takes to load Web sites you visit often. For example, if you start your day with the online version of the *Evansville Courier*, the network document is saved in the cache and, upon loading, Netscape simply updates the parts of the page that are different from the cached document.

To clear both the memory and disk cache, follow these steps:

1. Open the Preferences dialog by clicking Edit ➪ Preferences, and select Cache under the Advanced options category.

2. Click the Cache tab. Figure 32-3 shows the Preferences window with the Cache tab displayed.

3. Click Clear Memory Cache to clear the RAM cache.

4. Click Clear Disk Cache to clear the disk cache.

5. Click OK to close the Preferences dialog box.

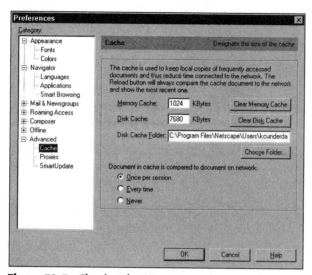

Figure 32-3: Clearing the Netscape memory and disk caches removes cached documents from your PC.

Making it private

Here is a summary of ways you can make your Internet experience as private as possible:

✦ Be aware of what you're doing. Remember that when you frequent sites, they may be gathering information about you.

✦ Set your browser to prompt you before it accepts cookies (although this may make some sites difficult to navigate efficiently).

✦ Avoid putting too much information in your e-mail signature.

✦ Use caution and common sense about how much personal information you put on your Web site.

✦ Think about the newsgroups you review or join — they say a lot about you.

✦ Clear out your history and cache files regularly.

✦ Request to be taken off some mailing lists. The messages aren't fun to read — especially because you didn't ask for them — but somewhere buried in there is a clue as to how you can get your name taken off the list.

Caution

Beware — requesting to have your name removed from a spammer's mailing list may sometimes actually worsen your spam problem. When you e-mail the spammer telling them to remove your name, this actually confirms to them that your e-mail address is correct — and many devious spammers will then send you more spam!

Other Internet considerations involve security—being able to transmit data safely over the Internet. Security issues are coming up later in this chapter.

Warding off hackers

"Shall we play a game?" croaked Matthew Broderick's computer in the 1983 film *Wargames*. With that, the public was introduced to the concept of computer *hacking*, wherein a skilled PC user can defeat electronic security measures and gain access to networked computer systems. Although this activity is considered criminal today, we view Broderick's character David Lightman as heroic because he illustrated the reality of this problem to almost anyone who uses a computer.

By accessing the Internet, your computer becomes part of the network. Every computer connected to the Internet is indirectly linked, in the same way that every driveway in America is linked via the highway system. And if you're not paying attention, a hacker can easily drive up and park in the driveway of your computer and steal things out of your virtual garage.

Fortunately, hacking into individual computers simply isn't practical in most cases, because most individuals still connect to the Internet through relatively slow modem connections. Thus, hackers are more likely to attack systems with faster connections or corporate networks where they are more likely to find something valuable.

If you have a faster connection, a computer that is continually connected to the Internet, or if you run a business with sensitive information on your company network, some added caution is called for. You can do something to protect yourself:

✦ If you have a network, restrict access to hard drives and other network resources so that a password is required for access.

✦ Consider disabling permanent connections during anticipated periods of inactivity.

✦ Use firewall software that more carefully restricts network access from outside sources.

✦ Install software specifically designed to monitor and block hacker attacks, such as BlackICE.

Note Even if you have a slow connection, beware that your system may include sensitive information about you. If a hacker knows exactly where to look for it, your privacy could be compromised even with a very slow dial-up connection.

BlackICE defender

Network ICE (http://www.networkice.com/) offers a countermeasure to hacker attacks called BlackICE Defender. BlackICE is a Windows program that runs in the background, continuously monitoring your Internet connection. Unlike many antivirus programs, our testing suggests that BlackICE has no measurable impact on system speed or performance, which makes it an attractive option.

BlackICE is not an antivirus program. Instead, it monitors your Internet connection and identifies — and more importantly, blocks — attempts by outside users to access your system via the Internet. It is configurable, enabling you to set the level of paranoia that you feel comfortable with. A trial version of BlackICE defender is available on the *Internet Bible* CD-ROM.

Once BlackICE is installed, an icon for the program will appear in the Windows system tray, as shown in Figure 32-4. To configure BlackICE, right-click the icon and choose Configure.

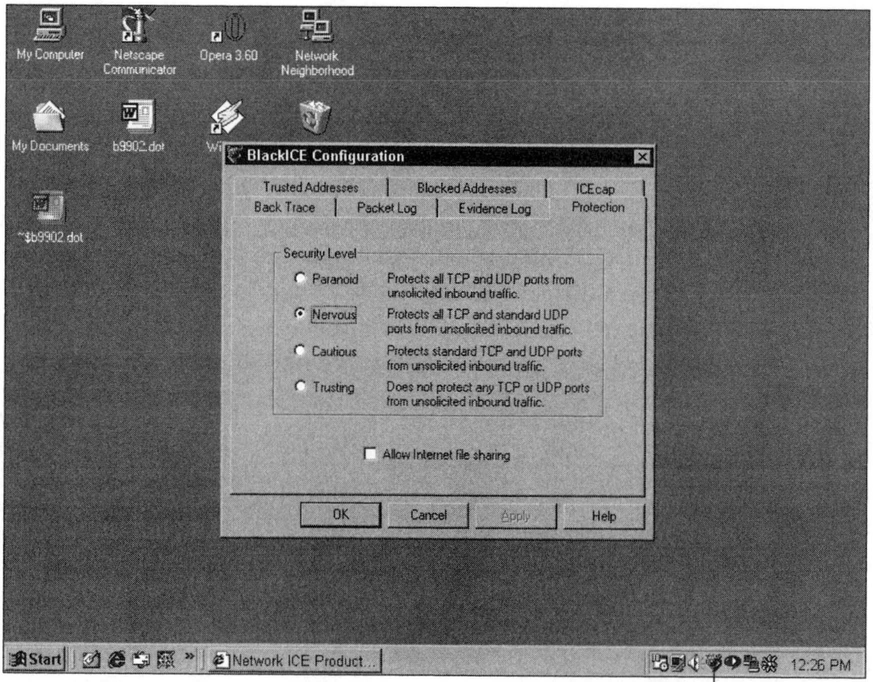

The BlackICE icon will flash red if an attack or probe is detected

Figure 32-4: BlackICE Defender protects your computer from hacker attacks via your Internet connection.

BlackICE can be set to four basic levels of protection, but for most applications we suggest the Nervous setting. If an attack or probe is detected, the system tray icon will flash red. Double-click the flashing icon to display a window similar to Figure 32-5, where you can learn more about the attack.

Most of the "attacks" that BlackICE detects are actually not attacks against you personally. Many novice hackers will perform widespread scans of thousands of systems simultaneously, looking for open TCP/IP (Transmission Control Protocol/Internet Protocol) or UDP (User Datagram Protocol) ports through which to access various systems. Figure 32-5 shows a report of just such a probe.

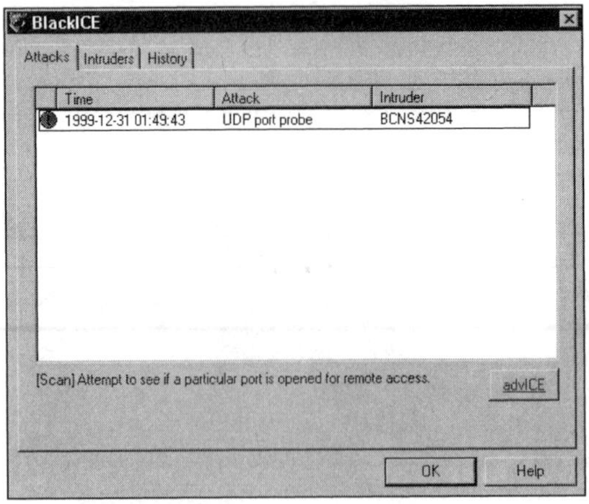

Figure 32-5: BlackICE Defender has identified a UDP Port Probe. Click advICE to learn more about any attack or probe you may receive.

BlackICE makes it easy for you to identify probes and attacks, learn more about them, and even pursue the offenders if you are so inclined.

Note   If you are using the Internet Connection Sharing feature available in newer versions of Windows, BlackICE will block the client computers from accessing the Internet. BlackICE identifies and blocks DNS port probes, an action necessary to facilitate connection sharing. You can work around this by listing the IP addresses of each networked computer on the BlackICE Trusted Addresses tab in the configuration dialog box. To learn more about doing this, see Chapter 7, "Getting Online with Your Small Network."

Industry responses

The concern over cookies and other privacy matters is not lost on the computer industry. Various companies are working on ways to ensure privacy and still enable e-commerce companies to gather the information they need in order to survive on the Internet.

TRUSTe (http://www.truste.org) is a nonprofit organization that is working on ways to resolve privacy issues. They have developed a Seal of Approval that participating sites display. This Seal of Approval tells Web visitors whether the participating site gathers information from users, what they do with the information, and whether they give out the information to third parties.

Managing Your Security

Security—keeping data safe and healthy—is an important part of your Internet experience. Even if you use the Internet only for fun and games, you need to protect your system against viruses. If you ever purchase anything online—whether you're buying books from Amazon.com or ordering music from Columbia House—you want the credit card number you give out to be seen by the merchant's eyes only, not spread around the Internet for a million wandering eyes to see.

Businesses have even greater needs where data protection is concerned. They still have viruses and credit card theft to worry about, but they have other assets to protect as well. Confidential communications, proprietary research, and so on, are valuables that companies spend a lot of time and resources safekeeping.

Setting up security in Internet Explorer

Internet Explorer enables you to set up different zones for Web sites you know to be either secure or risky. You choose the level of security you want to employ for each zone and then add the sites you know about to the appropriate zone. Table 16-1 provides a description of the security zones and shows you their security level.

	Table 32-1 **Internet Explorer Security Zones**	
Zone	**Description**	**Security Level**
Local intranet	Your in-house network	Medium
Trusted sites	Sites you deem to be trustworthy and add to the zone by clicking Sites.	Low
Internet	The entire zone encompassing all Internet sites	Medium
Restricted sites	Sites you specify as being potentially dangerous to security	High

Here's how you add a site to one of the security zones:

1. Open the Tools menu and choose Internet Options.

2. Click the Security tab.

3. Select the zone you want to adjust settings for in the upper half of the window (see Figure 32-6).

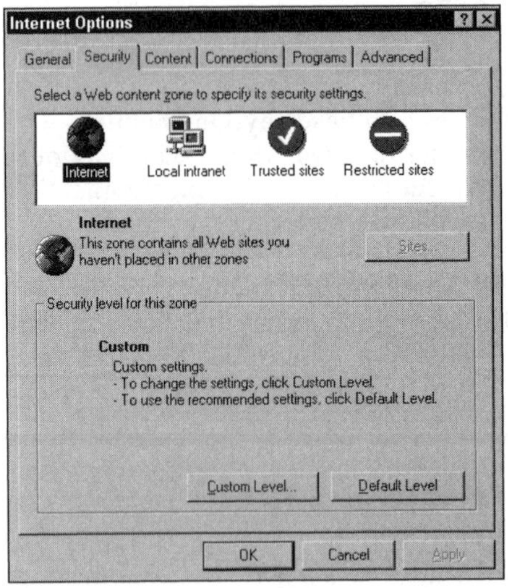

Figure 32-6: You can assign different security levels to zones and organize the sites you find trustworthy or suspicious.

4. Choose the zone you want. (For this example, you might choose Trusted sites zone.)

5. Click Sites. The Trusted sites zone dialog box appears, as Figure 32-7 shows.

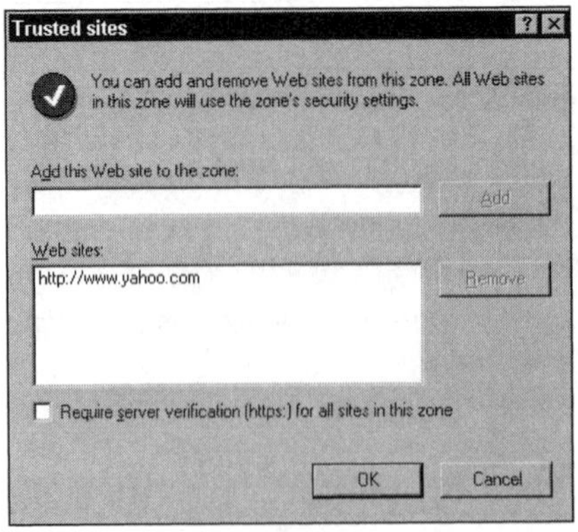

Figure 32-7: You add sites using the Trusted sites zone dialog box in Internet Explorer.

6. Enter the URL of the Web page you want to add to the Trusted sites zone and then click Add. The URL then appears in the Web sites box.

Note

If you cannot add a site to the Trusted list, remove the check mark next to the "Require server verification" option at the bottom of the window. This option enables you to specify that only sites on secure servers can be designated as trusted.

7. When you finish adding sites, click OK to close the Trusted sites dialog box and then the Internet Options dialog box.

Securing Netscape

Not to be outdone by Internet Explorer, Netscape Communicator also includes security features. Display the security options by clicking Communicator ⇨ Tools ⇨ Security Info (or just click the Security button on the Navigator toolbar) and choosing Navigator. The Navigator security settings appear, as Figure 32-8 shows.

The Navigator tab includes options that control when security alerts are displayed. If you want to be told when you are entering or leaving a secure server or you want to know when you are looking at a document that may be questionable in terms of its security, make sure that the first three options are checked. (Note: These options are checked by default, so, unless you have deselected them, they are currently in effect.) If you want to be alerted before you submit a form that is not secure, click the last option in the *Show a Warning Before* area. In the bottom of the Navigator tab are two options related to SSL.

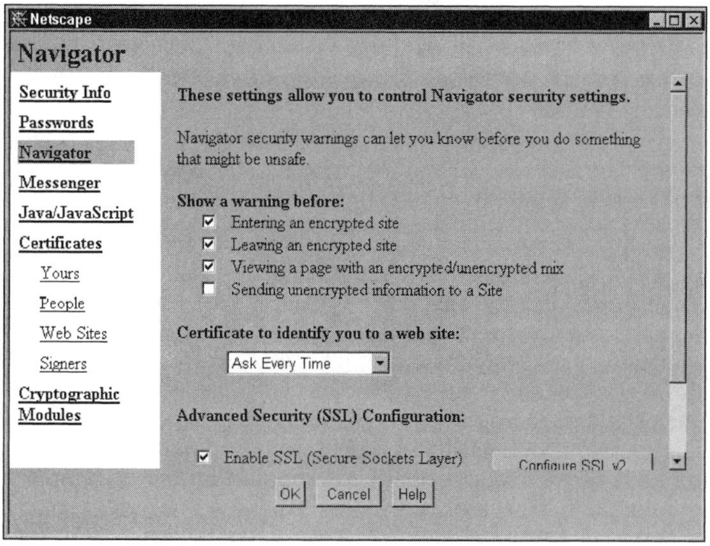

Figure 32-8: The Navigator security settings group enables you to make security decisions for your Netscape use.

Note   SSL (Secure Sockets Layer) is a protocol designed by Netscape that provides a secure method of transmitting data between your Web browser and servers you visit. The data that moves from one point to another is encrypted and preserved so that no changes are made during transmission. SSL is discussed in more detail later in this chapter.

The Passwords group, of course, enables you to set a password for use with Netscape. A password is a good idea if you share your PC with others or if your 16-year-old daughter is always looking for a chance to get in some chat time. You can enter a password and then choose how many times it's needed—when you begin for the day, after certain periods of nonuse, and in other situations.

Using Encryption

Encryption sounds like something that happens in James Bond movies, but it's worth considering if you're worried about keeping your communications secure. Encrypting your data may sound like a lot of hassle—and if all you're dealing with on a daily basis is a set of e-mails to and from your mom and Aunt Frieda, then you might not be too worried about whether or not you should encrypt your files. But encrypting can do more than just protect your privacy; it can also protect your data against theft, forgery, or corruption.

Defining encryption

Encryption is a procedure that turns regular text into coded text. You need a "key" to be able to "unlock" the code and read the text in its regular form again. Unlike a door key, an encryption key is a series of numbers—called *bits*—that must be used in the right order for the key to unlock the encryption. The more bits in the key, the harder the key is to decipher.

Encrypting methods

You can encrypt your files in two basic ways: single-key encryption and two-key encryption. When you use a single-key system, you use the same key to lock and unlock the file. The trouble with the single-key system is that you have to give the key to the recipient—and if that person is 5,000 miles away and you have to send the key over the Internet, how secure is that? Single-key systems are more reliable if you can walk down the hall and hand your coworker a slip of paper with the key written on it (remember to remind the coworker to eat the paper after he or she is done with it). But relying on the security of the Internet to pass along a key you need because you need better security on the Internet is a bit of a contradiction.

Two-key systems solve the problem of long-distance security. The first key is known as a *public key,* and you use it to encrypt files. If someone needs to send you an encrypted file, you simply send that person the public key, which they use to encode the file. When you receive the file, you use the *private key*, to decode it. That way, even if ne'er-do-wells out there in cyberspace intercept both your public key and the file itself, they can't do anything with the data because the key needed to unlock it all — the related but unique private key you create — is safely there on your PC.

Secure Socket Layers (SSL)

As mentioned earlier in this chapter, Netscape began addressing the encryption question with the SSL (Secure Sockets Layer) security protocol in its first incarnation. SSL version 3 is now the de facto standard for encryption models in the online world, primarily because all major browsers support it.

> **Note**
>
> Netscape includes a visual clue to tell you when you're working with a secure site. The little key or closed padlock in the lower left corner of the Netscape window shows you when you are in a secure area. The padlock is open (or broken, in the case of the key) when you are visiting an insecure site. Opera contains a similar padlock indicator in the lower left corner of session windows, and Internet Explorer indicates a secure site with a padlock indicator near the lower right of the screen.

When you first log on to a Web site, there are a number of communications of which you are probably unaware. During this opening conversation between browser and server, the browser makes sure that security-wise both parties are on the same page and a session ID number is assigned. When SSL has determined that the interaction is secure, digital IDs can be exchanged (these are also called certificates) to verify identities. A process of exchanging keys and generating premaster private keys occurs; then a secure transmission can take place.

Secure HTTP

Secure HTTP is another encryption standard that differs from SSL in that, rather than establishing a secure connection between two computers, it concentrates on securing individual messages. A Secure HTTP server can generally be identified by the protocol https://, and it can be used in conjunction with SSL.

Private Communications Technology

Private Communications Technology (PCT) is a security protocol introduced by Microsoft in 1995 and included in Internet Explorer versions 3.0 and later. The primary difference between PCT and SSL is in the number of transmissions that take place during the *handshaking* stage — when the browser and server are getting to know each other and making sure that a safe transaction is about to take place. However, PCT has not caught on because it is only supported by Internet Explorer. It is unlikely that you will find many sites using this encryption model.

Transport Layer Security (TLS)

Another security protocol, Transport Layer Security, has been introduced by the Internet Engineering Task Force (IETF). This protocol was based on the SSL standard but different enough that the two protocols (specifically, with SSL 3.0) were not compatible with each other. TLS has all but disappeared from the online world, but it is still supported by Netscape Navigator and Internet Explorer.

Employing Digital IDs

When you write a check at Wal-Mart, the checkout clerk may ask to see your driver's license. It's a fairly common way of making sure you are who you say you are — and that you're the one qualified to write the check. When you attach a digital ID to your e-mail messages, you are providing evidence that you are in fact you, and that you have the right to be participating in the current transaction, whether you are buying a car on the Web or trading sensitive information with overseas distributors.

In talking about encryption, we established that different keys are used to encrypt and decrypt data. In a two-key system, the public key is used for encryption and the private key is used by the recipient so the message can be decrypted on the other end of the transmission. A digital ID involves the use of a public key, a private key, and a digital signature, which is appended at the end of the message file.

Finding your digital ID

Like your John Hancock on documents requiring your signature, your digital signature is your "mark" made on an electronic document. You get your own digital signature from a third-party company. One place you can find a digital ID is VeriSign, at `http://digitalid.verisign.com`, the Web home of The Digital ID Center. VeriSign works with Microsoft and others in assigning and authenticating digital IDs. You'll find a link directly from Microsoft's Web page to the VeriSign site.

Another authorized Digital ID provider is GlobalSign NV-SA, available at `http://www.globalsign.net/`. Either one of these sites can help fix you up for digital IDs for Outlook Express or Netscape Messenger.

Getting your digital ID

Before you can use a digital ID to make sure your message transmissions are secure, you need to set up your e-mail program to work with a digital ID. This section explains how to do so using Outlook Express. The process may work differently if you are using another e-mail program.

1. Start Outlook Express.

2. Choose Tools and then Options. The Options dialog box appears. Click the Security tab, which is shown in Figure 32-9.

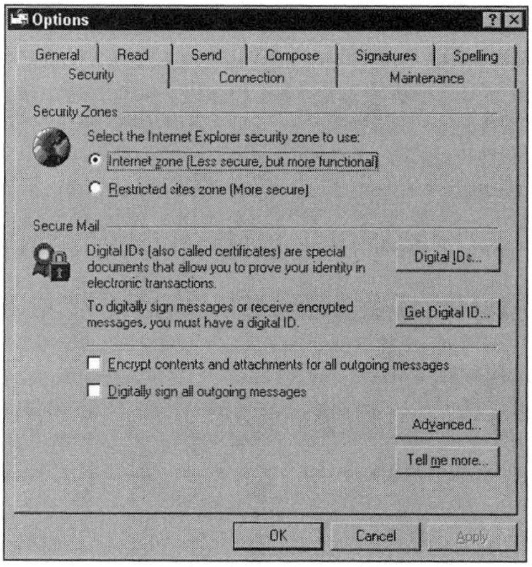

Figure 32-9: Go to the Security tab in the Options dialog box to get a digital ID for use with Outlook Express.

3. Click the Get Digital ID button and you are taken to the Microsoft Internet Explorer Digital ID Web site (see Figure 32-10).

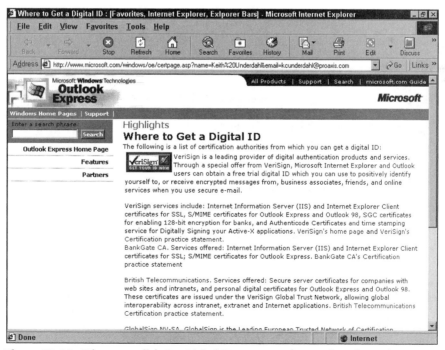

Figure 32-10: When you click Get Digital ID, you are taken to the Microsoft Internet Explorer Digital ID Web site.

4. Click the VeriSign link, or scroll down to GlobalSign to choose that ID provider if you prefer.

5. Follow the instructions on the ID provider's site to get set up with your digital ID.

Note

Netscape calls IDs certificates and gives you the option of obtaining one by choosing Communicator ➪ Tools ➪ Security Info and clicking the "Yours" link under the Certificates listing. When you click Get a Certificate (you may have to scroll down to see it), a wizard begins to help you obtain a personal certificate, or digital ID.

Setting up your digital ID

Once you get the digital ID, you must set it up to work with your e-mail program. Different programs have different procedures on how to do this, but here are the steps for Outlook Express:

1. Choose Tools ➪ Accounts. The Internet Accounts dialog box appears.

2. Double-click the e-mail account for which you want to configure an ID. The Properties dialog box for that service appears.

3. Click the Security tab, and then click the *Use a digital ID when sending secure messages* check box.

4. Click the Digital ID button and select your new digital ID from the list that appears.

5. Click OK to close the dialog box. You are now set up to use your digital ID on your e-mail messages.

Tip

If you only need to send encrypted e-mail occasionally, consider setting up an e-mail identity in Outlook Express exclusively for this type of communication. See Chapter 12, "Choosing an E-Mail Client and Using E-Mail," to learn more about configuring multiple identities in Outlook Express.

Using your digital ID

Now the only step that remains is to use your new digital ID. Simply create your normal e-mail message and, in Outlook Express, click the *Sign message tool* on the right side of the toolbar. This adds a red ribbon in the far right side of the message header. When the message is received in the recipient's Inbox, the message icon shows the small red ribbon, indicating that the message has been given a digital ID.

Caution

Remember, a digital signature only authenticates your identity to the recipient; the message can still be intercepted and read by unauthorized persons. If the message contains sensitive information, you should also use encryption.

Adding other digital IDs

It doesn't do much good to have a digital ID if you're the only person using one. When secure transmissions are important to you, encourage others you communicate with to get their own digital IDs. When you receive a digitally signed message from someone, you can add his or her digital ID to your address book in Outlook Express by following these steps:

1. Display the message.

2. Choose File ⇨ Properties.

3. Click the Digital IDs tab and click Add Digital ID to Address book.

Outlook Express then adds the ID to the user information, and a small red ribbon appears beside the entry in the Address book.

Summary

In this chapter, you've taken a look at the information—your own personal information—that may be splattered out there on the Internet without your knowledge or consent. You've also learned about the various ways you can reclaim and protect your online privacy. What's more, you've determined how you can make sure people are who they say they are on the Internet and ensure secure data transmissions and e-mail practices. This chapter also discussed Digital IDs, which you can use to make sure others know you are on the level.

✦   ✦   ✦

Protecting Your Kids on the Internet

When our children venture onto the Internet, they are exploring a place not unlike the streets of their own city or town, a world that's filled with valuable resources, new friends, and lots of fun. Yet, like the real world, the Internet also has dangers. For this reason, parents have cast a wary eye on their computers, increasingly worried about who or what their children may encounter in the world of cyberspace. Many are looking for ways to protect their children against online perils.

In this chapter, you'll learn how you can protect your children while still allowing them to enjoy the many wonderful things the Internet has to offer. You'll learn about filtering software that blocks offensive Web sites, rating systems that can determine which Web sites are safe for your children, and family-friendly Internet Service Providers that tailor their services for parents and kids alike. You'll also find other resources and information that can help you guide and protect your children while they are online.

Getting Involved: What You Can Do

The Internet may be new, and your kids may know more about it than you, but that doesn't mean there's nothing you can do to protect them while they're surfing the Web or visiting chat rooms. Here's what you can do:

   ✦ Involve yourself with your children's online activities and talk to them about what they do and who they meet.

   ✦ Invest in software that blocks access to sites known to be objectionable, or find an ISP that will block unwanted URLs for you.

✦ Become familiar with Web rating systems.

✦ Learn about the work of CyberAngels (`http://www.cyberangels.org/`), among others. These organizations offer help to parents who want to let their kids surf the Internet and who don't want to worry about objectionable content.

✦ To investigate the broader issues of blocking software, censorship, and free speech, take a look at the Electronic Frontier Foundation's (EEF)Web site (`http://www.eff.org/`). The EEF provides a clearinghouse of information on software that filters out offensive sites. It also alerts people to congressional action on Internet free-speech legislation, as well as fostering industry-wide roundtable discussions and advisory panels on these subjects.

Tip
If you want to learn more about issues surrounding free speech and the Web, check out the Electronic Frontier Foundation's Australian branch Web site at `http://www.efa.org.au/EFA/Issues/Censor/`.

Talking to your children

Even the staunchest advocate of blocking objectionable Web sites would agree that getting children to cooperate comes first. They need to understand how to have fun and learn on the Web, but not how to get into trouble. The first step is to talk to your kids:

✦ Place the computer in a family area and make the Internet a family activity. Talk to your children about what they do online.

✦ Ask your kids to show you where they go when they're online. Take a genuine interest in who their online pen pals are. Get a sense of who the new, unfamiliar "faces" are.

✦ Remind your kids not to talk to strangers. Tell them it's not unusual for people to lie about their identities and motives online. Your kids should never give out their real name, phone number, address, or any other personal information.

✦ Take a look at the phone bill. Be aware of prefixes that indicate a prepaid telephone service, such as adult bulletin boards and chat lines.

✦ Be really clear about the rules.

Here are some additional battle plans that require your child's cooperation:

✦ Have them tell you right away if someone sends them hate mail, mail of a sexual or suggestive nature, or something that just doesn't sit right with them.

✦ Set up online time limits.

✦ A period of trying times in the "real world" may cause children to seek extra solace in the world of their online friends. Be aware of your child's online dynamic and patterns.

Tip

Younger children tend to believe that if someone says something to them, there was a reason for it. A child would think that if they get singled out for special attention, good or bad, that they did something to deserve it. He or she will quite naturally assume that a random "message" appearing out of the blue would be intended just for them. Also, if someone makes an inappropriate suggestion online, children would tend to feel they had done something to deserve it, feel ashamed, and probably be too embarrassed to mention it to their parents. Parents need to get involved before something like this happens.

When it comes time to discuss Internet issues with your children, approach the subject in a friendly way and preferably before an incident occurs that makes such a discussion imperative — meaning, before the $200 phone bill, or before the handsome stranger shows up at your door looking for a romantic interest named "Gigi." Try to find out your child's opinion first, and determine their level of sophistication before you say what you think.

If they have other online friends in the neighborhood, they may have already explored chat rooms and such, and you might not have to explain what they are. As you go through the basic points you think are important, such as protecting their privacy and being cautious in talking to strangers, make sure they understand why you are bringing this up now. Be really clear about the rules you expect them to follow, and why.

Blocking Objectionable Web Sites

You can control your children's access to the Internet. Software is available that, once installed on your computer, prevents your children from accessing sites deemed objectionable. These programs are sometimes called blocking software or Internet filters.

Finding blocking software

Before you buy blocking software, take a look at the following criteria, which will help you find the right blocking software for you and your family:

✦ Do you want software that blocks out entire Web sites altogether, or only pages of those sites that are objectionable?

✦ Is it possible to "fine-tune" the way filtering software works? For example, is it possible to let a child research breast cancer on the Web, but still filter out sites where "breast" would indicate objectionable content?

✦ Do you trust a software company or rating system to fully decide which sites get blocked? How about software that enables you to add additional URLs to the "bad list," and likewise, enables you to "unblock" sites — in those cases where you believe the cyberpolice have overstepped?

✦ Do you believe ISPs should be able to block sites from being available to their customers?

✦ Do you want to configure filtering software for various family members, providing access to a few sites for younger children, and a broader range to older kids?

✦ Do you want safeguards against passwords, personal phone numbers, and addresses being given out? Do you want to limit the vocabulary that your children use in chat rooms when online?

✦ Do you want to block your kids from receiving e-mail from certain addresses, or from receiving e-mail containing objectionable vocabulary?

✦ Do you want to defend against online predators, such as pedophiles who misrepresent themselves and befriend children they meet on the Internet?

Using home-based filtering software products

Here are descriptions with plusses and minuses of some of the major filtering software packages available. We'll discuss what each product does and how each responds to objectionable content when and if it comes across the screen.

CyberSitter

CyberSitter costs $39.95 and is available from `http://www.solidoak.com` for a ten-day free trial. The program installs easily and works by blocking out sites with sex-related content, adult violence, gambling, illegal activities, and hate material. You can also add additional blocked sites to the list. When your child surfs the Web, CyberSitter will not allow pages to be shown that contain certain vocabulary, but is sophisticated enough to be able to tell if such words are being used in a harmless context, and such pages will not be blocked. If a page with offensive vocabulary is accessed, CyberSitter blanks out those words.

The program also enables you to restrict your child from using certain types of Internet tools, such as FTP sites, newsgroups, or AOL Instant Messenger. Note, however, that your child is able to type whatever he or she wants. "Output" is not blocked. In Figure 33-1, note that the Options dialog box is open. In this space, you can filter out files from sources you find objectionable. CyberSitter appears to not support profiles for multiple users at this time. E-mail is also monitored, although a password holder can turn off e-mail controls.

CyberSitter is currently available only for Windows 95/98/NT platforms.

WatchDog

WatchDog (`http://www.sarna.net/watchdog/`) is another control program that has received a number of favorable reviews recently. This program is somewhat simpler than most other filters, because it only controls the amount of time users spend online. It sets up a counter when the user logs on, and when the time has run out it either displays a log-in dialog box, restarts Windows, or shuts down the computer altogether, depending on how you configure it. WatchDog is available only for Windows 95/98, and if you decide to purchase it after the 30-day trial period, the cost is $25.

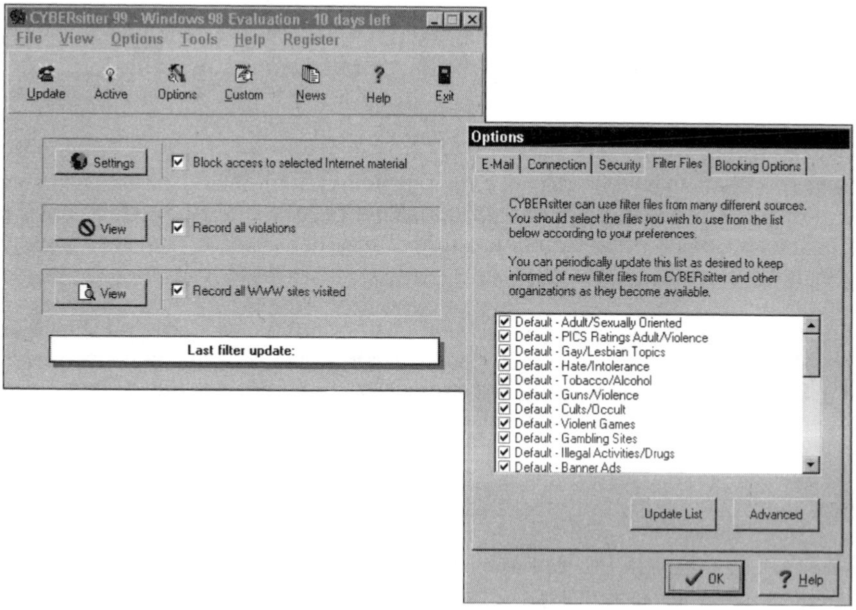

Figure 33-1: The CyberSitter main screen and the Filter Files tab of the Options dialog. Here you can select the types of sites you want to filter.

ISP-provided software

In addition to the products mentioned here, check with your ISP to see if they provide any special filtering software; many national ISPs do. Prodigy, for instance, provides a program called Cyber Patrol that provides a secure, easy to manage interface for filtering objectionable content. It also enables you to control when and for how long other users can access the Internet. Cyber Patrol is a free download offered to Prodigy members, available on their Web site in the Extras section.

MindSpring provides a browser plug-in called SurfMonkey that filters content within the browser. SurfMonkey places a special toolbar at the bottom of the browser window that includes links to a special online community. The SurfMonkey community offers a variety of services and even enables your kids to get their own SurfMonkey e-mail account. SurfMonkey can be downloaded from the MindSpring Web site, or you can find it on your MindSpring software CD in the Tools folder (run the program called Tasetup.exe in that folder).

Rating Web Sites

Web rating systems provide Webmasters and ISPs with a tool to determine which sites they might want to block from their more content-conscious customers, perhaps offering such customers the ability to block out all sites that rate poorly. Also, parents can deem off-limits those sites that rate as offensive (or are not rated at all).

Two main Web rating systems exist at the moment, one from the Recreational Software Advisory Council (RSAC, which also rates computer games), and another from SafeSurf. Rating is voluntary, and to date, fewer than 200,000 Web sites have been rated.

Under the RSAC's special Internet rating system, it's the Webmasters themselves that rate the sites, using four categories: violence, sex, nudity, and language. Each category receives a 0 to 4 rating. A rating of zero in a category means no offensive content is found.

Tip   It's easy to find out if a site has been rated or not. Go to a site and view it as an HTML document (In Navigator, click View ⇨ Page Source; in IE, click View ⇨ Source). If, near the top, you see references to a particular rating system (SafeSurf or RSAC) this means that the site has been rated. You might also find a clickable button somewhere on the page that enables you to view the site's rating.

The CyberAngels organization (`http://www.cyberangels.com/`), which is an offshoot of the Guardian Angels, has a Web site offering help of all sorts for anyone who is besieged by online predators. It offers counseling, prevention tips, suggestions for aggressive legal action against online predators, helpful links, as well as a staff that offers lots of peer support and general encouragement. Also, check out `http://www.netparents.org/` and `http://www.yellodyno.com/html/inetpeds.html`.

Using Family-Friendly ISPs

Although no solution to objectionable content is foolproof, perhaps one of the most complete options available to you is to select an Internet service provider that advertises itself as family friendly. Family-friendly service providers generally filter all of the content that passes through their servers, thereby protecting you (in theory) from objectionable content.

Of course, if your ISP is filtering the content you receive you won't have the option to turn the filter off, as you could with a software filter or other server-based filter. Still, it's a fairly thorough solution to objectionable content. What follows are brief descriptions of two popular filtered ISPs.

MayberryUSA

MayberryUSA (`http://www.mbusa.net/`) is a full-service national ISP with local dial-up numbers throughout the United States. Their filters claim to block pornography, hate groups, criminal skills, illegal drugs, and other offensive material. The service also hosts filtered chat rooms, homework help, and other family-friendly community areas.

Pricing is competitive with other Internet Service Providers, and their extensive network of dial-up numbers is impressive. If you don't have Web access yet, you can contact the MayberryUSA sales office at (800) 383-5854.

FAMILY.NET

FAMILY.NET (`http://www.family.net/`) is another popular filtered service provider catering to families, schools, libraries, and any other group or organization that might want filtered access. Although their network of dial-up numbers is not quite as extensive as MayberryUSA's, availability is still widespread and offers high-speed access in most locations. Pricing starts at $21.95 per month for unlimited access. The FAMILY.NET sales staff can be reached at (888) 905-0888.

Parent Soup

Although not actually an ISP, Parent Soup (`http://www.parentsoup.com/`) *is* a fascinating and supportive community for parents. If you have little ones (or not-so-little ones), there will be something of interest for you here. Like many other online communities, Parent Soup offers free e-mail, and interest areas are broken down into minicommunities that serve different parents with different needs. For instance, expecting parents and parents of teenagers have very different needs and concerns, so there are special areas designed for each.

Parent Soup also provides:

- ◆ Cyberfridges, which act as miniature personal Web pages for members. Show off pictures of your kids here!
- ◆ Chat groups that cover many parenting topics and include daily and ongoing discussions.
- ◆ Discussion groups that cover parenting topics in a newsgroup format so that posted messages can be read more easily.
- ◆ Parent Soup experts who are ready to answer your questions! Doctors and other knowledgeable folks often take part in special chats and discussion groups.
- ◆ Fun & Games that entertain parents and kids alike. Check out the Baby Name Finder and the Baby Name Scrambler!

Parent Soup provides an excellent archive of information about protecting your kids online, including links to literally hundreds of resources. And because of the community atmosphere of Parent Soup, it is a place you probably wouldn't mind visiting even when you aren't trying to learn about protecting your kids online. The forum areas of Parent Soup are also a good place to discuss your ideas and concerns about online safety with other parents. If you're looking for a safe, useful, and entertaining home page, this would be a good choice.

Looking Beyond Technology

Organizations such as the Electronic Frontier Foundation and American Civil Liberties Union object to the idea of software that blocks other software. Even the best-intentioned devices are subject to the predisposition of the designers. (One popular software filter goes as far as filtering out the Web sites of organizations that object to software filters!)

Practically everyone agrees that totally unfettered access to the Internet is not appropriate for all children, but who's responsibility is it to decide where your kids can or cannot go online? It's true, many software filters enable parents to create their own list of blocked sites. But parents often view these products as a way to avoid involvement in their children's Internet experience — they let the software become surrogate mothers and fathers.

The fact is, all the software in the world cannot replace interested and involved parents. For example, if a young man has deeply racist ideas, he may never express them around family and friends. If he did, they would most likely be criticized. But on the Internet, he can stumble upon a chat room of fellow believers, and suddenly he's got a small community of people who will help him articulate, and even act on, ideas that he used to be a bit ashamed of. Preventing such situations lies in the hands of family members and friends, not a computer program. If a 12-year-old girl types the words "Do you think I'm pretty?" to a man who, unbeknownst to her, is three times her age, this could only happen because a very important family conversation about the nature of the Internet did *not* happen. Ultimately, it's about common sense, not software.

Summary

This chapter reviewed how parents can have a positive effect on their child's online experience, and looked at some of the software, both PC- and server-based, that blocks unwanted Web sites. We discussed the various rating systems, and found out about organizations and Web resources that are helpful to parents who have kids that spend lots of time online.

✦   ✦   ✦

Spending Money Online Safely

The idea of shopping online is both exciting and frightening. With online commerce you can buy products or services from merchants almost anywhere in the world. No one has to be minding the store—you can shop in the middle of the night or whenever you get the urge. But at the same time, shopping over the Internet isn't exactly for the faint of heart. You need to consider all sorts of security issues so that your credit card number doesn't end up in the hands of thieves.

Investigating Online Commerce Security Basics

At one time, most merchants and customers knew and trusted each other. If you sent little Johnny down to the corner market for a quart of milk and a dozen eggs, you wouldn't have to worry that he wouldn't come back with the goods and correct change.

Today, of course, the world has changed. Few people shop at the corner grocery store—you're far more likely to shop at a huge store where no one knows you. If you want to buy something on credit, you probably use a credit card issued by a large bank. The world of commerce has become more impersonal and less based on individual trust.

Buying from an online merchant on the Internet, however, does require an awful lot of trust. Consider the following points:

✦ When you buy online, you have to trust that the merchant is reputable and not just someone who's trying to get your credit card number.

✦ Since you can't personally see and feel the products or services you buy online, you have to trust that the merchant is telling the truth about the quality of the items.

✦ The merchant has to trust that you will pay for what is delivered.

✦ Finally, both parties have to have confidence that the transaction is safe and secure.

Let's take a quick look at these items. Later in this chapter you'll see specific solutions that address each of these issues.

Knowing who to trust

Anyone can create an impressive Web site. In many ways, the Web is a great equalizer. A small one-room operation can look just as impressive as the largest corporate entity on the Web. It's difficult to discern whether Andy's Computer Mega-Mall is really the "world's largest computer discounter" or simply a one-man operation Andy runs from his basement in his spare time.

So how are you supposed to know who you can trust? How can you be sure a merchant is reputable and not a crook who wants to spread your credit card number around the world faster than you can blink?

One solution to establishing identities on the Internet is through the use of certificates — digital identity signatures that confirm a party's identity. If the certificate is valid, the identity is confirmed. Several Internet Certificate Authorities, such as VeriSign (`http://www.verisign.com`), provide these types of digital IDs.

Of course, even if an online merchant has a certificate, you still have no assurance that the merchandise is described accurately or that it is in stock. The support of your credit card company can help in this situation. Most credit cards include some form of purchase protection — if the merchandise turns out to be garbage, your credit card company will probably stand behind you and not charge your account.

Securing payment

Just as you want assurances that you can trust the online merchant, merchants need assurances that they'll be paid for their products or services. Of course, there are many different ways to pay for a purchase. Cash is one method, but it's difficult to pay cash for an online purchase. Instead, an electronic method of making payments is needed.

The most common method of payment for online transactions is to use a credit card. However, many people are wary of giving out their credit card number online, because it is possible for the number to be compromised by hackers or other unscrupulous people who intercept the card number while you complete your transaction. And, of course, if you are buying something from a private individual, they probably aren't set up to take credit card payments anyway.

Electronic money can solve many of the problems of online commerce. The merchant receives their funds, and the customer obtains their desired products while payment is sent securely to the vendor. One of the companies providing this secure form of payment is eCash Technologies (http://www.ecashtechnologies.com/). Electronic money goes beyond simply enabling you to make online purchases. Generally most forms of electronic online payment also protect your privacy and make shopping online less subject to abusive snooping, too.

Trusting the transaction

Both parties to an online transaction want the transaction to be secure. They need to be able to trust that any documents or data haven't been altered, and they need to be certain that confidential information — such as credit card numbers — remains confidential.

Web sites can use special protocols such as Secure Sockets Layer (SSL) or Secure HTTP (S-HTTP) to ensure the security of online transactions. These special protocols use encryption to create secure Web sites so that any messages you exchange with a secure Web site can't be viewed or modified by third parties. Netscape was the original developer of SSL, but now Microsoft and Opera also support SSL.

Using Digital IDs

Unless you know a local merchant well, you probably use some sort of ID for almost any noncash transaction. You may have a check cashing card, a driver's license, or some other sort of photo ID that identifies you and assures the merchant that you're the owner of the checking account or credit card being used for payment. Likewise, you want to be certain the merchant is who he or she claims to be.

Digital IDs give you the ability to prove your identity online, and they provide you the security and assurance that the people you are dealing with online are really who they say they are. Digital IDs provide:

✦ **Unique identities.** When you have a digital ID, no one else can pretend to be you. If you've given people your digital ID, they can verify your identity, and they can be certain that messages without a valid digital ID aren't from you.

✦ **Secure communications.** When a vendor uses a digital ID, you can be certain that no one has modified any messages or files the vendor has sent you. If you trust the vendor, you can trust the messages and files.

✦ **Automatic system and application updates.** If you've told your computer to accept items from a particular digital ID, you won't have to verify each update. Your system can even automatically verify that the digital ID is still valid.

Digital IDs are also called certificates. If you want to obtain a certificate of your own, a good place to start is with VeriSign (`www.versign.com`) or BelSign (`www.belsign.be`), leading providers of digital certificates.

Digital IDs and certificates aren't simply for personal identification. The VeriSign and BelSign Web sites provide information about other types of certificates. For example, at the VeriSign Web site you'll also find information on Server IDs (certificates that help provide for secure online commerce) and Secure Electronic Transactions (SET).

Obtaining your own digital ID isn't absolutely necessary, but carrying a photo ID might not be absolutely necessary when you go shopping at the mall, either. Both precautions, however, are a good idea.

Paying on the Internet

Obviously, traditional forms of money — dollar bills, for example — don't work for online transactions. Unless you meet with the merchant face-to-face, it's pretty hard to pay your bill if all you have is paper money. When you're buying stuff online, you need an alternative that's just as good as cash but can be transmitted over the Internet safely.

Using credit cards

Not surprisingly, credit cards are used for most online purchases today. But there are a number of reasons why you might not want to use a credit card. You may not like sacrificing your privacy by giving your name — and possibly a lot of other personal information — every time you buy something. And, of course, there are security concerns involved in giving your credit card number over the Internet. If someone intercepts your number it could be used for many unauthorized purchases.

Shelling out electronic money on the Internet

One alternative is electronic money. Electronic money is a unique series of numbers similar to the serial numbers assigned to cash by a country's treasury. These numbers are purchased from a participating bank, and sent to a vendor when you make a purchase. Serial numbers are encrypted and exchanged using a system of digital signatures to ensure that they won't be intercepted and used by someone else. Those numbers represent cash just as a check you write to a merchant represents cash the merchant can obtain from your bank.

Since all you need to send to the vendor is a serial number, you can maintain your privacy, while at the same time preventing some unscrupulous person from gaining access to your assets.

The eCash Web site, `www.ecashtechnologies.com`, is one of the best places to find out about electronic money. Here you can even see a demonstration of eCash — the software that enables you to use electronic money.

Another site you may want to visit is that maintained by the Smart Card Industry Association (`http://www.scia.org/`). There you can learn about *smart cards*, a credit card-sized electronic device that can be used to store electronic cash. Smart cards are handy because you can easily take your electronic money with you, and in the future you will even be able to use it for many "real world" purchases just like a regular credit card.

Unfortunately, electronic money still hasn't gained much popularity. This is because few banks are set up to offer electronic cash serial numbers, and most online retailers still don't accept it.

Charging on the Internet

Credit cards are probably the most common method of payment used on the Internet today. Credit cards and shopping on the Internet should be a natural match. The merchant doesn't need to know you personally — all he or she really needs is the assurance that your credit card is valid. Of course, the nature of the Internet complicates this simple transaction. Any message you send to someone across the Internet passes through several (if not dozens) of computers between you and the recipient. Are you really comfortable having your credit card number available to all those different systems? If not, you can easily understand why some people are reluctant to shop on the Internet.

Secure Electronic Transaction

As you can imagine, the credit card companies would like you to use your credit cards for online purchases, and as a result, they're concerned about security, too. Accordingly, Visa and MasterCard developed Secure Electronic Transaction (SET) as a method of protecting the security of your online credit card transactions. Visa claims that SET makes online transactions as safe as using your credit card at a local merchant. They even back up this claim with the assurance that you won't be at a greater risk from online SET purchases than you would be from any other credit card purchase.

Note   SET was developed jointly by Visa and MasterCard. Both companies, of course, have a great interest in ensuring the security of online credit card transactions. You may want to visit Visa's Web site, `http://www.visa.com`, to learn more about safely using your Visa credit card for online purchases.

SET is a messaging standard developed specifically for one purpose—to enable the secure use of credit cards electronically. Because of this narrow focus, SET can use the same encryption model worldwide. Other more general types of data encryption (such as SSL) are limited to a less secure encryption standard when used internationally. But since SET is used only for credit card data, it doesn't face the export restrictions that can reduce the effectiveness of more generalized encryption systems. The lack of restrictions enables SET to employ a single-use, 56-bit symmetric key further encrypted using public/private key pairs that are 1,024 bits long. Data encryption is a very complex subject, but just remember this simple concept—the longer the key, the harder it will be for someone to break the key and steal the data.

Using Electronic Wallets

You probably keep your driver's license or other ID, credit cards, and some cash in your wallet. The wallet serves as a convenient, secure place to keep all of these items together. Wallets on your computer work like the wallet you carry in your pocket. You place the items in the wallet—actually a software package that encrypts and stores your personal information—and control who can access those items. Storing all of that important information (digital IDs, credit card accounts, your address, and so forth) in your wallet is also convenient. Whenever you need to use the information, it's all ready to go without having to reenter it each time. And since the wallet contains your Digital ID, it helps positively identify you to online merchants.

Finding free wallets for everyone

Wallets work as a plug-in for your Web browser. Like most plug-ins, a wallet needs to be specifically designed for your browser. If you use Internet Explorer, you'll probably choose Microsoft Wallet. Netscape Navigator users may want to opt for the CyberCash Wallet. In both cases, the wallet software is free and available either as a part of the initial browser download or as an individual item you can add later.

If you happen to use a different browser such as Opera, you can find stand-alone Java-based wallet software programs that will work with your browser, too. You may want to look around a bit before you settle on one of these programs, however. Because wallet technology is relatively new, you'll want to make certain that the wallet software you choose is reliable and secure. Not surprisingly, the Visa Web site has quite a bit of information about wallets at `http://www.visa.com/pd/ ewallet/main.html`, including links to wallets offered by five different banks. The wallets listed here are actually tied to their own credit cards issued by the respective bank.

Regardless of the wallet software you choose, you'll find that using a wallet will make online commerce much more convenient.

Using a wallet

Before you can use a wallet, you must enter the information that makes a wallet useful. To enter credit card information in Microsoft Wallet:

1. Launch Internet Explorer. You don't need to be connected to the Internet to work with Wallet, so if Internet Explorer tries to connect to the Internet, cancel the connection.

2. Select Tools ⇨ Internet Options to display the Internet Options dialog box.

3. Click the Content tab.

   You might expect to find Wallet on the Security tab, but it's actually on the Content tab as shown in Figure 34-1.

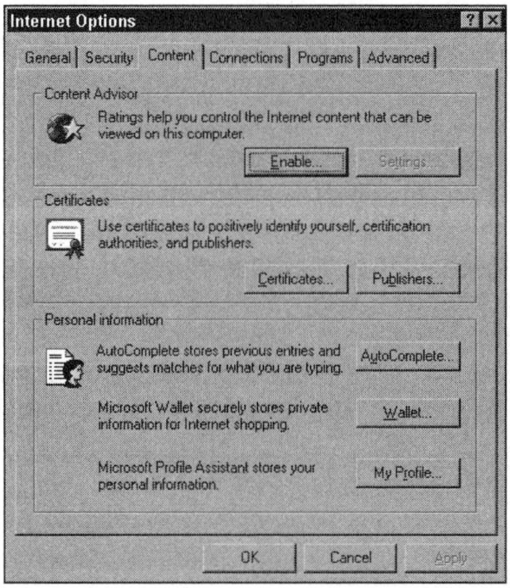

Figure 34-1: Microsoft Wallet is found in the Personal information section of the Internet Options Content tab.

> **Note**
> If Wallet isn't available, you may need to use the Windows Setup tab of the Add/Remove Programs dialog box to add the Wallet. You'll find the Wallet under Internet Tools.

4. Click the Wallet button.

   The Microsoft Wallet dialog box initially will be blank, and your only option will be to add a new credit card, as shown in Figure 34-2. The Addresses tab lets you enter billing addresses and such that you will need for some transactions.

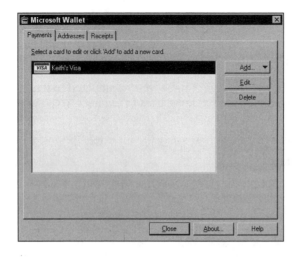

Figure 34-2: The Microsoft Wallet dialog box shows all credit cards you currently have in your wallet.

5. Click the Add button, and select a credit card type from the menu that appears.

You use the Add a New Credit Card wizard shown in Figure 34-3 to enter your address information. Follow the instructions on-screen to enter information about your credit card, including a billing address. You will also have to enter a password that will be used to gain access to the wallet.

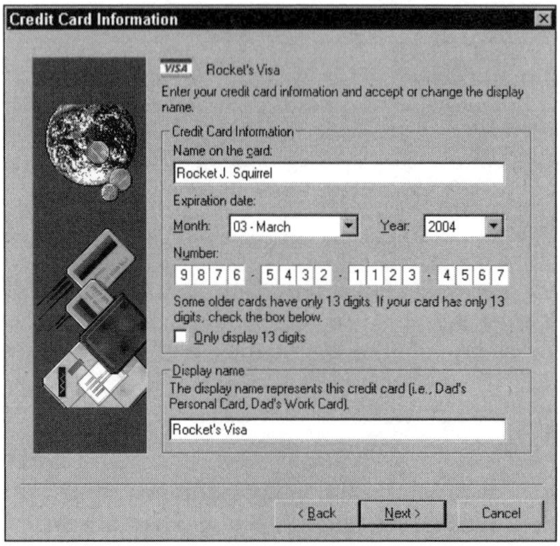

Figure 34-3: Fill in as much of the credit card information as possible to save time later.

6. Click Finish in the last wizard screen to return to the Microsoft Wallet dialog box.

If you want to add additional credit cards to your wallet, click the Add button again and continue adding cards.

7. When you're done adding new cards, click Close to return to the Internet Options dialog box.

When you visit Wallet-enabled Web sites, you'll be able to choose which card information to send by selecting the name from a list. If you have several similar credit cards in your wallet, be sure to enter a unique name in the Display name text box of the Add a New Credit Card dialog box so you can easily identify the card you want to use.

Securing Web Sites

One of the final stepping stones of online security—especially in regard to online commerce—is the secure Web site. If you've spent any time browsing the Web, you've probably seen message boxes from time to time that informed you when you were entering or leaving a secure Web site. You may have wondered about the meaning of these messages.

Note
If a closed padlock icon appears on the status bar of your browser—be it Internet Explorer, Netscape Navigator, or Opera—you're visiting a secure Web site.

Secure Web sites use a special protocol (generally SSL or S-HTTP) to encrypt all information exchanged between your Web browser and the Web site itself. These security protocols make certain that only the Web site and your computer have access to any information you provide. Any computers involved in forwarding the messages over the Internet see only the encrypted message—not the raw data.

Because secure Web sites use encryption, you can feel confident that the information you send is safe—up to a point. Your level of safety is directly affected by the version of the Web browser you use. Internet Explorer and Netscape Communicator both offer versions of their browser with 40-bit and 128-bit encryption. The following list explains why different versions are offered:

✦ **40-bit encryption.** US law prohibits export of data encryption technology with more than 40-bit encryption, so most Web browsers use the 40-bit encryption standard, which is also known as the "international" version.

✦ **128-bit encryption.** If you want a higher level of security, and you live in the United States, you can download the US domestic-only version of your browser, with which you can get 128-bit encryption. Since more data bits in the encryption key result in much higher security, you'll be much safer using this version if it is available to you.

When you begin to download a new version of Internet Explorer or Netscape, one of the first questions you will be asked is where you live. You probably won't be asked which level of encryption you want; if you answer that you live in the USA you'll get 128-bit encryption, and if you live anywhere else you'll have to settle for 40-bit.

Of course, U.S. export laws don't apply to software developers in other countries, and 128-bit encryption is legal in many parts of the world. Furthermore, there is no law forbidding U.S. residents from *importing* Web browsers that contain 128-bit encryption. That is why Opera (developed in Norway) is *only* available with 128-bit encryption. Since Norway has no law restricting the export of 128-bit encryption technology in Web browsers, Opera Software has no compelling reason to develop a less-secure version.

As online commerce on the Internet grows and matures, online security will become easier to use and more bulletproof. To stay informed about new developments in online commerce, visit the Electronic Commerce Guide at `http://e-comm.internet.com/`. This site generally contains some of the most up-to-date information you'll find on this subject along with hundreds of links to other related Web sites.

Summary

Feeling safe about spending money on the Internet can be a big step for most people. In this chapter, you've learned about the many different security methods to make you feel better about sending your credit card number to an online vendor. You've also learned how to protect yourself while making things a bit easier.

✦   ✦   ✦

Investing and Doing Business Online

If you like to research and manage your own investments, the Internet provides a tremendous amount of financial information and services. There are online investment guides, company news and research reports, stock quotes and charts, and a variety of online stock brokerage services.

There is so much free information available, you don't have to spend a dime to start following your favorite stocks or managing your portfolio online. Even companies that make their money selling research reports or financial articles will usually give you a few free reports or several free weeks of their service.

Many major brokerage firms already offer ways of letting their customers trade stocks on the Internet. If you have a brokerage account, you may be a phone call away from getting a user name and password that would enable you to manage your account and trade equities on the Internet, using your Internet browser.

This chapter helps you find some of the best resources for investing on the Internet.

Beginning Online Investing

With all of the financial services available on the Web, it is tempting to jump right in and start trading. "Who needs a broker?" you may think to yourself. Well, if you don't know anything about investing, Internet investing can just give you lots of power to lose money.

That said, there are many people who believe that if you learn about the tools of investing and do your research carefully, you can become a successful investor. This section describes some Web sites that provide you with general investment information, then follows that with some Web tools that help you evaluate how you should be allocating the funds you have to invest.

Getting online investment help

For the first-time investor, there are plenty of Web sites that are ready to help you get started. As part of their services, some financial sites on the Web offer guides to investment basics. There are also things like Frequently Asked Questions lists that will help answer your investment questions. Some excellent guides for beginner investors are described here.

> **Tip**   If you are truly new to investing, you should also consider getting some professional education on the subject. Many community colleges offer courses in investment and stock trading, and taking such a class could prove to be a valuable investment in yourself by introducing you to some basic financial concepts.

Motley Fool: 13 Steps to Investing Foolishly

One of the most popular and fun investment sites on the Web is Motley Fool (http://www.motleyfool.com). The philosophy behind Motley Fool is that, with some education, you can be the best person to manage your own investments. The information you find on the Motley Fool site will help you with that education, in an amusing way.

When you are new to a subject, you need to start with the basics. Click the School button, and the Motley Fool site displays topics that are of interest to the new investor. There are links to advice on determining the value of stocks and on dealing with taxes. The place they recommend first, however, is the Thirteen Steps to Investing Foolishly.

The thirteen steps present an approach to investing that covers more than just buying and selling stocks. In the steps, they question some of the traditional beliefs about investing. After that, they recommend ways of getting your own finances in order. Other steps describe how to set and track expectations, then suggest several different investment strategies.

To keep you engaged with the Motley Fool site, you can register to become part of the Motley Fool community (click Register from the Motley Fool home page). Once you register, you can participate fully in the special Motley Fool features.

Quicken Investment Basics

Continuing its tradition of helping people with their personal finances, Intuit offers a Quicken Investment Basics page (`http://www.quicken.com/investments/basics/`) covering a wide range of topics. Under Inside Basics, find out what an index fund is, how to buy on margin, and how to start investing with only a small amount of money. You will find book reviews of some of the best investment books available. You can also read an Expert Advice column from Marshall Loeb.

The Investment FAQ

When you begin almost anything new on the Web, there is usually a frequently asked questions (FAQ) list to help you get started. Investments are no exception. From the Investment FAQ (`http://www.invest-faq.com`), you can choose from about 20 categories relating to investing and personal finance. The topics cover stocks, bonds, insurance, technical analysis, taxes, and mutual funds.

The Investment FAQ has advice for beginners and descriptions of how to do analysis. If you want a more interactive way of finding investment information, the site offers tours for beginning, intermediate, and expert investors.

The Investment FAQ is also available from the USENET newsgroup service from a variety of news servers. For example, one location is the Internet FAQ Association (`http://www.faqs.org/faqs/investment-faq/`). The FAQ is divided into 17 parts (though the parts sometimes break in the middle of sections).

✦ **Part 1 (General)** — Provides general information about the FAQ and a table of contents.

✦ **Part 2 (Advice, and Analysis)** — The Advice section gives information that is valuable to beginning investors. It also contains suggestions about paying for investment advice and researching a company. The Analysis section describes annual reports, beta and alpha, book-to-bill ratio, computing compound returns, P/E ratios, and other valuable components for investment analysis.

✦ **Part 3 (Bonds)** — The Bonds section gives general information about bonds and describes different types of bonds, such as municipal bonds and treasury bills.

✦ **Part 4 (Bonds, Derivatives)** — A continuation of bonds is offered, including descriptions of U.S. Savings Bonds and zero-coupon bonds. Derivatives describes stock futures and options.

✦ **Part 5 (Exchanges, Financial Planning)** — Exchanges describes the different stock exchanges (such as the New York Stock Exchange and NASDAQ) and ticker tape terminology. Financial Planning describes basic planning and discusses such issues as whether to pay off a mortgage or invest your money.

✦ **Part 6 (Information Sources)** — Information Sources describes investment associations, the Internet, mailing lists, and several publications.

✦ **Part 7 (Insurance, Mutual Funds)** — Insurance describes annuities and life insurance. Mutual Funds describes the basics of mutual funds, average returns, and fees and expenses.

✦ **Part 8 (Mutual Funds, Real Estate, Regulation)** — The continuation of mutual finds describes money market funds, redemptions, and mutual funds versus stocks. Real Estate describes REITs and discusses renting versus buying a home. Regulation tells about such things as the U.S. Federal Reserve and the Securities and Exchange Commission.

✦ **Part 9 (Regulation, Retirement Plans)** — More Regulation issues are discussed, including information on surviving a bankrupt broker. The Retirement Plans section discusses 401K, Keogh plans, IRA and other investment tools.

✦ **Part 10 (Retirement Plans, Software, Stocks)** — Traditional IRAs are discussed, along with software to help you invest and manage your portfolio. After describing basics about investing in stocks, the section on Stocks describes different types of stocks and stock indexes.

✦ **Part 11 (Stocks)** — Continues the descriptions on stocks, including company repurchasing, shareholders rights, shorting, and splitting stocks.

✦ **Part 12 (Strategy, Tax Code)** — Strategy describes investment strategies, such as hedging, when to buy and sell, buying on margin, and dollar/value cost averaging. Tax Code discusses some basic tax issues for investors, including tax deductions for investors, capital gains, and gifts of stock.

✦ **Part 13 (Tax Code, Technical Analysis)** — Tax Code continues with tax swaps, and short-term versus long-term gains and losses. Technical Analysis describes different types of charting and tracking theories.

✦ **Part 14 (Technical Analysis, Trading)** — More charting and tracking theories are discussed in Technical Analysis. Trading describes after-hours trading, terms (such as bid, ask, and spread), and brokerage accounts.

✦ **Part 15 (Trading)** — This continuation of the previous part describes trading electronically on the Internet, insider trading, terminology, NASD licenses, and buying/selling without a broker.

✦ **Part 16 (Trading)** — The continuation of Trading describes such topics as pink sheet stocks, round lots of shares, account transfers, and selling worthless shares.

✦ **Part 17 (Trivia, Warning)** — The Trivia section describes Bull and Bear lore, getting rich quickly, and one-letter ticker symbols. The Warning section warns about dangerous types of investing and some services to avoid.

The Investment FAQ is a compilation by Christopher Lott. You can reach Christopher Lott at lott@invest-faq.com.

American Association of Individual Investors

There is a wealth of information available from the American Association of Individual Investors site (http://www.aaii.com). Figure 35-1 shows the AAII home page.

From the AAII home page, select Investing Basics to access articles that will help you get started with an investment plan and monitor your portfolio. There are also other articles of interest under the Education and Research headings on the AAII page. You can read about financial planning, mutual funds, stocks, fixed-income investments, broker issues, and more.

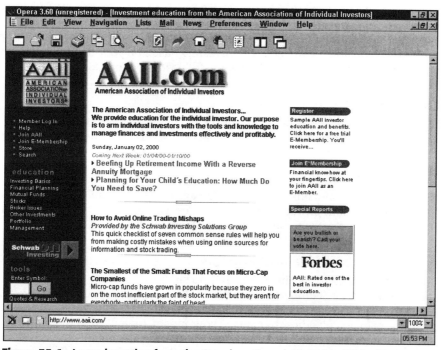

Figure 35-1: Learn investing from the American Association of Individual Investors.

Though some of the information on the site is accessible to everyone, you need to become a member to have full access to the site. For example, you need to be a member to access archives and participate in discussions on message boards. Basic AAII membership is $49, or you can obtain an E*Membership for just $39. Click the Join link for details.

MarketCentral Investment Guide

The Investment Guide available from MarketCentral (`http://www.mktctl.com/guide.htm`) is designed to give individual investors an understanding of economic and market issues they would need to become successful investors. Though the site is still under construction (at the time of this writing), it does contain some interesting articles on market economics, inflation, and forecasting. The site is designed to be used in conjunction with the Market Central newsletter.

Evaluating your financial position

As mentioned earlier, most online stock brokerages have a method for evaluating your financial status. So, if you already have a brokerage you are working with, you may want to start there to put together an investment strategy. If you want to get some advice on how to proceed with investing based on your financial position, try a few of the Web sites described in the following sections for help.

CNNfn

The CNNfn site (`http://cnnfn.com/markets/personalfinance/`) offers some excellent resources for managing your finances. Several selections from this site can help you evaluate your financial position and find the financial services that suit you.

One of the most useful links on the CNNfn page is the Tips and Tools link. It leads to information about protecting your assets, estate planning, cutting your debt, refinancing your mortgage, and keeping your credit clean.

American Express Financial Advisors

On the American Express Financial Advisors site (`http://www.americanexpress.com/advisors/assess`) you can use a set of tools to assess your personal financial situation, then create a personal financial profile to help you plan how to manage your money today and in the future.

With the tools, you can figure out your net worth, track your cash flow, determine your take-home pay (net-net pay), and work out how much you will need to save for retirement, college education, or for the future of your estate. Next, you can input information that creates a profile to help you manage your assets and set up an investment strategy that suits your level of risk tolerance and investment time frame.

Researching Investments Online

The Web holds a truly awesome amount of information to help you research your investments. Stock quotes are the most commonly available type of investment information on the Web. Along with stock quotes go a variety of different charting methods and news services that can give you information about each company.

If you are looking for more dynamic ways of doing investment research, you can choose from many different online chat rooms and message boards. Message boards, in particular, are a great way to share information on a company or industry with lots of other interested people.

Analyzing stock quotes and charts

If you don't mind a few minutes delay, you should never have to pay a cent to view stock quotes on the Internet. Many brokerage sites, search engines, and investment research Web pages let you enter a stock symbol and come back with a price quote and a variety of other information.

Because there are so many different sites offering stock quotes, you can be choosy about which ones you use. Don't limit yourself to just a stock quote when a service can also show you charts, analyst opinions, news stories, and a variety of statistical data about the stock. The following sections describe a few stock quote services.

InvestorGuide Public Company Directory

Why settle for one stock quote service, when you can choose from several? The InvestorGuide Public Company Directory (`http://www.investorguide.com/StockList.htm`) lets you choose a company you are interested in, then access stock prices, reports, and other information about that company from one page.

Type a ticker symbol for a company, and then click the here button. A page appears that lets you choose from several different types of sites that can offer you information about the company. This information includes stock and options quotes, charts, news and press, SEC filings, technical tools, historical data, earnings estimates, information about competitors, discussion boards, and more.

Quotes from My Excite channel

If you are like a lot of people who use a service such as Excite to personalize the home page that appears when you start your browser, you may already have a stock quote search tool right on your home page. In the case of Excite, the stock quotes are handled by Charles Schwab.

Go to the My Excite page (http://my.excite.com), type a stock symbol into the quote box, and then click Go. Standard data about the stock price quote appears (the last trade, price change, volume, and so on). However, from the page you can also access recent headlines about the company, charts of price history, descriptions of competitors, analysts buy/sell recommendations, financials, and other data.

Reading newsletters

Because there are so many financial newsletters available, we chose to provide you with information about where you can find and evaluate newsletters, rather than list a bunch of them. For just a big list of newsletters, try out the Yahoo! Market Newsletters index. To get an opinion on which are the better financial newsletters, check out the Financial Newsletter Network or Forbes/Hubert Investment Letter Survey.

Tip   Some experts suggest that you may not need to subscribe to a financial newsletter these days, given the huge amount of financial information that is available today for free.

The Yahoo! Market Newsletters displays links to more than 100 financial newsletters. To get this list from the Yahoo! home page (www.yahoo.com), select Business and Economy ⇨ Companies ⇨ Financial Services ⇨ Investment Services ⇨ Market Information and Research ⇨ Newsletters.

You can choose a newsletter for the industry you are interested in (such as Biotechnology) and the area it covers (such as Asia or Mexico), or one that simply looks for certain kinds of trends.

The Financial Newsletter Network (http://www.investmentletters.net) sifts through the thousands of financial newsletters available today to recommend which are the best. The site is maintained by Dick Davis Publishing Co., which for more than 18 years has followed the financial newsletter industry.

Joining discussion groups

Along with the popularity of online investing has come an increase in people's desires to discuss investment ideas with others. Online discussion groups are one of the best ways for people to share their knowledge, experience, or opinions about investments. There are dozens of discussion groups available on Internet-related investing. This section describes a few of them.

Caution   Because anyone can participate in discussion groups, you should be careful about the advice you get there. Use input from these groups as just one of many ways to evaluate the prudence of an investment.

The Stock Club

Hundreds of different discussion groups are available from the Stock Club (http://stockclub.com). Interactive discussions center around both investment topics as well as individual stocks. There are groups discussing companies involved in energy, financial services, industrial supplies and services, technology, utilities,and other topics. To participate in forums, you must become a Stock Club member. (Membership is free and is intended to provide a measure of responsibility to the discussions.)

Silicon Investor

There are more than 12,000,000 messages stored in the Silicon Investor (http://www.siliconinvestor.com/) online discussion group of technology stocks. Anyone can read the messages posted to Silicon Investor groups. However, you need to become a member to post your own messages, create customized stock groups, use tracking tools, participate in surveys, or send e-mail to SI members.

Click the link to SI Tour Page. This tour lets you tour the site for information related to the semiconductor company Intel. You can view a 100-day chart, make your own comparison charts, view the TechStocks 120 Indexes, and join a discussion group.

Choosing an Online Broker

Those brokers who have created online services that enable their customers to buy and sell stocks, do research, and track their investments have experienced tremendous growth in the past few years. Even larger investment houses that prefer doing business the old fashioned way have begun offering online brokerage services to keep up with the competition.

This section describes some services that are available for evaluating online brokers, then describes several of the top brokers on the Internet today.

Evaluating Online Brokerages

A couple of years ago there were only a few brokerages offering investment services over the Internet; now there are hundreds to choose from. Online brokerages are fighting for you business by offering cut-rate commissions for Internet trades, stock quotes, and research information. As an online investor, you want to balance good prices with quality of service (for example, does your trade happen on a timely basis and is the company reputable?).

As with most everything else on the Web, if there are enough companies doing something, there are people out there ready to tell you who is doing it best. Here are a few places that have ranked online brokerages.

Gomez.com

An Internet Broker Scorecard is offered by Gomez.com (`http://www.gomezadvisors.com`). The scorecard ranks more than 50 Internet brokers, based on ease of use, customer confidence, onsite resources, relationship services, and overall cost. The scorecard also rates the suitability of the services for different types of investors: life goal planner, serious investor, hyperactive trader, and one-stop shopper. Figure 35-2 shows the Gomez.com Internet Broker Overall Scorecard.

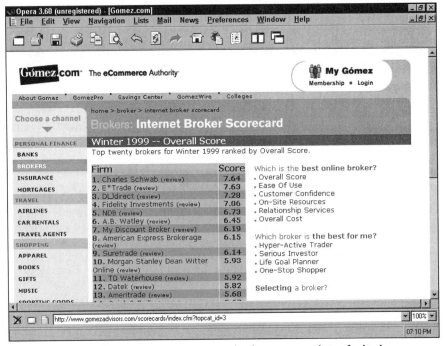

Figure 35-2: Gomez Advisors rates Internet brokers on a variety of criteria.

To find out more about one of the brokers, click the link to the broker shown on the scorecard. If you want to receive more information on a particular broker, click the Review link next to the appropriate listing on the card.

MONEY.COM

MONEY.COM offers a guide to online brokers at `http://www.pathfinder.com/money/broker/`. The site offers a basic scorecard that rates brokerages on ease of use, customer service, system responsiveness, products and tools offered to customers, and cost.

You can also tailor the scorecard to your specific needs. The main page has a list of questions that you can answer about your needs and desired investment strategy. When you answer the questions and click Continue, a list of brokers that fit your needs is produced, along with overall ratings for each. If you want more information about a broker shown on the MONEY.COM site, just click its listing on the scorecard.

Motley Fool Discount Brokerage Center

After making bold statements about your own ability to manage your investments, the people at Motley Fool offer a site where you can evaluate which brokerages l are for you (`http://www.fool.com/Media/DiscountBrokerageCenter/DiscountBrokeragecenter.htm`). From this site, you can get information such as how to choose a discount broker, and whether you want a full-service or a discount broker. This site also points you to "The Fourth Step to Investing Foolishly: Choosing a Broker" (which is part of their 13-step investing guide).

Finding popular online brokerage firms

Because most online brokerage firms let you trade standard equities, view stock quotes, and do at least some level of research, you may find it difficult to choose between them. Here are a few of the most popular brokerage firms and some descriptions of what sets each apart from the others.

DLJdirect

For over ten years, DLJdirect (`http://www.dljdirect.com`) has been offering online investing to its customers. Because DLJdirect is the online service of Donaldson, Lufkin & Jenrette Securities Corporation, subscribers of this service have access to research and initial public offerings available through that firm.

While DLJdirect doesn't offer the lowest pricing in the industry, its combination of good pricing with excellent customer confidence and onsite resources has resulted in excellent ratings among its competitors.

Datek Online

Datek Online (`http://www.datek.com`) prides itself on providing speed of execution and low commissions. Commission rates are as low as $9.99 per trade. If a marketable order takes more than 60 seconds, the trade is commission-free. If you think you have seen Datek somewhere on the Internet, you're probably right. Datek has been among the top Internet advertisers since the service came into existence in 1996.

E*TRADE Securities

While keeping commission rates low, E*TRADE (`http://www.etrade.com`) offers its account holders free market information, news, and analysis. E*TRADE offers a variety of account types, such as individual, joint, custodian (for minors), investment club, corporate partnership, sole proprietorship, and trust (estate and conservatorship) accounts. There are also different retirement accounts offered, such as IRA (rollover and simple IRAs), profit sharing plans, and money purchase plans.

Along with your account comes a variety of investment tools for doing research and getting stock quotes. E*TRADE routinely rates as one of the top online brokers.

Charles Schwab

By offering a full complement of services and an established reputation in online trading, Charles Schwab (`http://www.schwab.com`) has become one of the most popular online brokerage services. Commission rates fall between those of deep discount brokers and those of full-service brokers.

Within the Charles Schwab site are a variety of research tools. From the Schwab home page, select Quotes and Research. Choose from a variety of Quotes and Research services, such as delayed quotes, Market Buzz (news and research), daily audio newscasts, equity report cards, and a featured industry of the week. To account customers, features such as special company news and research, as well as market news, are also available.

Ameritrade

Ameritrade (`http://www.ameritrade.com`) focuses on low commissions to attract customer accounts. When you make an online equity trade with Ameritrade, the cost is $8 per trade, regardless of the price or number of shares you purchase. This service seems to be best for those investors who do their research from other Internet sites or in other ways, then simply want an inexpensive way to make the trades.

Tracking Your Investments

After you have made some investments online, you probably want to keep track of how they are doing. There are some wonderful services available on the Internet to let you set up your portfolio, then watch as it changes. You can also set up profiles that display how various markets and stocks are doing. Here are a few services you can use to track your investment portfolio.

Caution   Before you enter your very private portfolio information into some Web page on the Internet, check the privacy policy of the company providing the service. If you don't trust the company, don't enter any private information (or don't use the service at all). You can learn more about online security in Chapter 32, "Maintaining Your Online Privacy and Security."

My Excite channel stock portfolio

If investing in stocks and bonds is one of your interests, setting up your portfolio on your browser start page is a great way to track your investments. The My Excite channel page (`http://my.excite.com`) offers a service, provided by

Charles Schwab, that lets you enter your portfolio and have it displayed on your personalized Excite start page.

On the My Excite page, click the Full Portfolio link under the My Stocks heading. On the page that appears, enter your user name and password for My Excite. (If you don't have a profile with Excite, click the link to "create one now.") A generic portfolio of Internet stocks appears at first, but you can click Edit to modify the portfolio listing that appears there. For each stock you can enter the number of shares you own and the price you paid per share.

> **Tip** When you view the page to create your portfolio, you can choose what information is displayed for each investment. There are many different types of information, such as the current price, price change (and percentage), volume, average purchase price, gain/loss, and value.

After you have completed your portfolio, the next time you view your personalized My Excite channel page, you will see information about your portfolio. The latest market and stock prices will be displayed. Also, the gain and loss on each stock or mutual fund will be shown (both on a daily and on a total return basis).

Reuter's moneynet portfolio

Reuters moneynet (`http://www.moneynet.com`) has a nice service for tracking your portfolio, along with stock exchanges and indexes. From the moneynet home page, click the Portfolio Tracking link (look on the left column). The site will ask you to sign up for a free membership, after which you can enter your portfolio.

Figure 35-3 shows an example of a portfolio entered into the moneynet Portfolio tool. (Though the stocks and data shown are real, the actual portfolio was just created to try to make the author look smart.)

Figure 35-3 shows a portfolio with a holding of one stock. You can see the stock symbol, the company name, the type of currency used (USD is U.S. dollars), the current price of the stock, how much the stock price changed since yesterday (net change and percentage), and the total market value of each investment (based on the number of shares you entered). You can also see how much you have gained or lost today in dollars (it was a rough day) and your total profit or loss (in dollars and as a percentage). The Watch Items list is for displaying how the stock markets and indexes are doing, and it is also for following any stocks you want to keep an eye on. A complete summary of your portfolio is shown at the bottom of the page.

> **Tip** Unless your brokerage offers a better way of tracking your portfolio, the Reuter's moneynet portfolio tracker is an excellent central site for managing your portfolio. The links in the left column let you go beyond your portfolio to get quotes, news, company profiles, and a wealth of other information.

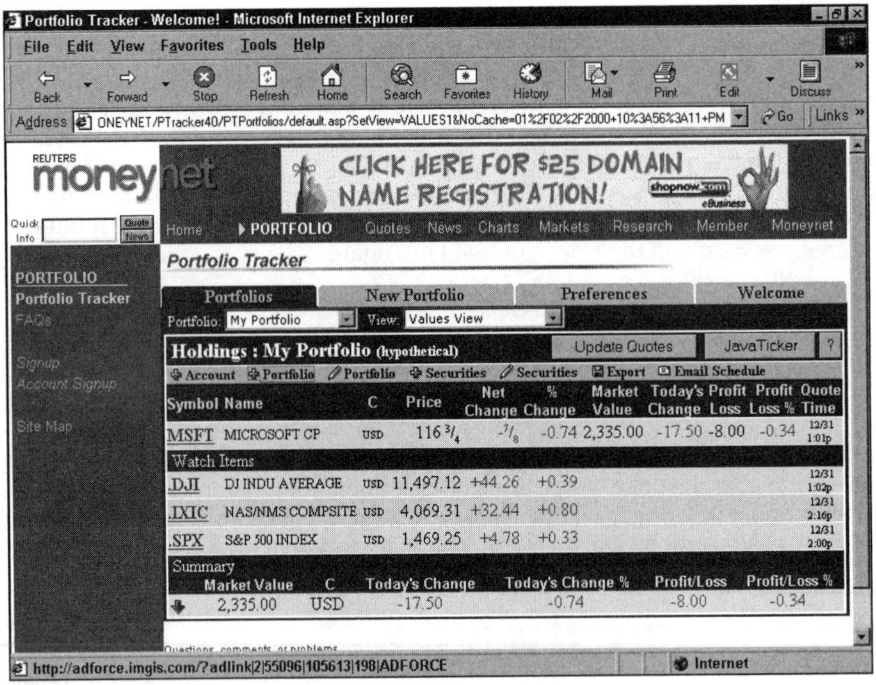

Figure 35-3: Track your portfolio with moneynet.

Summary

This chapter described how to use sites such as Motley Fool (http://www.motleyfool.com) to learn about investing strategies. The chapter also described ways to evaluate your financial position (using tools available on the Internet from Intuit and American Express). For those who are ready to start their own brokerage accounts, there are descriptions of Web sites that contain ratings of brokerage accounts, as well as descriptions of a few of the most popular online brokerages.

In the last section of this chapter, there are descriptions of a few different tools available for tracking your investment portfolios online. These include the Portfolio Tracker from Reuter's moneynet (http://www.moneynet.com) and services available from personalized news and information sites, such as My Excite channel page (http://my.excite.com).

✦   ✦   ✦

Gaming Online

The Internet is an inexhaustible resource for gaming. Without too much hunting, you can find literally thousands of games to download from the Internet. Games range from sophisticated graphical shoot-em-up games to strategy games to your favorite board and card games. Though tons of games exist that you can download and play by yourself at home, this chapter focuses on games you can play against others on the Internet. Believe it or not, at any time of the day or night, thousands of people are out on the Internet just waiting to play games with whomever shows up.

This brings several questions to mind. Where do you get Internet games? What do these games cost to purchase and to play? How do you find players to play against? Most Internet games are available on the Internet itself. Even games that are sold on CD-ROM from your local computer store often offer restricted or demo versions that you can download from the Internet and try out. If you know of a particular game you want, you can go right to its Web site. If you just want to try out a bunch of them, you can surf some of the Internet gaming sites and indexes described later in this chapter.

Getting Ready to Play

Requirements for playing games can vary a lot, depending on the type of game you are interested in. However, here are a few tips that can make your online gaming more pleasant:

✦ **Upgrade your hardware.** Computer games that are graphical (3D and virtual reality), can run poorly on inexpensive computers. If the graphics appear rough (jagged on the edges), you may need a better video adapter with as much video memory as you can afford, to display higher resolutions and show more colors. If the games perform slowly, you may need more random access memory (RAM) in the computer for the game to run effectively.

Specialized gaming hardware includes joysticks, driving wheels, 3D graphic accelerator cards, and game pads. Most games now make noise, so you need to have sound capability on your system. Higher quality speakers will make the experience more vivid. Try Ultimate Game Machine (http://www.gamespot.com/) for help with your gaming computer hardware.

✦ **Upgrade your software.** Some games require that you have some updated software drivers installed. Read the requirements from the download site or from the readme files that come with the game before you run it. In particular, some Windows games rely on the Microsoft DirectX drivers, which are used to improve 3D animation, sound, and other special effects. If you don't have the latest DirectX software installed, the game may not run at all.

Tip   If the game you are running fails because DirectX is not installed, you can get DirectX free from the Web. Go to the Microsoft DirectX site (http://www.microsoft.com/directx). Click the Download button, and then select the DirectX package (based on the type of computer you have) and a download site. Once DirectX is downloaded, run the executable file and the drivers will be installed.

✦ **Clear some disk space.** If you are near the end of your hard disk space, you will not have room for some of the fancier games available. Even demo versions of some of the best games can be around 20MB, and then expand to 40MB or more when they are installed. Huge hard drives are cheap, so upgrading is worth serious consideration.

✦ **Try before you spend.** As we mentioned, most (though not all) of the best games on the Internet are either sold retail or as shareware. However, almost all games have a demo version you can try. Usually these demos will only let you use certain characters, only visit parts of the virtual world, or limit the time in which you can play online.

Because some of the games cost around $50, it's best to know that it is a game you will use, before you buy it. Later in this chapter you'll find listings of sites where you can download free demos.

✦ **Get the latest versions.** Just because you find a game on the Internet doesn't mean you have the latest version. Downloading a game from the games home page (as opposed to using a site that gathers lots of games) is one way to be assured of the latest version.

✦ **Use a good ISP.** If you are playing online games that require quick response (such as many of the action/adventure games), a slow modem or a busy Internet Service Provider can have a negative impact on your play. The problem is referred to as *latency*, where a lag occurs between the time you make a move (or someone makes a move at you), and when that move actually reaches the game server. A fast connection and a responsive ISP are a must for serious gamers.

✦ **Look for patches.** Nobody's perfect. Even the best online games will have a glitch or two (or more). Usually the same place you find the games software download sites you will find patches you can download to correct bugs in the program. If you have trouble with a store-bought game, checking the game's Web site for patches, workarounds, or troubleshooting information can save you some frustration.

Reviewing and Downloading Games

If you have never played games on the Internet before, the shear number of games available can be a bit daunting at first. You can start by just randomly downloading games. However, a more efficient way is to check out some of the gaming review sites on the Web. Besides offering Internet gaming reviews, these sites often let you download gaming software.

Tip   Look for top-ten lists to start off with some of the best games from the following sites. If you know the name of the game you want to check out, see if the gaming sites have a search tool that lets you search the site for the game you want.

GameSpot

The ZDNet's GameSpot site (http://www.gamespot.com) contains the latest information about computer games and hardware. The site is organized by the game categories Action, Adventure, Driving, Puzzle, Role Playing, Simulation, Sports, and Strategy.

GameSpot offers more than just game reviews and links. The site serves as an online magazine, with articles about upcoming games as well as stories about game history and reader input. You will also find daily polls where you can vote on various topics and, of course, cheats. Games are reviewed using a 10-point rating scale, and, when possible, downloads are available.

Computer Games Online

If you are looking for reviews, previews, and downloads of lots of games, the Computer Games Online home page (http://www.cdmag.com) is a good place to begin. The game reviewers have obviously had their hands on a lot of games, making their evaluations and comparisons valuable. The site also gives a lot of attention to hardware, with many articles and reviews of technology to make your gaming more enjoyable.

If you need some help with a game, click the Cheats link. You can find cheat codes, strategy tips, hints, and walkthroughs for many online games. The site also hosts various forums, which you can access by clicking the (surprise!) Forums link at the bottom of the screen. Forums provide a space to ask questions and read others' posts on various game topics.

Games Domain

If you want to look up a review for a popular Internet game, you will probably find it on the Games Domain site (http://www.gamesdomain.com). The Games Domain site gives equal time to both PC and console games (Console games are those that run on game consoles such as Sony PlayStation and Sega DreamCast).

Tip   If you're only interested in console games, click the link for Console Domain (http://www.consoledomain.com/).

This site has an extensive "cheats" database. Click Cheats from the home page. Then select the type of hardware you have (for example, a PC) to find the game you are looking for. Like other gaming sites, the Games Domain also lets you download demos and patches for hundreds of games.

The Game Center

The CNET Game Center (http://www.gamecenter.com) is another good site for the first-time online gamer. Some of the feature articles from this site include a listing of the Game Center's top games, as well as a listing of the most popular downloads.

If you are interested in what games are on the horizon, click the Game News link. This link will direct you to articles about what the top computer gaming companies are working on. Click Tips and Tactics for information that will help you navigate your favorite online games.

GamePower

Hundreds of computer game reviews appear at the GamePower site (http://www.gamepower.com). As with other gaming sites, reviews and download information is contained in categories, such as Action, Adventure, Classics, Console, RPGs, Sims, Sports, and Strategy.

Of special interest to those playing games over the Internet is the Multiplayer department of GamePower. Besides having information about multiplayer Internet games, the Web page also has information about gaming services. Find out what different services offer and what they cost.

GameWeb

If you'd like to begin your exploration into games with a search, GameWeb is one of your best bets. From the GameWeb home page (http://thegw.com), the GameWeb search engine lets you enter keywords, select how many matching sites to return, and choose quick or verbose output.

Just below the title on the GameWeb site is a scrolling list of game titles and other topics. If you see a title you are interested in, click it as it scrolls by. In addition to game reviews and cheats, GameWeb also provides numerous links to game-related Web sites.

Snap! online games

From the Snap! home page (`http://home.snap.com`), click Games under the Web Directory. The result is a listing and descriptions of some of the best gaming sites available on the Internet.

For specific information about Internet games, click the link to Multiplayer & Online Games. You will see a list of game categories you can check out. Another selection from the Games page is a link to Gamers' Magazines. The Gamers' Magazines links that appear can connect you to articles, opinions, and links to a lot of information about online gaming.

Yahoo Internet Games

The games listed under Yahoo's Internet Games site (`http://www.yahoo.com/ Recreation/Games/Internet_Games`) are organized into dozens of categories. Select Interactive Web Games and more than 40 categories of games appear. From there, follow links to board games, where you can find lots of board games that you can play against others, such as chess, backgammon, or Battleship. Choose Multi-User Games to find links to games you can play against others, such as Web Paintball, Tank Battle, and Multi-player Web Poker.

Playing Console Games on Your Computer

Early console games like the Atari 2600, Activision system, and even the first Nintendo game systems stored their game software on ROM (Read Only Memory) chips inside proprietary cartridges. Even some early personal computers, such as the Commodore 64, used cartridges to store games. This scheme ensured that the games could never be played in anything but the game console they were designed for.

But when Sony released its PlayStation in 1995, things changed because the game software was stored on compact discs. It wasn't long before gamers wondered if they could place those CDs in the CD-ROM drives of their computers and play them on the PC.

As delivered, you cannot play PlayStation (PSX) games on your computer, but you can if you use a console emulator such as Bleem. Like most emulators, Bleem doesn't support all PSX features, such as sound and 3D graphics, but it is still an interesting package if you really want to play these games on your PC. You can learn more about Bleem and other console emulators at EmuGaming, online at `www.emugaming.com`.

Finding Free and Inexpensive Internet Games

Because so many free and inexpensive games are available on the Web today, it's hard to know where to begin. Instead of trying to get an exhaustive list (which you can find, if you like, on some of the indexes described earlier), this section describes some of the major types of online games and gives you an example or two of each.

Excite Internet games

The Excite Games site (`http://www.excite.com/games/`) is a good place to find games that you can play immediately. The site offers dozens of games, ranging from traditional card and casino games to arcade-style games. We got hooked on a game called Tube Runner for a while that is a fun little Pac Man–style game. Most of the games run in a Java applet, so, although you will need a Java-capable Web browser, the games are easy to play and take only a minute or two each for the applet download. If you're bored and have Internet access, this site provides many great ways to pass the time.

Note   Most games at Excite Games require you to log-in with an Excite Passport. If you haven't signed up for one yet, you will be prompted to do so when you try to join a game.

Board games

Most of the popular board games you grew up with now have their electronic equivalent available on the Internet. Not only is it easy to find these games, but it is easy to find someone to play with too. If you feel satisfied with these low-tech games, several gaming services await your exploration:

✦ **PlaySite.** If you want to play Chess, Checkers, Backgammon, Reversi, Go-moku, Tangleword, or Hearts (and have a Java-enabled browser), PlaySite (`http://www.playsite.com`) is a great site for you. Play is free and no special software is required. Just click the type of game you want to play, and then log in to the site.

✦ **World Opponent Network.** Play a variety of Hoyle classic board games from the Won.net site (`http://www.won.net`). This service is free, and includes a selection of many other games as well.

The following are a few board games you might want to try.

Chess

Chess was one of the first games played on the Internet. (In fact, one of the first newsgroups on the Internet was for chess, because the designers of Usenet liked to play.) These days, however, instead of sending moves back and forth by e-mail, beautiful, graphical game boards enable you to play live against worldwide competitors on the Web.

One site that allows you to play chess online and train with Grandmasters is chess.net (`http://www.chess.net`). Here you can play games using chess.net software that vary from one that provides a three-dimensional view of the board to a free two-dimensional "lite" version of the software. You can also play using a downloadable Java applet or even via telnet.

Another site is the Free Internet Chess Server, or FICS, online at `www.freechess.org`. This is another good place to play chess with other people, as well as read news and information from the world of chess.

Many, many more chess sites are available online. Go to any search engine and look for *chess servers*. Your search could produce hundreds of results.

Backgammon

Finding a place to play backgammon on the Web is not hard to do. Yahoo! (`http://dir.yahoo.com/Recreation/Games/Board_Games/Backgammon/`) lists numerous backgammon servers.

One place listed with Yahoo is the GamesGrid site (`http://www.gamesgrid.com`). Another good one is NetGammon (`http://www.netgammon.com/`), which claims to be the world's largest backgammon club. They offer a collection of free downloads, although there is a subscription fee that at this writing was $53 for one year.

Card games

If you like to unwind with a game of cards, but are getting a little tired of solitaire, try one of the many online sites for playing games. Some of these sites require no special software, because they rely on common Web technology (such as Java). As a result, you just have to go to the card game site and start playing in your Web browser.

Here are a couple of sites you can visit to play card games, such as hearts, spades, or bridge.

✦ **pogo.com.** You can play card games for free against competitors on the Web from pogo.com (`http://www.pogo.com/`). From this site you can play Euchre, Hearts, Spades, and more. The games are Java applets, so they work in your browser. If you have visited the Excite Games page, this site will look familiar because pogo.com hosts the games at Excite.

✦ **Yahoo! Games.** No special software is needed to play Hearts, Spades, Bridge, Poker, or other games against Internet opponents from Yahoo! Games (`http://games.yahoo.com/`). Yahoo! also offers multiplayer Go, Backgammon, Checkers, and Chess games. If your Web browser is Java-enabled, you can play these games right from your browser. If you have Java disabled, or if your browser doesn't support Java applets, you won't be able to play these games.

Playing Popular Online Action and Strategy Games

Featured in the following sections are some games that combine the best features of game playing with the capability to play against others on the Internet. Many more games are available than this chapter describes. However, trying out these games will give you a good idea about the state of the art and, even if you just run the demos, you'll have some fun.

Total Annihilation

If you like a game where thinking and planning is as important as shooting, Total Annihilation might suit you. The game sets two sides against each other: the Core, whose people had no bodies but transferred their minds into killing machines, and the Arm, whose physical bodies are protected by powerful combat suits. You can command either the Arm or the Core, with the object of both sides to totally annihilate the opponent.

Not only do you set armies in motion, but you must build the facilities that support your force. As the commander, it's your job to manage your army's resources (consisting of metal and energy). These resources are necessary to create the units you need to do battle. The units consist of such things as planes, ships, and tanks, as well as structures such as factories. The game is played across battlefields at sea, on land, and in the air. You start with your matter/antimatter backpack and build the units you need to take on your opponents.

Total Annihilation is developed by CaveDog (http://www.cavedog.com). The complete version of the game consists of numerous missions and maps, and the capability to play against multiple opponents on the Internet. To just try out the game, a demo version is available consisting of three missions taken from the full game.

To play the game, you can use a combination of mouse actions and keystrokes. Click any unit with the left mouse button. You will see the unit's build capabilities or the orders you can give it. These orders define how aggressive the unit is when an enemy attacks or actions the unit can take (such as capturing, patrolling, moving, guarding, or attacking). Click and drag the mouse to select a group of units, and then set them in motion to attack or defend.

WarBirds

With WarBirds (www.iencentral.com), instead of fighting against a computer as you do with many flight-simulator types of games, you are combating live opponents over the Internet. The virtual WarBirds world consists of four countries that are fighting an on-going battle to gain territory. You choose a country to fly for, and then battle against other "live" players.

Once you have mastered the controls, descriptions of maneuvers tell you how to fly the plane. Basic flight maneuvers tell you how to use the controls, such as break turns, barrel rolls, and loops. The air combat maneuvers section contains links to articles that describe how to use the controls strategically in battle.

The WarBirds gaming servers (hosted by iEntertainment Network) run every hour of every day. To play, you can download the software for free, and then pay an hourly fee for using the service. When you register with the iEntertainment Network, you get access to various games with their Premium account, including WarBirds, Kingdom of Drakkar, and Dawn of Aces. The site offers various account plans, ranging from $9.95 to $29.95 per month, plus a small hourly rate that varies depending on the rate plan you choose. The monthly subscription fee is applied to your hourly charges account. So, for example, if you only plan to play about five hours per month, choose the Silver account. It costs $9.95, and the hourly rate for WarBirds is $1.99. This means you can play up to five hours without accruing any additional charges.

Quake III Arena

By combining 3D interactive action (in the tradition of Doom) and a format based on completing missions, Quake III is one of the premier multiplayer Internet action games available today. In Quake, you travel through several 3D maps trying to complete the objectives of your mission. On the way, you encounter objects that will help you to your goal and, as you might expect, plenty of creepy creatures to blast out of existence. Features in the multiplayer game enable users to acknowledge each other by saluting, waving, or pointing.

Quake is published by Activision (http://www.activision.com/). Some of the services that support multiplayer Quake III include Mplayer (http://www.mplayer.com) and Heat.net (http://www.heat.net). Many ISPs also host Quake servers, so check there to see if one is available.

Joining Internet Gaming Networks

The Internet gaming networks are gathering places for those who want to play games with or against other Internet players. If you just want to play a simple card or board game, there are a number of sites where you can play for free or for small fees. Some of the sites that support high-speed action charge monthly or hourly fees.

The GameSpot site has an online gaming service list (http://www.gamespot.com/). This list shows the service name, pricing, and available games. Click the name of the service to get more information about it. Click the names of the games listed to view more information about that game. This is an excellent resource for choosing gaming services.

World Opponent Network (WON)

The World Opponent Network (http://www.won.net) is a free online gaming services that lets you compete in a large variety of games against opponents on the Internet. The site sells an extensive collection of games online, or you can download some free games.

Currently, more than 20 WON-enabled games are available. You can check for a current list of games by clicking the link for CD-based games. Games include: 3D Mini-Golf Deluxe, Civil War Generals 2, Sierra Sports Football Pro and Golf Pro, Hoyle games (Classic Board Games, Card Games, Blackjack, Poker, and Casino), Lords of Magic, Lords of the Realm II, MissionForce: Cyberstorm, Outpost 2, Red Baron II, The Time Warp of Dr. Brain, Trophy Bass 2, and Trophy Rivers.

To download the free and demo WON games, go to the site's download page. To use the WON service, just start up a game that is WON-enabled and choose Multiplayer or Internet game. When you choose Internet, you can play against the computer (if you select single player). With Multiplayer, you create a game or create a room and play against other players on the Internet who are waiting for you.

HEAT.NET Internet Game Network

Serious Internet gamers find what they are looking for at the Heat.net Internet Game Network (http://www.heat.net). This service supports most popular multiplayer PC games. To use Heat.net, you can get a free membership by clicking the New Users link. This membership doesn't limit the games or amount of times you can play. You can even get paid frequent-player points called *Degrees* simply by logging in and playing. However, you must be a Premium member to participate in premium member-only events. These include tournaments, challenge series, and various special events. Premium membership currently costs $49.99 per year. When we visited the site there were specials offered, such as free magazine subscriptions, if you signed up for a premium account for a whole year.

Kali

Kali (http://www.kali.net) claims to be the world's largest Internet gaming network enabling multiplayer Internet games for more than 275,000 players. Many of the most popular games are listed as supported by the Kali online gaming site. As an unregistered member of Kali, you can play any game it supports, but your play time is limited to 15 minutes per session.

To register as a Kali member for life, you pay $20. That entitles you to unlimited play forever and the Kali software (which you can download from the Kali site). Kali also boasts a very large international player representation.

To find the games you want to play, click Games in the menu bar on the left side of the window. This leads you to an introductory screen, where you can choose to browse the list of games at Kali, download demos, or perform a search.

Summary

Although the Internet is serious business to many people, nothing limits the amount of game playing available on the Internet. If you are new to Internet gaming, start by checking out many of the online gaming magazines. From those sites you can find out what the best games are and where to get demos.

✦   ✦   ✦

Finding the Best Deals on the Web

Shopping on the Internet might not be for you if you like to touch and smell and try on before you buy. But if you like to read specs, compare prices, and find cool and exotic stuff without leaving your seat, then Internet shopping may suit you perfectly.

About $20 billion in sales were generated during the 1999 holiday online shopping bonanza, according to estimates from Forrester Research (http://access.forrester.com/). This number astounded nearly everyone; it represents a twenty-fold increase over online sales as recently as 1996. New technologies and a dizzying range of available products have made Internet shopping both attractive and a bit scary to the first-time Internet shopper.

Although Web shopping has been around for a couple of years now, many people are still concerned about its safety and reliability. After giving you a rundown on what to look for in Internet shopping services, this chapter describes some of the ways you can improve the safety of your online shopping. If you haven't done so already, you should also read Chapter 34, "Spending Money Online Safely."

Before you buy, the Web has services that enable you to help you find the kind of product you are looking for by matching products to the specifications you enter. For example, you could enter the price range, style, size, and features of an automobile and a Web site can tell you which models meet your specifications.

Once you overcome your online shopping shyness, there are lots of excellent, reputable businesses on the Web that have a shopping cart ready for you. You can get travel bargains from Travelocity, flowers from 1-800-FLOWERS, or bid on almost anything under the sun at ebay. Those sites and others are described in this chapter.

Identifying Online Shopping Essentials

Just like shopping at a store in your neighborhood, successful online shopping depends on finding a vendor that will sell you a quality product at a fair price, and that will support you if you need help. With online shopping, however, you face some different challenges and opportunities.

This section describes what you can and should expect from the online stores with which you do business. Understanding how online shopping works and doing some homework before you buy is the best way to make sure you will be happy with your online purchases.

Shopping safely

Any place you shop online should use *Secure Sockets Layer (SSL)*, S-HTTP (an Internet protocol for sending secure messages), or other types of secure connection to encrypt the personal information (credit card numbers, addresses, phone numbers, and so on) you send over the Internet. While some believe there is little chance of someone stealing even unencrypted information sent over the Internet, the use of SSL shows a level of dedication to the security of your information.

When you enter the secure portion of a shopping site, a dialog box should appear, informing you that you are beginning a secure connection.

 Cross-Reference For an in-depth description of SSL and other online shopping security issues, read Chapter 32, "Maintaining Your Online Privacy and Security."

Assessing the integrity of online merchants

Just because there's little risk of a stranger grabbing your account numbers and emptying your life savings, that doesn't mean you're completely safe from being victimized. In fact, the greatest risk of someone cheating you comes from the Web site with which you are having the transaction.

Anyone who can create a Web account can call themselves an online store. There are those who try to sell things over the Internet who don't have an office, an address, or even a telephone number. If they take your money and never send you a product, it may be difficult or even impossible to find them again.

We strongly recommend checking out an online store before you buy anything. There are companies that rate the integrity and service quality of shopping Web sites. These rating services give you their assessment of the online shopping site, as well as the opinions of customers who have used the site. Examples of services that rate online shopping sites are the BizRate Guide and the Virtual Emporium, which are described later in this chapter.

If you know a company's reputation outside of its Web site, you can probably expect the same level of service that you would get if you shopped there in person. Many companies now maintain an online presence in addition to their traditional "storefront" operations. Although many have done this to protect their own market share in the face of new competition from Internet upstarts, you benefit from their real world presence and reputations.

Protecting your information

Some online companies have policies that help protect your personal information from being misused. For example, when you buy something through the AT&T catalog service, AT&T claims it does not store your credit card information for purposes other than the sales transaction itself. So, each time you make a purchase you need to resubmit your credit card number. (However, AT&T does support Wallet technology that lets you submit credit card information that is stored safely on your own computer.)

Tip — When you check out an online store using the BizRate Guide, the guide tells you whether the online store has a policy of protecting your personal information from further distribution.

Contacting customer service

It's important that a shopping Web site have good customer support. For example, if you purchase an expensive item, you want to make sure that there is someone who can help you if there is a problem with it or if you need to return it. In particular, check that the company has a customer support telephone number so you can personally speak to someone. While a customer support e-mail address might be helpful, there is no way to guarantee that anyone will ever get back to you. If you do get a hold of a customer support representative, keep track of who you talk to, when you talked to them, and what was said.

Most online stores that do a lot of business on the Internet should provide you with several different ways to contact them, including:

✦ A telephone number
✦ An e-mail address

✦ A fax number

✦ A street address

It may take a few mouse clicks to get this information. Often there will be an *Information* or *About the Company* link to customer support information. Though most online stores have telephone support, in general they would prefer that you not use it. It's this lack of personal interaction that helps make their online business profitable, but it can also be frustrating for you. If you find a site that offers low prices *and* generous tech support, consider yourself fortunate indeed.

Describing online shopping features

The best shopping sites on the Internet have a combination of advanced technology features designed to make your shopping experience easier. Here are some of the features, as well as some pitfalls, you should be aware of when you shop online:

✦ **Shopping Carts**. Online stores want to make it easy for you to browse and purchase as much as possible from their Web sites. Online shopping carts are buttons, usually in the form of a shopping cart or basket, that are placed next to each product. When you click the button, the item is added to the list of items you have chosen during this buying session. When you have made all of your selections, you can view the items in your shopping cart, change or delete items, and then go ahead and make your purchase.

✦ **Specifications**. Often products displayed from the online store are associated with links to detailed descriptions of the products. Sometimes you are able to compare the product to similar products, based on features and pricing. Other times links bring you to the Web sites of the product manufacturer for more information.

✦ **Personal Accounts**. Some shopping sites want you to have a personal account created before you shop their site. The account typically provides the business with your name, address, e-mail, phone number, and possibly credit card numbers. This information may be stored by the company, thereby speeding your shopping experience the next time you visit. However, if you decide you don't want the site to have this information, you may not be able to shop at the site.

✦ **Shipping and Handling**. Sometimes the price of a product looks really good, but when the final bill is totaled, it may cost you more than it would if you bought it down the street. Check if there are any shipping and handling costs associated with your purchase. In fact, it's best to know what the grand total is *before* you complete your purchase.

✦ **Samples and Specials**. Some online shopping sites offer free samples or special deals. For example, online music stores sometimes have audio samplings of the CDs they sell. Computer software is frequently offered with free trial periods or as a trial version with reduced features. Likewise, a patient Web shopper can dig out some great travel deals online.

✦ **In-Stock Items**. A great price won't do you much good if you need a product now and it's not in stock. Some shopping services tell you if a product is ready to ship before you order it. If availability is an issue for you, and that information is not noted when you order, you may want to call the customer service number to make sure. U.S. law requires that items be shipped within 30 days if the delivery date is not noted.

Caution

You may also want to find out if the site charges you for items that aren't in stock. If your credit card gets charged for an item that remains out of stock for a long period of time, you could have a hard time getting a refund if you decide to cancel the order.

✦ **Return Policy**. Especially in the case of large purchases, you want to know that you can get a full refund if you need to return the product. If the online store makes a mistake, they will often cover the charges for shipping for you to return the item.

If you find you like shopping online and do it regularly, you will surely encounter sites without shopping baskets, limited supported information, and even order forms without secure connections.

Shopping at Insecure Sites

So you have found that special widget or doo-hickey on the Web that you absolutely must have, but the site doesn't offer any of the security features that make online shopping relatively safe. Should you just give up the idea?

While we would never wholeheartedly recommend shopping at insecure Web sites, we have on occasion purchased items from an insecure site. Sometimes, the site asks you to send your credit card number, name, and address in an e-mail message to make your purchase. Though you shouldn't do that, there may still be a less risky way to buy the product.

If the site shows a company name and address, you can check with the Better Business Bureau to find out if the company is reputable. When you make your purchase, paying cash on delivery (COD) or by check can limit your risk.

If you still don't feel comfortable ordering blindly, ask the company if they sell their product at any retail outlets that are near you.

Finding Safe Shopping Sites

If you're shopping online because of its convenience, you probably won't find it convenient to spend days researching the integrity of every site at which you would like to shop. Luckily, there are services that have already done much of the research of the top online shopping sites for you.

Two such sites are the BizRate Guide and the Virtual Emporium Web sites. The BizRate Guide has very comprehensive evaluations of online shopping sites. It provides information about the type of services each site offers, the quality of those services, and feedback from customers who have used those services. The Virtual Emporium has a customer feedback forum and information about the type of payment methods available from each site.

BizRate Guide

The BizRate Guide (`http://www.bizrate.com`) touts itself as "the first People's Portal to e-commerce." BizRate looks like many search engines in that it provides a directory that links to hundreds of online shopping sites. But unlike other directories, sites cannot pay to be included in BizRate. Instead, companies must maintain a high level of customer service quality, determined largely by feedback from BizRate members.

From the BizRate Guide site, you can find lots of valuable information for evaluating and reaching some of the best shopping sites on the Web. You can search for an online merchant from the BizRate Guide site or find merchants from that site by browsing various categories.

Online shopping sites listed by the BizRate Guide are catalogued by overall rating and are organized under specific categories, such as these:

- ✦ **Store – View Report**. Links to a report on the site's performance, broken down into 11 criteria.

- ✦ **BizRater Rebates**. Discounts offered to BizRate members for clicking through from the BizRate Web site.

- ✦ **On-Time Index**. Provides a rating between zero (worst) and 100 (best) that represents the percentage of orders that are delivered on time.

- ✦ **Go Shop.** This link directs you to the site so that you can begin shopping, including information on any click-through discounts that may apply.

To use BizRate, you must register and become a BizRate member. The membership is free, and along with it you get a free BizRate e-mail address. You can use this e-mail address when you shop online, thereby keeping the spam that inevitably results from online shopping out of your normal e-mail account.

Virtual Emporium

The Virtual Emporium (http://www.virtualemporium.com) is another gathering place for links to and information about online shopping sites. Click "Lead me to the stores" to view a category list of shopping sites. The directory is organized in much the same manner as a directory you might find in a large department store (but, sadly, it won't tell you which floor the restrooms are located on).

Several links are common to each page at the Virtual Emporium. One is a link to seasonal shopping deals, and another lists Sales & Specials. This link is especially useful if you're a diehard bargain shopper.

As with BizRate, sites listed at Virtual Emporium must meet standards for customer service, security, and ease of use. If you have any feedback on a site you visit through Virtual Emporium, click the Feedback link at the bottom of each Virtual Emporium page to tell them about your experience.

Researching the Best Online Deals

If you like to research products before you buy, the Web offers opportunities to compare products, check out specs, and find the best prices. The potential for comparison shopping on the Web has just begun to be realized, but the comparison shopping services that are available today can give you a great feel for the possibilities.

Products, such as automobiles, are a natural for selecting and comparing specs and pricing (see the description of comparison shopping for automobiles just up ahead). Likewise, other high-ticket, technical products — such as computers and entertainment equipment — are well suited for comparison shopping on the Web.

Besides head-to-head comparisons, there are also services that gather reviews of the products or services in which you may be interested. Some offer search tools with which you can turn up articles and reviews about the products you are shopping for.

Personal Logic

Personal Logic (http://www.personalogic.com/) is another service for comparing and selecting various things is available from. This site links you to services that step you through the process of selecting cars, vacations, computers, colleges, mutual funds, bicycles, cities to live in, camcorders, or dogs.

To compare products or services, click on a category that interests you. Depending on the service, you can choose to answer a series of questions about your needs, or you can select specific products and compare them side by side. Some categories link you directly to outside sources. For instance, if you click on "Used Cars," you are linked directly to a site hosted by AutoTrader.com.

Personal Logic is a free service that makes its money from commissions earned by matching well-informed shoppers with vendors. The idea is that once someone goes through the process of selecting a product or servicebased on their exact specs, the company or organization that has a product that meets that need has a ready-made sale.

Consumer World

More than 1,800 consumer resources on the Internet are available from the ConsumerWorld site (`http://www.consumerworld.org`. In fact, some of the best information can be found right on the Consumer World home page by scrolling down a bit. Figure 37-1 shows a portion of the Consumer World home page.

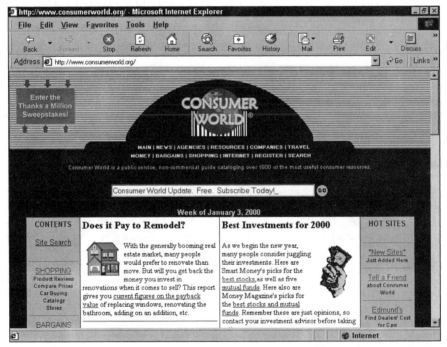

Figure 37-1: Find consumer resources from Consumer World.

Consumer World has a Price Checker that lets you scan several discount vendors for the best prices. Type the name of the product you want, select the category it falls under, then click Search. If there are any matches, the name of the vendor appears, along with the name of the product and the price. Click the price and you are taken to the site that sells the product . . . with that product added to your shopping cart!

Consumer World also provides other links to sites that evaluate online brokerage houses, discount stores, online shopping malls, and discount travel agencies, to name a few. If you have the time, you can find some excellent information and bargains at Consumer World.

Using Shopping Index Sites

Why settle for shopping at one online store at a time when you can shop at several online stores all at once? Some of the best places to do this are located at the various online search services available on the Web. This section describes some of the best online shopping indexes available on the Web.

Yahoo! Shopping Guide

The Yahoo! Shopping Guide (`http://shopguide.yahoo.com`) is available from the yahoo.com search site. Shopping categories are sorted into 17 different groups under the Find Products heading. When you select a category, the guide not only shows you to the online stores that fall into that category, but it also provides search tools for finding the products in which you are interested. Figure 37-2 shows the Yahoo! Shopping Guide site.

Figure 37-2: Find shopping sites and consumer information.

A neat feature of the Yahoo! Shopping Guide is that it helps you find stores in local area. Under the Yahoo! Resources heading, click "Search offline with Yellow Pages." This presents a category list similar to Yahoo!'s Web directory. Click on a category, enter your ZIP code, and continue clicking links until a nearby location is found. Business names, addresses, phone numbers, and even the mean distance from the ZIP code you entered are provided. And if you click the link for the business name, a MapQuest map shows you the exact location of the business.

Excite Shopping

The Excite Shopping Channel (`http://shopping.excite.com/`) is another excellent online shopping resource. In addition to the requisite shopping categories, Excite Shopping offers a list of quick links to Featured Merchants, as well as an area called Mini Shops. This is a place where smaller — but still reputable — online merchants can hawk their wares.

Go Shop

Infoseek hosts its own online shopping mall at Go Shop (`http://shop.go.com/`). From this site, you can easily find your way to thousands of online stores, as well as a Buyer's Guide that helps you learn about and compare products, and then figure out where the best place to buy them is.

LycoShop

Like many other shopping indexes, LycoShop (`http://shop.lycos.com/`) provides sensible links to various online shopping sites. When you select a category from the page, not only will you see a list of links directly to shopping sites, but also relevant online auctions, new products articles from LycoShop editors, and links to other related information. This emphasis on research and product information helps you be a more informed shopper.

World Best Buy

One of the newer online mega malls is World Best Buy (`http://www.worldbestbuy.com/`). Although it contains shopping categories like the other sites listed here, World Best Buy also places a significant emphasis on allowing private individuals to buy and sell things through the site. Click the Garage Sale link to view items that members have put up for sale. Registration is required if you want to sell an item, but you can browse as a shopper without providing any personal information.

Bidding for Goods Online

Online auctions have been one of the biggest "growth" areas for online commerce in the last couple of years. As with traditional auctions, individuals or businesses post items for sale, and prospective buyers can bid on them. When a specific period of time has passed, the sale is closed and the item is bought by the highest bidder (assuming, that is, the minimum bid was met).

eBay

eBay (`http://www.ebay.com/`) is the best known online auction site, primarily due to a significant volume of media attention. Some of the items that have been posted for sale on eBay are controversial, to say the least. Items put up for bid range from the illegal (such as drugs and human organs) to the outrageous (like a former Soviet Navy submarine). eBay has policies against illegal items being sold at their site, of course, but the sheer volume of items for sale—over three million items were for sale when we checked—means that some things are bound to slip through.

eBay provides a safe location to trade items online, thanks to several important features:

✦ You can instantly check the "reputation" of individuals and businesses in online transactions.

✦ Up to $175 insurance is offered to buyers in case they never receive an item they paid for.

✦ eBay offers an escrow service for very expensive items. A third party ensures that the seller and buyer receive the money and goods they are due.

✦ eBay's support staff are on hand to help resolve disagreements concerning transactions on the site. To learn more, click the SafeHarbor link at the bottom of eBay's main page.

eBay offers a list of shopping categories, but due to the volume of items for sale, you may have better luck performing a keyword search. When you get a list of items that matches your search criteria, each item will be listed by name, the current price, the number of bids, and the time remaining before the auction on that item ends.

If you wish to bid on something at eBay, you have to register. If you want to sell something, you must register and pay a an "insertion" fee to list an item, which can range from as little as 25 cents up to $50. Once the item is sold, an additional "Final Value Fee" is charged based on the final sale price. For a complete breakdown of eBay fees, visit the seller guide at `http://pages.ebay.com/help/sellerguide/selling-fees.html`.

Caution   We have seen a sharp increase in e-mail spam after registering with eBay. We suggest that you use a separate e-mail address when registering with eBay to keep spam out of your main inbox.

Yahoo! Auctions

Yahoo! Provides another popular online auction site at `http://auctions.yahoo.com/`. The site resembles Yahoo!'s shopping page, with categories and a search feature. As with eBay, the volume of items offered for sale at Yahoo! Auctions is large enough that you will probably find it more effective to perform a keyword search.

Yahoo! Auctions makes it easy for you to track specific auctions using your My Yahoo! Account. And unlike other auction sites, Yahoo! Auction is free to both buyers and sellers.

Searching for Travel Bargains Online

Given the bizarre nature of pricing in the travel industry, searching out bargains and booking travel arrangements on the Web is a popular activity. These days you can be your own travel agent, booking your own plane flights, car rentals, hotel accommodations, and dining reservations without leaving your computer. If you are patient, you can find tremendous travel bargains on the Web.

Best Fares Discount Travel Magazine

The Best Fares Discount Travel Magazine Online (`http://www.bestfares.com`) is one of those Web pages that lets you scroll down to see everything you might want to know on a subject. In this case, the subject is travel bargains.

The Best Fares site connects you to low discount plane fares as they become available (airlines are constantly changing their fares). Special hotel rates are available in cities around the world. Car rentals, train travel, and cruises are all offered at special rates.

To take advantage of Best Fares special travel promotions and other features, you need to subscribe to the magazine first. To learn more about what is available to members only, click the Subscriber Info link.

Travelocity

From the Travelocity site (`http://www.travelocity.com`) you can research and reserve your own plane flights, car rentals, cruises, hotel rooms, and lots of other travel arrangements. Set up your own account with Travelocity, book your travel, and just wait for your tickets to arrive in the mail.

When you book your travel reservations, you can search for arrangements based on prices, airlines, travel time, or several other criteria. Before you leave, Travelocity can provide you with weather information, maps to your destination, and news affecting the places you might be visiting around the world.

Shopping for Gifts Online

If you are a last-minute birthday or holiday gift shopper, there are some excellent ways to find that special present and get it to that special someone in the nick of time. Though there are many sites that feature specialty gifts, some of the best ones carry old favorites: flowers, candy, and perfume.

1-800-flowers.com

The 1-800-flowers.com site (`http://www.1800flowers.com/`) turns up on many of the top ten shopping site lists on the Web. In addition to flowers, you can also order balloons, gift baskets, gourmet goodies, and plants. Your gift can then be delivered to locations all over the United States and to about 15 foreign countries.

One of the best features of 1-800-flowers.com is that you can choose an occasion (birthday, Valentine's day, and the like), a category (flowers, balloons, and so on), and a price range, and then view the products available in the criteria you selected. When you find the one you like, just click the button below the picture that says Click to Buy. In most cases, orders placed before 2:00 PM can be delivered on the same day.

Godiva Chocolates

If you are going to give a gift that contains a lot of calories, it should at least taste like Godiva chocolates. The Godiva Chocolatier site (`http://www.godiva.com`) lets you order some of the world's finest chocolates and have it delivered to someone special.

Choose from cordial assortments, grande mints, all milk chocolate collections, deluxe assortments, and a variety of other fine chocolates. Chocolates are available for special occasions, such as weddings, birthdays, Valentine's Day, and even the birth of a baby (that is, chocolate cigars). The site also provides a store locator if you want to locate a store near you.

FragranceNet

FragranceNet (`http://www.fragrancenet.com/`) refers to itself as the world's largest discount fragrance store, offering more than 1,000 brand-name fragrances at discount prices. Fragrances are organized by women's fragrances, men's fragrances, and gifts & specials. A search tool lets you find the particular fragrance you want.

The FragranceNet membership lets you enter birthdays, anniversaries, and other important dates, and then notifies you in time for you to buy the fragrance you need for the occasion.

Buying CDs and Videos Online

Music, movies, and other entertainment products have made their way to online stores in great numbers. Music and videos offer one of the best try-before-you-buy opportunities: You can use the Web to preview thousands of music CDs and movies, read reviews of your favorite artists, and find links to newsgroups and chat rooms that discuss music and film.

Because so many music and video online stores have popped up, there is stiff competition for sales. Shop around before you buy. Chances are the music CD or film you're looking for is being discounted by someone.

CDNOW

At the CDNOW site (`http://www.cdnow.com`), you can search a database containing hundreds of thousands of sound clips. Besides CDs, the site also sells movies, music videos, cassettes, and laserdiscs.

In addition to buying music CDs, CDNOW also lets you purchase and download some individual songs. Downloadable music is provided in either MP3 format, or in a proprietary format used by Windows Media Player or Liquid Audio. If you plan to keep the music for a while, we suggest that you go for the MP3 format.

 Cross-Reference To learn more about downloading and playing audio files, take a look at Chapter 18, "Finding the Best Online Audio and Video Sites."

Mass Music

Besides carrying music on compact disc, Mass Music (`http://www.massmusic.com`) also sells movies, magazine subscriptions, and accessories for audiophiles. Follow links to reviews of your favorite artists, check out the bulletin board, and try out their online magazine.

Summary

The number and variety of shopping sites on the Web today is staggering. It's tempting to just jump in and start buying, but before you do, you need to think about security issues, guarding your personal information, and the integrity of online shopping sites.

There are several excellent Web sites that help you evaluate the quality of online stores (such as the BizRate Guide) and others that let you do comparison shopping on the Web (such as CompareNet). Before you make a purchase, get a feeling for the reliability of the site and whether or not you are getting a good deal.

✦   ✦   ✦

Holding a Meeting on the Internet

◆　◆　◆　◆

In This Chapter

Conducting
cybermeetings

Communicating with
NetMeeting

Making your point
with whiteboarding

Conferencing online
with friends and
associates

◆　◆　◆　◆

The Internet has become an integral part of the business world, and business communications in particular have been transformed by it. E-mail, intranets, and collaborative computing have changed, for better or worse, the way in which people work together. In many cases, it's no longer necessary for people to toil together in the same building — they telecommute instead. Yet regardless of the technological changes in the work place, one thing is still clear: There will always be the need for people to exchange ideas, discuss options, argue over the details, and decide on a plan; there will always be a need for meetings.

This chapter introduces you to the possibility of online meetings, giving you a few ideas for ways you can use the technology and a few practical suggestions for dos and don'ts. We'll also take a look at NetMeeting, Microsoft's online meeting software and experiment with a few different ways of communicating in real time across the airwaves and phone lines.

Conducting Cybermeetings

Today, companies large and small are using the Web as a huge whiteboard, scribbling Xs and Os, drawing game plans and editing layouts, planning marketing campaigns, and designing buildings. Team members from different parts of the country, or even in different countries around the world, use the Internet to meet and discuss business.

The connectivity of the Internet makes it possible for friends and business associates located in different parts of the world to meet and collaborate—not just one-on-one, through e-mail or by phone—but in a true conference or seminar setting. These *cybermeetings* happen in real time—although they require some up front planning, they can be highly productive and cost-efficient. When you consider the outlay of time and money business travel requires, cybermeetings are a viable alternative.

Considering online conferencing

With the pace at which technology—and specifically Internet technology—is changing, it can be hard to imagine how to take advantage of these new tools. Is cybermeeting, more commonly known as *online conferencing*, something that would benefit you? Here are a few ideas for meetings you might want to have on the Net:

✦ A group of salespeople in different regions gather online to discuss a new product announcement.

✦ The chairman of the board calls an emergency board meeting online.

✦ A professor holds an online lecture about communications technology.

✦ A team of designers meets online to critique a new ad campaign.

✦ Telecommuters stay in constant contact with the main office using an instant messaging program.

✦ A virtual book club holds a conference and invites a well-known author.

Planning a productive online meeting

In this chapter, you learn about a few different types of programs you can use to do online conferencing. But no matter which program you use, there are a certain number of things you can do to ensure that you are getting the most out of your meeting time.

✦ **Plan ahead**. Use e-mail to set up the meeting and distribute your agenda. Make sure everyone knows the meeting time (remember that different participants may be in different time zones), the agenda, the materials they need to have at hand, and how they will be expected to participate. Figure 38-1 shows an example of a setup memo circulated in preparation for an online meeting.

✦ **Do a trial run**. If you are unfamiliar with the conferencing software, be sure to try it out and get familiar with it in advance of the meeting date. You don't want to be messing with the speakers or figuring out why the microphone isn't working when you've got clients on three continents waiting to hear your voice.

✦ **Anticipate problems**. Because of the distance and the nature of the Net, it's possible that unexpected circumstances will arise. What happens if the server goes down? What if one of the participants can't get online? Be sure you have copies of the phone numbers of all participants and they have yours, so if worst come to worst they can join the conference by phone.

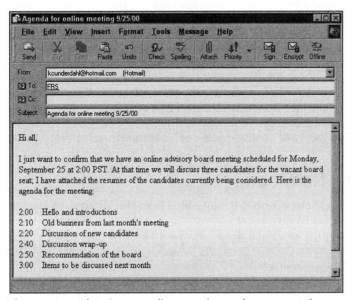

Figure 38-1: Planning an online meeting makes your conference time more productive.

✦ **Know what you want to accomplish**. Before you go into the meeting, have a goal in mind. "We will review and sign off on the layout for the January issue" is one idea for a goal. Or "This meeting will be a kick-off meeting for the new building plans" is another.

Communicating with NetMeeting

One of the most widely known and used online conferencing programs currently available is Microsoft NetMeeting. Version 3.0 of NetMeeting is covered here, and it represents a substantial improvement over its predecessors. Earlier incarnations of NetMeeting were slow, problematic, and confusing to learn and use. NetMeeting 3.0 is considerably simpler and more reliable, while maintaining its basic level of features that make it ideal for both business conferences and home users who simply want to make a video call over the Internet. This section explains some of the basics and the highlights of NetMeeting.

Describing NetMeeting

NetMeeting is a conferencing tool that enables you to meet online with coworkers, friends, and family members, no matter where in the world they are. You can include up to 32 participants in an online NetMeeting conference. To use NetMeeting, you and the other meeting participants need a Pentium computer running Windows 95 or higher, 16MB or more of random access memory (RAM), a sound board, a microphone, and speakers or headphones. And if you have a video camera hooked up to your computer, you can even see the person you're talking to. The quality of your audio and video connection will vary greatly depending on the type of hardware you have and the bandwidth available.

Tip   There are other conference products available, as you will see later in this chapter. One program that is comparable to NetMeeting is Intel Create & Share Video Phone. Both programs are compatible, which means that meeting participants using NetMeeting can communicate with participants using Video Phone.

Acquiring NetMeeting

NetMeeting is a Microsoft product, available from the Microsoft Web site at `http://www.microsoft.com/netmeeting/`. At the site, you find plenty of information about how to install and work with NetMeeting, plus a FAQ that will answer most of the questions you may have. The rest of this section walks you through a sample meeting with NetMeeting.

Installing and setting up NetMeeting

The process of getting and installing NetMeeting is simple. If you download the program from the Web site, elect to save the program as a file and install it later using Add/Remove Programs in the Windows Control Panel.

When you first launch NetMeeting (click Start ➪ Programs ➪ Accessories ➪ Internet Tools ➪ NetMeeting), a wizard leads you through a series of questions. Enter your information and click Next in each screen. When you are asked about logging onto a server, just accept the default setting.

NetMeeting will eventually come to a series of screens to help you configure your system for conferencing. The Audio Tuning Wizard, which is shown in Figure 38-2, will ask you to test the volume of your speakers. Whether you are using external speakers, stereo speakers build into your system, or a headset, you should be able to hear sound when you click the Test button. Adjust the Volume level to a point comfortable for you and then click Stop. When you are satisfied with the volume level, click Next to continue.

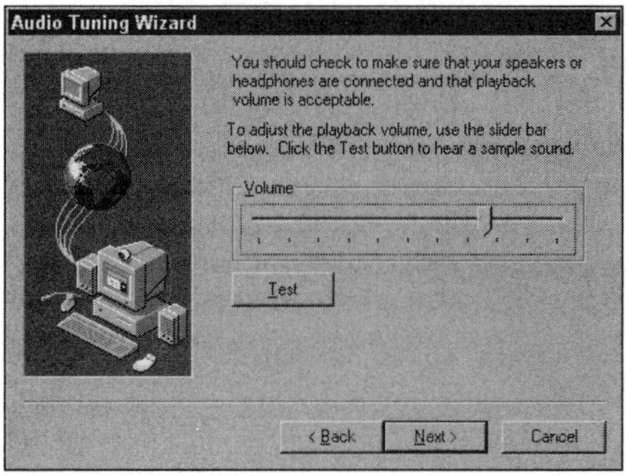

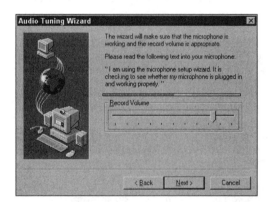

Figure 38-2: The Audio Tuning Wizard checks the sound level of your speakers so you can be sure you'll be able to hear participants.

Next, the Audio Tuning Wizard checks the volume of your microphone, as shown in Figure 38-3. Again, the microphone may be built into your system; it may be a standalone microphone; or it may be part of a headset. (If you are using an Internet phone hookup, the device may be your telephone handset.)

Figure 38-3: When you read the sample sentence, NetMeeting automatically checks the sound levels and adjusts it to make sure you sound as clear as possible.

Note You must have a sound card, a microphone, and speakers — or a headset or compatible phone unit — in order to use NetMeeting's audio capabilities. You need a video-capture card and a camera, or a video camera that can be connected to your PC's parallel or USB port, in order for other meeting members to see you.

Testing your camera

Once you have NetMeeting set up, you should test your camera (if you have one) to make sure it works with the program. Before you can view video of yourself, you must install and configure the camera according to the manufacturer's instructions. Once it's ready, launch NetMeeting and click View ➪ My Video. Make sure the camera is turned on, and click the Play button in the My Video window, which is shown in Figure 38-4. You will probably need to adjust the camera to make sure it is positioned correctly. You can also use this opportunity to adjust lighting in the room for a better picture.

Figure 38-4: Your author is ready to conference. Click the Stop button when you are done previewing.

NetMeeting Tips

Here's how to make your NetMeetings work smoothly:

✦ The faster your Internet connection, the better (56.6K or higher recommended).

✦ Faster computers will make video and voice work better.

✦ If you are experiencing "choppy" sound, try changing NetMeeting to half-duplex (full-duplex is the default and uses more bandwidth and processing power). To change to half-duplex, hang up from the current call, choose Tools ⇨ Options, click the Audio tab, and click the Enable Full Duplex Audio checkbox to clear it.

✦ If NetMeeting freezes when you start it, you may need to update your sound driver. Contact the manufacturer of your sound board to get the latest driver, which can usually be downloaded from their Web site.

✦ You can get online help for NetMeeting by opening the Help menu and choosing Online Support.

✦ NetMeeting 3.0 is the current version and your meeting will go smoothest if all participants are using that version. Although other meeting attendees can sometimes use earlier versions of NetMeeting, they will not be able to host the event.

✦ If your video is playing slowly or displaying odd colors, try shining more light on the person or area in the video. Poor lighting can slow processing and produce odd effects.

Performing a NetMeeting trial run

In this section, you will take a trial run using NetMeeting. If you have the software installed, fire it up and play along. If not, notice how simple it is to collaborate online using the various features of the program.

Once you establish your dial-up connection, you can start NetMeeting by either double-clicking the NetMeeting icon on your desktop, or opening the Start menu, pointing to Programs, and choosing NetMeeting from the displayed list. The NetMeeting window opens, which is shown in Figure 38-5.

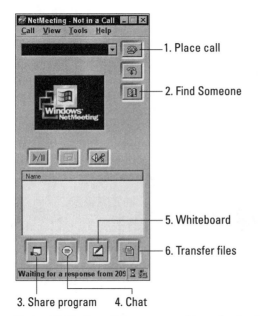

1. Place call

2. Find Someone

5. Whiteboard

6. Transfer files

3. Share program   4. Chat

Figure 38-5: Everything you need in order to start a meeting is right on the NetMeeting window.

Caution

We found that if any of the meeting participants are using software (such as BlackICE) that guards their Internet connection from hackers, the NetMeeting call will not be established. Users generally need to disable hacker countermeasures and firewalls before NetMeeting will work.

Contacting participants with NetMeeting

Connecting with your associates online may sound tricky, but it's actually quite simple, once you go through the process a time or two. However, it is a lot easier if you all have a MSN passport, which you can get by signing up for a free Hotmail account. This will list you in the Microsoft Internet Directory, the default directory used by NetMeeting.

Note To sign up for a free Hotmail account and MSN passport, go to the MSN Web site (www.msn.com) and click the Hotmail link.

To contact someone with NetMeeting:

1. Launch NetMeeting. On the NetMeeting window, click the Find Someone button.

2. When the Find Someone window opens, as shown in Figure 38-6, choose an address book or a directory from the Select a directory box. For our example, click on the Microsoft Internet Directory, and then click the link to log on to the MSN Messenger service (if necessary). Your MSN Messenger contacts list will be displayed. If you need to add some people to the contacts list, open Messenger and click Add to locate contacts.

Figure 38-6: The first part of contacting users is to find them in the MSN Messenger contact list. Your contacts must be online for you to call them.

3. A meeting participant must be online to make a call. Click their name in the list of Contacts Currently Online. It may take a minute and several tries to establish a connection.

When you have connected to the call, the names of the meeting participants will appear in the list in the lower half of the NetMeeting window. If they have audio and/or video capabilities, you should receive those signals now.

Tip If either caller has anything less than an ISDN-quality Internet connection, the connection quality will probably be poor. If you are having trouble communicating effectively with sound and video, click the Chat button at the bottom of the NetMeeting screen and use the chat window to type messages to the group.

Everyone who is currently in the call will be shown in the lower half of the window, as illustrated in Figure 38-7. Video may also be shown if there is enough bandwidth to allow it.

Figure 38-7: A call is underway in NetMeeting.

Selecting another server

NetMeeting only has one server configured in the program: Microsoft's Internet Directory. If you use another server, you need to have the address for it and enter it manually. Click Tools ➪ Options, and on the General tab type the address of the server in the Directory box.

Note Again, you'll find that it is much easier to make calls with NetMeeting if you simply use Microsoft's Internet Directory. The only drawback is that everyone must have an MSN Passport. At least they are free.

Making Your Point with Whiteboarding

The whiteboard gets its name from the big write-on/wipe-off board that you've seen used in many offices and classrooms. They are helpful for illustrating a point during a meeting. When you are sitting in a board room brainstorming with coworkers, for example, someone invariably has a colored pen and is writing ideas up on the board as you throw them out, or they are drawing pictures to better illustrate their point.

NetMeeting's whiteboard performs a similar function. While you are online, you can toss ideas up on the board and see which ones stick. When someone in the meeting starts the Whiteboard feature, it appears on everyone's monitor, like the one shown in Figure 38-8. Each person can contribute and all others can see what he or she has added.

Figure 38-8: Everyone involved in the meeting can see and work on the whiteboard.

To start Whiteboard, click the Whiteboard tool at the bottom of the Current Call window. If you prefer, you can open the Tools menu and choose the Whiteboard command.

If you wish to keep a copy of everyone's comments shown on the Whiteboard, save it by opening the File menu, choosing Save, and typing a name for the file. The default format for Whiteboard files is .nmw, which can only be used in the Whiteboard program.

Sharing Applications and Collaborating

Another tool available in the Current Call window of NetMeeting is the Share Program tool. This tool enables you to share an open application with other participants — whatever you display on your monitor is available on theirs, whether or not they have that application on their computers. The first time I used this feature, it blew my mind. For example, you can actually help design a new company logo using a copy of Photoshop that's running on a colleague's computer located in another state. Amazing.

Caution Again, just because you can use Netmeeting to share applications, that doesn't mean you always should. If some of the meeting members have slow connections or limited RAM, they could run into problems and even encounter a system crash.

To share an application using NetMeeting:

1. Launch the application you wish to share with the rest of the group. This can be any application, such as Word, Excel, Photoshop, or even Opera. Then open the file you plan to work on during the meeting.

2. Click the Share Program button at the bottom of the NetMeeting window.

3. Choose the name of the application you want to share from the Sharing dialog, which is shown in Figure 38-9. The application and the file appear on all participants' monitors.

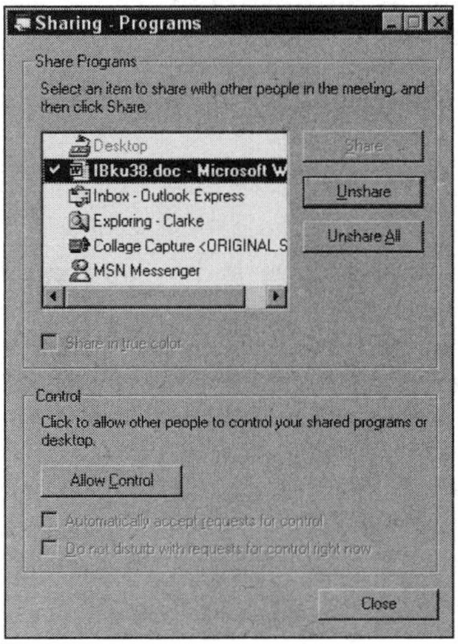

Figure 38-9: Select the program you want to share and click Share.

At this point, everyone can see the shared file, but only you can work on it. If you want to allow other meeting participants to edit the file during the meeting, click the Allow Control button in the Sharing dialog. Now anyone can edit the file — even if they don't have the application or the file stored on their computers.

When a file is being shared in this way, only one person can be in control of the pointer at any one time. The initials of the person in control of the pointer are shown beneath the pointer on everyone's screen. To take control of the pointer, click the mouse.

If bandwidth is limited, you may find that it is difficult to share applications effectively. Again, experiment to see what works well for you. When you are done sharing, click Unshare.

Chatting with the Group Online

Chatting has been around for quite a while on the Internet — it's fun, it's addictive, but is it businesslike? It's professional if you determine what you'll be chatting about in your meeting and stick to that. The Chat feature in NetMeeting works just like chat in Internet chatrooms: All the typed conversation scrolls in a window, so everyone can read what's going on.

To start a NetMeeting chat:

1. Click Chat after the Current Call window is displayed. The Chat window appears. The title bar tells you how many people are participating in your call.

2. Type your comments in the Message line and then press Enter. The message appears in the main portion of the Chat window, and your name is listed to the left of the text. The other participants will be able to see and respond to your comments in the same way.

Note

It is possible to send private messages to one person in the group rather than dis-playing everything it to the entire group. If you want to speak directly to a member, type your message in the Message box; but before you press Enter, click the Send to: down-arrow and choose the person's name from the displayed list. This will "whisper" to that person without the others looking on.

One of the great things about chat is that when you are finished, you can save the entire dialog as a text file and open it using a word processing program. This gives you a discussion log that allows you to save the text of your discussion. This is important if you don't want the great ideas spawned by your synergistic assembly to float away downstream.

Conferencing Large and Small

Even though NetMeeting is the online conferencing software used to demonstrate cybermeetings in this chapter, it's by no means the only program of its type out there. This section lists some other online conferencing programs you might want to check out.

Intel Video Phone

The Intel Internet Video Phone (http://www.intel.com/pccamera/), which is part of Intel's Create & Share Camera Packs, is a conferencing tool similar to Microsoft NetMeeting. Intel's video phone was designed to be used for person-to-person video calls over the Internet, rather than for meetings of large groups. If all you want to do is have a video call with one person — your grandchild across the country, for example — the Intel package is far simpler to use.

Figure 38-10 shows the Intel Video Phone window. As you can see, the interface is simple to use. As with anything that uses the Internet to transfer information, bandwidth will be your biggest limitation. If you plan to make video calls, try to get a high speed Internet connection.

Figure 38-10: Intel's Video Phone is very simple to use for one-on-one video calls.

The Intel Video Phone automatically uses a directory service set up by Intel. Because Intel provides you with an extra CD, you can use the Video Phone to call other people who don't have a Video Phone or the Create & Share package. The CD even comes with its own shipping envelope; just address it, affix postage, and send it to anyone who has a Pentium 166 MMX computer with 32 MB of RAM running Windows 95 or higher. Of course, you won't be able to receive video from them if they don't have a camera, but at least they will be able to see you.

Note   Not surprisingly, Intel recommends that the Video Phone only be used with a genuine Intel processor. However, we tested an Intel PC Camera Pack with USB camera on an AMD K6-2-400 system and it worked just fine.

To place a call using Video Phone:

1. Open the Intel Video Phone program and connect to the Internet. The person you plan to call must also be online and have their Intel Video Phone software running.

2. Click Call. In the Make an Internet Call dialog, enter the e-mail address of the person you plan to call and click OK.

3. A message should appear to let you know that the program is contacting the user. If they accept the call, sound and video should be established.

If you are having bandwidth problems, consider disabling the full video and simply conversing using audio. The Video Phone software lets you take and exchange snapshots during your call, which can be a good way to exchange pictures when a slow Internet connection won't allow full motion video. Figure 38-11 shows the snapshot window in Intel's Video Phone. To open this window, click Share ➪ Snapshots.

Figure 38-11: Snapshots let you exchange pictures even when limited bandwidth makes video impractical.

DataBeam's T.120 Toolkits

DataBeam (http://www.databeam.com/) doesn't replace NetMeeting as an online conferencing tool; the program extends NetMeeting's capabilities. The T.120 Toolkits provide additional security features, shared resources, help for hosting large online conferences, and increased flexibility.

HoneyCom

HoneyCom, by Honey Software (http://www.honeysw.com/), enables you to meet with other individuals or host a group meeting online. With support for voice, conferencing, video, chat, file transfer, and more, HoneyCom is a shareware program available for $29.95 after the free 30-day trial period.

TeleVu 2000

As its name suggests, TeleVu 2000 (http://www.televu.com/tv2000/default.htm) focuses on video communication and conferencing. TeleVu 2000 gives you the ability to capture full color images recorded by camcorders, VCRs, or digital cameras. You can also use graphics produced by scanners or imported from other graphics programs.

TeleVu 2000 uses what the manufacturer calls a 3-in-1 remote imaging system to provide image conferencing. TeleVu 2000 conferencing includes a whiteboard, personal communications, and remote access to other computers.

Mirabilis' ICQ

Mirabilis (http://www.mirabilis.com/)claims that ICQ is the Internet's largest online communications network.

One of the great things about ICQ is its ability to know when your coworkers are logged on to the Internet. If they are running ICQ while connected, an indicator on your desktop shows that they are online. You can then call them and invite them to chat. These things can be done impromptu or as part of a plan; you'll find a whole host of meeting places for your larger groups. What's the downside? Each person participating has to have the ICQ instant messaging program installed and running. The program is free, but it does require a sizable chunk of hard disk space and RAM as it runs.

Cross-Reference   To learn more about Mirabilis' ICQ and other instant messaging programs, take a look at Chapter 22, "Taking Time to Chat."

PowWOW

PowWOW (`http://www.powwow.com/`) is offered by Tribal Voice, a company that puts itself forth as supporting the management of Internet communities. The program offers voice messaging, chat rooms, bulletin boards, games, and more. The idea is built around the "virtual communities" concept, that people who gather in an Internet community share similar ideas, objectives, or interests. The program is available free of charge from the PowWOW Web site.

Summary

This chapter has explored one of the great uses of the Internet — bringing people together for online meetings. You learned how online meetings happen, how to contact people, and what types of programs help to facilitate an online meeting. You learned a bit about NetMeeting, the predominant online conferencing software in use today, and discovered its many online conferencing features, such as whiteboarding, program sharing, and chatting.

✦   ✦   ✦

Appendixes

What's This URL Stuff?

If you want to call someone on the telephone, what kind of information do you need to know before you can place that call? What if you want to send someone a birthday present? What information do you need before you send the parcel? In these cases, telephone numbers and street addresses provide critical information that help you make these things to happen. No phone number, no call. No street address? Return to sender.

On the Internet, too, each location must have a way of identifying itself, an address that cybersurfers can use to find their way there. This address is called a Uniform Resource Locator — URL for short — and is a critical piece of information that you'll need to find a resource on the Internet. The most familiar type of URL is a Web site address, which might look something like this:

```
http://www.yahoo.com/
```

These addresses have become ubiquitous during the last few of years; "dot com" is now part of our everyday speech, and children recognize Web addresses before they even learn how to read. But familiar or not, those of us who did *not* grow up hearing and seeing URLs for everything from soda pop to government agencies may have a hard time fully understanding what all those little symbols and letters mean. This section explains URLs so you can better comprehend their meaning and proper use.

Following Uniform Resource Locator Protocols

When we discuss URLs, most people immediately think of Web site addresses. This is misleading because such addresses are only one type of URL. Addresses for e-mail, newsgroups, and FTP sites all qualify as Uniform Resource Locators, and identifying each one is relatively easy. But how do you know what kind of URL you are looking at?

To answer this question, we need to understand the basic parts of the URL. Most URLs break down like this:

```
<protocol>://<domain>/<path>
```

Exceptions to this are e-mail and newsgroup addresses, but we'll get to those later. For now let's discuss the parts listed above. The first thing you see is the Internet *protocol*. Table A-1 lists the protocols that you are most likely to encounter.

Table A-1 URL Protocols		
Protocol	**Full Name**	**Description**
FTP	File Transfer Protocol	A basic method for transmitting files over the Internet. Sometimes used to download large files, such as shareware or technical documents.
Gopher	Gopher	Now something of a relic, Gopher sites used to be a common way to download files from government and educational institutions.
HTTP	HyperText Transfer Protocol	This is the most familiar type of URL used today. Most World Wide Web documents (such as Web pages) use the HTTP protocol.
Mailto	Electronic Mail	This protocol indicates an e-mail address. It is usually not seen by most Internet users.
News	Usenet News	Indicates a Usenet newsgroup. Like Mailto, this protocol is usually hidden.

Modern Web browsers let you access FTP, Gopher, and HTTP protocols directly. The protocol is the first thing listed in the address, and you can see this in the address bar of your browser. In Figure A-1, you can see that I have accessed an HTTP resource, in this case a Web page.

With FTP, Gopher, and HTTP, the protocol is separated from the rest of the URL by a colon and two forward slashes (`://`). It is important that you use the correct type of slash marks when typing a URL, because if you type in a back slash (\) it won't work.

Road Test Garage - Microsoft Internet Explorer
File Edit View Favorites Tools Help
Back Forward Stop Refresh Home Search Favorites History Mail Print Edit
Links Best of the Web
Address http://www.proaxis.com/~kcunderdahl/garage.htm
Go

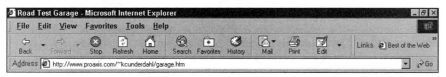

Figure A-1: The address bar shows that I have accessed an HTTP resource.

Using Domain Names

The next thing you will see after the `://` is the *domain*. The domain identifies what computer on the Internet you are trying to access. This computer is also sometimes referred to as the host. In Figure A-2, you can see that the host computer is called `ftp.proaxis.com` and that this is an FTP resource.

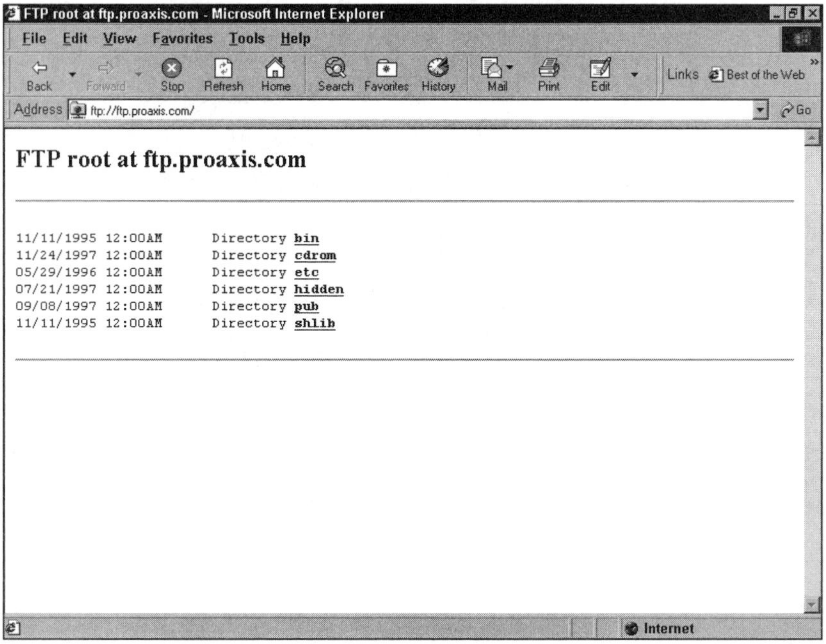

FTP root at ftp.proaxis.com - Microsoft Internet Explorer
File Edit View Favorites Tools Help
Back Forward Stop Refresh Home Search Favorites History Mail Print Edit
Links Best of the Web
Address ftp://ftp.proaxis.com/
Go
FTP root at ftp.proaxis.com
11/11/1995 12:00AM Directory bin
11/24/1997 12:00AM Directory cdrom
05/29/1996 12:00AM Directory etc
07/21/1997 12:00AM Directory hidden
09/08/1997 12:00AM Directory pub
11/11/1995 12:00AM Directory shlib
Internet

Figure A-2: The domain, or host computer, is `ftp.proaxis.com`.

One interesting thing to note is that the URLs shown in Figures A-1 and A-2 both appear to come from the same host (Proaxis). Although in this case they actually are on the same computer (although one is an FTP resource and the other HTTP), you should keep in mind that this is not always the case. For instance, if we go to `http://www.irs.com/`, we will see the Web site of a company called irs.com, an independent tax consultation service. But `http://www.irs.gov/` takes us to a Web site of the U.S. Internal Revenue Service, as shown in Figure A-3. That's because there are also different parts of the domain name.

In the domain `www.irs.gov`, the `www` stands for World Wide Web, and `irs.gov` refers to the actual domain. The suffix of the domain—in this case `.gov`—indicates the top-level domain (TLD) to which this domain belongs. TLDs are assigned much more liberally than they used to be, and for that matter many Web sites don't have `www` in front of them any more. The important thing is that if you want to visit a specific site, make sure you type the URL correctly or you may not get to the correct place.

Figure A-3: Although this page could easily be mistaken for almost any commercial Web site, the `.gov` suffix in the URL tells us that this is actually the Tax Man's Official Online Presence.

Tracing File Paths

Once you have determined the protocol and domain of the computer you are trying to reach, you must specify a path to the desired file. This tells your Web browser which directory on the domain to look in, and which file to retrieve. The path must be separated from the domain name by a single forward slash (/). Additional forward slashes might be used to indicate subdirectories in the domain.

Look at the address bar in Figure A-1. You can see that the page uses the HTTP protocol and is located on a computer identified by the domain name `www.proaxis.com`. Proaxis is actually an Internet Service Provider, and somewhere on the hard drive of the proaxis.com server is a directory that stores files for customer's personal Web pages. The name of the directory for this customer (yours truly) is `~kcunderdahl`, which you can see is separated from the domain by a /. This directory name is in turn followed by another /, and then the filename of the Web page (`garage.htm`). If I had created some subdirectories within the directory `~kcunderdahl`, they would each be separated by /. But as you can see, I just put this file in my main directory.

When typing a URL, you can sometimes leave off the filename. For instance, type the following into the address bar of your browser:

```
http://www.proaxis.com/~kcunderdahl/
```

Notice that you have only indicated a directory in the path, but not a filename. By default, the browser looks for a file with a name such as `index.html` or `home.html` or something like that. If none exists, you might see a list of files and subdirectories in that directory similar to what appears in Figure A-2. But generally speaking, Web publishers include a file in their root directory that serves as a home page, and that is what loads when the browser looks for `index.html` or `home.html`. Now try typing this:

```
http://www.proaxis.com/
```

Proaxis has its own home page, and that is what you should see if you type in this URL. In fact, most modern browsers let you leave off a lot of that address stuff, as long as you are looking for a site on the World Wide Web. To get to the Proaxis Web site, all you should really have to type is `www.proaxis.com` and then press Enter, and the browser fills in the `http://` and /. Sometimes it works this easily and sometimes it doesn't, so it's best to know the entire URL of a site you want to access.

Addressing E-mail Addresses

As you know, an e-mail address is really just another type of URL. The full syntax for an e-mail address looks like this:

```
mailto:<account>@<domain>
```

The `mailto:` indicates the protocol being used, and it is usually hidden. The only time you are likely to see it is if you are viewing the source code of a Web page. Figure A-4 shows what will happen if you click View ➪ Source for a Web page in Internet Explorer. A Notepad window opens showing the HTML coding that was used to create the Web page.

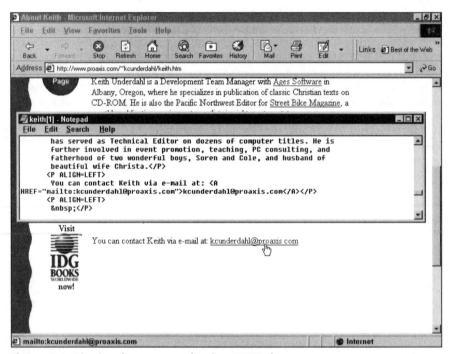

Figure A-4: Viewing the source code of an HTML document

At the bottom of the Web page shown in Figure A-4 is a link that viewers can click to send the site author an e-mail. To facilitate this process, an HTML instruction has been entered that starts with the protocol `mailto:` and then lists the e-mail address. While some of the first browsers were unable to interpret this instruction, modern software can identify a `mailto:` link and automatically launch an e-mail application such as Eudora or Outlook Express. When the e-mail window opens, the address listed in the source code should be automatically inserted in the To field.

Normally, you won't have to worry about the `mailto:` protocol stuff—it's something that happens behind the scenes while you work. However, you will need to know the rest of the address if you want to send e-mail to someone. Usually, the first part of the address is that person's account. In the case of my e-mail address, you can recognize that the name of my account with Proaxis is "kcunderdahl." The second part of the address follows the @ symbol and indicates the domain name of my ISP. Notice the similarities between my e-mail address and Web site address:

```
kcunderdahl@proaxis.com
http://www.proaxis.com/~kcunderdahl/
```

If you understand how URLs are constructed, but you only know my Web site address, it should be fairly easy for you to infer what my e-mail address will be, and vice versa. Most ISPs, even the larger national services such as MindSpring and Prodigy, construct their subscribers' e-mail and Web site URLs in a similar manner. Thus, as long as you know the person's account name and ISP, you should be able to figure out the rest.

Addressing Usenet Newsgroups

Now we come to the last URL protocol, news. The syntax for Usenet addresses is simple:

```
news:<newsgroup name>
```

Individual messages posted on a newsgroup have their own URL, as follows:

```
news:<message-ID>
```

As with the `mailto:` protocol, the `news:` is usually hidden. If your Web browser encounters a `news:` link, it should automatically launch your news reader program and show whatever newsgroup was specified in the link. Typically when you link to a newsgroup in this manner, your news viewer will not automatically subscribe you to the group. For more on using newsgroups, see Chapter 23, "Finding and Using Newsgroups."

✦   ✦   ✦

An Internet Primer

You've probably been hearing about the Internet for several years now. The newness has worn off, and this electronic phenomenon has pervaded into virtually every aspect of modern life. In spite of this, you may still have some questions about what exactly the Internet is and where it came from. We're not going to bore you with a lot of useless trivia, but we will tell you what you need to know to make the best use of this medium.

Looking Back at the History of the Internet

To begin with, let's take a look back at how the Internet began, and where it has come since then. If you were to create a timeline of technological innovations during the twentieth century, you'd have to start right at the beginning of the 20th century and consider the dramatic innovations in transportation, the most emblematic of which was the introduction of the automobile. Before then, one would move from one place to another by walking, riding a horse or carriage, or catching a train. People just didn't have the ability to go very far very fast. Now, at the beginning of the 21st century, the automobile and the airplane have become such integral parts of modern life that we think nothing of hopping in our cars and zipping down to the convenience store just for a jug of milk, or flying half way around the world in less than a day!

In the 20th century, the evolution of communication was no less dramatic. In 1900 the telephone and telegraph enabled relatively fast communication, but they were usually reserved for the wealthy and the fortunate. Letters written on paper still comprised the bulk of long distance communication. Today the telephone is almost ubiquitous in the developed world, and computers and the Internet are opening new avenues of communication just as the telephone did a century ago.

Computers made their first appearance at about the middle of the twentieth century. Those early computers were huge, unreliable, and slow, but they still did things that were almost impossible through any other means. Your modern wristwatch or microwave oven has many times the computing power of those early computers.

Personal computers came into being in the last quarter of the century. At about the same time a loose collection of government and university computers was creating the foundation for what we now call the Internet. PCs and the Internet didn't really meet until the mid-1990s with the appearance of the World Wide Web.

The Internet is evolving at a tremendous rate, so fast that what you knew about it yesterday may have changed by tomorrow. Still, some simple but useful descriptions of the Internet will give you a better understanding of all the hype.

✦ The precursor to the Internet began in 1969 as a project called ARPANET commissioned by the United States Department of Defense and conducted by Advanced Research Projects Agency (ARPA). The idea was to connect government and university computers so that, in the event of a nuclear war, messages could still be sent even if part of the network had been destroyed. This is the idea that makes the Internet work today — no one computer on the Internet is so important that it has much effect on the rest of the network if it fails.

✦ The *Internet* is a term used to describe the way millions of computers around the world are linked into a huge network so they can easily share files and communicate with one another.

✦ No one owns the Internet. No one giant company or government agency owns or controls the Internet. A number of independent standards organizations work toward making certain everyone can communicate using the same protocols, but that's a far cry from saying anyone controls the Internet.

✦ The reason you can't just connect to the Internet without paying for access is simple — you need to be able to connect to one of the *backbones* — essentially the actual network cables — that link the various servers on the Internet. Your Internet Service Provider (or ISP) has this type of connection, either directly or through a very expensive link. You probably connect to the Internet by dialing in to the computers at your ISP, and their computers forward your messages to the Internet.

✦ Information traveling over the Internet is transferred using a protocol called TCP/IP (Transmission Control Protocol/Internet Protocol). This protocol breaks data down into packets to minimize the chance that parts of the data will be lost. The packets are directed to the proper destination via routers that interpret Internet addresses and pass the packets along. A packet may pass through many routers on its way to its destination.

So if the Internet is really just a big network that no one owns, what good is it to you? How could anyone get excited about a bunch of computers that are hooked together?

If the Internet hadn't grown as explosively as it has in the past few years, the answers would be a whole lot different. A network of 50 or so computers (which is just about how the Internet started out) wouldn't do a whole lot for most of us—many large offices have more PCs than that on their local networks. But a worldwide network of millions of computers is a different story. With millions of computers online, your options are virtually endless. Consider just some of the things you can do with the Internet today:

✦ You can send e-mail to almost any computer in the world.

✦ You can access information in libraries, on government sites, and on commercial sites around the world no matter what the time.

✦ You can share your own information with people all around the globe at no expense beyond your basic Internet access charges.

✦ You can find music and entertainment to suit any taste.

✦ You can shop from the comfort of your home at any hour of the day.

✦ You can participate in discussion groups on thousands of different subjects.

✦ You can get exact directions from your house to anywhere you want to go, and even get information about any road construction you might encounter along the way.

Of course this list is really just the beginning—you'll find a lot more as you try out the Internet for yourself. (For a taste of what's out there, take a look at Part VI of this book, which presents a directory of various Web sites.)

Defining the World Wide Web

The World Wide Web (WWW) is actually just one of several parts of the Internet. It just happens to be the most popular part of the Internet, and a lot of people don't really know the difference.

Information has to be accessible in order to be useful—otherwise it's just data. If you're going to learn about ferrets, you need to know where to look for the information. Imagine for a moment that someone gave you a complete set of printed encyclopedias and that you wanted to look up ferrets in the 30 printed volumes. You'd probably start by looking at the spines on each volume until you found the one that covered the letter F because it would likely list ferrets. That is, you would make a link between the letter F on the spine and the subjects in the volume. Without that link you'd have to figure out for yourself where you might find the subject of ferrets in the thousands of pages of text.

The idea behind the Web is a similar one—you need useful links if you're going to be able to find the information you want among the millions of pages of online documents. On the Web these links are a special type of electronic connection, known as a hyperlinks. These hyperlinks provide a unique method of retrieving information—when you click a link the document associated with the link is displayed. For example, in Figure B-1 you can see that a link is highlighted (the mouse pointer has changed to a hand) on the IDG Books Worldwide Web site. If you click this link, the new Web page is displayed in place of the one currently on the screen.

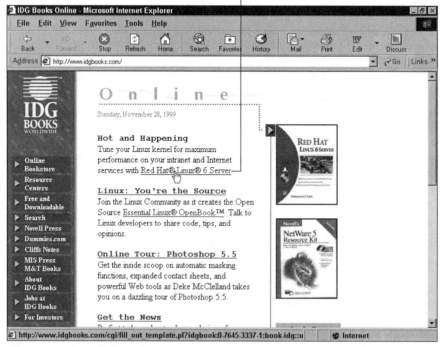

Figure B-1: Hyperlinks make information accessible on the Web.

Links are possible because all Web documents have a unique URL—Uniform Resource Locator. This is just a fancy way of saying that every document has an address that identifies its location on the Internet. Just as street addresses help you find your way to someone's house, URLs help you find your way to documents.

Cross-Reference   If you'd like to learn more about URLs, see Appendix A, "What's this URL Stuff?"

Discovering the beginnings of the Web

Even though the Internet has been around for over 30 years, the Web itself began with a proposal in March 1989 by Tim Berners-Lee at CERN, a physics lab in Geneva, Switzerland. The proposal was for a hypertext system—essentially a method of making documents available on the Internet using hyperlinks to locate those documents.

In March 1991 the first trials of the Web were begun, but it would be another two years before the first graphical Web browsers were available. One of these, Mosaic, was developed by Marc Andreessen at NCSA (the National Center for Supercomputing Applications) in Champaign, Illinois. Mosaic was really the browser that made the Web popular and available to the masses. In fact, in 1994 Marc Andreessen left NCSA and formed a company that produced a commercial version of Mosaic that you just may have heard of—Netscape Navigator.

What began as a proposal that would facilitate the sharing of information between members of the high-energy physics research community grew into what most people now think of as the Internet—even though the Web is really just one part of the Internet. With the Web's explosive growth, the Web became too much for CERN to manage. In July 1994 a new organization was formed to direct the future standards and growth of the Web. This organization, the World Wide Web Consortium—W3C for short—is responsible for setting the standards everyone uses when developing products for the Web. Figure B-2 shows the W3C Web site, `http://www.w3.org/`.

Understanding how the Web works

The Web is a part of the Internet that is based on pages programmed using *HTML*—HyperText Markup Language. HTML is a fairly simple computer authoring languages, and has a major advantage over some other programming languages— it doesn't require any specific type of computer to run. This means that you can view HTML pages on any computer that has a Web browser.

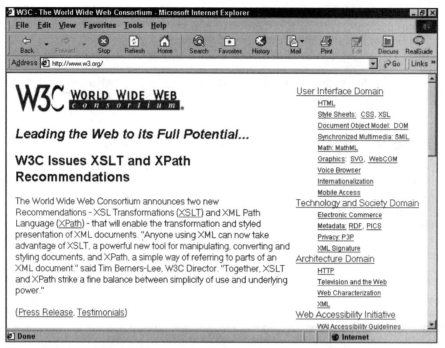

Figure B-2: To find out the latest official information about the Web, visit the W3C Web site.

In simple terms, an HTML document is similar to many of the old word processor documents that were common on personal computers in the days before *WYSIWYG* (What You See Is What You Get) displays became the norm. In those early days, you inserted codes into your documents to control how the document would print. For example, you might have added something like {BB} to start making text boldface, and {BE} to stop using boldface. Everything between the two codes would then appear boldface in the printout, but the "bold begin" and "bold end" tags wouldn't appear in the printout. HTML documents use a similar series of tags to begin and end attributes.

In an HTML document, certain keywords are used as tags. These keywords are part of the HTML language and are understood by all Web browsers. When a browser encounters a tag, the browser knows how to display the information that follows based upon the tag itself. For example, Figure B-3 shows some of the source code that creates the IDG Books Worldwide home page (as seen earlier in Figure B-1). The second line of the text contains a tag <head> that begins the page head, and the fourteenth line contains the tag </head> to end the page head. All HTML tags work the same way—a beginning tag is followed by an ending tag that includes a forward slash (/) just before the tag name. Of course, between the tags there can be a little or a lot of information.

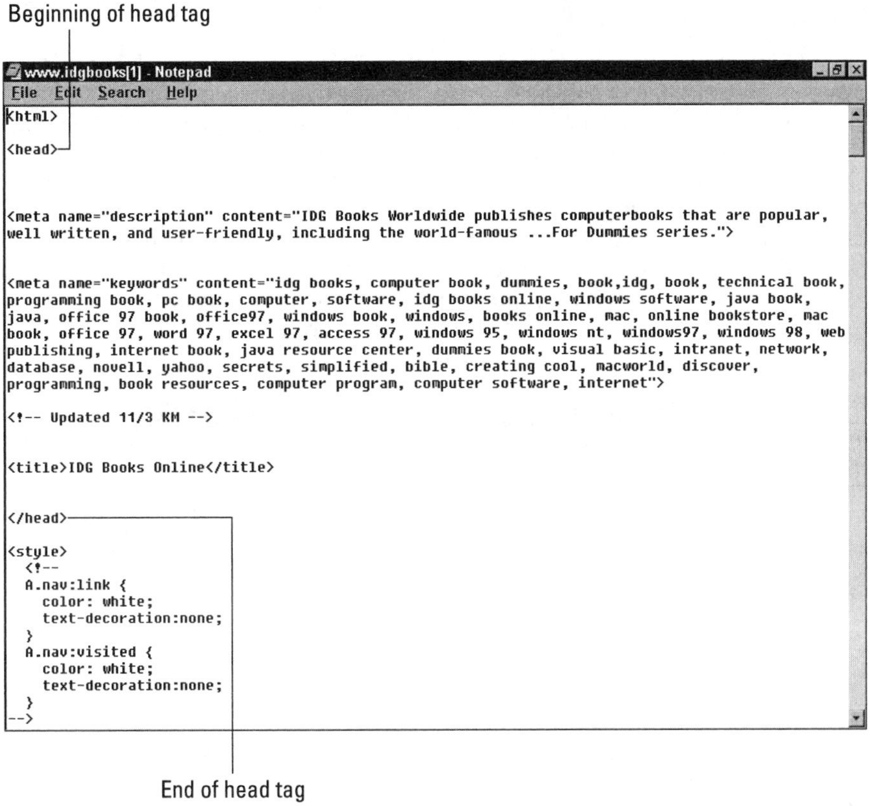
Beginning of head tag
www.idgbooks[1] - Notepad
File Edit Search Help
End of head tag

```
<html>

<head>


<meta name="description" content="IDG Books Worldwide publishes computerbooks that are popular,
well written, and user-friendly, including the world-famous ...For Dummies series.">


<meta name="keywords" content="idg books, computer book, dummies, book,idg, book, technical book,
programming book, pc book, computer, software, idg books online, windows software, java book,
java, office 97 book, office97, windows book, windows, books online, mac, online bookstore, mac
book, office 97, word 97, excel 97, access 97, windows 95, windows nt, windows97, windows 98, web
publishing, internet book, java resource center, dummies book, visual basic, intranet, network,
database, novell, yahoo, secrets, simplified, bible, creating cool, macworld, discover,
programming, book resources, computer program, computer software, internet">

<!-- Updated 11/3 KM -->


<title>IDG Books Online</title>


</head>

<style>
  <!--
  A.nav:link {
    color: white;
    text-decoration:none;
  }
  A.nav:visited {
    color: white;
    text-decoration:none;
  }
-->
```

Figure B-3: Web pages are created using HTML — a fairly simple authoring language.

Fortunately for you, your Web browser takes care of the task of converting the HTML code into the colorful and graphical Web pages you're used to seeing as you browse the Web. Even so, it's important to understand that this simple authoring language is what makes the Web possible. Because HTML was specifically designed to facilitate hyperlinks, your Web browser is able to load HTML documents from anywhere on the Web with just a click of your mouse button. When you consider how powerful a concept this is, you have to be amazed at how simply it works!

Discovering What's Hidden on the Internet

Although it may seem like all there is to the Internet is the Web, this is not the case. You'll actually find a lot of other interesting things on the Internet. You may have to search a little to find them, but you'll find some pretty interesting rewards for some of those searches.

Let's have a quick look at some of the things you'll find "hidden" on the Internet.

Usenet Newsgroups

Usenet newsgroups are essentially the talk radio of the Internet. They are discussion groups where anyone can jump in and ask questions, post comments, or even make rude remarks about another participant. Want to meet with a bunch of people from around the world who share your interest in ferrets? Want to learn how to keep your old Xerox computer running? Or maybe you'd like to learn all about the stars in your favorite sci-fi show? Or join a worldwide discussion on poetry? Or download MP3 music of your favorite bands? All of these are possible in Usenet newsgroups. For example, Figure B-4 shows just some of the newsgroups that have "computer" in their names. If you can't find a subject that interests you among the 100,000+ Usenet newsgroups, you're probably not trying very hard!

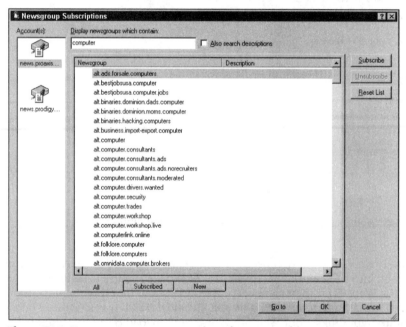

Figure B-4: Usenet newsgroups cover just about any subject you can imagine.

Caution   Unfortunately, newsgroups generally also include lots of postings of extremely rank, adult material that has nothing whatsoever to do with the newsgroup topic. You probably can't avoid this completely, but you can do the next best thing — ignore it.

Cross-Reference   Chapter 23, "Finding and Using Newsgroups," provides more information on Usenet newsgroups.

Mailing lists

Usenet newsgroups aren't the only Internet discussion groups. A lot of very useful information is exchanged through mailing lists. One huge advantage of mailing lists compared to most newsgroups is that many mailing lists are *moderated* — someone is responsible for what is and isn't posted to such lists. Although this can prevent some legitimate comments from being posted, it does tend to keep the discussion on the subject and reduces the level of rude or inappropriate content to an absolute minimum.

Another good thing about mailing lists is that they can be highly specialized. You may be interested in a Usenet newsgroup on poetry, but if your interest is narrower than that, how about a mailing list devoted to haiku poetry? Mailing lists make specialization easy.

Figure B-5 shows one typical mailing list, the Adaptec CD-R Users' List. This list covers all areas relating to CD recordable technology, and is an extremely useful resource for anyone interested in this subject.

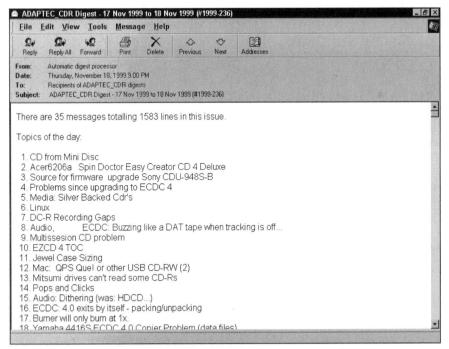

Figure B-5: Mailing lists provide well-focused discussions of the list topics.

You can find many mailing lists at Liszt, the mailing list directory at http://www.liszt.com/. In addition, you'll often find mailing lists you can subscribe to at various Web sites, such as one run by a hardware or software manufacturer.

FTP

FTP stands for File Transfer Protocol — a means of sending files across the Internet. FTP was around long before the Web, and remains an excellent means of quickly obtaining useful files from Internet FTP sites.

Although you can transfer files using your Web browser, FTP offers several advantages instead. Without the overhead of the Web, FTP file transfers are often much faster than transferring files using a Web browser. In addition, if you use software such as WS_FTP or Fetch, you can transfer a whole series of files at one time, rather than waiting for each download to complete.

Tip

When you visit the Microsoft FTP site at `ftp.microsoft.com`, be sure to start by downloading either `dirmap.txt` or `dirmap.htm` (the HTML version of dirmap. txt). These files provide a map of the FTP site and will help you find the files you'd like to download.

Cross-Reference

Chapter 17, "Finding Cool Software on the Web," provides much more information on using FTP.

Chat

Chat is probably best described as a community party line where you can get together and talk to other people from around the world. The conversations may extend over a broad range of topics, or they may be focused into a narrow area — such as a technical support chat about a specific product.

Figure B-6 shows a typical conversation you might encounter using Microsoft Chat — a chat program that uses comic characters to make chat sessions a little more interesting.

Cross-Reference

Chapter 22, "Taking Time to Chat," shows you how to use Chat and how to find Chat rooms that suit your interests.

Telnet, Gopher, and other delights

At one time the Internet was entirely text based. To access a remote computer you had to use *Telnet* — a terminal emulator that enabled your computer to act as if it were a terminal on a remote computer. If you wanted to find information on remote systems, you probably would have used *Gopher* — a network of archives of text-based information. You might have searched Gopherspace with search engines such as *Archie* or *Veronica* — but none of these was very easy to learn or use. As opposed to the user-friendly graphical environment of today's Web, all of these early Internet services were aimed directly at the dedicated computer nerd.

Figure B-6: Chat enables people to communicate with each other over the Internet.

The Internet is thriving, especially the World Wide Web. Older technologies inevitably fade in the shadow of the Web, and Gopherspace is one of them. These days the text-based Internet is all but dead. Oh sure, if you really want five-year-old weather forecasts you can still find them on some of the Gopher sites. But for all practical purposes, these relics of the past are pretty much gone.

✦　　　✦　　　✦

Using the Internet Bible CD-ROM

Using the Internet Bible, 2nd Edition CD-ROM

The *Internet Bible,* 2nd Edition CD-ROM contains a number of excellent applications. Some of those programs are freeware, and others are shareware and only free for a short trial period. This appendix discusses the different types of software on the CD-ROM, and we also tell you how to install and uninstall the various applications.

In addition to the freeware and shareware, we have included an HTML version of the Web Directory.

Freeware and Shareware

It is extremely important that we distinguish between the two types of software offered on the *Internet Bible,* 2nd Edition CD-ROM. The software roughly breaks down into two categories: freeware and shareware. *Freeware* is a compound word derived from the words *free* and *software. Free*, in this instance, means that you do not need to pay any money for its use, you don't have to register it, you won't be asked to provide your mother's maiden name to its authors, and you can continue to use it as long as you want. Freeware is generous, but it is also rare. Always check the license agreement for any software you plan to use to see whether it is free or not.

The rest of the software you will find on this CD-ROM is *shareware*. It is a simple fact of life that people need to make a living. That fact extends to software developers, who often have a hard time selling their products simply because no one knows about those products. So in an effort to "spread the word" about the great software they have to offer the world, many developers have embraced the concept of *shareware*. Shareware is distributed free of charge through a variety of methods, including book-related CD-ROMs such as this.

The most important fact to remember about shareware is that it isn't free. Usually, you are allowed to "test" the shareware for a specific period for free, presumably to decide if the software suits your needs or not. At the end of the period you must register the software and pay a specified fee to continue use. The trial period is usually enforced using one of several methods:

✦ Some shareware simply uses the honor system. This is the most trusting method, and it is entirely up to you to decide when to send in the fee. It is also not very common anymore.

✦ A warning message may appear after the trial period has expired. Sometimes, this message only appears when you first launch the program, but sometimes the warning message is prominent in every window of the program.

✦ At the end of the trial period, some shareware ceases to function. An internal counter records when you first installed the program, and at the end of the period the program no longer works. With other shareware, certain key features are disabled at the end of the trial period.

✦ Many shareware applications have fewer features than the full version, thus they only give you a "taste" of the fully featured version. These limited-feature programs are often referred to as "lite" versions.

Every shareware program is a little different, so you should always read the software's licensing agreement to find out exactly what is expected. Table C-1 lists the software applications that you'll find on the *Internet Bible,* 2nd Edition CD-ROM, both freeware and shareware.

Table C-1
Contents of the Internet Bible, 2nd Edition CD-ROM

Software Title	*Description*
1Jump	1Jump makes finding information on the Web much easier.
602Pro Personal Office Server	Out of the office? Have e-mail, faxes, and voice mail keep up with your hectic pace with Personal Office Server.
About My Cache 1.21	About My Cache analyzes your browser's cache, and gives you information about everything stored there.

Software Title	Description
Adobe Acrobat 4.05 for Macintosh	Acrobat allows you to view documents in the Portable Document Format (.pdf)
Adobe Acrobat 4.05 for Windows	Acrobat allows you to view documents in the Portable Document Format (.pdf)
Aladdin DropStuff 5.0 for Windows	This versatile tool allows you to compress and uncompress files in the ZIP or SIT formats.
Aladdin DropStuff 5.5 for Macintosh	This versatile tool allows you to compress and uncompress files in the ZIP or SIT formats.
BlackICE Defender	Is your machine really safe from security breaches? Make sure with BlackICE Defender.
CanOpener 1.0 for Windows	Emergency access to any file — even if the file type is unknown or the file is damaged!
CanOpener 1.0 for Macintosh	Emergency access to any file — even if the file type is unknown or the file is damaged!
Copernic 99 for Macintosh	Copernic allows you to simultaneously search multiple search engines and eliminates duplicate results.
Copernic 2000 for Windows	Copernic allows you to simultaneously search multiple search engines and eliminates duplicate results.
DownloadWizard Plus 2.5	DownloadWizard Plus can schedule downloads, check for updates, resume interrupted downloads, and help you install downloaded programs.
Dreamweaver 3.0	Are you dreaming of creating a great Web site? Make that dream a reality with Dreamweaver.
Dropit 3.4 (16- and 32-bit versions)	Dropit is used to quickly fill out those tiresome on-line forms, or anywhere else that you need to type the same information repeatedly.
EarthLink 5.0	EarthLink is one of the most popular Internet Service Providers. This software will help you get started. EarthLink 5.0 includes many additional features.
EarthLink Total Access 2.1.5 for Macintosh PowerPC	EarthLink is one of the most popular Internet Service Providers. This software will help you get started.
Eudora Pro Email v4.2.1 for Macintosh	Eudora Pro is a popular e-mail client for the Mac.

Continued

Table C-1 (continued)

Software Title	Description
Eudora Pro Email v4.2.1 for Windows	Eudora Pro is a fast and easy to use e-mail client.
GetRight (16-bit and 32-bit versions)	There is nothing quite like the frustration of losing your Internet connection after downloading 145mb of a 148mb file. With GetRight, you can pick up where you left off.
Go!Zilla 3.5	Go!Zilla is an easy-to-use download manager.
HomeSite 4.5	HomeSite is a high-performance Web page creation tool that is still easy to use.
McAfee Guard Dog	ActiveX controls can do serious damage to your data. Guard Dog protects you from hostile ActiveX code.
McAfee Virus Scan 4.0	McAfee Virus Scan is one of the most trusted names in antivirus software.
Microsoft Internet Explorer 5.0	Microsoft's Internet browser is probably the most widely used browser in the world.
MindSpring Internet Software 4.0 for MacOS 9	MindSpring is another very popular Internet Service Provider.
MindSpring Internet Software 4.0 for Windows	MindSpring is another very popular Internet Service Provider.
mIRC	MIRC is a very configurable chat client.
NeoTrace 2.12	How does data get from a Web site to your computer? Follow the route with NeoTrace.
Netscape Communicator 4.7 for Macintosh PowerPC	Netscape Communicator includes Netscape Navigator and many other add-ons.
Netscape Communicator 4.7 for Windows	Netscape Communicator includes Netscape Navigator and many other add-ons.
NetSonic 2.5	NetSonic stores Web pages you have visited on your computer so that when you return they are loaded more quickly.
Panda Anti-Virus Shareware	It's been said that 75 percent of the businesses that lose their data will go out of business. Viruses can make that nightmare a reality. Panda Anti-Virus is one of the leaders in virus protection.
Powermarks 3.07 Bookmark Manager	Bookmark Manager helps you to organize your bookmarks or favorites folders.
QuickTime 4.1	QuickTime allows you to play high-quality video clips on your computer.

Software Title	*Description*
ShrinkWrap	ShrinkWrap is used to creat an exact duplicate of files and directories or even whole disks.
Stuffit Lite for Macintosh PowerPC	Stuffit is a utility for creating and expandind SIT files.
WebPage Wizard 2.0	WebPage Wizard is an easy-to-use "WYSIWYG" (What You See Is What You Get) tool for creating Web pages.
WinZip 7.0	This is one of the most popular compression utilities available.
WS-FTP LE	Would you rather use the manual FTP commands to transfer files, or the graphical WS-FTP utility and save some typing? This is the "lite" edition.
WS-FTP Pro	Would you rather use the manual FTP commands to transfer files, or the graphical WS-FTP utility and save some typing? This is the full version.

As long as you don't think of it as free, shareware is actually a pretty good deal. Usually when you buy software, the only things you might have to go on are word of mouth and magazine reviews. And in most instances, after you've purchased software and opened the wrapper, you cannot return it for a refund. This is the simple fact of buying computer software today.

But shareware provides an interesting alternative. With shareware, you can try it out for yourself before you spend the money. If you decide you don't like it, you don't have to worry about trying to get a refund because you didn't pay anything for it in the first place. Shareware offers a simple and economical way for you to find out which software is the best for you. But don't make the mistake of thinking that all shareware programs are simple or second-rate. On the contrary; a number of them are powerful and robust. Some shareware programs, such as WinZip, are highly respected or industry standards. Give them all a go!

CD-ROM Installation Instructions

The software that's included with the *Internet Bible CD-ROM* is simple to install. Before you install anything, though, you must decide which programs you want (see the program list in Appendix C) and then find them on the CD-ROM. To browse the contents of the CD-ROM, follow these steps:

1. Insert the *Internet Bible* CD-ROM into your CD-ROM drive.

2. On your Windows' desktop, open the My Computer icon. When the My Computer window opens, find the icon for the CD-ROM drive (usually D:).

If you are using a Macintosh computer, simply look for CD icon on your desktop and click on it.

As you can see, the CD-ROM contains folders that correspond to programs on the disk. Each folder holds all of the files that are required to install that software. Once you decide which program you want to install, do the following:

1. Open the folder icon for the program you want to install.

2. What you see next varies depending on the software. If you see any files called "License" or "Readme," open them first. Double-clicking those files opens them using Notepad, a simple Windows applet for viewing and editing text documents.

3. When you finish viewing the Readme and License files (if there were any) you are ready to install the software. Browse through the contents of the program's folder until you find the installation file listed in Table C-1. It should be an executable file (ending in .exe).

4. Open the icon for the executable installation file. An easy-to-use installation wizard launches to guide you through the setup process. Each one is different, so just follow the onscreen instructions to complete the process.

Some programs on the *Internet Bible* CD-ROM do not contain an executable file in their folders. Some of them are contained in zip files. A zip file is a file that has been compressed using special software to save room on the disk. To decompress or "unzip" the file, you first need to install a program such as WinZip (also available on the CD-ROM). Once you install WinZip, simply open the zip file icon. WinZip launches automatically, and the contents of the zip file are shown. You can then open files directly from the WinZip window. Again, view any Readme.txt or License.txt files first, and then look for a file called Setup.exe or some other executable file.

Guilty by Association

Some programs will ask you if you want to associate certain file extensions with them. Associate in this case means that if you open a file of a certain type, it launches with whatever application it is associated with. For example, if HTML files are associated with Internet Explorer, Internet Explorer is launched whenever you open an HTML file.

Sometimes these associations are a good thing, and sometimes they aren't. In the case of shareware, we usually recommend that you choose "No" if you're asked about file association during the setup process. We say this because you may install the shareware and then decide a day or two later that you don't like it. While you may remember to uninstall the shareware application, there's a good chance that you will forget to undo the association thing (we always do), and the uninstallation wizard won't do it for you (life is harsh). Obviously, this can cause you some minor but annoying problems later on. And if you decide that you do like the shareware and want to keep it, it's usually a simple matter to associate those file types later on.

Note

Note that you don't need to have WinZip already installed to open the WinZip installation file itself; this file extracts itself automatically when you double-click it.

Again, every program's installation process will be a little different. Fortunately, once you find the file you want to open, installation wizards simplify the process.

Reading the Web Directory from Your CD-ROM

You've probably already been mesmerized by Part VI of the *Internet Bible*, 2nd Edition, the Web Directory. It lists countless educational, entertaining, informative, and just plain weird (and silly) Web sites all over the Internet in a simple-to-use format. To make your Web browsing experience even more enjoyable, we have included an HTML version of the Web Directory on the Internet Bible CD-ROM. You may find this a preferable way to view the directory, because you can easily link to the Web sites discussed.

Begin by opening the Web Directory HTML file with your Web browser. You can open it using several methods:

✦ Open Windows Explorer, browse to the file on the CD-ROM, and open its icon.

✦ In your Web browser window, enter the path to the Web Directory where the Web site URL usually appears (either the Address Bar or Location Bar, depending on what browser you are using). The path should be D:\Book\directory.html, where D: is the drive letter for your CD-ROM drive.

✦ Click Start ⇨ Run and browse to the file on the CD-ROM. Click Run to launch your Web browser and view the directory.

Whatever method you used to open the Web Directory, it should now appear in your Web browser window as one very large Web page. You can scroll through the document and read through the Web site descriptions at your leisure. When you see a site you want to visit, simply click the blue hyperlink listing the Web site's URL and you will be immediately transported to that site. Use your browser's Back button to return to the Web Directory.

Here's a good tip. Just in case you get lost on the Web, make it easy to get back to the Web Directory by bookmarking it first — before you wander off to the many Web links this directory brings you. To find out more about bookmarking (also called favorites), please see Chapter 15.

Uninstalling Software from the CD-ROM

If you no longer use some of the applications that you installed from the *Internet Bible* CD-ROM, it's a good idea to uninstall them. Not only will this create more free space on your hard drive and unclutter your Windows Start menu, but your system will run more efficiently. Furthermore, keep in mind that you need to uninstall any shareware applications that you decide not to register. To uninstall software, you may need to do one or more of the following:

✦ Click the Windows Start button and choose Settings ➪ Control Panel. Open the Add/Remove Programs icon and locate the program you want to get rid of in the list shown on the Install/Uninstall tab. Click Add/Remove and watch the magic unfold.

✦ Some installed programs will not show up in the Add/Remove Programs window. If this is the case, open the folder for the program in question and look for an icon titled "Uninstall . . ." If you see such an icon, open it and follow the instructions that appear in the uninstall wizard.

✦ A few very stubborn programs don't even come with an uninstall wizard. These you will have to delete manually. Open Windows Explorer by right-clicking the Start button and choosing Explore. Find the folder that was created when the program was installed and delete it.

Deleting files and folders from your hard drive is not something to be taken lightly. Dump the wrong file or folder and you'll turn your entire PC into a $2,000 paper weight faster than you can say, "Abort, Retry, or Fail." Before you delete any folders, make absolutely certain that they contain only files for the program that you mean to uninstall.

Even after you have removed the unwanted program, it may still show up in your Start menu. To get rid of unwanted links in your Start menu, open Windows Explorer by right-clicking the Start button and choosing Explore. Scroll down the folder list until you see the Start Menu folder. Expand it and browse until you find the links you no longer need. Click each one and choose Delete from the Explorer toolbar.

✦   ✦   ✦

Index

Continued

Continued

Continued

Continued

Continued

Continued

Continued

Continued

Web Site Credits

Anonymizer Web pages copyright Anonymizer, Inc.

CompuServe Web page graphics courtesy of CompuServe Interactive Services, Inc.

Construct Worlds Web pages copyright Construct Internet Design Co.

Copernic Web pages © 2000 Copernic Technologies, Inc.

eCash Web pages courtesy of eCash Technologies, Inc. © 2000 eCash Technologies, Inc. All rights reserved. eCash is a registered trademark of eCash Technologies, Inc.

Infoseek Web pages reprinted by permission. Infoseek, Ultrasmart, Ultraseek, Ultraseek Server, Infoseek Desktop, Infoseek Ultra, iSeek, Quickseek, Imageseek, Ultrashop, the Infoseek logos and the tagline, "Once you know, you know." are trademarks of Infoseek Corporation, which may be registered in certain jurisdictions. Other trademarks shown are trademarks of their respective owners. Copyright © 1994-2000 Infoseek Corporation. All rights reserved.

InfoSpace Web pages © 2000 InfoSpace, Inc.

Internet Movie Database Web pages courtesy Internet Movie Database, Ltd. (www.IMDB.com)

Kelly Blue Book Web pages © 2000 by Kelly Blue Book Co. All rights reserved.

Screenshots of MetaCrawler provided with the express permission of go2net, Inc.

Microsoft Internet Explorer screen shots reprinted with permission of Microsoft Corporation.

MindSpring Web pages © 2000 MindSpring Enterprises, Inc.

Portions copyright 1998 Netscape Communications Corp. Used with permission. All rights reserved. Netscape, Netscape Navigator, and Netscape N logo are registered trademarks of Netscape in the United States and other countries.

Reuter's MoneyNet Web page © 2000 Reality Online, Inc., A REUTERS Company, 1000 Madison Avenue, Norristown, PA 19403, USA. All rights reserved.

Tripod Web pages © 2000 Tripod, Inc. All rights reserved.

IDG Books Worldwide, Inc.
End-User License Agreement

READ THIS. You should carefully read these terms and conditions before opening the software packet(s) included with this book ("Book"). This is a license agreement ("Agreement") between you and IDG Books Worldwide, Inc. ("IDGB"). By opening the accompanying software packet(s), you acknowledge that you have read and accept the following terms and conditions. If you do not agree and do not want to be bound by such terms and conditions, promptly return the Book and the unopened software packet(s) to the place you obtained them for a full refund.

1. **License Grant.** IDGB grants to you (either an individual or entity) a nonexclusive license to use one copy of the enclosed software program(s) (collectively, the "Software") solely for your own personal or business purposes on a single computer (whether a standard computer or a workstation component of a multiuser network). The Software is in use on a computer when it is loaded into temporary memory (RAM) or installed into permanent memory (hard disk, CD-ROM, or other storage device). IDGB reserves all rights not expressly granted herein.

2. **Ownership.** IDGB is the owner of all right, title, and interest, including copyright, in and to the compilation of the Software recorded on the disk(s) or CD-ROM ("Software Media"). Copyright to the individual programs recorded on the Software Media is owned by the author or other authorized copyright owner of each program. Ownership of the Software and all proprietary rights relating thereto remain with IDGB and its licensers.

3. **Restrictions On Use and Transfer.**

    (a) You may only (i) make one copy of the Software for backup or archival purposes, or (ii) transfer the Software to a single hard disk, provided that you keep the original for backup or archival purposes. You may not (i) rent or lease the Software, (ii) copy or reproduce the Software through a LAN or other network system or through any computer subscriber system or bulletin-board system, or (iii) modify, adapt, or create derivative works based on the Software.

    (b) You may not reverse engineer, decompile, or disassemble the Software. You may transfer the Software and user documentation on a permanent basis, provided that the transferee agrees to accept the terms and conditions of this Agreement and you retain no copies. If the Software is an update or has been updated, any transfer must include the most recent update and all prior versions.

4. **Restrictions on Use of Individual Programs.** You must follow the individual requirements and restrictions detailed for each individual program in Appendix C of this Book. These limitations are also contained in the individual

license agreements recorded on the Software Media. These limitations may include a requirement that after using the program for a specified period of time, the user must pay a registration fee or discontinue use. By opening the Software packet(s), you will be agreeing to abide by the licenses and restrictions for these individual programs that are detailed in Appendix C and on the Software Media. None of the material on this Software Media or listed in this Book may ever be redistributed, in original or modified form, for commercial purposes.

5. **Limited Warranty.**

(a) IDGB warrants that the Software and Software Media are free from defects in materials and workmanship under normal use for a period of sixty (60) days from the date of purchase of this Book. If IDGB receives notification within the warranty period of defects in materials or workmanship, IDGB will replace the defective Software Media.

(b) **IDGB AND THE AUTHORS OF THE BOOK DISCLAIM ALL OTHER WARRANTIES, EXPRESS OR IMPLIED, INCLUDING WITHOUT LIMITATION IMPLIED WARRANTIES OF MERCHANTABILITY AND FITNESS FOR A PARTICULAR PURPOSE, WITH RESPECT TO THE SOFTWARE, THE PROGRAMS, THE SOURCE CODE CONTAINED THEREIN, AND/OR THE TECHNIQUES DESCRIBED IN THIS BOOK. IDGB DOES NOT WARRANT THAT THE FUNCTIONS CONTAINED IN THE SOFTWARE WILL MEET YOUR REQUIREMENTS OR THAT THE OPERATION OF THE SOFTWARE WILL BE ERROR FREE.**

(c) This limited warranty gives you specific legal rights, and you may have other rights that vary from jurisdiction to jurisdiction.

6. **Remedies.**

(a) IDGB's entire liability and your exclusive remedy for defects in materials and workmanship shall be limited to replacement of the Software Media, which may be returned to IDGB with a copy of your receipt at the following address: Software Media Fulfillment Department, Attn.: *Internet Bible,* 2nd Edition, IDG Books Worldwide, Inc., 10475 Crosspoint Blvd., Indianapolis, IN 46256, or call 1-800-762-2974. Please allow three to four weeks for delivery. This Limited Warranty is void if failure of the Software Media has resulted from accident, abuse, or misapplication. Any replacement Software Media will be warranted for the remainder of the original warranty period or thirty (30) days, whichever is longer.

(b) In no event shall IDGB or the authors be liable for any damages whatsoever (including without limitation damages for loss of business profits, business interruption, loss of business information, or any other pecuniary loss) arising from the use of or inability to use the Book or the Software, even if IDGB has been advised of the possibility of such damages.

(c) Because some jurisdictions do not allow the exclusion or limitation of liability for consequential or incidental damages, the above limitation or exclusion may not apply to you.

7. **U.S. Government Restricted Rights.** Use, duplication, or disclosure of the Software by the U.S. Government is subject to restrictions stated in paragraph (c)(1)(ii) of the Rights in Technical Data and Computer Software clause of DFARS 252.227-7013, and in subparagraphs (a) through (d) of the Commercial Computer — Restricted Rights clause at FAR 52.227-19, and in similar clauses in the NASA FAR supplement, when applicable.

8. **General.** This Agreement constitutes the entire understanding of the parties and revokes and supersedes all prior agreements, oral or written, between them and may not be modified or amended except in a writing signed by both parties hereto that specifically refers to this Agreement. This Agreement shall take precedence over any other documents that may be in conflict herewith. If any one or more provisions contained in this Agreement are held by any court or tribunal to be invalid, illegal, or otherwise unenforceable, each and every other provision shall remain in full force and effect.

Keep in touch

with family and friends

over the Internet!

The Intel® PC Camera
Pro Pack

Video Phone

Import Video from your

camcorder or VCR

Add video to your email

Make a movie in minutes

For more information please go to
www.intel.com/pccamera

intel.

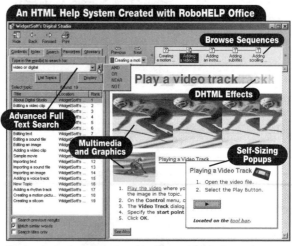

my2cents.idgbooks.com

Register This Book — And Win!

Visit **http://my2cents.idgbooks.com** to register this book and we'll automatically enter you in our fantastic monthly prize giveaway. It's also your opportunity to give us feedback: let us know what you thought of this book and how you would like to see other topics covered.

Discover IDG Books Online!

The IDG Books Online Web site is your online resource for tackling technology — at home and at the office. Frequently updated, the IDG Books Online Web site features exclusive software, insider information, online books, and live events!

10 Productive & Career-Enhancing Things You Can Do at www.idgbooks.com

- Nab source code for your own programming projects.

- Download software.

- Read Web exclusives: special articles and book excerpts by IDG Books Worldwide authors.

- Take advantage of resources to help you advance your career as a Novell or Microsoft professional.

- Buy IDG Books Worldwide titles or find a convenient bookstore that carries them.

- Register your book and win a prize.

- Chat live online with authors.

- Sign up for regular e-mail updates about our latest books.

- Suggest a book you'd like to read or write.

- Give us your 2¢ about our books and about our Web site.

You say you're not on the Web yet? It's easy to get started with IDG Books' *Discover the Internet*, available at local retailers everywhere.

CD-ROM Installation Instructions

The software that's included with the *Internet Bible* CD-ROM is simple to install. Before you install anything, though, you must decide which programs you want (see the program list in Appendix C) and then find them on the CD-ROM. To browse the contents of the CD-ROM, follow these steps:

1. Insert the *Internet Bible* CD-ROM into your CD-ROM drive.

2. On your Windows' desktop, open the My Computer icon. When the My Computer window opens, find the icon for the CD-ROM drive (usually D:).

   If you are using a Macintosh computer, simply look for CD icon on your desktop and click on it.

As you can see, the CD-ROM contains folders that correspond to programs on the disk. Each folder holds all of the files that are required to install that software. Once you decide which program you want to install, do the following:

1. Open the folder icon for the program you want to install.

2. What you see next varies depending on the software. If you see any files called "License" or "Readme," open them first. Double-clicking those files opens them using Notepad, a simple Windows applet for viewing and editing text documents.

3. When you finish viewing the Readme and License files (if there were any) you are ready to install the software. Browse through the contents of the program's folder until you find the installation file listed in Table C-1. It should be an executable file (ending in .exe).

4. Open the icon for the executable installation file. An easy-to-use installation wizard launches to guide you through the setup process. Each one is different, so just follow the onscreen instructions to complete the process.

Some programs on the *Internet Bible* CD-ROM do not contain an executable file in their folders. Some of them are contained in zip files. A zip file is a file that has been compressed using special software to save room on the disk. To decompress or "unzip" the file, you first need to install a program, such as WinZip (also available on the CD-ROM). Once you install WinZip, simply open the zip file icon. WinZip launches automatically, and the contents of the zip file are shown. You can then open files directly from the WinZip window. Again, view any Readme.txt or License.txt files first, and then look for a file called Setup.exe or some other executable file.